THE BLUE GUIDES

Austria
Belgium and Luxembourg
Channel Islands
China*
Corsica
Crete
Cyprus
Egypt
England
France
Germany
Greece
Holland
Hungary*
Ireland
Northern Italy
Southern Italy
Morocco
Portugal
Scotland
Sicily
Spain
Switzerland
Turkey: Bursa to Antakya
Wales
Yugoslavia

Boston and Cambridge
Florence
Istanbul
Jerusalem
London
Moscow and Leningrad
New York
Oxford and Cambridge
Paris and Versailles
Rome and Environs
Venice

Cathedral   s
Literary B
Museums
Victorian

D1355548

in preparation

Capital from the abbey church of Payerne, Canton Vaud (11–12C)

BLUE GUIDE

SWITZERLAND

Ian Robertson

A. & C. Black
London

W. W. Norton
New York

Fourth Edition 1987
Reprinted with corrections 1989

Published by A & C Black (Publishers, Limited
35 Bedford Row, London WC1R 4JH

© A & C Black (Publishers) Limited 1987

Published in the United States of America by
WW Norton & Company, Incorporated
500 Fifth Avenue, New York, NY 10110

Published simultaneously in Canada by
Penguin Books Canada Limited
2801 John Street, Markham, Ontario L3R 1B4

ISBN 0-7136-2837-5

A CIP catalogue record for this book
is available from the British Library.

ISBN 0-393-30368-3   USA

Maps and plans drawn by Andras Bereznay,
based on material supplied by. Bundesamt fur
Landestopographie, Wabern

Ian Robertson was born in Tokyo and educated in England. After
spending several years in publishing and bookselling in London, he
began working on *Blue Guides* when he was commissioned to rewrite
Blue Guide Spain in 1970. He has since revised the Blue Guides to
Ireland, France, Paris, Portugal and Switzerland, as well as writing *Blue
Guide Austria* and *Blue Guide Cyprus*. He has also written introductions
to reprints of Richard Ford's *Handbook for Travellers in Spain*, Joseph
Baretti's *Journey from London to Genoa* and Gleig's *The Subaltern*.

PREFACE

This fourth edition of *Blue Guide Switzerland* is virtually a new book, for several decades have passed since the last complete edition, edited by L. Russell Muirhead, and the separate volume describing *The Bernese Oberland and Lucerne*, were available, and very considerable changes have taken place during the intervening years.

So much has been done to modernise and extend the facilities available to the winter-sports enthusiast that the detailed information about ski lifts, mountain refuges, and the cost of guides, etc. provided in former editions would be superfluous. General introductory articles on skiing and mountaineering have been newly commissioned, but this book does not claim to be a climbers' guide: serious alpinists have their own more specialised sources of information. Among several shifts of emphasis has been the inclusion of an article on the botany and natural history of the country. The beauties of its landscape—in every season—require little commendation. More emphasis has been placed on Switzerland's cultural heritage. The range and quality of Swiss museums will surprise many travellers, while both the main cities and smaller towns contain numerous buildings and monuments of note. A new introduction to Swiss history has been written by *Clive Church*, which will provide a chronological framework.

Switzerland has long been known as 'the playground of Europe', and although other areas—particularly around the Mediterranean—have to a certain extent usurped its position, it still provides a range and quality of accommodation and service second to none. Most hotels still give value for money. Switzerland remains very 'tourist conscious', for it still relies to a large extent on this form of invisible export, and each town and region vies with others in exploiting its natural attractions. Tourist offices are competently staffed, and there is professionalism in the sensitive field of providing guidance and offering hospitality. Hotels and restaurants, which are found throughout the country, are no longer listed in this guide, for national, regional and municipal tourist offices can provide comprehensive and up-to-date information of this nature, together with details of the latest prices and facilities. Likewise, times of admission to monuments and museums are not included: to do so would inevitably misinform the traveller in a high proportion of cases, while tourist offices have current information.

Following the conventional formula adopted for the Blue Guides, the country is described in a series of routes following its remarkable network of well-engineered roads, although its railway system is also exceptional. It does not intend to be a fast motorists' guide. Towns are described for sightseeing on foot; many now contain pedestrian precincts.

A very considerable area of Switzerland has been covered in person during recent months by the Editor, but it is virtually impossible to visit every locality, every church, and every waterfall. Certain unintentional omissions are unavoidable, and the Editor, on whom the preparation of this guide has depended almost entirely, is alone responsible for all inexactitudes, shortcoming, inconsistencies, and solecisms. The readers' assistance is solicited: any constructive suggestions for correction and improvement will be gratefully welcomed and acknowledged by the Editor, for—as he knows from experience—things may change immediately he has turned his back, as indeed they did at Bellinzona, where the denuded facade of its main church, under restoration, became from one day to the next embellished by five huge statues which had been hoisted into position. Recommendations for the deletion of buildings, for example, which perhaps do not merit inclusion, would also be welcomed.

Selection remains the touchstone by which guidebooks are judged, and an attempt has been made to provide a balanced account of most aspects of Switzerland without being so exhaustive as to leave travellers no opportunity of discovering additional pleasures. The practice of 'starring' the highlights may come in for some criticism, but although the system is subjective and inconsistent, such asterisks do help the hurried traveller to pick out those things which the consensus of informed opinion (modified occasionally by the Editor's personal prejudices, admittedly) considers should not be missed. In certain cases a museum has been starred, rather than individual objects among those described, when the standard of its contents is remarkably high.

In an endeavour to acknowledge all obligations, the Editor must express his thanks to a number of directors and their assistants in the National, Regional, Cantonal, and municipal or local Tourist Offices, in particular to *Albert Kunz* and *Franz Blum* in London; to *Urs Eberhard* (and *Corinne Berger*) in Zürich; and *Matthias Adank* in Madrid. Among others whose help and hospitality are much appreciated, are: *Helga von Graevenitz* (Basle); *Marco Bronzini* and *Gabriella Regolati* (Bellinzona); *Marcel Grandjean* (Berne); *Walter Twerenbold* and *André Dähler* (Interlaken); *Marlène Chaperon* and *Christiane Campia* (Lausanne); *René Leuba* (Neuchâtel); *Viktor Borter* (Sion); and the Regional tourist office in Fribourg. Others whose advice and assistance has been helpful are: *Marianne Stalder* (Lausanne); *Luigi Bonalumi* (Locarno); *Nirvana Cattomio* (Lugano); *Emmi Hofer* and *Jean-Marie Gebel* (Lucerne); *Esther Alder* (St. Gallen); *Daniela Bonetti* (St. Moritz); *Norman Marxer* (Liechtenstein); and *Irène Dinten* (Zürich), in addition to numerous local tourist offices whose staff have almost without exception been helpful, among them *Lisbeth Schellenberg* at Schwyz, and *Bettina Pfeiffer* at Müstair.

Hanne Zweifel-Wüthrich, at **Pro Helvetia**, Zürich, has been especially considerate in easing the Editor's path in several ways in the cultural field, and has provided essential documentation, as has *Dr Hans Kunz* at the Swiss Embassy, London. Among the directors, curators, and their assistants at several museums and foundations, the following must be mentioned: *Dr Hans Braun* (Martin Bodmer Foundation, Geneva); *Dr Hans Christoph Ackermann* (Historisches Museum, Basle); *Miroslav Lazovič* (Musée d'art et d'histoire, Geneva); *André Kamber* (Kunstmuseum, Solothurn); *Roland Labarthe* (Nyon); *Dr Lisbeth Stähelin* (Oskar Reinhart Foundation, 'Am Römerholz', Winterthur); *Dr Eberhard Fischer* (Rietberg Museum, Zürich); *Dr Alain Grüber* (Abegg Foundation, Riggisberg); *Prof. Dr Margot Schmidt* and *Dr Gérard Seiterle* (Antikenmuseum, Basle); *Dr Alois Schacher* (Central Library, Lucerne); *Philippe Monnier* (University Library, Geneva); *Béatrice Buser* (Ballenberg); *Gertrude Borghera* (Villa Favorita, Lugano); *Regina Meili* and *Ursula Perucchi-Petri* (Kunsthaus, Zürich); *Jean-Pierre Jelmini* (Musée d'art et d'histoire, Neuchâtel); *Dr Christian Geelhaar* and *Franziska Heuss* (Kunstmuseum, Basle); *Dr François de Capitani* (Historisches Museum, Berne); *Charles Wirz* (Institut et Musée Voltaire, Geneva); *Pierre-Francis Schneeberger*, and *Frank Dunand* (Collections Bauer, Geneva); *Leonard Gianadda* (Martigny); *Dr Alex Furger* (Augst); and members of the staff at the Transport Museum, Lucerne; the Kunstmuseum, Berne; the Bührle Foundation, Zürich; and at the Museum at St. Gallen.

The Editor is also grateful to the following who have in several ways advised and assisted: *Fritz Wernli* (Ftan); *Gaëtan Cassina* (Archives cantonales, Sion); *Dr Ulrich Ruoff* (Archaeological Office, Zürich); *Werner Zimmermann* (Stadtarchiv, Zürich); *Dr Othmar Fries* (Lucerne); *Elizabeth Hussey* (Ski Club of Great Britain); *John Elliott* (Swissair, London); *Miss E.W.D. Steel* (Geneva); *Walter Frey* (Kümmerley & Frey AG, Berne); *Éduard Strebel* (Hallwag AG, Berne); *Dr Gian-Willi Vonesch* (Gesellschaft für Schweizerische Kunstgeschichte, Berne); *Hans-Uli Feldmann* and *Martin Roggli* (Federal Office of Topography, Wabern); *Dr H.R. Conrad, Sir John Wraight, J.E. Powell-Jones; Anthony Nind;* and *Richard de Willermin*. *Kümmerly & Frey A.G.*, Berne, and the *Federal Office of Topography,* Wabern, have offered cartographical facilities, generously providing base material for the maps and town plans included in the guide.

Arthur and *Marion Boyars*, and *Alain* and *Françoise Bertrand* have continued to provide welcome refuges to the Editor on his travels to and from Switzerland; my wife has again done all the driving in that country, so well provided with well-engineered roads; *Alta Macadam* has thrown light on the Swiss-Italian frontier area; and *Paul Langridge* and *Gemma Davies* have provided essential support and editorial guidance during the Guide's writing and production.

Please note that the *Alpine Museum* in Berne (p148) is likely to be closed until extended into the rest of the building and entirely reorganised and inaugurated. The remarkable *Antikenmuseum* in Basle has been reopened, and a more detailed description of its contents will be included in the next edition of this Guide. This will also include a revised description of the *Thyssen-Bornemisza Collection* in the *Villa Favorita* near Lugano. No precise information is at present available as to what will remain there after the projected redistribution of the collection takes place.

BLUE GUIDES: THEIR HISTORY

Prior to the outbreak of the First World War, the editors of the English editions of the German *Baedeker Guides*, marketed from 1908 by T. Fisher Unwin, were *Finlay* and *James Muirhead*. During 1915, with influential backing, the editors acquired the copyright of the majority of the famous 'Red' *Hand-Books* formerly published by *John Murray*, the standby of English travellers to the Continent and elsewhere for the previous three-quarters of a century. Indeed (according to Jack Simmons's informative Introduction and Bibliographical Note in the 1970 reprint of its first edition) the 'Handbook for Switzerland', written by *John Murray III* (1808–92), assisted by *William Brockedon* (1781–1854)—for Murray himself was no mountaineer—and first published in 1838, had already reached its 17th edition in 1886, and by the time the 18th edition (entirely recast by *W.H.B. Coolidge*, the alpinist) was published five years later it had sold almost 50,000 copies.[1] The last edition, the 19th, was issued in 1904 under the imprint of *Edward Stanford*. This almost coincided with the 20th English edition of *Karl Baedeker*'s 'Switzerland', which by 1928 had reached its 27th edition.

Muirhead had also bought the copyright of a series published by *Macmillan*, who were to market the new series, the first of which was announced for publication by *Muirhead Guide-Books Limited* by early 1916. In the following year an agreement for mutual co-operation with *Hachette et Cie* of Paris was entered into: the French house, which had previously published the *blue* cloth bound *Guides Joanne*—named after their first editor, *Adolphe Joanne* (1813–81), whose 'Itinéraire descriptif et touristique de la Suisse' was first published in 1841—were to handle a translation of a guide to London, which was in fact the first '**Guide Bleu**'; this, and other guides originating with Muirhead, were entitled **The Blue Guides** (further distinguishing them from the *red* Baedekers and Murrays). In 1921 an adaptation—not a direct translation—of Hachette's Guide Bleu to 'Paris et ses Environs' was published in London, another example of the collaboration between the two firms. In 1927 a new agreement was made; this lasted for six years and then lapsed.

Meanwhile, in 1931, the Blue Guides had been bought by *Benn Brothers*, and in 1934 *L. Russell Muirhead* (1896–1976), Finlay Muirhead's son, became editor. From 1954 he was assisted by *Stuart Rossiter* (1923–82), who succeeded him as editor in 1963, taking personal responsibility for the revision and compilation of several volumes, and under whom the present editor undertook the revision of his first Blue Guide in 1971. *Paul Langridge* was House Editor in the decade 1975–85, after which he was succeeded by *Tom Neville*. The series has continued to grow spectacularly, with over 30 titles currently in print.

In April 1984, a year after Benn Brothers had itself been taken over by Extel, their guide-book publishing side, *Ernest Benn Ltd*, was bought by *A. & C. Black*, who had themselves a long history of

[1]   The first edition was in fact bound in *blue*, being young Murray's preference, but his father then insisted on the uniform red binding throughout for the series.

guide-book publishing, beginning in 1826 with 'Black's Economical Tourist of Scotland', and including several written by Charles Bertram Black, eldest son of the firm's founder. The hey-day of Black's guide-book publishing was perhaps the 1890s, when more than 55 titles were in print.

Blue Guide Switzerland was first published in 1923; the second edition in 1930, and the third in 1948 (reprinted 1952), while a revised edition of the section on *The Bernese Oberland and Lucerne* only, was published in 1963.

While this fourth edition is not specifically written for mountaineers, it is perhaps appropriate to quote from Martin Conway's 'Mountain Memories', where he noted, after compiling a guide for them, that 'No sooner was the Pocket-book in the hands of climbers and in actual use than its deficiencies became apparent. I heard little from those who found themselves correctly guided, but was deluged with complaints from less fortunate individuals who had been insufficiently or wrongly directed. A list of obscurities requiring elucidation thus rapidly formed and grew. Scarcely was the ink dry on the first edition than materials were collecting for another'.

'Blue Guides' is a registered trade mark.

CONTENTS

12   CONTENTS

MAPS AND PLANS

EXPLANATIONS

Type. The main routes are described in large type, as are some sub-routes. Smaller type is used for most sub-routes, detours, excursions and ascents, etc.; for historical and preliminary paragraphs and (generally speaking) for descriptions of greater detail or minor importance.

Asterisks indicate points of special interest or excellence: two 'stars' are used sparingly.

Distances, total and intermediate, are measured in kilometres; total route distances are also given in miles. Road distances along the routes themselves record the approx. distance between the towns or villages, etc. described, but it should be emphasised that with the re-alignment of many roads it is almost certain that these distances will vary slightly from those measured on milometres.

Altitudes are measured in metres (m); as not all maps give the same altitude for the same place, pass or peak in most cases heights are those printed on the *Bundesamt für Landestopographie* maps.

Population figures are given in round numbers, and are based on the census of 1980, except for the main cities, which have been updated. These include those normally resident; tourists can swell the numbers very considerably in the seasons.

Anglicisation. Most place-names retain their usual German, French, or Italian form, although certain towns—such as *Biel/Bienne*, or *Murten/Morat*, which are on a language frontier—are given both spellings. *Basle, Berne, Geneva,* and *Lucerne* are anglicised, but their French or German forms (*Genève,* or *Genf,* for example) are given at the appropriate place, as are a number in Romansch. Each form is printed in the index.

Abbreviations. In addition to generally accepted and self-explanatory forms, the following occur in the guide:

C = Century
m = metres
R = Room
Rte = Route
St. = Saint (*Sankt* in German)
SNTO = Swiss National Tourist Office

BACKGROUND INFORMATION

Introduction to the History of Switzerland

By **Clive H. Church**

If 'practiced travellers' are reputed to 'think Switzerland is rather dull' they probably assume that its history is equally unworthy of attention. In fact, images of the present are a poor guide to the Swiss past; Switzerland has had many yesterdays. Each canton, of course, has had its own history. And, again contrary to legend, cantonal and national histories have not proceeded smoothly but in complicated and often contested ways. These fascinating and continuing stories of how diverse peoples did, nonetheless, come together to accept one political identity deserve to be better known and understood. Where the Swiss as a whole are concerned, the story is not one which can be traced too far back. The real beginning of the Swiss is in the folk movements of the Dark Ages. From then until the late 15C came the formative years in which cantonal communities emerged, joined together and carved out a place for themselves in Europe. Then, from the 16C, the new Confederacy rather turned in on itself because of its religious and social divisions. Not until 1798 was there a revolutionary redirection in Swiss development, leading to the creation and acceptance of a new federal state amidst rapid industrialisation and external challenges, ending with the Second World War. Since then, history has not stood still, for while political life has been untroubled, the country has gone through a social and economic transformation as dramatic as anything seen before.

While the lands which we now know as Switzerland were inhabited in prehistoric times, its peoples made little contribution to this process. They have, however, left some concrete reminders of their presence, such as the paleolithic caves like Wildkirchli in Appenzell, which testify to the existence of hunters during breaks in the long glacial eras. It is also clear that when, about 8000 BC, the glaciers retreated, mesolithic hunter-fisher peoples began to spread across the Plain to sites such as Mooseedorf in Berne and Wauwiler Moos in Lucerne until, about 2000 years later, they were assimilated or ejected by new peoples from the Middle East. The latter brought the neolithic revolution of settled villages and farms to the area. Sites such as Gächlingen in Schwyz and waterside villages like Cortaillod in Neuchâtel show that they were numerous. As time went on their stone tools gave way first to bronze and then to iron as more sophisticated and warlike tribes arrived, operating from forts like the Wittnauer Horn in Aargau. From about 750 BC fortified warehouses like that at La Tène brought Switzerland into the disturbed and fractious tribal world of the Celts with its warlords, advanced tools and crafts, and townships at Basle, Berne and Altstatten in Zürich.

At this point the Celts came into contact with the emerging power of Rome, often disastrously. One tribe, the Helvetii, were crushed by Julius Caesar in 58 BC and resettled in the west of the Plain as a sort of border guard. Romanisation increased between 47 BC and AD 15 when more of the Alps were opened up and colonies of veterans established at Nyon, Kaiseraugst and, eventually, Avenches. For the next 200 years the western and central parts of the area enjoyed an era of peace and prosperity, with upwards of three thousand large Roman-style farms producing the cereals, livestock, fruit and wine required by a growing population. There was also a host of cities, some large and impressive as the 5.7km of the walls of Avenches show, others small market towns like Berne-Enge. They shared in the active civic life and culture of the Roman Empire, with Celtic notables mixing with true Romans.

A new era opened after 253–59 when there was a series of devastating raids by German tribes. Although these stopped, and the Empire reasserted itself, Switzerland became much more of a frontier area. The population began to dwindle, especially in the east, and to seek refuge in the towns and castles. Although the times were such as to discourage trade and manufacturing, there was no sudden and complete ending of Roman influence, even after the legions were withdrawn.

The Formative Years of the Swiss (6–16C). From the 5C many parts of Switzerland were settled by the new Germanic tribes who are the real ancestors of the Swiss. The small communities they formed developed within the Empire until the 13C when they began to distance themselves and create a growing league of towns and rural corporations. In the 14th and 15C they developed further and played a dramatic role in Europe despite their own deep-rooted divisions. By the end of the period they had gained international recognition as a free Confederacy of an original kind.

The essential feature of the 'Dark Ages' was not the onset of barbarism but the way in which the present-day territory of Switzerland became divided between different cultures. In the W the Burgundians were settled as allies and merged with the Gallo-Roman peoples—and adopted their language and something of their way of life. Similarly, S of the Alps and in what was then known as Rhetia, the Lombards and Romanche peoples maintained much of the Latin legacy. In the less populated and more heavily forested centre and NE the pattern was different as small numbers of Allemani moved in and created new farms, small hamlets and villages. Their establishment took place over a long period and without much conflict. Where the land was already settled, the Allemani tended to halt, so the language frontier slowly emerged. Nonetheless, being more numerous than the Burgundians, having less experience of Rome and Christianity, implanted elsewhere and facing fewer natives, they kept and expanded their language and customs. It was from them, therefore, that much of the dynamism for the early history of the Confederation was to come.

Large parts of both areas were brought perforce into the Frankish Empire and gained from the Carolingian creation of monasteries. These began the process of converting the Allemani, thus giving a major boost to St. Gallen with its school of manuscript illumination. But the Empire then subsided into division and disorder throughout most of the 9th and 10C. Not until about 1050 did peace and order return with the Salian Emperors, and the rural communities began to expand and develop, with something like a third of the forests being cleared at this time. Meanwhile, the feudal magnates, who had emerged with the decline of the Carolingians, began to plant towns to establish their position and exploit the general European revival of the time.

In the pre-alpine regions of the centre and E farming often made special demands, because it needed a communal effort to organise the pastures in the valleys and the transit of the flocks to the Alpine meadows in summer. Hence, in many places, what were known as *Talgenossenschaft* began to develop to carry out these functions. Those which were found just S of the crucial St. Gotthard route, when it was opened about 1200, were to be particularly significant because they had access to the great cities of Lombardy which purchased their sheep and cattle. This produced well-to-do and self-confident livestock-rearing communities, who began to look to the Plains for the grain they needed to feed themselves. And, though rulers and magnates were keen to control the route to Italy and the revenues it produced, the valleys were a long way off and difficult to control, especially with the decay of the feudal nobility from which the towns of both E and W also profited. The area was thus freer and more self-reliant than other parts of Europe.

Yet if the empire was far away and if, by chance, no one magnate dominated the area, a number of houses sought to exercise control there. Rural communities and towns often had to look to them for protection, especially on the vital trade routes. The 13C was thus a period of conflict and changing alignments and not of self-conscious freedom movements amongst colonial peoples. Some towns and rural communities, like Uri in 1231 and Schwyz in 1240, sought to avoid domination by becoming directly responsible only to the Emperor. Others sought alliances with towns in similar circumstances as did Berne, Morat and Fribourg in 1243. A new complication came in 1273 when the energetic Rudolf of Habsburg, who had emerged, along with the counts of Savoy in the W, as one of the two major houses remaining in the area, was elected Emperor. While the towns and communities apparently adjusted to this, it did threaten their future development. On his death in 1291 many sought new partnerships to protect themselves in an uncertain future, one of which was the perpetual league between Uri, Schwyz and Unterwalden. This was a renewal of a now-lost earlier agreement—signed anywhere between 1230 and 1290—which declared that an attack on one would be considered an attack on all. It also provided that they would accept no outside judges and would resolve their disputes by their own mediation. There was here no mention of William Tell, of secret oaths or of social revolt.

The pact of 1291 was neither revolutionary nor unique. It did not envisage the creation of a modern nation nor did it guarantee military security. Yet, thanks to circumstances and the skills of the three communities, it lasted and prospered. By 1309 it had secured Imperial confirmation of their privileges. More significantly, when in 1315 the Habsburgs finally tried to punish the allies for rejecting the family's rights and its claim to the Imperial throne, the Habsburgs suffered a crushing defeat at *Morgarten*. The latter were forced to concede an amnesty and leave the three communities alone. In turn, the communities consolidated their entente by a new pact by which they bound themselves to accept no outside ruler and to agree on all matters of foreign policy.

Their successes had a marked effect on others in the region who were either threatened by the Habsburgs or involved in the St. Gotthard economy. The mountain communities, in fact, were increasingly concentrating on selling livestock and hard cheese in Lombardy, and buying grain from the towns N of the pass with their profits. On the basis of this economic and strategic identity of interest, a recognisable—although very loose—political community began to emerge during the 14C. There was nothing ineluctable about this process. Outside factors like the Black Death and the eclipse of feudal lords played a significant part. Nonetheless, as the dates of accession to the Confederation show, new members began to ally with the original three. Thus, in 1332 Lucerne signed an alliance in order to avoid having to fight her trading partners as demanded by her Habsburg overlords; twenty years later Zürich joined to preserve the freedoms won by its craft guilds and Berne to protect its interests in the Oberland from the mountaineers. Zug and Glarus were then more or less forced into an inferior alliance to protect connecting routes.

Such alliances were neither wholly binding nor wholly successful. The Habsburgs soon reasserted control over Zug and Glarus. But they did permit the consolidation of the network of alliances by agreements such as the *Priests' Charter* of 1370. This provided for cantonal jurisdiction over travellers and the Church. With similar leagues emerging in the Graubunden and Upper Valais the Habsburgs and their noble allies again took action against the cantons. Again they suffered exemplary defeat, this time at *Sempach* and *Näfels*, in 1386–88. The Habsburgs had to accept the loss of their lands to the cantons. The relationships between the latter became closer by the *Sempacherbrief* of 1393, which provided rules for the army of 100,000 men which they could then raise. So by this stage, the eight cantons of what the English called 'The Leagues of High Germany' were a significant if still somewhat unorganised political force.

In the 14C their potential had mainly been used defensively, but this changed over the next hundred and twenty years. Up to the 1460s there was a continual and often aggressive consolidation of League territories. Sometimes this was by purchase of lands from decayed noble families, sometimes by alliances with likely allies such as the town of St. Gallen, and sometimes by ruthlessly exploiting opportunities to invade Habsburg territories such as Aargau and Thurgau. The joint administration of these latter territories proved to be a much-needed bond to hold the leagues together in the face of the *Old Zürich War* of the 1440s. Zürich came to blows with Schwyz and the rest of the Leagues over the crucial Toggenburg inheritance. It then turned to its hereditary Habsburg enemy in order to try and break their stranglehold, but in the end it had to submit. The war showed that not even the most powerful member could go its own way, and that the whole was now greater than the cantonal parts.

The European trade revival was, meanwhile, benefitting the towns much more than the country. The resulting power and prosperity of towns, many of which were now manufacturing centres too, upset the values and balance of the Leagues. At the same time the benefits of prosperity were not equally distributed either inside towns or mountain communities, so that social divisions within as well as between the cantons increased. Hence, when after 1460 the Swiss began to use their military prowess abroad, either as mercenaries, or as part of the campaign to keep the door to western expansion open by defeating the rising power of Burgundy, tensions were aggravated. The booty won in the remarkable victories of *Grandson*, *Morat*, and *Nancy* led to bitter disputes. The problem was brought to a head when Solothurn and Fribourg applied to join the Leagues, as this threatened to marginalise the rural cantons. The crisis was only

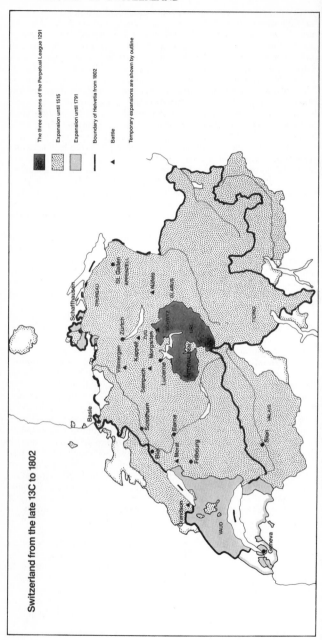

Switzerland from the late 13C to 1802

The three cantons of the Perpetual League 1291

Expansion until 1515

Expansion until 1791

Boundary of Helvetia from 1802

Battle

Temporary expansions are shown by outline

resolved by the mediation of the hermit Nicolas von der Flüe. Membership, both of these towns and then of Basle, Schaffhausen and, finally, Appenzell, was only agreed on condition that they played a mediating role in the affairs of what was by then effectively a free Confederacy rather than merely a set of Leagues. The Swiss also won *de facto* freedom from the Empire in the so-called *Swabian War* of 1499–1500.

Unfortunately, instead of enjoying the benefits of expansion and consolidation the Swiss then got involved in the struggle for power in Italy precipitated by the French invasion of 1492. Some cantons favoured France, some the Papacy; others were swayed by self-interest, which might take the form of being paid off as mercenaries and by the contractors who supplied them. While the Swiss won stunning victories, and at times created a virtual protectorate in Lombardy, they were riven by disagreements and came near to fighting each other. In 1515 a divided force rashly attacked the more modern French artillery and cavalry at *Marignano* and they suffered a signal defeat. Their answer was to sign a *Perpetual Peace* with France the next year which gave France virtual monopoly of mercenaries and bound the Confederacy to adopt a more passive policy in the future. This turned out to be part of a significant change in the fortunes of the Confederacy, just as it was apparently becoming a modern state.

By then it was also acquiring a reputation as the supplier of the almost invincible mercenaries depicted in the baleful engravings of Urs Graf and others. This reputation was not always an admiring one. The Milanese particularly resented their depredations and Sir Thomas More bitterly attacked their export of soldiers. However, this was perhaps no worse than the vision of a desolate hell which Switzerland had given many early English visitors. A Canterbury monk in 1188 described it as a 'place of torment indeed where the marble pavement of stony ground is ice alone and you cannot set down a foot safely'; Adam of Usk, escaping from Henry IV in 1402, had to be blindfolded before he could cross the Alps. But by then the country was beginning to develop a reputation for being able not just to defend its liberties but also to police its roads. And with its strongly walled cities, frescoed houses and rhapsodic fountains, not to mention its cultural liveliness, it began to figure in landscape painting and the activities of humanists like Erasmus.

Deadlock and Introversion (16–late 18C). Given this golden age of culture, the rapid development of political institutions and the enduring military potential, further political changes might have been expected. Instead, things became fixed, with no new members and no constitutional reforms being permitted for over 200 years. This unexpected stasis emerged as the only alternative to self-destructive religious conflict. Despite immense committment to the two confessions the Confederacy managed to stay together, albeit at the cost of its early dynamism and democracy. Only in the social and economic field did things change significantly. Even here the rise of new oligarchies and the partial solution of the religious problem did not lead to the political initiatives made necessary by the changing intellectual climate of the 18C.

Although the Reformation started outside Switzerland, it soon made itself felt throughout the Confederacy. Essentially, it involved replacing the rituals, traditions, and authority of the Catholic Church by new forms of worship and authority based on the Bible, the

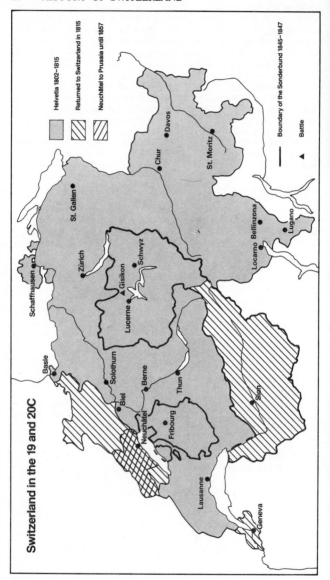

Switzerland in the 19 and 20C

individual believer, and the local community. This had a special appeal to urban artisans and elites who found the Church a barrier to their own development. Hence the Reformation was spread not only by inspiration, but also by urban governments. Partly for this reason it was also bitterly resisted in the rural areas, especially by those dependent on the profits of the mercenary service which Zwingli so criticised. With the spread of Protestantism there was immediate religious and political confrontation, both locally and centrally. In the latter case many good Catholics from central Switzerland felt that not merely their faith but also their influence in the Confederacy was at risk, particularly with Zwingli talking about reorganising the Confederacy under the leadership of Berne and Zürich. For a while compromise prevented the conflict becoming violent, but in 1531 war did come at *Kappel*, where, despite their superior resources the Protestant cities were defeated and Zwingli was killed.

Though the victorious Catholics did not seek to impose their creed on the Reformed cantons, so that a measure of tolerance persisted, they did assert their authority, and that of the rural interest, in the common balliages and in the Diet. So, despite being a minority, they obtained a veto on Confederal affairs. But this did not slow down the spread of Protestantism, especially with Berne helping to bring Geneva, Neuchâtel and its new conquest of the Vaud into the Reformed camp. In the 1550s things changed, despite the consolidation of Protestantism round Calvinist ideas and leadership, because of the development of the Counter-reformation. Conflict became more bitter and deep-seated as the Catholics not merely began to reform their own faith and discipline, but also to re-establish their position in disputed or threatened areas. With both sides getting drawn into the French Wars of Religion, and cantons like Glarus and Appenzell being rent apart, any kind of accommodation seemed almost impossible, although Appenzell and less formally, Glarus, were preserved from extinction by being divided into two separate half cantons.

The religious divide began to affect not just the political life of the Confederacy but its cultural and economic life as well. The whole period until the early 18C was dominated by it and without the integrating effects of shared economic and social interests such as those in the commonly administered lands and mercenary contracts the Confederacy might well have fallen apart. In domestic politics, although the Swiss proved willing to abide by their own rules, even when these were felt to be unfair and unwise, they could not agree on any new initiatives. No new members could be accepted in case they disturbed the balance of the confessions, or, in the case of Geneva, contaminated it. Similarly, there could be no rationalisation of the administration of the joint balliages because this would deprive the Catholics of the advantages won at Kappel. Ultimately, there were to be two Diets, one at Aarau for the Protestants and one at Lucerne for the Catholics. Even the old confederal oaths could not be renewed because they involved swearing 'by the saints', which the Protestants would not accept. Within individual communities the clash of beliefs often involved much violence, as with allies like Valais and, especially, the Graubunden, which was devastated by civil war during the Thirty Years War. A whole series of constitutional reforms were aborted because there was so little agreement within and between the religious camps, which often acted as separate states. This was especially the case with the Catholic Golden League.

Not surprisingly, all this affected foreign relations. Although the Confederacy could agree on renewing the alliance with France, and on staying formally outside the French and Thirty Years Wars, it could not achieve any consistency in policy. Each confession tended to do its own deals with associates and friendly foreign powers, as the Catholics did with Spain. This often gave foreign diplomats considerable influence in Swiss affairs and even led to mercenaries serving on opposing sides, as at Malplaquet in 1709 where they incurred heavy losses. Such inconsistency and division meant that attempts to create a common confederal military system did not succeed as well as they might. At the end of the Thirty Years War the Confederacy agreed on a scheme for raising a joint force to prevent war spilling over the borders, but once the crisis was over it proved impossible to obtain agreement on maintaining the arrangement. So the *Defensional of Wyl*, as it was known, became a largely Protestant venture. The negotiation of *de jure* independence of the Empire in 1648 was also undertaken in part as a Protestant initiative. Even the decision to try to avoid trouble by staying neutral, a term which was officially used from 1674, did not produce a united front. Hence, towards the turn of the century, when the Swiss were presented with new difficulties by the pressures of Louis XIV, which sent a flood of Protestant refugees to Switzerland, and by the disputed succession to the allied Principality of Neuchâtel, it was virtually impossible to obtain agreement. Thus the Protestant King of Prussia was invited to become Prince of Neuchâtel. Perhaps the remarkable thing was that Neuchâtel was *not* added to the list of territories which the Confederacy lost because of the religious schism, territories which included the Chablais, Gex, Rottweil, Strasbourg, and nearly Geneva as well.

The general peace and order of the country also continued to be disturbed by the religious divide. Even though Berne and Lucerne were able to combine in 1653 to put down a Peasant Revolt against post-war financial policies, within two years they found themselves on different sides in a new religious war. After clashes over the persecution of Protestants in the common balliages, and especially at Arth-Goldau, Zürich and Berne went to war. But they failed to use their military superiority and suffered a humiliating defeat at *Villmergen*. Cantonal rights in religious matters remained unchallenged as a result. Consequently, talk of reforming the constitutional provisions of the Helvetic body, as the Confederacy was by then called, came to nothing in the 1670s. It was not until the Abbot of St. Gallen tried to coerce his Protestant peasants in the early 18C that things changed. In a third religious war it was the turn of the Catholics to make crucial mistakes. Hence, after a second battle at Vilmergen, they conceded the Peace of Aarau which gave the Protestants their fair share of influence in the common bailliages and in confederal politics. Although the Catholics turned to France for further help this came to nothing and tensions very slowly began to subside.

By then, of course, much of Swiss life had been affected. Culturally the division between the two zones was clear. In Catholic areas there was a profusion of friars, ornate ceremonies and baroque buildings like the Stockalper Palace in Brig and the Jesuit Churches in Lucerne and Solothurn. In Protestant areas, after the iconoclasm of the early Reformation which had affected even artists like Graf, there was greater austerity and restraint, with higher literacy and awareness balanced by strict control over dress, morals and the theatre. Despite this and despite attacks on witches and Jews, the country maintained a high standard of education and scholarship from Paracelsus to the School of Schaffhausen.

Even the economy was affected to some extent because all parts were happy enough to use the new banking facilities of the Protestant cities. And Protestant exiles, both those in the early 16C and the Huguenots in the 1680s, played a significant part in helping to maintain Swiss manufactures in the face of local conservatism and contrary European trends. The cases of silk in Zürich and watch-making in Geneva are the classic ones. With this and the advantages of neutrality the country was able to deal better than most with the problems of depression. The Protestant cities were able to reassert their political power at the expense of the Catholic cantons, whose rural economies could no longer support their population, making them dependent on mercenary service.

This reassertion was part of a general shift towards social and political conservatism which had its roots in the way in which the wealth of both urban and rural cantons was increasingly concentrated in a few hands. The fears raised by depression and peasant revolt combined with a sense of divine ordination to make new elites assert increasing power and privilege. Hence, from 1674 to 1718 canton after canton made it impossible for newcomers, even religious exiles, to gain civic rights. And full citizens found themselves frozen out of the Great Councils which opened the way to political careers. Within the Councils themselves further barriers were erected, so that the number of families able to hold office fell continually until in the 1770s a definite limit to their numbers was imposed. A few patricians thus came to monopolise all lucrative offices and contracts, as well as arrogating to themselves all political power and even the status of nobles. People outside the charmed circle of a capital city and the patrician elites found themselves bearing a disproportionate share of taxes and dues with few political or economic rights.

This power was not used to reform the Confederacy because the rights of the old rural cantons still had to be respected by the 'Secret Councils' of Berne and Zürich which now dominated affairs. They were able to keep the country profitably out of the wars of the mid-18C yet, at the same time, their military weakness was such that they often had to turn to foreign powers to deal with disturbances on their peripheries, as they did in the Jura in 1740 and, especially, in Geneva in 1777. This almost prompted schemes of partition amongst some of the Confederacy's nominal allies. At home there was no real change either, but there was a surprising amount of unrest caused either by factionalism or resentment. Hence the apparent calm was disturbed by murderous struggles for power in some Catholic cantons while elsewhere there were crops of conspiracies against the patricians of the great Protestant cities and of violent rural challenges to their fiscality and denial of privileges and autonomy. And while this was an age of great cultural achievement, with the Swiss playing a leading part in the cosmopolitan thought and science of the Enlightenment, the patricians could also be fairly brusque with dissident artists like Fuseli and Angelika Kauffmann who had to spend much of their lives in exile in London. They were also unhappy about movements such as the new Helvetianism which brought Catholics and Protestants together in their concern for the nation as a whole.

To some extent these challenges reflected the way economic change was giving confidence to new classes. For while the growing population (it reached 1.6 million by 1800) and declining demand for mercenaries threatened to overwhelm the old economy, new possibilities began to emerge in manufacturing. In the W the Genevan watch industry was paralleled by an expanding new industry in the inhospitable Jura hills where, by the end of the century, thousands of peasants were working for new entrepreneurs. In cantons like Glarus, Aargau, St. Gallen and Appenzell A.R. a cotton industry also boomed, with 200,000 part-timers working in their own homes for entrepreneurs who supplied the materials and markets for an industry which was second only to that of Britain. Such development enabled many peasants to supplement their farm revenues and thus stay on the land without a decline in their standard of living. It also helped to destroy the old corporations and their hold on the country, especially when combined with expanding banking and increasing numbers of foreign travellers. The prosperity thus generated made people less willing to tolerate the constraints of patrician rule and culture.

Few visitors seem to have been aware of this transformation. As at the beginning of the period they were amazed by Switzerland's complicated republicanism and the way it preserved both formidable military strength and a high level of creature comforts. The first English ambassador was sent to seek a military alliance in the early 16C, while popular writers like Simler drew attention to the frugality and charity of the republics which made up, despite all their differences, a single polity. For Montaigne it was the comfort of glazed windows, tiled stoves and the baths in Baden, which impressed. The contrast between Swiss prosperity and cleanliness and other parts of Europe, noted by English travellers such as Fynes Morison, became even more marked during the Thirty Years War. Simplicissimus 'held this land for an earthly paradise' because of its freedom from plundering soldiery. Many English visitors in the 17th and 18C like Burnet and Addison, attributed this to the fervent Protestantism of the Swiss. This was something which had much impressed Cromwell and led to the regular stationing of an English envoy, and a growing use of Swiss soldiers in the wars against Louis XIV.

As time went on the country became a regular stop on the Grand Tour. People were drawn by the increasingly fashionable mountains, and the free, tolerant and cultured society they were alleged to produce. Roland thought the cantons the nearest thing to the ancient Greek republics and Rousseau had a love-hate relationship with them, since they both inspired his thinking and burnt his books for their 'presumption'. And if Goethe thought that the Swiss had degenerated and were now imprisoned by their customs and their pettiness, English writers like George Keate—who dedicated a laudatory account of the 'singularly curious' laws of Geneva to Voltaire—and Gibbon took a more generous view. Gibbon, one of a growing English colony in the Pays de Vaud, felt that but for the lack of political liberty allowed by Berne, he was in an earthly paradise. Yet, to an extent, it was the critics who were to be proved right by subsequent events.

Revolution and Redirection (1798–1945). From the late 18C the country was thrust by French invasion onto a revolutionary new course. After much conflict this led, in 1848, to the creation of a united nation, and then, as industrialisation developed further, to the democratic system which obtains today. In the course of this process the country established a new place for itself in the minds of European statesmen and visitors. Nonetheless, all was not plain sailing and Switzerland has been sorely tried in the present century, notably by the Second World War, just as it had been at the turn of the 19C.

At that time the Swiss Confederacy remained very much what it had been centuries earlier, a complex mosaic of communities with different rights, lacking a central government and an agreed foreign policy, and marked by mutual suspicion and the dominance of a patriciate which numbered perhaps 10,000 in a population of 1.8 million. This archaic Establishment provoked many of the less privileged to respond to the new ideology of the French Revolution, with libertarian demonstrations in the Bernese colony of Vaud and at Stäfa in the Zürich countryside. When the French finally invaded, the Establishment found itself unable either to stop areas like the Vaud declaring themselves independent or to gather its own forces together to resist the invasion. With some cantons refusing to mobilise the country was rapidly over-run and such resistance as there was in the Forest Cantons was bloodily put down.

Swiss of all shades of opinion then found themselves dragooned into a unitary republic designed by pro-French progressives. And though this set out to modernise archaic structures, its reliance on French military support and its abolition of cantons made it bitterly unpopular with both conservatives and moderates. It quickly degenerated into such anarchy that Napoleon came to see the Swiss as his most perverse and ungovernable subjects. In the end he brought them to their senses by withdrawing French troops and leaving them to their own disorders. This inclined them to accept his new Mediation settlement of 1803 which imposed new cantonal and confederal constitutions. As a result, the old elites regained some authority, but at the cost of accepting six new cantons and a central government structure which, for the first time, made the country definitely a Confederal state.

Partly as a result, the Napoleonic era was to be relatively prosperous and stable for the Swiss, despite French exactions and British industrial competition. But the new order was too liberal for the old elites who reasserted themselves as the Empire collapsed. It took the influence of Alexander I of Russia and Stratford Canning, the British envoy, to ensure that modernisation was not wholly abandoned in 1815. What emerged was a new Confederation, half way between the Mediation and the extreme looseness of pre-1798 days, in which three new cantons—Geneva, Neuchâtel and Valais—were included, and which was recognised as perpetually neutral by the Powers. Within it, the old elites re-established much of their control over cantonal politics. Not surprisingly, this was neither democratic nor united enough for many liberals, but once the post-war crisis was over the country settled down.

In the 1820s, however, the revolutionary impulse revived as petty-minded and unjust regimes came to seem increasingly unattractive in calmer times. Liberal reforms began and turned into a flood after the encouragement given by new revolutions in Paris and elsewhere in 1830. A popular 'Regeneration' took place in a majority of cantons as the middle classes of the smaller towns combined with peasants, artisans and intellectuals, and forcibly swept away the privileges of the old cities and elites who had so long denied them real political rights. Yet this did not lead to real social change nor to any revision of the Confederal constitution. So liberal governments came under pressure from a new Radicalism which sought to make Switzerland a single social democracy.

One reason for this was the way industrialisation had outgrown the old framework and frontiers with their internal customs barriers and differing weights and measures, which had made it easier to trade between Geneva and Constantinople than between Geneva and St. Gallen. In the eastern triangle of Aargau, Appenzell and Glarus the cotton industry was increasingly factory-based, although factories and workers alike were still a rural phenomenon. Such mechanisation had enabled the country both to cope with British competition and to develop its own engineering and chemical industries. Supported by silks, chocolate, straw weaving and watch-making, together with a more developed agriculture and the beginnings of tourism, the Swiss industrial economy began to expand dramatically, as seen in the new towns of Le Locle, La Chaux-de-Fonds and the rebuilt Glarus.

Yet it was actually to be religion which was the catalyst for change. Much Swiss opinion was still staunchly Protestant as well as democratic and responded fiercely to the militant and reactionary Catholicism generated by the French revolution. Attempts to control the Catholic Church by the 1834 articles of Baden, together with anti-clericalism in the mixed canton of Aargau, then prompted Lucerne to call in the execrated Jesuits to run the schools. And when radical 'hit squads' tried to attack them in Lucerne the Catholics formed a defensive league or '*Sonderbund*' to protect themselves. With the Radicals gaining a majority in the Diet through a series of cantonal revolutions the country moved towards civil war. This came in 1847 and resulted in a rapid and decisive Radical Protestant victory. The way was thus cleared for drastic constitutional change.

From 1848 Switzerland became a modern nation with a more Federal state structure including a central government and two directly elected houses representing the people and the cantons respectively. Power was shared between the Federal authorities and the cantons, but the balance was now distinctly different. If this was intended in a partisan manner it was actually implemented in a more open-minded way, permitting an eventual reconciliation between vanquished and victors. Admittedly, the Catholics were slow to warm to the new system, particularly when it was responsible for a new confrontation in the 1870s and '80s over the place of the post-Vatican Church in society. Yet in the end a compromise was achieved and the effects of population growth and the referendum enabled the Catholics to exert considerable political influence, and to block further changes of which they disapproved. For their part the Radicals, although superficially dominant, were actually divided and cautious, using their powers on matters like the development of railways to strengthen cantonal rather than central authority. There was a similar caution in their foreign policy because anti-clericalism and sympathy with liberation movements in Italy and Germany caused intense foreign irritation.

Nonetheless, the Radicals did consolidate the nation and in so doing their leaders built up power and links with banks in a way very different from what the peasants and lower classes had expected. So from the 1860s there was successful pressure for greater, and more social, democracy. Many cantons introduced popular constitutional and legislative referenda, direct election of governments and reforms in banking, education and taxation which soon produced federal demands for popular central control of the army, education, law and the legislative process. Catholics and decentralists such as the French-speakers feared that this would thrust them into a permanent minority situation. By a cynical policy of divide and rule the support of the French was won for a watered-down package in 1874. It was this which introduced the referendum into federal politics, thereby creating both the basis of the present-day constitutional system and a more integrated Federation.

Attention turned to the activities of the system, partly because the European depression of the time was forcing the economy away from agriculture and textiles to chemicals and machinery, boosted by an expanding railway network. Competition and falling prices exposed the agricultural community to great stress, and though many switched to dairying, others emigrated to the Americas or the towns. Conditions in the latter also deteriorated as industry adapted to competition, notably in watch-making, by concentration and mechanisation. The growth of heavy industry and the depression added a new element to Swiss society and politics in the shape of an urbanised, factory-based working class. By 1880 it had founded a trade union and eight years later came a socialist party.

This, together with further democratisation in the 1890s with the introduction of proportional representation at cantonal level and easier constitutional reform at the federal level, forced other groups to adapt. Employers, small businessmen and peasants all formed their own interest groups in the last 30 years of the century, just as other political movements turned themselves into organised parties, the better to campaign and to pressurise a federal government which was then playing a more active role, as the nationalisation of the railways by 1903 and the beginnings of health insurance show. With the threat from the left leading the Radicals to be more welcoming to the Catholic conservatives, to the extent of allowing them a seat in the government, the political system was almost the matter of compromise, coalition and consultation that it is today.

By then, not merely was the economic crisis over but the Switzerland of the Zürich railway-station and the Tell monument at Altdorf had become an accepted part of the European scene. This had not been so in the 1850s when she had been felt to be revolutionary and, indeed, had nearly gone to war to prevent the King of Prussia maintaining his rights in Neuchâtel. But the way the country there-after maintained a strict neutrality in 1859 and especially in 1870, when many French troops were interned, and dealt smartly with Bismarck's spies, convinced the powers that Switzerland was neither a threat nor a pushover. At the same time the sponsoring of many international agencies and conferences, like the Red Cross, the International Postal Union and the Alabama negotiations, meant that Europe began to appreciate the utility of its neutrality in the years before 1914.

This acceptance was probably helped by the increasing number of influential people who became familiar with, and fond of, Switzerland through the growth of tourism. Romantics like Wordsworth and Byron had made it fashionable by praising its resistance to the French and by evocations of the 'Prisoner of Chillon', while Schiller in 'William Tell', achieved the kind of rewriting of history that is normally associated with Shakespeare. Soon after the Napoleonic wars large numbers of English, among other visitors, began to arrive. Though they claimed that they were cheated—just as the Swiss claimed that the English were mean and too demanding—they continued to come. The formation of Alpine clubs, beginning with that of London in 1857, reflected the increasing amount of mountaineering then taking place, symbolised by Whymper's tragic conquest of the Matterhorn in that year. By then the first Cook's Tour had taken place, and the first Murray's 'Handbooks' and Baedeker's 'Guides' to Switzerland had been published.

With comfortable railways, good hotels, the promotion of the curative effect of a visit to the Alps, with the publication of such books as Leslie Stephen's 'The Playground of Europe' and the activities of travel agents such as Henry Lunn, more and more tourists flocked there. Some came to climb, others to indulge in various forms of winter sports which had been introduced during the 1890s; among those who stayed there for rest or recuperation were John Addington Symonds, Conan Doyle, Robert Louis Stevenson, and Thomas Mann. Many admired not just the rustic simplicity of still largely unspoilt villages like Davos, but also the social progress achieved by the Swiss. The relative absence of both distress and luxury, the stress on education and training, and the way the country was 'a perfect hive of industry', were all favourably commented upon. There were of course the scoffers, who disliked the 'golden mediocrity' of the new Switzerland, and claimed like Max Beerbohm that it had nothing to offer except for the non-existent 'William Tell', but generally comforting images prevailed and the impression developed that the country was not subject to the main currents of the times. But many leading Swiss novelists—among them Gotthelf, Keller, and Meyer—queried the direction their country was taking and, like the artist Ferdinand Hodler, sought inspiration in the past and in the landscape. And, in fact, Switzerland was to be very much tried and tested in the 20C.

Although Switzerland was not invaded during the First World War, it suffered deep divisions between French and German speakers whose over-enthusiasm often caused serious embarrassment. None of the belligerents wholly trusted the Swiss and their trade was kept under close surveillance. This compounded the economic problems caused by a loss of access to materials and markets, and the shortage of food and labour. This last was due to the need to maintain large numbers of unpaid soldiers on the frontiers and to support tens of thousands of internees and refugees (among the latter were James Joyce and Lenin). Urban workers suffered most from the consequent deprivation and, with the encouragement of the Russian Revolution, they staged a damaging General Strike at the end of 1918. This was dealt with by a combination of mobilisation and reform, including proportional representation and social improvement.

But class rivalries and fear of the Left persisted, especially with the Socialists being so strongly entrenched in Geneva and Zürich. At home this encouraged the growth of the Catholic conservatives and of a separate Peasant Party which, apart from ending the Radical Party's monopoly of government and parliament, kept the Socialists and labour movement at bay, until in the 1930s the former moved away from a radical Marxist posture to an acceptance of democratic pluralism. In 1937 the main union signed the famous no strike/no lockout agreement known as the *Labour Peace*, in order to prevent social conflicts facilitating the rise of Nazism. This may now seem a fanciful threat, yet, despite the stability of Swiss politics, the economic situation did contribute to a flirtation with fascism. After an export-led boom in the 1920s, the Slump struck hard in 1931–1932. Industrial exports were halved, wages and farm incomes dropped, and unemployment rose. Dozens of Nazi-type groups began to campaign for a complete revision of the constitution to remove an 'ineffective' government. This was defeated and eventually, after a surprisingly slow economic recovery, the situation began to improve. Nonetheless, the Swiss remained very aware of their exposure to Nazi influences at home.

In the field of foreign policy similar changes were occurring. Immediately after the First World War Switzerland had broken with tradition and chose to enter the League of Nations, albeit still maintaining its neutrality. This did not stop them from offering a home to the League in Geneva and at the same time maintaining a strong anti-Communist policy. But by the mid 1930s the requirement to impose sanctions on Italy after the Abyssinian invasion proved too much for Swiss neutrality. Their ban on arms exports to both sides was unpopular and, stepping back from the League, they reverted to 'integral neutrality'. They fell back on their own resources both culturally and more generally, a change expressed in the creation of Pro Helvetia—the Swiss equivalent of the British Council—and in the national exhibition of 1939. Similarly, the country voted to make Rheto-Romanche a national language and made greater use of Schweizer-deutsch in order to distance itself from Fascist pressures. Banks introduced numbered accounts to protect the savings of German Jews. Above all, much more was done in preparation for war, with arrangements to pay soldiers and their dependents, plans for placing the economy on a war footing, notably by assuring food supplies, and reforming the army.

All this was to be needed, particularly after 1940 when—unlike in 1930—the Swiss were totally surrounded by the Axis powers. Some elements felt that they should adapt to this unenviable situation, but the country at large—symbolised by Gen. Guisan and the army—insisted that they should fight to the last for their independence and plans were made to sacrifice the lowlands and fight on in their mountain fastnesses. This helped to dissuade the Germans from invasion both in 1940 and in 1942–43.

But being cut off and dependent on the Axis for access to the outside world, especially for raw materials, made the Swiss situation extremely difficult and several concessions had to be made—on the admission of refugees, the freedom of the press, the supply of manufactured goods, and in financial services. They also had to endure a freeze on rents, prices and wages, and food was rationed. A good number of spies were shot. Though some British officials appreciated the Swiss predicament, and were no doubt encouraged by the Socialist victory in the 1943 election, most Allied opinion was critical. The facts that the standard of life was so much better than elsewhere in Europe, that the Swiss were still trading profitably with the Axis, were providing credits and accepting Nazi gold and were slow to close down the Nazi party in Switzerland (whose strength was exaggerated), told against them. Allied pressures on their trade relations were resisted until 1943, when they scaled down, but only in 1944–45 were they finally halted.

Social and Economic Transformation (1945 to the present). The Swiss were not forgiven for staying out of the struggle against Fascism. Stalin, calling them swine, forced the resignation of a member of the government; there was even some fear of an Allied invasion. It was felt unwise to risk further humiliation by seeking to join the United Nations and again, as in the period after 1798, the outside world presented Switzerland with surprising problems. At the end of the war not only was Switzerland somewhat isolated diplomatically, it also suffered a wave of strikes in reaction to the austerity and constraints of the war period. Popular agitation for denazification was led by the left which preserved its electoral advantage until 1947 and was able to promote a number of social reforms such as old-age and health insurance. As domestic politics returned to normal, so international isolation began to diminish. Diplomatic relations with the USSR were resumed, the Geneva conventions were revised, and tourists returned. Yet in 1949 the Swiss still felt they had to stay out of the new Council of Europe.

Normalisation continued apace in the 1950s once the Swiss had been persuaded to play a mediating role in the Korean conflict. They went on to arrange conferences such as that on Indo-China in 1954. They accepted observer status in the United Nations (many of whose agencies returned to Geneva) and by 1955 were being held up by the Russians as a model for neutralised Austria. They became more active during international crises such as those in the Congo, Cuba and Cyprus, in line with a new policy of neutrality and solidarity, aiming to show that independence also carried responsibilities to others as well as advantages. Switzerland joined the European Free Trade Association and, in 1963, the Council of Europe. This led in 1972 to a free trade agreement with the European Community; the latter now absorbs half of Switzerland's exports and provides three-quarters of its imports. While not engaging in political liaisons with the Community, Switzerland plays an active part in technical co-operation.

The Swiss economy grew rapidly in the post-war period. By 1975 a very high level of output and productivity had been achieved and a great deal of the output was exported: 70 per cent in the case of machinery, and 80 per cent in that of chemicals, two main industrial sectors. The value of exports rose from 4000 million francs in 1950 to 22,000 million in 1970. Although imports were even higher (providing raw materials and the half of the country's food needs not met by a subsidised but increasingly modernised farming sector), there was a consistently high surplus largely due to the profits from services, large overseas investments and tourism. Thanks to these investments, to concentration on research and development, to unequalled labour relations—which kept the country totally strike free in some years—to adaptability and a more open economy, Switzerland managed to overcome increasing competition and the interruptions to growth caused by overheating in the 1960s. As a result inflation normally remained very low, and unemployment—despite the arrival of nearly a million foreign workers—hardly existed.

Such immense growth and prosperity showed itself in politics. The electorate moved away from state spending and social action; in 1953 a socialist minister resigned over opposition to tax increases to pay for such State action. The socialist party moved more to the centre, from 1959 forming a permanent coalition with the other three major parties. The Communists were marginalised, especially after the Hungarian uprising, which gave a considerable impetus to anti-communism. By the 1960s the government, though still subject to strict constraints, had become more active, taking on new powers and financing higher education and an impressive motorway network. The late sixties saw a surge of new parties and popular activity, encouraged both by the events of May 1968 and talk of a Swiss malaise. This was reinforced by the disturbing French-language activism over the failure of referenda to establish the independent canton of the Jura.

By the 1970s Switzerland had become more populous, more urbanised, more oriented towards the service sector than ever before, and also much richer. By 1980 its per capita income was 60 per cent higher than that of Britain. A high proportion of the population of 6.5 million (including hundreds of thousands of foreigners) is crowded into the towns of the Plain, with almost 40 per cent now living in the major conurbations, notably around Zürich. Since the war the agricultural labour force has halved, with only 6 per cent in industry and 55 per cent in services. An increasing number are now salaried rather than self-employed, often working for large firms including the many multinationals which now operate from Switzerland. With rising prosperity, Switzerland has moved away from the old divisions of religion and class. Divisions of age, regions and, especially, language, are now equally important.

Although heavily dependent on imported energy and materials, the country was less hit by the oil crisis than most. While growth was halted, output fell, the foreign-trade deficit doubled and inflation rose to 12 per cent, large-scale unemployment was avoided, in part by not renewing the contracts of 200,000 foreign workers. The situation had improved by 1977, and though there have been problems, for instance in the hard-pressed watch industry, by the mid 1980s the economy was again running competitively and healthily. The growth rate, at 2.5 per cent per annum, was far higher than the unemployment rate and almost as high as the inflation rate.

But the recession did introduce new strains into Swiss life, and questions have been asked concerning the extent of the country's neutrality in the face of increasing integration in the free-world economy. There has also been opposition to aspects of the militia army, while the occupation of the Kaiseraugst nuclear power-station site in 1975, the youth movements in Zürich and elsewhere in 1980–81 and the recent surge of interest in the preservation of environment are all redolent of a questioning of the new society. At the same time there has been nativist opposition, from the Schwarzenburg initiatives to limit the number of foreigners in the 1970s to present-day concern about Tamil and other refugees. And although the canton of the Jura was duly created in 1979, debate continues with regard to the way economic growth has strengthened the German-speaking community at the expense of French-speakers.

Although Swiss politics may appear remarkably stable there are subtle currents of change. Some feel that the present system is not sufficiently democratic, that an inordinate time seems to pass before positive decisions are taken, as with the question of female suffrage, or full constitutional reform, or entry into the United Nations when it took 20 years before the decision not to join was made. To some extent this is because virtually all the executive bodies, from communes to the Federal Council, are coalitions which can only progress by amicable agreement rather than according to the will of the majority, a fact which has led to the Socialists considering pulling out of the government. But the system remains highly federal and open to direct democratic influence. The 3000 communes still remain the basis of citizenship and political life, while the 26 cantons and half-cantons still function as mini-states with extensive rights of their own; they have an important role as executants of federal policy and considerable representation in the parliamentary and electoral processes. The Federal council has no police force of its own and no standing army. Instead it relies on a highly efficient militia army. Yet its weight in Swiss politics has increased in recent years and its relations with organised lobbies have been questioned, as has the inter-relationship of Parliament, lobbies and parties. There is still a great deal of direct democratic participation. Some bills must be submitted to referenda; all federal laws are subject to challenge at a referendum if 50,000 citizens so wish; constitutional amendments are voted on if 100,000 citizens demand it; and the number and frequency of such votes has increased greatly. At the same time there has been a distinct decline in the numbers voting in both parliamentary elections and at referenda, whether federal or cantonal. Not many initiatives succeed and decisions taken after scrupulous, if private, consultation often prevail. While this may annoy some Swiss, it is the price of a level of sensitive, federal democracy to which many states can only aspire.

There is also talk of problems in other fields: of an expensive health service, an incomplete welfare system (although old-age and health insurance had previously been introduced after long delays), an accommodation shortage, drug abuse and a high suicide rate, of environmental pollution and declining competetiveness, but these are neither unique to Switzerland nor so acute as in many other countries. Yet this concern with the imperfections of Swiss society is a reminder that prevailing images are not always a good guide either to Switzerland today or to its past. In both cases the reality deserves to be better known.

Ecology of Switzerland

By **R.G.H. Bunce**

It need hardly be emphasised that geologically Switzerland is dominated by the Alps, a series of mountains whose structure consists of two different masses of rock, the older and harder granites, schists, and gneiss, usually low in lime, and the much softer, younger, rocks such as shales and limestones, frequently rich in lime owing to the fossil shells they contain. Subsequent movement, currently thought to be due to the collision between the African and European tectonic plates, lifted the rocks and thrust them into the immense folds of the Alpine ranges, the original sequence in which they were laid down being distorted in the process. Thus the old crystalline complexes of Mont Blanc, Monte Rosa, Dent Blanche, Bernina and Silveretta have been worn down over vast periods of time prior to being covered by sediments, the order of which has in some cases been reversed by the mountain building, as in the formation called *Nappes*.

The effect of these overall processes has been to produce complex local patterns of rocks, often in close proximity. A major difference, ecologically, is that between the hard granites, for example, which give rise to acidic soils (on which species such as heather and rhododendron grow), and the calcium-rich soils formed by limestone rocks, which have very different plants, such as the lady's slipper orchid and lily of the valley. There are generally more species in the lime-rich areas, including orchids among many other interesting plants. Other important local factors include the grazing of the district, snow lie and availability of water. A geological map of Switzerland will display these different areas to the field botanist. However, it must also be remembered that many local variations are too fine for such a map.

Basically, the country consists of a relatively low-lying plateau bounded to the N by the Jura and to the S by the main mountain block of the central Alps. The latter is divided along the same axis by the valleys of the Rhône and Rhine, their heads separated by the St. Gotthard massif. There is a strong contrast between the rich valleys of the Mittelland (where the younger rocks predominate) and the rounded hills of the Jura, as opposed to the jagged peaks of the Oberland and Valais.

The orientation of the valleys and mountain chains is largely the result of the major movements in the uplift of the Alps, whose surface is the product of millions of years of weathering and denudation, processes still going on. The principal features are caused by reactions of the rocks under tectonic stresses and by fault lines. On the other hand the more detailed pattern of terraces and valley steps depends on the distribution and types of rock. Superficial features have been shaped largely by the action of ice. (It was the Swiss scientists Agassiz and De Saussure, who were amongst the first to study glaciology in the early 19C.) A series of ice ages started some 600,000 years ago and sheets of ice passed over the Alps, eventually—c 16,000 years ago—retreating to something approaching their present extent. At its greatest extent this ice would have covered all but the highest peaks. Its erosive power was such that vast quantities of boulders, gravel and fine rock particles were shifted and deposited in heaps. These features are termed moraines and are of many sizes. The ice-sheets also produced extensive local features such as the gravel deposits of the central plateau.

Apart from the deposition of such debris, glacial erosion caused widespread topographical modifications such as the U-shaped floors and hanging valleys seen along the side of the Lauterbrunnen valley. Other typical features are valleys with truncated cirques and spurs surrounded by sharp-edged ridges, such as the pyramidal peak of the Matterhorn. The glacially excavated valley floors are often unevenly deepened, depending on the thickness and velocity of the ice and the nature of the substrata, and a series of steps—as in the valley below Zermatt—may be formed. The action of water caused extensive erosion during interglacial periods, scouring deep troughs which were later refilled with ice; all of which added to a complex and inextricable variety of structural features. And where a more recently formed river encountered an interglacial river trench it would cut through the gravel in the form of rapids—a spectacular example being the Falls of the Rhine.

Switzerland contains a number of lakes which invariably originated in glacial activity. The larger were usually formed in valleys obstructed by morainic barriers, although the depth of each lake is largely determined by the extent to which the terminal basin was excavated by ice rather than by the height of the moraine. Other types of lakes are those found at higher levels in ice-eroded rock basins, often surrounded by peaks, or those formed temporarily in valleys obstructed by glacial drifts; kettle holes may be left by the melting of masses of stagnant ice (as at Lucerne).

The climate of Switzerland is moderately 'continental' (i.e. with cold dry winters and relatively hot summers, when most of the rain falls), although there are extensive and local variations, usually due to altitude. As this increases temperatures fall and rainfall is heavier. For example, in the Valais the high peaks have a climate comparable to Spitzbergen, while that in the valleys is moderate; around Sion and in parts of the Engadine the rain shadow effect of the mountains causes it to be about as dry as the steppes of eastern Europe. Local variations may be caused by the *Föhn*, a warm dry spring wind, or by the orientation of the valleys, while sudden storms of swirling mists and snow may spring up among the mountains. On their southern slopes, particularly in Ticino, the climate is virtually Mediterranean, with higher summer temperatures and more sunshine than elsewhere. In the NW of the Jura there are Atlantic influences, with higher humidity and rainfall.

In general the patterns are complex, even changing from one valley to the next, and this is reflected in the richness and variety of the country's flora and fauna. Olives flourish in the S, while alpine species are notable elsewhere. The climate is largely determinate, although the critical factor at the local level is the soil present in any given district. In the Valais and Ticino fruit groves and vineyards have been long established, while in the Mittelland the clearances have given way to arable land.

Low-growing trees such as birch and willow gradually established themselves on the retreat of the ice sheets and developed into forests filling the valleys, the tree line reaching between 2000–2500m, depending on exposure, etc. on good terrain. Much of this has been subsequently cleared for agricultural purposes but forests remain on some steeper slopes or have been left as protection against avalanches.

The vegetation cover can be divided into several characteristic zones, although these broad categories are somewhat arbitrary; those given below are intended to provide a framework for an understanding of the ecology of the country. Some plants are to be found in several different areas, but those listed are fairly typical. A table (below) lists the Latin names of the major species mentioned, although only the English names are printed in the text. Before describing these some ecological problems are outlined which the increasing pressure of leisure activities in Switzerland have precipitated (however these are problems experienced by other mountain areas of Western Europe due to similar activities). Extensive erosion can be caused by earthmoving equipment used to change the angle of ski slopes to increase snow lie, for example, while the winter-sports industry, particularly towards the end of the season, must have a destructive effect on vegetation emerging from the snow. Another form of erosion is caused by visitors taking short cuts, for the footpaths in the Alps are generally carefully sited and well maintained. Other problems are being raised by the increased level of detergents and sewage effluent in the lakes, but the effects on the hydrological system as a whole have yet to be fully assessed. There is no definitive evidence yet available on the damage caused to high mountain flora by acid rain, which it is claimed is already having a significant effect on some Swiss forests.

Springtime in the Gerschnialp above Engelberg.

Flora and Fauna. In the early days of alpine tourism the collection of plants was pursued with enthusiasm but with serious effects on certain species, such as the Eidelweiss. Times have changed and these plants and many other rare species are now rigorously protected (many are illustrated on posters displayed in alpine huts and hotels). Plant life should be respected at all times, whether in Nature Reserves or National Parks or not. Interest in the conservation of wild life has also increased, although in ecological terms there is little conflict between controlled culling and the maintainance of a balance which has been upset by man's destruction of the larger carnivores. Indeed, notably in the dense conifer plantations, certain species of deer are becoming too abundant and supervised shooting has been necessary to control the population. Meanwhile species such as the capercaillie have declined to such an extent as to be threatened with extinction.

Hunting in Switzerland is strictly controlled by the issue of Individual and District Licences. The former applies to most of the country, particularly in the French-speaking and more mountainous cantons, where the season begins towards the middle of September.

Different regulations apply, depending on the type of hunting involved. Those interested should contact a local tourist office or the Federal Forestry Office in Berne. The District Licence system, which largely applies in the NE of the country, is more restricted. Hunting is only possible if one is able to get the agreement of the District holder of the hunting lease to shoot as a guest in his district. Contact may be made by advertising in a Swiss shooting magazine.

There is free angling in many lakes, although a licence is required for fishing from a boat, and there are usually a number of local regulations. All are summarised in those leaflets handed to the angler with his licence, but in all cases one is advised to use substitutes for lead weights and to use nylon lines with great care.

Fishing waters range from low-lying lakes or fast-flowing mountain streams to the high-level alpine tarns, and the range of species which may be caught is equally wide. Further information may be obtained from Swiss National Tourist Offices and local tourist offices. It is advisable to make enquiries in advance.

Season. Switzerland offers much in every season, with the strong contrast of snow and dark forests in winter, or with autumn leaves turning russet on the hillsides, but it is in the spring and summer that the flora is seen at its most magnificent. The effects of altitude cause spring to be delayed at high levels and the period at which flowers may be seen to advantage is thus prolonged. Therefore a range of plants in flower is seen as one moves from the lower slopes to the high alps. In the lower valleys many of the better known alpines appear early, soon after the snow melts, and having flowered they are soon lost beneath the dense foliage of taller meadow plants. As the snow recedes, so these flowers appear at progressively higher altitudes, until by late June and early July they fill the alpine zone with colour. It is then that one has the benefit of a complete range of conditions from the lower meadows (some of which will not yet be cut for hay) to the higher pastures, where the flowers are at their peak and where the cattle have not yet grazed too heavily. By mid July one must climb higher still, the pleasures of finding flowers being enhanced by their scarcity and restriction to even smaller niches. By August the alpines are only to be found near the permanent snow line, and in reduced numbers, although there is often a second flowering at lower levels, notably after the meadows have been mowed.

These generalisations refer to the main mountain areas, for in the Ticino individual plants will be flowering long before those of the same species in central Switzerland. An orchid which flowers in May in the Ticino may not be seen until August in the Oberland, at 2500m. At a more local level, aspect causes considerable contrasts; for example a sunny slope, particularly in the S, will bring plants into flower at least a fortnight earlier. The orientation of the southern valleys is important and is reflected in the composition of the vegetation, since the S-facing slopes contain species from more southern climes. It is often rewarding to visit the same area at different seasons, its appearance being dependent on which plants are in flower at the time.

Some of the centres from which a range of plants can be seen are described in detail in Lionel Bacon's 'Mountain Flower Holidays'. This, together with the 'Guide to Alpine Flowers' published by Collins, will enhance the pleasure of travel in Switzerland during the spring or summer. A summary of some of the main recommended areas follows.

The Bernese Oberland. This massif forms the N side of the Rhône valley and the upper reaches of the Rhine; it contains all the main species of flora except the Mediterranean. The great range of plants is largely due to its complex geology, which includes extensive areas of limestone. Wengen and Kandersteg, for example, are good bases from which to explore the higher levels without much climbing from the valleys.

The Valais consists mainly of the Rhône valley and its tributaries, from the passes of the Simplon and Furka to Lake Geneva, and its ecology is comparable to the Oberland, except that limestone is less frequently found. Its alpine flora is perhaps the richest in the country as it includes a number of southern species. The centres of Zermatt and Saas-Fee provide ready access to high ground and a wide range of ecological conditions are found in their vicinity.

The Engadine, in effect the upper valley of the Inn, to the SE, has a somewhat different flora, more typical of the eastern Alps. Both Pontresina and Arosa are excellent bases, well known for their plant life and providing numerous high altitude walks.

There are of course a number of other districts throughout the country rich in a variety of flora—the yellow foxgloves and rampions in the woods near Winterthur, and the limestone pastures near Abländschen (near the Jaunpass) are among those which remain long in the mind.

Ecological zones often merge, depending on altitude, exposure and local climatic conditions, and their borders are arbitrary. The zones may be termed Forest, Grassland, and Alpine, apart from the agricultural and lakeland areas. In the intensively farmed Mittelland cereals are the main crop, while in the Jura, with its relatively high rainfall, pasture predominates. Around Lake Geneva the climate is condusive to the cultivation of vegetables, while in the Valais and in the Ticino Mediterranean influences are apparent, with the vineyards and mixed agricultural patterns typical of Italian landscapes.

The Forest zone may be divided into four sections; the Broadleaved (deciduous), the Coniferous (evergreen), Scrub, and Heath. The *Broadleaved* area, mostly low-lying, would have been covered formerly by forests, now largely cleared; only limited areas remain on more inaccessible slopes, usually on lime-rich soils and dominated by species such as beech and field maple, with alder and ash close to streams. Typical species among the ground vegetation are dog's mercury, yellow foxglove, and rampion. In the steeper valleys sycamore, wych elm, and ash are typical, rising above the tall broadleaved herbs such as hog's fennel and mountain ragwort. Often seen on sunny slopes are montane beech woods, frequently containing silver firs. Such woods are often on lime-rich rocks and the flora is exceptionally rich. Many orchids, such as the purple helleborine, and coral root, are present, together with the shrubby honeysuckle and spurge laurel among bushes. The Ticino is notable for its chestnut groves, typical of the warmer climate, together with cistrose and Spanish broom among other species of the degenerate forests.

The *Coniferous* forests are those most readily associated with Switzerland, with the green spires of the Norway spruce (or Christmas tree) finely contrasting with snowy backdrops. Although scenically attractive, their timber is also vital to the economy, and these forests are well conserved and managed, thinning and felling being carefully controlled. Avalanches and stone falls occasionally cut swathes through these forests, which fill a vital protective role, the trees are mainly spruce, although larch is found at higher levels, and the Arolla pine and its relatives cover extensive areas in certain districts. Among typical plants on the ground are bilberry, cowberry, chickweed wintergreen and alpine coltsfoot. Many ferns are also present, such as the hard and lady ferns, and a carpet of mosses can provide a haunting atmosphere when illuminated by shafts of sunlight. The roe deer is typical among the fauna, while bird species such as the crossbill, crested tit, and large woodpecker are seen.

Scrub; i.e. low-growing, often rather open, occupies a relatively small area, but is ecologically important in that it forms a transitional zone between the forests and the high alpine regions. Green alder, various willows and the mountain ash, together with tall herbs such as blue sow-thistle and wood stitchwort, are frequently seen near the watercourses and on the rich wet soils at these altitudes. Mountain pines are also found at the upper level of the coniferous forests, often together with heath, while the flora is a mixture of woodland plants such as the flowered wintergreen and Daphne on the one hand and mountain avens and mountain valerian on the other. Among the birds seen here are such species as the stonechat, whinchat, and wheatear, and raptors such as merlin and kestrel.

The main species found on the upland *Heaths*, where environmental conditions are too severe to allow tree growth, are the alpine rose or alpine rhododendron, but juniper is also widespread. On the poorer soils there is a series of species of the heather family such as the ling heather, cowberry, and bilberry, together with a well-developed moss layer, as well as grasses and sedges. Many alpine plants such as Arnica and burnt orchid are also present. The vegetation may have a more grassy appearance if heavily grazed.

The *Grassland zone*. The superb floral display of the hay meadows is certainly the first and often one of the more lasting impressions of Switzerland as they are crossed on ascending towards the higher alps. In contrast to many British meadows, broadleaved herbs predominate, as opposed to grasses, providing a bewildering array of species and colours. There is a marked sequence through the seasons, from the spring flowers, including several species of narcissi and crocuses. These are followed by meadow cranesbill, ox eye daisy, and bladder campion, which are widespread in Britain, but joined here by such distinctive alpines as the Martagon lily, great meadow rue, and yellow monkswood. There is some regrowth and flowering, particularly of members of the daisy family, after the meadows are cut. The hay meadows are usually on lower slopes, ease of access being important.

As the altitude increases, the meadows are less often cut, and there is a marked succession of flowers. In particular, plants appear after the melting snow, such as the dwarf snowbell, oxlip, and crocus. Later in the season burnt orchid, spring gentian and sulphur anemone will flower, followed by the taller plants such as the yellow gentian, white false helleborine, and spiniest thistle.

It is in this zone that marmots are usually seen, and also the chamoix and ibex, although they extend into the alpine zone. The bird fauna is limited, although distinctive, with several species of pipits, ravens and wheatears.

The *Alpine Zone*. In the moraines and screes are mountain sorrel, purple saxifrage and the alpine lady's mantle, but the majority of species are confined to alpine regions. Among these are the alpine toadflax, the alpine moon daisy and alpine buttercup, and also the Eidelweiss, now extremely rare. Niches among the rocks and cliffs provide restricted areas for plant growth, and these plants often form cushions to resist severe conditions. Among them are the moss campion, the livelong saxifrage, and Androsace, growing in tight cushions. Other plants have developed different methods of survival, the bulb of Lloyd's lily and the creeping stem of the alpine aster being examples. Distinctive snow-patch vegetation is encountered in hollows below the shelter of steep cliffs, where the snow lies long after it has melted elsewhere. The dwarf snowbell appears first, followed often by the coltsfoot. Other dwarf species such as the bilberry and dwarf willow, as well as several mosses and liverworts, may also be found. The snow bunting, alpine chough, and alpine accentor are among the birds inhabiting this rarified region, while the chamois and ibex may be encountered.

The flora of the lakes is distinctive, although many of the species are also found in Britain. They include the awlwort, quillwort, small bur-reed, common marsh marigold, starry saxifrage and golden mountain saxifrage, together with such alpine species as the alpine butterwort, pink primula and wild chives. Cotton grass, bog bean and sedges occur in the comparatively infrequent areas of bog.

The nomenclature in the appended list follows *Polunin* rather than the *Flora Europa*, since most readers are likely to use the former.

Latin and English names of Indicator plants for the descriptions of the zones given in the text.

FOREST ZONE
(a) *Broadleaved*
Lowland
Trees:
　Alder (*Alnus glutinosa*)
　Ash (*Fraxinus excelsior*)
　Beech (*Fagus sylvatica*)
　Field maple (*Acer campestre*)
Ground vegetation:
　Dog's mercury (*Mercurialis perennis*)
　Rampion (*Phyteuma spicatum*)
　Yellow foxglove (*Digitalis lutea*)

Steep slopes
Trees:
　Ash (*Fraximus excelsior*)
　Sycamore (*Acer pseudoplatanus*)
　Wych elm (*Ulmus glabra*)
Ground vegetation:
　Hog's fennel (*Peucedenum alpinum*)
　Mountain ragwort (*Senecio alpina*)

Montane beechwood
Trees:
　Beech (*Fagus sylvatica*)
　Silver Fir (*Abies alba*)

Ground vegetation:
　Coral root orchid (*Corallorrhiza rigida*)
　Purple helleborine (*Cephalanthera purpurea*)

Mediterranean
Trees:
　Sweet Chestnut (*Castanea sativa*)
Shrubs:
　Cistrose (*Cistusspp*)
　Spanish broom (*Spartium junceum*)

(b) *Conifer*
Trees:
　Arolla pine (*Pinus cembra*)
　Larch (*Larix decidua*)
　Norway spruce (*Picea abies*)
Ground vegetation
(British species):
　Bilberry (*Vaccinium myrtillus*)
　Chickweed wintergreen (*Trientalis europea*)
　Cowberry (*Vaccinium vitis-idaea*)
　Hard fern (*Blechnum spicant*)
　Lady fern (*Athyrium filix-femina*)

(Alpine species):
   Alpine coltsfoot
      (*Homogyne alpina*)

(c) *Scrub*
   Shrubs:
      Green alder (*Alnus viridis*)
      Willows (*Salix*)
      Mountain ash (*Sorbus
         aucuparia*)
   Ground vegetation:
      Adenostyles (*Adenostyles
         alliariae*)
      Blue sow thistle (*Cicerbita
         alpina*)
      Wood stitchwort (*Stellaria
         nemorum*)

   Tree limit
   Shrubs:
      Mountain pine (*Pinus
         mugo*)
   Ground vegetation:
      Daphne (*Daphne stricta*)
      Mountain avens (*Dryas
         octopetala*)
      Mountain valerian
         (*Valeriana murtena*)
      One flowered wintergreen
         (*Moneses uniflora*)

(d) *Heath*
   Shrubs:
      Alpen Rose (*Rhododendron
         ferruginum & hirsutum*)
      Juniper (*Juniperus
         communis*)
   Ground vegetation·
      Arnica (*Arnica montana*)
      Bilberry (*Vaccinium
         myrtillus*)
      Burnt orchid (*Orchis
         nigritella*)
      Ling heather (*Calluna
         vulgaris*)
      Shrubby milkwort
         (*Polygala chamaebuxus*)

GRASSLAND ZONE
(a) *Hay meadows*
   Early:
      Crocus (*Crocus albiflorus*)
      Spring snowflake
         (*Leucojum vernum*)
      Narcissus (*Narcissus
         stellaria*)
   British species:
      Bladder campion (*Silene
         cucubalis*)
      Meadow cranesbill
         (*Geranium pratense*)
      Ox-eye daisy
         (*Crysanthemum
         leucanthemum*)

Alpine species:
   Great meadow rue
      (*Thalictrummajus*)
   Martagon lily (*Lilium
      martagon*)
   Yellow monkshood
      (*Aconitum paniculatum*)

(b) *Grazed meadows*
   Early:
      Crocus (*Crocus albiflorus*)
      Dwarf snowbell (*Soldanella
         pusilla*)
      Oxlip (*Primula elatior*)
   Midseason:
      One flowered hawkweed
         (*Hypochaeris uniflora*)
      Spring gentian (*Gentiana
         verna*)
      Sulphur anemone
         (*Anemone sulphurea*)
   Main season:
      Spiniest thistle (*Cirsium
         spinosissima*)
      White false helloborine
         (*Veratrum albun*)
      Yellow gentian (*Gentiana
         lutea*)

ALPINE ZONE
(a) *Moraine and scree*
   British species:
      Alpine lady's mantle
         (*Alchemilla alpina*)
      Mountain sorrel (*Oxyria
         digyna*)
      Purple saxifrage (*Saxifraga
         oppositifolia*)
   Alpine species:
      Alpine buttercup
         (*Ranunculus glacialis*)
      Alpine moon daisy
         (*Bellidastrum alpina*)
      Alpine toadflax (*Linaria
         alpina*)

(b) *Rocks and cliffs*
   Alpine aster (*Astenal pinus*)
   Androsace (*Androsace
      alpina*)
   Livelong saxifrage
      (*Saxifraga cotyledon*)
   Lloyd's lily (*Lloydia
      serotina*)
   Moss campion (*Silene
      acaulis*)

(c) *Snow patches*
   Bilberry (*Vaccinium
      myrtillus*)
   Dwarf snowbell (*Soldanella
      alpina*)
   Dwarf willow (*Salix
      herbacea*)

WATER ZONE
Lakes:
Awlwort (*Subularia aquatica*)
Quillwort (*Isotes lacutris*)
Small bur-reed (*Sparganium minium*)
Golden mountain saxifrage (*Saxifraga aizodes*)
British species:
Marsh marigold (*Caltha palustris*)
Starry saxifrage (*Saxifraga stellaris*)

Alpine species:
Alpine butterwort (*Pinguicula alpina*)
Primula (*Primula minima*)
Wild chives (*Allium virale*)
Bogs:
Cotton grass (*Eriophorum angustifolium*)
Deergrass (*Trichophorum caespitosum*)
Lousewort (*Pedicularis palustris*)

Planning Excursions. Always take into account the abilities of the party, and the weather. Having said that, it is surprising what even the most modest party can achieve with careful acclimatisation.

Weather: always look at the local weather forecast, often obtainable in the local tourist office or hotel foyer. General weather patterns are accurately predicted. Thus, if heavy storms or continuous rain are forecast it is not advisable to go to high levels. Instead head for the lower valleys where the weather is likely to be better. Even so, it is always advisable to look out of the window in the morning as the threatened front may not have arrived or passed over quicker than expected. Local people may be able to point out local variations.

The mountains tend to make their own weather and conditions are thus infinitely variable. Such unpredictability has to be accepted, though weather does however vary consistently between centres—thus the Ticino and the Engadine have generally more settled weather than the higher mountains of Grindelwald and Zermatt. Of course it is disappointing when low cloud obscures the magnificent views but plant-hunters will find that the colour of flowers can still be appreciated. A good modern waterproof and a big umbrella, such as the guides often carry, provide protection from the worst of the weather.

At the start of a holiday short walks only should be taken, gradually building up during subsequent days. In this way people are frequently amazed at the distances that they can comfortably achieve by the end of a holiday. It is a good idea to have the odd day off, otherwise it is easy to overdo the exertion and spoil the remainder of one's stay. Look at local maps and work out a schedule for visiting different valleys and altitudes. Whilst one can get much pleasure planning in a general way at home, this is usually best left until arrival at the centre, because local conditions are often very different from how they appear in brochures! Use chairlifts to get to high altitudes so that more time can be spent at these locations—save these for guaranteed fine days, preferably towards the end of a holiday.

Tourist offices often sell local guides to plants; these provide useful local hints on identification. Suggestions are often provided for particularly good localities to visit and some valleys even have their own alpine gardens with labelled plants.

A number of organisations now offer holidays for people interested in plants. These tours provide a botanical guide to help with identification and to lead excursions. The Alpine Garden Society publishes regular bulletins and provides enthusiastic advice and encouragement.

Bibliography: E. Egli, *Switzerland, A survey of its land and people* (P. Haupt, Berne); E.A. Brugger, G. Furrer, M. and P. Messerli (eds.), *The Transformation of Swiss Mountain Regions* (P. Haupt, Berne). Useful for plant identification are: L. Bacon, *Mountain flower holidays in Europe* (The Alpine Garden Society); R.S.R. Fitter, *Grasses, sedges, rushes and ferns of Britain and Northern Europe*; C. Grey-Wilson and M. Blamey, *Alpine Flowers of Britain and Europe*; A. Mitchell, *A field guide to the trees of Britain and Europe*; O. Polunin, *The flowers of Europe: a field guide*; B. Slavik, *Colour guide to familiar mountain flowers*; S. Stefenelli, *Colour field guide to mountain flowers*. At present out of print, but useful, are T.P. Barneby, *European Alpine Flowers in Colour*; and A. Huxley, *Mountain Flowers in Colour*. The classic flora for the field is A. Binz and E. Thommen, *Flore de la Suisse* (2nd ed., F. Rouge, Lausanne), while the final authority is the *Flora Europea* (1964–80; 5 vols, CUP).

Other titles which may be found helpful are: M. Chinery, *A field guide to the insects of Britain and Northern Europe*; G. Corbet and D.W. Ovenden, *The mammals of Britain and Europe*; L.G. Higgins and N.D. Riley, *A field guide to the butterflies of Britain and Europe*; S. Keith and J. Gooders, *Collins bird guide—a photographic guide to the birds of Britain and Europe*; R. Peterson, G. Mountfort and P.A.D. Hollom, *A field guide to the birds of Britain and Europe*; R. Philips, *Mushrooms and other fungi of Great Britain and Europe*; and F.H. Pough, *Field guide to rocks and minerals*.

Skiing in Switzerland

By **Mark Heller**

It may be a surprise to many that of some 210 ski resorts in Switzerland, only seven are what may be called 'created' resorts of the French pattern, the 'third generation' ski resorts. It is an indication of the Swiss awareness of the problems associated with the conservation of the natural habitat of the skier.

For over 200 years the country had been catering for travellers and tourists curious to visit the Alps and their glaciers. During these years many simple mountain farming villages had built hostelries to accommodate them and when the tourists turned to winter visits to practice what came to be called winter sports these villages were able to adapt themselves easily to the expanded demand. Just as they had introduced alpinism, it was the British who were the first to experiment with winter sports in Switzerland. This can be accurately dated to 1864 when a party of 16 British and American visitors were persuaded to spend the entire winter in St. Moritz by Johannes Badrutt, in his Kulm Hotel. They enjoyed the promised sunshine, skated on the lake, tobogganned down the village street, and walked the snowy paths in the wonderful Engadine scenery.

Within 20 years a number of other mountain resorts followed this lead, greatly encouraged by the growing reputation of the Tuberculosis sanatoria in Davos and Arosa, where relatives of the patients discovered the pleasures of the currently fashionable winter sports. Skis had been introduced to Switzerland in 1859; in 1863 the Brangger brothers crossed from Davos to Arosa on ski, a trip they repeated with Sir Arthur Conan Doyle in 1894, which he reported in a dramatic article in the 'Strand Magazine'. The Bernese Oberland had been crossed from Meiringen to Brig by Dr Paulcke and his companions in 1897 and by the turn of the century a number of British had been skiing around Grindelwald and Saanenmöser, although travel to these mountain villages was long and arduous.

The rise of skiing towards its present dominant place in winter sports activity can be related to two quite different and contradictory developments. After the First World War, an increasing number of visitors, British, Dutch and German, were attracted to the excitement of day-long outings on the extensive skifields of Davos organised by the Richardson Brothers and the Ski Club of Great Britain. On the other side of Switzerland, in the Bernese Oberland, Arnold Lunn and friends were practising an entirely different kind of skiing, downhill only, with the grudging cooperation of the Wengen-Scheidegg-Grindelwald railway and the Almendhubel funicular in Mürren, which had been persuaded to continue to operate during the winter. Here the emphasis was on racing—both downhill and slalom, the latter a kind of obstacle race invented by Arnold Lunn. Skiing was regularly reported in the Press, and a sport which had been considered an eccentric pastime quickly became the leading winter-sports activity.

It was a painless transition and it was the railway which made it possible. Davos, Arosa and St. Moritz were directly linked to Chur; Gstaad, Villars and Château d'Oex had the Montreux-Oberland-Bernois railway and Adelboden and Lenk were close to the Lötschberg link. Funiculars lifted skiers from St. Moritz to Corviglia, from Engelberg to the Gerschnialp and from Unterwasser to Iltios. A funicular had been built specifically for skiers from Davos Dorf to the Weissfluh Joch to give 18km of uninterrupted downhill running to Küblis, where the train took the skiers back to Klosters and Davos. Despite all these aids they still had to climb for 20 minutes to get a minute's run on the nursery slopes, or hours from a funicular's end to the upper slopes. But in December 1934 Erich Konstam, an engineer from Zürich, installed and opened the first practical ski lift, the ubiquitous T-bar, on the slopes of the Bolgen nurseries in Davos. Within a year there were more than a hundred similar lifts all over the Alps. In due course chairlifts replaced the T-bar, and were in their own turn augmented by Von Roll's clever invention, the two-and four-seat gondolas. And finally, the cable car opened up the high peaks and glaciers to the skiers.

Even the Swiss had been converted to skiing after the privations of the war years and to serve their own special geographical requirements the small insignificant mountain villages with good skiing but no great mountain names joined the growing list of resorts. There are now organised skiing centres in all the Cantons, the majority being in the Grisons, Berne and the Valais, areas roughly coinciding with the main Alpine chain. Most of the ski villages lie between 1200m and 1800m and are separated from the upper grazing meadows by dense forest, through which paths zig-zag to the lower pasturages and the little dairy hutments, the *Maiensäss*. Above these, up to about 2800m, are the smooth grazing meadows providing ideal skiing country from early December to late March. With the tree-line averaging 1800m, there is clear skiing for a vertical drop of about 1000m and it is in this area that most skiing in Switzerland has developed. It is supported by the nursery slopes close to the village and the ubiquitous '*Schwendi*' (former cheese-making huts), often adapted to serve as restaurants.

From early December until late February there is little skiing above the open meadows where the snow cover comes early and lies late. It is only after February that the summits and glaciers, often served just by cable cars, are open for regular skiing which will continue until late April and, in some areas, throughout the summer; Zermatt, for example, around the Klein Matterhorn, the Corvatsch near St. Moritz, or on the Allalin glacier above Saas-Fee, now served by the new Felskinn funicular.

Much of the skiing in Switzerland could be classed as 'single mountain' skiing, the size of these massifs being such that they provide more runs than can be found in many linked resorts—uncommon in Switzerland. Owing to the height of the skiable mountains, a vertical drop of 2000m from summit to village is not uncommon and 1000m is the norm in early winter. For example, the Davos-Parsenn area, apart from eleven short-run lifts, gives a clear 2000m vertical from the summit of the Weissfluh (2844m) to Küblis (810m), or by a much steeper route, a 1300m vertical into Davos Dorf. Flims-Laax, half-an-hour's drive from Chur, with a maximum vertical of 1800m, has 31 lifts serving the Vorab and two subsidiary summits. The views—such as the panorama from the Gornergrat above Zermatt or the Bernina range from the Diavolezza restaurant and the incomparable Jungfrau, Mönch and Eiger which dominate every run one may take in Wengen, Grindelwald or Mürren—need hardly be stressed.

Not so well known are the many smaller, pre-alpine resorts which have grown up wherever the hills have provided adequate skiing; although not so well-visited by the tourist they provide excellent skiing for all grades and are much favoured by the Swiss skiers. Among these, easily reached from the main towns and well organised to satisfy the demands of family skiing, are such holiday villages as Wangs-Pizol, near Sargans, or Braunwald, a car-less settlement above Linthal near Glarus on a glorious sun-balcony only a hour away from Zürich, and perfect for small children; there is Flumser Berge, between Walensee and Sargans, a long-time Swiss family favourite, or Unterwasser and Wildhaus in the Toggenburg, equally accessible, with a plunging view from the Chäserrugg to the Walensee, 1000m below, with distant views of the Clariden and Glärnisch mountains.

The created, 'third generation' resorts have not enjoyed much success in Switzerland, with the exception perhaps of Verbier, loosely lift-linked to Super Nendaz and Thyon, and at the foot of very extensive skiing. Although popular with the British, there are few hotels and many ill-planned 'chalets' and long lift lines. Avoriaz, on the N side of the Rhône valley near Crans-Montana to which a lift link has long been promised, although well conceived, is taking time to popularise. Hochybrig, at the end of the Einsiedeln plateau, is a modern ski service station lacking both adequate skiing and reasonable snow cover.

Last, and by no means least, is the little-publicised cross-country terrain extending along the Jura range, S and E from Fribourg into the Gruyère valley and the Pays d'Enhaut. There are few specific resorts and the emphasis is on long nordic trails from village to village and from one isolated inn to some hospitable farmhouse. The routes are excellently signposted and maintained, taking the skier through attractive rural landscapes.

From the mid-winter tours that climb the grassy peaks of Glarus and the Sernftal, or the spring glacier tours of the Clariden, Susten and

Urner ranges, or the less frequented slopes of the Prättigau or Muottatal, the choice for the adventurous skier is wide indeed. For those who prefer their skiing mechanised, two hundred and ten ski resorts are more than a life-time of skiing can exhaust.

Mountaineering in Switzerland

By **Alan Blackshaw**

Anyone visiting Switzerland will certainly want to see something of the magnificent Swiss mountains, though whether just as a tourist, using mountain railways or téléphériques, or as a mountain-walker, rock-climber, alpinist or ski-mountaineer, will depend on the individual and his or her experience and inclinations. But whatever you want to do, Switzerland can provide it, and provide it extremely well.

The visitor interested in merely seeing the mountains should consider going to one of the main mountain resorts such as Zermatt, Grindelwald, or Pontresina. This introduction is for those wanting a more active acquaintance, but who may not be experienced alpinists—in short, for everyone from the beginner to those familiar with mountain-walking or climbing or ski-touring outside the Alps, but not yet in Switzerland.

The Beginnings. As long ago as the 16C men were exploring the higher passes such as the Theodule Pass, but until the middle of the 18C there were few ascents of high or snowy peaks.

The ascent of Mont Blanc from France in 1786 provided a spur to alpine exploration. The Jungfrau was climbed in 1811, and most of the peaks of Monte Rosa by 1842. Most of the first ascents in the Alps at that time were made by Continental climbers, such as the Meyers, Hugi, Puisuex, Desor, Agassiz, Ulrich, Zumstein, Vincent, Gnifetti, Studer and Dollfus-Ausset. British first ascents at that time included the Mittelhorn (1845), Strahlhorn (1854) and the main summit of Monte Rosa (1855). While John Ball produced a great guide-book to the Alps, J.D. Forbes made an ascent of the Jungfrau in 1841, notable because it was as much for sporting reasons as for the then customary scientific purposes.

Alfred Wills had a leading place among British climbers of the early 1850s and his ascent of the Wetterhorn from Grindelwald in September 1854 is often regarded as the beginning of alpine mountaineering as a sport. The Smyth brothers, E.S. Kennedy, Charles Hudson, the Mathews brothers, Hinchliff, Leslie Stephen, Moore, Fox, Adams Reilly, Tuckett, Tyndall and Edward Whymper, with their respective local guides, were only some of the good performers in what, between the late 1850s and 1865, was to become the Golden Age of Mountaineering.

The formation of *The Alpine Club* in 1857 stimulated enthusiasm and between 1858 and 1865 over eighty first ascents or first crossings were made of alpine peaks and passes of importance by those who were, or were to become, members of the Club. Some of these, such as the Jungfrau from the Rottal side (1864), were of considerable difficulty. The ascent of the Matterhorn on 14 July 1865 is generally accepted as marking the end of the Golden Age, as there were few of the great alpine peaks left to be climbed thereafter.

On the Rottal Glacier, c 1830; Watercolour by M. Disteli.

Since then the accent has been on the great ridges and faces and ski-mountaineering, and on rock-faces giving climbs of ever-greater difficulty. The guide-books (see below) for the respective areas give the details.

Planning Your Holiday. It is worth contacting the Swiss National Tourist Office to get information on the range of package tours available for walking or easy climbing, on the special arrangements made through the tourist offices in the Swiss mountain areas for weekly courses and the programmes arranged by the Swiss association of mountain schools.

With maps and guidebooks (see below), you will be able to plan a satisfactory trip relative to the strength and experience of yourself and your party, to obtain the necessary equipment (though it may be possible to hire an ice-axe or crampons, if you need them, in some of the Swiss mountain resorts), and then try to get yourself reasonably fit before going, so that you get the full benefit on the mountain. Try to find out also as much as possible about the various skills and techniques for mountain walking or climbing, from courses in your own country, and from technique books.

May is not too early in the lower areas. June probably gives the best combination of weather and conditions. July and August are more variable; and also more crowded. September may be very good, but the days are becoming shorter and colder. For ski-touring the season is March to May, according to altitude.

Equipment and Clothing. The equipment and clothing used for mountain-walking or climbing elsewhere is suitable for the Alps, subject to it being able to cover a wide range of temperatures, both cold in the morning and hot in the middle of the day. Mountain breeches with long wool stockings are normal, together with a flannel or wool shirt, a sweater, a windproof/showerproof anorak and a hat. Shorts can be useful when going up to huts. Take also some spare clothing (sweater, vest, gloves, socks) wrapped in a plastic bag unless your rucksack is really waterproof. A map (see below), compass, whistle, pen-knife, small first-aid kit and, possibly, a water bottle and a torch should also be taken. Two large plastic bags could prove a life-saver for any member of the party taken ill or suffering an injury in bad weather, until help comes.

Boots, whether for mountain-walking or climbing, must be comfortable, with rubber cleated soles in good condition, and will need a stiff sole if crampons (see below) are to be fitted. Gaiters keep out snow. **Crampons**, a framework of spikes fitted to the sole of the boot, are needed for snow and ice; they should fit precisely. An **ice-axe** is also essential for any snow or ice, with an adze for cutting steps in snow. **Hat**: a warm one for the morning and a cool one with a brim for mid-day. For mountaineering the use of a helmet is recommended where there is any risk of stone-fall.

Sun-protection is provided by dark glasses (possibly with side-pieces) or goggles, cutting out up to 80 per cent of the light, and by special high altitude sun-oil or cream and lip-salve with a high filtering effect, which should be applied early and regularly to all exposed parts. A camera will require a UV filter.

Ropes would normally be provided by the mountain school or guide. For rock-climbing, a 35–40m length of 11mm nylon *kernmantel* rope is normal, but for mountaineering the lighter 9mm version may be preferred, used double where necessary. A separate rope may be necessary for safeguarding the party on descents. A climbing harness and crevasse rescue devices are necessary for mountaineering, especially where glaciers are involved.

Try to obtain everything you need before you go as it may prove difficult to get just what you want in the Alps, when you are in a hurry, or the shops may be closed. Most of the bigger towns and the mountain centres in Britain have specialist mountain shops, and there are address lists and advertisements in the various mountaineering or outdoor magazines (titles may be obtained from your library or from the *British Mountaineering Council*).

Training and Guides. *The Alps are dangerous*, and the majority of alpine accidents occur in 'easy' places. Experienced hill-walkers should, nevertheless, have no difficulty below the snow line, provided that they keep to the tracks, and avoid steep grass or scree slopes. But if you and your companions want to do more than this and do not have the necessary skills and experience, you should go on a training course or take a guide.

Training is available from the Swiss mountain schools (addresses below), covering mountain-walking, summer climbing, and ski-touring. The *British Mountaineering Council* and some individual British mountain guides (see below) run introductory courses for alpine mountaineering; the *Ski Club of Great Britain* and the *Eagle Ski Club* run ski-touring programmes.

Guides. If necessary, consider obtaining the services of a qualified Mountain Guide for your introduction to alpine climbing, and in particular to introduce you to glacier techniques and other basic skills which can not be learned in Britain. Contact may be made through the Bureau des Guides (ask at the tourist office). Find out whether there is a party which you can join and thus spread the cost which may otherwise be high. In any case, establish the cost for what you have in mind before committing yourself. Make sure that there is no language problem and that he is the sort of person who will try to pass on his knowledge to you and not just treat you as someone to be got up a mountain regardless.

As well as the Swiss guides there are also British mountain guides who are equally qualified as members of the *International Association of Mountain Guides*. Details may be obtained through the *Association of British Mountain Guides*, or the *BMC*.

Mountain Huts. Throughout the Alps there are mountain huts or simple hotels, at convenient locations above the tree-line and usually below the permanent snow, to serve as a base for the main climbs or as overnight stops on hut-to-hut tours. There are also huts and bivouacs higher up in the mountains where necessary for particular, otherwise inaccessible, routes. These are owned either by the *Swiss Alpine Club* and other clubs or privately; they usually have a guardian who will supply simple meals, beverages and hot water, or cook your food.

Details of the huts and of their approaches are given in the guide-books, but there are changes from time to time and it is as well to check locally. Separate dormitories for men and women are the exception rather than the rule; wide alpine bunks, taking a dozen or more bodies at a time, with blankets but no sheets, are usual.

Membership of the Swiss Alpine Club, or other alpine clubs, entitles you to preferential treatment and reduced rates in the club huts. A reciprocal rights card providing reduced rates is also available from the British Mountaineering Council.

Many huts are on the telephone and it is courteous and prudent to book your places, especially for a group. For ski-mountaineering, check whether the hut, or a part of it (the winter-room), is open, and whether you need a key. Also whether a different approach is required to avoid avalanche risk.

Weather. Weather in the Alps follows the general pattern, but with local, usually adverse, variations. It is best to check the local forecast at the tourist office, or by telephone. Try to find out what the particular weather cycle is (e.g. one bad day, two good ones, one medium one, then another bad one) at the time, and get in step with it.

Generally, a wind from the N or E will give dry but possibly cold weather; while one from the SW or S is likely to bring rain and possibly a very warm air stream (*Föhn*), which make snow dangerously unstable.

Often the weather will be good in the morning but deteriorate after mid-day, leading to a severe local storm later in the afternoon; a good reason for starting early! Lightning can be a particular hazard during these storms, so try to be off high or exposed ground in good time.

Recognise that with each 100m of height gain it is about one degree colder.

Glaciers. Most of the higher Swiss alpine regions are heavily glaciated and these glaciers, slow-moving rivers of ice, often provide a natural route for mountaineers and ski mountaineers, properly trained and equipped to deal with the constant danger of crevasses. They should be avoided by the hill-walker, and tourist, unless accompanied by a guide or someone else with the necessary experience.

The glaciers start very high up in the mountains, where they are fed by the permanent snow fields and are themselves well snow-covered. Lower down, the surface snow will have disappeared on account of the greater warmth, so that the ice is exposed and the crevasses fully visible. The surface may also have a great deal of debris, and possibly water.

The size of the crevasses increases above ice-falls or other steep ground; and the glacier may become very contorted, with cliffs and pinnacles ('*seracs*') of ice and considerable danger of falling ice. There may also be big crevasses near the snout of the glacier.

Stone-Fall and Avalanches. The Alps are steep and loose stones are a danger at all times. Watch out for them in gullies or near moraines, and especially at the snout of a glacier which would normally be avoided for this reason. Choose sheltered or protected stopping places. If you happen to dislodge something yourself shout a warning to those who may be below.

Avalanches of sliding snow or ice are mainly of concern to the alpine climber or ski mountaineer. But the hill-walker, too, should beware of this possibility on warm or soft snow, and make a detour if necessary.

In spring there may also be a risk from big avalanches which have not yet come down from the high ground. These avalanches occur at the end of every winter, and the local tourist office should know whether any tracks are likely to be unsafe on account of them. See also p 73.

Insurance. The cost of a rescue party or helicopter in the Alps can be very high indeed and it has to be paid by the person concerned or his family. Doctors' bills and hospital treatment are also very expensive, and are not covered by the National Health Service (it is usually cheaper to fly home immediately at extra expense than to stay on the Continent for treatment). Some insurance cover against both rescue and medical costs is therefore advisable and there is also a case for insuring equipment which may prove surprisingly expensive to replace.

There are a number of standard accident policies which give a degree of cover for mountain-walking, but they normally exclude mountaineering or ski-mountaineering involving the use of ropes, so extra cover would be needed for this and for rescue costs. Membership of the British Mountaineering Council, or of one of the Continental alpine clubs, would enable you to use their special policies.

Guidebooks and Maps. *Guidebooks*. There are mountaineering and ski-mountaineering guide-books for each of the main areas, published by the Swiss Alpine club in French or German as follows:

Guide des Alpes Valaisannes
  Ferret-Collon
  Collon-Theodul
  Theodul-Mont Moro
  Strahlhorn-Simplon
  Simplon-Furka
Bündnerführer
  Oberland und Rheinwaldgebiet
  Südliche Bergellerberge un M Dizgrazia
  Bernina Gruppe
  Albula
Urnerführer
  Kaiserstock-Windgällen-Oberalpstock
  Urner Alpen West
Hochgebirgsführer Durch die Glarner Alpen

In addition, West Col Productions, in some cases in association with the Alpine Club, has the following series of English-language alpine mountaineering guidebooks:

Selected climbs in the Mont Blanc range
  Col du Geant to Trient
Selected climbs in the Pennine Alps
  Saas-Fee, Zermatt and Zinal
  Arolla and Western ranges
Selected climbs in the Bernese Alps
Central Switzerland
Engelhörner and Salbitschijen
Bregaglia West
Bregaglia East
Bernina

For mountain-walking, there will be local guidebooks for each of the main centres, with descriptions of the routes and sketchmaps. Kümmerly and Frey have an important series of guidebooks under the title *Guide Pedestre/Wanderbuch* covering the main Swiss areas and the Tour du Mont Blanc. Constable produces a mountain-walking guidebook, 'Zermatt and District'.

Maps. The Swiss Alpine Club publishes an excellent 1:500,000 map showing all its huts and the Swiss rescue posts, which may be useful for an overall view.

The guide-books usually contain diagrams of the climbing areas, but you will need the large-scale Swiss official maps (LK/CN) as well, preferably in the hard-wearing syntosil version. For all-round use the 1:50,000 scale is best (available also with ski-routes in most cases). The 1:25,000 maps are preferable for complicated areas, to supplement those at 1:50,000. the 1:100,000 maps are good for forming an overall impression of a range but do not give sufficient detail to show a complicated route.

Check the date when the map was last revised (so that you know which new roads, téléphériques, and reservoirs it shows) and if possible find out when the original survey was done (since a map which has been merely overprinted with new roads, etc. will not show important natural changes such as receded glaciers or snowfields).

Where to go Mountaineering. The notes below give an indication of the main characteristics of the various Swiss mountain areas. They are written from a mountaineer's standpoint and it is for you to rate yourself as a beginner, an experienced hill-walker or rock-climber, or an experienced alpine mountaineer, and to decide what to do accordingly, taking local advice and help as necessary.

Always remember the effects of altitude, which can make the peaks over 3500 particularly demanding even for experienced alpinists.

The Valais. This canton includes the whole of the Pennine Alps along the Swiss-Italian border between the Great St. Bernard Pass and the Simplon, plus the Lower Valais to the NW of the Great St. Bernard. It has more mountains over 4000m than any other alpine group and includes the highest summit shared by Switzerland (Monte Rosa, 4634m), and the highest one wholly in Switzerland (the Dom, 4545m). On the ordinary routes the technical difficulty of the rock climbing is not great but the length of the climbs necessitates a good deal of moving together in exposed positions on rock and snow and ice, and the higher routes tend to be serious.

The Mont Blanc group, W of the Great St. Bernard Pass, is only partly in Switzerland, and it would be worth making a visit to Chamonix (France) or Courmayeur (Italy) in order to see something of it. The Tour du Mont Blanc is a fine walking expedition, linking the Swiss, French and Italian valley approaches.

The main bases from W to E are as follows:

The Lower Valais. The mountains accessible from the Martigny area include the Aiguilles Dorées and du Tour, Mont Dolent, and the Grand Combin, with the Dents du Midi to the NW. There is a climbing school at La Fouly, near Champex in the Swiss Val Ferret.

Arolla is an excellent area for beginners, perhaps the best in Switzerland, with a mountain school. The peaks are not very high, nor are they difficult or complicated. The Pigne d'Arolla (3796m) is an easy snow climb and Mont Blanc de Cheilon offers an attractive traverse. The Petite Dent de Veisivi and the Aiguilles Rouges d'Arolla (longer) give pleasant rock climbing.

Zinal has some easy climbs, such as the popular Besso (3668m), and also a circle of bigger and more difficult mountains, e.g. the Ober Gabelhorn (4063m) the Zinal Rothorn (4221m) and the Weisshorn. The N ridge of the Rothorn is a most attractive climb of moderate difficulty.

Zermatt is overlooked by the Matterhorn and surrounded by 4000m peaks: indeed, most of the major peaks of the Pennines are easily accessible. There is little at low altitude but several of the high peaks are not difficult for experienced alpinists (e.g. Allalinhorn, Rimpfischhorn, Strahlhorn and Breithorn). The mountain railways and telepheriques enable the non-mountaineer to see some of the finest peaks in the Alps.

The Saas Valley gives good access to some of the E Zermatt peaks (Allalinhorn, Alphubel, Lenzspitze, Nadelhorn) and also has a range of peaks of its own including the Weissmies. There are several useful rock climbs at lower altitude such as the Jagigrat and the Portjengrat. Quite a good area for beginners. Saas-Fee is the best-known centre, but Saas-Almagell and Saas-Grund are better placed for some of the climbs.

Macunagna (Italy) is ideal for the big climbs on the Macunagna face of Monte Rosa, but they are also accessible in a long day from Zermatt.

The Bernese Alps. This range, N of the Rhône Valley, is rather lower than the Pennine Alps but has much to commend it. The climbing is not technically hard on the standard routes but the highest peaks are serious, largely because they get some of the worst weather in the Alps. The region is in two main parts.

The Western Bernese Alps. This area, from St. Maurice to the Lötschberg Tunnel, gives fairly gentle climbing, mostly at about 3000m. The main peaks are the Diablerets (3210m), the Wildstrubel (3244m) and the Balmhorn (3699m). There is low-altitude rock climbing in the Argentine, to the E of Bex, near St. Maurice. It is a good area for a first season.

The Eastern Bernese Alps has mainly 4000m peaks, including the Finsteraarhorn (4274m), the Aletschhorn, the Jungfrau and the Mönch. The Eiger is only slightly lower. It is often known among mountaineers as the 'Bernese Oberland', though strictly this is the whole area between Lake Thun and Canton Valais.

The area is bounded on the N by the huge wall from Scheidegg to Meiringen, which gives the extremely impressive north-face climbs on the Jungfrau, Mönch, Eiger, and Wetterhorn. The Engelhorner, S of Meiringen, have plenty of very steep rock climbs, mostly limestone. Grindelwald is perhaps the best centre, but it is also possible to enter from the S through the Lötschental or up the Aletsch glacier from Fiesch. The Baltschiedertal has some fine rock climbing above Visp. There are mountaineering schools at Rosenlaui, Meiringen and Fiesch.

Uri Alps and neighbouring areas. These areas, E of the Oberland and N of the Lepontine Alps, are rather lower than the main alpine areas and hence may be worth a visit for novices or in a bad season. Much of the climbing is fairly easy snow and ice but there is also a great deal of rock climbing, some of it very high standard and quality. There are plenty of huts, but in any case many of the rock climbs can be reached from the road. The main areas from SW to NE are as follows:

South of the Susten Pass. The Dammastock (3630m) and other peaks to the NE of Gletsch give snow and ice climbing and some very good rock climbs similar to those of the Chamonix Aiguilles though on a smaller scale. Further E there is excellent low-altitude rock climbing near Göschenen, NW of Andermatt, of which the best known is the Salbitschijen (2981m) with its classic S ridge and numerous harder climbs on good granite.

North of the Susten Pass (including the Engelberg). The main peak is Titlis (3238m) which though fairly easy by its ordinary route, also has hard limestone climbing. Engelberg is a central base.

Tödi Range. To the NE of Andermatt is a considerable range of fairly easy peaks of which the highest is Tödi (3620m).

The Lepontine Alps. This is the large area to the NE of the Pennines, between the Simplon Pass and the Splugen Pass (including the Ticino Alps). The highest peak is the Rheinwaldhorn (3402m) in the Ádula district, SE of the St. Gotthard Pass. In general there is not much of note for the climber but the scope for the hill walker is tremendous.

The Val Bregaglia and Upper Engadine. This part of SE Switzerland, to the S and N of St. Moritz, is lower and warmer, and usually has better weather, than the Pennine Alps or the Oberland. The Bernina and Albula groups are suitable for a first or second season since the climbing is fairly easy and the routes are not very complicated. The Bregaglia is more difficult, with many hard rock climbs. Details of the main groups from SW to NE are as follows:

Climbers in the Bernese Alps at the end of the 19C.

Bregaglia. The Sciora cirque includes the Piz Badile, with its N ridge giving a classic medium standard climb, and its NE face a high standard one. But the other areas to its E, notably the Forno, Albigna and Allievi cirques, give excellent climbing too, sometimes on snow as well as rock.

Bernina. In this area, S of St. Moritz, the main snow peaks are the Piz Bernina (4049m: the most easterly alpine 4000m peak), Piz Roseg, Piz Zupo, Bella Vista and Piz Palü. The Diavolezza lift provides a fine view-point. Separate from the main group is Monte Disgrázia (3678m). Pontresina is a good centre and has a mountaineering school.

Albula. N of St. Moritz and E of the Lepontine Alps. This area, of which Piz Kesch (3418m) is the principal summit, has plenty of easy climbing and glacier travel. It is, however, probably more worth while for the walker than for the climber.

Useful addresses, etc.

British Mountaineering Council, Crawford House, Precinct Centre, Booth Street E, Manchester M13 9RZ; *Ski Club of Great Britain*, 118 Eaton Square, London SW1 (for ski touring); *Association of British Mountain Guides*—as for British Mountaineering Council; *Association of British Members of the Swiss Alpine Club*, Mr J.W. Eccles, The Hon. New Members' Secretary, Albertine Cottage, 52 North Street, Marcham, Oxon, OX13 6NG.

There is an International School of Mountaineering at Leysin, and mountaineering schools at Andermatt, Champéry, Davos-Dorf, Kandersteg, Saas-Fee, Saas-Grund, Klosters, Riederalp, Thun, Fiesch, Grindelwald, Meiringen, Pontresina, Glarus, Les Collons, Zermatt, Urnasch and La Fouly.

Maps

Map references are given at the head of each route in this Guide, using the following abbreviations: M = **Michelin** Maps 216, 217, 218 and 219 (their most recent numeration) at 1:200,000; or BL = **Landeskarten der Schweiz** 26–48 at 1:100,000, published by the *Bundesamt für Landestopographie* (the equivalent of the British Ordnance Survey). In many regions the latter are supplemented by a new series at 1:50,000 which have been given a four-figure number beginning with 5, e.g. 5001, referring to the first sheet of some 20 so far published; in due course this series will cover the country (see below).

Travellers are advised to obtain in advance at least one of the following maps for general tour planning: *Michelin's* Switzerland (427) at 1.400,000; *Kümmerly & Frey's* Switzerland at the same scale; the *BL* Generalkarte der Schweiz at 1:300,000 (rather small print); *Orell Füssli's* Schweiz (same scale); or the *Hallwag* Switzerland at 1:303,000, among others. Also convenient is the *Kümmerly & Frey* map in *Atlas* form together with 35 town plans and index at 1:301,000 (unfortunately the town centre is frequently virtually hidden in the gutter of the double-page opening).

The *Michelin* 989 (France) is useful for those driving from the Channel ports to Switzerland.

The BL also publish several other series, covering the country: at 1:200,000, in four maps in a plastic folder; and among those at 1:50,000 some marked 'S' showing ski routes, and others marked 'T' showing pedestrian itineraries; and a series at 1:25,000. Among more specialised maps published by BL, which the traveller may well find of help in pinning down specific buildings and sites, are the *Karte der Kulturgüter* (at 1:300,000, containing 110 town or area plans on 48 pp), or—more detailed—the *Burgenkarte der Schweiz* or *Carte des Châteaux de la Suisse* (at 1:200,000 in four folders; unfortunately some of the booklets accompanying them are 'perfect bound' and tend to fall apart if used much); and a *Museumskarte der Schweiz* (1:300,000, showing the position of museums in the country and in the main towns).

The address of BL, the Bundesamt für Landestopographie (Office fédéral de topographie, or Ufficio federale di topografia) is simply 3084 Wabern (a S suburb of Berne, a few paces before the terminus of the No. 9 tram).

Kümmerly & Frey produce a series of *Hiking maps* (*Wanderkarte*), most of them either at 1:25,000 or 1:50,000; they also produce a *Rail-Map* (including funiculars, etc.) and a series of *Velokarte*, or *Cycling maps*. The same firm publish a '*Grand Atlas*' of the country and several town plans. *Orell Füssli* also publish town plans. Liechtenstein produce their own *Wanderkarte* at 1:50,000.

Many tourist offices will supply gratis local town plans of varying quality; most of them are some form of commercial publicity.

Most of the cartographical material listed above may be obtained at the better bookshops in Switzerland, together with those of a more specialised nature. The general maps listed should be available, or may be ordered, through

Stanfords, 12–14 Long Acre, London WC2; the AA, Fanum House, Leicester Square, London WC1, etc. Michelin maps may also be obtained from the Michelin Tyre Co. Ltd, Davy House, Lion Road, Harrow, Middx HA1 2DQ.

Bibliography

The number of books in English on Switzerland is large and the very brief list below (containing a few titles in French and German) does not pretend to be more than a compilation of works which may be useful for reference or in providing general background. Most of the volumes have been published within recent decades; if not the date of their first edition is given in brackets. Most contain comprehensive bibliographies for further reading. Some practical books are listed at the end of the introductory articles on Mountaineering and Natural History.

Topography and General: Murray's Hand-Book for Travellers in Switzerland (1838), reprinted 1970; W.A.B. Coolidge, Swiss Travel and Swiss Guide-Books (1889), The Alps in Nature and History (1908); James F. Muirhead, A Wayfarer in Switzerland (3rd ed. 1930); Arnold Lunn, Switzerland, her Topographical, Historical, and Literary Landmarks (1928), among several other works of unequal merit by the same author; Sir Gavin de Beer, Early Travellers in the Alps (1930), Alps and Men (1932; reprinted 1966), Travellers in Switzerland (1949); Speaking of Switzerland (1952); John Russell, Switzerland (1950; rev. ed. 1962); Edward Pyatt, The Passage of the Alps; Jonathan Steinberg, Why Switzerland?; Llewellyn Powys, Swiss Essays (1947); Samuel Butler, Alps and Sanctuaries of Piedmont and the Canton Ticino (1881); Christopher Herold, The Swiss without Halos (1948); John Wraight, The Swiss and the British (1987).

Mountaineering, etc. Ronald W. Clark, The Early Alpine Guides (1949); Claire E. Engel, Mountaineering in the Alps: an historical survey (rev. ed. 1971); V.H. Green, The Swiss Alps (1961); Martin Conway, The Alps from End to End (1895); John Tyndall, The Glaciers of the Alps (1871); A.F. Mummery, My Climbs in the Alps and Caucasus (reprinted 1947); Edward Whymper, Scrambles among the Alps in the years 1860–69 (1871 reprinted 1982); Leslie Stephen, The Playground of Europe (1871); Douglas Freshfield, Below the Snow Line (1923); J.D. Forbes, Travels through the Alps (2nd ed. 1900): A.G. Girdlestone, High Alps without Guides (1870); J.E. Tyler, The Alpine Passes (962–1250) (1930); Gerald Seligman, Snow Structure and Ski Fields (1936; reprinted 1962); Francis Gribble, The Early Mountaineers (1899); Claude Schuster, Men, Women, and Mountains (1931); Brian Spencer, Walking in the Alps; Geoffrey Winthrop Young, On High Hills (1927) and several works by Frank S. Smythe.

Among earlier works are: William Coxe, Travels in Switzerland (1791), Sketches of the natural, civil and political state of Switzerland (1779); T. Martyn, Sketch of a Tour through Switzerland (1737); Dorothy Wordsworth, Journal of a Tour on the Continent (1820; new ed. 1952); F.A. Pottle (ed.), Boswell on the Grand Tour: Germany and Switzerland, 1764 (1953); James Fenimore Cooper, Excursions in Switzerland (1836); Major Cockburn, Swiss Scenery (1820); William Beattie, Switzerland, illustrated by W.H. Bartlett (1835); W. Brockedon, Illustrations of the Passes of the Alps (1828), and Journal of Excursions in the Alps (1845). The first general guide to the country of any consequence was Johann Gottfried

Ebel's *Manuel du Voyageur en Suisse* (1805).

History: E. Bonjour, H.S. Offler, and G.R. Potter, *A Short History of Switzerland* (1952; rev. ed. 1954): Christopher Hughes, *Switzerland* (Nations of the Modern World); George Soloveytchick, *Switzerland in Perspective* (1954); Ludwig Pauli, *The Alps: Archaeology and Early History*; M.D. Hottinger, *The stories of Basel, Berne and Zürich* (Medieval Towns series, 1933; reprinted 1970); George Slocombe, *A mirror to Geneva*; E.W. Monter, *Calvin's Geneva*; P.G. Bietenholz, *Basle and France in the 16C*; J.M. Clark, *The Abbey of St. Gall as a centre of Literature and Art* (1926); M. Luck, *A History of Switzerland*; K.D. McCrae, *Conflict and Compromise*; G. Thurer, *Free and Swiss*; W. Martin, *Switzerland from Roman Times*.

Art and Architecture: Hans Jenny, *Kunstführer durch die Schweiz* (vol. 1, 6th ed. 1971; vol. 2, 5th ed. 1976; and vol. 3, 5th ed. 1982), published by Bucher-Verlag, who also publish several separate volumes covering specific cantons or districts; the *Gesellschaft für Schweizerische Kunstgeschichte*, Berne, issue a number of their descriptive booklets in English, and they have also contributed to the production of the *Karte der Kulturgüter* (see Maps, above).

Miscellaneous: C.E. Engel, *La Literature Alpestre en France et en Angleterre aux XVIIIe et XIXe siècles*; John McPhee, *The Swiss Army*; C.J. Allen, *Switzerland's Amazing Railways*.

PRACTICAL INFORMATION

Formalities and Currency

Passports are necessary for all British and American travellers entering Switzerland. Citizens of these countries do not require a visa. *European Community passports* are issued at the Passport Office, Clive House, Petty France, London SW1, and from certain provincial offices, or may be obtained for an additional fee through tourist agencies. *British Visitors' Passports* (valid one year), available from Post Offices in the UK, are also accepted.

Custom House. Except for travellers by air, who have to pass customs at the airport of arrival, or those travelling by international expresses, where their luggage is examined in the train, luggage is still liable to be scrutinised at the frontier (apart from intermediate frontiers). Provided that dutiable articles are declared, bonafide travellers will find the Swiss customs authorities are courteous and reasonable. Check in advance with Swiss Consulates or Tourist Offices for the latest regulations on the importation of firearms.

Embassies and Consulates in Switzerland. *British*, Thunstrasse 50, 3005 Berne, with Consulate-Generals at 37/39 Rue de Vermont, 1211 Geneva 20 and Dufourstrasse 56, 8008 Zürich. *Ireland*, Eigerstrasse 71, Berne; *Australia*, Alpenstrasse 29, Berne; *Canada*, Kirchenfeldstrasse 88, Berne; *South Africa*, Jungfraustrasse 1, Berne; and *USA*, Jubiläumsstrasse 93, Berne.

There are **Swiss Embassies** at 16–18 Montagu Place, *London* W1H 2BQ, with a Consulate-General at Sunley Bldg, Piccadilly Plaza, *Manchester* M1 4BH; and at 6 Ailesbury Rd, *Dublin* 4.

Medical advice. British travellers should check in advance with the DHSS with regard to health cover under form E111. There is *no* state medical health service in Switzerland, and medical treatment—which is expensive—must be paid for. It is advisable to take out some suitable form of *Insurance*, which is often an optional extra with any visit organised through a travel agent, from whom special winter-sporting policies are also obtainable.

Currency Regulations. There are no restrictions on the amount of sterling the traveller may take out of Great Britain, nor any limit to the amount of foreign currency which may be brought into and taken out of Switzerland by bonafide travellers, although other regulations may be in force in surrounding countries. The intricacies of 'numbered accounts' and similar banking facilities are beyond the scope of this Guide.

Money. The monetary unit is the Swiss *Franc*, which is divided into 100 *Centimes* (also known as *Rappen* in German-speaking Switzerland). Coins issued by the Swiss National Bank are of 5, 10, 20, and 50 centimes (or rather a ½Fr.), and 1, 2, and 5 Fr.; and notes of 10, 20, 50, 100, 500, and 1000 Fr.

Exchange (*Wechsel*). Banks are normally open from 8.30–16.30 from

SWITZERLAND
Main road and rail routes

▬▬▬▬▬ Motorways	⊙ Cantonal capitals
━━━━━ Main roads	○ Towns
▪▪▪▪▪▪ Roads with postal bus service	≍ Pass
━━━━━ Railway lines	✈ International Airports

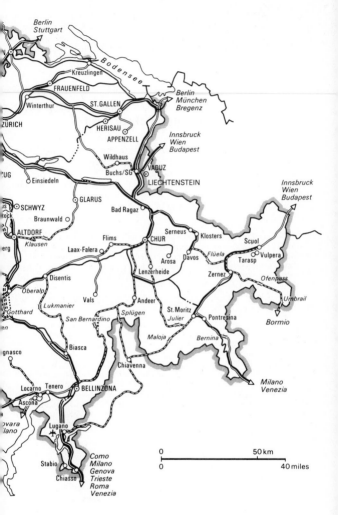

SNTO

Mon. to Fri. Facilities are also available at the main railway-stations and airports at other times and at weekends, but it is advisable to obtain a sufficient supply of Swiss change for incidental expenses before leaving home, and of other currencies to cover expenses en route.

Approaches to Switzerland; transport and motoring in Switzerland

Tourist Information. General information may be obtained gratis from the *Swiss National Tourist Office* (SNTO), Swiss Centre, 1 New Coventry Street, London W1V 8EE (between Picadilly Circus and Leicester Square). They can provide information on (but do not book) accommodation, entertainment, festivals, winter sports, transportation, Swiss Holiday Cards, and on all other forms of tickets available; they are unusually efficient.

The SNTO (head office: Bellariastrasse 38, CH-8027 *Zürich*) has branches in the *USA*, at Swiss Centre, 608 Fifth Ave, New York, NY 10020, 104 South Michigan Ave, Chicago, Illinois 60603, and 250 Stockton Street, San Francisco, CA 94108; in *Canada*, Commerce Court West, Suite No. 2015, Box 215, Toronto, Ontario M5L 1E8; in *Australia*, 203–233 New South Head Road, P.O. Box 82, Edgecliff, Sydney, NSW 2027; and in *South Africa*, c/o Swissair, Swiss House, 86 Main Street, P.O. Box 3866, Johannesburg; and in most important capitals throughout the world.

Switzerland is divided into eleven tourist regions (rather than on a cantonal basis), and each has its **Regional Tourist Office**. Their addresses are: (1, *Graubünden, or Grisons*), Hartbertstrasse 9, 7001 Chur; (2, the *NE, and Liechtenstein*), Bahnhofplatz 1A, 9001 St. Gallen; (3, *Zürich*), Bahnhofbrücke 15, 8023 Zürich; (4, *Central*), Alpenstrasse 1, 6002 Lucerne; (5, the *NW*), Blumenrain 2, 4001 Basle; (6, *Bernese Oberland*), Jungfraustrasse 38, 3800 Interlaken; (7, *Fribourg*, and the *Jura*), 4 Rue de la Carrière, 1703 Fribourg; 9 Rue du Trésor, 2001 Neuchâtel; 12 Pl. de la Gare, 2800 Delémont; and 26 Ave de la Poste, 2740 Moutier; (8, *Geneva and Lac Léman*), Ave Mon Répos 3, 1005 Lausanne; (9, the *Valais*), 15 Rue de Lausanne, 1951 Sion 1; (10, the *Ticino*), Villa Turrita, 6501 Bellinzona; (and 11, *Bernese region*), Im Bahnhof, Postfach 2700, 3001 Berne.

Almost all towns and resorts of any size have an official **Tourist Information Office** (*Verkehrsbüro*, in German), the staffs of which have a far more professional approach to travellers' queries and problems than those in some other European countries, and are almost invariably helpful when their advice is sought on accommodation, transport, local events, times of admission to museums, and general facilities. Some main stations and airports have such offices, with hotel reservation facilities. In most cases they will speak English.

Numerous and frequent **Passenger and Car Ferry Services** operate between England and the Continent. For the latest information on services contact the *Car Ferry Centre*, 53 Grosvenor Gardens, London SW1. *Hovercraft* services may be erratic in adverse weather conditions.

The *British Rail Travel Centre*, Rex House, Lower Regent Street, London SW1, provides travel tickets, sleeping-berth tickets, seat reservations, etc. on Continental as well as British transport services, while *Swiss Federal Railways*, Swiss Centre, New Coventry Street,

London W1V 8EE, can provide full details of the services available, together with their cost, and information on half-fare season tickets; Senior Citizen's (Rail Europe Senior, or RES); Young People's, Student, Group, Family tickets, and Regional Holiday season tickets, etc. See also Swiss Holiday Card, p 63.

TGV (*Trains à Grande Vitesse*) run from Paris (Gare de Lyon) to Geneva and Lausanne. Trains for Basle and Zürich leave from the Gare de l'Est.

Luggage registered through by rail from the UK to stations within Switzerland require a green 'Customs Declaration' form, which may be completed and handed in at the time of registration, obviating the need to make any declaration at the Swiss frontier. A normal amount of luggage may be taken on trains without charge in Switzerland, while heavy baggage can be registered between any two stations, and to destinations of the principal lake-boats, and stops on Post-bus services. There is a standard charge per piece. Special rates are applicable for sports equipment. On the *Post-buses* 50 kg of luggage per passenger are allowed free; excess luggage is transported at the applicable rates.

There are several regular **Bus or Coach** services from the UK to various destinations on the Continent, and details may be obtained from Victoria Coach Station, London SW1, British Rail Travel Centres, etc.

Motorists driving to Switzerland will save much trouble by joining the *Automobile Association* (Fanum House, Basingstoke, Hants RG21 2EA), the *Royal Automobile Club* (83 Pall Mall, London SW1), the *Royal Scottish Automobile Club* (17 Rutland Square, Edinburgh), or the *American Automobile Association* (8111 Gatehouse Road, Falls Church, Virginia 22042), etc. These organisations can provide any necessary documents, as well as information concerning rules of the road abroad, restrictions on caravans and trailers, and arrangements for delivery of spare parts, insurance, etc. The insurance facilities offered by *Europ Assistance* should be considered. Motorists who are not the owners of their vehicle should possess the owner's permit for its use abroad.

The two main Swiss Automobile Associations are the TCS (*Touring Club Suisse/der Schweiz/Svizzero*; affiliated to the A.A.), with its head office at Rue Pierre-Fatio 9, Geneva, and with offices or branches in the main centres; and the ACS (*Automobil-Club der Schweiz*; affiliated to the R.A.C.), at Wasser-werkgasse 39, Berne.

Motorists are advised to equip themselves with a good map; see p54. The most direct and fastest roads from the Channel ports are the following recommended routes. Those preferring to use motorways should note that there are tolls to pay on those of France, Belgium, and Italy, although in Germany they are free. See below for Switzerland.

Motorways (autoroutes) **in France** may be entered near *St. Omer* (E of Boulogne and SE of Calais), and at Dunkerque. These converge not far E of *Arras*, whence the A26 strikes SE to approach *St. Quentin*. It will be continued, by-passing *Reims* and *Troyes* to meet the A31 just W of *Langres*. Hence, depending on one's objective, either the N19 via *Vesoul* and *Belfort* may be followed, and then the D419, to enter Switzerland at *Basle* (for Berne, Lucerne, or Zürich); alternatively, one may fork left just S of Langres onto the D67 via *Gray*, to *Besançon*, and then follow either the N57 to *Pontarlier* (for Lausanne, Geneva or Neuchâtel, for Berne).

Those approaching from *Paris* may follow the A6 SE to *Beaune*, thence the A36 NE to *Besançon* and *Belfort* (or alternatively the main road to the S of *Dole* towards *Pontarlier*). Other roads to *Geneva* are the N5 from *Dijon* and *Poligny*, later crossing the Col de la Savine and Col de la Givrine, to reach Lac Léman near *Nyon*, N of Geneva; or via the Col de la Faucille and Gex, but neither are recommended in winter, when the following are suggested. Until the A40 motorway is completed (which will diverge from the A6 at *Mâcon*, by-pass *Bourg-en-Bresse*, and then veer NE via *Nantua* towards Geneva), one may turn off the A6 at *Tournus* to follow the D975 to *Bourg*, and then the N75. After 20km the N75 meets the N84; turn left for *Nantua*, and just prior to *Bellegarde* take the A40 for *Geneva*.

Another rapid (but expensive) route is the A4 from Paris (which may be joined from the NW at *Reims*), by-passing *Metz*, to approach *Strasbourg*, there following the main road S via *Colmar*, to *Basle*; or alternatively, by crossing the Rhine at Strasbourg, and taking the A5 autobahn S past *Freiburg*.

Travellers entering Switzerland from the SW will follow the N84 from *Lyon*, or the A43 from Lyon to *Chambéry* and *Annecy*, or the main roads running roughly parallel to the latter.

From Germany, one may take either the A5 S from *Frankfurt*; the A81 from *Stuttgart*, later turning off via *Singen* to enter Switzerland at *Schaffhausen*; or from Ulm one may strike S to skirt the E end of the Bodensee by traversing *Bregenz*, there crossing the Rhine for *St. Gallen*, or *Chur*.

From Italy, the main approaches are from *Aosta* to *Martigny* via the *Grand St. Bernard* tunnel; from *Domodóssola* to *Brig* via the *Simplon*; from *Milan* via *Como* for *Lugano*; or from the N end of Lake Como via *Chiavenna* to *St. Moritz*. The Grisons may also be entered from *Merano* at *Müstair*.

From Austria, the most direct approach is by crossing the Rhine between *Bregenz* and *Feldkirch*, while from *Landeck*, the Unter-Engadine may be entered via the Inn valley.

Motoring in Switzerland. The wearing of seat-belts is compulsory in front seats, while children under 12 must be in the back seats. Driving with side lights only is no longer permitted, and the use of headlights, dipped headlights or twin fog-lamps is compulsory in heavy rain or poor visibility. Dipped headlights are obligatory in road tunnels. It is advisable but not compulsory to carry a warning triangle in case of breakdown. The laws concerning speed limits, lighting, and seat-belts, etc. are strictly enforced and police are authorised to collect on-the-spot fines. The speed limit is 50km per hour (31 mph) in built-up areas; 80km per hour (50 mph) on open roads unless otherwise indicated, and 120km per hour (75 mph) on motorways. Restrictions also apply between November and April for vehicles using chains (which may be compulsory), which may be hired on the spot, or studded tyres.

Motorways (*autobahns, autoroutes*, or *autostradas*). In January 1985 the Swiss authorities sensibly introduced a general blanket tax or charge of 30 Swiss Francs on all vehicles (and double for trailers and caravans) using a motorway or limited access highway. This, when considering the contour of the country, and its remarkable network of roads, tunnels, and viaducts, is a negligible imposition. Visitors can pay on entry (at the Customs' point or near by) or in advance from a SNTO. One is then provided with a motorway vignette or sticker, valid from 1 December of the preceding year to 31 January of the one following the year printed on the vignette. There are otherwise no toll roads (except a few private roads), apart from the tunnel below the Grand St. Bernard pass.

The roads in Switzerland are in general very good and well-engineered. Drivers not used to steep gradients should engage a low gear in good time when descending mountain roads. Road sides are marked by coloured posts in all areas likely to require such demarcation during winter snows. Vehicles ascending always have priority, as do Post-buses, on Alpine roads. Black ice may be a hazard.

The sensible baffle-walls flanking motorways when in the vicinity of built-up areas will be noticed, and likewise—particularly in strategic sites—the position of barriers or tank-traps on the road. Not so noticeable, but a fact, is that all bridges and viaducts are also provided with facilities for their destruction at short notice!

A curiosity which briefly baffled the Editor was the frequent sight of several tall posts or sticks clustered together not far from the road-side, and surmounted with cross or angle-bars, until he was enlightened . . . they show the provisional position of a projected building, and are erected first, should there be any complaints!

Parking can often be a problem, although the major centres are provided with a number of sites, both above and below ground. The sign '*Parking reserviert für Cars*' means '*No* Parking', incidentally. Tourist Offices and hotels can advise on the local problem. More patience than usual is required when waiting at semaphores or 'lights' in towns.

Another hazard which motorists (or pedestrians) may well encounter arises from the fertilisation of fields by careful manuring. Unusual stenches sometimes arise but this invigorating application has long been the practice in rural areas: indeed Murray, writing a century and a half ago refers to it in a choice description: 'The drainings of dunghills, cow-houses, and pigsties, are not allowed to run to waste, but are carefully collected in a vat by the farmer, and at a fit moment carried out in carts to the fields, and ladled over them, very much to their benefit, and to the equal disgust of the olfactory nerves of all who pass; the air, far and near, being filled with this truly Swiss fragrance'.

The yellow **Post-Bus** or **postal coach** network in Switzerland is very comprehensive and reliable. There is hardly a hamlet which is not visited by them, and travellers without their own transport are strongly advised to use them—in conjunction with the equally widely-spread network of **railways**—when exploring the country. Branches of the SNTO can provide a **Swiss Holiday Card**. This document (for which your passport number is required) makes possible—at a considerable saving and without buying numerous separate tickets—travel around the country on railways, post-buses and lake-boats.

All that is necessary, or at least preferable, is to book in advance on post-buses, which is done simply and at no extra charge through any Post Office or Railway Station. This document also enables one to use many funiculars and cableways at discounts of up to 50 per cent. They are available for 4, 8 and 15-day periods, or for one month. They may also be purchased from most travel agents, British Rail Travel Centres, at the railway information offices at Zürich and Geneva airports, and at Swiss border stations. Children from 6–16 travel at half-price. Holiday season tickets or weekly season tickets are also available on the post-buses. Season tickets are usually available for most lake-boats.

Travellers staying any length of time in one of the major cities should enquire at the Tourist Office about any tourist or season tickets available for local transport. There are also various automatic *ticket-vending machines*, for which small change is required, for they do not normally give change. It is essential to obtain a ticket prior to entering a bus or tram, and have it punched on the machine provided, otherwise an on-the-spot fine may be incurred.

Tourist Offices can also advise on the availability of seasonal ski-passes for funiculars, cable-ways, ski-lifts, etc., if the particular resort is specified.

This Guide gives only an indication of the facilities available in numerous areas, and the particular form of 'lift' is not always specified; up-to-date information may be obtained at the resort concerned. Apart from several cog-wheel or rack-and-pinion railways mounting to considerable heights (such as to the Jungfraujoch, or Gornergrat), the following are in operation:

English	French	German	Italian
Funicular	Funiculaire	Bergbahn	Funicolare
Cableway	Téléphérique	Luftseilbahn	Funivia
Gondola	Télécabine	Gondelbahn	Telecabina
Chair-lift	Télésiège	Sesselbahn	Seggiovia
Ski-lift	Téléski	Skilift	Sciovia

Mountain Passes. Several of the routes described in this Guide are impassable during winter months, and during. this period it is advisable to check in advance on the condition of the roads concerned. *The major passes listed below are likely to be* **closed** *at any time during the months of November to May/June,* as are a number of minor passes not listed. High passes normally kept open throughout the year, though chains or studded tyres may be required, are the *Bernina, Flüela, Julier, Ofen,* and *Simplon.* Vehicles may also be transported on car-carrying railway lines through the following tunnels: *Lötschberg* (Kandersteg–Brig); *Simplon* (Brig–Domodóssola); and *Furka* (Oberwald–Realp); for details of services available and their cost, enquire at stations or tourist offices.

The name of the pass is first given, followed by the total distance in kilometres of the ascent and descent and the maximum height in metres. The *Grand St. Bernard, San Bernardino,* and *St. Gotthard* now have **road tunnels** below them, enabling communication to be maintained on these three routes.

Albula (Tiefencastel–La Punt)	23	2312
Furka (Gletsch–Andermatt)	28	1778
Grand St. Bernard (Martigny–Aosta)	79	2469
Grimsel (Meiringen–Gletsch)	33	2165
Klausen (Altdorf–Glarus)	47	1948
Lukmanier (Disentis–Biasca)	48	1916
Marchairuz (Le Brassus–Rolle)	18	1447
Nefenen (Ulrichen–Airolo)	36	2478
Oberalp (Andermatt–Disentis)	32	2074
San Bernardino (Hinterrhein–Mesocco)	32	2065
St. Gotthard (Andermatt–Airolo)	27	2108
Splügen (Splügen–Chiavenna)	39	2113
Susten (Meiringen–Wassen)	46	2224
Umbrail (Val Müstair–Bormio)	33	2501

Regular **Air Services** between Great Britain and Switzerland are maintained by **Swissair**, working in conjunction with **British Airways**. Full information regarding flights from London (Heathrow) to Geneva, Basle/Mulhouse, and Zürich airports may be obtained from *Swissair,* Swiss Centre, 3 New Coventry Street, London W1V 4BJ, and from

British Airways, 75 Regent Street, London W1. There are also direct flights from Manchester and Dublin (also with *Aer Lingus*) to the three main Swiss airports. Apart from First Class, Business Class, and Economy Class fares, there are a variety of 'Eurobudget', Excursion, Pex, and Apex fares available.

Dan-Air provide a service from Gatwick to Berne and Zürich.

Swissair have offices at The Rotunda, New Street, *Birmingham*; 78 Vincent Street, *Glasgow*; 12 John Dalton Street, *Manchester*; and 54 Dawson Street, *Dublin*.

The main offices of Swissair in Switzerland are at Bundesbahnhof, *Basle*; Hauptbahnhof, *Berne*; Gare de Cornavin, *Geneva*; and Hauptbahnhof and Bahnhofstrasse 27, *Zürich*, with their Head Office at Zürich airport.

In the USA they have offices at Atlanta, Boston, Chicago, Dallas, Hartford (Connecticut), Houston, Los Angeles, Miami, Minneapolis, Clifton (NJ), New York, Philadelphia, San Francisco and Washington DC. There are offices in Canada at Montreal and Toronto; and in most important centres in Europe, and elsewhere in the world.

There are bus or train services from airports (*Flughafen* or *Aéroport*) to town terminals, and vice versa, while taxis will also meet planes, and many car-hire firms have offices at airports. All Swissair booking-offices equipped with world-wide PARS reservation system also have access to HORIS, an electronic Hotel Reservation and Information System.

Apart from internal or domestic flights between the three airports, there are frequent and reliable **train connections** between Basle and Berne, and Zürich airport; between Berne and Geneva, and Zürich airport; between Geneva and Berne, Biel/Bienne, Brig, Fribourg, Gstaad, La Chaux-de-Fonds, Lausanne, Montana/Crans, Montreux, Neuchâtel, Sion, Solothurn, Verbier, Vevey, Villars, Yverdon, and Zermatt; and between Zürich airport and Aarau, Arosa, Baden, Basle, Bellinzona, Berne, Biele/Bienne, Brig, Chur, Davos, Engelberg, Fribourg, Grindelwald, Interlaken, Lenk, Locarno, Lugano, Lucerne, Neuchâtel, Olten, St. Gallen, St. Moritz, Schaffhausen, Solothurn, Thun, Wengen, Winterthur, and Zug.

Geneva airport was linked directly to the rail network in 1987.

Apply at offices of *Swissair* for detailed information about fare reductions for infants, children, young people, group travel, etc., and likewise concerning flights during the winter-sports season. They can advise on the forwarding of luggage, insurance, etc.

Among the several **Travel Agents** with specific experience of Switzerland are *Kuoni Travel Ltd*, Dorking, Surrey RH5 4AZ (0306 885044), and *Swiss Travel Service Ltd*, Bridge House, Ware, Herts SG12 9DE (0920 3971), with an office at 54 Ebury Street, London SW1 for personal callers. The *Ski Club of Great Britain*, 118 Eaton Square, London SW1W 9AF (01-235 1038) is also able to provide Club flights, etc.

Among advantages of travelling by plane and rail is the ability to forward luggage from Basle, Zürich and Geneva airports for a comparatively small fee per piece, knowing that it will be delivered safely and on time. Those returning from holiday may use the same facilities from c 100 Swiss railway and postal-coach stations to their flight destination.

For more detailed information with regard to these and all other services and facilities available, do not hesitate to enquire at a SNTO.

Postal and Other Services

Most **Post Offices** are open from 7.30–12.00 and 13.45–18.00 from Mon. to Fri; on Sat. they close at 11.00 except for a few main offices in the cities, where they will close later. Facilities are usually available at main stations, and at airports. Correspondence marked 'Poste Restante' or 'Postlagernd' (to be called for) may be addressed to any post office (giving the postal district when applicable), and it is handed to the addressee on proof of identity (passport preferable). The sender's name should be written on the back of the envelope.

The main post offices in the principal cities are:

Postpassage 5, 4051 Basle	Bahnhofplatz 3, 6003 Lucerne
Schanzenpost, 3001 Berne	Via della Posta, 6900 Lugano
Hauptpost, 7000 Chur	Gare, 2000 Neuchâtel
Ave Tivoli 3, 1700 Fribourg	Bahnhofplatz 5, 9000 St. Gallen
18 Rue du Mont-Blanc, 1201 Geneva	Pl. de la Gare, 1950 Sion
Marktgasse 1, 3800 Interlaken	Sihlpost, Kasernenstrasse 95–99, 8021 Zürich
Pl. de la Gare, 1003 Lausanne	

Telephones are to be found in post offices, apart from public cabins, etc. All places in Switzerland, and most places elsewhere in Europe, may be reached by automatic STD dialling, and the charges are governed by time and distance bands. There is usually a surcharge on calls made from hotels. A list of essential telephone numbers (bank, insurance company, family, etc.), including area code numbers, should be carried as a precautionary measure.

The following numbers may be dialled for information, etc.:

110 Telegrams; **111** Enquiries about subscribers' numbers within Switzerland, also nearest doctor, chemist, etc.; **114** calls abroad not dialled direct; **117** police in case of emergency; **118** fire; **120** tourist information bulletin and winter snow report; **140** motoring assistance; **161** time; **162** weather report and, in winter, avalanche bulletin; **163** road, pass and general traffic conditions; **191** information on telephoning abroad and foreign subscribers' numbers.

Hotels and Restaurants

Availability of accommodation is not indicated in this Guide, for all forms and categories can be found throughout Switzerland, and National, Regional and local or municipal Tourist Offices can provide lists of hotels, etc. The usual European star system of categorisation is followed, charges varying according to the season. As tourism is such an important part of the economy the general standard of Swiss hotels is high, and the service provided is remarkably good. It is of course advisable to book in advance if intending to visit a town during a festival or festive season, apart from summer or winter-sports resorts, and it is sensible to check in advance the exact situation of the establishment, as it may be further from the centre than expected.

Murray, writing particularly about the canton of Berne a century and a half ago in his 'Hand-Book for Switzerland', remarked that 'the inns, even in the small and remote villages, are patterns of neatness, such as even fastidious travellers may be contented with', and this remains true of accommodation throughout the country. Hotels vary considerably, from quiet family hotels, international 'congress' hotels, those catering for tours and groups, the massive establishments of the later 19C (refurbished and modernised), or those concentrating on providing suitable accommodation for sportsmen, winter or summer. English is spoken in practically all hotels frequented by tourists.

The Swiss Hotel Association publish an annual *Swiss Hotel Guide*, valid from 1 Dec of each year, giving details of all hotels belonging to the Swiss Hotel Association. They also publish special brochures on accommodation for 'Senior Citizens', for the Disabled, One-star budget hotels, and hotels specially suitable for families. These guides may be obtained from a SNTO and from travel agents. Guides for specific areas may be obtained also from Regional Tourist Offices.

Note that a *Hotel garni* offers only bed and breakfast and that establishments listed as 'alcoholfrei' do not sell alcoholic drinks. Travellers preferring a *Gasthof* or *Pension* will find local tourist offices helpful. *Gratuities are now included in hotel bills.*

A department dealing with the complaints of guests may be contacted at the Swiss Hotel Association, Complaints Service, P.O. Box 2657, 3001 Berne.

The SNTOs do *not* make hotel reservations, but can supply a list of agents in the UK representing a proportion of hotels. Accommodation may be booked in advance either direct with a hotel or through a travel agent, or local tourist offices can provide advice on arrival. Some main railway stations and airports have reservation facilities; see p 65. The SNTO can also provide lists of contacts for those wishing to *rent* a chalet, house, flat or furnished apartment; also a *Guide to Swiss Spas, Private Clinics and Sanatoria*, etc., and a list of *Swiss Youth Hostels* (of which there are more than 90). A *Camping Guide* is published by the Swiss Camping and Caravanning Federation and the Swiss Camping Association, and may be purchased from them.

Travellers should acquaint themselves with the hotel's obligations and liabilities, and their own in cases of non-fulfilment of contract.

Restaurants and **Cafés** are found throughout the country (and in the Ticino, '*Grotti*'), except perhaps in the smallest villages, and there is usually someone to hand who can explain the menu to the non-German, French or Italian speaker. The quality of service is usually high, even if occasionally slow. Helpings are often on the large side, and it is quite in order for a couple to request one dish and two plates.

Wines tend to be expensive; travellers should ask for the locally produced wines (*vins du pays, Landweine*, or *offene Weine*), from the vineyards on the N banks of Lacs Léman and Neuchâtel, for example, while the Valais likewise produce several good wines. There is a considerable variety available throughout the country, at a price. The several well-known eaux-de-vie—Kirsch, Williamine, Pfümli, Marc, etc. hardly require commendation. Swiss beer of a lager type is ubiquitous.

Among specialities based on cheese are of course the *Fondue* and *Râclette*, the latter originating in the Valais, consisting of toasted cheese scraped onto a plate and eaten with baked potatoes or bread and gherkins. The basis of the fondue is the cheese of the Emmental, Gruyère, and Vacherin cooked in an earthenware pot kept warm over a heater, into which cubes of bread are dipped. Both are usually tasty and filling. In the Grisons one will find the air-dried beef, or *Bünderfleisch*; while two ubiquitous dishes are the *Berner Platte*, a plate of sausages, ham, bacon (occasionally boiled beef), with Sauerkraut, green beans or potatoes, and the *Rösti* (potatoes which have been boiled, diced, fried and then baked). In Zürich—and elsewhere—*Kalbsbratwurst*, veal sausages, and *geschnetzeltes Kalbsfleisch*, minced veal or calf's liver and cream, will be found on most menus (and in the French-speaking areas as *Émince de Veau*).

Gratuities are included in the bill. Local tourist offices can usually provide a list of local restaurants.

Visiting Churches, Museums, Schlösser or Châteaux

Comparatively few people think of Switzerland as a country of museums, although the recent tour of part of the Thyssen-Bornemisza collection has given the subject of such collections wider publicity. The number of institutions listed in guides to museums approaches 600, but a high proportion are local (*Heimatmuseums*) or municipal museums of comparatively slight general interest, although there are several outstanding exceptions. It need hardly be said that the Editor, although endeavouring to visit most of the important museums of the country, may well have overlooked a few, and would welcome information from those who have been impressed by the quality of others not listed.

Much has been done to modernise and reform the museums of Switzerland: those at Zug, Fribourg, the Museo Civico at Bellinzona, the Rätische Museum at Chur, that in the Ancien-Evêché at Lausanne, the Musée romain at Nyon, that at Avenches, and the Archaeological Museum at Sion are a few which come to mind. The process continues, and some are certainly due for essential attention, while in the last decade or so several important new museums have been inaugurated. In certain cases one has the impression that more money has been lavished on the 'frame' than the 'canvas' deserves, while in other cases the reverse applies. Most museums are *closed on Mondays*; check at local tourist offices for precise opening times for several museums are closed out of season or for refurbishing, or are only open for special exhibitions.

A complete list of museums will be found in the 1984 edition of the 'Schweizer Museumsführer' or 'Guide des musées suisses', published by Verlag Paul Haupt, while a fairly up-to-date list may be found together with the *Museumskarte der Schweiz*, published by the Bundesamt für Landestopographie. A booklet published by the SNTO, 'Ancient Castles and Historic Mansions in Switzerland', has a map at the back showing the approx. position of some 90-odd buildings. Several have been put to commercial use—housing a restaurant or a local museum, etc.

The following short list, partly reflecting the Editor's own judgement and tastes, contains a number of museums, collections and foundations, which should not be overlooked:

Ballenberg (near Brienz): the *Swiss Outdoor Museum* (rural architecture)

Basle: *Antikenmuseum*; *Paper Museum*; *Historisches Museum*; *Kirschgarten collection;* and *Kunstmuseum*

Berne: *Kunstmuseum; Alpine Museum*

La Chaux-de-Fonds: *Horological Museum*

Chur: *Rätisches Museum*

Geneva: *Collection Baur* (Oriental ceramics); *Musee d'art et d'histoire; Horological Museum;* and the *Martin Bodmer Foundation* at Cology

Lucerne: *Transport Museum; Wagner House* (Tribschen)

Lugano: the *Thyssen-Bornemisza collection* at 'Villa Favorita', Castagnola

Neuchâtel: *Musée d'art et d'histoire*

Riggisberg (S of Berne): *Abegg Foundation*

Schaffhausen: *Allerheiligen Museum*

Winterthur: the Oskar Reinhart collection at '*Am Römerholz*', and the *Oskar Reinhart Foundation* in the town centre

Zürich: *Kunsthaus;* the *Landesmuseum; Rietberg Museum* (Oriental antiquities); the *Bührle Foundation; Zunfthaus zur Meisen* (ceramics).

Many Churches and Cathedrals are open most of the day, but by no means all, particularly those of the Protestants. Some of these are closed except during services, when it is difficult to explore, or—as with the *Münster* at Basle, for example—only open during certain fixed hours at the convenience of the ecclesiastical authorities. Much has been done to restore the fabric of churches throughout the country during recent decades, together with the uncovering and touching up of murals and frescoes painted over with whitewash during the period of Protestant iconoclasticism, etc. It is all the more unfortunate that so much was done under the aegis of Albert Knoepfli, for too many buildings have been irretrievably spoilt even if they have been stripped of 'the clutter of piety of three centuries'. The amount of cement used is immeasurable; stonework has had its patina removed, or has been replaced, even if its original mason's marks and dates have been *recarved* on it; sculptures have been replaced by copies; and the addition of new glass, furniture, organ-cases, and other fittings has too often impaired their character. This over-restoration is to be condemned: the work of preservation should be restricted to the *structure* of the buildings concerned, without destroying their atmosphere. As Christopher Hughes has said, the authorities have 'striven for ... boldness, whiteness, decorated with a few choice examples or naïve curiosities (as in a rich man's house of good taste)', and have imposed 'a swissness and unity on buildings', a 'federal style'. One can only hope that more discrimination is used in future.

A torch, and a pair of binoculars, will often be found useful equipment when exploring the darker recesses of churches, etc.

The **Cantons; Demography.** There are now 26 cantons or half-cantons in Switzerland, making up the Confederation. They are listed below in alphabetical order together with their German names, and the year in which they were admitted to the confederation. This is followed by their area in km², their permanent resident population late in 1987, and the name of their capital.

Aargau (1803)	1405	478,000	Aarau
Appenzell (divided 1598)			
Ausser Rhoden (1513)	243	49,600	Herisau
Inner Rhoden (1513)	172	13,200	Appenzell

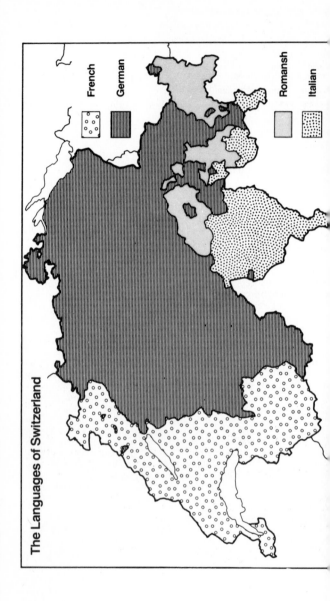

The Languages of Switzerland

French
German
Romansh
Italian

Basle (divided 1833)			
Land (1501)	428	226,900	Liestal
Stadt (1501)	37	192,800	Basle
Berne (1353)	6049	928,000	Berne
Fribourg/Freiburg (1481)	1670	197,200	Fribourg
Geneva/Genf (1815)	282	365,200	Geneva
Glarus (1352)	685	36,700	Glarus
Grisons/Graubünden (1803)	7106	167,100	Chur
Jura (1979)	837	64,800	Delémont
Lucerne (1332)	1492	308,500	Lucerne
Neuchâtel/Neuenburg (1815)	797	157,400	Neuchâtel
St. Gallen (1803)	2014	407,000	St. Gallen
Schaffhausen (1501)	298	70,000	Schaffhausen
Schwyz (1291)	908	104,800	Schwyz
Solothurn (1481)	791	222,400	Solothurn
Thurgau (1803)	1013	194,600	Frauenfeld
Ticino/Tessin (1803)	2811	279,100	Bellinzona
Unterwalden			
Nidwalden (1291)	276	31,500	Stans
Obwalden (1291)	491	27,900	Sarnen
Uri (1291)	1076	33,400	Altdorf
Valais/Wallis (1815)	5226	235,500	Sion
Vaud/Waadt (1803)	3218	556,700	Lausanne
Zug (1352)	239	83,100	Zug
Zürich (1351; actually 1450 or 1452, but backdated)	1729	1,136,700	Zürich

The total area of the country is 41,293km²; or—to make a comparison—half that of the island of Ireland); its maximum extent from N to S is 220km, and from E to W 348km. Its most southerly point is latitude 45°49'8"; its most northerly 47°48'35". Its most westerly point is 5°27'24" longitude E, and its most easterly is 10°29'36".

Switzerland is not usually thought of as a densely populated country, but it has an average of 159 inhabitants per km²; taking into account that large areas are uninhabited, the density increases to 250 per km², unequally spread, with the majority concentrated on the central plateau. But as Bp Burnet noted in 1687, 'Switzerland is extremely full of People, and in several places, in the Villages as well as in the Towns, one sees all the marks he can look for Plenty and Wealth; their Houses and windows are in good Case, the Highways are well maintained, all People are well clothed, and everyone lives at his Ease'.

The first census to cover most of the country (1798) lists ten communities with a population of over 5000 inhabitants: Geneva (24,000), Basle (15,000), Berne (12,000), and Zürich (10,500) leading, and then Lausanne, St. Gallen, Herisau, Altstätten, Schaffhausen, and Fribourg, with La Chaux-de-Fonds nearly approaching this figure. By 1850 the population of Geneva had risen to 31,000; Basle and Berne to 27,000 each, and Lausanne and Zürich to 17,000 each, with St. Gallen, Lucerne, and La Chaux-de-Fonds between 10,000 and 12,000 each. At this date the total population was 2,392,750, of which only 6.4 per cent lived in towns with over 10,000 inhabitants (by 1920 this had risen to 27.6 per cent, and in 1970 to 45.3 per cent). It was not until after its boundaries had been extended in 1893 that Zürich came to the top of the list, where it has since remained.

By 1941 the permanent resident Swiss citizen population had risen to 4,265,700; by 1960 to 5,429,050; and by late 1987 to 6,566,900. It is estimated that 60 per cent of the population live in towns, and less than 4 per cent live above the

1000m altitude line.

Of the total, 65 per cent speak *German*—or rather *Schweizerdeutsch*—as their first language, slightly over 18 per cent speak *French* and almost 10 per cent speak *Italian*; one per cent speaks *Romansch*. (The rest, largely foreigners, speak other languages.)

As far as **Religious confessions** are concerned, the balance is about equal, any recent increase among Roman Catholics being attributed to Italian and Spanish workers, 70 per cent of whom are Catholics. Of Swiss citizens, some 50 per cent are Protestants and 44 per cent Catholics, the latter predominant in the more backward rural areas of the original forest cantons, Appenzell, the Valais, and the Ticino, and in the cantons of Jura, Fribourg, Lucerne, and Zug.

General Information

Climate. The following table gives long-term averages in temperature (celsius) and annual precipitation (in cm).

	Jan	July	year	precip.
Basle	0	18	9	79
Davos	-6	12	3	100
Geneva	0	18	9	93
Lucerne	-1	18	9	115
Lugano	2	21	12	172
Zürich	-1	17	8	112

There are considerable differences in levels of precipitation within a matter of a few kilometres, depending on altitude, etc. For example, Monte Generoso (near Lugano) has 206cm (Lugano itself having 172cm); at Montreux it is 129cm, and 257cm at adjacent Rochers de Naye. Precipitation as snow is of course much heavier at high altitudes, while in certain areas, notably in the Valais and Engadine, there are deep rain shadows. Much rain is brought to the Jura by the W wind; while the warm S wind, the *Föhn*, blows sporadically down the N/S rift (for instance in the Haslital from the Grimselpass during some 79 days a year, and further E, at Altdorf, for 48 days a year), melting the snow and shrinking the glaciers. From the NE blows the biting *Bise*, notable along the axis of the Jura range, to which Geneva is also exposed.

These factors, and its varied relief, provide a multitude of regional microclimates, making it practically impossible to give any accurate description of the Swiss climate in general. Daily weather reports covering some 25 resorts are displayed outside post offices and at all major railway stations, while by dialling 120 and 162 one may obtain snow reports and weather reports, etc.

Glaciers. One of the most characteristic features of Swiss scenery is the Glacier (German *Gletscher, Ferner*; Italian *Ghiacciaio* or *Vedretta*; Romansch *Vadret*), which may be defined as a stream of ice fed by snow falling above the summer snow-level. The size and length of glaciers depend mainly on the extent of their snow-reservoirs and on the amount of snow that falls on these. The snow is gradually formed into ice by pressure, and the plastic ice-mass finds its way down the hollows of easiest channel. It is estimated that there are about 1200 glaciers in the Alps, of which half are within Switzerland.

As it moves the glacier undergoes a perpetual process of destruction and renovation, until its snout or lower end reaches a point where heat conquers cold, and the glacier discharges in a turbid stream of dirty-white or milky colour (due to the fine stone-dust carried down by the glacier).

The hard, granulated snow, on the upper part of a glacier, is known as *Firn* or *Névé*. The breaks or fissures in a glacier are named *Crevasses* or *Schründe*; and, as these are often concealed by treacherous snow-bridges, no one should venture to cross even the most innocent-looking glacier without expert guidance or advice. Roping is generally necessary. *Bergschrund* is the chasm or gulf between the head of the glacier and the snow that remains attached to the rock. *Moraine* is the name of the beds of stone, dirt, and rubbish that accompany most glaciers and disappoint travellers by obscuring the white face of virgin ice that they expect to see. They are divided into *Lateral, Terminal,* and *Medial Moraines,* the last occurring in the middle of large glaciers formed by the junction of two smaller ones. *Sérac* is the term applied to the fantastic crags, obelisks and towers of ice caused by the fractures due to an abrupt change of level. *Glacier Tables* are slabs of rock on pedestals of ice, due to the protection afforded by the rocks against the melting power of the sun. *Glacier Mills (Moulins, Mühlen)* are an exactly opposite phenomenon, caused by the extra heat transmitted by stones or other substances too small to repel the sun's heat. *Roches Moutonnées* are boulders polished by glacier action.

Avalanches (German *Lawinen*) are accumulations of snow precipitated from mountain to valley, either by their own weight or by the loosening effect of the sun's heat. They are often very destructive to both life and property, though this danger has been greatly diminished by the use of barricades and protective works of various kinds. The roar which accompanies their descent is often audible for long distances. Many avalanches have an habitual channel, down which they slide with almost periodic regularity. Few fall between June and October. The blast of air which accompanies them extends their destructive effect to a considerable distance on each side.

The *Staublawinen* or Dust Avalanches consist of loose, fresh-fallen snow, caught up by the wind; they are dangerous from their suddenness and incalculability. The usual spring avalanches, known as *Schlaglawinen* or Stroke Avalanches, are more easily guarded against but more destructive on account of the compact and viscid character of the snow. The *Grundlawinen* or Ground Avalanches are a secondary form of these, bringing down earth and rubbish. The avalanches seen and heard by summer-tourists near Mont Blanc and the Jungfrau are really fragments of glaciers, broken off by the melting power of the sun. An avalanche is frequently set in motion by thunder or other local noise; Swiss guides often request complete silence in passing dangerous spots.

Sports. Mountaineering and hiking, and winter sports, are the subjects of introductory articles. Switzerland is also well provided with facilities for several other sports, and numerous resorts have their own golf-courses, indoor and outdoor swimming-pools, tennis-courts, etc. There are water sports of various forms on many lakes and rivers—sailing, wind-surfing, water-skiing, canoeing, etc. The *Swiss Hotel Guide* (see p 67) indicates those hotels maintaining their own saunas, gym-halls, bowling-alleys, etc. Lists of facilities for hang-gliding, and the whereabouts of riding schools and golf-courses, etc. may be obtained from a SNTO. They can also advise on facilities

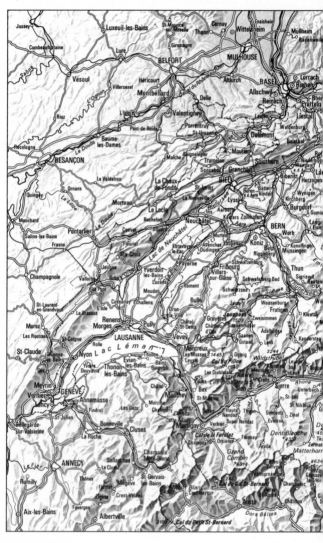

0   10   20   30   40   50 km

SWITZERLAND
General

© KÜMMERLY + FREY, BERN

for fishing and angling, and on the hire of equipment in general, including the hiring of bicycles at stations, etc.

Music Festivals, etc. Travellers planning to take in such festivals as those held in Lucerne, Ascona, Gstaad (or Saanen), Meiringen, Lausanne, Locarno and elsewhere, and jazz festivals at Montreux, Berne, Zürich, etc., should enquire some time in advance from SNTOs about inclusive dates and booking procedures, and are advised to secure accommodation in good time.

The SNTO publish a booklet covering forthcoming events, exhibitions, sporting tournaments and trade fairs—everything from carnivals to wrestling and yodelling contests is included, apart from numerous miscellaneous manifestations of folklore or its commercialisation. Several brochures listing other forms of entertainment are produced by all the main cities and larger centres and resorts, and are readily obtainable at local tourist offices.

Public Holidays. 1 Jan, Good Friday, Easter Monday, Ascension Day, Whit Monday, and 25–26 Dec. Several cantons also observe such dates as 2 Jan, 1 May, Corpus Christi, and 1 Aug (National Day).

Shops and offices are normally open from 8.00–12.00, and from 14.00–17.00 or (shops) 18.00 from Mon. to Fri. Shops may remain open until 16.00 on Sat., but often remain closed on Mon. mornings.

Chemists, which operate a night and Sunday rota system, will when closed display notice giving the address of the nearest one open.

Symbols. The national flag of the Federation is a white cross on a red background, often seen in the form of hanging banners, as are the several flags of the cantons, the colours and symbols of which are ubiquitous in their own territories, whether it be the bear of Berne, the bull of Uri or the ram of Schaffhausen. Shutters and tiled roofs often display the colours of the canton concerned: blue and white for Zug, Zürich and Lucerne; red and white for Solothurn; red, white, and green for Neuchâtel; red and blue for the Ticino, etc.

Clothing. In general, the same clothing should be taken as one would wear in a similar season in Great Britain, but obviously additional sweaters will be needed in the Grisons and Jura, etc. in winter, and after sunset in most high-lying resorts. A windcheater and light raincoat should not be overlooked, and at least one pair of strong walking-shoes. Those taking part in winter-sports or any form of mountaineering are advised to acquire the necessary clothing and equipment in advance, although this can usually be hired on the spot or bought—at a price.

Crossing streets. Care should be taken when crossing streets, particularly those in which trams or streetcars run. There is generally more discipline shown than in some other countries; streets are crossed at street-crossings, and jay-walking is frowned upon.

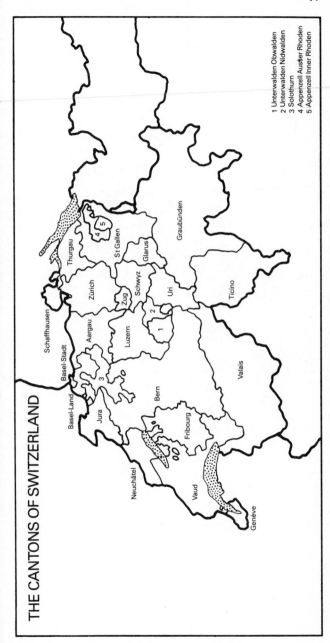

THE CANTONS OF SWITZERLAND

1 Unterwalden Obwalden
2 Unterwalden Nidwalden
3 Solothurn
4 Appenzell Ausser Rhoden
5 Appenzell Inner Rhoden

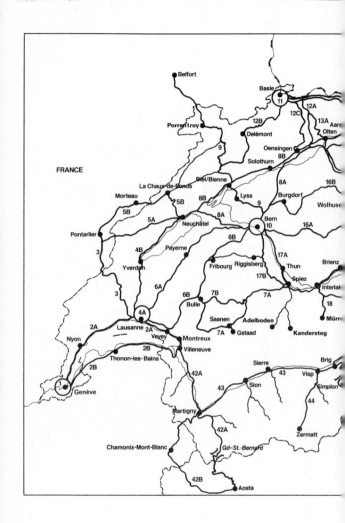

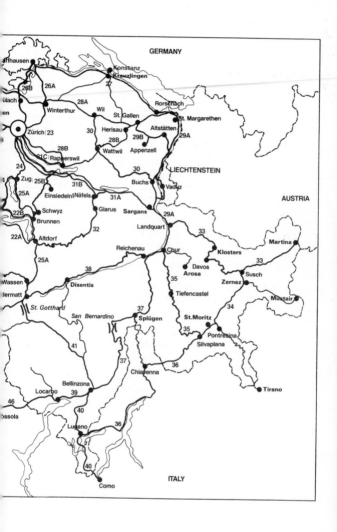

1 Geneva and Environs

Maps: M 217; BL 40.

GENEVA (as anglicised; 375m; 169,000 inhab.; 70,350 in 1880; 29,950 in 1837), *Genève* in French; *Genf* in German; and *Ginevra* in Italian, is finely sited at the SW extremity of Lac Léman. It ranks third in size among the cities of Switzerland, after Zürich and Basle, and is the opulent capital of the small canton of the same name, almost surrounded by French territory. Voltaire scoffed at its diminutive size, claiming that the whole republic would be powdered when he shook his wig! It is now the economic centre of 'La Suisse Romande', French-speaking Switzerland, having long been its cultural and intellectual capital. After the end of the First World War it enjoyed the credit of being the seat of *The League of Nations*, and since 1946 has been that of the European offices of *The United Nations* (also known as ONU), among several other international organisations. Some 54,500 of its inhabitants (35 per cent) are foreigners, most of them in some way connected with these Alliances, Councils, Associations, Bureaux, Centres, Commissions, Federations, Institutes, Leagues, Societies, Unions, and what-have-you, which makes it expensive, and likewise it is the most cosmopolitan and least 'Swiss' of its cities.

Nevertheless, it has several attractions, not least of which is the older town built on a height above the S bank of the Rhône as it issues from the lake, and it contains a number of important museums, while its quays on the right bank command a famous distant view of Mont Blanc. Geneva has been noted since 1587 for its watches, and jewellery, which are still features of its window-displays, while facades fronting the quays ostentatiously advertise banks and in-surance companies. Some would still insinuate, as did the Duc de Choiseul, that 'If you see a Genevan banker leap from a five-storey building, follow him with confidence. You cannot earn at it less than five per cent', which by the time it was repeated by Stendhal had grown to ten per cent; while there is more than a grain of truth in Voltaire's observation that 'There, one calculates, but never laughs'.

The principal railway station is the *Gare de Cornavin*, at the W end of the Rue du Mont-Blanc; the *Gare des Eaux-Vives* lies some distance to the E of the Quai Gén. Guisan. The Airport of *Genève-Cointrin* lies 3.5km NW of the centre, to which it is now connected by rail. Motor-launches, etc. ply on the lake.

Julius Caesar records that *Genava* or *Genua* was the last oppidum of the Allobroges and the nearest to the Helvetian border, and the Roman remains found near the cathedral confirm that it was a place of some importance. It was promoted to the rank of civitas c 300 and the hill was surrounded by a wall, the first of several during its history. It was a bishop's see from the 4C, and later a residence of Burgundian kings, but in 1032 it passed, with the rest of Burgundy, into the hand of the Emperor Conrad II, becoming an imperial city under the local administration of its bishops, who became princes of the Empire in 1162. From the 12C they were constantly feuding with the Counts of Geneva and Dukes of Savoy, a rivalry which the citizens turned to their own advantage, and a party known as the Confederates (*Eidgenossen* or *Eidgenots*, whence possibly Huguenots) made an alliance with the Swiss cantons of Fribourg (1519) and Berne (1526), compelling the Duke of Savoy (whose adherents were derisively known as 'Mamelukes') to recognise the independence of the city (1530). This settlement was emphasised by the adoption of Protestantism in 1535, and Jean Calvin, who first visited it the following year as a guest of Guillaume Farel, and returned to it permanently in 1541, succeeded in establishing a rigid theocracy here. This 'Rome of Protestantism' sheltered many refugees from other countries, among them John Knox. The 'Geneva Confession' (1536) and the 'Geneva Catechism' (1545) were well-known subordinate standards of Calvinist theology. Geneva defrayed the expenses of printing the 'Geneva' or 'Breeches' Bible (1560), the first English version to have numbered verses and to be printed in Roman type, mainly the work of the refugees William Whittingham, Anthony Gilby, and Thomas Sampson. A number of incunables had been printed in Geneva, by Steinshaber, Cruse, Belot, et al, and the city continued to be a great centre of printing and publishing.

But, intolerantly, Calvin brooked no opposition to his severe and stiff-necked rule. In 1543 thirty-one people were executed for 'witchcraft', and Michael Servetus, among others, was tried and burnt (1553) for merely publishing a book contesting Calvin's views. When Calvin died in 1564, he was succeeded by the milder Théodore de Beza (or Bèze; 1519–1605, who died here), but the austere stamp of Calvinism was firmly impressed on the town for several generations.

In 1561 the Venetian envoy to France reported that it was 'full of refugees', and that 'The quantity of money being sent secretly from France to help the French in Geneva, is incalculable'. By 1564 at least 1500 French families had made their home here, and the flow of Huguenots continued, with over 2000 more arriving after the Eve of St Bartholomew (1572); to a large extent they set up the Genevan watch-making industry. The Dukes of Savoy did not surrender Geneva without a struggle, and the frustration of their last *coup-de-main* under Charles-Emmanuel I, known as the '*Escalade*' (11–12 Dec 1602), is still commemorated. There was a further influx of Huguenots after the Revocation of the Edict of Nantes (1685).

Diderot and D'Alembert's 'Encyclopédie' was largely printed here (1777–79), together with several other important works prohibited in France. The French Revolution led to a Genevan version of the Reign of Terror, and the virtual end of its tyrannical oligarchy (although Dickens, in 1846, still referred to its 'insolent little aristocracy'), and in 1798 it was annexed to France, regaining her liberty with the downfall of Napoleon. By the turn of the century M. Pictet of Geneva was translating Maria Edgeworth's 'Practical Education' for his 'Bibliothèque Britannique'. The author visited Geneva in 1820.

Geneva joined the Swiss Confederation in 1814, since when it has become the classic neutral ground for the meeting of international conferences, etc., much to its material advantage. Its old gates were demolished in 1831–41. The '*Red Cross*', adopting as its badge the flag of Switzerland with the colours transposed, dates from the *Geneva Convention* of 1864. The first plenary gathering of the *International* took place here in 1866. Here in 1872 the '*Alabama*' *claim* was settled.

From 1920–46 it was the headquarters of the ineffective *League of Nations*, replaced by the European offices of the *United Nations*, while in 1953 it became the seat of the *Centre européen de recherches nucléaires* (CERN). Also based here are the *World Health Organisation*, the *International Telecommunication Union*, and the *International Labour Organisation*.

Among its numerous distinguished natives were: Jean-Jacques Rousseau (1712–78); Rodolphe Töepffer (1799–1846), author of 'Voyages en zig-zag', and caricaturist; Henri-Frédéric Amiel (1821–81), the diarist and critic; the dramatist Adolphe Appia (1862–1928); and Robert Pinget (1919–). Among artists, Jean-Étienne Liotard (1702–89), Jacques-Laurent Agasse (1767–1849, in London, where he had settled in 1800); François Diday (1802–77); Barthelémy Menn (1815–93); Pierre-Louis De la Rive (1753–1817); Wolfgang-Adam Töepffer (1766–1847); Jean Huber (1721–86); Jean-Pierre Saint-Ours (1752–1809); Jean-Jacques Chalon (1778–1845, in London, where he was known as John); Édouard Castres (1838–1902); and the sculptor James Pradier (1792–1852).

Among others were Isaac Casaubon (1559–1614), the classical scholar, buried in Westminster Abbey; Sir Théodore Turquet de Mayerne (1573–1655), physician to Charles I; Jacques Necker (1732–1804), the financier, and father of Mme de Staël; Horace Benedict de Saussure (1740–99), author of 'Voyages dans les Alps'; Henri Dunant (1828–1910), the philanthropist and founder of the Red Cross; Pyrame de Candolle (1778–1842), the botanist; Sismondi (1773–1842), the political economist and historian; Émile Jacques-Dalcroze (1865–1950), creator

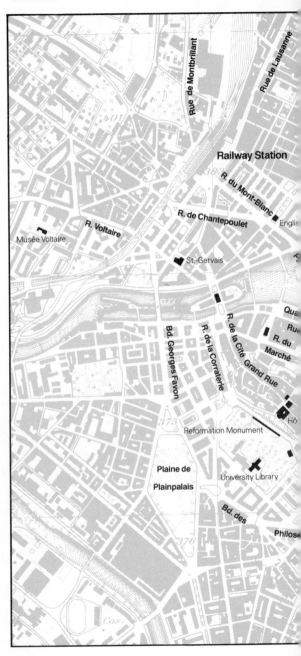

GENEVA

0 m 300

N

Quai Gustave Ador

Jardin Anglais

Rive

R.P. Fatio

Ave Pictet de Rochemont

R. A. Lachenal

Musée d'Art et d'Histoire

Nat. History Museum

Helvétique

Musée

Rte de Malagnou

des Tranchées

blanc

369

372

373.6

378

399

of Eurhythmics; the composers Ernest Bloch (1880–1959), and Frank Martin (1890–1974); and the actor Michel Simon (1895–1975). John Roget, a native of Geneva, was the father of Peter Mark Roget (1779–1869), born in Soho, and author of the 'Thesaurus of English words and phrases' (1852).

Agrippa d'Aubigné (1552–1630) died here, where he had spent the previous decade; also the violinist Rodolphe Kreutzer, in 1831, the Empress Elisabeth of Austria (1837–98; assassinated), and Robert Musil (1880–1942), author of 'The Man without Qualities', having emigrated to Zürich in 1938.

Among residents or visitors were—notably—Voltaire (see p 93), who in 1769 received several visits from Adam Smith; Fynes Moryson, who met Théodore de Beza here in 1595; Milton in 1639; Robert Boyle in 1641, and John Evelyn in 1646, who also visited the learned Giovanni Diotadi here; Francis Godolphin, and Robert Hoblyn, the book-collector, in 1737; Horace Walpole in 1739; Gretry in 1766–67; Dr Charles Burney in 1770; Gibbon; Byron and Shelley (see p 95); Turner, for the first time in 1802 (on the first of several tours in Switzerland between then and 1844); Bonington; Ruskin; Liszt, in 1835, with the Comtesse Marie d'Agoult; George Eliot in 1849–50 (at Rue Pélisserie); Tolstoy in April 1857, who had relatives there; Dostoevsky in 1867–68; Bakunin in 1869–70; Lenin, first in 1904; Joseph Conrad in 1906. Francis Danby, the artist, lived in the vicinity between 1829 and 1841, some of the time at Montalegre; Samuel Egerton Brydges (1762–1837), the bibliographer and editor, lived there from 1818; in 1814 Michael Faraday first visited Switzerland, staying at Geneva with Sir Humphry Davy (1778–1829), who is buried in the Plainpalais Cemetery; William Beckford spent a year and a half here from 1777, when completing his education, and lived in the Vaud during several periods in subsequent years.

In 1792 it was notably full of English, among them Charles Wilkins, the authority on Sanskrit, apart from such social luminaries as Georgiana, Duchess of Devonshire, Lady Henrietta Duncannon, Lady Caroline Ponsonby (later Lady Caroline Lamb), and Mary, Viscountess Palmerston. A later benefactor of the city was Daniel Fitzgerald Pakenham Barton (1850–1907), consul here from 1886–97, who built the Victoria Hall in 1890, founded a cricket club, and introduced the Genevese to the pastime of sailing on Lac Léman; his wife, the eldest daughter of Sir Robert Peel (junior; 1822–95), who had been Chargé d'Affaires in Berne in 1846–50, was a distinguished hostess.

A. The Left Bank, or Vieille Ville

A good general view of the quays may be had from the *Pont du Mont-Blanc*, the longest (260m) and northernmost of several bridges crossing the Rhône, built in 1862 and later widened, also providing a view of the *Ile Rousseau*, with a seated statue of Rousseau by Pradier (1835), connected by a footbridge with the *Pont des Bergues*. In the opposite direction, beyond the yacht basin and the two granite rocks known as the *Pierres du Niton* (one of which was taken as the basis for the triangulation of Switzerland), is the *Jet d'eau*, a fountain occasionally shooting water to a height of some 145m, dating from 1886.

From the S end of the bridge one may turn right, shortly passing near (left) the Pl. du Molard, with a flower-market, and further W the parallel Pl. de la Fusterie, with an 18C church. Beyond the *Pont de la Machine*, we reach the *Ponts de l'Île*, with the *Tour de l'Île* (13C), at the foot of which the patriot Philibert Berthelier was beheaded in 1519. Adjacent is the *Tourist Office*.

Turning S, we cross the Pl. Bel-Air and ascend the Rue de la Cité, which is continued by the Grand-Rue, traversing the **Vieille Ville**, with its numerous dignified 18C houses. No. 24 (1707) in the Rue de la Cité was the home of De Saussure, the savant and mountaineer. In the Rue des Granges, parallel to the S, are several notable 18C mansions, including the *Hôtel de Sellon*, containing the *Comtesse Tatiana Zoubov Foundation*, a collection of objets d'art and furniture, and portraits by Vigée-Lebrun, Gérard, and J.-B. Lampi, father and son, which may be seen on a guided visit.—Further along the street stands *St.-Germain*, rebuilt in the 13C on the site of a much earlier basilica, and restored in 1810.

No. 11 in the Grand-Rue is the *Residence de France*, with an interior courtyard of interest. At No. 13 Ferdinand Hodler had his studio in 1881–1902; while at No. 40 (rebuilt) Rousseau was born, in the house of his grandfather. His 'Émile' was burnt by the public executioner in front of the Hôtel de Ville in 1762.

The **Hôtel de Ville** itself, to the S at the main cross street, is a heavy Renaissance building, largely of 1556–78, in the courtyard of which is a square tower containing a paved ramp instead of a staircase.

In the Salle de l'Alabama, opening off the court, the Alabama Claim was settled in 1872; it contains a portrait of Adm. Winslow, USN, who in 1864 sank the ship. Here too were signed the first two conventions of the Red Cross (in 1864, and 1906, respectively).

To the N is the arcaded *Arsenal* (15–17C; restored), now containing Archives.—A few steps beyond, No. 6 in the Rue du Puits-St.-Pierre is the *Maison Tavel* (13–14C), restored to house collections concerning the history of Geneva formerly in the Musée d'art et d'histoire.—To the left further downhill is the site of Calvin's residence, rebuilt.

A turning to the E leads into the Cour St.-Pierre, overlooked by the *CATHEDRAL*, the history of which is complex. The present edifice was built in 1160–1232, onto the SW corner of which the *Chapelle des Macchabées* was added in 1397–1406 by Card. de Brogny, while the somewhat incongruous neo-Classical W front replaced the Romanesque facade in 1752–56. At the E end are two dissimilar towers, between which is a late 19C spire in the position of an early 16C bell-turret, which had replaced the original spire.

Extensive archaeological excavations were inaugurated in 1976 both in the cathedral itself, and its vicinity, some of which may be made visible to the public by 1987. The first Christian church (late 4C) stood just NW of the present building, while soon after a baptistery was built in what is now the W end of the nave. The original church (or northern cathedral) was then enlarged (42m by 17m) on a basilical plan, while on and just W of the present Maccabean chapel another (southern) cathedral was erected, and the two episcopal sanctuaries were joined by several dependencies. Later, but still during the 6C, sacristies were added to the apse of the southern cathedral, together with a heated room against its S wall, the floor of which was covered with 45 square panels of mosaic paving. The city was destroyed by fire in 500–1 during internecine wars, and a major reconstruction of the episcopal buildings was begun. A new church was erected, with three irregular apses to the E of the first baptistery, on the site of the present nave. This was enlarged at the beginning of the Romanesque period (10–11C), and a circular crypt built, the vault of which was razed about 1160, when work started on the present cathedral under Bp Arducius de Faucigny, a friend of St. Bernard. The chancel was completed by c 1200, and the towers by c 1291. During the medieval period it experienced the usual disastrous fires, that of 1334 also damaging the cloister on its NW side, while the roof was destroyed in 1349, and restored, and serious destruction was caused by a third fire in 1430. Conrad Witz's altarpiece (see p 88–9) embellished the main altar in 1444.

On accepting the Reformation in 1535, it suffered from the proclivities of iconoclasts, following the example of the people of Berne, and little but its bare walls, its clustered columns with their grotesque and other capitals, and happily the stained glass of the chancel, remained; and also the pulpit, from which Farel, Calvin, and Beza preached.

The neo-Classical front, designed by Count Benedetto Alfieri—and looking more like that of a Bourse—later replaced the old facade, which was in danger of collapsing, and the cloisters were swept away, to be replaced by the *Mallet House* (by Blondel; 1721). At the Reformation the Maccabean chapel was turned into a warehouse, and at the end of the 17C into an auditorium for the Academy, and not restored until 1878 in the neo-Gothic taste (after the designs of Viollet-le-Duc), while some buttresses were added to the main fabric of the cathedral in 1890–95.

The few stalls preserved in the S aisle may have been the gift of Florentine merchant bankers in Geneva; the statue of Duc Henri de Rohan, slain at Rheinfelden in 1638, and the leader of the French Protestants in the time of Louis XIII, is a late 19C version of the damaged original. Théodore de Beza was buried in the cloister, as was Agrippa d'Aubigne (the grandfather of Mme de Maintenon), whose tombstone was later moved to the S wall of the cathedral; Émilie de Nassau, the daughter of William of Orange, was also buried here. The Organ is an unfortunate addition of 1965.

A few steps to the SE, opposite the S transept, stands the *Auditoire Calvin*, formerly the church of N.-D.-la-Neuve, itself on the site of a 5C bishop's chapel. Here Calvin lectured, and Knox preached as pastor of the English community in 1554–59.

From near the apse a covered stairway, known as 'Les Degrés de Poule', descends steeply to the Rue de la Fontaine; see below.

From the Cathedral we may ascend to gain the Rue Hôtel de Ville, in which No. 8 is the *Maison Turrettini* (1618), once the residence of Francesco Turrettini (1547–1628), a refugee from Lucca, who founded the Grande Boutique, the biggest Genevan silk company of its time, in 1593. In the courtyard of No. 11 are the remains of the Roman enceinte.

We now reach the characteristic PL. DU BOURG DE FOUR, probably on the site of the Roman forum, and a mediëval market-place. It was perhaps also the site of a Burgundian castle destroyed in 1320.

Hence the Rue de la Fontaine descends to the N to *La Madeleine*, a Gothic church with a Romanesque tower, built on the foundations of an 11C church, itself on a paleo-Christian site.—To the NE the Rue Verdaine descends past (right) the *Palais de Justice* (1706–12), formerly a hospital. 'Amiel' died at No. 15 in 1881.

The Rue des Chaudronniers (at No. 18 in which Étienne Liotard, the portrait-painter, died in 1789) leads E from the Pl. du Bourg de Four to meet the Rue Théodore. A few steps to the left brings one to the *Collège St.-Antoine*, founded by Calvin in 1559, but which soon became the stamping-ground of foreign nobility, causing a pastor to complain a century later of those that came 'in great numbers ... who live in great licence'.—A bridge, crossing high above the Blvd Jacques-Delcroze (formerly Rue des Casemates), connects the Promenade de St.-Antoine (with a sculpture by Henry Moore) with the Rue Charles-Galland, dominated by the white quadrilateral of the **Musée d'Art et d'Histoire** (see below).

By turning right (S) on reaching the Promenade, one may shortly bear right along the old Rue Beauregard to reach (left) the *Athénée*, where exhibitions of contemporary art are held.

In a room of this building was formed the International Committee of the Red Cross (1863), which, although composed of citizens of Geneva, has been officially recognised by all foreign governments.

To the right at Nos 20–22 Rue St.-Léger are the relics of the mid 14C *Hôpital de la Trinité*, with a restored chapel.

To the W, above the NE corner of the Promenade des Bastions, stands the *Palais Eynard*, a neo-Grecian building of 1820, once the property of J.-G. Eynard (1775–1863), the Philhellene; it was acquired by the city in 1891.

Steps (right) descend to the ***Monument de la Réformation** (1909–17), built with funds collected in Protestant countries and designed by Lausanne architects in the form of a 100m-long rampart wall with a narrow moat of water below it.

In the central group are statues (by Paul Landowski, and H. Bouchard) of Calvin, Farel, Beza, and Knox; to the left are Frederick William of Brandenburg, William the Silent, and Adm. Coligny; to the right Roger Williams (minister at Boston in 1631), Cromwell, and Stephen Bocskay, the Hungarian Protestant leader. In the spaces between are low reliefs, depicting the Compact of the Mayflower, and inscriptions. The dates of 1536 and 1602 refer to the formal acceptance of the Reformation and to the Escalade (see p 81). Luther and Zwingli are commemorated merely by detached blocks carved with their names.

To the S, on the far side of the PROMENADE DES BASTIONS, formerly a Botanical Garden, stand the *University Buildings* of 1867–71. The University was reconstituted in 1873, being formerly an Academy, founded by Calvin in 1559. It has some 11,000 students, a third of whom are foreigners, and comprises seven faculties.

The **Library**, accommodated in the SE wing, contains some 1,200,000 volumes, 15,000 MSS; 45,000 prints; and 23,000 maps. On the Ground Floor are two rooms named after Ami Lullin (1695–1756), a benefactor of the library, in which are collections devoted to the Reformation, and to Jean-Jacques Rousseau. The items displayed deserve better presentation.

Numerous MSS, first and early editions, and memorabilia of famous Genevois may be seen; among them a copy of the 'Roman de la Rose' of Guillaume de Lorris and Jean de Meung (mid 14C); the 'Demandes de Charles VI' by Pierre Salmon (1412); Bonivard's Missal (mid 15C), and a Request by Vladimir Oulianoff (Lenin) to become a member of the Société de lecture. Among other bibliographical rarities are a copy of the Geneva Bible of 1560, printed by Rowland Hill; a French Bible (Geneva, 1588) intended for Henri IV, with his arms, but never sent as he had abjured; a copy of the Augsbourg Confession presented to Charles V; and a letter sent by Benjamin Franklin to Horace-Bénédict de Saussure from Passy ten days before the signing of the Treaty of Independence.

In the second room are a Death-mask of Rousseau, modelled by Houdon; a copy of 'Émile' annotated by Voltaire; an autograph MS of the first version of 'The Social Contract'; Rousseau's watch and coffee-pot, etc., and a Portrait of Mme de Staël as Corinne, by Mme Vigée-Lebrun.

A few minutes' walk to the S, off the Blvd des Philosophes, at No. 4 Rue de l' École-de-Chimie is the **Collection Barbier-Müller*, with several fine examples of the art of Africa and Oceania, which will interest the specialist.

The *Musée d'ethnographie* (with good collections from Mexico, Peru, and Colombia, etc.) is at No. 65 Blvd Carl-Vogt, some ten minutes' walk further W, on the far side of the PLAINE DE PLAINPALAIS, a large diamond-shaped open space. The museum has an annexe at No. 7 Chemin Calandrini, in the SE suburb of *Conches*, concentrating on Swiss folk art, etc.

Walking NW from the University Library, we shortly reach the PL. NEUVE, with an equestrian statue of Gén. Dufour (1787–1875), Victor of the 'Sonderbund' war in 1847, and flanked by the *Conservatoire de*

Musique, the *Grand Théâtre* (1879), and adjacent *Musée Rath*, a Classical building now used for temporary exhibitions.—By following the Rue de la Corraterie alongside the last we may regain the Pl. Bel-Air.

B. East of the Vieille Ville

The Rue Charles-Galland is dominated by the ***MUSÉE D'ART ET D'HISTOIRE**, a large quadrilateral erected by Camoletti from 1903 and inaugurated in 1910. Its collections have outgrown the building and several departments have been or will be moved to other sites, such as the *Maison Tavel*, which will be devoted to the history of Geneva. The collection of clocks and watches may be seen at the *Villa de Malagnou*, and ceramics at the *Musée Ariana*. The bulk of the collections will remain in the building, and one is recommended to start a visit by ascending to the First Floor (Paintings) before traversing the rooms devoted to the Decorative Arts (Ground Floor), and, in the Basement, the Classical Antiquities and Archaeological collections.

On the Staircase are several cartoons by *Hodler* depicting 16C Swiss

Konrad Witz, Christ Walking on the Water, with Geneva in the background

mercenaries, and the battles of Marignano, and Morat.—**R401** displays: *Konrad Witz*, Wings of the high altarpiece for the cathedral of Geneva (1444), with Christ walking on the water (the background being the waterfront at Geneva, with the Petit-Salève, the Môle, and in the distance Mont Blanc), and The deliverance of St. Peter, on the reverse of which are, respectively, The Adoration of the Magi, and the donor (the bishop of Geneva) kneeling before the Virgin; *Patinir*, St. Jerome in the desert; *Master of the Female Half-lengths*, Landscape with a hunting scene; *Jan de Flandes*, Beheading of the Baptist; *Corneille de Lyon*, Portrait of Laurent de Normandie; *School of Fontainebleau*, Sabina Popea; *Nicolas de Neufchâtel*, Portrait of Wenzel Jamnitzer, the goldsmith; *Nicolas Régnier*, Card players; Two Savoyards playing a triangle (Dutch; c 1650); *Philippe de Champagne*, The Visitation.—**R402**: *Avercamp*, Winter scene at Isselmuiden; *Wouwerman*, Cavalier; *Fabritius*, Old lady reading the Bible; *Patinir*, Virgin and child in a landscape; *Willem de Poorter*, Vanity; *Gonzales Coques*, The visit; *Nicolas Maes*, Portrait of Mme Adriana Brasser; The spinners (*anon.*; Delft school); *Pourbus the Younger*, Portrait of the Archduke Albrecht of Austria.

*R403: *Jean Étienne Liotard*, Self-portrait of 1749, another with his hand on his throat, and also one laughing; Portraits of Richard Pococke in Turkish costume (1738–9), of Mme d'Épinay, and one presumed to be Mary, Countess of Coventry, née Gunning, Women à la turque.—**R418**: *Maurice Quentin Delatour*, Self-portrait, Portraits of a negro, two of the Abbé Jean-Jacques Huber (one when reading), and Rousseau, and of Mme de Charrière; *Dmitri Levitski*, Portrait of Diderot.—**R417**: *Thomas de Keyser*, Male portrait; *Pieter Brueghel the Younger*, Dance round the Maypole; *Hobbema*, The forest of Haarlem; *Van Ravesteyn*, Portrait of Pieter van Veen with his son.—**R420**: *Fuseli*, Beaufort frightened by the ghost of Gloucester.—**R404**: *Jean-Pierre St.-Ours*, The Olympic Games, and other Classical scenes, Portrait of Louis Herpin and his family, of the enamellist Abraham Lissignol, and of Princess Porcia.—**R405**: *Adam-Wolfgang Töepffer*, Landscapes, Collecting apples, Fishing; also Landscapes by *Pierre Louis De la Rive*.

R406: *Jacques Laurent Agasse*, Equestrian portraits of Lord Heathfield, and Lord Rivers, A negro girl, Two hounds, Leaving Brocket Hall for the hunt, F.S. Audeoud and his horse, Children playing (an almost identical painting is in the Reinhart Foundation at Winterthur), and other works.—**R407**: Mountainscapes by *Alexandre Calame*, and *François Diday*.—**R422**: Numerous pastel *Portraits by *Liotard* including Maria Theresia of Austria and her children, and others by *Joseph Petitot*; and *Houdon*, Busts of Dr Théodore Tronchin, Jacques Necker, and Rousseau (in 1778).—**R421**: *Henriette Rath*, Portrait of J.-B. Isabey; *P.-L. Bouvier*, Portrait of Laline, the engraver, and works by *Daniel Favas*.—**R423** is at present closed.—**R408**: *Corot*, The Moulin de la Galette at Montmartre in 1845, Young bather, Female nude reclining, and other works; *Barthelemy Menn*, Self-portrait, and Landscapes; *Pradier*, Bust of Rousseau.—**R409**: *Ferdinand Hodler*, Young girl, Self-portraits, Portraits of Sophia and Louis Weber, and a Bust of Hodler by *Auguste Rodo*.—**R410** is devoted to Landscapes by *Hodler* and contains furniture by *Josef Hoffmann*.

In **R216** on the GROUND FLOOR are an *anon.* View of the Promenade at Geneva; two Views of Geneva in 1778 by *S. Malgo*; View of Geneva by *Momper the Younger*; and the Forge of La

Jean-Étienne Liotard, Richard Pococke in Turkish Costume

Corraterie, by *John Chalon*.

To the left of the entrance vestibule are rooms devoted to temporary exhibitions. Beyond are those displaying examples of DECORATIVE ART, in **R202** collections of Goldsmiths' work.—**R204**: Arms and Armour, including a Trophy made up of weapons used in the 'Escalade' of 1602.—**RR206–7**: Renaissance furniture and bronzes.—**R209**, a panelled room (1805) from the Château de Cartigny, near Geneva, carved by *Jean Jaquet* (1754–1839).—**R210**, with panelling from the council-chamber of the Tour Baudet in the Hôtel de Ville, and with portraits by *Largillière*, *Nattier*, and *Hoppner* (of Lady Louisa Manners).—Stairs ascend to **R306**, with collections of pewter.—**R305** has late 17C panelling and furniture from Zizers in the Grisons, including the table on which the alliance between Zürich, Berne, and Geneva was signed in 1584. More furniture is displayed in the following rooms, including several poêles or stoves manufactured at Winterthur.—**R302** contains more pewter; from it we descend to **R212**, with late 15C stained glass from the cathedral of Geneva.

R218, to the right of the entrance vestibule: Archaeological collections from Geneva and its vicinity.

Among BASEMENT ROOMS (descend to the right) are **R115**, with fine collections of bronzes, the Treasure of Martigny, and sculptured heads including that of Trajan's father (AD 117); a bust of Alexander Severus (AD 230), and of an anon. matron; collections of glass, glyptics, jewellery, coins, and sarcophagi, among them one decorated with garlands; also Bacchic masks, a stele depicting a repast, and sculptured fragments, etc.—**R114**: Etruscan funerary vases and their supports, including one known as 'de Canosa' (3C BC); also a cult plate of the 6C BC.—**R113**: Greek vases, red- and black-figure ware; a Crater depicting the myth of the Danaides (4C BC); jewellery and diadems, etc.; cameos and intaglios; coins; a marble seated nymph (2C); busts of Hermes and Apollo addorsed, an antique replica; a Cnidian Aphrodite, an antique copy of one by Praxiteles; funerary urns and steles; a crater depicting Hercules strangling the Nemean Lion, c 520 BC, etc.; amphorae; terracotta statuettes; Geometric pottery; Cycladic idols; a Cypriot Centaur, other figurines, and a collection of ceramics.—**R112**: Bronzes from Luristan and ceramics from Iran; bits, etc.; bracelets and pins; a female idol from Amlasch; terracottas; reliefs; bronze and silver figurines from Syria (2000–1000 BC); fard and ungent boxes (Syro-Hittite; 8C BC).—**R111**: Seals and scarabs; cylinder seals; a duck-shaped weight (2000 BC); cuneiform tablets and rolls; amulets, etc. Among recent donations (by M. Jean Pozzi) are a collection of some 330 Islamic miniatures.

The building also houses a Library.

Exhibitions of prints, etc. are occasionally held in the *Cabinet des Estampes*, at No. 5 Promenade du Pin, in the block of buildings immediately to the SW.

SE from this point the Rue St.-Victor bridges the Blvd Helvétique. At No. 2 is the **Petit Palais**, built on the ramparts.

This contains a curious mélange of paintings hanging higgledy-piggledy on the walls of several rooms and passages, labelled after a fashion, belonging to the collection of M. Oscar Ghez. Many are of slender merit, but the collection includes examples of work by Guillaumin, Caillebotte, Monet, Renoir, Cézanne, Foujita, Utrillo, Chagall, Kisling, Van Dongen, Maurice Barraud and Marie Bracquemond.

By walking E along the Rue Charles-Galland from the Musée d'Art et d'Histoire, we pass (left) at No. 23 Rue Lefort—adjacent to the *Russian Church* (1866) with its gilded domes—the *Musée d'Instruments anciens de musique*. This is a remarkable collection assembled by Fritz Ernst, founded in 1927 and acquired by the city and inaugurated in 1969. Most of the c 250 instruments are in perfect condition; they are used in concerts of early music which take place occasionally in the same building.

At No. 8 Rue Munier-Romilly, S of the Rue Charles-Galland, is the **Collection Baur**, a remarkable Oriental collection formed by Alfred

Baur (1865–1951), and opened to the public in 1964. GROUND FLOOR. **RR1–4**: Ceramics of the T'ang (618–906), Sung (960–1279), Tüan (1260–1368), and Ming (1368–1644) periods.—**R5** displays a collection of Jades (17–19Cs), some carved; also carved crystals and hardstone bottles.—**R6** is reserved for temporary exhibitions, and contains reference catalogues of the collection.—FIRST FLOOR. **RR7–9**: Ch'ing (1644–1911) of great variety, and a series of Screens.—**RR10–11**: Japanese ceramics of the Tokugawa (1615–1868) and Meiji (1868–1912) periods, and a collection of short swords and their guards (tsuba); lacquered inrō (boxes); netsuke (pron. netski); glazed stone tea-caddies; tobacco-pipes; etc. Also displayed are a selection of prints and costumes, etc.

By turning left in the Blvd des Tranches, immediately to the E, we approach the crossroads of the Pl. Sturm, on the far side of which stands the **Natural History Museum** (1965), founded in 1820 with earlier collections, and well displayed on four floors, the upper containing fossils and minerals.

Immediately behind is the *Musée de l'horlogerie et de l'émaillerie, housed in the *Villa de Malagnou* since 1972. In addition to an outstanding collection of watches and clocks, the majority of them made in Geneva (by Pierre Duhamel, Jacques Sermand, Barthelemy Soret, Jean Rousseau, et al), échappement mechanisms, chronometers, etc., are rare collections of art nouveau jewellery; boxes by Antoine Tavan; and a reconstruction of a watchmaker's workshop (that of Louis Cottier of Carouge), with his instruments. Notable are an astronomical clock of 1712 by André Millenet, a mechanical pendulum clock of 1711 by J.-M. Labaume, and a clock of 1806 by L.-A. Bréguet.

Among the paintings on enamel and miniature paintings for which Geneva was also well-known, are several remarkable works by *Jean I Petitot* (1607–91), of Mazarin, and Anne of Austria; by *Jacques Bordier* (1616–84); *Jacques Thouron* (1749–89), of Necker; and by *Abraham Constantin* (1785–1855), among many other artists.

In the Rue Adrien-Lachenal, descending from the Pl. Sturm, is the *Maison de Verre* (1932), by Le Corbusier and Pierre Jeanneret. We cross the Carrefour de Rive and the PL. DES EAUX-VIVES, at the far end of which the Rue Versonnex leads left to the Quai Gén.-Guisan, flanked by the *Jardin Anglais*.

C. The Right Bank

This sector of Geneva is of comparatively slight interest and is here divided into two. The S half is described first.

From the W end of the *Pont du Mont-Blanc* the Rue du Mont-Blanc soon passes (right) the *English Church* (1853), containing a monument to Gen. Sir George Thomas Napier (1784–1855; governor of the Cape of Good Hope in 1837–43), among others.—Hence we turn left along the Rue du Cendrier to reach the Pl. St.-Gervais, facing the N side of the *Ponts de l'Île*.—In the Rue du Temple, to the W, stands the *Temple St. Gervais* (open on Sun.), built in the mid 15C, containing a chapel decorated with frescoes and, below the choir, a chapel of Carolingian foundation.

Continuing W, we pass below the railway and ascend the Rue

Voltaire. At the next main junction turn left into the Rue des Délices, on the W side of which is No. 25, the ***Institut et Musée Voltaire** (adm. Mon.–Fri., 14.00–17.00).

The house (1730–35) was bought by Voltaire in 1755 and was his principal residence for the next four years, remaining his property until 1765. The building was acquired by the city in 1929. In 1954 the Institut et Musée Voltaire was officially inaugurated, thanks to the initiative of Theodore Besterman. The *Library* contains some 20,000 books and periodicals and c 2000 MSS by or concerned with François-Marie Arouet de Voltaire (1694–1778), while the *Museum* contains some 275 objects. Among them, apart from MSS, letters and first editions, etc., are *Largillière's* Portrait of Voltaire aged 44; *Jean Huber's* painting of Voltaire getting dressed; Views of Cirey, donated by Nancy Mitford; two of his desks, his watch, and some clothing; the original terracotta statue of him seated, by *Houdon*, and two busts of Voltaire, one taken only a week before his death; also a Portrait of the Marquise Du Châtelet attrib. to *Nattier*. See also *Ferney-Voltaire*, p 95.

D'Alembert spent five weeks here in 1756, his controversial article on Geneva being published in the 7th volume of the Encyclopedia the following year.

The return to the centre may be made by following the Rue de Lyon to the NE and bearing right to pass (left) *Notre-Dame* (1859), just N of which is the main *Railway Station* (Gare de Cornavin); continue downhill to regain the *Pont du Mont-Blanc*.

A few paces to the N is the Quai du Mont-Blanc, from which there is a distant *View* of the Mont Blanc massif (given good visibility; best on clear evenings). It was near here that the Empress Elisabeth of Austria was stabbed to death by the 26-year-old anarchist Luigi Lucheni on 10 September 1898, when walking from the Beau Rivage Hôtel to the steamer quay.—To the left is the Pl. des Alpes, disfigured by a *Monument to Duke Charles II of Brunswick* (1804–73).

Dethroned in 1830 and living exiled in Paris, he moved to Geneva in 1870 on the approach of the Prussians. He left his considerable fortune to the city on condition that a mausoleum would be erected to him in the style of the Tomb of Cansignorio Scaliger in Verona, but the equestrian statue was found to be too heavy to surmount it and stands on a separate pedestal.

The longer walk towards the Pl. des Nations (approached also by buses F. and G. from the Gare de Cornavin) may be followed hence, after passing the new *Casino* (1980), and in the Quai Wilson the *Palais Wilson*, formerly a hotel, which served as the headquarters of the League of Nations from 1920 to 1936; in it took place the Disarmament Conference of 1931. On the terrace wall is a monument to Woodrow Wilson (1856–1924). It is now the *Bureau International d'Éducation*.—The quay ends at the *Parc Mon Repos*, extended by *La Perle du Lac*. Here the *Musée d'Histoire des sciences* is at present closed but may be visited on special request. It contains several scientific instruments invented by H.-B. de Saussure.

Further N is the *Parc Barton*, in which stood the Hôtel d'Angleterre, of great repute in the early 19C.—To the right on reaching the PL. ALBERT-THOMAS, are the massive offices of G.A.T.T. (General Agreement of Tariffs and Trade), installed in the former building (1925) of the International Labour Office, which has since 1973 been accommodated in new buildings some distance W; see below.

Hence we may follow the Ave de la Paix to the W, passing (right) the *Botanical Gardens* and *Conservatoire botanique*, containing an important library and *Herbarium*, etc., and busts and portraits of famous botanists.—On crossing the railway the *Parc Ariana* is reached, and later the PL. DES NATIONS.

The **Palais des Nations** (right) was built for the League of Nations in 1929–36 by a team of international architects, each member state contributing to the cost. It passed to the *United Nations* (ONU or UNO) in 1946 after the last General Assembly in April of that year, and has since been enlarged. Parts of the complex may be visited on a guided tour, when one may see Bas-reliefs by *Eric Gill* in the Lobby of the Council Chamber, an Assembly Hall decorated with paintings by *Édouard Vuillard* and *Maurice Denis*, among others, and the Council Chamber, embellished with murals by *José Maria Sert*. The Library was the gift of John D. Rockefeller, Jnr; it contains the Archives of the League of Nations.

Adjacent to the W is the *Musée Ariana*, containing important collections of Ceramics, both European and Oriental, and with a noteworthy selection of porcelains from Nyon and Geneva (at present closed for reformation). The building, in an Italian Renaissance style, and its contents were bequeathed to the city in 1890 by Gustave Revilliod, and named after his mother, née Ariane de la Rive.

To the N, at No. 18 Chemin de l'Impératrice, approached by the Ave de la Paix (which curves N here), is the *Musée des Suisses à l'étranger*, largely concerned with the exploits of Swiss mercenaries from the 15–19Cs and with other Swiss celebrities abroad.

W of the Ave de la Paix are the buildings of the C.I.C.R. (Comité International de la Croix-Rouge, or *Red Cross*). The offices of the collaborating Ligue des Sociétés des Croix-Rouges lie some distance further S at No. 17 Chemin des Crêts.

To the W are the buildings of the O.M.S. or W.H.O. (Organisation mondiale de la Santé, or *World Health Organisation*), founded in 1948; and to the NW, those of the B.I.T. or I.L.O. (Bureau international du Travail, or *International Labour Organisation*), since 1973. Further W is the seat of the C.O.E. (Conseil oecuménique des Églises, or *World Council of Churches*).

SW of the Pl. des Nations is the building of the O.M.P.I. or W.I.P.O. (Organisation mondiale de la propriété intellectuelle, or *World Intellectual Property Organisation*), and beyond, that of the O.M.M. or W.M.O. (*World Meteorological Organisation*). SE are those of U.I.T. or I.T.U. (*International Telecommunications Union*), and A.E.L.E. (Association européenne de libre-échange).

From a point not far E of the Pl. des Nations, we may turn right off the Ave de France via the Rue de Montbrillant to regain the Gare de Cornavin.

D. Short excursions from Geneva; by car

The Bodmer Foundation and Cologny. From the Quai Gén.-Guisan, we follow the Quai Gustave-Ador NE past the *Jet d'eau* (see p 84), and the *Parc des Eaux-Vives*, with the manor of *La Grange*, and château, built in the mid 18C. This was the home of Marc Lullin, and from 1801 of the Favre family. Louis Favre (1826–79) was the constructor of the Gotthard tunnel. Relics of a Roman villa of the 1–4C were discovered in the park in 1919.—At the PL. DE TRAÎNANT, some distance beyond, turn right and ascend the Rampe de Cologny to the village of *Cologny*. To the right, at No. 19 Route de Guignard, is the ****Bibliotheca Bodmeriana**.

The Martin Bodmer Foundation was opened to the public in 1971, soon after the death of its founder, who over a period of fifty years assembled an imposing collection of MSS and printed material concerning the dissemination of human ideas. Part of the collection may be viewed on Thursdays from 14.00–18.00.

In certain ways it is a collection of literary milestones, or at least items symbolic of their period, including papyri, cylinder seals, and Roman cameos and coins, apart from some 2000 autographs, 300 illuminated MSS, 300 incunables, etc., making a total of some 160,000 items. A selection of some of the most important objects is on display, among them numerous examples of the work of early printers, most of them of historical significance.

Just N of the village is the *Villa Diodati* (1711), where the third canto of 'Childe Harold' was written in 1816, and where Byron was visited by 'Monk' Lewis, and Hobhouse. Below lies the 'crystal face' of Lac Léman which, as Byron noted, sometimes reflects distant Mont Blanc. The house takes its name from Giovanni Diodati (1576–1649), whom Milton visited here (in an earlier building) in 1639, and John Evelyn a few years later.—Further N, at *Montalegre*, stood the Maison Chapuis, the villa in which 'Claire' Clairmont, Shelley, and Mary Godwin were living in 1816, and where the last commenced 'Frankenstein'. Francis Danby later resided here.—For the district beyond, see the last section of Rte 2B.

Carouge. From the Pl. Neuve (see p 87) one may drive S, shortly following the Rue de Carouge to cross the Arve, on the far bank of which is the industrial suburb of *Carouge* (13,100 inhab.), with a centre of Roman origin. It was later in Burgundian hands, and then part of Savoy, and it still retains what has been described as 'a quasi-Italian impress'. Several 18C houses of the planned town are preserved, while the Rue St.-Victor leads S to the Pl. du Temple, with an early 19C Protestant church, and beyond, in the Pl. du Marche, that of *Ste-Croix*, largely of 1777–1824.

C.E.R.N. Just beyond *Meyrin* (18,800 inhab.), 6km W of Geneva, approached by car (or bus X from the Cornavin railway station) via the Rue de la Servette (immediately S of the Gare de Cornavin) and its continuation, is the *Centre Européen de Recherches Nucléaires*, inaugurated in 1955. It may be visited at 9.30 and/or 14.30 on Saturdays only, on application preferably at least ten days in advance.

The villages of *Russin* (8km SW of Meyrin), and *Epeisses*, beyond, on the far bank of the Rhône abutting the frontier, preserve characteristic features.

From *Meyrin*, one may drive NE, shortly crossing the frontier (Customs) to visit **Ferney-Voltaire** (6400 inhab.), where in the much-altered *Château* Voltaire lived from 1758–78, enjoying the social liberty of France together with the political liberty of Geneva. Here in 1764 he was visited by James Boswell, by John Wilkes the following year, and in 1770 by Charles Burney. Voltaire's bedroom and ante-chamber contain their original furniture, and a pastel portrait of Voltaire by *Quentin Delatour*, etc. A disused chapel may be seen, with the inscription 'Deo erexit Voltaire'. In the course of his quarrel with

with the republic of Geneva he set up a rival colony of watchmakers at Ferney; here too he began his series of polemical protests on behalf of the oppressed.—Bearing SE (Customs), we tunnel below the runway of *Geneva Airport*, to approach the Pl. des Nations (see above), descending thence to the Quai Wilson, skirting the W bank of Lac Léman to the Pont du Mont-Blanc.

For the road from Geneva to *Lausanne* and *Montreux*, see Rte 2A; and for that along the *S bank of Lac Léman* to Montreux, Rte 2B, in reverse, and also *Blue Guide France*; likewise for *St.-Claude* (61km NW) and *Chamonix* (83km SE), for which see also Rte 42B.

2   Lac Léman

A. Geneva to Montreux via Ouchy or Lausanne

Total distance, 86km (53 miles). No. 1 14km *Coppet*—9km **Nyon**—27km *Morges*—11km *Ouchy* or **Lausanne**—No. 9 18km **Vevey**—7km **Montreux**.

Maps: M 217; BL 40, 41.

LAC LÉMAN, the Roman *Lacus Lemanus*, or *Lac Genève* (or the *Lake of Geneva*), 372m above sea level and the largest of the Alpine lakes, divides SW Switzerland from French Savoy. Roughly crescent-shaped, with a perimeter of 167km and an area of 581km², its N shore is 72km long, and its greatest breadth (between Rolle and Thonon) is 14km, while its greatest depth is 310m. It is fed by the Rhône, which has dug a distinct channel through its bed, entering at its SE extremity, and with its exit flanked by the quays of Geneva. Its SW horn, known as the *Petit Lac*, is slightly separated from the *Grand Lac* by the bar or strait of Promenthoux (some 3.4km wide), named after a promontory just E of Nyon, opposite which lies Yvoire.

Its water is much bluer than that of other Swiss lakes, and more transparent in winter; its surface is generally calm, but is exposed to violent winds. It is subject to arbitrary fluctuations of level known as *Seiches*, in which the whole mass of water sways rhythmically from shore to shore, a phenomenon apparently caused by sudden changes in the wind and atmospheric pressure. The longitudinal seiches, most marked at Geneva, have lasted over an hour; the transverse seiches usually between 5–10 minutes. Fish found in Lac Léman include lake-trout, Omble-chevalier, and Lotte (on which Rousseau's Julie made a repast, described as 'une espèce de barbeau, assez fade, peu cher, et commun').

Several tours of the lake, or sections of it, may be made during the season from the jetties of Geneva and other lake-ports such as Nyon, Morges, Ouchy, Montreux, etc. Details may be obtained from local tourist offices, who can also provide information on the hire of motor-boats and other craft.

Seen from the lake—here described in a clockwise direction—the N bank is largely covered by the vineyards and orchards of the Vaud, rising to the ridges of the Jura, with the prominent summits of La Dôle (NW of Nyon) and Mont Tendre, due N of Rolle. From near Morges there is a fine view S towards the Mont Blanc massif. On the most northerly arc of the lake lies Ouchy, with Lausanne rising steeply above its quays, beyond which are the slopes of Lavaux, producing some fine wines. On nearing Vevey, Mont Pélerin and Les Pléiades are prominent, while the banks become steeper at the lake's E end, rising abruptly in an amphitheatre of snowy peaks to the Rochers de Naye behind Montreux. Notable feats of engineering are the viaducts of the motorway clinging closely to the rock face high above the lakeside and the Château of Chillon, which is seen to advantage before the motorway descends to the valley floor S of Villeneuve. To the S, W of the Rhône valley rises the seven-peaked massif of the Dents du Midi, while on its E side is the Grand Muveran. W of the alluvial flat through which the Rhône enters the lake—its widely visible course here of a muddy grey, and known as *'La Bataillière'*—rises Le Grammont, and further S is part of the barrier range between the Valais and Savoy. Returning along the S shore, we pass St. Gingolph, the frontier village, SW of which, beyond the quarried cliffs of Meillerie, rises the Dent d'Oche, and inland from Évian-les-Bains, Mont Billiat. After passing the alluvial delta formed by the Dranse, the Château de Ripaille is seen, beyond which is Thonon-les-Bains. Yvoire on its promontory is next reached, before bearing SW to approach Geneva, with the Jura, Mont Salève, and the Voirons rising to the W, S, and SE respectively.

Although the N1 motorway provides the more rapid approach to Lausanne, running roughly parallel to but at some distance inland from the lake-side No. 1, it is the latter which this route follows, as it passes through several places of interest.

Driving due N from Geneva, we shortly diverge right to by-pass *Pregny*, the residence in exile of Leopold III of the Belgians (died 1983), and traverse *Genthod*, with several 18C mansions, among them the home of H.-B. de Saussure, the alpinist (1723; designed by Blondel), and in 1955 that of President Eisenhower. The actors Georges and Ludmilla Pitoëff are buried here. Bronze Age lake-dwellings and Roman relics have been unearthed at (8km) *Versoix*, a village which, when it belonged to France, Choiseul tried to develop as a rival to Geneva. We now imperceptibly enter the canton of Vaud.

6km **Coppet** (pron. Cop-é), a comparatively unspoilt lake-side village with a church of c 1500, is famous for its 18C *Château*, of ancient foundation, a short distance behind the S end of the main street. In 1784 it was purchased by Jacques Necker, Louis XVI's Minister of Finance, and here he lived in retirement from 1790 until his death in 1804. He, his wife Suzanne Churchod (1739–94; born at *Crassier*, 7km W of Nyon), and their daughter Germaine, later Mme de Staël (1766–1818), are all buried in a chapel some distance W of the château. Here, over the years, took place the exacting and seductive philosophical and literary salon constantly attended by Benjamin Constant (from 1794), August Wilhelm von Schlegel (from 1804), Sismondi, Mme Récamier, Chateaubriand, Bonstetten, et al, and here Mme de Staël was visited by Byron in 1816.

From April to October several rooms are open; they contain souvenirs of Mme de Staël, her parents and entourage, together with furniture of the period, including her piano. Among portraits are those of her by *Mme Vigée-Lebrun*, and *Baron Gérard*, of Necker and his wife by *Duplessis*, and of Mme Necker by *Liotard*; the bust of Buffon is by *Houdon*.

To the NW, beyond the French spa of *Divonne-les-Bains*, rises the viewpoint of La Dôle (1677m), the second highest peak of the Swiss Jura, and marking the frontier, which here bears away from the lake.

9km **NYON** (12,850 inhab.; 6050 in 1950), the successor of Roman

Noviodunum, a small lake port, was the birthplace of John William
Fletcher (de la Flechere; 1729–85), vicar of Madeley and a friend of
the Wesleys; and of Alfred Cortot (1877–1962), the pianist. The 16C
Castle, at the NE corner of the upper town and once the seat of the
Bernese 'baillis', is of 12C foundation. It contains a *Collection of
'Porcelaines de Nyon'*, manufactured here between 1781–1811, in-
cluding the remarkably complete 'Queen of Naples' dinner-service,
and a series of pharmacy jars.

A short distance SW in the Rue Maupertius is the *Roman Museum*,
with imaginatively displayed collections of artefacts, inscriptions,
sculptures, mosaics, and architectural elements excavated in the town
and environs, while on the wall of an adjacent building is a trompe
l'oeil perspective drawing of the 1C Basilica which stood on this site.

The line of an Aqueduct has been traced to Divonne, some 10km
SW. The Forum stood further W, on a site now crossed by the Grande
Rue, in which Nos 22 and 24 are notable, near the S end of which
stands *Notre-Dame*, largely 15C.—To the S are 2½ Roman columns set
up on the *Terrace* above the town walls. The terrace commands a good
view, and from it one may descend to the lake side, with (left) the *Tour
César* (10–11C) and (right) the *Lac Léman Museum*, devoted to the
history, natural history, and navigation of the lake, with models of the
former lanteen-sailed fishing-boats, etc.

FROM NYON TO ST. -CERGUE AND LA CURE (20km). The No. 90 leads NW,
after 2km crossing the motorway, 3km beyond which a left-hand turning bears
through *Gingins*, with a château of 1440—from which a steep mountain road
ascends towards the summit of *La Dôle* (see above)—to (4km) the *Abbey of
Bonmont*, the relic of a Cistercian foundation of 1124, its church preserving an
attractive portal.—The main road commences the steep zigzag ascent to St.
-Cergue (1041m), a well-sited little resort on the crest of the Jura, providing a
fine panorama of the Alps, one that Thomas Arnold 'never saw surpassed'.—A
minor road leads E through (6km) *Arzier*, likewise with extensive views, before
descending via *Begnins* towards Lac Léman and regaining the main road at
Rolle.—Another road turns N below Arzier to ascend via *St.-George* to the *Col
du Marchairuz* (1447m), some 7km NE of which rises *Mont Tendre* (1679m),
before climbing down into the *Vallée de Joux* and *Le Brassus*; see Rte 3.—The
main road from St.-Cergue bears W to cross the *Col de la Givrine* (1228m) to reach
(7.5km) the frontier village of *La Cure* (Customs). The massif of *Le Noirmont*
(1568m) rises to the NE of the col, also commanding a splendid view of the
Alps.—*Morez* lies 11km N of La Cure, and *St.-Laurent-en-Grandvaux* 12km
beyond, for which, and for *Champagnole* (22km N of the latter) and *Lons-le-
Saunier* (48km NW), see *Blue Guide France*.

Shortly beyond Nyon we pass (left) the *Château de Prangins* (1723;
briefly occupied by Voltaire in 1755, and by Joseph Bonaparte in
1814). The *Villa Prangins* was the residence of the exiled ex-Emperor
Karl of Austria in 1919–21 before he left for Madeira, where he died
the following year. The mansion of *La Bergerie* was the property of
Prince Louis Napoleon.

The road regains the lakeside after by-passing (left) *Gland*, and later
passes the 18C *Villa Choisi* (where Winston Churchill spent his first
post-war holiday, in 1946) prior to entering (12km) **Rolle**, Roman
Rotulum, with a castle dating from the 13C, rebuilt in the 16C, with
a detached tower of c 1476. Col Henry Bouquet (1719–65), pacifier of
the Red Indians in British America in the 1760s, was a native of Rolle.
On a neighbouring islet stands an obelisk to Gén. César de la Harpe
(1754–1838), a patriot to whom the canton of Vaud owed its independence from Berne (1798). A short distance inland rises the
view-point of the *Signal de Bougy* (707m).

The main road veers E, passing between Rolle and Aubonne several vineyards producing some of the best Vaudois wines, known as *La Côte*; while the view across the lake comprises the gulf of Thonon, the valley of the Dranse d'Abondance, and the snowy head of Mont Blanc peering over the mountains of Chablais; further E appear the rocks of Meillerie and the entrance to the Valais.—5km *Allaman*, with an old castle restored in the style of an 18C château.

3km inland, on higher ground, is seen the pleasant little town of **Aubonne**, crowned by the conspicuous 13C tower of its castle, and (according to Byron) commanding 'by far the fairest view of the Lake of Geneva'. The *Château* was occupied in turn by Baron Jean-Baptiste Tavernier (1605–89), the traveller in Asia and the Orient, and by Adm. Duquesne (1610–88), who has a monument in the 16C church.

Etoy is shortly by-passed; here in 1921 Rilke lived in a former Augustin priory.—At 5km the charming little lakeside village of *St.-Prex*, retaining its ancient defensive entrance-gate, is passed before reaching (5km) **Morges** (13,050 inhab.; 6450 in 1950), a lake port and the ancient *Morgia*. It was the birthplace of the Spanish novelist 'Fernan Caballero' (Cecilia Bohl von Faber; 1796–1877), and the one-time residence of both Paderewski (1860–1941), the Polish statesman and pianist, and Igor Stravinsky (1882–1971).

Its massive square *Castle* (now containing a *Military Museum*) was built in the 12C, and in 1420 was Duc Amadeus VII's refuge from the plague. The adjacent quay provides fine distant views of the Mont Blanc massif and of Lausanne to the E. No. 54 in the parallel Grand-Rue is the 16C *Maison Blanchenay*, containing the local *Musée Alexis Forel*, with collections of paintings and antiquities. The *Hôtel de Ville*, with a staircase-tower of 1520, has a portal of 1682; the *Temple*, at the end of the street, dates from 1770.

Some 2.5km inland rises the 15C castle of *Vufflens*, said to have been founded in the 10C by Queen Bertha. It is an imposing white-brick building with a tall square keep, and four deeply machicolated subsidiary towers.—3km NW is the château of *Chardonney*.

The main road N from Morges leads to (16km) *L'Isle* (660m), with a château of 1696, beyond which it ascends the *Côte de Mont-la-Ville* to (10km) the *Col du Mollendruz* (1180m; views), descending thence to (2km) the cross-road of *Pétra-Félix*, where the left-hand turning leads shortly into the upland *Vallée de Joux*; that to the right descends below the *Dent de Vaulion* to (13.5km) *Romainmôtier* to gain the main road from Vallorbe to Lausanne; see Rte 3.

After 4km the lakeside road by-passes *St.-Sulpice*, with the restored choir, transepts, and belfry of its 11C **Church*. The view hence towards the Dent d'Oche and the Savoy mountains is imposing.—Regaining the main road, we shortly pass (left) the extensive new buildings of the *École Politechnique Fédérale de Lausanne* to meet the junction for the road ascending to the centre of (7km) **Lausanne**, and that continuing to skirt the lake side via the Roman site of *Vidy* to *Ouchy*; see Rte 4.

Beyond Ouchy, we follow the road No. 9, shortly by-passing *Lutry*, with an interesting 16C church and castle with a 17C gateway, and later, *Cully*, the birthplace of the novelist Charles-Ferdinand Ramuz (1878–1947), above which rise the steep vine-clad heights of *Lavaux*. Between *Rivaz* and *St.-Saphorin* stands the *Château de Glérolles*, once the summer retreat of the bishops of Lausanne; Strindberg's son Hans was born in 1884 at *Chexbres*, to the N.

To the NE rises *Mont Pélerin* (1080m); across the lake to the S is the mouth of the Rhône, with the Dents du Midi in the background. We cross the Veveyse and enter (18km) *Vevey*, between which and Chillon is now little more than a continuous succession of hotels and villas, etc., straddled by the motorway.

VEVEY (16,150 inhab.; 13,650 in 1910), Roman *Vibiscum*, a well-sited lake-port at the mouth of the gorge of the Veveyse, commands a fine view of the lake and its mountains. It was described by Victor Hugo as 'white, clean, English, and comfortable', and as a resort many would still find it preferable to others in its vicinity.

Several English Regicides sought refuge here, including Nicholas Love (1608–82), the town refusing to surrender them to the vengeance of Charles II. Edmund Ludlow lived here from 1662 until his death in 1693, placing on his house the inscription (slab now in England) 'Omne solum forti patria, quia Patris'. Andrew Broughton (died 1687), who read the death-sentence to Charles I, is buried in St. Martin's church. The International Brotherhood, the first Russian anarchist organisation, was formed here by Bakunin in 1867.

During both European wars interned British prisoners were hospitably received by the town, and almost 100 are buried here; see below.

The artist Alexandre Calame (1810–64), Ernest Ansermet (1883–1969), the conductor, and Mme de Warens (1700–62), the protectress of Rousseau from 1729–42, were born here, as was John Pentland Mahaffy (1839–1919), the classical scholar and provost of Trinity College, Dublin (in neighbouring Chapponnaire). Sir Roderick Murchison (1792–1871), the geologist, lived here in 1816; it was visited by Hazlitt in 1825; Thackeray wrote part of 'The Newcomes' here; Gogol's 'Dead Souls' was begun here; Arnold Bennett's 'The Card' was written here in 1911; it was the scene of Henry James's 'Daisy Miller'; Elisée Reclus lived here in 1871–3; Sienkiewicz, author of 'Quo Vadis', died here in 1916 (body removed to Warsaw in 1924). Charlie Chaplin (1889–1977) lived at *Corsier*, to the N, from 1952 until his death. He was buried in the cemetery of *St. Maurice* at Corsier; his tomb was soon after desecrated.

Vevey is the scene of occasional 'Fétes des Vignerons', and is reputed for its thin cigars. *Nestlé* have their headquarters here, in a green glass building W of the town.

From the PL. DE LA GARE the Rue des Communaux leads E towards the *Russian Church* with its gilded dome, erected as the gift of Prince Schouvalow. Opposite is the *Musée Jenisch*, described as being 'agreeably promiscuous in its collections'.

Hence one may cross the railway-line and ascend to 12C **St. Martin's**, conspicuous on its terrace, remodelled in 1496 and restored in 1900 and 1932. Here are buried Ludlow and Broughton (see above), with a tablet with a Latin inscription erected by the wife of the former, and adjacent, a more recent tablet to John Phelps, joint-clerk of the court with Broughton, placed by his American descendants.—In the *Cemetery* behind, in secteur 53 (near its upper left-hand corner) are the graves of interned members of British forces who died in Switzerland.

Walking S from the station, we shortly reach the lake-side Grande Place, with its old granary, *La Grenette* (1808), behind which, near the *Theatre*, is the *Auberge de la Clef*, where Rousseau lodged in 1730, while Mme de Warens resided at No. 2 (just to the E, off the Place). The characteristic streets of the older town extend to the E, traversed by the Rue du Lac, leading shortly to the *Hôtel de Ville* of 1710 and *Tour St.-Jacques* (1755), on the site of an earlier chapel. A few paces NW in the Rue Simplon is the *Préfecture* or *Cour du Chantre* (1746); to the E is *Ste-Claire*, a restored chapel founded in 1425.

A few minutes' walk N from Ste-Claire brings one to the *English C*
Saints (1882), in the Route de Blonay. In the village of **Blonay** itself
620m) is its imposing 16C *Château* with a tower of 1175, while not far
road between Vevey and Blonay is the mid 18C château of *Hauteville*
Paul Hindemith (1895–1963) is buried in the graveyard of *St.-Legier-La Ch.*
to the N.

Adjoining Vevey is *La Tour de Peilz*, so-called from its old château
the towers of which were once, according to tradition, roofed with
skins (peilz). Gustave Courbet (1819–77), who sculpted the head of
Liberty on the fountain in the Market-place, died here in exile, but
his remains were removed to Ornans, his birthplace in the French
Jura, in 1919.

On approaching Clarens the road passes near the *Villas Dubochet*,
in one of which died President Paul Kruger (1825–1904), who
provoked the Boer War, while León Gambetta often visited the
neighbouring mid 19C *Château des Crêtes*, supposed to occupy the
site of Rousseau's 'Bosquet de Julie'. Further on at a higher level is
the *Château du Châtelard* (1440).

Clarens, which now merges imperceptibly with Montreux, is
inextricably associated with Rousseau's 'La Nouvelle Héloïse', but as
the author warns us, the scenes he so sentimentally describes are
'grossièrement altérés', and it is vain to attempt to identify them.

Byron briefly visited the place in 1816; Tolstoy made the excursion in May–June
1857, and Tchaikovsky in 1877; Stravinsky lived here in 1911–14, where he was
visited by Diaghilev; Henri Duparc (died 1933) retired here; Henri-Frédéric
Amiel (1821–81), author of 'Journal Intime', is buried in the cemetery.

Late nineteenth century photograph of Montreux

A road zigzags up to (8km) *Les Avants* (968m), a small resort with fields of
narcissi in May, above which one may continue NW to the *Col de Sonloup*
(1149m), or E to the *Col de Jaman* (1512m) below the pointed *Dent de Jaman*
(S; 1875m).

ge *Congress-hall* (1973), the venue of music festivals, etc., is ed on approaching (7km) **MONTREUX** itself (19,700 inhab. with adjoining communes; 17,850 in 1910; 6500 in 1880), a resort which s attracted numerous visitors and residents in the past due to the mildness of its spring and winter climate and its proximity to several ski slopes such as those at *Glion, Caux*, and *Les Avants*, approached without difficulty by cable-car, funicular and rack-and-pinion railway, etc. These lie on the W slope of the massif culminating in the *Rochers de Naye* (2042m). Rainer Maria Rilke (1875–1926) died in the clinic of Valmont at Glion; Oskar Kokoschka (1886–1980) died at Montreux. 'The village of Montreux is prettier in itself and its situation than even Clarens ...', wrote Murray, adding (perhaps with his tongue in his cheek) 'the statistical researches of Sir F. d'Ivernois have shown that Montreux is the place in the world where there is the smallest proportion of deaths and of imprudent marriages'. It has not improved since castigated by John Russell in 1950 as an example of 'with what ease the amenity of nature may be destroyed by the cupidity of man ... a pleasure-resort, with all the deserts of ennui and fatuity which that phrase must evoke'. The modern town, now embellished with several tower blocks, of slight interest in itself, is threaded by the Grand Rue and Ave du Casino. The *Casino*, on a tree-shaded promontory, was inaugurated in 1881, and rebuilt in 1975 after a fire. To the W is the PL. DU MARCHÉ, from which the Rue du Marché leads into the older centre, with the *Musée du Vieux-Montreux* installed in the former Convent of Sâles. *St. Vincent*, at *Les Planches*, dates from 1509. Further E, in the once fashionable suburb of *Territet*, is the *English Church* of *St. John's*.

A picturesque path leads up the *Baye du Montreux* (a rivulet passing through the centre of the town) to the wooded *Gorge of the Chauderon*, beyond which it climbs steeply to *Les Avants*; *Glion* may also be approached hence, or from the suburb of *Veytaux*, inland from Territet, as may *Caux*. Caux, also reached by a steeply climbing road, provides extensive lake and mountain views, including the conical *Dent de Jaman* to the NE.—A path ascends to the *Rochers de Naye* (2042m), commanding a *View which comprises the whole basin of Lac Léman, the Savoy Alps, the chain of Mont Blanc, and the Alps of Berne and the Valais. There is an *Alpine Garden* some few minutes' walk from the station of Rochers de Naye.

The most frequented excursion from Montreux is that to *Chillon*, 3km S of the centre, which is described here; but for the main road S into the *Valais* see Rte 42 and for that along the *S bank of Lac Léman* to Geneva see Rte 2B, below.

On an islet, connected to the shore by a wooden bridge, rise the reddish-brown roofs and conically capped towers of the strategically and picturesquely sited ***Castle of Chillon**, with its water-lapped walls, guarding what is still a narrow passage (with its road and railway) along the lakeside below the sheer mountain slope. In spite of the glamour cast over it by Byron's poem 'The Prisoner of Chillon', it is one of the better preserved medieval castles of Europe. It is often crowded with trippers.

Excavations confirm that it was a Bronze Age and Roman site. It was first mentioned in 1150, when it was held by the counts of Savoy, but it owes its present form mainly to Pierre II (from whom the Savoy in London takes its name), who flourished a century later. It is possible that Master James of St. George, the architect of several castles on the Welsh border, worked here earlier in his career. It was long used as a prison and several early Reformers were mewed up within its walls, among them François Bonivard (1493–1570),

The Castle of Chillon with the Dents du Midi in the background

lay prior of the Cluniac house of St. Victor, near Geneva, who, actively rebelling against the Duke of Savoy, was legitimately seized and confined here in 1530–36. For four years he languished in an underground dungeon, being set free with others when the Bernese captured the castle. Bonivard then became a Protestant, and apparently 'married' four times. Until 1733 it was the residence of the 'baillis de Vevey', and in 1798 passed to the canton of Vaud. It was here too that Julie, the heroine of 'La Nouvelle Héloïse', is described as rescuing one of her children from drowning, afterwards dying from the shock of immersion.

Its fame in literature made it the subject of numerous Romantic lithographs during the 19C, and apart from Byron and Shelley in June 1816 (Byron's name carved on a pillar of Bonivard's prison is a forgery), it was visited by Alexandre Dumas père, Hans Andersen, Hugo, Flaubert, Dickens, et al, during the next three decades (when the chapel was not shown, as it then served as a powder-magazine). The first tram in Switzerland ran between Vevey and Chillon (1888). The building was painstakingly restored by Albert Naef and others from 1892, occasionally over-restoring; in 1903 the moats were cleared. Major repairs had taken place in the late 16C, after damage caused by the earthquake of 1584.

B. Montreux to Geneva via Évian-les-Bains

Total distance, 80km (50 miles). No. 9 for 6km—6km
Porte-du-Sex—No. 21. 9km *St. Gingolph*—N5. 17km
Évian-les-Bains—9km **Thonon-les-Bains**—16km *Douvaine*—17km
Geneva.

Maps: M 217; BL 40, 41.

For sub-routes off the N5 skirting the S shore of Lac Léman, see the
latter part of Rte 130 of *Blue Guide France*; for Lac Léman itself see
Rte 2A, above.

Passing (3km) the **Castle of Chillon** (see above), the road shortly skirts
Villeneuve, Roman *Penneloci*, one of the oldest lakeside towns in spite
of its name, and during the medieval period an important stage on the
road from Italy to Gaul via the Grand St. Bernard pass. It preserves
remains of its walls and a battered 13C church. Romain Rolland lived
here in 1921–38, and Kokoschka was also a one-time resident.

Just S of the town, which lies at the E extremity of the lake, we turn
right off the main road (see Rte 42) to (3km) *Noville*, with a restored
church containing traces of 14C frescoes, which lies on the flat alluvial
estuary of the Rhône, crossed 4km further SW. Ahead is an unattractive view of quarries and cement-works above *Porte du Sex* and
Vouvry, for which, and the road S to *Monthey*, see Rte 42. The former
has an old fort guarding the defile below *Le Grammont* (2172m) and
the *Cornettes des Bises* (2432m), the latter marking the frontier.

We turn right to traverse (5km) *Le Bouveret*, where John Evelyn,
on his return from Italy in 1646, contracted smallpox by turning the
innkeeper's daughter out of her bed and taking her place. The debris
of a gigantic landslip in 563 is still noticeable near the outflow of the
Rhône here. According to Gregory of Tours the landslip overwhelmed
the Roman station of *Tauretunum* and caused the river to overflow in
a destructive flood.

The French border is reached at *St.-Gingolph*, 4km beyond
(Customs).—7km *Meillerie*, a quarry village, was a centre of
Resistance in 1944, when burnt by the Germans. It was the romantic
retreat of St. Preux in Rousseau's 'Le Nouvelle Héloïse' (where St.
Preux and Julie sought refuge in a tempest). Here Byron and Shelley
were in fact overtaken by a storm in 1816, but they were able to make
the harbour at St.-Gingolph. Inland rise the *Pic de Mémises* (1677m),
and beyond, the *Dent d'Oche* (2222m).

The road passes through several lakeside villages to enter (10km)
Évian-les-Bains (6100 inhab.), an old and once fortified town whose
waters have for a long time been internationally famous. 14C
Ste-Marie, W of the *Casino*, has a conspicuous tower, while its
colourful lakeside gardens are attractive. Lausanne may be seen on
the far bank. William Beckford resided here in 1792. The road next
crosses *Amphion-les-Bains*, fashionable under the Second Empire
when frequented by Count Walewski, and after 7km passes a
right-hand turning to the ***Château de Ripaille**, incorporating four of
the seven tall machicolated towers (c 1434) which defended a
residence of Amadeus VIII (1383–1451), the first count to assume the
title of Duke of Savoy, in 1416.

He was elected Pope, as Felix V, although not in orders, by the Council of Basle
in 1439, but he abdicated both dukedom and papacy in 1449. Both he and his

father, Amadeus VII (1360–91; the 'Comte Rouge') died here. The life of
indulgence that he is reputed to have led gave rise to the expression 'faire ripaille'
(to be in clover). The castle was burned by the Swiss in 1589, and until 1793 was
a Carthusian monastery, for which additional buildings were erected.

We shortly enter *Rives*, the lake-side suburb and harbour of **Thonon-
les-Bains** (28,200 inhab.), an attractively situated spa, once the capital
of the Chablais. It was the occasional residence of Kropotkin in the
1880s. In the Grande Rue is a *Church* of 1429, built above a
Romanesque crypt and enlarged in 1698. St. Francis de Sales
preached the Counter-Reformation here in the 1590s. Nearby is the
Musée, of local interest, and further N, a Place on which stood a castle
demolished in 1626.

After 9.5km the main road reaches a junction.

The right-hand turning follows the shore to (6.5km) *Yvoire*, a picturesque walled
village with two gateways and an early 14C waterside castle, there bearing SW
through *Messery*—and opposite Nyon, at the entrance of the Petit Lac—to
approach (13km) the frontier village of **Hermance** (Customs). Its walls were built
by Aymon II de Faucigny after 1247, while the keep dates from 1338; 13C
St.-Georges was rebuilt in 1679. Adjacent is the 15C *Mestral*. Hermance was
incorporated into the canton of Geneva in 1814. Coppet lies on the opposite bank
of the lake here.

The main road continues W, the wooded slopes of the *Voirons* rising
to the S, and the *Grand Signal* (1480m), to (6km) *Douvaine* (French
Customs). The frontier is crossed after c 6km, with the ridge of *Mont
Salève* (1375m) to the S, and to the W the main ridge of the Jura (*Mont
Colomby de Gex*; 1689m). After 3km we bear right to meet the
lakeside road. The left-hand fork at this junction continues SW for 4km
to enter *Cologny* (see Rte 1D) before descending to the main road
skirting Lac Léman to enter the NE suburbs of **Geneva** itself; see Rte
1.

3   Pontarlier to Lausanne via Vallorbe

Total distance, 67km (41 miles). N57 and No. 9. 27km
Vallorbe—12.5km *Croy* (**Romainmôtier** lies 1.5km W)—11.5km
Cossonay—16km **Lausanne**.

Maps: M 217; BL 35, 40, or 5020.

Pontarlier (18,800 Pontissaliens), some 60km SE of *Besançon* (for the
roads hence see *Blue Guide France*) takes its name from *Pons
Ariolicae*, a bridge over the Doubs. Here in 1871, Bourbaki's Army of
the East, under Gén. Clichant, made its last futile stand against the
Prussians before retreating into Switzerland, the subject of several
paintings.

St.-Bénigne, S of the main street, has a Flamboyant portal, but its
facade was reconstructed after a fire in 1736 which ravaged the town.

For the roads from Pontarlier to **Neuchâtel** and on to **Berne** see Rtes 5 and 8A
respectively.

The *Cluse de Pontarlier* is threaded to (4km) the *Fort de Joux* (right).

In 1755 the younger Mirabeau was imprisoned in the old fortress by a 'lettre de
cachet' obtained by his father. He escaped the following year, accompanied by

Mme Thérèse de Monnier. The negro patriot of San Domingo, Toussaint-Louverture (1743–1803) died a prisoner here. Gén. Dupont was held here after his capitulation at Bailen, in Spain, in 1808. The fort was blown up in 1877.

The N57 continues S, passing near (right) the *Lac de St.-Point*, and traverses (14km) *Les Hôpitaux-Neufs* and (2km) *Jougnes*. The frontier (Customs) is 4km further, beneath *Mont d'Or* (right; 1463m).

A new motorway leads due E above the left bank of the Orbe river to meet the N1 between Orbe and Yverdon, providing a rapid approach to Lausanne (and, when the project is completed, to Berne). It is intended to extend the motorway to the NE along the S bank of the Lac de Neuchâtel past Estavayer to meet that section between Murten and Berne; see Rtes 6A and 8A.

A minor road leads in the same direction, traversing (3km) *Ballaigues*, a small resort on a terrace above the Orbe at the foot of extensive pinewoods commanding a view of the Alps. *Mont Suchet* (NE; 1588m) is the highest of several peaks near the frontier ridge which may be ascended hence.

The main road descends to (3km) **Vallorbe** (769m), a small industrial town standing astride the deep valley of the Orbe, the picturesque source of which, c 30 minutes' walk to the W, is in fact the reappearance of the subterranean outflow from Lac Brenet; see below. The town is dominated to the SW by the precipice of the *Dent de Vaulion* (1483m). A *Musée de Fer* has been installed in the 'Grandes Forges' here, in operation since 1495. On crossing the river we make an abrupt turn to the E; see below.

FROM VALLORBE TO (8km) LE PONT, FOR THE VALLÉE DE JOUX OR ROMAINMÔTIER. The road leads W along the steep N bank of the Orbe, rising to the frontier ridge. It climbs above its source below the *Dent de Vaulion*, to skirt the diminutive *Lac Brenet* (right) and then approaches *Le Pont*, a small resort named from the causeway over the channel connecting Lac Brenet to the **Lac de Joux**. The latter extends 8.5km to the SW and is 1.5km wide, the largest lake in the Swiss Jura. It lies between the frontier ridge of *Mont Risoux* and a parallel ridge culminating in *Mont Tendre* (1679m) to the SW.—2km SW lies the hamlet of *L'Abbaye*, where the massive tower of the former Premonstratensian Abbey of *Lac de Joux* (1126–1536) is conspicuous.—The road circles the lake. 4km beyond its far end is *Le Brassus*, a watch-making village being developed as a resort like others on the lake-side (among which is *Le Sentier*, with the *Le Coultre* factory). A road climbs SE from Le Brassus to the *Col du Marchairuz*.—2.5km SE of Le Pont is *Pétra-Félix*, 2km NW of the *Col du Mollendruz*. From the same junction one may turn NE below the *Dent de Vaulion*, which may be ascended hence, through (5km) *Vaulion*, with views to the right, later climbing down to (8.5km) *Romainmôtier*, 1.5km W of *Croy*, on the main route. See below for Croy, and for a description of the abbey-church.

From Vallorbe we follow the right bank of the gorge of the Orbe, with *Le Suchet* (1588m) rising beyond its far bank, shortly passing (left) *Clées*, with its restored 11–12C château, to (12.5km) *Croy*.

1.5km W, in a sequestered valley, lies the village of **Romainmôtier**, with its remarkable •*Priory-church*, founded in the 5C. The present building is essentially a Romanesque work of the 10–11Cs, with a 13C narthex and 14–15C choir. Notable are the huge piers on square bases and its mutilated statues. On its site stood 7th and 8C chapels, while the present church once had a Gothic cloister. The lamps and glass are unfortunate additions.

6km NE of Croy lies **Orbe** (479m), Roman *Urba*, and once the capital of 'Petite Bourgogne'—the name commemorates the ancient duchy of Upper Burgundy. It fell to the house of Savoy and in 1475 was captured by the Swiss after a desperate resistance by the garrison of its castle, of which only the towers now remain. The *Church*, mainly 15C, with a turreted tower (18C), contains fantastic carvings and a monument to Pierre Viret (1511–71), the reformer and a native of Orbe. The *Hôtel de Ville*, by Samuel Jeaneret, dates from 1789.

At *Boscéaz*, 2km N, on the road to Yverdon, several notable 3C *Roman mosaics* may be seen, and at *Mathod*, 4.5km beyond, a late 18C château.—At *Montcherand*, 3km NW of Orbe, the church has a 12C apse containing contemporary murals, restored.

Driving S from Croy, the main road (which may be regained 6km S of Orbe) commands several views of the Alps.—At (6km) *La Sarraz* is a 15–16C castle, founded in the 11C, containing collections of furniture and antiquities. In the chapel of *St.-Antoine* is the *Tomb of François de la Sarraz* (d 1363) surrounded by praying figures of his wife and (armed) children. In dependencies of the castle is an *Equestrian Museum*.

Beyond (5.5km) *Cossonay*, with a large 11th and 15C church, the road climbs down into the valley of the Venoge, from which one may either continue SE to approach (16km) **Lausanne**, or join the N1 motorway (off which the N9 bears SE), depending on which part of the town one is making for (see Rte 4A).

A minor road leads SW from Cossonay via (11.5km) *Vufflens* and (6.5km) *Aubonne* to meet the lakeside road for Geneva at (6km) *Rolle*; see Rte 2A.

4   Lausanne to Neuchâtel

A. Lausanne

Map: BL 5020.

LAUSANNE (485m; 123,700 inhab.; 75,900 in 1930; 29,350 in 1880; 14,100 in 1837), capital of the French-speaking canton of *Vaud* (*Waadt* in German), the fourth largest canton. 'ill-built in a delightful landscape', in the words of Gibbon, it sprawls along the steep and irregular slopes of Mont Jorat, at the foot of which lies the contiguous lakeside resort and port of Ouchy; see below. While it contains comparatively few monuments of great interest, it does provide—when visibility is good—extensive views across Lac Léman, and its commanding site has attracted numerous English and other foreign residents in the past. The TGV train now brings it within 3½ hours of Paris.

Neolithic remains have been excavated at *Vidy* (immediately W of Ouchy). This later became an extensive Gallo-Helvetic settlement (*Lousonna*), which was removed during the late Roman period (?4C) to the more defensible hill where the cathedral now stands. But the importance of Lausanne dates from 590, when Bp Marius transferred his see here from Avenches. It was thereafter identified with the increasing power of the bishops, who became princes of the Empire in 1125. The episcopal territories were overrun in 1536 by the Bernese, who introduced Protestantism, and the bishopric was translated in 1663 to Fribourg. The Bernese continued to control the area until 1798, in spite of the romantic uprising lead by Major Davel in 1723. In 1803 Lausanne became the capital of the new canton of Vaud.

Since 1874 it has been the seat of the Federal Court of Justice, while it later became known for its several educational and medical establishments, for its École Hotelière (now at Châlet-à-Gobet, Epalinges, to the NE), and for the École Polytechnique Fédérale de Lausanne, whose extensive premises lie some distance W of the town. In 1922–23 it was the scene of international conferences on the Near East, dominated by Lord Curzon, which resulted in a treaty between Greece and Turkey and restored British prestige in Turkey.

Among natives of Lausanne were: J. L. Burkhardt (1784–1817), the first European explorer to enter Mecca (see p 155); Benjamin Constant (1767–1830); Alexandre Vinet (at Ouchy; 1797–1847), the essayist; and the artists Théophile Alexandre Steinlen (1859–1923), Félix Vallotton (1865–1925); and René Auberjonois (1872–1957).

The tragedian John Philip Kemble (1757–1823) lies in the cemetery of *La Sallaz*. John Lisle (c 1610–64), the regicide (cf. Vevey), seeking asylum in Switzerland, was murdered in Lausanne by Sir James Cotter M.P. of Carrigtwohill, Co. Cork.

Edward Gibbon (1737–94) lived in Lausanne in 1753–58 (Chez Pastor Pavillard, who weaned him from Roman Catholicism). During this period he first met Voltaire and was briefly engaged to Susanne Churchod (afterwards Mme Necker). In 1763–64 he resided Chez Henri Crousaz at the Château de Mézery-Bellecour, where he wrote his 'Lausanne Journals'. In 1763 he was visited by Henry Temple, second Viscount Palmerston and between 1783 and 1793 he lived Chez Georges Deyverdun at La Grotte, where he completed his 'Decline and Fall of the Roman Empire' (27 June 1787). It was in 1783 that Gibbon complained that 'the fashion of viewing the mountains and Glaciers, has opened us on all sides to the incursions of foreigners'. Beckford's 'Vathek' was first published here in 1787; in 1792–94 Beckford bought a number of books from Gibbon's library. It was Sir William Wickham's base in 1795–97, when he was Pitt's envoy in Switzerland at this crucial period; he visited the country again in 1799–1802. Lausanne was visited by Byron and Shelley in 1816, by Southey the following year, and by Wordsworth in 1790 and 1820. Dickens resided here at 'Rosemont' in 1846; he began 'Dombey & Son', wrote 'The Battle of Life', and was visited by Tennyson, Thackeray, Marc Isambard Brunel and William Harrison Ainsworth; he visited Lausanne again in 1853. Ruskin heartily disliked the place, but by the later 19C it had a large English colony. Stravinsky's 'L'Histoire du Soldat', in collaboration with Ramuz (its decor by Auberjonois, and conducted by Ansermet), was first performed here, in September 1918. T.S. Eliot recuperated here in 1921–22, where 'The Waste Land' was partly written—'there you feel free'.

Some idea of the slope on which Lausanne lies may be gained from the following altitudes: lakeside Ouchy stands at 377m, the church of St. François at 475m, the view-point of Le Signal, N of the cathedral, is at 647m, while Mont Jorat itself rises to 927m.

19C view of Lausanne

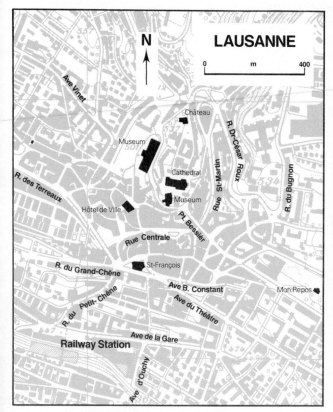

The old, irregularly shaped, enceinte lies N of the main centre, the
PL. ST. FRANÇOIS, on a terrace some distance above the *Railway
Station*, from which it is approached by ascending the steep Rue du
Petit-Chêne.

The church of **St. François** was until 1536 that of a Franciscan
foundation of the mid 13C, but it has been much rebuilt and altered
since, and contains curious relics of stalls. The tilt of the choir will be
noticed. Its dependencies formerly extended to the S across the
present street, forming a bastion in the town walls, and here later stood
La Grotte, the house in which Gibbon lived after 1783. The site is now
occupied by the *Post Office*. The summer-house in which he completed 'Decline and Fall of the Roman Empire' stood in a garden later
belonging to the *Hôtel Gibbon*, demolished in 1921 to make way for
a bank.

From just N of the church, the Rue de Bourg climbs E. At the Rue
Caroline turn left to the *Pont Bessières* (1910), spanning the Rue
Centrale, built over the bed of the Flon torrent, which once divided
the Bourg from the upper Cité. From its N end we ascend to the
cathedral, first passing (left) the former *Hôpital de Nôtre-Dame*, an
18C building now a college.

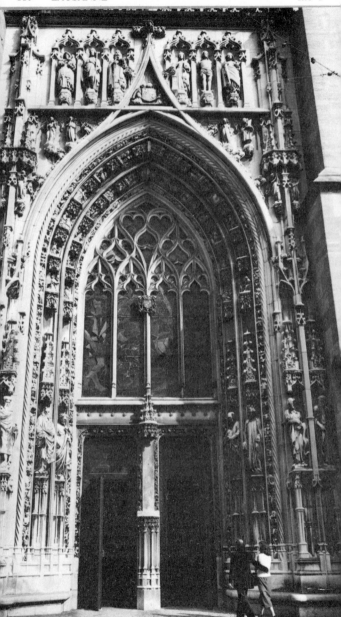

The W portal of Lausanne Cathedral

The ***Cathedral** is an imposing pile, dating largely from 1190 (E half of the nave and choir) to 1232, when the heavily buttressed W end, with its SW belfry tower, was erected, showing the possible influence of those at Laon in France; the NW tower was never completed.

It stands on the site of an earlier and much smaller edifice of c 1000, itself erected above a Carolingian cathedral. It is possible that a late Roman camp and then a fortified palace previously stood here, but archaeological researches are not completed. The cathedral was consecrated in 1275 by Gregory X in the presence of Rudolf of Habsburg. Between the W end of the nave and the tower stood the 'Great Bay', an open archway (more noticeable when seen from the interior) filled in at the beginning of the 16C. Indeed the 'Westwerk' block was almost the equivalent of the gateway of the upper town, to the E of which was a roadway.

Charles le Téméraire attended mass here before the battle of Morat (1476); and here took place the Disputation held by Calvin, Farel and other eminent Reformers in 1536, heralding their break with the Catholics and the eventual removal of the bishopric to Fribourg.

On the S side is the small *'Painted Portal'*, with sculptures representing the Death and Assumption of the Virgin below a mandorla supported by two angels and containing a Christ in majesty. The large W Portal, or 'de Montfaucon', added in the early 16C, is embellished with numerous statues, freely restored, as was the whole building after 1873, at the instance of Viollet-le-Duc, who died at Lausanne in 1879. The ambulatory dates from 1160–75, and the apse is flanked by two low towers, while the crossing is surmounted by a spired lantern. The conservation of the cathedral, due to the friable nature of the stone, continues to present a problem.

From the W, we traverse the narthex, with its apses, part of the monumental portal, and a vestibule, to enter the 'Great Bay'. The memorial by Bartolini to Sir Stratford Canning's first wife, née Harriet Raikes (died 1817), will be noted. In the *St. Maurice chapel* (N) are elaborately carved canopied stalls of 1509, arranged thus in 1914. With the introduction of Protestantism and the consequent destruction and removal of many treasures, reliquaries and ornaments, the interior is bare, but impresses by the height of its vaulting; above the varied arrangement of the piers and vaulting shafts in the nave is a triforium, continued round the transepts and apse, while in the nave is a clerestory range of triple lancets. Some 13C stalls are placed against the S wall of the nave. The capitals on the NW pier of the crossing and in the N transept are remarkable. The raised apsidal choir is surrounded by an ambulatory; on the left is the tomb of Otho of Grandson (slain in a judicial duel in 1328), one of whose poems was translated by Chaucer. In the ambulatory and S transept are the mutilated tombs of 13–14C bishops. Note the *Rose-window* in the S transept, which was sketched by Villard de Honnecourt when passing through Lausanne in c 1235; its early 13C glass is probably by Pierre d'Arras. A door in the N transept leads to the former cloister. (The crypt contains several Merovingian and Carolingian sarcophagi, and the tombs of miscellaneous bishops.)

A few paces to the SW of the cathedral is the old *Evêché*, now housing the **Cathedral Museum** and historical collections. It contains several of the original painted statues from the S portal, relics of stalls, 13C glass, a 13C bishop's tomb, early 16C statues of sundry saints and photographs of the excavations of the former cloister abutting the N side of the cathedral. Upper floors display views of picturesque old

Lausanne, among them one by John Dobbin, a Plan of the town by David Buttet (1638), collections of pewter, etc., and the original figure of Justice from the fountain in the Pl. de la Palud.

Bearing round to the N of the cathedral, we see (left) the buildings of the old *Academy* (1587), now part of the *University*, at which Sainte-Beuve (in 1837–38), Mickiewicz and Alexandre Vinet lectured. Its School of Theology was established in 1537. In 1890 the Academy was converted into a university, when a medical faculty was added. It now has six faculties, and other schools, and is attended by some 5000 students. A plaque commemorates Alexandre Yersin (1863–1943), discoverer of the plague bacillus.

The Rue Cité-Devant leads N to the Pl. du Château, overlooked by a square stone building with a projecting top storey and corner turrets of brick, erected in 1397–1431 for the use of the bishops, and now occupied by cantonal authorities. It may be visited to view its 15–16C frescoes, etc. On its S facade is a monument to Major Davel (1670–1723), who was executed at Vidy after his abortive attempt to liberate Vaud from the domination of Berne.

Some minutes' walk to the N is the *Fondation de l'Hermitage*, the venue of art exhibitions in a well-furnished mid 19C villa.

From the Pl. du Château one may walk down the Rue Cité-Derrière (at No. 17 young Gibbon lodged in 1753) to reach the N transept of the cathedral, near which is the *Chapter-house*, and the *Jacques Schmied Museum*, devoted to tobacco pipes and the smoking of that weed.

From immediately W of the cathedral, covered steps, the *Escalier de la Cathédral*, and a second flight, the *Escalier du Marché*, referred to by Rilke, descend to the PL. DE LA PALUD, the scene of colourful markets. On the W side of the Place is the fine mid 15C *Hôtel de Ville*, built over arcades, with a later facade in Renaissance style.

Hence we ascend the Rue Madeleine to the N to enter the spacious PL. DE LA RIPONNE, dominated by the huge **Palais de Rumine** (1898–1904), named after Gabriel de Rumine (died 1871), the Maecenas who left money for the construction of a building of public utility. The neo-Florentine confection is flanked by two columns bearing a chimera and sphinx. It contains the headquarters of the University and several cantonal and municipal museums, among them *Geological, Palaeontological*, and *Zoological collections*. Notable is the skeleton of a Mammoth of c 10,300 BC found near Le Brassus (SW of the Lac de Joux) in 1969. The collections of *Archaeology*, include artefacts of the La Tène culture and Hallstatt period; a copy of the golden bust of Marcus Aurelius, discovered at Avenches in 1939; finds from Burgundian cemeteries at St.-Prex, St.-Sulpice, and Bel-Air; also from Gaulish cemeteries; buckles, plaques, and arms, many from lake sites near Morat and Neuchâtel; Roman glass, bronzes, and statuettes; metalwork, and ceramics, etc. There is a good 'Cabinet des Médailles'.

Few Swiss artists are represented in the **Musée des Beaux-Arts**. It contains examples of the art of Renoir, Bonnard, Utrillo, Vlaminck, Marquet, Vuillard (including a Portrait of Dr Auguste Widner, Mme Widner, and three others), and *Henri Martin* (1860–1943); and drawings by *Félix Jeanrenaud* (1882–1954). The whole deserves a thorough restoration.

The **Collection de l'Art Brut**, displayed at the *Château de Beaulieu* (1767) in the Ave de Bergières, is reached by ascending steps on the W side of the Place, and following the Ave Vinet to the NW, a walk of about 10 minutes.

Jean Dubuffet (1901–85) began collecting in 1945. His extensive collection was offered to and accepted by the City of Lausanne in 1971. Among the work shown are examples by Madge Gill, Pascal Maisonneuve, Émile Ratier, Michelle Cassou, Gérard Sendrey and Gérard Lattier.

Opposite the entrance is the pile of the *Palais de Beaulieu* (1920), an extensive complex of congress and exhibition halls, etc., the scene in September of the trade fair known as *La Comptoir Suisse*, among others.

From the SW corner of the Pl. de le Riponne, the Rue Haldimand descends to (right) *St. Laurent* (1719), on the site of an 11C church, whence, following the Rue St.-Laurent and its continuation to the W, we shortly reach the *Tour de l'Ale*, an outwork of earlier fortifications.—Turning S here, and then left, the Rue des Terreaux leads past the Pl. Bel-Air, to the *Grand-Pont* (1844)—with a view of the viaduct of the *Pont Chauderon* to the W. From here we can return to the Pl. St-François.

A short distance W, approached by the Rue du Grand-Chêne, lies the *Promenade de Montbrenon*, commanding a fine view of Lac Léman and the mountains to the S. Here stand the *Palais de Justice* of 1886 and the *Casino*, with the *Cinémathèque Suisse*.—To the NE we have a view of the cathedral; beyond is the bulk of the new cantonal *Hospital*, the object of much criticism.

In the Rue du Grand-Chêne is the upper station of the 'Métro' descending to Ouchy; see below.

In the opposite direction, one may walk from the Pl. St-François up the Ave Benjamin-Constant past the *Hôtel de la Paix*, later bearing off to the right along the Rue Étraz, to reach the *Parc de Mon Repos*, in which stands an early 19C villa, replacing an 18C manor-house in which Gibbon saw Voltaire act in his own plays.—On the slope behind it is the 110m-long facade of the *Tribunal Fédéral*, the main law-courts of the Confederation, completed in 1927.

Ouchy. The funicular 'Métro' from just W of the Pl. St.-François, descends to Ouchy, with intermediate stops. Alternatively, follow the Ave d'Ouchy, descending from the E end of the Ave de la Gare. The Ave d'Ouchy shortly passes (left) the Ave Dr Tissot, in which Dickens lived in 1846, and then (right) the *English Church* (1878; after designs by George Edmund Street) to reach the crossroads of the Ave de Cour (right; leading to the *Botanical Gardens*), and the Ave de l'Élysée, in which No. 18 is the *Musée de l'Élysée*, a mansion of 1781 containing important collections of engravings and photographs, etc.

At the foot of the Ave d'Ouchy stands the 13C tower of the *Hôtel du Château*, part of an old episcopal castle demolished in the 17C. Strindberg stayed here in 1884. To the S are the lake-steamer quays. To the E is the *Hôtel d'Angleterre* (considerably modernised), formerly the *Ancre Inn*, in which Shelley and Byron stayed, storm-bound, in June 1816: here Byron, in two days, wrote the 'Prisoner of Chillon'. In 1893 the Swiss Hotel School was founded here. Further E is the *Hôtel Beau-Rivage* (1861), in which the Treaty of 24 July 1923 was signed, assuring the independence of Turkey. The property was in English hands from 1828–57.

The first paddle-steamer in Switzerland, the 'Guillaume Tell', plied between Ouchy and Geneva from 1823, built by Church, the first of several constructed by British engineers during the next thirty years.

The important site of **Vidy**, ancient *Lousonna*, lies c 2km NW, immediately SW of a roundabout at La Maladière and the start of the motorway for Geneva, which now covers part of the excavated area. Recently laid out as a 'Promenade archéologique', it displays the forum, a Gallo-Roman temple and a 1C basilica, and the quays, etc., of the town. Many of the portable artefacts from the site are in the *Museum*, further to the NW, reached by a tunnel below the motorway.

B. Lausanne to Neuchâtel via Yverdon

Total distance, 70km (43 miles). No. 5. 32km **Yverdon**—38km **Neuchâtel**.

Maps: M 217; BL 35, 36, 40, or 5020.

The N1 motorway provides a rapid route to the SW extremity of the Lac de Neuchâtel to a point just beyond Grandson.

The old road, which we follow, provides good retrospective views as it ascends onto the plateau behind Lausanne, at 8km by-passing (right) *Morrens*, the birthplace of Major Davel (1670–1723).—7km **Echallens**, with a restored 13C *Château* and *Hôtel de Ville* of 1781, among other 18C buildings.—At *St.-Barthélemy*, 3km W, is an attractive château.

17km **YVERDON** (435m; 20,800 inhab.; 9700 in 1930), a small industrial town, lies close to the SW end of the Lac de Neuchâtel and at the mouth of the Orbe (or Thielle). It inherits the site and name of Gallo-Roman *Eburodunum*. Its waters, known to the Romans, were rediscovered in the 16C and are still exploited in the Parc Thermal. Sir Frederick Haldimand (1718–91), who distinguished himself at Ticonderoga and was governor and commander-in-chief in Canada in 1778–85, was from a local family, and returned here to die. Numerous volumes of Diderot's 'Encyclopédie' were printed here in 1770–80; see also Geneva.

In the town centre stands the **Castle**, erected in 1260–78 by Pierre II of Savoy and later modernised. Once encircled by a moat, now largely filled in, it is a quadrangle with four cylindrical pepperpot towers. Here Pestalozzi established his educational institute in 1806–25, but he was an indifferent practical schoolmaster and it failed. Friedrich Frobel also worked here in 1808–10. One tower contains a room devoted to Pestalozzi; other rooms are occupied by a local *Museum*, which contains such unlikely items as Queen Victoria's slippers, spectacles and pen, preserved by a household servant, Mlle Tschumi, and deposited here at her death.

The adjacent Place is flanked by the *Hôtel de Ville* of 1773, and the Classical facade of the *Reformed Church* of 1757, while there are several characteristic houses in the neighbouring streets. At No. 5 Rue du Four is a *Musée de L'Utopie* or *'d'Ailleurs'*.

At *Ursins*, 7km SE of Yverdon, the 12th and 18C church is built on the site of a 2C Roman temple, itself erected above a Gallic sanctuary.

FROM YVERDON TO STE-CROIX (19km). From just N of the town a road forks left, at 4km passing (left) *Champvent*, its 13–14C castle with four conspicuous towers.—At 4.5km a left-hand turning leads 3.5km to *Baulmes*, on the site of a prehistoric settlement, above which rises the *Mont de Baulmes* (1285m).—The main road starts to climb in steep zigzags above the *Gorges de Covatannaz* to (10.5km) **Ste-Croix** (1069m), a curiously situated resort in an hollow close to the summit ridge of the Jura, with musical-box factories. It commands a good distant view of the Alps, as does the summit of the Mont de Baulmes, 4.5km S, reached by a track.—The return to the *Lac de Neuchâtel* (25km), gained just E of *Grandson*, may be made by following a picturesque minor road to the E via *Les Rasses* (view), above which rises the *Chasseron* (1607m), commanding an extensive panoramic *View, and *Mauborget*.—Bearing N from Ste-Croix, one may cross the *Col des Étroits* and descend to the NE down the *Vallon des Noirvaux* on the N flank of the Chasseron ridge to meet the main road between Pontarlier and Neuchâtel at (13km) *Fleurier*; see Rte 5A.

FROM YVERDON TO AVENCHES (37km). The S shore of the Lac de Neuchâtel is followed, passing near several neolithic menhirs, to (8km) *Yvonand*, a village of Roman origin.—11km beyond is **Estavayer-le-Lac**, a picturesque little walled town on a terrace above the lake, with a 13–15C stone and brick *Castle* entered by a barbican and covered bridge. In *St.-Laurent* (1379–1525) the carved stalls (1522), and wrought-iron choir screen are notable. Near the far end of the Grand-Rue, the chapel of the *Dominican convent* contains a triptych by Hans Geiler (1520); near by is the 15C *Maison de la Dîme*, with a local *Museum*.—*Payerne* lies 8km SE; see Rte 6A.—Continuing E, the road veers away from the lake, traversing (8km) *Ressudens*, its 13C church containing late 14C murals.—6km beyond Ressudens the road bears right for (4km) *Avenches*; see Rte 6A.

From Yverdon the main road follows the vine-clad N shore of the **Lac de Neuchâtel**, 430m above sea level, and by far the largest entirely Swiss lake (218km²; 37.5km long and extending to 8km in width, with a maximum depth of 153m).

4km **Grandson**, a large village, possesses a well-restored baronial **Castle** (13C), on the site of its mid 11C predecessor, and with two later towers. It contains a collection of *Veteran Cars*, and several rooms in the fortress may be visited. The chapel preserves a Virgin by Jan Metsys. It also houses the *Institut suisse d'armes anciennes*.

The church of *St.-Jean-Baptiste*, a short walk uphill to the SW, dates from the 12C, with a 15C choir, and originally belonged to a Benedictine priory. It contains several remarkable carved capitals surmounting monolithic Roman columns.

The *Battle of Grandson* took place further NE, between Corcelles and Concise.

In 1476, after a brave resistance, the garrison of Grandson surrendered to Charles le Téméraire of Burgundy who treacherously put them all to death. Two days later (2 March) the Swiss Confederates, 18,000 strong, defeated Charles and his army of 30,000 in the first of their three great victories (with Morat and Nancy) in which the ambitious duke lost successively his treasure, his morale and his life ('Gut, Mut, und Blut'). He is said to have fled across the mountains with only five followers, while among the spoils of his camp were the ducal tent with its costly hangings, his military chest and other treasure, 120 pieces of cannon and 600 standards.

6km *Onnens*, with 14C frescoes in the choir of its church.—2.5km *Concise*, with a good Romanesque church tower, beyond which we enter the canton of Neuchâtel.—5km *Vaumarcus*, its 15C château with a wing of 1773, is traversed, and beyond (2.5km) *St.-Aubin-Sauges* the château of *Gorgier* (13C; rebuilt 1564) is by-passed.

The road shortly veers away from the lake, with a view to the right of the church-tower of *Cortaillod*, site of a neolithic lake-village, which gives its name to a red wine, to enter *Boudry*, birthplace of Jean-Paul Marat (1743–93), the revolutionary, and of Philippe Suchard (1797–1884), the chocolate manufacturer. The 14–16C château contains a *Wine Museum*. We cross the Areuse, the gorge of which may be followed by a path to *Champ-du-Moulin* and beyond; see Rte 5A.

The motorway follows the lake side hence to (10km) **Neuchâtel** (see Rte 5A), while the inland road bears left past the château of *Vaudijon* (1807) through *Colombier*, with a 15–16C castle on Roman foundadations, containing a *Military Museum*, partly devoted to the de Meuron regiment (see p 117).

It was a favourite residence of the outlawed Jacobite George Keith, 10th Earl Marischal of Scotland (?1693–1778), during his governorship of Neuchâtel; it was also the home from the 1770s of Mme de Charrière (1740–1805), an intimate of Benjamin Constant.

The main road by-passes *Auvernier*, with old houses in its Grande-Rue, and a château of 1559. On the outskirts of Neuchâtel lies *Serrières*, with Chocolat Suchard factories (founded 1826), a 16C château and the church in which Farel first preached Reform in December 1529.—For **Neuchâtel**, see Rte 5A.

5   Pontarlier to Neuchâtel

A. Direct

Total distance, 53km (33 miles). N57. 5km—D67bis. 7km *Meudon*—No. 10. 41km **Neuchâtel**.

Maps: M 217, 216; BL 35, 36.

For **Pontarlier** and *La Cluse* see Rte 3.

At 5km we turn left to reach the frontier at (7km) *Verrières-de-Joux* (Customs), below the *Grand Taureau* (1323m), and Swiss *Les Verrières* (931m), surrounded by pine-forests, where in February 1871 Bourbaki's army and other French forces—some 80,000 in all—led by Gén. Clinchant, retreated ignominiously before the Prussians, to be interned in central Switzerland.

The road soon begins the descent of the wooded but industrial VAL DE TRAVERS, watered by the Areuse and noted for its asphalt-mines.

From (10km) *Fleurier* a road forks left, climbing to cross a ridge via the small resort of *La Brévine* to (28km) *Le Locle*; see Rte 5B.—We by-pass **Môtiers**, preserving several characteristic old houses, a 15C church, partly Romanesque, and the dependencies of a Benedictine convent founded in the 11C but secularised in the 16th. Rousseau occupied a house here from July 1762 to September 1765, after his banishment from Geneva. The desk at which he wrote the 'Letters de la Montagne' and the peep-holes in the upper gallery through which he could inspect the passers-by are shown. Here, in 1764, he was visited by James Boswell. On the ground floor is a small *Forestry Museum*. An *Artisanal Museum* has been installed in the 18C *Maison des Mascarons*. To the S is a 14–16C château.

At 2km a left-hand turning climbs steeply across a ridge of the Jura to (8km) *Les Petits Ponts* in the parallel valley, from which one may continue NE via (10km) *La Sagne*, with a 15–16C church and several characteristic old houses; it was the birthplace of the horologist Daniel-Jean Richard (1665–1741). The road leads on to *La Chaux-de-Fonds*.—The left-hand turning at Les Petits Ponts ascends to cross the ridge of *Sommartel*, rising to 1337m, prior to descending to (12.5km) *Le Locle*; see Rte 5B.

3km *Noraigue* (right), from which one may explore the *Gorge of the Areuse*, where a path descends to a cascade near the *Pont-Dessus* and a house near *Champ-du-Moulin* occupied by Rousseau in September 1764; while from the *Ferme Robert* one may enter the remarkable limestone cirque of the *Creux-du-Van*.—Traversing a tunnel, the main road begins the descent (views) towards the W suburbs of (17km) Neuchâtel.

NEUCHÂTEL (*Neuenburg* in German; 34,000 inhab.; 22,650 in 1930), the French-speaking capital of its canton, is an old town attractively situated below a ridge to the W, crowned by its castle and the collegiate church, while along the lake side newer quarters have been built on reclaimed land. Several yellow sandstone buildings have been well restored recently and the town contains two or three museums of some interest.

The countship of Neuchâtel, of Celtic and then Roman foundation (*Novum castellum*), was part of the kingdom of Upper or Transjuran Burgundy, but in the 11C it was transferred to the German Empire. In 1288 it was nominally under the suzerainty of the Burgundian house of Chalon (although the counts and their subjects paid them very limited obedience) and allied itself to the free towns of the Swiss Federation. A number of French Protestants sought refuge here after the Revocation of the Edict of Nantes in 1685. When the house of Chalon became extinct in 1707 on the death of the Duchesse de Nemours, Frederick I of Prussia (as the nearest descendant in the female line) was chosen overlord from fifteen claimants. This was largely due to the machinations of Abraham Stanyan (c 1669–1732), the English diplomat, in conjunction with Runkel, the Dutch envoy. Stanyan later published 'An Account of Switzerland' (Tonson; 1714). In 1752–60 George Keith, the Jacobite 10th Earl Marischal of Scotland, was Governor of Neuchâtel, due to his friendship with Frederick the Great. Brandenburg domination lasted until 1848 (although Neuchâtel was formally incorporated in the Swiss Confederation in 1815), apart from the period when Marshal Berthier ruled under the title of Prince de Neuchâtel (1806–14). The De Meuron regiment from Neuchâtel fought at the storming of Seringapatam in 1799. The revolution of 1 March 1848 established a republican constitution, and in 1857 the King of Prussia, yielding to the mediation of the Great Powers, renounced his claim even if he retained the title of prince.

Among natives were Robert de Meuron (1823–97), the artist; Jean Piaget (1896–1980), the child psychologist; and Denis de Rougemont (1906–1985). Maximilien de Meuron (1785–1868), the artist, died here.

The vineyards flanking the N bank of the Lac de Neuchâtel are largely devoted to producing the Chasselas wine, but there are several other good varieties under the Neuchâtel label.

Most main roads converge on the wide Ave du 1er Mars, just E of the centre, in which No. 26 is the *University* (since 1909; formerly an Academy), with about 2000 students studying at four faculties. Between the W end of the avenue and the small lake-port is the **Musée d'Art et d'Histoire**.

The GROUND FLOOR displays material of local interest, including portraits of Neuchâtelois, among them one by Rigaud; Views of the town and vicinity; collections of ecclesiastical silver; watches; coins; furniture; peasant ceramics; jewellery; costumes; playing-cards; arms; glass, including work by Gallé; cotton-printing machines, etc. But the highlights of the museum are the three ***Automata** made by *Pierre Jaquet-Droz* (1721–90) and his son *Henri-Louis* (1752–91), assisted by *Jean Leschot* (1746–1824), which whirr into action at 14.00, 15.00, and 16.00 on the first Sunday afternoon of each month; otherwise by special arrangement.

The automata are: the *Writer* (1769), with his quill, which can be set to write any text of not more than 40 letters or signs; the *Musician*, and the *Draughtsman* (both 1773)—the latter can make four different drawings.—They will fascinate even those who may otherwise disparage mechanical puppets.

The Writer; an automaton by Pierre Jaquet-Droz, and its mechanism

On the FIRST FLOOR, the decoration on the staircase to which is by *Clement Heaton* (1904), are the paintings of the collection, including representative works by *Calame, Anker, Hodler,* the *Maître à*

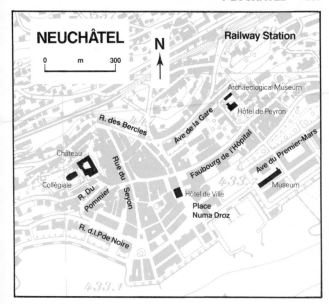

NEUCHÂTEL N Railway Station

0 m 300

Archaeological Museum

Hôtel de Peyron

R. des Bercles

Ave de la Gare

Faubourg de l'Hôpital

Ave du Premier-Mars

Château

Rue du Seyon

R. Du Pommier

Collégiale

Museum

Hôtel de Ville

Place Numa Droz

R. d.l.P.de Noire

L'Oeillet, and The 'Ile St.-Pierre' (cf.) painted in 1825 by *Maximilien de Meuron*. The Amez-Droz collection contains works by *Corot, Lebourg, Lépine, Monet, Pissarro, Renoir*, and *Sisley*.

Further W, beyond the *Hôtel des Postes*, on the S side of the Pl. Numa-Droz (with the Tourist Information Office) is the *Municipal Library*, in which numerous letters and some MSS by Rousseau are preserved.—From the Quai Osterwald, a few paces S, there is—with good visibility—a distant view of the snow-clad crests of the Bernese Oberland and the Mont Blanc range.

The Rue de l'Hôtel-de-Ville leads N past the *Theatre* of 1769 and adjacent colonnaded *Hôtel de Ville* of 1790.—Hence the Rue du Faubourg de l'Hôpital (note Nos 8, 21, and 24) leads E to the imposing *Hôtel de Perou (left), built in 1768 for P.A. de Perou, a friend of Rousseau. A building to its rear contains the *Archaeological Museum*, of interest for its finds from lake-dwelling sites and others of the La Tène and Hallstatt cultures discovered in the vicinity.

The Rue de l'Hôpital leads W from the Hôtel de Ville to cross the Rue du Seyon to the parallel Rue des Moulins (right) and (left) the Rue du Trésor. The last leads S past (right) a small courtyard containing a fine Renaissance stair-tower, hidden until recently uncovered, the 15C *Maison du Tresor* and the picturesque *Maison des Halles* of 1570.

Turn right at the PL. PURY , with a statue by David d'Angers of David de Pury (1709–86, in Lisbon), a benefactor of the town, and right again in the Rue du Pommier, which with the Rue du Château winds steeply uphill to the **Château**, a picturesque pile, the old residence of the counts of Neuchâtel, founded in the 12C (see blind arcade of the W wing), but dating almost entirely from the 16C. It is now occupied by cantonal offices, but the courtyard may be entered and several rooms may be visited on request.

Adjacent rises the **Collegiate Church**, a late 12C building enlarged in the following century and restored in 1869–75 when the spire and NE tower were erected. The triple apse is notable. It suffered by fire in 1450 and was damaged during the Reformation (1530), instigated by Guillaume Farel (1489–1565), a statue of whom stands near. To the N are relics of cloisters with 12C blind arcading, rebuilt in 1450. The choir contains an unusual *Cenotaph of the Counts*, with 15 painted life-size effigies (from 1372–c 1478), restored in 1840. Several capitals, among other features, are noteworthy.

By walking W, with the 11C *Tour des Prisons* to the left, crossing a footbridge and traversing a small park, we approach via the Rue Jeanne-de-Hochberg the entrance to the *Ethnological Museum. It was founded in 1834 with the earlier collections of Gén. Charles-Daniel de Meuron; among several others is that of Charles-Joseph Latrobe (1801–75; later governor of the province of Victoria, Australia), who had married a Neuchâteloise. During the years after 1824 he had climbed several passes and peaks previously unexplored by Englishmen, and he was the author of 'The Alpenstock, or Sketches of Swiss Scenery and Manners' (1829), etc. The collection has been extended very considerably since, particularly with material from Black Africa, and Bhutan. A modern annexe embellished with a mural by Hans Erni is the site of a variety of exhibitions.

From the château one may descend flights of steps past the *Tour de Diesse* (10C; rebuilt in the 18th) and the little Place in which stands the *Banneret Fountain* of 1581, to regain the junction of the Rue du Tresor and the Rue des Moulins.

B. Via Morteau and La Chaux-de-Fonds

Total distance, 75km (46 miles). D437. 31km *Morteau*—D461. 14km **Le Locle**—No. 20. 8km **La Chaux-de-Fonds**—22km **Neuchâtel**.

Maps: M 216; BL 30, 31.

From **Pontarlier** (see Rte 3) we follow the D437 NE through *Montbenoît*, with a remarkable 13–16C *Abbey-church* with a small cloister, and containing well-carved stalls and misericords of 1527.—17km further NE, beyond a defile of the Doubs, lies *Morteau*, with a 13–18C priory church, where we turn SE (D461) to (6km) *Villers-le-Lac*.

From just beyond this village an alternative road forks left to cross the frontier to (4km) *Les Brenets*, from which the *Saut du Doubs* may be visited. The Doubs, threading a fissure in the Jura limestone, and here marking the frontier, expands to form the *Lac des Brenets* (or *de Chaillexon*; 4km long and 500m wide), immediately downstream from which is the waterfall, some 27m high. It may also be approached by a road N of La Chaux-de-Fonds; see below.—The main route may be regained SE of Les Brenets, just W of Le Locle.

Bearing right beyond Villers-le-Lac, we meet the frontier at (6km; Customs) the *Col des Roches*, and veer NE to (2km) **Le Locle** (916m; 12,050 inhab.; 10,400 in 1880), the oldest watch-making town in Switzerland, rebuilt after a devastating fire in 1833. The *Church*, with a tower of 1521, was reconstructed in 1759.

It was here in 1705 that Daniel-Jean Richard (1665–1741; he made his first watch at Neuchâtel in 1681) settled and taught the art of watch-making to his brothers, his five sons and other pupils, by whom the industry was carried to La

Chaux-de-Fonds and other centres.

A sign-posted road climbs steeply N above the town to the 18C *Château des Monts* (not Montre), containing a fine *Horological Museum*, including the Maurice Sandoz collection of automata (normally only open between May and October).

The main road ascends steeply before levelling out on approaching (8km) **LA CHAUX-DE-FONDS** (984m; 37,250 inhab.; 35,250 in 1930), the surprisingly sited centre of the Swiss watch-making industry, introduced here in the early 18C from Le Locle; see above. It was also ravaged by fire, in 1794, and rebuilt on a grid plan, its main thoroughfare being the long Ave Léopold-Robert, named after the local artist (1794–1835).

Other natives were Pierre Jaquet-Droz and his son Henri-Louis (1712–90 and 1752–91, respectively), the watch-makers and constructors of automata (see Rte 5A); Édouard Jeanneret-Gris ('Le Corbusier'; 1887–1965), the artist and architect; 'Blaise Cendrars' (Frédéric Sauser; 1887–1961), the author; Édouard Kaiser (1855–1931) and Madeleine Woog (1892–1929), artists.

In the Rue des Musées, SE of the centre, is the remarkable sub-terranean **Musée International d'Horlogerie**, inaugurated in 1974. Time must be put aside to give the collection other than the most cursory perusal. It supersedes an earlier museum incorporated in the buildings of the School of Horology, founded in 1865.

Over 300 watches and clocks are imaginatively displayed in the underground site, consisting of several open-plan areas connected by steps and ramps. The exhibits are shown in roughly chronological order, from archaic forms—sundials, etc.—to the most recent developments in the field: quartz-crystal, atomic, and electronic time-keepers. A ground plan and catalogue are available at the entrance.

The first level contains exhibits up to the modern era, with numerous outstanding examples of watches of all types, from several countries, and all periods, including a notable display of Neuchâtel clocks. The upper level is concerned with more recent clocks and watches and is more technically orientated, describing forms of escapement, horological instruments, etc., and displays examples of recently produced watches. A large *Carillon*, of which the museum is in-ordinately proud, may be seen and heard, while the exhibition or conference room contains paintings by Hans Erni representing the 'Measurement of Time'. An extensive *Library* and *Documentation Centre* may be visited; departments specialising in valuation and restoring are also housed here.

Adjacent is the **Musée des Beaux-Arts**, with several notable paintings by *Édouard Kaiser*, *Léopold Robert*, *Madeleine Woog* and *Charles Humbert* (Le Locle, 1891–1958), including his portrait of Madeleine Woog, who he married in 1920. The rest of the collection, although extensive, contains comparatively few works of great merit.

Above, in the park, is the *Musée historique et médaillier*, with local collections.

FROM LA CHAUX-DE-FONDS TO BIAUFOND (13km). The road ascends steeply to the NE over a ridge of the Jura, off which a left-hand turning leads below the viewpoint of *Pouillerel* (1276m) to *Les Planchettes*, to approach the *Saut-du-Doubs* from the E; see p 120. The main road descends steeply to skirt the Doubs, crossed at the frontier village of *Biaufond* (Customs).—*Maiche*, 17km beyond, lies on the main road between Morteau and *Montbéliard*, 42km further N; see *Blue Guide France*.

FROM LA CHAUX-DE-FONDS TO DELÉMONT (58km). The No. 18 bears left
5.5km E, running parallel to the Doubs across a high-lying forested region known
as *Les Franches-Montagnes*, noted for its sturdy 'Freiberger' ponies, to (25km)
Saignelégier, after *Le Noirmont* passing below the *Spiegelberg* (1T08m),
crowned by castle ruins. The 18C *Préfecture* of Saignelégier is notable; several
villages in the area conserve characteristic Jura houses. There is a border
crossing at *Goumois*, 8.5km W on the Doubs; 9km over the ridge to the SE lies
Tramelan, on the road to *Tavannes*, 9km beyond; see Rte 9.—The route continues
NE to (6km) *Montfaucon*. Hence one may follow alternative routes to the main
road, which forking right after 8km descends through *Glovelier* to (19km)
Delémont; see Rte 12B.—The left-hand fork follows the *Corniche du Jura* (views)
for 11km to meet the No. 6, descending to the SE through *Develier* to (16km)
Delémont, while a picturesque road climbs in steep zigzags N over a ridge from
Montfaucon, descending to *Soubey*, on the Doubs, thence diagonally crossing
another ridge forming a long tongue circled by the river, which is re-crossed at
(22km) **St.-Ursanne**. This ancient little town preserves two medieval gateways
and sections of ramparts. The restored collegiate *Church* (12–14C) has a
sculptured and polychromed S doorway, finely carved stalls and pulpit, and a
cloister of interest, off which is a *Musée lapidaire*, containing several 7–8C stone
sarcophagi. Beneath the altar are the remains of Ursicinus, a 7C hermit and
companion of Columbanus, who inhabited a neighbouring cave.—A steep climb
to the E brings one in 5.5km to the No. 6, whence one may descend SE through
Develier to (16km) *Delémont*.—There is a frontier crossing 9.5km W of St.-
Ursanne, beyond which the road follows the valley of the Doubs to (23km)
St.-Hippolyte, 30km S of Montbéliard; see *Blue Guide France*.

FROM LA CHAUX-DE-FONDS TO BIEL/BIENNE (45km). Ascending E we bear
right after 5.5km, descending the long *Vallon de St.-Imier*, watered by the Suze,
passing (right) the ruins of the 11C castle of *Erguel*, to enter (10.5km) **St.-Imier**
(793m), a watch-making town since 1770. Its 12C collegiate *Church* is of interest,
as is the Romanesque *Tour de la Reine Berthe* attached to *St.-Martin*.—To the
N rises *Mont Soleil* (1291m); to the SE, the ridge of the *Chasseral* (1607m). Both
are fine viewpoints, and the summits of both are nearly approached by steeply
climbing roads (that to the Chasseral partly toll).—The main road continues down
the valley through *Courtelary*, with an old church rebuilt in the 17–18Cs, to meet
the No. 6 at (15km) *Sonceboz*. We now thread a picturesque wooded defile by
an improved road, and bear right for *Biel/Bienne*; see Rte 9.

The main road S from La Chaux-de-Fonds shortly climbs round a
shoulder of the Jura range, ascending to (7km; 1283m) the *Vue des
Alpes*, a col between *Mont d'Amin* (E; 1417m) and the *Tête de Ran*
(1422m). From there it climbs down through *Boudevilliers* to pass (left
after 10km) **Valangin**, an old village with a medieval gateway and
church of 1506, commanded by a 12C castle, enlarged in the 15C,
reconstructed in 1772, and now containing a regional museum.

We descend rapidly through the thickly wooded *Gorge of the Seyon*
to meet suddenly the W suburbs of **Neuchâtel**; see Rte 5A.

6   Lausanne to Berne

A. Via Payerne, Avenches, and Murten/Morat

Total distance, 91km (57 miles). No. 1. 23km *Moudon*—21km
Payerne—10km **Avenches**—9km **Murten/Morat**—N1. 28km **Berne**.

Maps: M 217; BL 40, 35, 36 or 5020, 5016.

The road climbs steeply NE from central **Lausanne** (see Rte 4A), passing below the N9 motorway; see Rte 6B.—At *Epalinges* we by-pass the new site of the Swiss *École Hôtelière*, with the wooded ridge of *Mont Jorat* beyond, and shortly obtain a good distant view of the Alps. The road later descends into the valley of the Broye, at 19km leaving to our right a road to (5.5km) *Rue*, an old village with a picturesque castle rebuilt in the 17C.—23km **Moudon** (513m), an ancient little town of Roman origin (*Minnodunum*), fortified in the 12C and once the capital of the Pays de Vaud Savoyard. Gothic *St.-Étienne* (founded in 1011 but rebuilt in the late 13C) preserves well-carved choir-stalls and misericords of 1502, and relics of murals; the modern glass is unfortunate. The belfry with its 17C spire is in fact part of the town defences. Several 14–17C houses may be seen in the Rue du Château, traversing the upper town, among them the *Maison d'Arnay* (No. 34), with a huge gable, the four-square *Broye Tower* (1120) and 16C *Château de Rochefort* are notable.

The main road skirts a nuclear power-station, and at 5.5km passes (left) *Lucens*, a small industrial town overlooked by an imposing partly 13C *Castle*, once belonging to the bishops of Lausanne. It contains a reconstruction of the study of the indubitable 'Sherlock Holmes', with souvenirs of Sir Arthur Conan Doyle (1859–1930; cf. Davos).—At *Curtilles*, to the right, is an 11C church with 15C murals, and ogival vaulting in its choir.

CURTILLES TO FRIBOURG VIA ROMONT (32km). The road ascends the plateau to (16km) **Romont** (780m), a little walled town founded in the early 10C, picturesquely situaced on the summit of an isolated hill (*rotundus mons*). It possesses two curious cylindrical *Towers*, their entrances high above the ground and with openings facing the cardinal points placed just below their roofs. One stands outside the walls; the other, much altered, forms part of the *Castle* (10th and 14Cs) and now houses a small *Museum*, with a section devoted to glass. The nave of the *Church* dates from 1296; the choir, with good woodwork, was rebuilt after a fire in 1434.—The route continues NE above the valley of the Glâne. The serrated crests of the Fribourg Alps are seen to the right, and we later cross the N12 motorway to meet the old main road just short of **Fribourg** itself; see Rte 6B.

10km *Granges-près-Marnand* (left) preserves a restored early Romanesque church with Gothic additions.—At 6km Payerne lies 2km N (left); the right-hand turning provides a pleasant approach to *Fribourg*, 19km E, and commands several fine views of the Bernese Oberland.

PAYERNE (458m), Roman *Paterniacum*, now a small industrial town, was once the capital of Transjuran Burgundy, and the seat of a Cluniac abbey founded in the 10C by Queen Bertha, wife of Rudolf II, and whose alleged tomb is in the Protestant Temple. In 1536 it passed from the house of Savoy to Berne.

Daniel Beat Christin, who emigrated hence to England in 1788, was the ancestor of John Christie (1882–1962), founder of the opera-house at Glyndebourne.

The ***Abbey-church of Notre-Dame** is an imposing Romanesque edifice, mainly 11–12C, with five apses and a tower over the crossing surmounted by a 15C spire (twisted). Its nave is on the site of a 10C church, built over that of a Roman villa. It was long used as a warehouse, and its restoration did not start until 1926. It preserves several interesting capitals and 13–15C wall-paintings; the N side splays from the parallel to meet a chapel added in the 14C. To the S is the rebuilt chapter-house.

The 14C *Château*, now municipal offices, was built in 1640 on the site of conventual dependencies; it contains good 17C decoration.

Estavayer-le-Lac lies 8km NW; see Rte 4B.

The main road is regained 3km NE, beyond *Corcelles*, with an 11C church.

Avenches; the château and Roman amphitheatre

7km **AVENCHES**, on its hill (480m), succeeds *Aventicum*, originally a town of the Helvetii, which became the most extensive Roman colony in Helvetia.

The present village occupies only the W corner of the walled enceinte, some 5km in circumference, several stretches of which are visible. This was virtually destroyed in 260 by the Alemani, and in the mid 4C overrun by the Huns.

At the N end of the village is the 16C *Castle*, probably successor to the 7C stronghold of a Count Wivilo, just E of which is the *Roman Amphitheatre* (100 by 90m). This is overlooked by a medieval tower occupied by the ***Musée Romain** which contains many of the antiquities found here and a copy of the gold bust of Marcus Aurelius discovered in 1939 near the *Cigognier*. The latter, a once-solitary Corinthian column, so-called from the stork's nest which long crowned it, stands at a lower level some 5 minutes' walk to the E, and was part of a temple. Not far beyond it is the *Roman Theatre*.—Some 15 minutes' walk NE of the latter is the *East Gate* of the Roman town, with the best-preserved portion of the wall adjoining. The partly excavated grid pattern of its streets is conspicuous on either side of the main road which we follow to the N to (5km) *Faoug*, on the **Murtensee**.

The lake (9km by 3.5km) is drained into the Lac du Neuchâtel by the river Broye. Several remains of lake-dwellings have been discovered on its shores, such as those at *Greng*, close to Murten. Louis Agassiz (1807–73), who in 1847 became professor of zoology and geology at Harvard, was born at *Môtier*, below *Mont Vully* (653m) on the far bank.

4km **•Murten** (**Morat** in French; 453m), on the German-language frontier and by-passed by an extension of the N1 motorway, is one of

Murten battlements: the wall walk

the best-preserved medieval towns in Switzerland. Standing on a terrace above the lake, it is still surrounded by its 15C walls which for thirteen days withstood Burgundian artillery in 1476.

At the battle (22 June) the besieging army under Charles le Téméraire was routed with immense slaughter (some 10,000 Burgundians are said to have been left on the field) by Adrian of Bubenberg and his Bernese garrison. The Swiss force attacking impetuously from heights to the SE are said to have been armed with portable culverins, then a comparatively new invention.

Murten was the birthplace of 'Jeremias Gotthelf' (Albert Bitzius; 1797–1854), the novelist.

From near the *Castle* (13–15C), with a local *Museum*, the arcaded HAUPTGASSE, preserving 17–18C houses, leads to the *Berntor* of 1778, with its clock-tower. The German *Protestant Church* (rebuilt 1710) retains good late 15C woodwork and uses a rampart-tower as a belfry. The *Ramparts* are accessible from here and elsewhere. The *French Church*, at the NE corner of the town, dates from 1481.

The left-hand turning 2km beyond Murten leads NE to (17km) *Aarberg*; see Rte 9.—The right-hand fork—from which the N1 motorway, providing a rapid approach to Berne (24km E) may be entered—later skirts the S side of the *Wohlensee*.

At 9km a right-hand turning leads 5km to *Laupen*, with a hilltop *Schloss*. Near-by took place the battle of 1339, in which the Bernese defeated a coalition of Burgundian counts and bishops.—Crossing the Saane, *Mühleberg* is shortly reached, to the N of which, on the far side of the N1, is a nuclear power-station. The motorway is crossed prior to traversing the *Bremgartenwald* and entering the W outskirts of **Berne**; see Rte 10.

B. Via Bulle, and Fribourg

Total distance, 106km (66 miles). N9. 22km—N12. 26km—*Bulle* lies 3km S—25km **Fribourg**—33km **Berne**.

Maps: M 217; BL 40, 41, 36 or 5020, 5018.

FROM LAUSANNE TO BULLE VIA ORON (40km). We turn off to the right just before reaching the N9 motorway (see below), and bear E to (19km; 700m) *Oron*. The village is dominated by its *Château*, containing several rooms of interest; it dates largely from the second half of the 13C, and is built on the site of an earlier castle.—At 14km the road descends to meet the main road and N12 motorway, the former bearing E to (7km) *Bulle* itself; see below and Rte 7.

The N9 is conveniently entered by ascending NE from central **Lausanne** (see Rte 4A). The road bears SE along the upper vine-clad slopes high above *Lac Léman*, threading several short tunnels, and providing extensive views across the lake towards Meillerie and the Dent d'Oche, of the mouth of the Rhône valley, and of the Rochers de Naye, beyond Montreux. The road likewise commands a number of plunging views of the lakeside resorts, notably *Vevey* and *Montreux* (see Rte 2A). The latter is approached some 4km beyond the entry to the N12, behind Vevey, to the N of which rises *Mont Pelerin* (1080m).

The N9 continues SE and then S in a series of remarkably engineered viaducts below the steep face of the massif rising to the

Rochers de Naye, which is pierced by a tunnel below Glion. The lakeside *Castle of Chillon* is well seen as the road descends to the valley floor beyond *Villeneuve*; for the road beyond, into the *Valais*, see Rte 42A.

The N12 climbs NE away from the lake, along the flank of *Les Pléiades* (1397m) and above the valley of the Veveyse past (left) *Châtel-St.-Denis*, with its castle, a 13C foundation, on the old road from which one may ascend steeply to (5km) *Les Paccots*, a small resort dominated further E by the *Dent de Lys* (2014m).

Both the N12 and No. 12 now circle to the NE below the *Niremont* (1514m) and *Les Alpettes* (1413m), the N12 by-passing both *Vaulruz* (left), with a castle of 1302 rebuilt in the 15–16Cs, and *Vuadens* (right), with a Guigoz Milk factory.—**Bulle** is best approached from the next exit (for *Echarlens*), 3km N of the town (see Rte 7A, and likewise for *Gruyères*, some 6km further SE).

Both the main road and motorway turn N above the W shore of the artificial *Lac de la Gruyère* past *Vuippens*, with a castle, to the NW of which rises the *Gibloux* (1206m).—After 25km we reach the N exit for **Fribourg**, 2km S.

Some distance E of the reservoir rises *La Berra* (1719m), which may be ascended from *La Roche*, 9.5km NE on the minor road from Echarlens to *Fribourg*, 17.5km beyond.

Those following the old road may visit, by turning right beyond (20km) *Posieux*, the *Abbaye of Hauterive* or *Altenryf*, in an elbow of the Sarine, founded in 1138 by monks from Charlieu in France, who were here until 1848; it was returned to the Cistercian Order in 1940. The 12–14C *Church*, with its barrel vaults, preserves notable 15C stalls, stained-glass of 1320–40, and relics of murals. The Romanesque *Cloister* has an upper storey added in the 15C. The S gallery was destroyed in a fire. The abbey was largely rebuilt in the Baroque style in the 18C.

At *Châtillon-sur-Glâne*, at the confluence of the river Glâne and the Sarine, a settlement of archaeological interest is being excavated.

FRIBOURG (**Freiburg** in German; 629m; 37,400 inhab.; 21,550 in 1930), capital of its canton, and lying on the language frontier, was one of the more picturesque towns of Switzerland, and parts of it remain so. This is partly due to the curious irregularities of its site on the W bank of a meander of the Saane or Sarine, on which the lower town stands, and the several old defensive towers surmounting the surrounding cliffs.

Its modern history begins in 1157, when Berchtold IV of Zähringen, founder of Freiburg-im-Breisgau (in Germany), established the town on its defensible site. It later passed to the Counts of Kyburg (1218–77) and then, until 1452, to the Habsburgs, and its expansion was marked by successive lines of fortifications. In 1452 it accepted the protection of the Dukes of Savoy, but the Fribourgeois took the Swiss part in the battles of Grandson and Morat (1476) and in 1481 at the Diet of Stans they were admitted to the Federation. Erasmus lived here in 1529–35 before returning to Basle.

But Fribourg always stubbornly resisted attempts at Reform and remained a bastion of Roman Catholicism, which it still is. The bishop of Geneva settled here in 1612, and in 1663 that of Lausanne. Numerous religious orders established themselves here in addition to earlier ecclesiastical foundations. The town stagnated and duly joined the reactionary Sonderbund in 1846. Since 1889 it has been the site of a Catholic university.

It was taken by Marshal Brune in 1798 and its oligarchic regime was interrupted until 1815. This weakened in the 1830s and its constitution was revised in 1857. Its textile manufacturers once flourished, but Addison, when he passed through, noted only that its snails were reputed.

The artist Jean Tinguely (1925–), known for his 'constructions', was born here.

Clementina Walkinshaw (?1726–1802), mistress of Charles Edward, the Young Pretender, died here, and is buried in St. Nicholas.

Several roads converge on the PL. NOTRE-DAME, just NW of the cathedral.

The church of **St. Nicholas**, a *Cathedral* since 1924, dates from the late 13C, the choir being completed in 1343; the early 15C nave was surmounted by its imposing Flamboyant 76m-high *Tower* in 1490. The late 14C relief in the tympanum of the main portal depicts the Last Judgment, but the statues on either side are copies of the originals. The sculpted and polychromed group of the *Entombment* (1433) in the SW chapel is notable, as are the pulpit of 1515 and font of 1499. The wrought iron screen and choir-stalls are 15C; the (enlarged) early 19C organ is reputed for its quality.

From the Grand-Rue, parallel to the S and flanked by several 16–18C mansions, we turn right to reach the *Hôtel de Ville*, an early 16C building with a later double exterior staircase; the octagonal belfry dates from 1642. It is supposed to occupy the site of a 12C castle. The adjacent *Corps de Garde* dates from 1782; the *Fountain* (1525) is by Hans Geiler, who was responsible for several others in the town.

Hence one may descend to the left along the Rue de la Grand'-Fontaine into the suburb of *Neuveville* or *Neustadt*, following flights of steps (left) to reach the Rue de la Neuville, in which are several characteristic Gothic houses, and cross the *Pont de St. Jean* (1746), providing curious views of the cliffs of houses to the N.

In the Quartier de Planche here are a *Church* founded in the 13C, that of a Commandery of the Knights of St. John, a quaint 18C granary, now an armoury, and several other 18C building.

Energetic visitors may climb from the W end of the triangular Place, formerly the cattle-market, to the *Porte de la Maigrauge*, beyond which is the *Abbaye de la Maigrauge*, a 13C foundation. To the SE the road passes the Capuchin *Convent of Montorge* (founded 1626), and later the *Loretto chapel* (1648; by Hans-Franz Reyff) on a terrace commanding a remarkable view of the town. A main road is reached some distance beyond the *Porte de Bourguillon*, where we turn left, passing the *Tour Dürrenbühl* (1385), and then either descend in zigzags to the *Pont de Berne* (see below) or cross the *Götteron suspension bridge* (view). By following the latter course, we bear round to the left past the 13C *Tour Rouge*, below which are the *Tour des Chats* and the *Porte de Berne* (13th and 15C), joined by a rampart. A good retrospective view is commanded by the *Zähringen Bridge* of 1922, which is next crossed; it replaced the famous suspension bridge thrown across the valley in 1835 by the French engineer Chaley. The cathedral may be regained a short distance from the far end of the bridge.

From the *Quartier de Planche* one may cross the *Pont du Milieu*, rebuilt in 1720, to reach the low-lying tongue of land known as the Auge, dominated by precipices to the S and E. The old covered wooden *Pont de Berne*, mentioned as early as 1275, lies a short distance NE. From the quaint PL. PETIT-ST.-JEAN, with Gothic houses both here and in the adjacent Goldgasse or Rue d'Or, we climb NW up the Rue de la Samaritaine, passing near (right) the former Augustinian church of *St. Maurice* (13C; altered in the late 18C), and continue the steep ascent up to the Rue du Stalden to reach the lower end of the Grande Rue. The *Zähringen Bridge* lies a few paces to the right of their junction.

The PL. NOTRE-DAME, with its *Samson Fountain* of 1547 by Hans Gieng, is flanked to the N by its basilican *Church*, rebuilt in the 18C but preserving Romanesque windows of 1201 in its tower and early 16C stalls.—A few paces beyond stands the **Franciscan Church** of a convent founded in 1256, likewise rebuilt in the 18C with the exception of the choir and sacristy which date from the original edifice. Notable in the church are an *Altarpiece of the Crucifixion* by the 'Master of the Carnation' (after 1480), a fine gilt wood *Triptych* of the early 16C (Crucifixion; Adoration of the Magi, and of the Shepherds) and the *St. Anthony altarpiece* (1506; by Hans Fries).

To the right in the Ave des Cordeliers is the **Musée d'art et d'histoire**, installed in the *Old Préfecture* of 1583. Among collections displayed on four floors of the main building are a number of medieval statues, some polychromed and several of them carved by Martin Gamp; Paintings by *Hans Fries*; carved plaques; a Plan of the town in 1606; Views of Fribourg in the 17C; and local archaeological collections.—A tunnel leads to the modern extension in which several of the original statues from the cathedral are displayed; also ecclesiastical silver; 16C figures from fountains; and a collection of paintings by local artists of the 19–20Cs.

The Rue de Morat continues N past (right) the *Church of the Visitation* (1653; by Hans-Franz Reyff), with its cupola, and the *Capuchin Church* (1622) to the *Porte de Morat*, a tall 15C N gateway of the old town. To the right beyond the gate is the Palladian *Château de la Poya* of 1701.—W of the gate is the cylindrical *Tour des Rasoirs* (1410), from which a path leads round to a huge semi-circular bastion of the fortifications, dating from 1490. Hence one may continue S to the Pl. Georges-Python; see below.

Turning S from the Museum, fork right and turn right before reaching the Rue de Lausanne, one of the main thoroughfares. Steps shortly ascend to the conspicuous *Collège de St.-Michel*, in Jesuit hands from 1585–1773 and again in 1818–48, with a church of 1613 containing later Rococo decoration. Turn left a few paces beyond to reach the Pl. Georges-Python, at the W end of the Rue de Lausanne, with the mid 17C *Ursuline convent-church* by Hans-Franz Reyff on its SE side. There is a belvedere a short distance to the S, while the Rue St.-Pierre leads W to the Grand-Places, with the *Tourist Office*.

Further W is the *Station*; some distance to the NW, abutting the medieval *Tour Henri*, a survival from the ramparts, are the *University buildings* of 1940.

FROM FRIBOURG TO THE SCHWARZSEE (27km). The road ascends due E to (5km) *Tafers*, with a church founded in 1148, preserving a 15C Pietà. Here turn right and follow the valley of the Sense to (15km) *Zollhaus*, an old custom house, where we bear right up the Warme Sense to (7km) the *Schwarzsee* or *Black Lake*, at the NW foot of the *Kaiseregg* (2185m). A path to the SW ascends to the *Col de la Balisa* (1414m), descending thence towards *Charmey*, while other walks lead S over the *Euschelspass* (1567m) to *Jaun*; see Rte 7B. Between the two rise the *Dents Vertes* (*Schopfenspitz*; 2104m) among other peaks which may be easily ascended.

From Zollhaus, a mountain road circles to the NE, climbing steeply up to *Schwefelbergbad*, the starting-point for the scramble up the *Ochsen* (S; 2188m) and several other ascents in the area. These include the *Bürglen* (2165m) and *Gantrisch* (2175m), further SW, between which is a pass (1959m) leading over to *Weissenburg*. The road continues up the Kalte Sense valley to a point (1594m) below the *Selibüel* (W; 1750m) and the *Gurnigelberg* (1548m), to the NE, to (27km) *Rüti*, below the *Gibelegg* (1133m)—all of which may be climbed for the views they command—and 5km beyond, **Riggisberg**; see Rte 17B.

FROM FRIBOURG TO RIGGISBERG VIA SCHWARZENBURG (31km), for Thun, 12km beyond. From *Tafers* (see above) we follow the attractive cross-country road, bridging the Sense and climbing steeply to (11km) **Schwarzenburg**

(792m), a cheese-making village with a 16C castle. The chapel has a quaint shingled spire, the design of which may be due to the Sudeten glass-workers who immigrated here in the 15C. The much-rebuilt parish church is at *Wahlern*, 1km NE, while to the NW are the ruins of the 12–15C castle of *Grasburg*. For **Riggisberg**, 12km further E, see Rte 17B.

On quitting Fribourg, the N12 crosses the *Schiffenen See*, an expansion of the Sarine, on the far bank of which are the two Schlösser of *Vivy* and *Barberêche*, and veers to the NE past (right) *Düdingen*, noted for its cider. We later cross the Sense valley, with the Jungfrau and other peaks of the Bernese Oberland appearing in the distance to the right, and after 27km reach the main exit for **Berne**; see Rte 10.

The old route No. 12 climbs NE from Fribourg, after 14km passing 2km W of *Ueberstorf*, with an early 16C *Schloss*, and after descending into the valley of the Sense, closely follows the motorway towards central **Berne**, also commanding occasional distant views of the Oberland.

7   Bulle to Interlaken

A. Via Château d'Oex, and Gstaad

Total distance, 113km (70 miles). 4km. **Gruyères** is 1km to the right—23km **Château d'Oex** is to the left—No. 11. 12km *Saanen*. **Gstaad** is 3km S.—14km *Zweisimmen*—34km *Spiez*—N8. 18km **Interlaken**.

Maps: M 217; BL 36, 37, 41, or 5004, 5009.

Bulle (771m), a small industrial town and the main focus of traffic of the Gruyère region, a rich pasturage district widely known for its cheeses (although that known to us as 'Gruyère' is really made in the Emmental), is attractively situated 3km S of the motorway between Lausanne and Fribourg; see Rte 6B. To the N of the central marketplace is *St. Pierre-aux-Liens*, rebuilt in 1805 after a fire; to the SE stands the 13C *Château*, later modified, near which is the *Musée Gruérien*, with several collections of interest.

Near *Riaz*, 3km N, the early medieval cemetery of *Tronche-Bélon*, with some 400 graves abutting a Roman temple, was excavated in 1973–76; some 5km SW is the former Carthusian monastery of *La Part-Dieu*, founded in 1307.

Driving SE, we pass at adjacent *La Tour-de-Trême* a large 13C Keep, and approach (4km) **Gruyères**. Its hilltop *Castle*, at 830m, is reached by following a road to the right, later climbing to a car park near the entrance to the walled enceinte. Because it is so steeply and picturesquely perched on its isolated hill, it is often uncomfortably crowded. Many of the old houses—several of the 15–17Cs—display the crane (*grue*) used by the counts in their coat-of-arms. The so-called *Maison de Chalamala* (14C) is said to have belonged to the count's jester. From the far end of the wide main street or central oval Place, one may ascend to the well-preserved 12–15C *Castle*, a former residence of the Counts of Gruyère, in which several rooms may be visited. Note the Copes of the order of the Golden Fleece, part of the spoils taken by the Swiss at Murten, and four landscapes by Corot, while the chapel preserves relics of murals. The walled village commands superb views: of the *Moléson* (2002m), ascended from the village of *Moléson*, to the SW; the *Dents de Broc* (1829m), to the E; and *du Bourgo* (1909m), S of the last, etc.

Regaining the main road, we ascend the valley of the Sarine, passing close to *Grandvillard* (left), with several old houses and a waterfall at the foot of the *Vanil Noir* (2389m), to reach (12.5km) *Montbovon* (described by Byron as 'a pretty, scraggy village, with a wild river and a wooden bridge'), where we meet the railway from Montreux after it has tunnelled below the Col de Jaman.

A mountain road ascends beside it up the Hongrin valley to the SW to the peak-encircled *Lac de l'Hongrin*, from the E end of which one may regain the main road S, between Château-d'Oex and Aigle; see below.

Good walkers may cross from Montbovon to *Montreux* over the *Col de Jaman*, a route which Byron, who followed it—in the other direction—with Hobhouse in 1816, described as 'beautiful as a dream'. From the *Col* (1512m; views), from which the steep *Dent de Jaman* (1875m) may be scaled, the descent is made via *Les Avants* and the *Chauderon Gorge*.

Beyond Montbovon the road turns abruptly E, threading the *Defile of La Tine* to enter the pastoral *Pays d'Enhaut*. Skirting the small *Lac du Vernex*, *Rossinière* is traversed, with a huge wooden chalet of 1754 with 113 windows, among others of note, lying at the foot of the *Pointe de Cray* (2070m), a fine view-point.

At 8.5km we turn left for (2km) **Château-d'Oex** (pron. d'ex; 958m), well-sited on the N side of the open valley of the Sarine, an old resort of scattered chalets backed by pine-woods. It is named after its former castle, the site of which is now occupied by a church in which some of its masonry is probably incorporated. There is a regional *Museum*. The father of Vincent Perronet, 'the archbishop of Methodism' was a native.

Several pleasant excursions may be made in the neighbourhood, among them to the *Vallon des Morteys*, 'a curious basin to the N, known for its rare flowers, between the *Vanil Noir* (2389m) and the *Dent de Brenleire* (2353m), further NE.

Château d'Oex is a good base from which several ascents may be made, apart from those peaks listed above, among them the *Laitemaire* (NE; 1678m); the *Pointe de Paray* (N; 2374m); the *Dent de Folliéran* (2340m; close to the *Dent de Brenleire*); to the NE the *Dent de Savigny* (2252m) and *Dent de Ruth* (2236m), for experienced climbers only; further N, the *Hochmatt* (2152m), noted for its edelweiss; and to the SE, the *Rubli* (2284m), easily ascended from Rougemont.

FROM CHÂTEAU-D'OEX TO AIGLE (32km). The No. 11 threads the wild *Gorges du Pissot* to enter the *Vallée de l'Étivaz*, through which flows the torrent of the Tourneresse, below the *Rocher du Midi* (2097m) and the *Douve Gummfluh* (2458m) further E, a striking and conspicuous peak, and towards the *Arpilles* (2133m). After 8km we turn W, climbing steeply to (3.5km) *La Lecherette* (1379m), close to the *Lac de l'Hongrin*, and ascend to the *Col des Mosses* (1445m), an open plateau from which *Lac Lioson* and the *Pic Chaussy* (SE; 2351m) may be reached. To the W rises *Mont d'Or* (2175m). The road climbs down, with a view ahead of the *Chamossaire* (2113m) to meet that from *Les Diablerets* (see below) at *Les Planches*, just E of (10.5km) *Le Sépey* (974m), a small resort on the steep N slope of the *Ville des Ormonts*, commanding a fine view of the Dents du Midi to the SW.—A rough mountain road climbs S from Les Planches via *La Forclaz*, with old houses, to the *Lac de Chavonnes*, and *Bretaye*; see p 307. To the N the *Col de la Pierre du Möellé* (1661m), named after a huge erratic boulder, is crossed by a path leading to the *Lac de l'Hongrin*; see above.—The larger resort of **Leysin** (1315m), approached by a road from Le Sépey, lies high up on the sunny S slope of the *Berneuse* (2048m), and was formerly a centre for the sun-treatment of tuberculosis. There are several comparatively easy ascents immediately above

Leysin; more difficult are the *Tour d'Aï* (2331m) and *Tour de Mayen* (2326m), further N, each commanding an extensive view.—The main road descends steeply SW from Les Planches above the turbulent Grande-Eau, with a view ahead of Aigle, surrounded by vineyards, near the valley floor, and of the frontier range rising abruptly on the far side of the Rhône.—8km **Aigle**; see Rte 42.

The main road leads due E along the right bank of the Sarine, spanned beyond *Les Granges* by the bold *Pont de Geignez.*—7.5km **Rougemont** (1007m), an attractive village of wooden chalets, and with a restored *Castle* founded in the 11C but dating largely from the 16th, adjacent to which is its late 11C **Church*, until 1555 dependent on a Cluniac priory. To the S rises the *Rubli*.

We shortly enter the canton of Berne and cross the language frontier to traverse (4.5km) **Saanen**, a small resort of large wooden houses with characteristic overhanging eaves. Its mid 15C *Church*, with a top-heavy octagonal spire, was rebuilt after a fire in 1942. It has a deep barrel-vaulted roof, a good font, and repainted frescoes of the legend of St. Maurice, etc. Saanen is known for its Vacherin cheese, and a music festival organised by Yehudi Menuhin.

Gstaad (1050m), 3km SE, at the junction of the valleys of the Saane, Turbach and Lauibach, has developed into a fashionable summer and winter resort with all the usual facilities, but consists mainly of one long street in which is the much-restored chapel of *St. Nicolas* (1402). It is a good centre for excursions into the surrounding valleys, among them the LAUENENTAL, in which (6.5km SE) lies *Lauenen*, a pleasant village with a 16C church and a house of 1765, a notable example of local craftsmanship. Hence one may ascend to the charming *Lauenensee*, with the *Spitzhorn* (2807m) rising to the SW, and to the S, the *Wildhorn* (3248m). Beyond the lake are the *Dungelschuss* waterfalls. Easy ascents from Lauenen are the *Lauenenhorn* (2477m) and *Giferspitz* (2542m), both to the NE.—*Gsteig* (see below) may be approached from Lauenen by the easy *Krinnen Pass* (SW; 1659m).

FROM GSTAAD TO LES PLANCHES VIA THE COL DU PILLON AND LES DIABLERETS (32km). The road leads S along the Saane valley, with the *Mittaghorn* (2579m) rising ahead, past *Grund* (whence the ascent of the *Gummfluh* may be made via the *Col de Jable* at 1884m, to the W) and N of the *Wittenberghorn* (2350m).—From (6km) *Feutersoey* one may follow a path up the TSCHERZISTAL to the *Arnensee* (1542m), below (W; 2211m) the *Arnenhorn*.—4km **Gsteig**, a small resort finely sited in an amphitheatre of mountains, conspicuous among which are the pointed *Spitzhorn* (SE; 2807m) and the precipitous *Schluchhorn* (S; 2579m); other adjacent ascents are the *Walighürli* (NW; 2050m), the *Oldenhorn* (S of the Col du Pillon; 3123m), the *Sex Rouge* (2971m) and, beyond to the SW, the *Diablerets*, rising to 3210m. A path ascends S from Steig past the cascade of the *Sanetschfall* to cross the range to the *Col du Sanetsch* (2251m) for *Sion*; see Rte 43.—The road now climbs SW to (7km) the **Col du Pillon** (1546m) from which the Oldenhorn and Diablerets massif (see above) may be approached. The *Tsanfleuron glacier* descends from the massif. To the N of the col lies the little *Lac de Retaud*. The road descends past cascades to (4km) the scattered village of *Les Diablerets* (1162m), situated in full view of the range known as the *Creux de Champ*.—A steep mountain road climbs SW to the *Col de la Croix* (1778m), between the *Tête de Meilleret* (1939m) and, to the SE, the *Culan* (2789m), climbing down to (17km) *Villars*; see Rte 42A.—The main road continues the descent of the valley of the OTMONT-DESSUS to (11km) *Les Planches*; see p 131.

From Saanen, the main road climbs through (4km) *Schönried*, to the NW of which rises the *Hugeligrat* (1899m), and to the SE the *Hornflue*

(1949m) and *Horntube* (1993m), best approached from (2.5km) *Saanenmöser*, a small resort on the pastoral watershed between the Saane and the Simme. We traverse pine forests to (7.5km) **Zweisimmen** (941m), the main village of the SIMMENTAL, at the confluence of the Kleine Simme and the Simme, a broad valley of rich alpine meadows with their hay-drying racks. It contains several examples of the decorated wooden houses characteristic of the valley, well known also for its breed of dun and dappled cattle. The 15C church contains a wooden ceiling, murals and 15–16C glass. There is a small regional museum. To the W rises the *Hundsrügg* (2047m) and to the S the *Rinderberg* (2079m), both easily ascended and commanding wide views.

FROM ZWEISIMMEN TO LENK (13km); THE SIMMENTAL. We shortly pass *Blankenburg*, with its 18C *Schloss*, and *Ried*, with a church of some interest, beyond which a path ascends SW into the TURBACH VALLEY, for *Gstaad*. We soon have a view of the *Wildstrubel* (3243m) to the left beyond **Lenk** (1068m), a ski resort and mountaineering centre also known for its sulphur springs, while the *Betelberg*, to the SW, is noted for its alpine flora.

Among the main ascents in the area is that of the *Wildstrubel*, perhaps more easily tackled from *Adelboden* (see Rte 17B). It may be approached by climbing SE via *Oberried* and the *Simmenfälle* (above which is the *Glacier de la Plaine Morte*); from near the latter a fatiguing path leads E across the *Ammertenpass* (2443m) to *Adelboden* via *Engstligenalp*; another path leads from Lenk to Adelboden via the *Hahnenmoospass* (1956m). *Lauenen* (see above) may be reached by crossing the *Trütlisbergpass* (2038m) to the SW.—The descent from the Wildstrubel may be made via the *Gemmipass* to *Leukerbad*; see Rte 43.—Other ascents are the *Iffigenhorn* (2378m), to the SW, reached via *Poschenried*, the *Iffigenfall* and *Iffigenalp* (1584m). To the S of the peak is the *Iffigensee*; to the SE of Iffigenalp is the *Rawilpass* (2429m), from which the descent may be made to *Sion*; see Rte 43. The summit of the *Wildhorn* (3248m) may also be approached from this direction; it commands a very extensive view. Easier ascents include the *Mülkerblatten* (SW of Lenk; 1936m), the *Albristhorn* (NE; 2762m) and the *Niesenhorn* (2776m), W of the Iffigensee. From Iffigenalp good walkers may also ascend to the NE below the *Oberlaubhorn* (1999m; view), descending E to the chalets of *Rezliberg* and circling down to *Oberried* for *Lenk*, passing the source of the Simme at the *Sieben Brunnen*, which gives the upper valley its local name of SIEBENTAL.

Driving N from Zweisimmen, we pass (right) *Mannried*, near the ruined *Mannenberg castle*, traversing narrows as (8km) *Boltigen* is approached, just before which the road from the *Jaunpass* (7.5km SW; see below) joins our route. A track climbs NW across the *Kaiseregg pass* to the *Schwarzsee* (see p 129) between the *Widdergalm* (NW; 2174m) and the *Schafberg* (W; 2235m).

The NIEDER SIMMENTAL bears E, and the road traverses (8km) *Därstetten*, an old village with several charming wooden houses, notably the *Haus Knutti* (1756). Adjacent to the N is the old spa of *Weissenburgbad*, in the wooded ravine of the *Bunschen*. A track leads NE hence to ascend the *Stockhorn* (2190m), noted for its flowers and commanding an almost complete view of the Thuner See. The peak and the *Stockhornsee* are also approached with ease from (6.5km) **Erlenbach**, which is soon reached. The village contains several attractive wooden houses, and 15C murals in its church, founded in the 10–11C but much rebuilt. The 18C parsonage was the starting-point of the ascents graphically described in his 'Alpenstock' by Charles J. Latrobe (1801–75).—At 2km *Latterbach is traversed*.

Hence the pastoral DIEMTIGTAL may be entered, shortly passing *Diemtigen*, a village preserving several old houses, beyond which the road ascends to the

SW alongside the Fildrich via *Zwischenflüh* to (14km) *Grimmialp* (1214m), a hamlet surrounded by mountains. Among them are the *Seehore* (W; 2281m), commanding a wide view; the *Spillgerte* (2476m; a difficult ascent to the SW); the *Mannliflue* (SE; 2652m; extensive panoramic view), and—better climbed from Adelboden—the *Gsür* (2708m) and *Albristhorn* (2762m) to the S.—From Grimmialp a track leads SW to the *Grimmi pass* (1970m; views), whence one may descend the green FÄRMELTAL to *Matten* below *Lenk*. From the hamlet of *Fildrich*, SE of Grimmialp, a path climbs E to the *Otterepass* (2278m), from which the descent may be made into the valley below *Adelboden*; see Rte 17B.

The road continues E from Latterbach through a defile known as the *Port*, beyond which (2km left) lies *Reutigen*, and to the right, *Wimmis*; for both see Rte 17B. Between the two is a short section of motorway, which after 3km meets the N6 just W of *Spiez*. To the S rises the *Niesen* (2362m). We turn right above the *Thuner See*, which is skirted to **Interlaken**, 18km E; see Rte 18.

B. Via Charmey, and the Jaunpass

Total distance, 81km (50 miles). 11km *Charmey*—10km *Jaun*—15km *Reidenbach*—No. 11. 27km *Spiez*—18km **Interlaken**.

Maps: M 217; BL 36, 37, or 5009, 5004.

Bearing SE from *Bulle*, with a view of the castle of *Gruyères* on its height to the S (see Rte 7A) we traverse (4km) *Broc*, with a medieval bridge, and a large Nestlé chocolate factory founded by Alexandre Cailler in 1898, with the *Dent de Broc* (1829m) rising ahead. To the left is the S extremity of the *Lac de la Gruyère*.

Turning right, the road climbs above the artificial *Lac de Montsalvens*, below its ruined castle.

After 6km a minor road climbs NE to (5.5km) the Carthusian monastery of *La Valsainte*, founded in 1295, most of the dependencies of which date from the 18C (which may only be visited by men). A path leads E across the *Col de la Balisa* (1414m) to the *Schwarzsee*.

The main road traverses *Charmey*, an attractively sited village, to the E of which rise the *Dents Vertes* (1813m), approached via *Vounetse*.—We bear SE up the gorge of the Jogne below a ridge to (11km) *Jaun*, with a ruined castle and a waterfall, from which a path leading N crosses the *Euschelspass* (1567m) to the *Schwarzsee*; to the S is the jagged *Gastlosen* (1935m), well-known to rock-climbers.

A road circles S to *Abländschen*, on the E side of the ridge, from which a path ascends S, later descending towards *Saanenmöser* and *Gstaad*.

Passing through a defile the road climbs to (7.5km) the *Jaunpass* (1509m; views). Hence we descend steeply NE to meet the main road at (7.5km) *Reidenbach*, in the valley of the Simme; see p 133.

8   Neuchâtel to Zûrich

A. Via Berne

Total distance, 170km (105 miles) without detours. No. 10.
26km—N1. 21km **Berne**—34km. **Solothurn** lies 5km W.—28km.
Olten lies 5km N.—12km. **Aarau** lies 7km N.—25km. **Baden** lies
2km N.—24km **Zûrich**.

Maps: M 216, 217; BL 27, 31, 32, 36, or 5005, 5016, 5019.

The No. 10 skirts the NE end of the *Lac de Neuchâtel*, briefly following
the completed section of the N5, off which, after 9.5km, we bear SE
above (on the lakeside) *St.-Blaise*, with several 17C houses and a
church-tower of 1516. The adjacent hamlet of *La Tène* has given its
name to the Iron Age culture of the 5–1Cs BC, which followed that
of Hallstatt, remarkable remains of which were discovered there in
1856, many of which may be seen in the museums of Neuchâtel and
Biel/Bienne.

Immediately after crossing the canalised Zihl—joining the lake to the *Bieler See*
(see Rte 8B)—a left-hand turn leads 3km to (left) the former Benedictine
monastery of *St.-Johannsen*, founded in 1100, with a choir of 1390, and
containing ancient tombstones.—2km beyond lies *Erlach*, an old village sited
below a ridge running down to the lake of Biel. The late 11C castle here was
the ancestral home of Rudolf von Erlach, the victor of Laupen.—Hence the
Heidenweg traverses a tongue of land reaching out to the **St.-Petersinsel** (or Île
Saint-Pierre), a small wooded island on which Rousseau took refuge in the
building of a former Cluniac foundation in Sept–Oct 1765. His room is preserved
in the hotel, together with the trap-door to the garret, through which he escaped
to avoid the importunities of curious visitors. The obstreperous William Pitt, 2nd
Baron Camelford (1775–1804) was in the event unable to be buried here, as he
had wished.—The main road may be regained at *Ins*, 5km S of Erlach.

The No. 10 crosses the low-lying isthmus between the lakes to (5.5km)
Ins, birthplace of Albert Anker (1831–1910), the artist. From Ins a
right-hand fork leads 11km S across flats to **Murten**, on the *Murtensee*,
with *Mont Vully* to the W; see Rte 6A. The main road continues SE
to (8km) *Kerzers*, which may be by-passed by turning right to join in
3km the N1 motorway just before the town.
    The exit for **Berne** is reached 18km E; see Rte 10.
    The recommended route hence is the N1 motorway, bearing NE,
with exits after 19km for **Burgdorf** (5km E; see Rte 16B) and, 15km
beyond, **Solothurn** (5km W; see Rte 8B) with the main ridge of the Jura
rising ahead.

FROM BERNE TO SOLOTHURN VIA THE NO. 12 (36km). The old main road
drives N. In a wooded loop of the Aar to the NW, after passing below the
motorway at *Tiefenau* and prior to crossing the river, a Celtic fort and Roman
settlement stood until the 4C, several relics of which, including an amphitheatre
(close to a modern church) may be seen.—Traversing (7km) *Zollikofen*, we fork
right; the left-hand fork leads shortly to *Münchenbuchsee*.—At 4km, after
Moosseedorf, where remains of lake-dwellings of two different periods have
been found, we bear left onto the No. 12; the No. 1 veers NE; see below.—4km
Jegenstorf, with a large 13C *Schloss*, baroquised in the 18C.—4.5km
Fraubrunnen, where Enguerrand de Coucy's French troops were nearly an-
nihilated in 1376, is traversed, and 5.5km beyond at *Bätterkinden*, with an 18C
church, we pass (2km right) near *Schloss Landshut*, at *Utzenstorf*, now housing
a *Hunting Museum*.—At *Bucheggc* c 2.5km W, is a regional *Museum*.—8km

Biberist, where the art gallery of the *Moos Flury Foundation* is largely devoted to artist from Solothurn; for **Solothurn** itself, shortly entered, see Rte 8B.

FROM BERNE TO OLTEN VIA LANGENTHAL (64km). The No. 1 is followed past *Zollikofen* (see above), where we bear right through (16km) *Hindelbank*, with its Baroque *Schloss*. *Burgdorf* is 7km E; see Rte 16A.—*Utzenstorf* (see above) lies 6km N of (6km) *Kirchberg*.—15.5km *Herzogenbuchsee*, with a church of 1728, on a Roman site, from which a 1C mosaic has been removed. William Wordsworth spent the night in his voiture here rather than pay six francs for a bed!—At 4km we by-pass (right) *Thunstetten*, with a notable early 18C *Schloss*, and 4km beyond leave **Langenthal** (13,400 inhab.), a small industrial and textile town with a regional museum, to our right.—4km At *Roggwil*, 2km right, is the 13–16C *Schloss Mammertshofen*, while at adjacent **St.-Urban** stands a former Cistercian abbey (1194–1848), the fine Baroque *Church* of which (1711–15; by Franz and Johann Michael Beer, two Austrian architects), preserves remarkable choirstalls by Peter Frölicher, Viktor Wüest and Rochus Frey.—At *Wynau*, N of the main road, is a Romanesque church with a 14C choir containing relics of murals.—We shortly reach and skirt the Aare and cross the N1 to enter (10km) **Aarburg**, dominated by a conspicuous 17C *Castle*, on the site of a much earlier fort. A small museum is housed in a mansion of 1750, but the town was largely rebuilt after a fire in 1840.—4km **Olten**; see p 168.

B. Via Biel/Bienne, Solothurn, Olten, and Aarau

Total distance, 154km (95 miles). N5. 34km **Biel/Bienne**—No. 5. 24km **Solothurn**—34km **Olten**—13km **Aarau**—No. 25. 11km *Lenzburg*—No. 1. 10km *Wohlen*—6km *Bremgarten*—22km **Zürich**.

Maps: M 216; BL 31, 32, or 5005, 5016, 5019.

See Rte 8A for the first 9.5km, after which veer NE, passing (right) oil-refineries dating from 1966, at a junction of the Karlsruhe–Marseille pipeline, and at 5km an exit for adjacent **Le Landeron**, just S of the motorway, founded in 1325 and preserving two town-gates, a long central Place and a 15C *Hôtel de Ville*.

The road shortly crosses or by-passes **La Neuveville** (or *Neuenstadt*), an old town founded by the prince-bishops of Basle. It overlooks the SW end of the Bielersee and preserves several medieval rampart-towers, and a market-place traversed by a rivulet, and with gate-towers at either end. Near the upper end is the *Hôtel de Ville*, with a fine 17C hall and local *Museum*. To the E of the centre is the so-called *Église Blanche*, founded in the 11C, with 15–17C murals, restored, and tombstones of interest. The town is overlooked to the N by the *Schlossberg* with its late 13C *Castle*.

A road (partly toll) ascends via *Lignières* and (10km) *Nods* to cross the W flank of the *Chasseral* (1607m), the highest summit of the Bernese Jura, descending thence to *St.-Imier*; see Rte 5B.

The main road skirts the vine-clad slopes to the N of the **Bielersee**, some 14.5km long and 3.5km wide, with a view of the *St.-Petersinsel* (see Rte 8A). Several remains of neolithic lake villages were brought to light with the lowering of the water-level by the construction of the *Aar Canal* (from its S shore to Aarberg) in 1878. Following the railwayline along the lake-side, we shortly cross *Ligerz*, with a conspicuous late 15C Gothic *Church*, then adjacent *Twann*, here crossing the language frontier, and 9km beyond, at the head of the lake, enter **Biel/Bienne**; see Rte 9.

The main road continues NE below the steep ridge of the Jura through (14km) **Grenchen** (16,800 inhab.), an industrial and watch-making centre, to approach (11km) **SOLOTHURN (Soleure** in French; 15,800 inhab.; 7550 in 1880), the capital of its canton, a small industrial town largely on the N bank of the Aare. It preserves a partly walled centre of considerable charm, with a number of medieval buildings of interest, and is dominated by its white stone cathedral.

Founded on the site of a Roman settlement of c 370 (*Castrum Salodurense* or *Salodurum*), it became a free imperial city in 1218, at first controlled by the secular canons of the cathedral, from which its citizens freed themselves in 1252. In 1481, together with surrounding rural districts, they joined the Swiss Federation. From 1554 to 1791 the city was the official residence of the French envoy to the Confederation and became a centre of enlistment for recruits into the Swiss regiments of the French army, and later an asylum of French emigrés. Since 1828 Solothurn, largely German-speaking, has been the residence of the Roman Catholic bishop of Basle. Among its natives was Cuno Amiet (1868–1961), the artist. 'Charles Sealsfield' (Karl Anton Postl; 1793–1864), author of 'Austria as it is' (1828), resided here after returning from America in 1837. Thaddeus Kosciuszko (1746–1817), the Polish patriot, died here.

The *Rötibrücke* crosses the Aare immediately E of the enceinte, which one may conveniently enter by the *Baseltor* (1508), N of which is a promenade constructed round the bastion of *St. Ursus*, the main relic of the mid 17C fortifications, laid out at vast expense and largely levelled after 1835. Passing through the town gate, we reach the **Cathedral of St. Ursus**, a massive but not unhandsome Italianate Baroque building of 1762–73, erected by G.-M. Pisoni of Ascona, which occupies the site of a church founded by Queen Bertha c 910. Its *Treasury* may be visited by applying to the Sacristy, 75 Hauptgasse.

A few paces W in this street, bordered by several attractive 17C houses, is the *Jesuitkirche* or *Professorenkirche* (1680–1705), radically restored in the 1950s. Adjacent (No. 60) is the entrance to the former cloister, containing a lapidary collection; while just beyond, over-looking the market-place with a *Fountain* of 1561, is the *Zeitglockenturm*, a mid 13C clock-tower with a jaquemart of 1545.

From the W end of the Hauptgasse we may work our way N along the Staden, through the Friedhofplatz, preserving a fragment of the original Roman castrum, and up the Schmiedengasse to reach the *Bieltor* (1535), at the W end of the Gurzelngasse which contains several notable mansions. Passing through the gate and turning right, we reach the *Burristurm* (1535). Bear right through gardens laid out on the former glacis, past the *Reformkirche* and a *Concert-hall*, to reach the ***Kunstmuseum**.

Notable paintings include: *Hans Asper*, Portrait of Peter Fuessly, Wilhelm Froelich and Anna Froelich-Rahn; *Anton Graff*, A Polish lady; *Hans Holbein the Younger*, The Virgin of Solothurn, flanked by Saints Ursus and Nicholas of Myra; *Rigaud*, Portrait of Gérard Edelinck; *Frans Snyders*, Still life with ape and parrot; *Tiberius Wocher*, Self-portrait; *Caspar Wolf*, A cavern; *Antwerp Master of c 1520–30*, Triptych of the Crucifixion; *Master of the Paradise-garden*, Virgin of the strawberries (c 1425); *Albert Anker*, Young girl with a red background; *Johann Jakob Biedermann*, The Rheinfall near Schaffhausen; *Alexandre Calame*, View of Lac Léman; *Frank Buchser*, The sunshade, Portrait of Johann August Sutter; *Cuno Amiet*, Snow-scene, Anna Amiet in a green hat, Breton girl, Portrait of Arthur Honegger in 1935; *Ferdinand Hodler*, The avalanche, William Tell, and several other works; *Hans Berger*, A peasant; *Cézanne*, Three skulls; *Van Gogh*, The warden at St.-Rémy; *Klimt*, Goldfish; *Max Liebermann*, Hunter and dogs; *Matisse*, Nude at a window in Nice; *Félix Vallotton*, Nude; *Otto Vautier*, Seated woman with a pink; Landscapes by *Otto Frölicher* (Solothurn, 1840–90); and representative works by *Renoir, Braque, Utrillo, Rouault*, and *G. Giacometti*.

Walking SW, the old town is re-entered near (left) the *Franziskanerkirche*, which dates in its present form from 1664, although mentioned in 1280. On the S side of its Platz is the *Rathaus*, with a facade of c 1700 and a tower of 1476 containing a winding stair of curious workmanship added in 1632, and flanked by two lower domes.

A few paces E stands the *Old Arsenal or *Altes Zeughaus*, a massive gabled building of 1614 dominating its Platz, embellished by the *St. Maurice Fountain* of 1556. It contains—on three floors connected by spiral stairs—an extensive collection of Arms, Armour, Uniforms, numerous standards (some of which are genuine) captured by the Swiss in their campaigns against the Burgundians and Austrians, and decorations from Charles le Téméraire's tent, taken at Grandson; also a group of armed figures arranged by Disteli to represent the Diet of Stans, at which Solothurn was admitted to the Federation in 1481. Murray remarked that some of the armour was for sale in the 1830s.

Turning S, we shortly regain the cathedral and continuing downhill reach the KLOSTERPLATZ, to the E of which is the 17C chapel of *St. Peter*. No. 2 in the Platz contains *Natural History collections*, including several fossil turtles of a kind only found in this district.—To the SW is the *Palais Besenval* (early 18C), beyond which is the *Landhaus* of 1723.

In the old transpontine suburb approached by the *Wengibrücke*, further W, is the *Church* (1736) of an old hospital, SW of which is the *Krummeturm*, a mid 17C bastion surmounted by a twisted spire.

Among places of interest in the vicinity of Solothurn, apart from several convents (16–20Cs) are—N of the centre—the 18C *Schloss Blumenstein*, containing the town's *Historical Museum*, including a collection of musical-boxes; and, further NE the *Schloss Waldegg* (late 17C), with terraced gardens.—From between the two, a path ascends a romantic gorge to the chapel of *St. Verena*.

4km NW of Solothurn lies *Oberdorf*, with a church of Carolingian foundation rebuilt in the 17C, from which one may take a chair-lift to the *Weissenstein* (1284m) or follow the steeply climbing road to the summit. This crest of the Jura range commands a splendid distant view of the Alps from Mont Blanc to the Santis; in front are the peaks of the Bernese Oberland, with (from left to right) the Schreckhorn, Finsteraarhorn, Mönch, Eiger, and Jungfrau; while to the right are the lakes of Biel, Neuchâtel, and Morat. Still more extensive views may be obtained from either the *Röti* (E; 1396m) or the *Hasenmatt* (W; 1445m).

The recommended route hence is the N1 motorway, entered 5km E, with its main exits at 20km, for **Basle**, and 10km beyond, for **Lucerne**; after a further 10km **Aarau** lies 7km N; see below. The motorway may be regained 7km E of Aarau for (16km) **Baden** and **Zürich**, 24km beyond; see Rtes 14 and 23.

FROM SOLOTHURN TO OLTEN AND AARAU VIA THE NO. 5 (47km). We bear NE through (10km) *Wiedlisbach*, a characteristic little town, 2km S of which, beyond the motorway, lies *Wangen an der Aare*, likewise conserving several medieval features, including a covered bridge.—7km *Oensingen*, with the 13C

Schloss Neu-Bechburg.—15km **Olten**; see Rte 13A. *Schönenwerd*, 8.5km beyond, has a fine collegiate church several times altered since the 12C, and a *Museum of Footwear*, part of the Bally establishment.

4.5km **AARAU** (15,800 inhab.; 5900 in 1880), the busy capital of its German-speaking canton (*Aargau*, or *Argovia*), the least mountainous of Switzerland. Until 1798 it was subject to Berne, but then became the capital of the short-lived Helvetic Republic, and since 1803 has been a separate canton of the Confederation. Thomas Lever (1521–77) was minister to the English community here in 1556–59. It was the residence for many years of Heinrich Zschokke (1771–1848), the historian and novelist, who died here. The Altstadt preserves several concentric streets of character, flanked by 17–18C houses with painted gables. The 18C *Rathaus* is built round the older tower of the Counts von Rore, a few paces SW of which is the *Stadtkirche* (15C), with a fine organ, modern glass, and a 17C belfry. A short distance S of the *Obertorturm* (13th and 16C), on the S side of the enceinte, is the *Aargauer Kunsthaus*, with a representative collection of the works of Swiss artists, together with a few French canvases.

FROM AARAU TO ZÜRICH VIA LENZBURG AND BREMGARTEN (48km). An alternative to the motorway is the old No. 1, driving due E to (11km) **Lenzburg**, an ancient little town dominated by its feudal *Castle*, once the property of the Habsburgs and Bernese, and now containing a cantonal *Museum*. Frank Wedekind (1864–1918) was living here in 1886 (his family had settled here in 1872), as was Strindberg, whose second wife, Frieda Uhl, was later to live with Wedekind. To the NE, between the town and the motorway, and discovered in 1964 during the construction of the latter, are remains of a 1C *Roman Theatre*.—We shortly bear SE, after 8.5km turning left for (1.5km) **Wohlen** (11,700 inhab.), a small industrial town formerly the centre of Swiss straw-hat making.—*Villmergen*, 1km right of this junction, was the centre of the so-called 'Villmergen Wars' in 1656 and 1712, during the religious disputes between Catholics and Protestants, the former losing in the second war the advantages gained in the first.—**Muri**, 10.5km SE of the crossroads, was the site of a powerful Benedictine abbey, founded in 1027 and suppressed in 1841; the *Church*, baroquised by Caspar Moosbrugger in 1695, preserves good stalls, two notable Baroque organs (restored) and an 11C crypt. The stuccowork is by Giovanni Bettini, the frescos by F.A. Giorgioli. The cloister, restored, and containing Renaissance glass, dates from 1534; other dependencies were rebuilt after a fire in 1889. Muri was the birthplace of Caspar Wolf (1735–83), the artist.

Bearing SE from Wohlen, the road descends into the valley of the Reuss, with a good view of **Bremgarten**, a little medieval town, its rampart towers rising above the far bank, the river being spanned by a covered wooden *Bridge*. At the E end of the upper town is a 16–17C *Castle*. The Protestant theologian Heinrich Bullinger (1504–75) was a native, as was the humanist and translator Niklas von Wyle (c 1410–78/9). It was also the home of the Middle High German poet Walther von Rheinau.—At *Hermetschwill*, 2.5km S, on the E bank, is a Benedictine house founded in the late 12C, its church rebuilt in the early 17C, the date of its present dependencies.—The road climbs steeply NE from Bremgarten over the flank of the *Heitersberg* (views), descending to meet the No. 3 after 12.5km, just E of *Dietikon* (cf.), later joining the motorway in the industrial NW suburbs of **Zürich**; see Rte 23.

9 Belfort to Berne via Porrentruy, Tavannes and Biel/Bienne

Total distance, 126km (78 miles). N19. 19km *Delle*—No. 6. 14km **Porrentruy**—13km. *St. Ursanne* lies 5.5km SW.—7.5km *Glovelier*, where turn left for 1.5km, then right through the *Gorges du Pichoux*. Turn left at 7km for (5.5km) *Bellelay*—7.5km *Tavannes*—No. 6. 18km **Biel/Bienne**—11km *Lyss*—22km **Berne**.

Maps: M 216; BL 26, 31, 36 or 5016.

We turn onto the N19 not far S of **Belfort** (see *Blue Guide France*), and later cross the Rhine–Rhône Canal prior to reaching *Delle*, the frontier town (Customs). Entering the canton of *Jura*, so denominated in 1979 and formerly part of the canton of Berne, the road ascends the wide valley of the Allaine to (14km) **PORRENTRUY** (443m; **Pruntrut** in German), a small industrial town on its right bank.

It is overlooked by the old Palace of the prince-bishops of Basle (from 1529–1792), a picturesque pile of various dates. The town prospered particularly during the incumbency of Bp Blarer, from 1575–1608. During the Revolutionary period it was the capital of the department of Mont-Terrible (see below), and in 1815 was incorporated into the canton of Berne by the Treaty of Vienna.

Below the *Château* is the *Porte du France* (1536), while the Rue Pierre-Péquignat leads S, continued beyond the Pl. de l'Independence by the Grand-Rue. In this main street stand the *Hôtel des Halles, Hôtel de Ville*, and *Hôtel-Dieu* or hospital, all built in the 1760s by Pierre-François Pâris. The last houses the *Tourist Office* and a local *Museum*. To the E is *St.-Pierre*, dating from the early 14C; further S is the early 17C *Jesuit church*. In the Rue des Annonciades, parallel to and W of the Grand-Rue, is the *Hôtel de Gléresse* (1750), with the *Public Library*, containing several MSS and incunables of interest, and archives.—*St.-Germain*, a short walk E of the Pl. de l'Independence, is of various dates from the 12th to the mid 17C.

From (4.5km) *Courgenay*, a minor road ascends S over a ridge to **St.-Ursanne**—which is better approached from crossroads 8.5km further along the main road—which climbs steeply along the N side of *Mont Terri* (804m). Mont Terri was the site of a Roman fort which briefly gave its name, somewhat deformed, to the former department; see above. St.-Ursanne (see p 122) lies in the valley of the Doub, reached by a road descending abruptly to the right at the hilltop crossroads.

The main road climbs down to the SE to (16km) **Delémont**; see Rte 12B. Our route bears right; the 'Corniche du Jura' shortly forks right from it to (25km) *Saignelégier*; see p 122. We climb down through (5.5km) *Boécourt*, and 2km beyond, at *Glovelier*, turn left and then right after 1.5km to ascend the picturesque ***Gorges du Pichoux**, traversed for 7km.—From its upper end a minor road bears E to (c 10km) *Moutier* (see Rte 12B) via the *Col des Écorcheresses*, below the *Moron* (1336m).

Turning sharp right, the road leads past (5.5km) the former Premonstratensian *Abbey of Bellelay* (931m), founded in 1136 and occupied until 1797. Most of its conventual buildings, now an asylum, date from the 1C BC, while the ***Church** of c 1710 is an imposing if bare Baroque edifice.

Hence we turn S to descend to (7.5km) *Tavannes*, crossing which, we climb over a ridge to the SW, close to which is the *Pierre-Perthuis*, a natural opening enlarged to facilitate the movement of Roman legions, and with a partly defaced Latin inscription. The road climbs down to meet that from St.-Imier at (5km) *Sonceboz*, and threads a picturesque wooded defile before bearing right for *Biel/Bienne*.

BIEL, or **BIENNE** (437m; 53,800 inhab.; 16,600 in 1880), a bilingual industrial and watch-making town founded c 1230, lies at the NE extremity of its lake and below a ridge of the Jura. It has comparatively little to interest the traveller apart from its quaint Altstadt and a museum. Robert Walser (1878–1956), the author, was born here.

At the S end of the Aldstadt is the Bourgplatz, from which one may enter the old enceinte, of which several towers remain on the NW side. Here is the *Rathaus* of 1676. A short street to the right leads to the *Ring*, a picturesque arcaded square with the 15C *Stadtkirche*, a turreted Renaissance house (rebuilt) and a fountain of 1546. At the upper end of the arcaded Obergasse is the *Gasthaus zur Krone* (c 1582; restored), where Goethe put up in 1770; facing it is another quaint fountain.

To the SW, at No. 50 Seevorstadt, is the **Museum Schwab**, named after its founder, Col Friedrich Schwab (1803–69), and largely devoted to the archaeology of the several lake-villages discovered in the vicinity during the last century. The collection includes artefacts from La Tène (cf.).

FROM BIEL/BIENNE TO MURTEN VIA INS (32km). We traverse *Nidau*, with a 12C castle rebuilt in the 14C, and skirt the S shore of the *Bieler See*, with a view of the *St.-Petersinsel* to the W; see Rte 6A. Near (7km) *Mörigen* a lake-village has been discovered with important remains of the early Iron Age (800 BC); adjacent *Täuffelen* shows traces of Roman occupation. Beyond Täuffelen we cross the Hagneck Canal and veer away from the lake shore to (14km) *Ins* (see p 135), and **Murten/Morat**, 11km beyond, see Rte 6A.

At *Buren an der Aare*, 11km due E of Biel/Bienne, is a 17C castle.

The recommended route from Biel to Berne is the motorway, recently completed, which roughly follows the old main road through (11km) the small industrial town of *Lyss* (by-passed), 5km SW of which lies *Aarburg* (see p 136), while c 5km SE of Aarberg is the former Cistercian monastery of *Frienisberg*, founded in 1131, with a 13C church.

A further 13km brings us to *Münchenbuchsee*, birthplace of Paul Klee (1879–1940), with a church containing good glass of c 1300, beyond which we meet the No. 1 at *Zollikofen*, 7km N of **Berne** ; see Rte 10 and p 135.

10 Berne

BERNE (in its anglicised form; **Bern** in German; 548m; 136,300 inhab.; 163,150 in 1960; 111,800 in 1930; 45,750 in 1880), is the mainly German-speaking capital of its canton, and the comparatively centrally sited political capital or '*Bundesstadt*' of the Swiss Confederation, although fourth in size (after Zürich, Basle and Geneva) of its cities. Its characteristic old centre, largely built of a greenish-grey sandstone, is picturesquely situated on a high peninsular bluff within a narrow loop of the Aare, which flows below it in a deep ravine. The river is spanned by several lofty bridges connecting the old centre with more modern quarters. With its buttressed '*Lauben*', or arcades, which flank its ancient streets and its numerous carved and gaily painted fountains (many attributed to Hans Gieng), old Berne retains more of a medieval aspect than any other city in Switzerland, while it commands several superb distant views of the snow-clad Alps.

The canton of Berne is second in size (after the Grisons), and in population (after Zürich), and comprises three main divisions, the Seeland, to the NW, which until 1979 included that area now the canton of Jura; the so-called Mittelland, embracing the foothills of the Alps and the country around Berne itself, including the fertile Simmental; and the Bernese Oberland, or high Alps, to the S and SE, culminating in the Jungfrau and Finsteraarhorn.

Mid nineteenth century view of Berne

Although a small amphitheatre and other Roman remains have been uncovered at *Tiefenau*, some 3km to the N, it appears that Berne itself, 'youngest and haughtiest of the famous towns of the Swiss', was founded in 1191 as a military post on its easily defended site by Berchtold V, Duke of Zähringen. Its name may be derived from the German *Bär*, a bear; at all events the bear is its heraldic device and was used on its oldest known civic seal (1224), and is ubiquitous; see also p 146. Berne became a free imperial city in 1218, and its independence was finally confirmed by the victories of Dornbühl and Laupen (in 1298 and 1339 respectively).

The first enceinte reached as far W as the Zeitglockenturm, or Clock Tower, in its original form dating from 1218–20; by 1250 the town had extended to the present Käfigturm or Prison Tower and by 1350 to the Christoffel Tower (which stood near the Heiliggeistkirche, but was dismantled in 1865). Much of the medieval timber-built town was destroyed in a devastating fire in 1405, and then rebuilt in stone.

In 1353 Berne joined the Swiss Confederation, of which it was soon to take the lead; it likewise later became one of the main champions of the Reformation in Switzerland, which it accepted in 1528. Although always aristocratically inclined, its patricians ('Leurs Excellences les Messieurs de Berne') became an extremely powerful oligarchy, against which the revolts of its citizens in 1470 (as described by Thüring Frikart), of Major Davel in 1723, and Samuel Henzi in 1749, made little headway. The first effective shock to their entrenched control of affairs came with the French occupation in 1798, when the city's Treasury was plundered. Since 1831 Berne has been a stronghold of political progress and in 1848 it became the capital of the Federation. It has since, apart from being the site of foreign embassies, become the seat of several international bodies, among them that of the *Universal Postal Union* (1874), and the *Central Office for International Rail Transport*. The *Berne Convention of International Copyright* was signed here in 1886.

Among natives of Berne have been the artists Niklaus Manuel (Deutsch; 1484–1530), also a propagandist for the Reformation; Johann Grimm (1677–1747); David Morier (?1705–70), who emigrated to England in 1743, and known for his equestrian portraits; Franz Niklaus König (1765–1832); Joseph Werner the Younger (1637–1710); Abraham von Bonstetten (1796–1879); Ferdinand Hodler (1853–1918); Oscar Lüthy (1882–1945) and Otto Mayer-Amden (1885–1933). And in other fields, Albrecht von Haller (1708–77), poet and physician; Johann David Wyss (1743–1818), author of 'The Swiss Family Robinson'; Karl Viktor von Bonstetten (1745–1832), the political economist and friend of Thomas Gray and Mme de Staël; Mme Marie Tussaud (née Gressholz; 1760–1850); Théodore Emil Kocher (1841–1917), the surgeon, and Gottfried von Einem (1918–), composer.

Hermann Hesse (1877–1962) lived here in 1912–19; Michael Bakunin, the anarchist, died in the hospital of Berne on 1 July 1876.

A. Old Berne

Several main roads converging on the city from the W lead to the BAHNHOFPLATZ, a busy hub of communications, dominated to the N by the extensive modern complex of buildings (1970) erected over the *Railway Station* (dating from 1857) and containing the *Tourist Office*.

Underground parking facilities are available to the N of this complex, approached off the Schanzenstrasse, the first main street to the W. This ascends past the main *Post Office* and across the railway lines to the University quarter on the hill known as the *Grosse Schanze*, occupying the site of the main bastion of the fortifications of Berne, demolished in 1840.

The *Terrace*, reached by a flight of steps opposite the *Law Courts*, commands a fine *View over the city and towards the distant Alps of the Bernese Oberland; but see Kleine Schanze, below. To the N are the *University Buildings* (1905). The University, refounded as such in 1834, consists of seven faculties and contains c 7000 students. To the NE is the *Institute of Physical Research*, housing the *Observatory*.

Immediately W of the Bahnhofplatz, at Bubenbergplatz 4, stands the *Burgerspital*, or hospital, of 1742, with its two courtyards.—To the E rises the **Heiliggeistkirche** (of the Holy Ghost), a Baroque building of 1729 by Niklaus Schiltknecht, its interior stuccowork by J.A. Feichtmayr.

An escalator descends to the vast underground subway and shopping area below the square where the preserved remains of the mid 14C outer wall of the old city, including the foundations of the *Christoffelturm*, can be seen.

The short Christoffelgasse leads S to the viewpoint of the *Kleine Schanze*, with gardens laid out on the site of 17C fortifications. The peaks normally in view are (from left to right): the Wetterhorn, Schreckhorn, Finsteraarhorn, Eiger, Mönch, Jungfrau, Gletscherhorn, Ebnefluh, Grosshorn, Breithorn, Gspaltenhorn, Blümlisalp, Doldenhorn, Altels and Balmhorn.

To the left, on buttressed cliffs overlooking the Aare, rises a range of buildings comprising the **Bundeshaus**, or *Federal Palace*. Its W wing, of 1857, accommodates ministeries; the central block (1901; by Hans Wilhelm Auer), surmounted by a lofty dome and two subordinate cupolas, and inscribed 'Curia Confoederationis Helveticae', is the seat of the *Swiss Parliament* or *Bundesversammlung*. The interior may be inspected on an accompanied visit.—The *Bernerhof*, built as a hotel in 1859 immediately E of the gardens, houses the Federal Finance

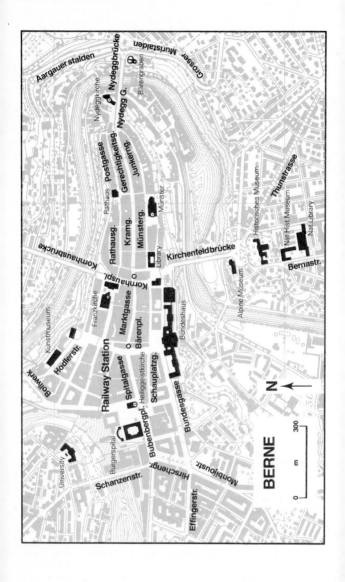

and Customs Department.

From the Bahnhofplatz, the arcaded Spitalgasse—a busy shopping street—leads E. With its continuations, it forms the main thoroughfare traversing the peninsula under several names to the Nydeggbrücke, at the far end of the old town. The restored *Pfeiferbrunnen* or *Bagpiper Fountain* (1545) will be noticed.

We now reach the BÄRENPLATZ, dominated by the *Käfigturm* or *Prison Tower* (1642), on the site of the W gate of 1256, and used as a prison until 1897. The Platz itself, together with the BUNDESPLATZ, dominated by the *Federal Palace*, and the WAISENHAUSPLATZ to the left, are the sites of colourful markets on Tuesday, Thursday (in summer) afternoon and evening, and Saturday mornings. Here also, on the fourth Monday in November, takes place the Onion Market, which ends in a bear-like Carnival with 'Zibelegrinde'. For the area to the N see p 149.

Passing through the tower, we enter the arcaded Marktgasse, leading E to the Zeitglockenturm. The *Seilerbrunnen* is notable, with a figure said to be that of Anna Seiler, founder of Berne's first hospital (later known as the Insel Hospital), but perhaps an allegory of Moderation. The original sculpture of 1549 (now in the Historical Museum) was replaced by a copy in 1968. Further down the street, but not in its original position, is the *Schützenbrunnen*, or *Musketeer Fountain* (1543).

To the left at the next main crossroad, in the KORNHAUSPLATZ, is the horrific *Kindlifresserbrunnen* or *Ogre Fountain* (c 1544), in which a figure is shown devouring a child. Whether this is some reference to the myth of Cronus, or to the spurious allegation of Jewish ritual murder said to have been committed in the late 13C (for the statue was once painted yellow), is debatable.

Further N, on the W side of the Place, is the *Kornhaus* or *Granary* of 1718, rebuilt in the 1890s, in an upper floor of which is the small *Gutenberg Museum*, illustrating the history of printing.—Behind the building stands the *Französische Kirche* or *French Church* (late 13C), that of a former Dominican monastery, the W front and S aisle of which date from 1754, but the whole has been frequently restored.—Beyond the Kornhaus is the *Stadttheater* of 1903, and the *Kornhausbrücke* (1898) which leads N to the suburb of *Altenberg* and the *Kursaal*. Its span is 115m; it stands some 58m above the Aare, and provides a good view.

S of the Kornhausplatz is the *Theaterplatz*, in which is the *Hôtel de Musique* (by Niklaus Sprüngli; 1770), later much altered; and facing the end of the street, the collonaded *Alte Hauptwache* or *Guardhouse* (1768), by the same architect.—A few paces W of the latter is the *Marcuardhaus*, a mansion of 1765..

The **Zeitglockenturm**, which dominates the area, was in its original form (c 1191) the first W Gate of the enceinte. It later grew in height, and in the late 15C was transformed into more or less what we see today, although several alterations were made in 1770–71, and it has been restored since. The clock itself, by Kaspar Brunner, dates from 1530. On the E side of the tower is an astronomical clock, adjacent to which is an amusing Jaquemart, with jester, cock, bears, etc., which whirrs into action 4 minutes before each hour. It is still the 'object of wonder to an admiring crowd of gaping idlers', in the words of Murray.

The Zibelgässli leads N. No. 20 is the *Haus zur Glocke* (1581; later heightened), on the corner of the arcaded Rathausgasse, to the N of which is the old Brunngasse.—S of the Clock Tower is the *Erkerhaus* (1505), with its oriel window, while No. 87 in the arcaded Kramgasse, which we now follow, dates from 1564, although frequently altered.—For the Münstergasse, parallel to the S, and the Münster or Cathedral, see below. No. 72 Kramgasse, the *Haus de Grenus*, has a facade of 1740; near it is the *Zähringerbrunnen*, a fountain of 1542, raised in memory of the city's founder and displaying 'Mutz', the heraldic bear wearing a visored helmet surmounted by a gilt orb.—No. 62, the *Kirchbergerhaus*, dates from 1719.—The upper floor of No. 49 was the *Home of Albert Einstein* in 1903–05, and may be visited; it contains momentoes of the scientist. No. 54 (opposite), dates from 1743; No. 45, the *Zunfthaus*, or Guildhall of the Butchers, from 1770. We now reach the *Simsonbrunnen* or *Samson Fountain* (1544), with a replica of the original statue, possibly donated by the butchers. Among other mansions of note are Nos 29 (1722), 9 (1770) and 2 (the *Rathausapotheke*, a pharmacy since 1571, with a facade of c 1720).

From this point the street changes its name to Gerechtigkeitsgasse, in which Nos 81 and 79 (the *Zunfthaus zu Distelzwang*) date from 1768 and 1702 respectively.

Rather than continuing E, one may make a brief detour to the N (left) into the small Rathausplatz, in which now stands the *Vennerbrunnen*, or Ensign Fountain, the statue a replica of the original of 1542. The **Rathaus** or *Town Hall*, its most notable feature a double exterior staircase, was built in the early 15C after the fire of 1405, but was radically altered when not rebuilt in 1939–42.—At No. 72 Postgasse, which we follow to the right, is the *Staatskanzlie* (1535; with a portal of 1784); Nos 64/66 is the late 17C *Posthaus*; No. 57, opposite, the back of the former *Crown Inn* (until 1858) of 1630; No. 62 is the *Chapel of the Antonines* (1505; rebuilt 1940).

Hence we may follow a passage to the right to regain the Gerechtigkeitsgasse, in which Nos 52 (1760), 42 (1734) and 33 (opposite; 1608; with a facade of 1740), are notable. No. 62, the *Klötzlikeller*, is one of several ancient wine-cellars in the area. The *Gerechtigkeitsbrunnen* or *Fountain of Justice* (1543), will be noted. No. 7, the *Golden Eagle Inn*, dates from 1766.

The three main streets of the medieval town now converge at the W end of the Nydeggasse, but it is worth while bearing downhill to the left, passing the **Nydeggkirche** (1341–1500), partly built on the site of the original Zähringen fortress destroyed in c 1270, the well of which was rediscovered in 1960. Steps descend to the Mattenenge, in which No. 5 is the 13C *Ländtetor*, on the site of an older river-gate. Hence we may turn N to reach the Läuferplatz, with its *Messenger Fountain*, a replica of the original of 1545. The *Untertorbrücke* (1489), on the site of a mid 13C wooden bridge, and several times rebuilt, crosses to the *Felsenburg*, a relic of the late 13C bridge-gate on the far bank.

Ascending to the right, we approach, on the S side of the Nydeggbrücke, the **Bärengraben**, or *Bear Pit*. Since 1480 or 1513, except for a brief interval when the French removed them to Paris in 1798, several shaggy lumbering representatives of the genus *Urs* have been kept at the city's expense, and this pit dates from the 1850s. The antics of the bears and their cubs, presumably not too unhappy in such bare surroundings, can be amusing.

On the hill-slope to the NE are *Rose-gardens*, commanding a fine view over the older town.

The *Nydeggbrücke* (1840) which one crosses some 25m above the Aare, provides a view of the *Matte*, a riverside quarter. A short distance beyond fork left along the Junkerngasse, a characteristic old street, in which No. 33 was rebuilt in 1555, and since reconstructed. Nos 43 and 32 date from 1785 and 1740 respectively. No. 47, the *Erlacherhof*, is an imposing mansion of 1746–52, designed by Albrecht Stürler. Since 1832 it has been the seat of municipal government and for a decade after 1848 that of the Federal Council. Excavations have revealed foundations of late 12th and 13C buildings below the main structure and in the courtyard. Another fine patrician mansion is the *Béatrice von Wattenwylhaus* (No. 59), mid 15C; its upper floors date from 1560 and 1705, when the S wing was added.

We now meet the Münstergasse, in which Nos 2 and 6 date from 1718 and 1559–1609 respectively, to reach the apse of the ***Münster** (sometimes erroneously yet understandably referred to as the *Cathedral)*,which Addison described in 1701 as 'perhaps the most magnificent Protestant church in Europe out of England'.

It was begun in 1421 by Matthäus Ensinger from Ulm, who had worked with his father, one of the builders of Strasbourg cathedral. It was not entirely vaulted until the close of the 16C, there having been a hiatus with the acceptance of the Reformation in Berne in 1528 when the minster was the object of iconoclastic destruction. A smaller 13C church which previously stood on the site was not demolished until c 1450. The 100m-high tower—one of its main features—was not completed until 1893, with the addition of an octagon and spire designed by August Beyer.

Regrettably, the friable nature of the sandstone has necessitated the restoration of the fine *West Portal*, with its numerous replicas of statues, and, in the tympanum, the Last Judgement sculpted by Erhart Küng, a Dutch Westphalian, in which over 200 figures are depicted; the Wise and Foolish Virgins will be noted.

The *Interior* is in a good state of preservation, but somewhat cold and bare, although relieved by stained-glass depicting coats of arms in the clerestory and elsewhere (15–20C). Some of the earlier glass, in S windows, was twice shattered by hailstones. There is some good 15C glass in the choir (N side), the 19.4m-high vaulting of which, completed by Peter Pfister in 1517 and said to have been painted by Niklaus Manuel, is dissimilar to that in the 20.7m-high nave, designed by Daniel Heintz (1573), with 14 key-stones displaying the arms of patricians of Berne. The openwork stair-turret to the left of the choir will be noted, and also the well-carved stalls of 1523. The pulpit dates from 1470. The 18C organ has been several times altered.

Opposite the entrance stands the *Tscharnerhaus* (1735), and to the SW the *Chapter-house*, dating from 1755, after designs by Albrecht Stürler, built on the site of a former house of the Teutonic Knights. Hence we may turn onto the well-buttressed, chestnut-planted *Plattform* or terrace, providing an interesting view over the weir of the Aare and of the Bernese Oberland (see p 143).

The Münstergasse continues W from the Platz. No. 61, built as a granary in 1760, accommodates the *City and University Library*, where occasional bibliographical exhibitions are held. Among its treasures are a 9C bestiary of the School of Rheims, and Diebold Schilling's 'Spiezer Chronik'.

We shortly enter the Casinoplatz, dominated by the ponderous edifice of the *Casino* (1909), a few paces SE of the Clock Tower.

B. The district of Kirchenfeld

The *Kirchenfeldbrücke* (1883), 230m long and 38m above the Aare, leads S from the Casinoplatz to the HELVETIAPLATZ, providing several views: of the Oberland (see Kleine Schanzel), of the heavily buttressed *Münster Plattform*, and *Federal Palace*, etc.

To the left of the Helvetiaplatz is the *Kunsthalle* (1918), the venue of temporary art exhibitions; to the right the *Alpine Museum*, on the GROUND FLOOR of which is installed the *P.T.T.* (or Swiss Post, Telegraph and Telephone) *Museum*. This latter contains several items of interest in the development of postal and telephone communications in Switzerland, and a comprehensive philatelic collection. The original postal coach from St. Gallen to Heiden will be noted. It is expected that the P.T.T. collections will be moved to new premises in the Helvetiastrasse, near the Landesbibliothek; see below.

The *Alpine Museum preserves a most interesting collection of material on every aspect of the Alps. Sections are devoted to photographs and paintings showing glacier movement; minerals and crystals; relief models of mountains and ranges, etc.; historical collections of climbing implements—ice axes, alpenstocks, crampons, snow-shoes, and skis, etc., including the most modern equipment; photographs of early alpinists, together with their books and notebooks; paintings, watercolours and lithographs by *Gabriel Matthias Lory* (1784–1846), *Samuel Birmann* (1793–1847), *Niklaus Sprüngli* (1725–1802), *Caspar Wolf, J.S. Weibel, C.L. Hackert* and later artists.

The upper floor displays numerous early Maps (including reproductions), among them those of Thomas Schoepf (1577), Gabriel Walser (1770), and of Hermann Kümmerly (1897/8), etc., and several more topographical reliefs at various scales, including one of the whole of Switzerland (by Charles Eugene Perron at 1:100,000; c 1900), and collections of theodolites and other cartographical instruments. Also several mountainscapes by *Alexander Calame*, among other views and lithographs (some by *Maximilien de Meuron*) and a number of Panoramas. Among other collections are those of model Alpine chalets; wood-carvings and distaffs, masks from the Lötschental and costumes, etc.

The offices of the *Swiss Alpine Club* (S.A.C.), founded in 1863, are also here.

On the S side of the Place, beyond the *International Telegraph Union Monument* (1922), is the **Historical Museum**, in an only-too-solid edifice in a mock medieval Bernese style (1894 and 1922). Work has started on the long overdue modernisation of the museum, which will probably take several years to complete.

To the right of the entrance vestibule are the *Archaeological collections*, including Neolithic, Bronze Age, Roman and Celtic finds, among them objects of the Hallstatt period; statuettes, glass, ceramics, bronzes and mosaics; jewellery; arms and armour; utensils and implements, etc. Notable is a bronze vessel from Meikirch (11km NW of Berne).

Stairs descend to the MEZZANINE FLOOR, with a relief plan of Berne in 1800 at 1:500; depictions of bear-hunting in 1584–86 by Humbert Mareschet; Portraits by Emanuel Handmann, etc.; collections of porcelain, silver and furniture, and the Salon Portalès

(1765).—The BASEMENT contains original statues from the W portal of the Münster; costumes, glass, ceramics, and other models. A collection of arms and armour from the Middle East may also be seen.—Several reconstituted panelled rooms containing furniture of their period are likewise displayed. Notable is a copy—on a reduced scale—made in 1649 of the 24 pictures of the Dance of Death which were on the exterior wall of the Dominican monastery at Berne, the originals of which, of 1516–17, were by Niklaus Manuel.

On the stairs are a collection of 18–early 19C paintings depicting Swiss types, and a huge carved bust of St. Christopher which once embellished the Christoffelturm.

Following the Bernastrasse to the W of the museum, we shortly pass the *Schützenmuseum*, devoted to Swiss sharpshooters, to reach the **Natural History Museum**, the main interest of which lies in its collections of quartz crystals and other minerals from the Bernese Oberland and numerous dioramas displaying the fauna of Switzerland and elsewhere. The stuffed body of 'Barry', a St. Bernard dog which saved many lives in the early years of the 19C, will be noted.

Further on is the *Landesbibliothek*, or *Swiss National Library*, with a comprehensive collection of books, pamphlets and maps, mainly relating to Switzerland.—Beyond, to the right, is the *Mint* (Eidgenössische Münzstätte). We now reach the Kirchenfeldstrasse, traversing a residential quarter in which there are several embassies.—Not far to the W are the *Federal Archives*; to the E the street passes the *English Church* (*St. Ursula*; 1906) to reach the Thunplatz, with the *British Embassy* on its W side. The Thunstrasse leads diagonally NW to the Helvetiaplatz.

Just S of the church is the *Dählhölzli*, a park leading down to the Aare, with a small *Zoo* at its SW corner.

C. The Kunstmuseum

From the Käfigturm we may turn N into the Waisenhausplatz—overlooked (right) by the *Höllanderturm*—off which, in the Aarbergergass, stands the *Ryffli Fountain* of 1545. Ryffli was a captain of archers who after the battle of Laupen shot Jordan von Burgistein.—At the N end of the Platz stands the former *Waisenhaus* or *Orphanage* (1786; by L.E. Zehender), now Police Headquarters. Turning left, we follow the Hodlerstrasse, off which are slight remains of the 15C *Town Wall*, to reach (right) the Kunstmuseum.

The ***KUNSTMUSEUM** or *Art Gallery*, inaugurated in 1879, has been recently modernised, some sections being open-plan. GROUND FLOOR: **R1** *Ferdinand Hodler*, Portrait of Albertine Bernard, and Night, among several other works by this artist; *Max Buri*, Portrait of his daughter, Hedwig.—**R2** Several *anon*. *Italian* paintings of the 14–15Cs; *Duccio*, Maesta (1290); *Fra Angelico*, Madonna and child.—**R3** *anon*. Saints Christopher and Peter (1480); *anon*. S German Nativity (1465); the *Bernese Master of the Carnation*, Triptych of the Life of the Baptist (c 1490); and other works of the Bernese School of c 1500.—**R4** *Niklaus Manuel*, the St. Anne altar (1515); the St. Antony altar (1520); Decapitation of the Baptist; Martyrdom of the 10,000 on Ararat; the Conversion of Saul, etc.; *Hans Asper*, Portrait of Marx

Roeist.—**R5** *Joseph Werner the Younger*, several miniature portraits, etc.; *Joseph Heintz the Elder*, Male and Female portraits; *Johann Ludwig Aberli*, Landscapes; also several by *Casper Wolf*; *Franz Niklaus König*, Waterfall in the Lauterbrunnental; *Vigée-Lebrun*, Alpine fête (1808/9); and a terracotta plaque by *V. Sonnenschen*.

R7 *Albert Anker*, Portrait of Marie, the artist's daughter.—**R8** *Arnold Böcklin*, The mermaid; *Alois Erdtelt* (1851–1911), Portrait of the artist Gustav Vollenweider.—**R9** canvases by *Pissarro, Monet, Millet, Courbet* and *Delacroix*.—**R10** *Pissarro*, Peasant girl; *Cézanne*, Self-portrait in 1879; *Renoir*, Mme Renoir and her son; *Van Gogh*, Female peasant, and Sunflowers; and works by *Utrillo*, and *Sisley*.—**R11** Works by *Braque* and *Matisse*.—**R12** *Vuillard*, Portrait of Vallotton; *Félix Vallotton*, Self-portrait, and Woman reading; *Toulouse-Lautrec*, Mme Natanson at the piano; 'Varlin' (Willy Guggenheim; 1900–77), Portrait of Hugo Lötscher.—**RR14–16** are devoted to the art of *Hodler*, with numerous portraits, landscapes and huge allegorical canvases.

FIRST FLOOR: **R1** *Picasso*, Three figures; *Modigliani*, Elvira naked, and Portrait of Pinchus Krémegne; *Kemeny*, Mother and child.—**R2** *Cuno Amiet*, Self-portrait, Hodler in his coffin; three bronze nymphs, by *Maillol*.—**R3** *Picasso*, Mother and child (1901), The drinker (1902) and Seated woman (1922).—**R4** Works by *Braque* and *Juan Gris*.—**R5** Works by *Léger* and *Le Corbusier*.—**R6** Works by *Chagall*, *Soutine* and *Jawlensky*.—**R9** *Otto Mayer-Amden*, Portrait of a young girl; *Oscar Lüthy*, Variation of the 'Pietà of Avignon' by Enguerrand Quarton.—**R9** is devoted to *Kandinsky*.

RR10–11: Paul Klee; the Foundation preserves 42 canvases, 170 watercolours, 2300 drawings and other works by the artist.—**R12** displays works by *Jean Arp, Max Ernst, Miro* and *André Masson*.—**R13** *Magritte*, Souvenir de voyage, etc.; and *Dali*, Colossus of Rhodes, etc.—**R14** *Rothko*; sculpture by *Chillida*; and on the landing, more works by *Kemeny*.—**R15** *Poliakoff* and *Victor Passmore*.—**R18** *Lucio Fontana*, et al.

Among canvases not apparently at present on display are: *Marc Duval*, Portrait of Jeanne d'Albrecht; *Ambrosius Benson*, Male portrait; several portraits by *Johannes Dünz*; *Rigaud*, Portrait of Nicolas Boilau (?); *Emanuel Handmann*, Portrait of John Burnaby, British envoy in Berne (1748); *Liotard*, Portrait of Katherine, Countess of Guildford, and of Simon Lutrell in Turkish costume; *J.H. Tischbein the Elder*, Portraits of the artist's two wives; several landscapes by *Alexandre Calame*; *Henri Rousseau*, The tiger-hunt; *Lovis Corinth*, Self-portrait; *Frank Buchser*, Portraits of Gen. Sherman, Gen. Robert Lee, etc.; and *Madeleine Woog*, Self-portrait.

The Print Room is rich in 18C Swiss drawings, prints, and watercolours, and works by 19C French artists.

Bearing right on making our exit, we may walk a few paces along the *Lorrainebrücke*, with a view (right) of the former curtain wall and *Blutturm*, on the river bank. The bridge dates from 1930 and leads across to the *Botanic Garden* (right). The Bollwerk climbs S from the bridge towards the Heiliggeistkirche and the Bahnhofplatz.

A popular excursion from Berne is to the *Gurten-Kulm*, a hill (858m) to the S, providing extensive views, reached by a No. 9 tram (for *Wabern*) from near the Station. A funicular ascends from near the tram's penultimate stop.

For roads from Berne to **Murten/Morat**, see Rte 6A; for **Neuchâtel**, Rte 8A; for **Biel/Bienne**, Rte 12B, and for **Solothurn**, Rte 12C: all these in reverse. For Berne to **Lucerne**, see Rte 16; and for **Thun**, and **Interlaken**, Rte 17.

11   Basle

BASLE (as anglicised; in French **Bâle**; in German **Basel**; 273m; 171,700 inhab.; 148,050 in 1930; 61,750 in 1880 and 21,250 in 1837), after Zürich the second largest city in Switzerland, is strategically sited in the proximity of the French frontier at a right-angle bend of the Rhine and between the barrier ridges of the Jura and the Black Forest, a position which has fostered a lucrative transit trade over the centuries. It is divided into *Gross-Basel* and *Klein-Basel* (to the SW and NE respectively), and with a few adjoining communes the city forms the half-canton of *Basel-Stadt*; that of *Basel-Land* largely extending to the SE. It was a bishopric from the 4C until 1525, and since 1460 has been the seat of a University, in the following century becoming one of the great cradles of Humanism, maintaining a tradition alien to the concepts held in Geneva. Its Cathedral or Münster, of red sandstone like many of the city's buildings, rises picturesquely over the older town on a ridge overlooking the left bank of the Rhine. Its museums are notable; its important chemical works (Ciba-Geigy, Sandoz, Hoffman-La Roche, etc.), among other industries, are extensive; its fairs make it a focus of commercial activity; and since 1929 it has been the seat of the *Bank of International Settlements*.

The airport of *Bâle-Mulhouse* lies on French territory just N of the border. For boat trips on the Rhine, apply at the Tourist Office.

Basle originated in a settlement of the Celtic *Rauraci*, but first appears in history as a fort established in AD 374 by the Emperor Valentinian I, when it was called *Basilia*. Its importance was increased by the destruction of neighbouring *Augusta Raurica* by the Alemanni in the 5C and the erection by the bishop of Augusta of a new palace beside the fort. In 917 Basle was destroyed by the Huns. The 'Drei Könige' hotel occupies the site of a house where the Emperor Conrad II, his son Heinrich (afterwards Heinrich III) and Rudolf III, the last king of Burgundy, met in 1026.

The young Emperor Frederick II, Hohenstaufen, held his first 'court' at Basle in 1212. Its fortunes were firmly established in the early 13C, when Bp Heinrich of Thun built a bridge across the river and, although devastated by earthquake and fire in 1356, it was chosen as the meeting-place of the Ecumenical Council of Basle (1431–49). The secretary of the bishop of Fermo at this council was AEneas Sylvius Piccolomini, who later, when Pope Pius II, founded the University. The stimulus to trade given by the presence of the council increased the powers of the guilds, and in 1501 they joined the Swiss Federation. The bishop retired to Porrentruy in 1525 and (in 1528) to Solothurn.

The impulse of the Renaissance was strongly felt at Basle, and the teachings of Erasmus and Johannes Oekolampadius (1482–1531), among others, paved the way for the Reformation, the party for reform finally gaining the mastery in 1529, when the Mass was abolished. John Foxe resided in Basle from 1555 until 1559, employed as reader to Oporinus, who first published 'The Book of Martyrs' here in the latter year. Sebastian Castellio's influential 'De haereticis' (on whether heretics should be persecuted), was published here in 1554.

The Counter-Reformation brought many skilled tradesmen to Basle as refugees from France and Italy, the lace industry being brought from Lorraine by Antoine Lascailles in 1573. But the growth of oligarchic rule and the rigidity of the Church checked the development of the city and eventually (in 1831) led to a revolt in the rural parts of the canton. It has been suggested that an additional adverse effect was caused by a tendency to exclude newcomers from citizenship, and it is recorded that between the 1550s and 1650s the average numbers granted this honour annually fell from 45 to about 10.

Basle's industries were the making of dyes, chemicals, silk ribbons, and the brewing of beer, but these have been much diversified. It became an important

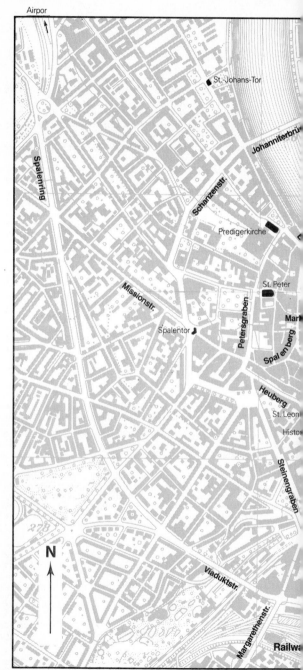

Airpor

St.-Johans-Tor

Johanniterbrü

Spalenring

Schanzenstr.

Predigerkirche

Missionstr.

St. Peter

Petersgraben

Mar

Spalentor

Spal en berg

Heuberg

St. Leon

Histo

Steinengraben

N

Viaduktstr.

Margarethenstr.

Railwa

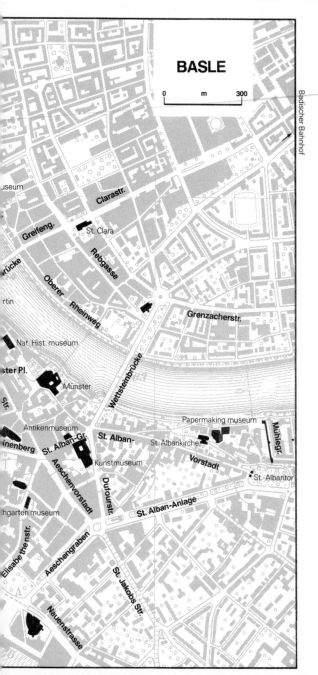

BASLE

0   m   300

Badischer Bahnhof

useum

Clarastr.

Greifeng.

St. Clara

Rebgasse

rücke

Oberer Rheinweg

rtin

Grenzacherstr.

Nat. Hist. museum

ster Pl.

Wettsteinbrücke

Münster

Papermaking museum

Mühleg.

Antikenmuseum

St. Alban-Gr.

St. Albankirche

inenberg

St. Alban-

Vorstadt

St.-Albantor

Kunstmuseum

Aeschenvorstadt

Dufourstr.

St. Alban-Anlage

hgarten museum

Elisabe the nstr.

Aeschengraben

St. Jakobs Str.

Nauenstrasse

hub of rail communication, gaining for itself the title of 'the Clapham Junction of Europe'. It was on 15 June 1844 that the first train steamed into Basle from France, but a regulation of the time insisted on the gate in the still existing fortifications being closed each evening after the last train had gone! 'Whistle-blowing' has continued in the pharmaceutical field. Its river-port (which may be visited) handles a high proportion of Swiss foreign trade.

Basle is the home of the *Schola Cantorum Basiliensis*, founded in 1926, and directed by Paul Sacher from 1933. Among natives of Basle have been Boniface Amerbach (1495–1562), the lawyer; Leonhard Euler (1707–83), the mathematician; the Bernouillis family in the 17–18Cs, several members of which, refugees from France, achieved eminence as mathematicians; the artists Hans Hug Kluber (1535/6–78); Joseph Heintz the Elder (1564–1609); Johann Rudolf Huber the Elder (1668–1748); Peter Birmann (1758–1844); Matthäus Merian the Elder (1593–1650), the engraver of topographical views; and Arnold Böcklin (1827–1901); Sir Luke Schaub (1690–1758), the diplomat; Johann Peter Hebel (1760–1826), the poet; Johann Jakob Bachofen (1815–87), whose 'Mutterrecht', a study of matriarchal societies, was influential; Jacob Burckhardt (1818–97), author of 'The Civilisation of the Renaissance in Italy', etc.; John James Heidegger (c 1659–1749), operatic manager to George II; Auguste Piccard (1884–1962), the physicist; Karl Barth (1886–1968), theologian and philosopher; and the pianist Edwin Fischer (1886–1960).

Zwingli studied in Basle in 1502–06; Hermann Hesse (1877–1962) spent his childhood here, where he worked in the book trade in 1899–1904 and resumed his Swiss citizenship in 1923; Hans Holbein the Younger (1497–1543, in London) was in Basle in 1515 and again in 1518–24 and 1528–32; Theophrastus Paracelsus was 'professor' of medicine here, briefly, in 1527; Friedrich Nietzsche held the chair of classical philosophy here in 1869–79; Heinrich Wölfflin, the art historian, followed Burckhardt as professor here in 1893. Desiderius Erasmus (1466–1536) settled in Basle in 1521, where many of his works were published by his friend Johann Froben (c 1460–1527) who had set up his business here in 1491. Andreas Vesalius (1514–64), the physician, visited Basle in 1542; Johann Jakob Grynaeus (1540–1617) was professor of theology here from 1575.

Among others who lived and died here were the artists Konrad Witz (1400–44/5) and Urs Graf (1485–1529); Konrad von Würzburg (c 1225–87), the Middle High German poet; Pierre-Louis Moreau de Maupertius (1698–1759), the French scientist; Sebastian Munster (c 1489–1552), who produced the 'Cosmographia Universalis' in 1544; Thomas Lovell Beddoes (1803–49), the poet and physiologist; Hans Arp (1887–1966), one of the founders of the Dada movement in Zürich in 1916; and Karl Jaspers (1883–1969), who held the chair of philosophy here from 1948.

Prince Charles Edward, the Young Pretender, under the alias of 'Dr Thompson', lived here in 1754–56 with his mistress Clementina Walkinshaw (who separated from him in 1760) and their daughter Charlotte Stuart (legitamised 1784).

A. Kunstmuseum; Münster

Several main roads converge on the *Bahnhof* or *Railway Station*, not far S of the early 17C enceinte of the city. A few paces to the E stands the cylindrical headquarters (1977) of the *Bank of International Settlements*, which has been compared to a colossal pile of coins.—Walking diagonally N across the adjacent gardens, we shortly reach the Elisabethenstrasse, in which No. 27 (right) is the ***Kirschgarten Haus**, now a museum.

The mansion, begun for Johann Rudolf Burckhardt-De Bary in 1775 to the design of Johann Ulrich Büchel, accommodates several well-displayed collections of quality on four floors. The rooms to the left of the entrance are devoted to an extensive collection of faïence and porcelain, etc., including Meissen, Ludwigsburg, Frankenthal and

Hoechst ware. This is continued in the basement, with examples of Strasbourg, Lunéville, Hanau and Winterthur ware, and a further collection of poêles or stoves, together with ironwork, shop-signs, grilles, etc. Also, on the ground floor, a small collection of glass.

From the well-proportioned Hall, stairs ascend to the FIRST FLOOR and a series of rooms; some have their original decoration, others have been transferred here from other sites. They contain a good collection of furniture and tapestries; also a spinet by Johann Heinrich Silbermann and, in the chapel, a late 17C organ. A collection of silver from Basle, and Kirschgarten porcelain may be seen. The kitchen is displayed on an upper floor.

One room is devoted to Johann Ludwig Burckhardt (John Lewis; 1784–1817, in Cairo), born in Lausanne and the son of the original owner of the house. He had visited England in 1806 and studied Arabic at Cambridge. He then travelled and explored extensively in the Middle East, disguised as 'Sheikh Ibrahim' and discovered Abū Simbel (in 1817) and the cliff city of Petra, and was the first European to make the pilgrimage to Mecca (1815). He also travelled to Palmyra, Baalbek, Jeddah and Abyssinia.

The Summer-house will be noted. The adjacent building now contains important collections of Clocks and Watches.

Beyond, to the left, is the *St. Elisabethenkirche* (1865), erected at the expense of Christoph Merian, a local Maecenas, to replace a medieval church.

We shortly reach a junction, the Bankenplatz, marking the S boundary of the medieval ALTSTADT. The old Aeschenvorstadt (sharp right), in which No. 15 is notable, is extended to the N by the *Freiestrasse*, a busy commercial street leading through the town to the Marktplatz.

Attic red-figured cup by the Tarquinia painter (470–460 BC), Antikenmuseum, Basle

We bear half right along the St.-Alban Graben, in which No. 5 is the *Antikenmuseum, with important collections of Greek and Roman Antiquities, opened in 1966, and in the process of extending into the adjacent building (No. 7); the mansion itself dates from 1828.

Many of the works of Classical art displayed come from the donated collections of Giovanni Züst, Robert Käppeli, and Peter and Irene Ludwig. Among the more remarkable objects are a marble grave relief of a Greek physician (c 480 BC); a bronze Mirror supported by a female figure, of the same date; a marble relief of a Banquet of the Dead (c 350 BC); the Medea Sarcophagus (Roman; AD 190); a Pithos decorated in relief (7C BC); several outstanding Archaic vases; an Attic black-figure amphora of c 540 BC decorated by the Amasis Painter; a red-figure amphora depicting Athena, by the Berlin Painter (490 BC); a collection of Vases from Apulia (2nd half of the 4C BC), and a remarkable collection of bronze figurines, etc.

Mention should be made of the extensive collection of Plaster Casts assembled at Mittlere Strasse 17, near the University.

A few paces beyond (right) stands the **KUNSTMUSEUM (1936; by R. Christ and P. Bonatz), containing one of the more important collections of Switzerland, with its entrance at the far end of the courtyard containing a cast of Rodin's Burghers of Calais. In the Vestibule are Félix Vallotton, The old concierge, and Bathers, and sculptures by Rodin.

To follow the chronological order of the paintings ascend to the First Floor.

GROUND FLOOR (left); Ferdinand Hodler, Portrait of Marc Odier, and numerous other portraits, landscapes, etc.; Amiet, Garden scene; Arnold Böcklin, Portrait of the artist's mother, Pan frightens the shepherd, The Isle of the Dead (first version of 1880), Self-portrait, etc.

MEZZANINE FLOOR: Gauguin, Garden at Auvers, Nafea faa ipoipo, and Self-portraits, etc.; Renoir, Portraits of Gabrielle, of Mme Jules Le Voeur, and Bust of Coco; Degas, Girl washing herself; and representative works by Manet, Monet, Sisley, Pissarro, Van Gogh, and Cézanne, and Odilon Redon, Portrait of Jeanne Chaire.

FIRST FLOOR: **R1** Circle of Luis Borrassá, Crucifixion; ascribed to Fernando Gallego (?), The mass of St. Gregory.—**R2** School of Konrad Witz, Nativity; Basle Master of 1460, Birth of the Baptist; Konrad Witz, St. Christopher, and Saints Joachim and Anna.—**R3** Follower of Konrad Witz, St. Martin, and St. George; Martin Schongauer, Virgin and Child.—**R4** Michael Pacher, Rest on the Flight into Egypt; several sections of the Mary altarpiece, by Hans Fries (1512)‚ Hans Holbein the Elder, Death of the Virgin (two versions); Gerard David, Virgin and Child, and Christ's farewell to Mary.—**R5** Bernhard Strigel, Portrait of Maximilian I; Lucas Cranach the Elder, Portraits of Luther, and of Luther's wife, Katherina von Bora, and of Friedrich of Saxony.—**R6** Cranach, Virgin and Child, and Judgement of Paris; Niklaus Manuel, Aquinus and St. Louis, Judgement of Paris, and Pyramus and Thisbe; Hans Baldung Grien, Deposition, and Nativity; Urs Graf, Lovers embracing, St. George and the dragon.—**R7** Hans Leu the Younger, Orpheus; Altdorfer (?), The Resurrection; Mathias Grunewald, Crucifixion; Niklaus Manuel, Beheading of the Baptist; Hans ·Baldung Grien, Death and the Maiden, Death and the Lady, Portrait of Adelberg III von Bärenfels.

Lucas Cranach the Elder, Judgement of Paris

R8 (a gallery round a courtyard) attrib. to *Memling*, St. Jerome; *Dutch Master of 1500*, Mother and child; *Ambrosius Benson*, Virgin and Child with Saints Andrew and Francis; *Isembrandt*, Nativity; *Jakob Cornelisz*, Nativity; *Van Orly*, Virgin and Child; *Braunschweiger Monogrammist*, Golgotha; *Herri met de Bles*, Holy Family and St. John; and a selection of Drawings by *Hans Holbein the Younger*, including a sketch of Thomas More and his family, but due to the delicate condition of such works they are only shown in rotation.—**R9** *Holbein the Younger*, Christ in the tomb, Adam and Eve (with munched apple), altarpiece of the Passion.—**R10** *Ambrosius Holbein*, Portraits of children, and of Hans Herbster von Basel; *Hans*

Hans Holbein the Younger, Portrait of Boniface Amerbach

Holbein the Younger, Portraits of Boniface Amerbach, of Erasmus in
1523, of his wife and eldest children, of an Englishman (1540), two
small portraits of Erasmus, and panels from the organ of the
Münster.—**R11** Drawings by *Hans Leu the Younger*; *Hans Holbein the
Younger*; *Hans Leonhard Schäufelein*; *Schongauer*; *Wolf Huber*,
Schloss Aggstein; *Altdorfer*; *Hans Fries*; *Hans Baldung Grien*; *Dürer*,
Young woman, and Portraits of Matthias von Wallenberg, etc. A
section is devoted to landscapes by *Caspar Wolf, Peter Birman, W.A.
Töepffer, Calame*, et al.

SECOND FLOOR: **R2** *Picasso*, The two brothers (1905), Harlequin
seated, The Poet (1912), and other works.—**R3** Paintings by *Bonnard*
and *Matisse*.—**R4** *Modigliani*, Marie; *Chagall*, My fiancée with black
gloves; *Rouault*, Portrait of Verlaine.—**R5** Works by *Gris* and
Braque.—**R6** *Klee, Robert Delaunay* and *Antoine Pevsner*.—**R7** *Le
Corbusier* and others.—**R8** *Léger*.—**R9** *Alberto Giacometti, Munch,
Emil Nolde, Kokoschka*, The tempest.—**R10** *Alberto Giacometti*,
mostly sculpture.—**R11** is devoted to *Paul Klee*; **R12** to *Mondrian*; **R13**
to *Arp. Kandinsky, Miró, Ernst, Tanguy* and *Dali*.—**R15** *Tapies,
Dubuffet* and *Poliakoff*; **R16** *Rothko*.

Among works not at present on view are: *Henri Rousseau*, The poet and his muse
(Apollinaire and Marie Laurencin), and Jungle scene (with negro attacked by
a leopard); also several paintings by *Mierevelt* and of the 17C Dutch and Flemish
Schools; by *Tobias Stimmer, Goya, Emanuel Handmann, Caspar Wolf, Rigaud,
Fuseli* and *Ensor*.

Of considerable importance are the *Library* and **Collection of Watercolours and Engravings**, including numerous examples of the work of *Hans Holbein the Elder,* and *the Younger, Hans Baldung Grien, Dürer, Urs Graf, Ambrosius Holbein, Stimmer* and *Niklaus Manuel,* apart from masters from the 17th to 20Cs.

Immediately E of the museum is a junction, from which the *Wettsteinbrücke* leads across the Rhine; see p 164, and for the area to the E.

We turn left along the Rittergasse, flanked by several imposing 18C mansions with remarkable iron-work. A lane on the right approaches the *Hohenfirstenhof* and *Ramsteinerhof.*

To the left is the Bäumleingasse, in which No. 18 (left) is the 15C *Haus zum Luft* in which Erasmus died (1536). It is still devoted to the sale of books. At the corner of this street (No. 10 Rittergasse) is the *Haus zum Delphin;* No. 12 is the *Eptinger Hof;* No. 16 the *Haus zum Höfli.*

We have now entered the Gallo-Roman enceinte, dominated by the *Münster,* or former *Cathedral,* a picturesque red-sandstone pile with a roof of variegated pattern, its W Front surmounted by two slightly dissimilar towers with their crocketed spires. Regrettably the interior of the building is not always easy of access, and it is hoped that its hours of opening will be extended.

The first church on this commanding site, perhaps dating from as early as the 7C, was destroyed by the Huns in 916, and its successor was erected with the aid of Heinrich II and consecrated in the presence of the Emperor in 1019. Little remains visible of this building, destroyed by fire in 1185, except the lower part of the N tower and part of the crypt, although recent excavations have revealed its foundations between the lines of pillars of the present edifice. Its reconstruction was carried out in a style partly Romanesque and partly Gothic, but the earthquake of 1356, in which the tower over the crossing fell, necessitated further rebuilding and a new vault, and by 1363 the high altar was reconsecrated. The building suffered the usual depredations of iconoclasts at the Reformation. Several alterations were carried out in the 18C, and the whole structure was in the hands of restorers in the 1850s, 1880s, and again more recently.

At the bases of the *St. Martin's Tower* (completed 1500) and *St. George's Tower* (completed 1472) stand equestrian statues of their

The Münster of Basle in 1764

respective saints, the latter (late 14C) impaling his dragon. The W
Portal, with well-carved archivolts, contains statues, probably placed
there after 1356, of Heinrich II and his wife, Kunigunde, and a Foolish
Virgin with her worldly Seducer. Several of these statues are copies
of the originals. Above this is a balustrade, together with another at
a higher level, connecting the two towers, between which the
triangular gable is notable. At the angles of the facade are statues of
Saints Peter and Paul.

On the N transept is the *St. Gallus Portal in its rectangular frame,
a naïve Romanesque composition of c 1180, depicting in the
tympanum Saints Peter and Paul interceding on behalf of the
founders, while in the lintel below are Wise and Foolish Virgins. The
buttress-like projections, relieved by colonnettes and statues of the
Baptist (? and St. Stephen), and the Evangelists with their symbols,
will be noted. Above is seen the Rose, or rather Wheel-window, with
several details of interest, and likewise the apse, which retains parts
of the Romanesque original, including some capitals, etc. The pavement shows the site of a former outer Carolingian crypt (?).

Detail of the west door of the Münster, Basle

The tree shaded bastion, providing a good view over the Rhine and
towards the Black Forest, is known as the Pfalz. Hence one may
continue round past a chapel to enter the extensive Cloisters and an

arcaded hall, off which opens the *Chapter-house*, partly Romanesque, but remodelled or added to in the 14–15C. Numerous tomb and memorial slabs may be seen, while here—among other divines and former city worthies including burgomaster Johann Rudolf Wettstein (1594–1666)—is interred Johannes Huszgen or Husschin, better known as Oekolampadius, a leader of the Reformation.

Interior. Emphasis is given to the general Transitional effect of the building by the Romanesque triforium gallery surmounting the main Gothic arcade. In the nave is the elaborate *Pulpit* of 1486 and, beyond, the raised *Choir*, from which steps descend to the *Crypt*, preserving some late Romanesque murals. On the N side of the choir is the altar-tomb and effigy of Gurtrude Anne of Habsburg (died 1281) and her infant son, Karl (died 1276). Note the capitals of the arcade between the choir and ambulatory.

At the E end of the N aisle, in the *Schaler chapel*, is an *Epitaph to Erasmus*, re-buried here in 1928; the adjacent *Relief of St. Vincent* (c 1100) will be noted. Further W are the recumbent monuments to Bp Arnold of Rotberg (died 1458), and Count Rudolf of Tierstein (died 1318), among several others of note. In the S transept is the *Font* of 1456, while at the E end of the S aisle, in the *Fröwler chapel*, is a relief of six apostles (c 1100). Several well-carved fragments of the late 14C choir-stalls, etc., are also to be seen. The organ of 1955 is unfortunate.

At the N end of the MÜNSTERPLATZ is the entrance to a *Museum of Swiss Folk Art*, while in the adjacent Augustinergasse is the **Museum of Natural History and Ethnography**, with extensive collections (over 200,000 objects), notably from Central and South America, among them a reconstructed 16m-high Culthouse from Papua, New Guinea, and numerous examples of fabrics, basket-work, ceramics, masks, feather-headdresses, etc.

The street is continued by the narrow Rheinsprung, passing the imposing 18C *Weisses Haus* and *Blaues Haus*, and (No. 11; right) the old *University building* (17C). Among those educated here were Sir Francis Walsingham (1555), Secretary of State to Elizabeth I, and Thomas Bodley (1578), founder of the Bodleian Library.

Steps ascend (left) to *St. Martin* (13–15C), on the site of a 6C church. The first Protestant services in Basle were held here by Oekolampadius.—The local *Archives* are preserved in another mansion in the Martingasse, flanked by the gateway to the Blaues Haus.

B. NW of the Marktplatz; the Historical Museum

Steps descend W from the Martinsplatz along the side of the Rathaus to the MARKTPLATZ, the main square of the Altstadt. It is dominated by the ruddy **Rathaus** or *Town Hall* of 1512, on the site of an earlier building, but radically altered at the end of the 19C and again recently. Several rooms may be visited.—No. 13, adjacent, is the *Geltenzunft*, the guildhouse of the wine-merchants (1578).

The Eisengasse bears right (NE) to the *Schifflände* or quay, at the W end of the *Mittlere Rheinbrücke* to *Klein-Basel*; see p 164. A few paces to the N is the *Tourist Office*, adjacent to which is the *Drie*

Könige Hotel, of ancient foundation, in which Theodor Herzl stayed
in 1897 when attending—as President—the First Zionist Congress.

Hence we may follow the Spiegelgasse and Schneidergasse S,
passing (right) the *Stadthaus* of 1775, next to which climbs the
Totengässlein, in which No. 3, the *Haus zum Sessel*, home of the
Amerbach family, now houses a *Pharmacy Museum*, containing
historical collections from the 16–19Cs.—Continuing S, the street
climbs the Spalenberg to the right past No. 12, the *Spalenhof*, to reach
(right) the characteristic Nadelberg, which one may now follow,
passing (left) the late 18C *Rosshof*, the 17C *Zerkindenhof, Schöner Hof*
and *Engelhof* (part 15C), behind which is the 17C *Schönes Haus*, to
reach the church of **St. Peter**, late Gothic on pre-Romanesque
foundations, containing the tombs of the Bernoullis and of
Froben.—The Petersgasse continues N to the Blumenrain, where we
turn left past (right) the *Seidenhof*, to reach the TOTENTANZ-PLATZ,
where at No. 2 the poet Johann Peter Hebel (1760–1826) was born.

The St. Johanns-Vorstadt leads N hence past the 18C *Erlacherhof* (Nos 15–17),
in which Goethe stayed; No. 22, site of Hans Holbein's residence, and No. 27,
the *Formonterhof* (1722) to—some minutes' walk beyond—the *St. Johanns-Tor*
(14–16C).

W of the Totentanz-Platz rises the restored **Predigerkirche**, the former
church (consecrated 1261) of a Dominican convent, with a belfry of
1423 and a Gothic choir beyond a rood-screen, and containing relics
of murals. The Silbermann Organ (reconstructed) is dated 1769.

Hence one may turn S along the Petersgraben past the *Cantonal
Hospital*, beyond which (right) is the Hebelstrasse, with several
buildings of note, among them the late 16C *Markgräfischer Hof* (Nos
2–6), and No. 32, the rococo *Holsteinerhof*.—A short distance S of the
latter is the *University Library*, preserving important collections of
Reformation MSS and printed books, etc.—SE of the library, past the
Botanical Gardens of the University, and at the SW corner of the
PETERSPLATZ, is the *Stachelschützenhaus* (partly 16C), the ancient
home of the Society of Archers. No. 12, on the N side of the square,
is the *Wildt'sche Haus* of 1763; on the S, the *University Buildings* of
1940, erected on the site of the former *Arsenal*. The University, the
oldest in Switzerland, with 5500 students and five faculties, was
founded in 1460; see History. Benjamin Britten wrote his 'Cantata
Academica' for its 500th anniversary.

To the SW of the Stachelschützenhaus rises the early 15C **Spalentor**,
the finest of the remaining town gates. Nietzsche lived at No. 47 in
the adjacent Schützengraben between 1869–79.

Hence the Missionstrasse leads NW. No. 21 Missionstrasse contains a *Missionary
Museum* and No. 28 a *Museum* devoted to *Sport*.

From the gate one may follow the old Spalenvorstadt past a copy of
a 16C *'Bagpiper' Fountain*, said to be after designs by Holbein and
Dürer, to reach (left) the *Gewerbe Museum* (1892), devoted to the
Industrial Arts, of which there are occasional exhibitions.

At No. 8 Kornhausgasse, a few minutes' walk to the S, is the **Swiss Jewish
Museum**, with an interesting collection of cult objects, documents, etc., among
them a Hebrew Bible printed in Basle in 1546; a 14C Pentateuch; Chanukka
lamps, and Torawimpels, etc. Almost 10,000 Jews entered the country during
the first half of 1942, until mid August, when those still arriving from France were
turned back at the frontier.

Continuing E, we traverse the characteristic Heuberg, in which the *Spiesshof* (No. 7) has Renaissance decoration, to reach a small square (view over the old town), dominated by the *Leonhardskirche (1481–1528), a well-vaulted church on the site of an earlier building consecrated in 1033, of which the crypt remains. The choir is separated from the nave by a rood-screen. Some 16C glass, relics of murals, and several tombs and epitaphs of interest may be seen in one of the least-visited of Basle's churches. The organ of 1718 (by Andreas Silbermann) has been re-sited.—The massive *Lohnhof*, adjacent, was once part of the SW defensive bastions, overlooking a moat. To the W of the square is a *Funerary hall*.

At No. 8 Leonhardstrasse, a short distance W, is the *Sammlung alter Musikinstrumente*, an extensive and important collection of early instruments (at present only open on Sun.), the majority assembled by Wilhelm Bernoulli (1904–80). The collection is particularly rich in brass, but also includes several pianos by Stein, Streicher and Graf, and Jenny Lind's piano; a 17C viola da gamba by Tielke, and Beethoven's flute (once owned by Weingartner), etc.

Steps descend from the Leonhardskirche to the BARFÜSSERPLATZ, a hub of communications, dominated to the E by the 14C *Franciscan* or *Barfüsserkirche* (renovated in 1975–81), housing a very fine *HISTORICAL MUSEUM. A mid 13C church stood slightly S of the present edifice, which is 80m long. It was used as a storehouse for salt and other goods for a century or more prior to its conversion into a museum in 1894.

The *Nave* now contains a curious congregation of carved Stalls and other furniture; collections of Glass; Pewter tankards; the original 'Bagpiper' Fountain (see above), among others; relics of murals, wood-carvings, and implements; metalwork; a carved Samson and Delilah (16C); the bronze Votive-plaque of Isabel of Burgundy; tombstones; and ecclesiastical silver, including several crucifixes.—In the *Choir*, carved, painted, and gilt plaques (including one of the Last Supper); sculptures (St. Catherine, and a Virgin and Child); a Palmesel (Christ on ass-back, used at Easter processions); a winged altarpiece from Rodels bei Thusis of c 1507, painted on the reverse, and—in a central position—another of the late 15C; stone sculpture from the Münster of the Virgin and Child of 1400, etc. On the walls are several Hangings (covered by protective blinds; press button to raise). Other objects include a Reliquary from Rheinau (1440); and the Altar of the Passion from Oberrhein (1520), flanked by the Virgin and the Emperor Heinrich II (1356).—In the former *Sacristy*, to the right, are a collection of reliquaries, including those of St. Pantalus (1270) and St. Ursula (1254); the Monstrance of the Apostles; a late 14C reliquary with silver plaques; the Hallwyl reliquary (Strasbourg; 1470); the Dorothea-oder Offenburg Monstrance (1433), and other Gothic monstrances.

In the *Crypt* are a collection of 17C Meisterkranz (floral crowns); a replica of a silver-smith's workshop; Owls; a Portrait of Wenzel Jamnitzer (1508–88), goldsmith of Nuremberg; Bronze figurines and 15–17C carved plaques; a carved boxwood Adam and Eve by Hans Wydyx the Elder, of c 1505; and collections of medals and coins. Other sections contain painted and panelled rooms displaying furniture; arms and armour; an alabaster relief of Erasmus; the Nautilus tankard of Burgermaster Wettstein (1649); and the *Amerbach Cabinet*. Largely collected by Basilius Amerbach (1533–91), this became the property of the University of Basle in 1662; three bronze statuettes in niches are notable.

Also in the basement are archaeological collections; bases of pillars; explanatory models; and miscellaneous antiquities.

One may ascend to the *Rood-screen*, rebuilt since its demolition in 1843. On it is a 16C positive organ. Relics of the Dance of Death frescoes from the Predigerkloster may be seen below.—On the right of the nave are several carved chests and boxes; tiles from poêles; and more hangings.

Above the nave is a section devoted to Bells from Basle of the 11–17Cs, and the *Silver Treasure* from Kaiseraugst (cf.), including a miniature sculptured Venus combing her hair, but this hoard may not be on permanent exhibition.

From just S of the apse, we may ascend and cross the Steinenberg to the new THEATERPLATZ, with a *Fountain* by Tinguely (1977), to the S of which is the *Theatre* of 1974, overlooked to the E by the *St.-Elisabethen-Kirche*; see p 155.

C. Klein-Basel and the Sankt Alban Tal

From the *Schifflände* (see p 161), we cross the *Mittlere Rheinbrücke* (1905). A small chapel on the bridge is the only relic of the picturesque wooden Alte Rheinbrücke, which stood on stone piers, and dated back to 1225. The view of the Münster and Altstadt on its ridge—the Münsterhügel—is impressive from the far bank.—A short distance N is the *City and Cathedral Museum*, adjacent to the former convent of *Klingental* (founded 1270); the choir of its church and a few Gothic rooms survive. The museum contains a model (at 1:400) of central Basle according to the Merian Plan of 1615–42, among others.

The Oberer Rheinweg, skirting the river S of the bridge, leads directly to the N end of the Wettsteinbrücke, but either of the next two parallel streets leading off the Greifengasse—in which (right) stands the much frequented *Café Spitz*—are characteristic of this quarter. The first, the Rheingasse, with its continuation, the Lindenberg, and the second, the Utengasse, both lead to the late 16C *Hattstätterhof* and to the St. Theodorekirche; see below.

The Greifeng leads shortly to the *Clarakirche*, a somewhat stark 13C building, frequently altered.—The street continues towards the *Trade* or *Sample Fair Buildings* (Mustermesse) and beyond to the *Badischer Bahnhof* (1913; by Karl Moser).—The Rebgasse leads SE from the church to *St. Theodorskirche*, 15C but of 11C foundation. Just to the W, between it and the bridge, are relics of an early 13C *Charterhouse*, now an *Orphanage* (Waisenhaus). The *Wettsteinbrücke* (1879) crosses back towards the Kunstmuseum; see p 156.

Hence the St. Alban-Vorstadt, with a number of old houses, leads E to the **St. Alban-Tor**, one of the remaining 14C town gates. A lane, the Mühlenberg, forks off this street past the old *Pfarrhaus* to the riverside embankment and church of *St. Alban*, in part late 13C, but dating from the 11th, with relics of its former convent.—Further E is the *Museum für Gegenwartskunst* (Contemporary Art) in a suitably modern building (1980; by K. and W. Steib).

Adjacent is a well-restored **Paper-mill** (Basler Papiermühle), with an interesting *Museum* devoted to paper-making of all periods; papers may be seen being manufactured.

On the river bank itself is the restored *Goldener Sternen* inn, and near by are several characteristic 17–18C houses, also restored. A few steps further E brings one to the *Letziturm* and a short stretch of the medieval walls, originally 13–14C, but later strengthened, and in part reconstructed. They are seen to advantage behind their dry moat.

The *Zoologischer Garten*, some minutes' walk to the W of the main station, is better than most and worth visiting.

At *Bottmingen*, some 4km SW of Basle, is a moated castle (15C); some 10km beyond, at *Mariastein*, is a notable mid 17C church.

7km NW, in France, is the *Airport of Bâle-Mulhouse*. Mulhouse itself is 36km from Basle and *Colmar* 69km. *Altkirch* is 31km W, and *Belfort* is 34km beyond (see *Blue Guide France*). *Frieburg* (*im Breisgau*), in Germany, lies 64km N—slightly more by the autobahn. *Titisee*, in the Black Forest, lies some 68km NE, and 31km E of Freiburg.

For roads from Basle to **Berne** via the motorway, via **Delémont**, and via **Solothurn**, see Rte 12; to **Lucerne**, Rte 13; to **Zürich** via Brugg and Baden, Rte 14; to **Winterthur** via the Rhine Valley, Rte 15.

12 Basle to Berne

A. Via the Motorway

Total distance, 94km (58 miles). N2. 40km—N1. 20km. **Solothurn** lies 5km W—34km **Berne**.

Maps: M 216; BL 26, 27, 31, 32, or 5016, 5019.

The N2 is entered immediately E of Basle, bearing SE after 11km, passing (left; on the Rhine) **Augst**; see Rte 14. After piercing a ridge, at 10km we cross the No. 2 (see Rte 13) and ascend the narrowing valley of the Diegter. Later, traversing a tunnel below the *Botchenflue* (1123m), part of the main ridge of the Jura, we have a view of the chain of the Alps on making our exit and veering downhill to the SW. The No. 5 is crossed 8km W of *Olten* (see Rte 13A), to meet the N1.

Berne lies 54km SW. The turning for **Solothurn** bears W after 20km; see Rtes 8A and B, and Rte 10 for *Berne* itself. The turning for **Lucerne** is 10km E, just beyond (left) **Aarburg**; *Lucerne* lies 46km SE, for which see Rtes 13 and 21.

B. Via Delémont, Moutier, and Biel/Bienne

Total distance, 125km (77 miles). No. 18. 40km. **Delémont** lies 2km right—No. 6. 11km *Moutier*—19km *Tavannes*—18km **Biel/Bienne**—11km *Lys*—22km **Berne**.

Maps: M 216; BL 26, 31, or 5016, 5019.

The No. 18 is followed due S to (8km) *Reinach*.

A left-hand turning crosses the new motorway, to (2km) **Arlesheim**, on the far side of the valley. The ornate Baroque *Church, begun in 1650, with twin belfries, dominates the dignified square below. It is flanked by the canonical residences of the cathedral chapter of Basle, who inhabited the place between 1678 and 1792. Its rococo stucco decoration of 1759–61 is notable, and the organ is by Johann Andreas Silbermann.

At a higher level are the ruins of *Reichenstein*, a 13C fortress partly destroyed by an earthquake in 1356, as were several others in the district. At a battle (22 July 1499) fought between here and *Dornach* the Swiss secured a decisive victory over the Emperor Maximilian I, forcing him to recognise the independence of the Federation.

Turning S from the square, after c 1km we approach, on a hill to the left, the monumental ferro-concrete structure (1924–28; the successor of an earlier edifice which burnt down) known as the **Goetheanum**. This is the headquarters of the Anthroposophical Society, a sect founded in 1913 by Rudolf Steiner (1861–1925) who designed the building. Several other houses in the area are similar in style.—On a height to the SE are the ruins of the castle of *Dorneck*, burned by the French in 1798. P.-L. Moreau de Maupertuis (1698–1759), the mathematician, is buried in the church of adjacent *Dornach*.—Continuing S past (left) the ruins of 14–16C *Schloss Angenstein*, we regain the main road just beyond *Aesch* and enter the *Gorge of the Birs*, a romantic ravine below thick forests, with narrow rocky defiles alternating with open meadows. Passing below (right) the ruins of *Schloss Pfeffingen*, the road veers E through *Zwingen*, with a 14C *Schloss*, enlarged in the 16–17Cs, to enter *Laufen*, 3km beyond.

Laufen, a small industrial town, formerly fortified, retains three gateways, two of them at either end of the Hauptstrasse. The late 17C *Katharinenkirche* contains rococo decoration by the Moosbrugger brothers.

The road continues to follow the narrow ravine of the Birs, passing occasional cement-works, after 13.5km reaching French-speaking *Soyhières*.

A minor road leads 12.5km NW to a frontier-post 2km beyond *Ederswiler*, from which a track climbs to the ruins of the 13–14C castle of *Löwenburg* and dependencies of the abbey of *Lucelle*. This once influential abbey, founded by St. Bernard of Clairvaux in 1123, now houses archaeological remains found in the vicinity; see below.

We enter more open country and reach the E suburbs of (3.5km) **Delémont** (432m; 11,700 inhab.; 6400 in 1930), a small industrial town (watch-making and precision instruments), once a residence of the prince-bishops of Basle and since 1979 the capital of the newly constituted canton of Jura. The early 18C *Château* was the episcopal residence until 1815. The former Grand-Rue (now du 23 Juin) leads W to the *Porte Monsieur* or *de Courtételle*, just N of which is the *Musée Jurassien*, displaying extensive collections of archaeological and historical interest from the region.

Travellers entering the Jura from *Altkirch* may follow the French D 4325 via *Ferrette* (see *Blue Guide France*) to cross the frontier (Customs) at *Lucelle* (see above), 13.5km NW of *Develier* (4.5km W of Delémont), on the direct road (No. 6) from *Porrentruy*; see Rte 9.

At *Vicques*, 4km SE, are the relics of a 1–3C Roman villa.

Driving S, we pass through *Courrendlin*, its belfry-tower with an exterior staircase, and enter and thread the gorge of *Val Moutier* or *Cluses des Roches* to approach (11km) **Moutier** (529m), a small industrial town which grew up round the abbey of Moutier-Granval, founded c 640 by Germanus of Treves, a disciple of St. Colomba. Its stones were probably used to build the *Château* (16C; enlarged in the 18th). The town preserves several 16–17C houses, among them the *Hôtel de Ville*. At No. 9 in the Rue de l'Hôtel-de-ville is the *Musée jurassien des beaux-arts*.

The Romanesque cemetery-chapel of *Chalières*, 1km W, contains early 11C frescoes.—To the S rises the *Graitery* (1280m); to the NE, *Mont Raimeux* (1302m).

From a point c 8km SE a mountain road turns off the No. 30 to *Balsthal*, 17km E, to approach the col of the *Weissenstein* (1284m); see p 138.

The No. 6 now bears SW, traversing the defile of the *Cluse de Court* to (7.5km) *Court*, there veering due W.—The valley of *Chaluet*, to the E, was inhabited by the industrious French-speaking descendants of Anabaptists expelled from Berne in 1708–11.

At (4.5km) *Bévilard-Malleray*—from where the forested flank of the *Montoz* (1328m; views) may be climbed—there was a skirmish in 1367 in which the prince-bishop of Basle was beaten by troops from Solothurn and Berne.—4km *Reconvilier*, birthplace of Adrian Wettach, better known as 'Grock', the famous clown (1880–1959), is crossed, and *Tavannes* is entered 3km beyond; see Rte 9, and for the road beyond.

C. Via Liestal, and Solothurn

Total distance, 100km (62 miles). No. 12. 17km **Liestal**—30km *Oensingen crossroads*—No. 5. 17km **Solothurn**—No. 12. 36km **Berne**.

Maps: M 216; BL 26, 27, 31, 32, or 5016, 5019.

The No. 12 is followed to the SE, at 6.5km passing (right) **Muttenz** (16,900 inhab.), an industrial suburb (chemical works), but of ancient origin. Its Romanesque and Gothic church of *St. Arbogast*, with early Renaissance murals in a chapel, stands within a fortified enclosure. There are several castle ruins on the hill above.

Pratteln, another industrial suburb (15,750 inhab.), with a 13–15C *Schloss*, is bypassed; to the N lies **Augst** with its Roman remains; see Rte 14.

The Roman road connecting Augst (*Augusta Raurica*) with Avenches (*Aventicum*) ran via Liestal and Balsthal.

Liestal (12,150 inhab.) is the industrial capital of the half-canton of *Basel-Land*, which has been separated from Basel-Stadt since 1833. In 1831 the then rural districts of the canton of Basel (1501) revolted against what they considered the undemocratic rule of the urban trade guilds. The citizens of Basle were twice defeated in the field before they acquiesced to the division of the canton. Johann Bernhard Merian (1723–1807), the philosopher, and the poet Carl Spitteler (1845–1924), were born here.

Only one tower remains of Liestal's ramparts. The centre of the older town is traversed by the Rathausgasse; the *Rathaus* is mid 16C, but the decoration of its facade dates from 1901. A cup of Charles le Téméraire, taken at Nancy in 1477 is held here. The archaeological collection in the *Cantonal Museum*, in the old *Armoury* (Alten Zeughaus), is of some interest.—For *Lausen*, to the SE, see Rte 13A.

We turn right 2km SE of Liestal, ascending the FRENKENTAL to (12km) *Waldenburg*, with relics of its fortifications, above which are the ruins of the 12C castle of the Counts of Frohburg. Waldenburg was the birthplace of Emanuel Handmann (1718–81), the artist. The road continues to climb, crossing the *Oberer Hauenstein pass* (731m) to (5km) the small resort of *Langenbruck*. There are relics of a Benedictine monastery at *Schönthal*, 2km N, founded in 1145, with an interesting W door to its church. The *Belchenflue* (1123m), to the E, may be climbed for the view.

The road descends to the SW below the ruins of the 12–14C castle of *Neu-Falkenstein*, to (8km) *Balsthal* (484m). Its old parish church was built on the site of a Roman villa. A small *Museum* has been installed in a paper-mill of 1773.

We shortly meet a road from *Moutier* (see Rte 12B) and turn left. On a height to the E is the 12–13C castle of *Alt-Falkenstein*, damaged by fire in 1798, and now containing a small local *Museum*.

The road threads the defile of the *Klus* in the main ridge of the Jura to meet the No. 5 just W of *Oensingen* and an entrance to the N1 motorway, where we bear left.

At 13km **Solothurn** lies 5km to the W; see Rtes 8A and B, and for the road to Berne, in reverse. For **Berne** itself see Rte 10.

13   Basle to Lucerne

A. Via Olten

Total distance, 95km (59 miles). No. 2. 42km **Olten**—5km **Aarburg**—5km *Zofingen*—19km. **Sursee** lies 2km E.—22km **Lucerne**.

Maps: M 216; BL 26, 27, 32, or 5019.

The old main road (No. 2) is followed past **Liestal** (see Rte 12C), and continues SE via *Lausen*, its church containing mid 15C murals, to (4km) *Sissach* (also rapidly reached by the N2), where the *Schloss Ebenrain* (1775) is notable. The road now follows the line of the railway, climbing to (11km) *Läufelfingen*, beyond which it ascends steeply over the *Unter Hauenstein pass* (691m).

The view-point of the *Frohburg* (820m) rises to the E and commands a distant view of the chain of the Alps.

We make a steep descent to the W through the wooded slopes of the Jura before turning SE to (10km) *Olten*.

Olten (19,000 inhab.; 13,500 in 1930; 3900 in 1880) is a busy industrial town and railway centre. It lies on the Aar, here crossed by a covered wooden *Bridge*. Olten was the birthplace of the artist and caricaturist Martin Disteli (1802–44), and the Swiss Alpine Club was founded here in 1863.

Little remains of the old centre which grew up around the early 16C

Stadtturm. N of the early 19C *Stadtkirche* is the *Kunstmuseum*, which has an extensive collection of paintings and drawings by Disteli, Landscapes by *Alexandre Calame; Cuno Amiet*, Breton girl; *Hodler*, The Mönch; and *Félix Vallotton*, Nude.—At No. 7 Konradstrasse, nearby, is a local *Museum.*

For **Aarau**, 13km NE in the Aare valley, and for alternative routes from Aarau to **Lucerne**, see p 139 and below; for **Aarburg**, 5km S, see p 136.

The No. 2 bears SE across the N1 to (6km) **Zofingen**, a small industrial town founded in the late 12C, which is supposed to have succeeded Roman *Tobinium*—mosaics from a Roman villa may be seen near the Romerbad hotel on the Lucerne road. The town was in Habsburg hands from 1251 and its ramparts were besieged by the Bernois in 1415. *St. Maurice* dates from the 12C, although later enlarged and with a 17C tower. Behind it is the former *Latin School* (1602). The *Rathaus* dates from 1795; the municipal *Museum* contains a numismatic collection, autograph letters of Swiss Reformers, etc.

Driving S up the valley of the Wigger, at (4.5km) *Reiden* the remains of a Commandery of the Knights of Malta (13C) are passed; 3.5km beyond, *Dagmersellen* is entered.

A right-hand turning leads across the N2 past (right) *Altishofen*, with its church rebuilt in 1772 by Jakob Singer, and a 16C *Schloss;* then on to *Aberswil*, with castle ruins and the Kasteln mansion, built for Heinrich von Sonnenberg in 1682, and (12km) *Willisau;* see Rte 16B.

We now veer SE past (7.5km) *Knutwil*, with a church-of 1826 by Josef Singer, and cross the motorway, after 3.5km turning left for (2km) *Sursee*; 1.5km to the right is the little *Mauensee*, with an early 17C *Schloss* on an island. **Sursee**, an attractive old town, lies close to the N end of the *Sempacher See*, and its surviving Gatehouse still displays the double-headed eagle of the empire. The *Rathaus* dates from the mid 16C, while the church of *St. Georg* is a fine Baroque edifice of 1641. There are several streets in the vicinity with characteristic 16–17C houses. On the Aarau road (N) is the *Kapuziner Kloster* (1608), its church containing Baroque decoration; a small *Museum* is devoted to the Capuchin order in Switzerland.

The main road to Lucerne, 19km SE, is regained a short distance S of the town. It skirts the SW bank of the lake, with a view of the Alps ahead, before climbing through *Neuenkirch*. However, the more interesting minor road follows the NE shore via (7.5km) *Sempach*, and is approached by turning right just prior to crossing the motorway; see below.

From this point one may also take in *Beromünster*, 7.5km NE, by following the No. 23, which climbs up beyond the motorway, later passing the German-language Broadcasting-station. **Beromünster** (642m), an old town which grew up around a monastery (Münster) founded in 981 by Bero von Lenzburg, has a fine collegiate *Church of the 11–12C, which was baroquised in the late 17C. Its tower has a 14C spire and the early 17C stalls are notable. Adjacent are several mansions of the 18C or earlier. Off the Hauptgasse is the so-called *Schloss*, now a *Museum*, in which Elias Helie probably printed the first book in Switzerland (1470); Ulrich Gering (1440–1510), a native of the town, later set up the first printing-press in France, at the Sorbonne. Several incunables, illuminated MSS, etc., are preserved here among other antiquities.—*Sempach* may be reached via *Neudorf*, with a late 17C church, and *Hildisreiden*, 7.5km S of Beromünster.

Sempach, on the SE side of its lake, retains a section of its ramparts and a characteristic main street. At the Battle of Sempach (9 July 1386) on the hillside to the NE—a chapel marks the site—a small Swiss force commanded by Arnold von Winkelried and Peter von Gundoldingen defeated Herzog Leopold III of Austria, who was killed in the mêlée.

At *Kirchbühl*, 1km N, the 13–16C church of *St. Martin*, built on Roman foundations, dates in part from c 1000, and contains 14C murals, amongst others.

One may either turn due S past an Ornithological station to regain the No. 2 below (4.5km) *Neuenkirch*, 10.km from Lucerne, or follow the N2 SE. Both routes provide views ahead of the Rigi (left), and Pilatus (right). For **Lucerne** see Rte 21.

FROM AARAU TO LUCERNE. Several alternatives may be followed by travellers taking in Aarau en route. The most westerly is the No. 24, driving due S along the *Suhre valley* to (27km) *Sursee.*—The No. 23, bearing SE along the *Wina valley* via (11.5km) *Unterkulm*, where the restored Romanesque church contains early 14C murals, and later passing industrial *Reinach*, leads to (14.5km) *Beromünster*. See above for the roads beyond Sursee and Beromünster.

Further E, reached by turning right off the Lenzburg road after 7km, is the No. 26, which enters *Seon* in the so-called SEETAL after 5km. Several relics of the Hallstatt culture have been excavated in the vicinity.—4km *Boniswil*, 1km E of which is moated *Schloss Hallwil*, the seat until 1847 of the family of which Hans von Hallwil, the hero of Morat, belonged. The road skirts the W shore of the *Hallwiler See* (some 10km^2 in area) below the *Homberg* (789m), with a view ahead of the chain of the Alps. We veer SE to (13.5km) *Gelfingen*, on the NE bank of the smaller *Balgegger See*. Above stands *Schloss Heidegg* (17C on 11C foundations) and to the N is *Hitzkirch*, the site of a former Commandery of the Teutonic Knights from 1236; to the SE are the 13C ruins of '*Nünegg*' at *Lieli*.—The main road continues S above the lake to (5.5km) *Hochdorf*. Its church, referred to in the 10C, was rebuilt in the Baroque taste by Jakob Singer in the mid 18C.—At *Hohenrain*, 3km NE, is a former Commandery of the Knights of St. John, founded in 1180 and rebuilt in 1694.—5km *Eschenbach*, with a Cistercian monastery founded in 1285 and rebuilt in the 16C.—**Lucerne** is entered 13km beyond; see Rte 21.

B. Via the Motorway

Total distance, 98km (61 miles). N2. 40km—N1. 8km—N2. 23km. **Sursee** lies 1km S.—8km. **Sempach** lies 1km right—15km **Lucerne**.

Maps: M 216; BL 26, 27, 32, or 5019.

The easiest and most rapid route is the N2 motorway, at least as far as the *Aarburg* exit, 5km S of *Olten*; see Rte 12A. For **Aarburg** itself, see p 136; for **Olten**, Rte 13A.

The motorway veers SE from Aarburg to by-pass (left) *Zofingen*, and later bears E briefly to the **Sursee** exit, beyond which it skirts the NE bank of the *Sempacher See*, for all of which, and for **Sempach** itself, see the latter part of Rte 13A.—Regaining the motorway just E of Sempach we continue S, with a view ahead of the Pilatus, to by-pass *Emmenbrücke* (right) and approach the centre of **Lucerne**; see Rte 21.

14 Basle to Zürich via Brugg, and Baden

Total distance, 73km (45 miles). No. 3. 18km **Rheinfelden**—25km **Brugg**—10km **Baden**—20km **Zürich**.

Maps: M 216; BL 27, or 5005.

At **Augst**, 11km E of Basle, is an important Roman site, easily approached either by the motorway or by the No. 5 skirting the left bank of the Rhine. Turn left immediately after passing below a railway bridge to reach the *Romerhaus* (left), a reconstructed and furnished Roman villa. There is a *Museum* adjacent, which displays the remarkable 4C *Silver Treasure* found in 1962. On the plateau here (and N of the motorway) is the extensive site of **Augusta Raurica**, founded c 44 BC by Munatius Plancus, and destroyed by the Alemanni c 260. Just S of the museum is the *Theatre*, built to hold c 8,000; it has undergone several reconstructions. To the E stood a *Forum*, the *Curia*, and a temple; further S was another *Forum*, and some distance beyond, the relics of an *Amphitheatre*. Other temples stood to the W, while a grid of streets was laid out to the E; beyond are the remains of walls.—To the N, on the bank of the Rhine, is the site of the Roman fortress of *Kaiser-Augst*; it was built c 300 by Constantius Chlorus—with material from Augst—to protect the bridgehead here. Relics of its walls can be seen; at the SW corner of these the silver hoard (see above) was discovered. Nearer the river are remains of the *Thermae*, and further E, a late 4C *Baptistery* (key at vicarage).

The main road follows the line of the Roman road to skirt the river to (7km) **Rheinfelden**, an ancient town originally constructed with the debris of Augusta Raurica, and strongly fortified. Parts of the inner wall and several gate-towers remain, together with a picturesque *Bridge* over the Rhine (Customs), which rests on a rocky island where the castle of Stein once stood. In the Marktgasse, parallel to the river, is the *Rathaus* (1533), several times restored, and with a Baroque facade of 1767. A short distance beyond is the local *Museum*. The late Gothic *Church* was refaced in 1770. The Duc de Rohan (1579–1638) was mortally wounded at a battle here during the Thirty Years' War. Its brine springs were only discovered in 1845. In the Rindergasse is a collection of some 60 models of Swiss towns at 1:200; in the *Kurpark*, a collection of Veteran cars.

The road now crosses a wide bend of the Rhine; nearby are the remains of a Roman lookout tower. It then passes through (9km) *Mumpf*, with a 17C church, the birthplace of 'Rachel' (Elisa Félix; 1821–58), the actress, born while her parents—Jewish pedlars—were staying at the inn.—At (2km) *Stein* a bridge rebuilt in 1799 spans the Rhine to *Bad Säckinger* (Customs). Here we fork right; for the riverside road see Rte 15.

Passing below the motorway, we approach (8km) *Frick*, in the FRICKTAL, the last Habsburg possession in Switzerland (ceded 1802).

1km beyond, a right-hand turning leads across country to *Aarau*, 15km S; see Rte 8B. The road ascends to the low *Bözberg pass* in the Jura (views) before climbing down into the valley of the Aare to enter (14km) Brugg. On the far bank rise the castles of *Habsburg* (see below) and *Altenburg* (16C, on the site of a late Roman fort).

Brugg, an old town, stands on the Aare close to its confluence with the Reuss. It was the birthplace of the artist Johannes Dünz (1645–1735), and J.G. von Zimmermann (1728–95), the philosopher and author of 'On Solitude', and physician to Frederick the Great, who was appointed His Britannic Majesty's Physician at Gottingen in 1768. Pestalozzi died here in 1827 and is buried at *Birr*, a village some 6km S.

Close to the bridge is the 11C *Schwarze Turm*, partly built with stones from the ruins of Roman *Vindonissa*, an important military and civil station under occupation between AD 9–260, and with a fortified camp designed to protect their territory against German incursions. The *Museum* of relics from Vindonissa may be visited in Brugg itself, but the site of the oppidum lies further SE, beyond the railway lines, on a neck of land above the Reuss; its W gate is just N of the main road. This skirts (right) the site of the *Forum*, a short distance S of which is the *Amphitheatre*, the largest in Helvetia, which would have held 10,000 spectators. A subterranean aqueduct has also been brought to light.

N of the *Westtor* stood the former abbey of **Königsfelden** (suppressed 1528 and now an asylum), founded in 1310 by the Empress Elizabeth on the spot where her husband Albrecht of Habsburg was assassinated in 1308. After the death of Elizabeth in 1313, Queen Agnes (widow of Andreas III of Hungary) became protectress of the convent and lived there until her death in 1364. Its 14C church contains curious contemporary stained-glass windows, while several members of the Austrian imperial family, including Agnes and Leopold, who fell at Sempach (cf.) were first buried in the vault here.

FROM BRUGG TO LENZBURG (14km). The No. 5 leading SW, is soon commanded by the partial ruins of the ancient castle of *Habsburg* or *Habichtsburg* ('Hawk's Castle'), built in 1020 by Bp Werner of Strasbourg and his brother Count Radbot, and the cradle of the House of Austria until its demise in 1918. The tall square keep stands above a dungeon and adjoins the 16C residential wing.—Bearing S, we pass the little spa of *Schinznach-Bad*—formerly one of the most frequented watering-places in Switzerland—and then *Wildegg*, with a 13C castle above. The castle belonged to the Effinger family for 400 years, and now contains a *Museum* preserving part of the Swiss national collections.—*Aarau* lies 11km W, and *Lenzburg* 4km S; see pp 139, 170 and 139 for roads to *Lucerne*, and *Bremgarten*.

The main road crosses the Reuss, on the left bank of which, further N, is modern *Windisch*, and circles to the N along the hillside overlooking the confluence of that river with the Limmat, to (10km) *Baden*.

BADEN (383m; 13,850 inhab.; 4050 in 1880), an ancient town and spa—not to be confused with its namesakes in Germany and Austria—and now an industrial centre, lies on the left bank of the Limmat above an abrupt bend. The old centre was once protected by the lofty castle of *Stein*, several times destroyed and rebuilt.

Its warm saline and sulphur waters were known to the Romans, who called it *Thermae* or *Aquae Helveticae*, while the miracles claimed to have been performed here by St. Verena (buried at Zurzach) brought it again to notice. Once a Habsburg stronghold, between 1426 and 1712 it was the meeting-place of the Confederate Diet. Poggio, papal secretary at the Council of Constance, describes the Public Baths in 1417 as being a place where 'you will see innumerable women of surpassing beauty, without husbands, without relatives, with two maids and a page, or with some little old duenna, to whom it costs less to give the slip than a decent meal ...'. It does not seem to have much changed when visited by Thomas Coryate in 1608, who 'saw many passing faire yong Ladies and Gentlewomen naked in the bathes with their wooers and favorites in the same. For at this time of the year many wooers come thither to solace themselves with their beautiful mistresses. Many of these yong Ladies had the haire of their head very curiously plaited in locks, and they wore certaine pretty garlands upon their heads made of fragrant and odoriferous flowers. A spectacle exceedingly amorous'. No wonder the waters of Baden also had the reputation of an 'admirable efficace to cure the sterilitie of women ... a matter verified and certainly confirmed by the experience of many'. Fynes Moryson, who had passed through some years earlier, in 1592, refers to the fact that 'many having no disease but that of love ... come hither for remedy, and many times find it'. Montaigne spent five days here in 1580.

In 1714 Prince Eugene and Marshal Villars signed the treaty in the Rathaus which ended the War of the Spanish Succession as far as France and the Empire were concerned. The line between Baden and Zürich was the first railway entirely *in* Switzerland to be opened (1847). It was known as the 'Spanisch-Brötli Bahn' from a kind of cake made here. In 1891 the Brown Bovari works were established by Charles Brown, a British engineer. Baden's wines are reputed.

To the N, in gardens overlooking the Limmat, stands the *Kursaal* of 1875 and *Theatre* of 1952. To the S is the *Stadtturm*, a 15C gate-house with bell-turrets, and SE of this stands the *Parish church* (15C, but with its interior much changed). Adjacent is a Renaissance structure, on the wall of which is a group of Christ in the Garden (1624).—Below, to the E, a covered wooden *Bridge* of 1809 crosses to the *Landvogteischloss*, the 14C bailiff's castle, now housing a local *Museum*.

Immediately to the S is a high-level bridge over the Limmat, crossed to approach adjacent **Wettingen** (18,400 inhab.; 8500 in 1930). Wettingen is overlooked to the NE by the *Burghorn* (859m; view); to the SW (between the railway and river) stands the former *Cistercian abbey* (1227–1841), its church containing the 14C stone coffin of Albrecht of Habsburg (see Königsfelden, above), good early 17C choir-stalls and, in the cloister, fine Renaissance stained-glass.

The recommended approach to Zürich, some 20km SE, is the motorway, gained just S of Baden, which follows the valley of the Limmat past (right) **Dietikon** (21,750 inhab.; 7150 in 1950). It is traversed by the old main road, where Masséna's French army crossed the river in 1799 before capturing Zürich. Notable in industrial *Altstetten*, the NW suburb of Zürich, is the *Telephone Exchange* of 1980, by Theo Hotz, with its huge cowls. For **Zürich** itself, see Rte 23.

15 Basle to Winterthur via the Rhine Valley

Total distance, 100km (62 miles). No. 3. 18km **Rheinfelden—**11km **Stein—**No. 7. 25km *Koblenz—*27km (*Eglisau/Bülach* crossroads) —19km **Winterthur**.

Maps: M 216; BL 27, or 5005, 5010.

For the road to *Stein*, see Rte 14. Here bear left onto the No. 7, skirting the left bank of the Rhine through (9.5km) *Laufenburg*, a picturesque little town with a ruined 13C castle, and baroquised church. It is named from the former rapids or *Laufen* here, much modified by blasting, and now the site of a power-station. In the churchyard are buried the last Lord Montague and his tutor, who were drowned when attempting to swim the Rhine at this point for a wager, and coincidentally on the same day that the family mansion, Cowdray Castle in Sussex, was burnt down (9 October 1793).

After crossing (10.5km) *Leibstadt*, near which is a nuclear power-station, we approach (7km) **Koblenz**, lying close to the confluence of the Aare and the Rhine, and 2km S of German *Waldshut* (Customs), deriving its name, like that of its more famous namesake, from this 'confluentia'.

The road then veers SE through (6.5km) **Zurzach**, once a Celtic and Roman fort (*Tenedo*, or *Forum Tiberii*), controlling the bridgehead of a highway that here crossed the Rhine. In the neighbouring suburb of *Kirchlibuck* are the foundations of a late 5C baptistery. Kirchlibuck was later the site of an important leather and linen fair, while nearby are extensive salt-workings. The *Church*, built in the 10C, and containing the tomb of St. Verena, with an effigy of 1613, has a lofty choir of c 1347. The nave was later baroquised.

Near (6.5km) *Rümikon* is a restored 4C lookout tower, 4.5km beyond which **Kaiserstuhl**, an ancient fortified town of some character, is passed. At 9.5km crossroads are reached 3km S of *Eglisau*, on the road from Zürich to *Schaffhausen*; see Rte 26B.—Passing below the *Rinsberg* (567m), with castle ruins, we descend the *Toss valley*, after 16km crossing the N1 motorway to enter **Winterthur** 3km beyond; see Rte 26A.

16 Berne to Lucerne

A. Via Langnau: the Emmental

Total distance, 91km (56 miles). No. 10. 30km *Langnau*—39km *Wolhusen*—22km **Lucerne**.

Maps: M 216, 217; BL 32, 36, 37, or 5008, 5016.

The No. 10 climbs SE out of the Aare valley to (10km) **Worb** (11,100 inhab.), with 13th and 18C castles, some 2km S of which, at *Schlosswil*, is a 17C mansion incorporating a late 12C keep.—7km. *Grosshöchstetten*, 4km S of which lies *Konolfingen*, birthplace of Friedrich Dürrenmatt (1921-), the dramatist.—Passing through (2km) *Zäziwil*, the road later descends into the EMMENTAL, a pastoral valley some 40km long, noted for its neat and prosperous farms, its cattle, and particularly its cheese.

11km **Langnau** (670m), the main market-town of the Emmental, has been known for its dairies and—since the 18C—its potteries. The *Church*, of 1673, by Abraham Dünz, preserves a fine contemporary pulpit. A 15C house contains a small regional *Museum*.

The road ascends the narrowing valley of the Ilfis to (5.5km)

Trubschachen.—From here a by-road climbs NE up the valley of the Treub and *Fankhausgraben*, at the head of which rises the *Napf* (1408m), providing extensive *Views.*—6.5km *Wiggen.*

5km S lies *Marbach*, from which the *Lochsitenberg* (1484m; views) may be ascended.—*Schangnau*, 4.5km SW, is in the upper valley of the Emme, which is followed by a road to (8km SE) *Kemmeriboden*, a small spa situated between the *Hohgant* ridge (SW; 2197m), the *Schibengütsch* (NE; 2037m) and the *Tannhorn* (SE; 2221m), overlooking the *Brienzer See*; see Rte 19.

The main road circles NE to (3km) *Escholzmatt* (853m), a dairying village on the watershed between the Emmental and the long pastoral vale of the ENTLEBUCH, here overlooked by the *Beichlen* (SE; 1770m).

At 6.5km a minor road climbs S up the WALD EMME valley to (7km) *Flühli* (883m), a small centre for mountain excursions. NE of Flühli rises the *Fürstein* (2040m; extensive views). The road continues to (8km) *Sörenberg* (1159m), a resort at the foot of the *Brienzer Rothorn* (2350m; it may be ascended by cable-car for the Views); see Rte 19. The road continues to climb to the *Glaubenbüelen pass* (1611m), then descends in zigzags to (21km) *Giswil*, on the main road 6km SW of *Sacheln*, on the *Sarner See*; see Rte 19.

Schüpfheim (719m), the main town of the Entlebuch, is soon reached and then (4km) *Hasle*, where the ossuary contains a 17C Dance of Death. 2km beyond, the village of *Entlebuch* itself is entered. It is built on a moraine hill, and has a classical *Church* of 1784 by Jakob Singer, with rococo decoration; adjacent is a medieval tower.

In 1375 the peasants of Entlebuch defeated a band of some 3000 Free Companions pillaging in the neighbourhood of *Buttisholz* (some 8km N of Wolhusen; see below), riding home on steeds and clad in armour they had captured. The Free Companions, largely a contingent of English troops, formed part of a numerous and splendidly equipped force which had invaded Switzerland under Enguerrand de Coucy (husband of Catherine, daughter of Edward III) to claim his Habsburg inheritance. They were nick-named 'Guglers' from their high-crowned iron caps, and it is said that the bones of those that fell are below a mound at Buttisholz, known as the *Englischer Grabhügel* or 'English Barrow'.

A mountain road climbs SE to the *Glaubenbergpass* (1543m) and then descends to (31km) *Sarnen*; see Rte 19.

10km *Wolhusen*, on the KLEINE EMME, also has a Dance of Death (of 1661) in its cemetery chapel. Here we meet the No. 2A, and turn right through (2.5km) *Werthenstein*, where on a rock stands a former Franciscan convent. Its 17C *Church* has two octagonal chapels on either side of the facade and is almost surrounded by a cloister-walk, while the cloister is adorned with frescoes of 1779 by Joseph Reinhart.

One may shortly join the motorway leading due E to approach (19.5km) **Lucerne**; see Rte 21. To the S are the unfrequented slopes of a range of hills, beyond which rises the Pilatus; see p 204.

B. Via Burgdorf, Huttwil, and Willisau

Total distance, 100km (62 miles). N1. 19km—No. 23. 5km **Burgdorf**—10.5km *Ramsei*—19.5km *Huttwil*—14km **Willisau-Stadt**—No. 2A. 10km *Wolhusen*—22km **Lucerne**.

Maps: M 216; BL 31, 32, or 5016, 5019.

The N1 motorway is followed NE for 19km, there turning right for
Burgdorf (15,400 inhab.; 6550 in 1880), a flourishing industrial town
built on an eminence above the Emme. Its *Castle*, founded in the 7C
and several times enlarged, contains a local *Museum*. It was the home
of Pestalozzi's first regular school (1798), before his removal to
Yverdon in 1804. The *Church* dates from 1471-87. Max
Schneckenburger (1819-49), author of 'Die Wacht am Rhein', died
here. The Swiss national ball-game of 'Hornussen' (which has been
described as 'a combination of a rough sort of golf, cricket and lawn
tennis') is said to have originated here.

We now bear SE up the lower EMMENTAL past (left at 8km)
Lützelflüh, where from 1832 the novelist 'Jeremias Gotthelf' (1797-
1854) was pastor.—After 2.5km turn left through (5km) *Sumiswald*
(700m). The road later circles to the E to approach (14.5km) *Huttwil*,
a small industrial town, and, 7km beyond, *Zell*, with a church of
1803.—3.5km *Gettnau*, just E of which the left-hand fork leads to
(12km) *Sursee*; see Rte 13A.

Bearing right, **Willisau-Stadt** is soon entered, with a picturesque
HAUPTGASSE, at either end of which are 16C town gates. Just
outside the *Obertor* (W) is the charming *Heiligblut chapel* (1675), and
on a height just within stands the *Parish-church*, rebuilt in a neo-
Classic style by J. Purtschert in 1801 but retaining its 13C tower.
Further up the hill is the former *Schloss* (late 17C).

The road then continues SE to (10km) *Wolhusen*, for which see Rte
16A, above, and for the road E to (22km) **Lucerne**.

17 Berne to Interlaken

A. Via Thun, and Spiez

Total distance, 54km (33 miles). No. 6. 28km **Thun**—11km
Spiez—No. 8. 15km **Interlaken**.

Maps: M 217; BL 36, 37, or 5018.

The most rapid route is that following the N6 motorway, leading SE
up the AARE VALLEY. There are several fine views of the Alps of the
Bernese Oberland, among them the *Stockhorn* (S; 2190m) and the
pyramidal *Niesen* (2362m). After 25km fork SE to (4km) *Thun*.

The No. 6 runs parallel to and E of the motorway via (9km) *Rubigen*,
near which is the church of *Kleinhöchstetten*, of Merovingian foundation.—4km *Münsingen*, has a medieval and 16C *Schloss* and an 18C
church, in the vicinity of which a Celtic cemetery and a Roman villa
have been found.—7km *Kiesen*, with a *Dairying Museum* housed in
an old Emmental cheese factory.

4km NE, at *Oberdiessbach*, the 16C church contains a monument to Albrecht
von Wattenwyl, who in 1668 built the *Schloss*, one of the best-preserved of its
type. To the SE rises the *Falkenflue* (1196m).

The main road soon reaches *Heimberg*, noted for its pottery since the
18C, and then by-passes (left) **Steffisburg** (12,550 inhab.), where the
church, rebuilt in 1681, retains its Romanesque tower.

8km **THUN** (560m; 36,900 inhab.; 16,500 in 1930; 8350 in 1880) lies at the N extremity of its lake, the Thuner See, the older enceinte on and E of an island site in the Aare, dominated by its Schloss on the hill above. Commanding a good view of the Eiger, Mönch, Jungfrau, Blümlisalp and Doldenhorn, and of the Niesen and the Stockhorn in the foreground, it was once considered *the* starting-place for those visiting the Bernese Oberland. 'There is not a more picturesque town in Switzerland than Thun', wrote Murray in 1838, 'thronged with a constant succession of travellers through the whole summer', even if 'within its walls there is nothing worth notice'. A small iron steamer plied on its lake from 1835.

It became a dependence of Berne in 1375, and was long an important garrison town. The future Napoleon III was a student at the Artillery School here from 1830. Heinrich von Kliest spent the spring of 1802 here; Matthew Arnold was much taken by a young lady here in 1865; Brahms composed his 'Double Concerto' and 'Thuner Sonata' in the suburb of *Hofstetten* during the summers of 1886–88; and Ludwig Spohr spent the summers of 1816–17 at *Thierachern*, just to the W.

From the Rathausplatz, on the E bank, with its 16C *Rathaus*, one may follow the arcaded OBERE HAUPTGASSE, with a characteristic pavement over the projecting street-level shops. From near the far end covered steps ascend steeply to the *Stadtkirche*, founded in 933 but dating in its present form from 1738, with an octagonal tower of the 14C surmounting a porch containing contemporary wall-paintings. The churchyard commands a fine view of the peaks of the Oberland.—A few paces to the SE stands the *Burgitor*.

Walking NW from the church we approach the massive, steeply-roofed *Schloss, built after 1182, with its picturesque corner-turrets (c 1230), and early 15C additions. It houses a somewhat miscellaneous collection including local antiquities, arms and armour, tapestries and ceramics—some from local potteries established c 1730.

Flights of covered steps descend from near the entrance, by which one may regain the Rathausplatz.

On the W bank of the Aare, near the lake side, is the church of *Scherzlingen*, with a Romanesque nave and choir, 14C tower and notable 13–16C wall-paintings.—Just beyond is the mid 19C *Schloss Schadau*, built on the site of a medieval fort. A building in the park (views) contains a panorama of Thun and its environs in 1800, painted by Marquard Wocher.

FROM THUN TO INTERLAKEN VIA MERLIGEN (23km). The road skirting the NE bank of the *Thuner See* traverses the suburbs of *Hünibach* and *Hilterfingen*, which merge with **Oberhofen**. Here, a medieval *Castle*, once the property of Albrecht of Habsburg, now houses material from the *Historical Museum* at Berne, including arms and armour, toys, musical instruments and marquetry panelling of 1607, the period it was in the possession of the Erlach family. There is also Empire furniture once belonging to the archduchess Anna Fedorovna of Russia, resident in Berne from 1813–60; the chapel, dating from 1473, contains murals. In the *Alpine Garden* is a statue of Winston Churchill.—8km *Gunten*, almost opposite Spiez (see below), on a sunny slope above which lies the ancient village of *Sigriswil*, with a church rebuilt in 1679 by Dünz. To the NE rises the *Sigriswiler Rothorn* (2050m).—The road next passes through *Merligen*, at the mouth of the JUSTISTAL, beyond which, at *Beatenbucht*, a cable railway ascends to *Beatenberg*; see below. We round the promontory known as the 'Nase', with the Faulhorn and Schwarzhorn prominent ahead. Above us rises the *Niederhorn* (1950m) and several other fine view-points approached from Beatenberg, extending along the upper slopes of the range, and also ascended to from Interlaken. We shortly pass the *Beatushöhlen*, a series of caves (the

Beatenbach gushes from the lowest), one of which is said to have been the hermitage of St. Beatus, an 8C Irish missionary.—At *Neuhaus*, the original landing-place at the end of the lake, we bear right and cross the Aare Canal, with the ruined castle of *Weissenau* to the left, to reach the main road immediately W of **Interlaken**; see Rte 18.

The motorway circles W of Thun and may be regained just N of the town, or at *Spiez*, 11km S on the No. 6. This, the old road, first traverses *Gwatt*, with a tower of a Strattligen fortress. It was the ancestral home of the Guelph, Count Rudolf, who founded the kingdom of Transjuran Burgundy in 889.—We cross the small delta of the Kander, which here flows through a conduit of 1714, designed by Samuel Jenner, an Englishman, to reach *Einigen*, with a tiny Romanesque church (10–13C; restored), preserving a carved wooden ceiling, and overlooking the Thuner See.

The **Thuner See** or *Lake of Thun* is 18.5km long, 3.6km across at its widest point and 48.4km^2 in area. It commands several splendid views of the lofty summits of the Bernese Alps beyond its S shore, among them the Stockhorn and the pyramidal Niesen, standing like sentinels at the entrance of the valleys of the Simme and the Kander. Behind these is the long array of snowy peaks of the Blümlisalp, and the massif of the Jungfrau, Mönch and Eiger, with the Schreckhorn and Wetterhorn rising further E.

11km **Spiez** lies on and above a small bay dominated by its *Castle* (15–16C; with an 11C tower), successively owned by the Strättligers, Bubenbergs, and from 1516–1875 by the Von Erlachs, whose chevrons are everywhere in evidence. On its S side are 18C extensions. Several rooms may be visited, including the Baroque Festsaal of 1614 by A. and P. Castello.—The adjacent Romanesque *Church*, with a spire of c 1625, altered in 1670 and restored in 1950, contains 11C murals and further wall paintings of c 1500 in the apse; those in the crypt are fragmentary. The Erlach family monuments are notable.

To the N is the *Spiezberg* (687m), providing a view of the Jungfrau peeping over the Morgenberghorn and Schwalmern.

For roads hence to *Adelboden* and *Kanderstegg*, see Rte 17B.

We traverse adjacent *Faulensee* to join the N8 skirting the Thuner See, with a view across to Beatenberg on the slopes of the Niederhorn (see above), to *Leissigen*, with an old church, above which rises the *Morgenberghorn* (2249m), and beyond, the *Därliggrat* (1890m).—8km **Interlaken**, also by-passed to the S by a short tunnel, off which turns the road to *Grindelwald* and *Lauterbrunnen*; see also Rte 18.

B. Via Riggisberg and Wimmis (for Adelboden and Kandersteg)

Total distance, 55km (34 miles). 7km *Kehrsatz*, where turn right—12km **Riggisberg**—7km *Wattenwil*—8km *Reutigen*—3km *Wimmis*—3km *Spiez* crossroads (for *Frutigen, Adelboden* and *Kandersteg*)—No. 8. 15km **Interlaken**.

Maps: M 217; BL 36, 37, or 5018, and 41, 42, or 5009.

We follow the main road S on the left bank of the Aare through the suburb of *Wabern*, above which rises the view-point of the *Gurten*

(858m), and shortly reach the turning to the *Airport*. The main road drives along the GÜRBETAL from Wabern to (18km) *Kirchenthurnen* (where the church, of 1673, preserves its medieval tower), 3km NE of Riggisberg. An alternative and preferable route is found by briefly following the airport road and turning right over the main road and then left. This—the *Längenberg-Höhenstrasse*—runs parallel to, but higher than, the main road and provides more extensive views of the Bernese Alps beyond the Thuner See; see Rte 17A.

Riggisberg, where the castle was occupied by the Von Erlach from 1387–1799, is a pleasantly sited village. 1km NE (well signposted) is the ****Abegg Foundation**.

The collection of the late Werner Abegg constitutes one of the most important of its kind, concentrating as it does on every aspect of textile design, including objects of antiquity in which the history of the design of fabrics is depicted. The building, the gardens of which also provide a splendid view towards the Oberland, houses a specialised *Library* of some 80,000 books, and a *School of Restoration*. Because of the delicate nature of most of the materials, only a selection is shown in rotation. The exhibitions usually concentrate on specific forms or periods of design or on textiles from geographical areas.

Note that the Foundation is normally only open from 14.00–17.00 from mid May to mid October; intending visitors should enquire first at the Tourist Office in Berne.

The objects listed are those which are likely to remain on display; in the case of fabrics, they will in all probability be replaced by other items from the very extensive collection, the scrupulous conservation of which—continually being increased by the donation and acquisition of rare textiles—is the main preoccupation of the enterprising director.

Notable are several Statuettes and an axe-head from Luristan; the head of a Cycladic idol; Persian Ivories (8C BC); a Rhyton of lapis lazuli (5C BC); a bronze Falcon (the god Horus) and Egyptian reliefs. There are also bronzes and alabaster reliefs; a rock-crystal amphora with gold fittings; Byzantine silverware and ivories; Limoges enamels; Romanesque portals, capitals and carved altarpieces; examples of Egyptian, Coptic, Persian, Chinese, Hispano-moresque and Byzantine textiles, apart from those of medieval and Renaissance Europe, and more recent fabrics of quality, including Tapestries and Costumes. The Paintings include a triptych by *Roger van der Weyden*; *Crivelli*, Resurrection; *Fra Angelico*, Adoration of the Magi; and *Botticelli*, Portrait of Aquinus. A room is also devoted to 17C painted wallpapers.

The main road W leads to (12km) *Schwarzenburg*, passing to the right after 4km *Rüeggisberg*, with remains of a Cluniac priory founded in 1070. To the SW of Riggisberg rises the *Gibelegg* (1133m; views); see the latter part of Rte 6B.

Continuing S and shortly forking left below the *Burgistein* (1021m), with an old castle, the cradle of the Wattenwyl family, we reach (7km) *Wattenwil*, with a church of 1683 by Abraham Dünz.—Ferdinand Hodler (1853–1918), the artist, was born at *Gurzelen*, 3km NE.

From (3.5km) *Blumenstein*, an old spa, where the 15–18C church has early 14C glass in its choir, the *Stockhorn* (S; 2190m) may be ascended.—4km *Oberstocken*, 3km E of which, by its little lake, is the old castle of **Amsoldingen**. The Romanesque **Church* has a saddle-back tower and blind arcading on the exterior. The original Roman columns from its fine crypt were removed to Thun in 1876. The 14C mural of St. Christopher and the font (the oldest in the Oberland)

should be noted.—Regaining the main road, bear SE below the
Stockhorn and turn right at the junction beyond *Reutigen*, where the
medieval church has wall-paintings of some interest, and then left at
the entrance of the SIMMENTAL (see Rte 7A) for **Wimmis**, overlooked
from the S by the pyramidal *Niesen* (2362m). Below the 15C *Schloss*
stands restored *St. Martin*, with a triple apse and Romanesque choir,
largely 10C, on the site of a 7–8C church, and 14–mid 15C murals.

For *Spiez*, some 3km NE beyond the N8 for **Interlaken**, and for the road thence,
see Rte 17A.

FROM SPIEZ TO (13.5km) FRUTIGEN, FOR ADELBODEN, AND
KANDERSTEG (15.5km SW and 12.5km S, respectively). Bear S up
the FRUTIGTAL, the pastoral valley of the Kander, with a view ahead
of the glistening white massif of the *Blümlisalp*, to (7km) *Mülenen*,
from which a funicular ascends the **Niesen** (W; 2362m). This peak
commands one of the finest *Views in the Bernese Alps, and may also
be ascended by bridle-paths from Wimmis or Frutigen. The morning
and evening views are best (before 8.00 and after 16.00). The steep
Fromberghorn (2394m) may be reached via the ridge to the SW of the
Niesen.

A steep road climbs NE from Mülenen to (2.5km) *Aeschi*, a village finely situated
on a ridge overlooking the Thuner See, and with a 16C church. From here a track
ascends the SULDTAL to the SE, from which one can walk across the *Tanzbödeli*
or *Renggli pass* (1879m) between the *Morgenberghorn* (N; 2249m) and the
Schwalmern (2777m), with the *Dreispitz* (2520m) rising to the SW, to descend
to *Saxeten*, SW of *Wilderswil*; see Rte 18.

The main road shortly skirts the village of *Reichenbach*, at the mouth
of the wooded KIENTAL, at the head of which rises the *Blümlisalp* and
the *Gspaltenhorn*.

A road climbs 7km from here to the village of *Kiental* (958m), a base for
excursions and climbs: to the SW rises the *Gehrihorn* (2130m); to the E, the
Dreispitz (2520m). The same minor road, keeping to the right, continues to climb
to (6.5km) *Griesalp* and *Gorneren*, small mountaineering centres within a cirque
of cliffs among which are several cascades. To the W and SW rise the *Ärmighorn*
(2742m) and *Dündenhorn* (2862m). Other ascents to be made from here include
the *Blümlisalp* (3663m), approached via the *Hohtürli pass* (2778m) to the S, from
which one may descend to *Kandersteg* via the *Öeschinensee*, and the
Gspaltenhorn (SE; 3436m), with the finest escalade of rocks in the Bernese
Oberland. There is also the *Bütlasse* (3192m), crowned with a pyramid of ice;
to the E leads the *Sefinen Furgge pass* (2612m), below the *Schilthorn* (2970m),
to *Mürren*; see Rte 18. SW of the Gspaltenhorn, and at the head of the *Gamchi
Glacier*, opens the *Gamchilücke* (2837m), a passage for experts only, leading to
the *Tschingel Pass*.

Beyond Reichenbach we bear SW up the valley of the *Kander*,
spanned by several characteristic covered bridges, and follow the line
of the railway to the *Lötschbergtunnel*; see below.—6.5km **Frutigen**
(803m), a village, lies at the confluence of the Kander and Engstligen,
the terrace of its 18C church providing a fine view of the
Blümlisalp massif. The *Steinschlaghorn* (2321m) and the
Mäggisserehorn (2347m), to the NW, and the *Gehrihorn* (E; 2130m)
are easily ascended from here.

FROM FRUTIGEN TO ADELBODEN (15.5km). The road ascends
SW up the romantic *ENGSTLIGENTAL, into which fall several
torrents descending from the chain of mountains on the right,

while the snow-capped *Wildstrubel* (3243m) is frequently in view ahead. Continuing to climb, *Boden* is reached, a village of scattered chalets in a level basin of lush Alpine meadows, from which the final steep pull brings one to **Adelboden** (1353m), a resort occupying a sunny position at the head of the valley, where several tributary valleys meet. The dominant feature of the view is still the Wildstrubel, and the striking *Engstligen Falls* in its lap. The ridge sheltering the village on the E is formed by the *Lohner* (3049m) and the *Bunderspitz* (2546m), and to the NW is the forest-clad slope of the *Teschentenalp* (2026m), with the *Gsur* (2708m) rising beyond. The *Church* at Adelboden dates back to the 15C, while the exterior S wall displays a 16C mural of the Last Judgement. The churchyard gates were presented by Allied servicemen interned here in 1943–45.

Among the several excursions which may be made from here a favourite is that to the *Engstligenalp* (1964m), a plateau to the S, and the base for a number of ascents. It is reached from *Unter dem Birg* by cable-car or footpath. To the SW rises the *Wildstrubel* (3243m), below which the high-level and fatiguing *Ammertenpass* (2443m) leads SW across to the *Simmefälle*, above *Oberried*, SE of *Lenk*; this is also approached direct from Adelboden via the *Hahnenmoospass* (1956m). The *Gemmipass*, for *Leukerbad*, may be reached via the *Engstligenalp* via a pass at 2610m, between the *Steghorn* (3146m) and the *Felsenhorn* (2782m), descending to the W bank of the *Daubensee*, see p 320.—Kandersteg, to the E, may be approached by a pass at 2385m, S of the *Bunderspitz* (2546m), from which one descends into the *Üschinertal*.

FROM FRUTIGEN TO KANDERSTEG (12.5km). The road up the KANDERTAL ascends almost due S, shortly passing below (right) the ruins of the castle of *Tellenburg*, once the residence of the bailiff or 'Amtmann' of the district; to the E rises the *Gehrihorn* (2130m). The railway line later crosses the road in the first of a series of remarkable double spiral loops, and we skirt the *Blausee*, a small transparent tarn, to the left of which is the ruined tower of *Felsenburg*. The straggling village of **Kandersteg** (1176m)—its name derived from the earliest foot-bridge or *Steg* over the stream—is a beautifully situated resort and mountaineering centre of long standing. There is much level land in and around the village, and the valley has always been known for its breed of cattle, which graze on the high pastures. It is also rich in wild flowers, and the Cistopteris montana (fern) grows here and on the Gemmi. It was an important base for the crossing of the range into the Valais prior to the piercing of the *Lötschberg railway tunnel* in 1906–12 (14.6km long and rising to 1244m). Kandersteg is the N terminus for the car-carrying shuttle-service to Goppenstein or Brig, in the Valais. It is still a good centre for excursions and ascents.

Above are seen several glaciers descending from the snow peaks of the Blümlisalp, the Fründenhorn, and the Doldenhorn to the SE. To the W rises the ridge of the Bunderspitz and Lohner, separating Kandersteg from Adelboden. To the NE is the *Bire* (2502m); to the SE, the *Fisistock* (2787m); and to the S the curiously shaped *Gällihorn* (2284m).
  Easily reached is the *Oeschinensee*, to the E, first passing three waterfalls. It is a beautifully sited oval lake overlooked by the snowy summits of the *Blümlisalp* and the *Fründenhorn* to the SE, from where one may cross the *Hohtürli pass* (2778m) to *Griesalp*; see p 180.—The road, later a track, continues S from Kandersteg, to near the *Klus*, a gorge of the Kander, and ascends SE up the wild GASTERENTAL to *Gasteren*, SW of which rises the *Balmhorn* (3699m); and to the S, the *Lötschenpass* (2690m), whence one may descend to *Ferden* in the Lötschental; see Rte 43.—A path ascends NE from Gasteren to approach the

approach the *Kanderfirn*, with the *Mutthorn* (3035m) rising above; beyond, the *Tschingelfirn* descends; see *Mürren*, Rte 18.—From just short of the Klus, a track ascends SW up the ÜSCHINENTAL towards the *Felsenhorn* (2782m), from where one may gain the *Gemmipass*, while off this track a path climbs W to a pass (2385m) below the *Bunderspitz* (2546m), from which one may descend to *Adelboden*.

FROM KANDERSTEG TO THE GEMMIPASS. A path and lift climb S from below the Klus past the *Schwarzbachfall*, with a view up the GASTERENTAL. Beyond *Spitalmatte*, a stoney pasturage ravaged in 1895 by the fall of a huge section of the *Altels Glacier*, which destroyed a herd of cattle and six herdsmen, we cross into the Valais to approach the solitary *Schwarenbach Hotel* (2060m). The *Balmhorn* (3699m), the principal peak of the region, can be climbed from here via the *Schwarz Glacier* and a long snow ridge. The nearer *Altels* (3629m) is more difficult, with much loose rock and shingle. The *Rinderhorn* (3453m) rises to the SE; NW, the *Felsenhorn* (2782m) is remarkable for its flora. The path skirts the dreary *Daubensee*, surrounded by limestone rocks, frozen most of the year, and with a subterranean channel to the Rhône valley. Just S of the lake is the *Gemmipass* (2314m), abounding in wild flowers in June, and commanding a superb view of the Alps from the Bischabelhörner and Monte Rosa to the Matterhorn, the Dent Blanche, and the Weisshorn. To the W rises the *Wildstrubel* (3243m), ascended via the LÄMMERNTAL, which opens to the W of the pass, and the glacier at its head. The *Steghorn* (3146m), to the NW, the *Schneehorn* (W; 3178m) and the *Rinderhorn* (see above), may also be ascended from the pass. Then one can descend on foot or by cable-car to *Leukerbad*; see Rte 43. The Gemmipass was described in Maupassant's 'Boule-de-Suif'.

18   Interlaken to Grindelwald, Wengen and Mürren: the Jungfrau

Interlaken to **Grindelwald**, 20km; Interlaken to **Lauterbrunnen** (12km), for *Wengen* and *Mürren*.

Maps: M 217; BL 37, 42, or 5004.

Interlaken (563m), so-called from its position 'between the lakes' of Thun and Brienz, lies on the *Bödeli*, an alluvial flat formed by the torrents descending from the valleys of Grindelwald and Lauterbrunnen. The *View* of the snow-clad Jungfrau from the *Höheweg*, the main thoroughfare, is famous, but perhaps because it is one of the oldest and most popular of Swiss resorts and has much expanded during the last century, it is now of slight interest in itself, although preserving a few quaint houses, mostly on the N bank of the Aare. Murray suggested that its beautiful position and closeness to numerous interesting sites, and its reputation of being inexpensive, had 'converted it into an English colony, two-thirds of the summer visitors, on a moderate computation, being of our nation, who have converted the place into a sort of Swiss Margate'.

The town originally grew up around an Augustinian monastery; the *Church*, founded in 1133 and deconsecrated in 1528, only the 14C chancel survives; the nave dates from 1909, when it was re-opened for services. The E wing of the cloister and the Chapter-house of 1445 also survive, and remains of conventual dependencies are incorporated into the adjoining *Schloss* (1747), now cantonal offices. They are situated just beyond the E end of the central park or Höhe-Matte, flanked to the N by several palatial hotels enjoying the view of the Jungfrau.

From the Central Platz, at the W end of the Höheweg, the Marktgasse crosses the railway and a narrow island in the Aare to reach the suburb of *Unterseen*, with a small *Museum*, and a *Church* rebuilt in 1674, and restored in 1850, but retaining its old tower. Several houses in the area date from the 17C.

Roads from here climb to the high-lying villages of *Beatenberg* (NW) and *Habkern* (NE); from the latter a path leads along a ridge to the summit of the *Augstmatthorn* (2137m). From Beatenberg, itself commanding a fine panorama of the Alps from the Schreckhorn to the Niesen, one may ascend the *Niederhorn* (1950m) to enjoy an even more extensive view. One can follow the ridge to the NE to the *Burgfeldstand* (2063m) and, beyond, the *Gemmenalphorn* (2061m).

From near the E end of the Höheweg in Interlaken a funicular ascends the tree-clad slopes of the *Harderkulm* (1323m), also providing a notable view of the Bernese Alps.

For roads from Interlaken to **Lucerne** via *Brienz* and *Sarnen*; and to **Andermatt** via *Meiringen* and the *Sustenpass*, see Rtes 19 and 20 respectively.

FROM INTERLAKEN TO GRINDELWALD (20km). Follow the main road S to *Wilderswil*, a small resort with several old chalets; a short distance NW is a 16C ruin, the traditional seat of Byron's 'Manfred'. The *Parish church*, rebuilt in 1673, on the right bank of the Lütschine, is reached by a covered wooden *Bridge*.

A road ascends SW to *Saxeten*, a village from which the *Sulegg* (SE; 2413m) may be climbed for the magnificent view. The *Schwalmere* (S; 2777m) is a more difficult climb, while to the SW is a pass (1879m) leading into the SULDTAL, below the *Morgenberghorn* (2249m); its NE ridge, the *Därlinggrat*, should only be attempted by experts.

From Wilderswil one may also take the rack-and-pinion railway climbing E to the *Schynige Platte* via *Breitlauenen*, with a good view of the lakes of Thun and Brienz, prior to piercing the ridge, where the whole chain of the Bernese Alps breaks into view. The **Schynige Platte** (2100m) commands one of the finest views in the Oberland, best seen from the *Daube*, a terrace at a higher level, reached by an easy path from the station. An *Alpine Garden* here can also be visited. Walkers may take an easily followed route E hence to the *Faulhorn* (2681m) see p 185.

From Wilderswil the road ascends the wooded valley of the Lütschine to *Zweilütschinen*, a village at its confluence with the Schwarze Lütschine, where we turn left: for the road to **Lauterbrunnen** see p 188. The Wetterhorn soon comes into view as the road climbs steeply and later the valley opens out as we approach **Grindelwald** itself (1034m), straggling over a sheltered and sunny slope, and one of the more attractive resorts and mountaineering centres of its size, with the majestic peaks of the *Wetterhorn* (E; 3701m), the *Mättenberg* (SE; 3104m, the lower part of the Schreckhorn ridge), and the *Eiger* (SW; 3970m) in its immediate vicinity.

Its name is first recorded in 1146. William Burnet, FRS, visited the place in 1708, and in 1765 Thomas Pennant, the naturalist, passed that way. Archdeacon William Coxe, the historian, noted in 1785 that the glacier had receded by 400 paces since he had first seen it in 1776. (Karl Viktor Bonstetten considered Coxe's 'Sketches of the Natural, Political, and Civil State of Swisserland' (1779) as 'not only dull, but writ in an ordinary pert stile'.) Southey visited it in 1817. Dr W.A.B. Coolidge (1850–1926), the Alpinist, who referred to a colony of English here in January 1888, died here and is buried in the cemetery. Skis were introduced to Grindelwald by Gerald Fox, an Englishman, in 1891. In the following year the village was seriously damaged by fire. Sir Henry Lunn founded the Public Schools Alpine Sports Club here shortly after.

Mountaineers on the Grindelwald Glacier in 1905

The one inevitable excursion is that to the glaciers which stream down on either side of the Mättenberg. The upper or *Oberer Gletscher* is the finer of the two: less energetic visitors may be content with a distant view of the lower. Both are explicitly mentioned in 13C charters, and began to arouse scientific interest in the 17C (being described in the 'Philosophical transactions' of the Royal Society in 1669). But it was not until the beginning of the 19C that certain bold spirits ventured to explore them. When first heard of they descended to a much lower level, but they have since receded considerably. In 1723 Sir Horace Mann reported that the services of an exorcist had been considered in order to drive the glacier back! The upper glacier may be approached by foot in 1½ hours from the *Railway Station* by following the main street to just beyond the *Church* (1793) and from that point taking a path to the right. The upper glacier is visible practically all the way from this turning. On reaching the *Wetterhorn Hotel*, follow a path to the right to the *Chalet Milchbach*, near the foot of the glacier (described by Byron as a 'frozen hurricane'), from which a steep ascent to the ice-grotto is made.—A path from the Wetterhorn Hotel leads in 1½ hours to the *Mättenberg bridge* and the lower glacier;

while a chair-lift ascends from near the church to *Pfingstegg*, on the path between the two glaciers.

For the *Gletscherschlucht* (or Glacier Gorge), and the lower or *Unterer Gletscher*, leave the main street between the *Adler Hotel* and the *Church*. The road descends to the Lütschine and crosses the Mättenberg bridge. Beyond a second bridge is the entrance to the Gorge, where a hanging path skirts the ravine above a deafening torrent and then tunnels through rock to a narrow cleft between sinister cliffs, with the huge ice wall of the lower glacier beyond.

Among numerous ascents in the neighbourhood, one of the easiest, and providing one of the finest views, is the **Faulhorn** (2681m), to the NW. The ascent is considerably shortened by taking the First-Sesselbahn or chair-lift, which rises to 2168m; then marked paths are followed past the *Bachsee*. The Faulhorn, with flora of interest, owes its name (faul = rotten) to the friable nature of its shaly slopes. The inn there was built in 1830, and in its early days was visited by Mendelssohn, Matthew Arnold and Prince Albert, among others. The summit commands a view of most of the main peaks of the Bernese Alps at close range, although some consider the view superior from its slightly higher neighbour to the S, the *Rötihorn* or *Reeti* (2757m). This includes the Schwarzhorn (E); the Wetterhorn, Schreckhorn and Finsteraarhorn (SE); the Fiescherhörner, Eiger, Mönch and Jungfrau (S); and the Gspaltenhorn and Blümlisalp (SW). The view also includes the lakes of Brienz (N) and Thun (W), Neuchâtel (NW) and Lucerne (NE).—The return to Grindelwald is often made by following a path diverging to the right at a stone hut a little below the summit and crossing the *Bussalp*. For the descent to the *Schynige Platte*, see p 183; to the *Grosse Scheidegg*, see below. The descent to *Giessbach*, on the Brienzer See, leads E via the *Hagelsee* and *Tschingelfeld* to *Axalp*; see p 192.

The **Wetterhorn**, due E of Grindelwald, one of the most striking summits of the Alps, consisting of a long knife-edge seen endwise as a sharp-pointed cone, has three peaks: the *Hasli Jungfrau*, the Wetterhorn proper (3701m); first climbed in August 1844, and in June 1854 by Eardley Blackwell (Alfred Wills, who later presided over the trial of Oscar Wilde, ascended the peak in September of the same year and thought he was the first, as described in 'Wanderings in the High Alps'); the *Mittelhorn* (3704m; first climbed by Stanhope Templeman Speer in July 1845); and the *Rosenhorn* (3689m; also first ascended in 1844).—The **Streckhorn** (4078m), SW of the Wetterhorn, and the adjacent **Lauteraarhorn** (4042m) demand expert knowledge, the first being conquered by Leslie Stephen in 1861, who called it 'the grimmest fiend of the Oberland'; the first winter ascent was made in 1879 by Coolidge. Leslie Stephen (1832–1904), the father of Virginia Woolf and the first editor of the Dictionary of National Biography (1882–91), was President of the Alpine Club in 1865–68.—Some distance further S rises the mighty **Finsteraarhorn** (4274m), the highest peak in the range, first ascended in 1829. Between the Wetterhorn and Schreckhorn rises the *Bärglistock* (3656m); almost due S of Grindelwald is the **Fiescherhörner** (4049m).

FROM GRINDELWALD TO MEIRINGEN VIA THE GROSSE SCHEIDEGG, one of the most frequented foot-paths in the Alps. From the *Wetterhorn Hotel*, a good track ascends beneath the tremendous precipices of the Wetterhorn (see above), which seem to overhang the route, although its base is some distance away. The path becomes steeper as we mount to the ***Grosse Scheidegg Pass** (1962m), formed by a col joining the Wetterhorn to the Schwarzhorn, but in fact it is 99m lower than the *Kleine Scheidegg* (see below): the epithet applies to its width and general extent. The retrospective view, with the contrast between the green pastures of the valley of Grindelwald and the bare walls of the Wetterhorn, is very striking. Above the village on the left rises the sharp crest of the Eiger, which is best seen from this point.

The *Schwarzhorn* (NW; 2928m), the highest peak of the Faulhorn range, is easily ascended, with a view perhaps finer than the Faulhorn itself (see above), which may also be approached from the Schwarzhorn, or from the hamlet of *Alp Grindel* (W of the pass) via the *Bachsee*; there are pleasant alternative and less steep descents to Grindelwald via Alp Grindel, or the First-bahn.

From the pass the path descends to *Schwarzwaldalp* (1454m), a little below the *Lower Schwarzwald Glacier* (right), which is of the type known as 'restored' (remanié), being composed of fragments of ice welded together by snow avalanches from the Wetterhorn. We now descend steeply into the ROSENLAUTAL, passing the little resort and climbing centre of *Rosenlaui*, rather shut in by trees, and situated close to a cascade of the *Reichenbach* at the foot of the *Wellhorn* (3192m). Here also is the seat of the *Swiss National Climbing School*.

To the E is the *Gletscherschlucht*, a gorge ascended by a rock-cut path, from the far end of which a track leads up to a point overlooking the retreating *Rosenlaui Glacier*. Above rise the *Dossenhorn* (3144m) and the *Renfenhorn* (further S; 3259m).

Beyond Rosenlaui the road crosses *Gschwantenmad*, a green level commanding a charming view of the Wetterhorn, the Wellhorn and the craggy peaks of the *Engelhörner* (2855m), one of which is named after Gertrude Bell, who was the first to scale it. The valley then contracts, its walls forming the backdrop for several waterfalls, and we descend steeply in zigzags to *Willigen*, on the main road just S of **Meiringen**; alternatively, one may follow a bridle-path to the left, leading shortly to the *Reichenbachfälle*; one can then climb down, or take a funicular; see Rte 20. If making the excursion in the reverse direction, from Meiringen to Grindelwald, the descent is more gradual.

FROM GRINDELWALD TO THE KLEINE SCHEIDEGG, FOR WENGEN AND LAUTERBRUNNEN, AND THE JUNGFRAUJOCH. The rack-and-pinion railway (inaugurated in 1893) descends to the valley floor, and starts the slow climb through meadows towards the Eiger through *Alpiglen*, with retrospective views of the Faulhorn (N), the Wetterhorn and the Grosse Scheidegg to the E, and down into the valley towards receding Grindelwald itself, and, to the NW, of the Männlichen. The train skirts the W buttress of the Eiger to approach the col of the **Kleine Scheidegg** (2061m). Among the first party of tourists to cross it, in 1771, was the Rev. Norton Nicholls (died 1809; a friend of Thomas Gray and a witness to Gibbon's will), also in the group were Karl Viktor von Bonstetten and Jakob Samuel Wyttenbach. The first hotel at Kleine Scheidegg was built in 1834 by Christian Seiler.

It is the starting-point for the ascent of the Jungfraujoch (see below), and commands one of the noblest *Views in the Alps, including the above-mentioned peaks and (above the Grosse Scheidegg) the Titlis, the Schreckhorn (S), the Eiger itself and the Mönch (SE), the Jungfrau, Schneehorn and Silberhorn (S), the Tschingelhorn (SW), the Schilton (W, beyond Mürren), and the nearer *Lauberhorn* (NW; 2472m).

The last, an easily ascended peak, was the scene of the first British downhill ski races (in 1921); the *Männlichen* (2343m), N of the Lauberhorn, is likewise climbed with ease, although the walk to the plateau is fairly steep, and the descent may be made to either Wengen or Grindelwald, also approached almost direct by cable-car. A shorter excursion is that to the Eiger Glacier; see below.

The **Eiger** (3970m), the N Wall of which is some 2300m of almost vertical rock, was first ascended by an Englishman named Barrington in August 1858; the first winter ascent was made in January 1890. The NE face was first climbed in August 1932, but the NW section of the N Face, *the Nordwand*, was not conquered until July 1938, by the Austrians Fritz Kasparek and Heinrich Harrer together with the Germans Andreas Heckmair and Ludwig Vörg, and for the first time in winter, in March 1961.

The North face of the Eiger

THE JUNGFRAU RAILWAY: FROM KLEINE SCHEIDEGG TO THE JUNGFRAUJOCH. The expedition may of course be made from either Grindelwald or Lauterbrunnen (see below) to the *Kleine Scheidegg*, where trains are changed. The journey to the summit takes 50–60 minutes, with three brief intermediate stops, and the trip may be broken at any station. Warm clothing is advisable. There is little point in making the ascent unless it is practically certain that there will be good visibility at the top; the transit of the long tunnel takes fully 30 minutes.

This, the highest railway in Europe, was constructed in 1896–1912 from the designs of Adolph Guyer-Zeller of Zürich at a total cost of £714,000. It attains a height of 3454m, while the terrace above (reached by lift) is at an altitude of 3573m (11,720ft), thus bringing the most unathletic into the upper regions of the expert mountaineer. The line, 'metre guage', is on the rack system (Strub's patent), with overhead trolleys. The steepest gradient is 1:4. The power is generated near both Lauterbrunnen and Burglauenen, and transmitted by high-tension lines. The first section is in the open air, but beyond Eigergletscher it runs through a long tunnel piercing the limestone and gneiss rock of the Eiger and Mönch.

The train first crosses pastures, with views of Wengen to the right, and after a short tunnel passes kennels of Eskimo dogs introduced here in 1913, to reach

Eigergletscher (2320m), at the W base of the Eiger. A short path leads to the *Eiger Glacier*, with its artificial grotto, but tourists should not go further without a guide. The glacier is crossed to approach the *Guggi Hut*, from which the **Mönch** (4099m) and the *Silberhorn* (3695m) are scaled; the former was first climbed in 1857; the latter by E. von Fellenberg and Karl Baedeker in 1863.

The train now enters a long tunnel which bears to the E, rising steeply to the station of *Eigerwand* (2864m), with a windowed gallery cut into the rock providing a remarkable view of Grindelwald over 1800m below, and also the Faulhorn, the Thuner See, and the distant ranges of the Jura, the Black Forest and Vosges. The tunnel now curves SW under the Eiger to the station of *Eismeer*, with a plunging view of the glacier, to which a shaft descends. The view extends over the *Grindelwald Fiescherfirn*, with its séracs and crevasses, while above tower the Wetterhorn, Schreckhorn and Fiescherhorn. The final pull up to the *Jungfraujoch*, the terminus, climbs at a gradient of 1 in 4. It stands on the slope of an icy ridge known as the *Sphinx*, situated between the Jungfrau and the Mönch. Galleries connect it with the snow plateau of the Joch.

The *Views* are naturally more extensive than from the lower stations. The *Jungfrau Glacier*, the upper part of the *Grosser Aletschgletscher*, the most extensive in the Alps, stretches away to the S, framed between the Mönch and the Jungfrau itself, and backed by the Lepontine Alps. Several peaks in the vicinity may be climbed by the experienced. The **Jungfrau**, or 'Virgin Peak' (4158m), lost its claim to such a title as far back as 1811. To the E rises the *Trugberg* (3933m), or 'Mount of Illusion', so named because mistaken by Agassiz's guides for the Jungfrau on its first ascent in 1841. On the summit of the Sphinx stands a meteorological and astronomical *Observatory*, perched there in 1937, to which a lift ascends. Its terraces and enclosed verandah are open to visitors. Caverns cut into the ice may also be visited from the station.

From Kleine Scheidegg, the railway descends gently through flowery pastures to the SW to *Wengernalp* (1874m), where Byron is supposed to have conceived his 'Manfred'. It is famous for its close *View* of the Jungfrau, down the precipices of which numerous avalanches fall into the deep ravine of the *Trümmelbach*, especially on sunny mid-days. The panorama includes the Eiger, Mönch, Schneehorn and Silberhorn, and the Giessen, Guggi and Eiger glaciers. The train, circling N, continues to descend along the flank of the *Lauberhorn* to **Wengen** (1275m), a well-appointed resort lying on a wide mountain terrace, and commanding a view of the Tschingelhorn, Breithorn, Mittaghorn, and the Jungfrau. The LAUTERBRUNNEN VALLEY is seen far below like a trench; the Staubbach is reduced to a thread, and its upper fall and its course, before it makes the leap, are exposed to view. The rack-and-pinion railway shortly turns S to climb down the valley side, with a view of the *Staubbachfall* to the SW, to reach its terminus at *Lauterbrunnen*; see below.

FROM INTERLAKEN TO (12km) LAUTERBRUNNEN, FOR WENGEN AND MÜRREN. For the road to *Zweilütschinen* see the first part of the Interlaken to Grindelwald sub-route, above. Here the road ahead up the valley of the Weisse Lütschine is followed, shortly passing (right) a bridle-path ascending to the beautifully situated hamlet of *Isenfluh* (1081m), commanding one of the best views of the Jungfrau and her sister peaks. Isenfluh may also be approached by a road from Lauterbrunnen via the *Sansbach Gorge* (wild flowers abundant), and is the usual starting-point for the rock-climbing hazards of the *Lobhorner* (2566m) to the SW.

The *Sausbachfall* (right) is next passed on ascending the narrow LAUTERBRUNNEN VALLEY, with the Hunnenfluh rising to the E, to reach the scattered resort of **Lauterbrunnen** itself (795m), deriving its name ('nothing but springs') from the innumerable 'wreaths of dangling water smoke' hanging from the rampart-like sides of the valley, often looking—when the clouds are low—as if they were bursting from the sky. Its most famous waterfall is the *Staubbach, which at its best appears like a veil of lace suspended in front of a precipice 305m high, and likened by Byron to the 'pale courser's tail' of the Apocalypse. In a dry season it hardly justifies its reputation.

View of the Lauterbrunnen Valley.

For **Wengen**, on a terrace to the NW, approached by the rack-and-pinion railway from Lauterbrunnen to the Kleine Scheidegg and Grindelwald (described in the reverse direction), see above.

Mürren (see below) inaccessible by car, is reached by cable-car from Lauterbrunnen to *Grütschalp*, thence by light railway, which mounts gradually, crossing several torrents en route, but those who can should walk (1½ hours). The old direct bridle-path from Lauterbrunnen to Mürren may also be used, except during the winter.

The *Mountain View* from Grütschalp is one of the finest in Switzerland, with the Lauterbrunnen valley at our feet, and the snowy crests of the Eiger, Mönch, Jungfrau and Silberhorn marshalled to the E. As we near Mürren, the Jungfrau vanishes behind the dark precipices of the Schwarzmönch, but the Gletscherhorn, Äbeni Flue, Grosshorn, Breithorn, Tschingelhorn and Gspaltenhorn carry on the dazzling procession.

The main road continues up the valley, off which a path to the left shortly leads to the *Trümmelbachfälle, fed by the combined snows of the Jungfrau, Mönch and Eiger, pent up within a cavernous gorge. The thunderous noise and the awesome drop are impressive, one of the falls issuing almost horizontally from the rock in a tremendous jet, while occasionally a rainbow can be seen in the spray.

The upper part of the valley exhibits scenery of the highest order, but the road ends at the hamlet of *Stechelberg*, at the mouth of the SEFINENTAL, prior to which cable-cars mount in three sections to *Gimmelwald* and *Mürren* (1638m), and then via *Birg* (2677m) to the summit of the *Schilthorn*; see below.

Mürren, a superbly situated resort, lies on a wide shelf above the precipices overhanging the Lauterbrunnen valley. It has a comparatively long history of winter-sports while in the summer botanists will be amply rewarded.

It was recorded as Mons Murren in 1257, but it was the English who in the 1840s and '50s first placed its few poor chalets on the map. Among them were Frederic Harrison, the author and positivist, John Addington Symonds, Frederick Locker-Lampson, and Tennyson. E.W. Benson, the future Archbishop of Canterbury, visited the place in 1880, and was severely critical of the English who were playing lawn-tennis in sight of the Jungfrau. The *English Church* dates from 1915. In 1922 the 'modern' slalom, invented by Arnold Lunn, was given its first trial here, and in 1924 the Kandahar Ski Club was founded at the Palace Hotel, while in 1928 the first 'Inferno' race from the summit of the Schilthorn down to Lauterbrunnen—an aggregate descent of some 2170m—took place.

The panorama of peaks visible from Mürren has few superiors. It includes the Wetterhorn (just visible to the NE), Eiger, Mönch, Jungfrau (partly masked by the precipices of the Schwarzmönch), Gletscherhorn, the Äbeni Flue (with its flattish top), Mittaghorn, Grosshorn and Breithorn (due S), Tschingelhorn, the sharp Gspaltenhorn, Bütlasse and Schilthorn (W; but not prominent). The view is best enjoyed from the *Allmendhubel*, a hill just N of the village, reached by cable or by foot via the BLUMENTAL, with good flora.

The principal excursion is the ascent of the *Schilthorn* (2970m), now easily reached by cable-car, later passing above the *Grauseeli*, a tiny tarn, above which is a monument to Alice Arbuthnot, killed here by lightning when on her honeymoon in 1865. The view from the summit, now embellished by a revolving restaurant, includes the Bernese and Valais Alps, with the Blümlisalp to the SW a particularly fine feature. Mont Blanc (c 130km away) is visible on a clear day from a point to the NW, a few minutes below the summit.

Among other ascents usually made from Mürren are the *Lobhörner* (NW; 2566m), the *Schwarzbirg* or *Bietenhorn* (2756m), the *Wyssbirg* (2621m), all to the NW, the *Hundshorn* (SW; 2928m), and *Spitzhorn* (2210m), to the S.

From the smaller resort of *Gimmelwand*, to the S, a path ascends the wild SEFINENTAL, passing several cascades, to the foot of the *Kilchbalm Glacier*, at the base of the *Gspaltenhorn* (3437m) and *Bütlasse*; (3192m); another path descends to *Stechelberg*. From the last village, paths ascend the Weisse Lütschine near a number of spectacular waterfalls to enter a *Nature Reserve*, and approach the hamlet of *Obersteinberg* (1778m), with a view of the Jungfrau, the Tschingelhorn and Breithorn glaciers and the Schmadribach fall.

Among passes which may be crossed by experienced hikers and with guides between Mürren and Kandersteg (see Rte 17B) are those from Gimmelwäld via the *Stefinenfurke* (2612m) and *Hohtürli* (2778m) passes to the *Öeschinensee*; or from Obersteinberg across the *Tschingel pass*, between the Blümlisalp and Mutthorn into the upper GASTERETAL; see p 181.

19   Interlaken to Lucerne via Brienz and Sarnen

Total distance, 70km (43 miles). No. 6–11. 16km **Brienz**—2km. **Ballenberg** lies to the left.—4km No. 4.—26km **Sarnen**—No. 8. 12km *Stansstad* crossroads—N2. 10km **Lucerne**.

Maps: 216, 217; BL 37, or 5004, 5008.

An extension of the N8 motorway under construction above the SE shore of the Brienzer See between Interlaken and *Brienzwiller* (5km E of Brienz) will provide a rapid route to Meiringen and the Sustenpass (see Rte 20), and also to Lucerne. It will pass *Iseltwald* (already reached by a narrow road along the lakeside) and *Giessbach*, at the mouth of its gorge and waterfalls, among the most beautiful in the Alps, which are for the time being best approached from Brienz.

The present main road follows the NW bank of the **Brienzer See**, almost 14.5km long, some 2.5km wide, and with an area of almost 30km^2. Crossing the Aare, *Goldswil* is traversed, dominated by the Romanesque tower of a ruined church (note grotesque figure), and then *Ringgenberg*, where the 17C church is embedded in a medieval castle perched above the dark blue lake, formerly reputed for the beauty of some of its oarswomen. The road provides several attractive views across towards Iseltwald, and of the Faulhorn (see Rte 18) among other summits of the range.

10km *Oberried*, with several characteristic old wooden houses, is crossed, and we circle the N end of the lake to enter (6km) *Brienz, birthplace of Heinrich Federer (1866–1928), the author. A large and notably attractive village worth leisurely exploration, it is a centre of the wood-carving and souvenir industries, apart from having an important school for the manufacture of stringed musical instruments (*lutherie*). A number of its houses have fruit trees and vines climbing their walls. It occupies the sloping field of a medieval landslide (1350). The *Church*, with an old tower, altered in the 17C by Dünz (and again in 1883), standing on rocky foundations, provides a fine view from its churchyard. Byron stayed at the *Hôtel Kreuz*. In the background are waterfalls descending from the *Brienzer Rothorn* (2350m), the summit of which is nearly approached by a rack-and-pinion railway of 1892.

The view from the summit embraces the Bernese Alps, and the mountains of the Valais, Uri and Unterwalden, with charming glimpses of several lakes, among them the tiny *Eisee* to the NE. A cable-car now descends N to the main road some 2.5km SE of *Sörenberg*, on the way to the *Glaubenbüelenpass*; see p 175. An excellent path (the 'Höheweg') leads E via the *Wilerhorn* (2004m) to the *Brünigpass*; see below.

From *Schwanden*, the adjacent village to the E of Brienz, a sign-posted road turns left towards *Hofstetten* and (c 3.5km) the entrance to the **Swiss Open-Air Museum** at **Ballenberg** (or *Schweizerisches Freilichtmuseum für ländliche Bau- und Wohnkultur*), open 9.00–17.00 from April to October.

This most interesting display of rural architecture, which deserves an extended visit, is a collection of buildings which have been brought from their original sites and re-erected in similar surroundings, or at least in surroundings compatible with their original environment. They are furnished as they would have been formerly, admirably exhibiting agricultural implements, domestic utensils and other by-gones. The buildings are seen to great advantage in a charming well-wooded district, in which the architectural units are laid out in roughly geographical order, the Jura group—one of 13—being at the W, while the Grisons will be towards the E entrance. The Museum was inaugurated in 1978 and is being extended as planned. A plan showing the distribution of the buildings and detailed explanatory books in English are available at the entrance.

Near the NW entrance (from Brienz) is the Bernese Mittelland unit, with No. 311, the early 19C 'Alter Baren' (Old Bear) inn from Rapperswil, with its large hip roof, now the restaurant. Slightly to the W stands No. 321, a huge shingle-covered multi-purpose house of

1709 from Madiswil, containing both living-quarters and farm buildings, with its adjacent Granary and Well-house; to the SE is No. 331, an impressive farmhouse from Ostermundigen, of 1797, with its characteristic *'Runde'*, or semicircular protective covering to its collar trusses.—Some distance NE, beyond a small lake, is the Eastern Mittelland unit, containing several characteristic half-timbered houses, among them No. 611, from Richterswil, of c 1780, near which is No. 621, from Uesslingen (17–18Cs). These, together with many more buildings, several containing the equipment and machinery of the pre-industrial period, and where several rural trades and crafts may still be seen in operation, are only a few of those which merit detailed inspection.

Regaining the main road, we continue E into the HASLITAL, a wide valley. The valley floor and the canalised Aare may be followed by turning right after 4km for **Meiringen**; see Rte 20.

A minor road leading due S from Schwanden bears round the end of the lake to approach *Giessbach*, with its waterfalls (see above), and the little high-lying resort of *Axalp* (1535m), a base for ascents of the Faulhorn and Schwarzhorn (for both see Rte 18) and the walk E below the *Oltschiburg* (2233m) to the *Oltschibachfall*; see Rte 20.

Our road bears left through *Brienzwiller*, and climbs steeply to (5.5km) the wooded *Brünigpass* (1008m), an ancient pass over which the road was constructed in 1861, providing retrospective views over the Aare valley to the Faulhorn (SW), the Engelhorn (S) and of Meiringen (SE).

A minor road turns right just before reaching the pass, which winds through the woods and pastures of the *Hasliberg*, and continues above the cliffs that shut in the vale of Hasli, passing through the village resorts of *Hohfluh, Wasserwendi* (from which a cable-car ascends to *Käserstatt*, below the *Hochstollen*; 2481m) and *Reuti* (from where cableways climb, one to and beyond *Unterstafel*, below the *Glogghüs*; 2534m), NE of *Meiringen* (to which a path and cableway also descend; see Rte 20).

The main road climbs down, with a fine distant prospect of Pilatus and Lake Lucerne, before turning E to (5km) *Lungern*, a village and resort on the small *Lungernsee* (now the storage basin of hydro-electric works), the E bank of which we skirt prior to descending to (6.5km) *Giswil*. A section of the N8 being constructed above the W bank will by-pass Giswil and meet the present motorway S of Sarnen.

The old village of Giswil was swept away by the Lauibach torrent in 1629, but an isolated 17C church (enlarged in 1823), with an ossuary of 1660, stands on a hill beyond the Aa. For the road to the *Glaubenbielen pass* to the W see p 175.—Skirting the *Sarnersee*, at 6km **Sachseln** is entered, an attractive village with a 17C church containing the tomb (1518) and relics of Nicolas von Flüe (1417–87), born at *Flüel-Ranft*, a hamlet 3.5km NE.

Known to the peasantry as 'Bruder Klaus', he is one of the popular heroes of Switzerland. At about the age of fifty he retired from his farm 'beside the cliff' (whence his name) to a hermitage in the Ranft, a neighbouring gorge, and by his sanctity and sense' (notably at the Diet of Stans) so influenced his pious countrymen that he was eventually (in 1947) canonised.

3km **SARNEN** (471m; 7500 inhab.), pleasantly situated on the Sarner-Aa at the lower end of the *Sarnersee*, is the capital of the Forest Canton of *Obwalden*; the valley of the Engelberger-Aa to the E forms in part the canton of *Nidwalden* (capital *Stans*); together they are known as *Unterwalden*. In August 1291 Nidwalden, with Obwalden joining a little later, formed the 'Everlasting League' with the cantons of Uri and Schwyz. Arnold Biedermann, in Scott's 'Anne of Geierstein', came from Unterwalden.

There are several portraits in the *Rathaus* of 1731 (by Georg Urban), including one by Wyrsch of Nicolas von der Flüe (1744), and also a relief map of the canton. The archives contain the 'Weisses Buch', the earliest document (c 1470) wherein the legendary history of the origin of the Swiss Confederation is found. The town contains two modern churches (1967 and 1966 respectively), that of the convent of *St. Andrew*, founded in 1615, and that of a Benedictine college, further S. To the N, a regional *Museum* is housed in the old *Arsenal* (1599).

On the opposite bank of the river is the *Landenberg*, with the white *Schützenhaus* (1752), once crowned by a castle of Heinrich von Landenberg, the Austrian bailiff, which is said to have been destroyed in the popular rising of 1308. Here the *Landsgemeinde* of Obwalden meets on the last Sunday in April to elect their magistrates.

To the SW, nearer the lake, is the large twin-towered *Church* of St. Peter, rebuilt and baroquised by Franz and Johann Anton Singer in 1739–42, adjoined by an ossuary of 1501.

FROM SARNEN TO STÖCKALP (15km). From *Kerns*, E of the motorway, with an early 19C church by Joseph Singer, we turn S up the pastoral MELCHTAL, shortly passing (left) *St. Niklausen*, its 14C *Church* containing contemporary murals and interesting woodwork. The village of *Melchtal*, with a Benedictine convent, claims to be the birthplace of the legendary Arnold an der Halden, one of the conspirators of the Rütli (cf.). A cable-car ascends E to *Rüti* (1338m), from which the *Storegg* (NE; 1742m) and *Juchli passes* (the latter to the SE at 2171m, and just N of the *Huetstock*; 2676m) provide routes into the ENGELBERGTAL; see Rte 22A. The road goes on up the valley to *Stöckalp* (1075m), from which a track and cable-car ascend to *Melchsee-Frutt*, a tiny resort amid alpine pastures on the N bank of the *Melchsee* (1891m). To the W rises the *Hochstollen* (2481m), below which a pass leads to *Käserstatt* (see above) for *Meiringen* and, to the S, the *Glogghüs* (2534m). Another path ascends E via the *Tannensee* and *Tannen* to *Engstlenalp*; see Rte 20.

Beyond Sarnen we enter (or by-pass on the N8) *Alpnach*, Roman *Alpeniacum*, with an early 19C church by Joseph Singer, and adjacent *Alpnachstad*, the lower terminus of the Pilatus railway (see Rte 21). We briefly skirt the N bank of the *Alpnacher See* and traverse a tunnel below a spur of the Pilatus to approach the S suburbs of **Lucerne**; see Rte 21.

20   Interlaken to Andermatt via Meiringen, for the Sustenpass (and Grimselpass)

Total distance, 92km (57 miles). No. 6–11. 16km **Brienz—**13km. **Meiringen** lies to the left.—6km *Innertkirchen*—No. 11. 28km *Sustenpass*—18km *Wassen*—No. 2. 11km **Andermatt**.

Maps: M 217; BL 37, or 5001, 5004.

For the road to 6km E of **Brienz** see Rte 19. Here turn onto the road following the wide floor of the HASLITAL, a characteristic alpine valley, and parallel to the canalised Aare. The view ahead is of the group of peaks of the *Mährenhorn*, in the Trift massif. The *Oltschibachfall* and other 'mare's tails' are passed to the right.

Meiringen (595m) is an ancient town which grew with the increasing traffic passing through it from the Grimsel, Susten, Brünig and Joch passes, and to a lesser extent from the Grosse Scheidegg. Few old houses survived the disastrous fires of 1879 and 1891. Hilaire Belloc was horrified by its tourist touts when he passed this way. Gertrude Bell stayed here in 1902, just before her nightmare experiences on the Finsteraarhorn. King Albert of the Belgians, an enthusiastic rock-climber, was a regular visitor.

The main object of interest is the *Church*, with a fine detached late Romanesque tower (14C) surmounted by a wooden spire. On the exterior of the SW corner of the church are 15C paintings of Saints Paul and Michael. The church also retains the W wall of its predecessor, with 14C frescoes of Old Testament scenes. A lower church (11–12C) may be visited; this was no doubt that of 'Magiringen' presented by the Emperor Heinrich VII in 1234 to the monks of St. Lazarus. The building has more than once been overwhelmed by floods from the Hasliberg, notably in 1762, and several different periods may be traced in its architecture. A Romanesque censer and reliquary found here are now in the British Museum. Near by is a regional *Museum*.

One of several sign-posted excursions from Meiringen is that E to the *Aareschlucht*, an imposing gorge or cleft in the limestone with perpendicular and even overhanging rock walls, the whole length of which may be threaded. The path beyond ascends to meet the main road above *Innertkirchen*; see below.—N of the church a zigzag path (and cable-car) climbs up to *Reuti*, on the *Hasliberg* (see Rte 19), providing a fine view of the Alpbach waterfall.—The *Reichenbachfälle*, S of the town, is well seen from the upper terminus of a funicular, and a path leads from here to the impressive **Kessel* or *Upper Fall*, the most remarkable of the five cascades formed by the stream. It was once suggested to Conan Doyle that should he wish to get rid of Sherlock Holmes this would be a convenient spot, but in the event he was reprieved! The path goes on to meet the *Rosenlaui* road; see p 186, and for the route to Grindelwald via the *Grosse Scheidegg*, in reverse.

Passing through the village of *Willigen*, the road ascends over the *Kirchet*, a limestone hill with scattered blocks of granite left by an ancient glacier, and zigzags down its far side, with a view of (6km) **Innertkirchen**, a scattered village and mountaineering base.

To the SW opens the URBACHTAL, partly traversed by a road commanding fine retrospective views of the cleft of the *Aare gorge* and views (right) of the *Engelhorner* precipices. A track continues to the *Gauli Hut* (2205m), with the *Ritzlihorn* (3282m) rising to the E, and, to the W, the *Hangendgletscherhorn* (3292m); to the SW descends the *Gauli Glacier*, scene of the rescue of passengers from a wrecked aircraft in 1946, and the *Ewigschneehorn* (3329m).

The road over the **Grimselpass**, connecting the Bernese Oberland with the upper valley of the Rhône, is one of the grandest and most frequented of the Alpine passes, and also one of the most ancient, unlike the Susten, which is rarely mentioned in early accounts. It was used by the Bernese for the invasion of the Valais as early as 1211. Later, in connection with the Gries Pass, it became a commercial thoroughfare to Italy. The well-engineered road dates from 1895 but some parts of its course have since been altered with the construction of hydro-electric works and reservoirs.

FROM INNERTKIRCHEN TO GLETSCH VIA THE GRIMSELPASS

(31km). We follow the No. 6, ascending SE below (left) the steep slopes of the *Banzlaui Stock* (2530m), traversing a defile and passing through two or three tunnels.—9km *Guttannen* (1057m), the highest village on this side of the pass, on a wild site. To the N rises the *Mährenhorn* (2923m); to the NE, the *Steinhüshorn* (3121m); to the E, the *Diechterhorn* (3389m); while to the W is the *Gallauistöck* (2869m), and, towering to the SW, the *Ritzlihorn* (3282m). A further 5km brings one to *Handegg* with a hydro-electric power station and (right) the *Handeggfall*, an impressive cataract. Beyond is the *Gelmersee* reservoir, and the *Tieralplistock* (3383m) and, further S, the *Gärstenhorner* (3189m). To the SW is the *Alplistock* (2877m). The road next skirts the *Raterischbodensee*, a storage reservoir occupying the bed of an ancient natural lake, shortly beyond which is a right-hand turning for the *Grimsel Hospiz*, standing on a rock known as the *Nollen* and overlooking the *Grimselsee* (1909m above sea level, and which covers the site of the old hospice, first mentioned in 1397). It is the most conspicuous part of the Oberhasli hydro-electric undertakings; all around are walls and slopes of grey granite, on which the marks of ancient glaciers are seen high above the present bed of the valley. In the distance the lake is backed by the *Finsteraarhorn* (4274m), among other peaks.

Due W of the reservoir is the foot of the *Unteraar Glacier*, remarkable for its evenness and symmetry, formed by the confluence of the *Lauteraar* and *Finsteraar* glaciers, with the rocky promontory of the *Abschwung* between them, rising to the *Lauteraar Rothörner* (3466m). Louis Agassiz made important observations here in 1840–41, and built on the glacier the stone shelter known as the 'Hôtel des Neuchâtelois', the remains of which have been carried down some distance. The *Lauteraar Hut* (2392m), W of the reservoir, is the usual base for mountaineers, and it was from here (then known as the Pavillon Dollfuss) that in 1902 Gertrude Bell and her two guides began the ascent of the NE face of the Finsteraarhorn, a hazardous climb resulting in a two-day struggle against the elements.

The road now ascends in zigzags to the **Grimselpass** itself (2165m), a broad and dreary saddle, on the W of which rises the *Sidelhorn* (2764m), to the N of which a road leads to the *Oberaarsee reservoir* (2303m), fed by the *Oberaar Glacier*, at the foot of the *Oberaarhorn* (3673m). The pass, defended by Austrian troops, who used the wooden hospice for fuel, was forced in August 1799 by Gén. Gudin; a later hospice was overwhelmed by an avalanche in 1838.

To the right of the road is the *Totensee*, a sullen tarn, near which an old paved track descends to *Obergestein*; see Rte 45.

The main road descends in zigzags, intersecting the older road, with a view of the snow peaks of the Valais and, to the NE, of the *Rhônegletscher*. It continues down a slope known as the *Meienwang*, noted for its alpine 'roses' and other flowers, to the hamlet of **Gletsch** (1757m), to meet the Furka road, for which, and for the *Rhône Glacier*, see Rte 45.

At Innertkirchen we turn left through the hamlet of *Wiler* and immediately begin the ascent of the lower valley of the GADMENTAL.

At 4km we pass the road (left) ascending the GENTAL to (14km) *Engstlenalp*, near the *Engstlensee*, a good base for several ascents and overlooked to the NE by the *Graustock* (2662m). Further to the E is the *Jochpass* (2207m), easily reached by a path across pastures; see Rte 22A. Beyond rise several peaks, including the rounded snow-capped *Titlis* (3238m).

The road now climbs to *Gadmen* (1205m), the main village in the valley, with several old wooden chalets. It is situated in a green basin under the rocky wall of the *Gadmerflue*, rising to the *Wendenstöcke* (3042m) and, beyond, the *Titlis* (3238m).

Most of the main road beyond this point was completed in 1945, largely by refugees from warring countries beyond the Swiss frontiers; an inscription on a rock near the *Steingletscher* reads: '1938–45. In times of stress lay the foundations of peace'. The remarkably engineered road threads numerous short tunnels, including one at the watershed, as it climbs in zigzags through the woods, passing several splendid view-points, later winding above a deep ravine, inevitably named the *Hôlle*, to the *Steinalp*. There is a fine view S of the *Stein Glacier*, dominated by the *Tierberg* (SW; 3447m) and the prominent *Gwächtenhorn* (3420m); likewise SW down the valley towards the peaks of the Wetterhorn and towards the *Sustenhorn* (3503m), to the SE, the highest summit in this region.

From the *Steingletscher Hotel* the road ascends in steep zigzags to the head of the **Sustenpass** (2224m), named from 'Sust', a toll or custom house, a tunnel piercing the watershed itself, at 2259m. The track over the pass was made after the Valais had been added by Napoleon to the French Empire in 1810, in order to enable the Bernese to convey their produce to Italy through Swiss territory. The prospect is limited, but there is a fine array of serried peaks and ridges in view, with the fitly-named *Fünffingerstöck* (3023m) prominent to the N. Snow lies throughout the year on this E slope.

The descent into the Forest Canton of *Uri* is made in another series of steep zigzags, before bearing SE into the MEIENTAL below the *Grassengrat* (2940m), by-passing the hamlet of *Färnigen* on the old road, and crossing *Meiendörfli*, with its protective palisades against avalanches. The *Meienschanz*, a redoubt built in 1712 to guard Uri from the Bernese and destroyed by the French in 1799, is passed.

The descent continues, with interesting glimpses ahead of the St. Gotthard railway and its bridges, to **Wassen** (916m), a village on the old main road (No. 2) from Altdorf to Andermatt, and, just beyond, the N2 motorway. The old road climbs steeply to the right (S) via *Göschenen* (1106m) to (11km) **Andermatt** (1447m), while the N2 enters the *Gotthardtunnel* at Göschenen; see Rte 25A, also Rtes 38, 41 and 45.

21   Lucerne

LUCERNE (as anglicised; or **Luzern**; 439m; 63,300 inhab., largely German-speaking; 47,050 in 1930; 17,750 in 1880), the capital of its canton, is finely situated on both banks of the Reuss, at the NW extremity of its lake, correctly the *Vierwaldstätter See* (see Rte 22A), the foreground overlooked from the SW by *Pilatus* (2120m), by the *Burgenstock* (1128m) to the SE, and the *Rigi* (1797m) to the E, but only fitfully visible. Its position has made it the focus of tourists for well over a century, and it was patronised in particular by the British (Queen Victoria visited it for a month during the summer of 1868 under the name of the 'Countess of Kent'). It remains a good centre for the exploration of the area for those preferring a large town as a base. The quaint covered wooden bridges spanning the Reuss and the line of medieval walls and watch-towers defending the N side of the old centre provide picturesque propitiatory touches. Its *Transport Museum* is important, while the *Wagner Museum* at Tribschen preserves a period atmosphere.

Lucerne grew up around a Benedictine convent founded c 750, which became in the 9C a 'cell' of the Abbey of Murbach in Alsace and was dedicated to St. Leodegar (St. Leger). It increased in importance when the first bridle-path was made over the St. Gotthard pass and its prosperity long depended on the traffic on this route; travellers frequently set sail from here (unless from Küssnach or Brunnen), for there was no road along the lake-side until the construction of the Axenstrasse in 1856. In 1291 the abbot of Murbach sold his possessions here to Rudolf of Habsburg, and this gave rise to the alliance of the Forest Cantons, which were joined by Lucerne in 1332. The town and canton had, like other conservative peasant enclaves, remained a Catholic stronghold, becoming the seat of the Papal Nuncio. Obscurantist Lucerne took a leading part in the formation of the reactionary 'Sonderbund', in spite of the Liberals being in control of the town in 1831. Indeed the Jesuits were invited to 're-convert' the canton.

Although 19C scepticism questioned the existence of some of the traditional heroes of Central Switzerland, there is no doubt that the shores of the Lake of Lucerne nurtured the men who began the long struggle for the independence of the country. Their combatative nature and experience of poverty caused them to seek service abroad under many flags and the back-to-the-wall bravery of the Swiss Guards in defence of the royal family of France in 1792 is commemorated in the famous 'Lion Monument'. With the development of lucrative tourist traffic in the second half of the 19C, Lucerne flourished, and this is still a major source of income, the tour of the lake and the ascent of the Rigi and Pilatus being other promoted 'lions'. Since 1938 a summer music festival has been held here.

Few natives of Lucerne have risen to any prominence, but these include the artists Robert Zünd (1827–1909) and Hans Erni (1909–). Rachmaninoff spent the summers of 1935–43 here; the conductors Mendelberg and Furtwangler spent their last years here, from 1946–51 and 1947–54, respectively.

A. The South bank of the Reuss

Many of the main roads entering Lucerne converge on the *Railway Station*, just S of the Bahnhofplatz and a few paces from the S end of the *Seebrücke* (1870), the main bridge across the Reuss. It provides a good view E over the W arm of the lake; to the NW is the many-towered *Museggmauer* and W is the famous *Kapellbrücke*; see below.

Immediately E of the Station, overlooking the quays from which steamers have been plying the lake since 1838, stands the **Kunst-und Kongresshaus** (1933), containing a concert-hall with notably fine acoustics, and the main *Art Gallery*.

Among the paintings displayed are: *anon.* Lamentation of 1500; *anon.* Visitation of c 1504; *anon. Lucerne Master*, Legend of St. Ursula, and Martyrdom of the 11,000 (both 1517); *Martin Moser* (c 1500–c 1570), Death of the Baptist, Dives and Lazarus, and The Last Judgement (1557); *Brussels Master H.B.*, Adoration of the Kings (c 1520); *Johann Melchior Wyrsch*, Self-portrait, Portraits of the De Bauffremont children, and others; *Fuseli*, Beatrice listening to Hero and Ursula; *J.-L. Agasse*, Lord Heathfield on horseback; *Xaver Schwegler* (Lucerne 1832–1902), Landscape; *Johann Gottfried Steffan* (1815–1905), Landscape; *Robert Zünd*, The Lake of Uri, and forest scenes, etc.; *Böcklin*, Portrait of Arnoldo, his son; *Édouard Castres*, Bourbaki's army retreating into Switzerland (see

below); *Hodler*, Watchmaker's workshop (Madrid, 1879), and The Breithorn;
Josef Reinhardt (1749–1824), groups in Swiss costumes, c 1800.

View by Matthäus Merian of Lucerne (1642)

The wide Pilatusstrasse leads SW from the Station, passing a few
paces N of the *Central Library* (1951), with important collections,
including some 2500 MSS and 800 incunables, and the profusely
illustrated 'Luzerner Bilderchronik' by Diebold Schilling (1513); the
'Etterling Chronicle' of 1517; a rare collection of 16C stage directions;
the second version of Wagner's 'Death of Siegfried', etc.

On the N side of the street is the *Tourist Office*.

The Hirschmattstrasse leads shortly to the apse of the restored
Jesuit Church of St. Franz Xaver, an imposing building, best seen
from the far bank, dating from 1669 (by Michael Beer or Michael

Thumb, superintended by Christoph Vogler). It was decorated in the Rococo taste in 1750. Its two onion-domed towers were added in 1892.

It lies at the E end of the old quarter of triangular shape known as the *Klein-Stadt*, formerly walled. Adjacent to the W is the *Regierungsgebäude*, originally the *Ritter'sche Palast*, begun by Giovanni Lynzo of Trento in the Florentine Renaissance style. It now accommodates cantonal offices, and its courtyard contains the original fountain of 1481 from the Weinmarkt; see below.—The *Archives*, opposite, the former Jesuit College, preserve an important numismatic collection and the gold seal of Charles le Téméraire, carried off among booty from the field of Grandson.

The **Franciscan Church** of St. Mary, a few paces S, of c 1300, is a plain Gothic building, altered in 1551–63 and enlarged in the 17C when stucco-work was added to certain chapels. Above the chancel arch is a 15C wall-painting of the Crucifixion and above the nave are copies of painted banners captured in the struggle for independence. The elaborately carved pulpit (1625), organ-loft and choir-stalls should be noted, and also the iron grilles.

To the NW, at the angle of the Rütligasse and Burgerstrasse, stands the 'Chinese Rococo' *Fideikommisshaus Segesser von Brunegg* (1752). Following the Pfistergasse NW, we turn right to the riverside

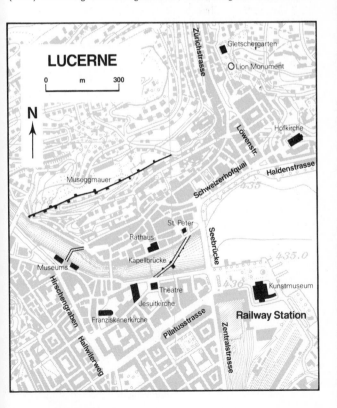

Korporationsgebäude of 1670, and then follow the Reusssteg W to the *Zeughaus* or *Arsenal* (1568), being restored to house an *Historical Museum*. Just beyond the Kasernenplatz is the *Natural History Museum*, better than some, on the first floor of which are archaeological collections.

B. The North bank of the Reuss

This of course may equally well be explored from the N end of the Seebrücke, but by following the itinerary described above we cross the *Spreuerbrücke, a covered wooden bridge of 1408, hung with some 56 early 17C paintings of the Dance of Death (restored) by Caspar Meglinger, to reach the MÜHLENPLATZ, just N of which the Löwengraben marks a line of inner defences of 1400.

The St. Karli-Quai follows the river bank to the W, to the westernmost gate-tower of the outer **Mauerring**, a range of nine tall and eminently picturesque towers of the 14C ramparts, between which and the Platz stands the *Museggmagazin*.

Turning right and then left off the E end of the Mühlenplatz, we enter the *Weinmarkt*, with a fine stone house of 1530 and a copy of a Gothic Fountain surmounted by a figure of St. Maurice; see below. Note the elaborate '*Zu Metzgern*' inn-sign.—From the NE corner of the square the HIRSCHENPLATZ is reached. Here the *Göldlinhaus* (No. 12) has an interior courtyard in Renaissance style; the Rococo *Zum Hirschen* and the *Adler*, at which Goethe put up, both have old inn-signs.—From its SE corner the *Kornmarkt* is entered, dominated by the **Altes Rathaus** (1607; by Anton Isenmann), flanked by a tower enlarged in the first decade of the 16C, but probably on foundations of one of the towers of the 12C wall. The exterior has murals which have been described as 'of idiosyncratic crudity'.

Adjacent is the *Am Rhyn-Haus* (1618), containing the *Picasso Museum*, or Rosengart Donation. Perhaps the 'Déjeuner sur l'Herbe' (after Manet; 1961) and the artist's aquatint of 'Venus and Cupid' (after Cranach; 1949), are the most notable items in this small collection, apart from several lithographs and other representative works.

A few paces further E is a Chinese restaurant, formerly *Dubeli's Bierhalle*, one of Wagner's haunts; while the Kapellgasse, leading off the NE corner of the Kornmarkt, one of the main shopping-streets, traverses the E half of the *Gross-Stadt*.

From the Rathaus, one may cross a footbridge, providing a good view of both the S facade of the Rathaus and of the Jesuit Church, to reach the *Theatre* (1924). It brings one to the S end of the quaint *Kapellbrücke, now 200m long. This roofed wooden bridge of 1333 crosses the river diagonally and forms one of the most characteristic features of Lucerne. Until demolished (in 1834–54) it extended 400m further E (where the Schweizerhofquai now runs) to the foot of the hill on which the Hofkirche stands; it was known as the Hofbrücke. Until the construction of the Seebrücke it was the uppermost bridge on the river.

In the 112 triangular paintings (by Hans Wagmann and his son Hans Ulrich; c 1600) hung from its rafters are recorded the lives of Saints Leger and Maurice, the town's patrons, and the deeds of Lucerners and men of the Forest Cantons. Towards its S end rises the picturesque octagonal *Wasserturm* or *Water Tower*, a bastion of the 13C fortifications, once used as the town treasury. The derivation of the name Lucerne from a lantern (lucerna) hung here is improbable.

Near the N end of the bridge stands the *Zur Gilgenhaus* (1510), with a tower, altered in 1731. Victor Hugo lodged here in 1839 when it was a pension. Adjacent is the *Peterskapelle*, 12C, but much altered in the 18th.

C. North-East Lucerne

From the N end of the Seebrücke and the busy Schwanenplatz the *Schweizerhofquai* skirts the lake. It is dominated by the palatial *Schweizerhof Hotel*, where in July 1857 Tolstoy stayed and wrote his story entitled 'Lucerne'; Wagner spent five months here in 1859 (29 March–7 September), and completed 'Tristan and Isolde'; see also *Tribschen*, below.

At the far end of the promenade, with its chestnut avenue, cross over to the Leodegarstrasse and turn right to ascend a broad flight of steps past the *Marienbrunnen* of 1603, and several 18C houses in its close, to approach the W front of the ***Hofkirche** (of Saints Leodegar and Mauritius), conspicuous with its twin tapering spires surmounting early 16C towers. The church, the seat of a college of secular canons since 1456, replacing a monastery of 8C foundation, was largely rebuilt after a fire in 1633. The porch of 1641 is by Niklaus Geissler, responsible also for the stalls, pulpit and font. The altars at the end of the aisles, the wrought-iron choir-screens, the organ of 1650 by Hans Geissler of Salzburg and a late Gothic altar representing the Death of the Virgin in the N side-aisle, are notable. The Baroque altarpiece of the Agony in the garden was painted by Giovanni Lanfranco. The arcaded churchyard, similar to an Italian Campo Santo, commands a good view of the lake.

On descending, turn right along the Löwenstrasse to the Löwenplatz, on the S side of which is a *Panorama* by Édouard Castres depicting the retreat into Switzerland of Gén. Bourbaki's French army in 1871 (see p 116). The W side of the Platz is dominated by the huge domed building (1914) of the *Federal Insurance Office* (SUVA).

The Denkmalstrasse leads N to (right) the ***Löwendenkmal** or *Lion Monument*, commemorating the 786 officers and men of the Swiss Guards who died in the defence of Louis XVI and Marie-Antoinette during the attack of the Revolutionary mob on the Tuileries in 1792. Designed by Thorvaldsen, the mortally wounded lion was carved out of the quarry wall in 1821 by Lukas Ahorn, from Constance.

A few paces further on is the entrance to the ***Gletschergarten** or *Glacier Garden*.

Its geological curiosities were discovered in 1872. The polished and striated face of the sandstone rocks are the result of the movement of a glacier, which, extending from the St. Gotthard, once covered the area, while the potholes were scoured by the vorticular force of melt-water under pressure. At the base of the potholes lie several worn erratic boulders which survived the turbulence. The adjacent *Museum* contains collections of fossils and minerals, a relief of central Switzerland completed by Gen. F.L. Pfyffer in 1786 (who was twice arrested as a spy when making the necessary observations!), together with another by J.E. Müller (1818), and a model of a battle in the Muotatal (1 October 1799) between the French under Lecourbe, and the Russians under Suvarov; also old maps and prints of the area and collections of furniture, etc

The Lion Memorial

Hence one may return to the Löwenplatz. Bearing right, the quay may be reached either via the Alpenstrasse or by turning right along the Museggstrasse past (left) the *Mariahilfkirche*, the 17C church of a former Ursuline convent, the ramparts can be examined more closely. The *Schirmertum*, above gardens, commands a view over the town and surrounding mountains.

To the NE of the Hofkirche and approached by roads ascending thence, is the Capuchin convent of *Wesemlin*, founded in 1584, with an important library and 16C church containing glass from the Franciscan church of St. Mary.—Further E, at *Dreilinden*, is the *Conservatory of Music* (View), and beyond, at Bruchstrasse 5, *Utenberg*, the *Trachten Museum*, with a collection of national costumes.

Two EXCURSIONS of interest which may easily be made from the centre are those to the *Swiss Transport Museum* or *Verkehrshaus*, reached by a No. 2 bus, skirting the N bank of the lake, and to the *Haus Tribschen*; see below.

The bus passes—not far E of the Hofkirche—the former *English Church* (St. Mark's; 1894), where services are still occasionally held, although the building has been sold to another ecclesiastical body.

The remarkable **Swiss Transport Museum**, or complex of

museums, was inaugurated in 1959 and has since grown rapidly to be Europe's largest museum of its kind, thanks to significant contributions from industries associated with it. Further extensions are projected. The main sections are concerned with Road transport, Rail transport, Aviation, Astronautics, Postal services, Telecommunications, Navigation and Tourism; in addition there are the 'Longines' *Planetarium* (1969) and the Hans Erni museum.

A well-illustrated descriptive catalogue depicts numerous models, replicas, or original vehicles, including early bicycles, motorcycles and motor cars, among the last several of Swiss manufacture, such as the Popp (1898), Berna (1902), Ajax (1908), Fischer (1913), Pic-Pic (1919), etc. Among locomotives are the support tender 'Genf' of 1858, the Brown tender-locomotive of 1881, which first traversed the Gotthard tunnel the following January, a cogwheel locomotive from the Vitznau-Rigi railway of 1873, and early trams, amongst many others. There were already 40 cogwheel railways operating in Switzerland by the end of the 19C.

Aeronautics are represented by the Dufaux bi-plane of 1910, a Blériot of 1913, a Haefeli of 1919, together with several other originals and more modern machines. An original Mercury space capsule, a Gemini spaceship which made 43 orbits of the earth in July 1966 (John W. Young and Michael Collins up), the Apollo space-suit worn on the moon by Edgar Mitchell in February 1971, etc., may also be seen. The history of Postal and Telecommunication services are well displayed, together with the development of Swiss broadcasting, television, and other services.

Numerous model ships, including one of the first paddle-steamer on Lake Constance in 1823, may be seen, together with the original steamship 'Rigi' (1847), constructed by Ditchborne and Mare, London, in service on Lake Lucerne until 1952; also models of Rhine shipping, and of the harbour at Basle, etc.

*Haus Tribschen may be approached by buses 6 or 7 driving S to the Wartegg stop, and then a short walk.

Richard Wagner had first visited Lucerne briefly in August 1850, having lived in Zürich as a political exile from May 1849. His fourth visit was in 1859, when he stayed at the Schweizerhof Hotel; see above. He returned to Lucerne to live there (from 1 April 1866 until 22 April 1872) at 'Haus Tribschen', this time accompanied by Cosima von Bülow, Liszt's daughter. They were eventually married at St. Matthew's church, Lucerne, on 28 August 1870. Here, on 25 December of the same year, Wagner's 'Siegfried Idyll', first called 'The Tribschen Idyll', was first performed. His 'Die Meistersinger von Nürnberg' was composed here, 'Siegfried' completed, and 'Götterdämmerung' commenced. Then he moved to Bayreuth. Among his numerous guests during this period, one of the more frequent was the young Nietzsche, who visited Tribschen 23 times. Others of note were Villiers de L'Isle Adam, Catulle Mendès, and Judith Gautier. The property was purchased by the town in 1931, and the *Wagner Museum* was later established.

The numerous mementoes of the composer include many photographs and letters, etc. Also of note are: his Erard grand piano; lithographs of Gluck, Haydn, Mozart and Beethoven which hung in his study; a Death mask by Augusto Benvenuti; a bronze Bust of Wagner c 1880 by Friedrich Schaper, of Cosima (a copy of that by G.A. Kietz; 1873) and of Mathilde Wesendonck (1828–1902), by L. Keiser (1860). A copy is displayed of the MS of 'The Siegfried Idyll', which the composer had given to Hans Richter; also Cosima's bonnet, made in Lucerne, and Wagner's velvet jacket and beret, and silk work-jacket.

On the first floor is a collection of *Musical Instruments*, among them a Wagner Tuba, a Regal of 1644, an Alphorn, and Trumscheit (marine trumpet), etc.

For roads from Lucerne to **Altdorf** see Rte 22, below; to **Basle**, Rte 13; to **Berne**, Rte 16; to **Interlaken** via Sarnen and Brienz, Rte 19; and to **Zürich** via Zug, Rte 24, the last four in reverse.

22   Lucerne to Altdorf

A. Via Stans: the South Bank of Lake Lucerne

Total distance, 43km (27 miles). No. 2. 13km **Stans**—30km **Altdorf**.
Maps: M 217; BL 37, or 5008.

The *Lake of Lucerne, properly the *Vierwaldstätter See*, or *Lake of the Four Forest Cantons* (Uri, Unterwalden, Schwyz and Lucerne), by which it is surrounded, is still one of the most beautiful of Europe, largely because of the grandeur of its mountain scenery and the charming irregularity of its shape, which constantly opens up new vistas to the traveller. Hopefully these will not be affected by further building along its shore.

The lake is formed by the river Reuss, descending from the St. Gotthard and the Furka to its head near Flüelen, at its SE extremity. The Reuss flows out at Lucerne. Several other streams and mountain torrents also enter it, including the two rivers Aa to the SW, and the Muota at Brunnen. It is 434m above sea level; its total area is 114km² and its length is 37km, but its breadth varies considerably, with two narrows (at Vitznau and Brunnen), while between Küssnacht and Hergiswil it is 14.5km across, forming two separate arms, themselves named lakes or *Seen*. Capricious and sometimes violent winds blow down the long reaches and the *Föhn* or S wind, sweeping down from Flüelen to Brunnen, may sometimes be dangerous to light craft.

On the lake are several saloon steamer services with restaurants on board and smaller motor-launches plying regularly across to specific points on its shore, although services are restricted in winter. Details are obtainable at all the lake ports. The views from these boats are not described, but as the roads following its banks are, this should be sufficient for travellers to pick out objects of interest on their cruise.

THE EXCURSION TO THE SUMMIT OF PILATUS is described first. This long rugged ridge, a mountain of gloomy, precipitous character, although rich in flora and with several peaks, the highest rising to 2128m, was known until the 15C as the *Frackimünd* (*Fractus Mons*). Although pious tradition chose to connect its name with Pontius Pilate, it is more probably a corruption of *Pileatus*, 'capped' with clouds, which it often is: a round cloud-cap may be a sign of fine weather, while a long stratified cloud presages rain.

The best path for walkers—who should keep to the marked paths—mounts from *Hergiswil*; others start from *Kriens*, and *Alpnachstad*. **Kriens** (21,100 inhab.; 3km SW of Lucerne) is also the terminus of a cable-car to near the summit via *Fräkmünt*. This may also be approached by cogwheel railway climbing steeply from Alpnachstad, to the SE of the mountain, beyond Hergiswil. The view-point of the *Esel*, near the hotels on the ridge, can provide—should visibility be good—a fine panorama, particularly of the snow-clad peaks of the Bernese Oberland to the S, and over the lake to the E.

Driving S from central Lucerne, one may follow either the No. 4 or the N2 motorway, the latter providing a more rapid route by piercing a buttress of Pilatus to reach *Alpnachstad*, see above. The old road traverses suburban villages and *Hergiswil*.

After c 10km the roads veer E to cross the narrows of the *Alpnacher See*, on the SE shore of which are the ruins of the castle of *Rozberg*, said to have been taken by the Confederates on New Year's Day 1308. The story goes that one of the attacking party, keeping a midnight tryst with a damsel in the castle, smuggled in a score of companions by his rope ladder.

To the left lies *Stansstad*, with a tower of 1280, from which a road climbs NE to the **Bürgenstock** (1128m), a scarped and wooded massif overlooking the main lake. The private property of several exclusive hotels, it may be visited for the views it commands.

To the S, in a broad fruit-growing valley at the foot of the Stanserhorn, lies **STANS** (5700 inhab.), the capital of the half-canton of *Nidwalden* which, with that of Oberwalden, comprises Unterwalden, and which in August 1291 formed the 'Everlasting League' with Uri and Schwyz. It was the birthplace of Arnold von Winkelried, the hero of Sempach (1386), but the house pointed out as his dates only from 1561.

It was at the Diet of Stans (1481) that the dissensions which arose over the division of the Burgundian spoils and the question of admitting Fribourg and Solothurn to the Confederation were settled by the sensible advice of Nicolas von Flüe (see p 192), although he did not appear in person. The tavern sign 'zum Eintracht' (concord), common in the region, is a reference to this event. The *Landsgemeinde* of Nidwalden still meets here on the last Sunday of April.

The *Church*, retaining its Romanesque tower, was rebuilt in 1647, and contains a 17C font and organ-loft. The adjoining *Ossuary* (c 1560) preserves a wall-painting of the Descent from the Cross. A tablet commemorates the lives of over 400 inhabitants of Nidwalden slaughtered in a hopeless stand against the French commanded by Gén. Foy in 1798, after which Pestalozzi established a home here for the orphans. Several buildings date from the 18C (although the town was ravaged by fire in 1713), including the *Rathaus*, rebuilt after the disaster, while an old storehouse of c 1700 accommodates the local *Museum*, in which several portraits by Melchior Wyrsch are notable.

The *Stanserhorn* (1898m), to the SW, a fine pyramid clothed to the summit in woods and pastures, may be ascended by funicular and cable-car from Stans, providing pleasant retrospective views, and views towards the Titlis massif to the S; see below.

FROM STANS TO ENGELBERG (20km). The road turns S, following the Engelberger Aa past *Dallenwil*, the lower terminus of several cable-cars.—7km *Wolfenschiessen*, a small resort where Conrad Scheuber (1480–1559), related to Nicolas von Flüe, was buried. His wooden hermitage was moved in 1568 to its present position adjacent to the *Church*, rebuilt by J.A. Singer in 1775. The *Höchhaus*, on the left bank of the Aa, is a fine building of 1586, restored.—A road climbs steeply SE to *Oberrickenbach*, from which cable-cars ascend to

Urnerstafel and other points near the *Bannalpsee reservoir*, overlooked to the S by the *Wallenstöcke* (2572m) and *Rigidalstock* (2593m),
and to the SE by the *Ruchstock* (2814m). The valley gradually narrows.
Beyond *Dörfli*, with a ruined 13C castle, the *Fallenbachfall* is passed
to the right before reaching (4.5km) *Grafenort*, with a striking chapel
of 1689 and mansions of the same date; the chapel of *St. Joder*, on a
height to the E, stands near the spot where Baumgarten killed the
bailiff of Wolfenschiessen, as told in Schiller's 'William Tell'. To the
SW rise the crags of *Wallenstöcke* (2593m).

The road gets steeper before the valley (described by Henry James
as 'grim, ragged, rather vacuous, but by no means absolutely un-
beautiful') opens out and the imposing massif of the Titlis and the
rocky pinnacles of the Spannörter come into view as **Engelberg** is
approached. The resort and mountaineering centre (1004m),
developed since 1905, lies in a sheltered basin. It originally grew up
round a Benedictine abbey named 'Mons Angelorum' by Pope
Calixtus II, from the German form of which it takes its name. The
'Alpine glow' is frequently observed in the neighbourhood.

The stately **Abbey**, founded c 1120 and three times burnt down,
stands at the E end of the village. The present building, erected in
1730–37 after the last conflagration, reflects more the hauteur than the
humility of the Church. The abbey was responsible directly to the
Pope, to whom the whole valley was subject until 1798; its revenues
were somewhat diminished by the French invasion. The large
Baroque Church, built by Johannes Rueff on the plans of Caspar
Moosbrugger, contains decoration by several of the best artists of the
period, among them Feuchtmayer, and is embellished by perhaps the
largest organ in Switzerland.

The *Treasury* preserves an early 13C cross-reliquary and an embroidered
surplice presented by Agnes of Hungary on her visit in 1325; the *Library*, which
conserves valuable illuminated MSS and Swiss incunables, is regrettably rarely
open. Adjoining the abbey are warehouses for cheese. When Queen Victoria
visited Engelberg she attended a Roman Catholic service for the first time in her
life, the propriety of which seriously exercised Sir Henry Ponsonby, her private
secretary.

For a nearer view of the Titlis and Spannörter follow the road SE at least as far
as the *Tätschbachfall*. The track continues to ascend below the *Klein Spannort*
(3140m), *Gross Spannort* (3198m) and *Schlossberg* (3133m), later circling to the
N towards the *Stierenbachfall*, to approach the *Surenenpass* (2291m), above
which rise the *Blacken Stock* (2980m) and *Uri-Rotstock* (2928m), among other
peaks. A steep descent may be made to *Altdorf*, with a fine retrospective view
of the Titlis.

Another good view of the massif may be gained from the high-lying hamlet
of *Schwand*, NW of Engelberg; while the road up the *Horbistal* (NE) leads to a
grand rocky cirque, its cliffs surmounted by glaciers.—A funicular ascends SW
to *Gerschnialp*, whence one may take a cable-car to the *Trübsee* (1796m),
commanding a splendid view of both the valley and of the Titlis; another lift
continues the ascent to 3028m, the *Klein Titlis*, not far below the rounded
snow-capped summit of the **Titlis** (3238m), the first snow-peak in Switzerland
to be climbed, in 1744. It is a superb view-point, looking down the GADMEN-
TAL, with the road climbing up to the *Sustenpass*, and towards the Finsteraarhorn, Wetterhorn, and Eiger, with the peaks of the Valais beyond; to the N the
Jura and Black Forest may be discerned. To the W is the *Jochpass* (2207m),
likewise ascended from just S of the Trübsee; from it a path leads almost due
W across pastures to *Engstlenalp*; see p 195.

Leading E from Stans, the motorway drives below the *Buochserhorn*

(1807m) and by-passes **Buochs**, the birthplace of Johann Melchior Wyrsch (1732–98), the portrait-painter. The artist, who became blind, was shot dead by a French soldier. The church, of Romanesque origin, was rebuilt at the beginning of the 19C.—Adjacent to the N is *Ennetbürgen*, below the Bürgenstock.—The road continues E above the lake, with a view of its narrows, the *'Nasen'* (or noses), and the Rigi rising beyond its far bank, and by-passes **Beckenried** (but see below), a lakeside resort with a late 18C neo-Classical church. Hence a cable-car ascends to *Klewenalp* (1593m), above which rises the *Schwalmis* (2246m).

An interesting EXCURSION is that across the *Seelisberg* (1108m) from Beckenried, approached by driving E under the motorway and climbing through *Emmetten* on its terrace opposite Gersau, then descending the E side of the *Seelisberg peninsula* past a little tarn (*Seeli*). We shortly reach the remarkably sited village of **Seelisberg** itself (846m).—Then the road climbs down very steeply N to lakeside *Treib*, with a quaint old inn, reconstructed. It is also reached by funicular. To the E of Treib, opposite Brunnen, is the isolated crag known as the *Mythenstein* or *Schillerstein*, inscribed in honour of the author of 'William Tell' (1804), which is now the chief buttress of the legend.

A path descends from Seelisberg in c 30 minutes to **Rütli** (perhaps best visited by boat, being only a short distance above the landing-stage). The Rütli (or *Grütli*, meaning 'a clearing in the forest') is the sacred meadow—in some ways the equivalent of Runnymede—where, according to chroniclers, took place the meeting at which a solemn oath was sworn by Walter Fürst (baron of Attinghausen in Uri), Werner von Stauffacher of Steinen in Schwyz and Arnold an der Halden of Melchtal in Obwalden, to defend the inherited liberties of their valleys against the tyrannical rule of Austria.

Known as the *Eidgenossenschaft*, the 'Oath Fellowship of the Confederation', the Charter (the only remaining copy of which, in Latin, may be seen in the Archives at Schwyz) does not mention any place of solemnisation and bears no signatures (only the seals of the communities of Uri, Schwyz (lost), and Nidwalden). It is dated the beginning (1st?) August, 1291. It has been suggested that the meeting at Rütli may have been a later confirmation, which took place on 10 November 1307. More certain is the *Morgartenbrief*, or Pact of Brunnen (where it was drawn up and sworn on 9 December 1315, three weeks after the battle), written in Middle High German, reiterating the substance of the former agreement, but also providing for a common 'foreign policy'. The field was bought by the State in 1859. A certain sanctity was given to the legend on 25 July 1940, when Gén. Guisan here addressed his officers when announcing his plan of resisting any possible German aggression by the defence of a central redoubt rather than the frontiers of Switzerland.

Not far E of Beckenried the motorway plunges into the *Seelisberg tunnel* (1980), 9.5km long, which veers SE below the *Niederbauen Chulm* (1923m), reappearing near the head of the *Urner See* (or Lake of Uri) opposite Flüelen, where we turn E across the alluvial flats of the canalised Reuss and bear right to **Altdorf**; see Rte 25A, and also for the roads ascending S to **Andermatt**.

To complete the CIRCUIT of the Lake of Lucerne, turn left (N) at the junction for Altdorf and thread the *Axenstrasse* to **Brunnen**; see Rte 22B, in reverse.

B. Via Weggis and Brunnen: the North Bank of Lake Lucerne

Total distance, 56km (35 miles). No. 2. 14km **Küssnacht**—No. 2B. 7.5km *Weggis*—5.5km *Vitznau*—14km **Brunnen**. (**Schwyz** lies 6km NE)—No. 2. 15km **Altdorf**.

Maps: M 217; BL 32, 37, or 5008.

We follow the No. 2 along the N shore of Lake Lucerne (see Rte 22A), shortly passing the *Swiss Transport Museum* (see p 202), and circle the promontory of *Meggenhorn*, passing (right) *Neu-Habsburg*, a 19C neo-Gothic *Schloss*. In its park is a 13C tower of a Habsburg stronghold destroyed by the Lucerners in 1352. The Rigi dominates the far bank of the *Küssnachtersee*, which the road now skirts, to traverse *Meggen*. On approaching Küssnacht a chapel is passed, commemorating Queen Astrid of Belgium, killed here in a motor accident in August 1935.

Küssnacht, Roman *Cosseniacum*, at the head of its bay, is of comparatively slight interest, although preserving several old houses and a restored 18C church.

About 1 km NE, passing a tower on the right supposed to be a relic of Gessler's castle, is the so-called *Hohle Gasse* or 'hollow lane', where Gessler, according to the legend, was ambushed and shot by William Tell. Tell's chapel, rebuilt in 1638, is decorated with frescoes.

For the old road from Küssnacht to *Arth* and *Zug* see Rte 24 in reverse.

A rapid alternative to the lakeside road described below is the N4 motorway, entered 2km N of Küssnacht. It leads SE between the *Rigi* and the *Zuger See*, after 11km by-passing *Goldau* (see also Rte 25A), where one may take the Rigi cogwheel railway to the *Rigi-Kulm* (opened 1875); see below. It then circles the N shore of the *Lauerzer See*, with at 7km an exit for *Schwyz* (3km SE; see Rte 25B), and another 3km further S for adjacent **Brunnen**; see below.

Turning S along the E bank of the lake, we pass a cable-car mounting to *Seebodenalp* ·(1031m), from which a path ascends to the *Rigi*; but see below.—*Greppen* is shortly traversed, with a church of 1647, to enter (7km) Weggis, just E of the promontory of *Tanzenberg*. Here in the 'Villa Serar' at *Hertenstein* Rachmaninoff lived in 1931–39 and composed his 'Rhapsody on a theme of Paganini'.—**Weggis**, a popular resort rebuilt since being devastated by a landslide in 1795, and with a view across the lake to the cliffs of Bürgenstock, is the lower terminus for a cable-car to *Rigi-Kaltbad*, there changing to the rack-railway for *Rigi-Kulm*; but see also *Vitznau*, below.

The **Rigi**, one of the famous view-points of Europe, is an isolated steep-sided and scarped mountain, rising to a long grassy ridge with several summits, the highest of which is the *Rigi-Kulm* (1798m), and the length of the saddle enhances its advantages as a natural platform. Its name has been derived with painstaking scholarship from '*Mons Rigidus*', '*Regina Montium*', etc., but it is more probably merely corrupted from a dialect word signifying 'bands' or stripes.

There is little point in making the ascent unless it is fairly certain that visibility will be good by the time one reaches the top; it is not infrequently hazy, cloudy, or misty. The hours of sunrise and sunset (when warm clothing is advisable) are the ideal times for viewing, and there are several hotels near the summit to accommodate   trippers: Mark   Twain's   description—when   tramping abroad—may be recalled. The first inn was built here in 1816 and within two decades Murray was able to write of it: 'During the height of summer . . . the Culm inn is crammed to overflowing every evening; numbers are turned away . . . . The house presents a scene of utmost confusion, servant maids hurrying in one direction, couriers and guides in another, while gentlemen with poles and knapsacks block up the passages . . .', etc. (Presumably it was out of season when visited by Wagner. On hearing the alphorn on the Rigi, he was inspired to compose the cor anglais tune for the herdsman's air at the start of the third act of 'Tristan'.) Muirhead, more recently, referred to the 'thousands of visitors yearly—far too many for comfort, on occasions', who flocked there and to the Pilatus; see Rte 22A. Tourists may ascend by one route and descend by another, and circular tickets are issued at Lucerne in connection with steamers and railways, etc.

The *Views hence gain in general effect from the isolation of the Rigi; details may be made out with the aid of an indicator or panorama. The two sharp peaks of the Mythen, the landslip of the Rossberg, the snowy summit of the Titlis, the gloomy ridge of Pilatus and the distant Jungfrau, are among the objects of most interest. A fine walk leads SE along the *Höhenweg* to the *Rigi-Scheidegg* (1662m), providing a view only a little less extensive than from the Kulm; from there cable-cars descend.

The station at Vitznau, the terminus of the Rigi rack-and-pinion railway, in 1880

Continuing to skirt the lake, at 5.5km **Vitznau** is reached, a sheltered resort facing W. It is the terminus for the cogwheel railway to the *Rigi-Kulm*, the oldest mountain railway in Switzerland, inaugurated in 1871; the gradient reaches 1 in 4, the first part of the line being the steepest. The road now circles the *Obere Nase*, facing the *Unterer Nase*, a promontory of the *Bürgenstock* (see Rte 22A), the strait between them only 800m across, and bears E to (6km) *Gersau*, a lakeside village which between 1390 and the French invasion formed an independent state, undoubtedly the smallest in Europe, its entire territory consisting of an alluvial slope leaning against the mountainside, with scarcely a level stretch of ground. Its church dates from 1812. Across the lake rises the Seelisberg.

We continue along the shore to (8km) **Brunnen**, situated at an elbow of the lake at the mouth of the Muota and commanding fine vistas of its two long stretches and their encircling mountains, the most spectacular being that looking S up the *Urner See*, while across the lake lies *Treib*, and the isolated *Schillerstein*; see p 207. The early *Baroque chapel* (1632), a few paces from the waterfront and landing-stage, was built by the Reding family.

It was at Brunnen in 1315, after the battle of Morgarten, that the three Forest Cantons confirmed their previous alliance (cf. Rütli), and here in 1798 that Alois Reding raised the standard of resistance against the French. Brunnen was the goal of Shelley's ill-fated visit to Switzerland in August 1814 with Mary Godwin and 'Claire' Clairmont, but they stayed there only two days. The composer Othmar Schoeck (1886–1957) was a native.

Morschach, a high-lying village (646m) on a terrace below the *Fronalpstock* (1922m), may be approached by a steep road immediately S of Brunnen; while only 4km NE of Brunnen lies the interesting town of **Schwyz**; see Rte 25B.

The narrow *Axenstrasse (named after the pastures of the *Axenberg* above it), a masterpiece of early engineering, was constructed in 1863–64 above the precipitous E bank of the *Urner See*, impassable before that date. Like the railway, it goes through numerous tunnels pierced in the rock and offers several splendid view-points, the first being across the lake towards the Rütli, below Seelisberg; see last paragraphs of Rte 22A.

4km *Sisikon*, a village with a church dating from 1447, lies at the mouth of the *Riemenstaldenbach*, whose deep gorge briefly breaks the line of cliffs.

Riemenstalden, a hamlet 3.5km E with an 18C church, is a convenient base for the ascent of the *Rossstock* (2461m) and other peaks in the hinterland.

At 3km we reach the *Tellsplatte*, a spur projecting into the lake from the foot of the Axenberg, where it is said that William Tell sprang ashore from the boat in which Gessler was carrying him to prison. One may descend to a chapel built here in 1879 on the site of that traditionally erected only thirty years after the hero's death.

On the far shore is the hamlet of *Bauen*, while the great snow-peak of the *Uri-Rotstock* (2928m) rises to the SW. It may be ascended from *Isenthal*, approached by following a narrow road along the W bank of the lake from *Seedorf*, W of Altdorf. From the head of the romantic ISENTHAL a track leads up to the *Schönegg Pass* (1924m) leading W to *Wolfenschiessen*; see Rte 22A.

The *Bristen* (3072m) towers in front as we approach the head of the lake, and (4km) *Flüelen*, the port of the Canton of Uri and a small resort lying below the crags of the *Eggsberg* (reached by cable-car), rising steeply from the alluvial flat formed by the Reuss. The castle of *Rudenz*, a heavy gabled edifice (14th and 19C) was once a fief of the Attinghausen family, while the restored church is an early Baroque building.

After 1km a right-hand turning is reached, which leads to the N2 motorway, which, if wishing to make the CIRCUIT of Lake Lucerne, we follow to the NW; see Rte 22A in reverse. **Altdorf** lies 2km S of this junction; see Rte 25A, and for the road to **Andermatt**.

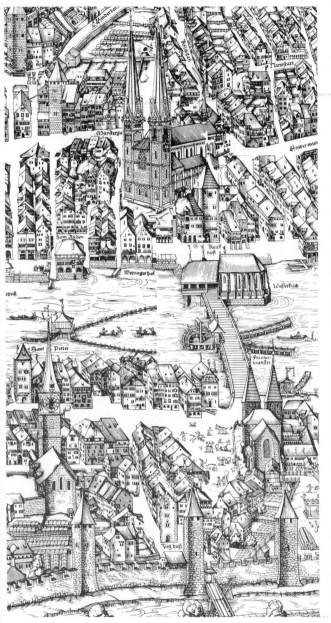

View of Zürich in 1576 (detail)

23   Zürich

ZÜRICH (Zurigo in Italian; 411m; 346,500 Züricher; 215,500 in 1910),
the largely German-speaking cosmopolitan capital of its canton, the
largest city and financial capital of Switzerland, is well situated at the
NW extremity of the Zürichsee, on both banks of the Limmat, and its
tributary, the Sihl. In clear weather a distant panorama of the Alps is
visible from its quays. It was long as famous for its silk production as
Lyon, but in recent decades other industries have grown rapidly with
diversification. Much of the characteristic ancient town survives and
its several important museums make it an interesting centre in which
to spend several days.

The earliest amphibian inhabitants were lake-dwellers, and Zürich's name is
probably derived from the Celtic 'Dur' (water), although the personal name
Turus, later *Turicum*, is also documented, among others. The Helvetian set-
tlement with its fort fell to the Romans in c 58 BC, who garrisoned the Lindenhof.
Christianity was introduced in the 2–3C, and the Alemanni controlled the place
until ousted by the Franks, who established residence here in c 800.
Charlemagne founded the cathedral and Louis the German (son of Le
Débonnaire) founded the monastery of Fraumünster (853). The medieval
Teutonic town grew up around these foundations and a settlement of 'free men',
mainly Alemmanic, on the Zürichberg.
   In 1218 Zürich became a free imperial city, but still showed Austrian
inclinations. In 1351 it threw its lot in with the Swiss Confederation, largely due
to the shrewdness of Rudolf Brun, its patrician burgomaster, who had already
admitted the guildsmen to a share in local government. The acession of this
thriving city to the Confederation had a far-reaching influence on its history, and
Zürich reached its greatest political importance in the 15C under Hans
Waldmann (burgomaster in 1483–89), who had made it the virtual capital of the
'Everlasting League'. In 1515 Henry VIII sent Richard Pace to Zürich to incite
the Swiss against François I.
   It was the vigorous adherence of Zürich to the Reformation that secured its
dominant position in Confederate counsels, with Zwingli preaching in the
cathedral from 1519 until his death in 1531, while in 1525 mass was abolished.
It was a refuge for many English Protestants banished under Mary, and Miles
Coverdale's first entire translation of the Bible and Apocrypha (from the German)
is believed to have been published here in 1535. The friendship of Heinrich
Bullinger (1508–75, in Zürich), Zwingli's successor, was remembered by Lady
Jane Grey on the scaffold. The 'Zürich Consensus' of 1549 marked the
ascendency of Calvinist theology in the Confederation. Persecuted Protestants
from Locarno were given asylum here; one of them, Evangelisto Zanino (died
1603) establishing the first large-scale textile manufactories, mainly for producing velvets.
   In August 1608 it was visited by Thomas Coryate, who observed 'Many ...
bitter brunts ... this Citie hath often endured before the time of the confederation
and since, having beene tossed to & fro from one Lord to another, as if shee had
beene Dame Fortune's tennis ball. But at this day by the gracious indulgence
of the heavenly powers, it enjoyeth great peace and a very halcedonian time with
the rest of the Helveticall Cities under that happy league of union, being subject
neither to king nor kaysar'. John Pell, the mathematician, was resident here
between 1654 and 1658 as Cromwell's diplomatic representative to the
Protestant Cantons.
   The town shared in the political reactions of the 18C, which ended in the
temporary overthrow of the Confederation in 1798, while Masséna, after a defeat
by the Archduke Charles at the first Battle of Zürich, gained a victory over the
Russians in 1799. Its medieval defences were progressively demolished during
the second and third decades of the 19C, and in 1863 the Bahnhofstrasse was
laid out. Its University (replacing Zwingli's 'Carolinum') was established after
a referendum in 1833; in 1854 the Federal Polytechnic (now the Institute of
Technology) was inaugurated. The Central Station was not opened until 1871,

although the first entirely Swiss railway had been laid down between Zürich and Baden in 1847. In 1893, with the redrawing of the city boundaries, its population leapt overnight from 28,000 to 121,000.

The 'Cabaret Voltaire' was founded here in 1916 by Hugo Ball (1886–1927), inaugurating the 'Dada' Movement, while in the 1930s the 'Pfeffermühle' was celebrated. A few bombs fell on the city in 1942–45, owing to its proximity to Germany. It then expanded rapidly as a centre of German culture with the temporary eclipse of Munich and other towns, and it has since become the main base of the great *Verbände*, the industrial and financial pressure-groups of modern Switzerland.

James Joyce in Zürich

Among famous natives have been: Hans Leu the Younger (1485–1527/8, and Hans Asper (1499–1571), artists; Caspar Waser (1565–1625), the philologist and Orientalist; Ludwig Senfl (1486–c 1543), the composer, although Basle claims to be his actual place of birth; Konrad Gessner (1516–65), the polymath (see below); Salomon Gessner (1730–88), author; Johann Caspar Lavater (1741–1801), physiognomist and essayist; Johann Jacob Scheuchzer (1672–1733), author of the 'Itinera Alpina'; Johann Heinrich Pestalozzi

(1746–1827), the educationalist; Johann Jakob Breitinger (1701–76), the scholar and friend of Johann Jakob Bodmer (1698–1783), the 'Dioscuri of Zürich'; John Gaspar Scheutzer (1702–29), the physician, buried in Chelsea Old Church; Johann Heinrich Füssli (known in England as Fuseli; 1741–1825, in Putney), who visited London in 1765 and settled there permanently in 1780; Gottfried Keller (1819–90); Conrad Ferdinand Meyer (1825–98), the poet; Max Frisch (1911–), novelist and dramatist; Hans Sturzenegger (1875–1943), artist; and Rolf Liebermann (1910–), composer.

Richard Wagner lived here sporadically as a political exile during the years 1849–58 and several of his works were first performed in Zürich; Ferrucio Busoni (1866–1924) lived here in 1915–18; Arthur Honegger (1892–1955) was a citizen of Zürich, although born in Le Havre; Barbara Schulthess-Wolf (1745–1818), the friend of Goethe, lived here, as did the poet Thomas Lovell Beddoes in 1835–41; and Lou Andreas-Salomé (1861–1937), who read theology at the University, was an influence on Nietzsche from 1882, and on Rilke from 1897; Einstein lectured here in 1901–13; Lenin lived here from February 1916 to April 1917 (Spiegelgasse 14).

James Joyce arrived in Zürich from Trieste in June 1915, remaining here until 1919 (Universitätstrasse 38), during which period much of 'Ulysses' was written, and returned here in December 1940 from Vichy (the Swiss authorities first requiring a bank deposit and financial guarantees, and a detailed declaration of his personal fortune!). He died here on 13 January 1941 and is buried in the Flünntern cemetery. Georg Büchner (1813–37), author of 'Dantons Tod' and 'Woyzeck', died at Spiegelgasse 12; Thomas Mann (1875–1955) died in the Cantonal hospital; and Carl Gustav Jung (1875–1961), who introduced the words 'extrovert' and 'introvert', died here, as did Johanna Spyri (1827–1901), author of 'Heidi', and the conductors Otto Klemperer (1885–1973) and Erich Kleiber (1890–1956).

It was *Konrad Gessner* (see above) who wrote: 'I will each year climb some mountains, or at least one, at the season when the flowers are in bloom, in order that I may examine these, and provide noble exercise for my body as well as delight for my soul'. His posthumous 'Opera botanica' (1753–59) does indeed contain evidence of first-hand observation, while his 'Historia animalium' (1551–58) is considered to be the most important zoological treatise of its epoch. These were only two aspects of his learning.

A. West bank of the Limmat

The BAHNHOFPLATZ (with the *Tourist Information Office*), immediately S of the *Railway Station* (1871), with regular rapid trains to the *Airport of Kloten* (1949), is one of the city's main centres. Immediately to the N of the Station is the **Schweizerisches Landesmuseum**, the *National Museum* (see Rte 23C).

The broad **Bahnhofstrasse**, the main commercial and banking thoroughfare, leads S to the lake. In itself it is of slender interest to the slender pursed.

The only object of interest to the W of this street is the *Ethnographical collection* of the University in the *old Botanical Gardens*, approached by the Pelikanstrasse, just beyond which the Schanzengraben indicates the line of the 17C fortifications of the city.

Before reaching this turning, one may fork left along the Rennweg, and half-way along it, turn up to the left and then climb right to the top of the tree-shaded *Lindenhof*, the site of the early settlement of Zürich, which provides an interesting panorama of the city. Descending from its S side, we reach a characteristic part of the older town on this W bank.

A short distance W, near the Bahnhofstrasse, is the late 13C *Augustinerkirche*, secularised in 1525, and later housing the Mint. It was recently radically restored.

Bearing S, we soon reach the restored church of **St. Peter**, dominated by its huge clock-face of 1534 (almost 8.7m in diameter); the base of the tower is 13C and although much altered in 1705 the church is one of the earliest foundations of Zürich. It contains the grave of Johann Caspar Lavater, pastor here for 23 years, who was gratuitously shot by a brutal French soldier when their forces, under Masséna, entered the town. He died a lingering death some three months later.

Hence we descend to the Storchengasse and turn right to enter the MÜNSTERHOF, where, to the left, is the attractive **Zunfthaus zur Meisen**, a mid 18C guildhall, built by David Morf, the first floor of which contains a very fine display of Zürich porcelain, part of the National Museum collection. The factory at *Schooren*, near Bendlikon, was founded in 1763 with the cooperation of Salomon Gessner, but it had ceased work by 1803. Collections of Strasbourg, Lunéville, Künersberg and Meissen ware are also to be seen.—On the NW side of the square is the *Zunfthaus zur Waag* (1637).

The S side is overlooked by the **Fraumünster**, a much-modernised 13C building, founded in 853 by Louis the German (Ludwig dem Deutschen) as a convent for noble ladies, with his daughter Hildegard as its first abbess. Her successors acquired many rights over the town, and in 1234 the title of princesses of the empire. The convent was suppressed in 1534. Some relics of the original building may be seen in the crypt, while the base of the Romanesque tower preserves 12C blind arcading. To the S are remains of its cloister. The rectangular choir has a screen of 1470; glass by Chagall and A. Giacometti now embellishes the transept, notable for its keystones.

Mid nineteenth century view of Zürich

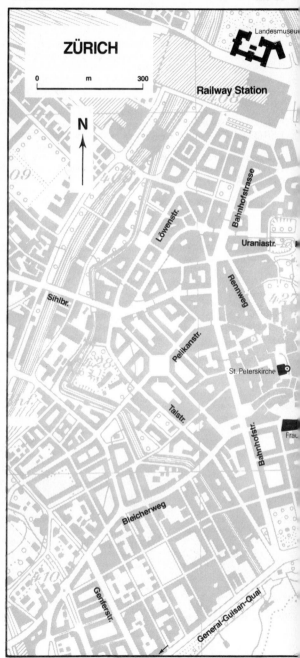

ZÜRICH

0   m   300

N

Landesmuseum

Railway Station

Bahnhofstrasse

Löwenstr.

Uraniastr.

Rennweg

Sihlbr.

Pelikanstr.

St. Peterskirche

Talstr.

Bahnhofstr.

Frau

Bleicherweg

Genferstr.

General-Guisan-Quai

Rietbergmuseum

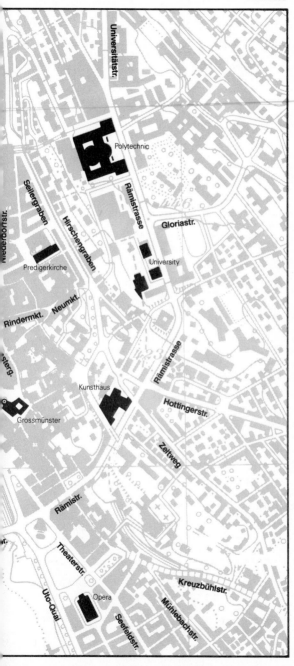

Universitätstr.

Polytechnic

Rämistrasse

Gloriastr.

Sellergraben

Hirschengraben

Niederdorfstr.

Predigerkirche

University

Rindermkt. Neumkt.

Rämistrasse

sterg.

Kunsthaus

Hottingerstr.

Grossmünster

Zeltweg

Rämistr.

Theaterstr.

Kreuzbühlstr.

Uto-Quai

Opera

Mühlebachstr.

Seefeldstr.

B. East bank of the Limmat

From the Münsterhof one may either follow the river bank S to the lake-side Bürkliplatz (see p 223, and for the district further S), there crossing the Limmat by the *Quaibrücke*, or cross by the *Münsterbrücke*. The latter provides a good view of the 18C *Helmhaus*, abutted by the **Wasserkirche** (1478–88), on the foundations of an earlier church, but secularised in 1521, and from 1631–1917 housing the City Library. It was reopened as a church in 1942 and displays glass by A. Giacometti.

On a terrace immediately to the E rises the ***Grossmünster**. Its conspicuous twin towers are surmounted by octagonal sugar-castor lanterns, which in 1786 replaced the former spires, the northernmost of which had been damaged by lightning. On the S side of the Romanesque part of the S tower is a replica of a statue said to be of Charlemagne, the earlier (late 15C) example of which is now in the crypt. On the N side of the N tower is an equestrian figure of c 1180. The present church was begun c 1100 on the site of an earlier building and was largely completed by 1230. It was the scene of Zwingli's preaching of the Reformation, and in August 1815 of an assembly which adopted the Confederate Constitution. The N portal, several times restored, has been provided with bronze doors by Otto Münch (1950).

The *interior* is notable for its height, its unrestored capitals and some 12C bas reliefs. The *Crypt* preserves relics of murals by Hans Leu the Elder, of c 1500. The upper *Choir*, with its blind arcading, contains glass by A. Giacometti.—The glass-covered **Cloisters**, entered to the right on making our exit from the church, at No. 6 ZWINGLIPLATZ, should not be overlooked. They survived entire demolition in the mid 19C and have been incorporated into a building which is now the Theological Faculty of the University. Their **Capitals* are remarkable.

In the Platz stands the *Haus zum Loch* of c 1300.

For the districts further SE see p 224.

The Kirchgasse (in which Nos 27 and 48 are notable) ascends E directly to the Hirschengraben, while the Münstergasse leads N, traversing the older town. But it is recommended to descend first to the Limmatquai and turn N, passing the following guild-houses: the *Zunfthaus zu Zimmerleuten* (1708; of the wood-workers); the *Gesellschafthaus zum Rüden* (1659); the *Haus zur Kerze* (Rüdenplatz 2; Chandlers); the *Haus zur Haue* (No. 52 on the quay); and the *Zunfthaus zur Saffran* (1723; spice-merchants).—Opposite stands the **Rathaus** (1698), on the site of its predecessor of 1398. In the council-hall here Austria renounced her claim to Lombardy in 1859.

Turning right here, and then left, we reach (right) the *Zunfthaus zur Schmiden* (Smiths), and turn right again to follow the characteristic Rindermarkt, the former cattle-market, to a small square, off which to the right is the Spiegelgasse; at No. 12 Lenin lived prior to his return to Russia in 1917; it contains other houses of some interest.—Nos 11, 8 and 4 in the Neumarkt, leading E, are among other buildings of note.—The Untere Zäune climbs SE from the Spiegelgasse to the Hirschengraben, in which Nos 20 and 22 are notable.

Turning right, one shortly reaches the Ramistrasse; turn left and left again to the entrance of the Kunsthaus.

The ***KUNSTHAUS** or *Art Gallery*, on a sloping site to the W of the Heimplatz, originated in a building of 1910 by Karl Moser. It has several times been enlarged, most recently in 1976 when a ribbed concrete and glass extension by Erwin Müller was erected. To the right of the entrance, abutting the facade, is *Rodin*'s 'Porte de l'Enfer' (or Gate of Hell; 1917), while in adjacent gardens are several sculptures, including works by *Lipchitz, Marini, Bourdelle, Maillol* and *Henry Moore*.

Although spacious, the internal layout can be confusing to the visitor, who should ascend to the FIRST FLOOR and turn right to enter **R2**, containing: *Hans Fries*, Adoration of the Magi (c 1500); the *elder Bernese Master of the Carnation* (? Paul Löwensprung), Presentation in the Temple; the *younger Bernese Master of the Carnation*, The Baptist in the desert, and on the reverse, his Beheading; the *Zürich Master of the Carnation* (? Hans Leu the Elder), Adoration of the Shepherds, and on the reverse, Saints Barbara and Catherine.—**R3** *Master of the Munich Dom Crucifixion*, Deposition (c 1440); *Master of the Munich Marientafeln*, Nativity.—**R4** *Cuyp*, Saul's vision; *Rubens*, Portrait of Philip IV; *Jan Verkolje*, Musician and his family.—**R5** *Hals*, Male portrait; *Verspronk*, Female portrait; *Rembrandt*, Simon the apostle; Landscapes by *Hobbema*, and *S. Van Ruisdael* (On the ice near Dordrecht); *J. van Ruisdael*, View near Haarlem; *Van der Velde*, Storm at sea; *Van Goyen*, View near Haarlem; *Jan van de Cappelle*, Harbour view.—**R6**, *Van Cleve*, Death of Lucretia; *Cranach the Elder*, Female portrait; *Pieter Coecke van Aelst*, The artist and his wife; *Jan Prevost*, Adoration of the Magi; *Patinir*, two Landscapes.

R7 Two views by *Bellotto*; Venetian scenes by *Guardi*, and *Canaletto*; *El Greco* (?), Portrait of Card. Charles de Guise; *Matteo di Giovanni*, The House of Levi; *Stomer*, Christ and the Samaritan, and Peter and the angel; *Pannini*, Interior of St. Peter's, Rome; *Moroni*, Portrait of Vittorio Michiel; *Preti*, Christ and the woman taken in adultery.—**R9** Several canvases by *Jan Brueghel the Elder*; *Memling*, Male portrait; *P. Wouwerman*, Soldiers on the march, and Landscape; *Momper*, Landscape, with figures by *David Teniers the Younger*; *Jan Wynants*, Landscape; *Van Goyen*, Harbour scene, View of Arnhem, Seascapes, etc; *Pieter Claesz*, Still life; *F. Snyders*, Still life with parrot; *Rubens*, St. Peter; *Van der Velde the Younger*, Ships; *Govaert Flink*, Girl with a dog; *Nic. Berchem*, Landscapes.

R11 *Arnold Böcklin*, Portrait of Gottfried Keller.—**R12** *Fuseli*, Falstaff in the linen-basket, Puck, Nude listening to music, and several other paintings of interest; *Giovanni Segantini*, Die bösen Mütter, a version of that in Vienna.—**R13** *Hans Asper*, Portraits; *Anton Graff*, Self-portrait, and of Salomon Gessner; *Angelika Kauffmann*, Portrait of J.J. Winkelmann; *Anna Waser* (1679–1713), Self-portrait; *J.C. Füssli*, Still life.—**R14** *Johann Heinrich Wuest* (1741–1821), the Rhône glacier in 1795; works by *Segantini*; *Albert Anker*, Pestalozzi and his children at Stans.—**R15** *Karl Stauffer-Bern* (1857–91), Portrait of Gottfried Keller; *Anselm Feuerbach*, Self-portrait.—**R18** *Ferdinand Hodler*, Self-portraits, Portrait of Mlle Léschaud, and several other Portraits and Landscapes, continued in **R19**.—**R8** on this floor contains works by *Giovanni Giacometti*, and others.

In the new extension are several examples of the art of *Magritte, Ernst, Miró, Mondrian* and *Tanguy*; a Head (muse endormie), by *Brancusi*, and numerous sculptures by *Alberto Giacometti*.

On the staircase, *Egon Schiele*, City of the Dead.

SECOND FLOOR, **R1** *Kokoschka*, Portraits of Adèle Astaire, Helen Kann, Else Kupfer, 'Candide' (1943), and Women in blue.—**R2** *Max Beckman* (1884–1950), Portrait of Max Reger (1917); *Max Liebermann* (1849–1935), Beergarden; *Lovis Corinth*, Self-portrait, etc.; *Edvard Munch* (1863–1944), Portraits of Albert Kollmann, Ellen Warburg, Dr Wilhelm Wartmann, and Else Glaser, and other works; *James Ensor*, Le Jardin d'Amour, Christ's entry into Brussels, Les poissardes mélancoliques, and Le grand juge; *Kokoschka*, Mountainscape, and Lovers with a cat; *Rodin*, Orpheus (1892).—**R3** *Courbet*, Trout, and The source of the Loue; *Manet*, Portrait of Albert Wolff; *Van Gogh*, Hollyhocks; *Renoir*, View off Guernsey, Roses, and a Female portrait; *Pissarro*, two Landscapes.—**R4** *Gauguin*, The gate, The first flowers, Race-horses, and Quarry near Pontoise; *Toulouse-Lautrec*, The bar.—**R5** *Félix Vallotton*, Summer-evening bathe, Nude with a book.—**R6** *Adolf Dietrich* (1877–1957), Winterscape.—**R7** *Cézanne*, Still lifes, Landscape, and Near Auvers; *Seurat*, The gardener; *Van Gogh*, Midday, Near St. Remy, Near Auvers; *Jongkind*, Honfleur; *Manet*, Rowing-boat; *Corot*, Mother and child, and Landscape (La Cervera), and *Rodin*, The martyr; *Monet*, Water-lilies, Man with a parasol, and other works; *Bonnard*, Portrait of Ambroise Vollard with cat, etc.; *Vuillard*, Interiors; *Signac*, Landscape.—**R8** Works by *Paul Klee*, and (in **R9**) *Kandinsky*, and (in **R10**) *Chagall*.

R11 *Picasso*, The kiss, Grand nu (1964), Woman with a hen (1938); works by *Robert Delaunay*, and *Léger*; sculptures by *Hans Arp*, and *Henry Moore*, Knife-edge (1962).—**R12** Sculptures by *Renoir*, *Picasso* (Fernande, 1906), *Matisse*, *Maillol*, *Henri Laurens*, *Marini*, *Bourdelle* (Bust of Beethoven, 1902); *Rodin*, Kneeling woman (1882), and *Balzac* (1891/7); and a painting by *Van Dongen*.—**R13** *Picasso*, Harlequin 'au loup' (1918), and works by *Vlaminck*. Also, among sculptures, works by *Chillida*; *Henry Moore*, Reclining figure; *Francis Bacon*, Three studies of the male back; *Tapies*, Pyramidal.

Also normally on view are *Henri Rousseau*, Pierre Loti with a cat, and Walking in the wood.

Extensive collections of prints, drawings, engravings and wood-cuts are held here, a selection of which are usually on view in the *Graphischen Sammlung*. It is rich in works by *Dürer, Stimmer, Saloman Gessner, Caspar Wolf, Fuseli, W.A. Töepfler, Calame, Hodler, Cézanne, Van Gogh, Rodin, Klimt* and *Schiele*. The *Library* is comprehensive.

To the SE is the *Schauspielhaus*, a theatre of 1889, modernised in 1978, near which, at Zeltweg 13, lived Wagner.—Turning N along Heim Strasse, we pass (right) Florhofgasse, in which Nos 2, 4 and 7 are of some interest, to regain the Hirschengraben, noting Nos 28, 40 (the *Haus zum Rechberg*, of 1759) and 42.—The Künstlergasse turns right. Passing between the last two buildings, we climb to reach the huge pile (completed 1914) of the **University**, with its 65m high tower and cupola, and, further N, the domed Swiss or **Federal Institute of Technology** or E.T.H.Z., designed by Gottfried Semper in 1864, but several times enlarged. It was founded in 1854, and now has some 7000 students and 12 departments. The *Cabinet of Engravings*, with its entrance at Rämistrasse 101, contains a comprehensive collection of graphic work of all periods, and is particularly rich in Dürer, Rembrandt, Schongauer, Goya and Félix Vallotton. Occasional exhibitions are held here.

The University, with its main entrance at Rämistrasse 71, comprises six faculties attended by c 14,000 students. Several faculty buildings lie further N and many have their specialised collections, such as those of *Medical History* (entrance Rämistrasse 71), and of *Zoology* and *Palaeontology* (entrance Künstlergasse 16).

In the same building as the last is the *Archaeological collection*, where, well displayed, are Etruscan finds, including lamps, glass, etc; Egyptian portrait-masks from mummies; a Relief of Assurnasirpal II from Nimrod (883–59 BC), and of Tiglat-Pilesar III (744–27 BC); statuettes of gods and goddesses; jewellery, scarabs and cylinder-seals; Roman bronze statuettes and terracottas; Black- and Red-figure ware; a bronze urn adorned by four bulls' heads (2nd half of 8C BC); Cycladic idols (2700–2100 BC); Bronze helmets and greaves; and a sculpted marble figure hanging by his wrists.

At Schönberggasse 15, to the S, a mansion of 1665, once the home of J.J. Bodmer, are the *Thomas Mann Archives*, with a reconstruction of his study at Kilchberg (cf.); opposite the University are the extensive buildings of the *Cantonal Hospital* (1945–51).

From the W end of the Künstlergasse steps descend to the Hirschengraben, and the Seilergraben, parallel at a lower level. Off the latter leads the Brunngasse, skirting the side of the **Prediger-kirche**, that of a former Dominican convent founded in 1230, a Gothic structure in which *Archives* now congregate. Adjacent is the *Central Library*, with some 18,500 MSS and incunables, among them the first book printed in Switzerland (Beromünster, 1470) and a large collection of maps, prints, etc., some of which are occasionally exhibited. Thomas Hollis, an Englishman who had travelled in Switzerland in 1748, donated to the library a complete set of works against the Jesuits as a delicate compliment; he likewise gave books to the libraries of Geneva, Basle and Berne. From the N side of the square one may follow the Zäringerstrasse N, skirting a somewhat unsalubrious district to reach the busy CENTRAL, and cross the river to regain the Bahnhofplatz.

C. The Swiss National Museum (Schweizerische Landesmuseum)

The Museum was installed in 1898 in a cumbersome castellated edifice by Gustav Gull, erected immediately N of the Station. It was intended to summarise several disparate styles of Swiss architecture, and its rambling layout is confusing. A notable feature is the number of rooms which have been bodily removed from medieval or Renaissance buildings throughout the canton and reconstructed within the museum. Its entrance lies to the left of the courtyard, besides which stands the old St. Gotthard diligence.

GROUND FLOOR. **RR1–2**, devoted to the medieval period, are at present closed for reformation. Some objects at present displayed elsewhere will probably be returned here in due course.—**R4** has on its ceiling 65 copies of the 153 painted panels of the church at Zillis (1130; cf.) and displays 14–15C stove tiles; carved and painted reliefs from a mid 15C altarpiece; a carved and painted Christ from Chur (c 1500), and Carrying the Cross (c 1515, from the high Valais; notice the man with a goitre).—**R5** 13C terracottas.—**R8** Panels by *Hans Leu the Younger*; carved stalls from St. Wolfgang at Zug (1486), and painted wooden figures of Christ on ass-back, known as a 'Palmesel', formerly used in Easter processions, including one of c 1200.—**R9**

Collections of Pewter.

In BASEMENT ROOMS reached from this point are displayed the furniture and equipment of a *Smithy* and the workshops of a *Wheelwright*, etc., with ploughs, butts, and also horn and leather-work; a flour-mill, cider-press, etc. and objects from the 17C arsenal of Zürich.

R14 Views of Zürich c 1502 by *Hans Leu the Elder*. This room, the panelled Council-chamber of Mellingen (1467), contains stained-glass windows displaying the arms of the Empire and of the first eight cantons of the Confederation.—**R15**, arcades from the Predigerkloster, Zürich (mid 13C), and good 15C glass.—**R19** contains a collection of 16C furniture and two portraits by *Hans Asper*.—**R22**, furniture and fittings from the Dispensary of the Benedictine abbey of Muri (18C).

Stairs ascend to the FIRST FLOOR and **R23**, with a display of watches and clocks, a terrestial globe of 1595; the room has a late Gothic ceiling from Arbon (1515).—**R24**, one of a series with panelling from earlier buildings, notable among which are **R26**, from the Casa Pestalozzi at Chiavenna (1585), and **R29**, from the Haus zum alten Seidenhof at Zürich (c 1615), with a poêle of 1620 from Winterthur. Good stained-glass and furniture is displayed in **R31**.

From **R32** stairs ascend to a tower containing several rooms devoted to collections of costumes, toys, ecclesiastical silver, etc. Returning to the FIRST FLOOR we enter **R42**, with Goldsmiths' work, off which opens **R43**, a panelled and painted reception room from the Lochmanhaus in Zürich (17C), containing a series of 54 portraits of members of the court of Louis XIII and their European con-temporaries.—**R44** is entered through an arch from the Castel Grande, Bellinzona.—**R45**, a Rococo room, with more Goldsmiths' work.—**R46** contains painted furniture and an organ of 1811.—**R48**, painted and engraved glass (16–18C); tiles; ceramic collections; and a poêle of 1698; carved, gilt and painted retables; a carved Virgin and child from Sempach (c 1180) and another from the Valais (Raron; c 1150), a Pietà from the Grisons (c 1330) and a Virgin and child from the canton of St. Gallen (c 1430).—**R49** Medals; tankards; a Gobelins tapestry depicting the renewal of the alliance of the Confederates with Louis XIV at Notre-Dame, Paris, in 1663 (after cartoons by Lebrun and Van der Meulen); an old map of the canton of Zürich; a poêle from Winterthur (1698); a 17C wooden penitentiary cell from Baden; a wrought-iron Gate of 1770.—**R50**, a large central hall or *Salle d'Armes*, devoted to heraldic stained-glass, uniforms, banners, arms and armour, etc. Collections of uniforms and regimental colours or of cantonal contingents are continued in the following rooms, among them the banner of the Anglo-Swiss Legion.

Turning left, we cross to the EAST WING, displaying *Archaeologi-cal Collections*, including (in **R69**) relics of the Roman occupation at Vindonissa, etc.—**R71** contains bronze arms and armour, and pottery and glass; an embossed golden bowl from Zürich-Altstetten of the Hallstatt period (6C BC), discovered in 1906, and the Celtic Treasure discovered in 1962 at Erstfeld (Uri) of the 4C BC, including a gold arm-ring, bracelets and necklaces.—**RR72–3** contain collections of ceramics; figurines from Avenches; a sculptured Romulus and Remus; Bacchus, parts of a bull (from Martigny); cult figures, etc.—**R74** Glass and jewellery; Langobardic or Burgundian fittings (6–7C); an Ostro-goth helmet (6C), and crested bronze helmet of the 1C BC from Gubiasco (Ticino); buckles and costume accessories; an ivory diptych of the consul Areobindus (AD 506), etc.

Rooms on the floor below display finds from the Neolithic era and Bronze Age, including a 10m-long dug-out canoe found in the Bielersee; and photographs showing excavated sites, etc.

Some minutes' walk to the NW, approached by crossing the Zollbrücke adjacent to the railway, is the *Kunstgewebenmuseum*, Ausstellungsstrasse 60, devoted to the applied arts, and inaugurated in 1875. It is the venue of occasional exhibitions of interest.

D. SW Zürich; the Museum Rietberg

The *Rietberg Museum* may be approached from the Bahnhofstrasse by taking the 7 or 10 tram travelling S beyond the *Bahnhof Enge* stop to the *Rieter Park*, to the W of the Seestrasse, from which the Gablerstrasse ascends to the museum.

The energetic may walk from the Bürkliplatz (at the S extremity of the Bahnhofstrasse), with a quay for lake-steamers, thence following the Gén. Guisan-quai, leading SW past the *Tonhalle* and *Kongresshaus* of 1939 to the *Arboretum*. Continuing S past the yacht harbour abutting the Mythen-quai, the *Belvoirpark* is reached. The *Rieter Park* lies further uphill, on the far side of the Seestrasse.

The ****Rietberg** (pron. Reetberg) **Museum** was founded in 1952, its basis being the collections, largely Oriental, donated to the city by Baron Eduard von der Heydt (1882–1964), a former German banker, although a Swiss citizen since 1937.

Several parts of his collection had been on loan to other museums for years. Among them were several Chinese works of art, including the larger stelae, which in 1950 were exchanged from a deposit in East Berlin for the tea glass, tea strainer and butter-knife used by Lenin in 1916–17 when he was living in Zürich. Other dispersed collections of non-European art which were not a victim of the war and occupation reverted on request to Von der Heydt, with the exception of those in the United States, which were *not* returned although *not* the property of the museums concerned.

The collection was installed in the *Villa Wesendonck* in the Rieterpark, the home from 1857, when it was built, to 1871 of Otto and Mathilde von Wesendonck, the latter an intimate of Richard Wagner, who, when their guest, occupied a garden pavilion which stood near the present late 19C *Villa Schönberg*, on the other side of the Gablerstrasse. Wagner's Forest Scene in 'Siegfried' is said to have been directly inspired by birdsong heard during his rambles in the Sihlwald.

The Museum's holdings have been increased by the C.A. Drenowatz collection of Chinese paintings and the anonymous donation of a fine collection of Rajasthani and Pahari miniatures; by the Alice Boner collection of Indian sculptures; Dr Rudolph Schmidt's collection of over 200 Luristan bronzes, and the Willy Boler collection of Japanese woodblock prints, etc. Work is going ahead with the extension of the display area and adjacent buildings will be approached hence by an underground passage. It is therefore likely that the present layout of the museum will be slightly changed.

By turning right from the entrance-hall one will in turn visit the following collections: the *Vestibule* itself contains objects from the ancient Near East, including a pair of seated figures from Sakkara (c 2400 BC); a votive statue from Cyprus (6C BC); Luristan bronzes (8–6C BC), etc.—**R2** is primarily devoted to the arts of Central America, that of the Maya and Incas and their predecessors, amongst other cultures, including an Aztec Coiled rattlesnake in basaltic lava (13C) brought back from Mexico by Alexander von Humboldt.—**RR3–5** and **11–12** contain a remarkable collection of Buddhist sculpture from India and SE Asia, including a figure of Umā (Khmer culture, Cambodia, early 10C) and another from Prasat Andet (Pre-Ankor style; late 7C), the divine mother. Also notable is Shiva dancing, from S India (11C).—**RR6–9** and **13–14** are devoted to the arts of China, including a fine Maitreya, or Buddha guarded by lions (Honan province; early 6C); a Buddhist votive stele (early 6C; late Northern Wei dynasty); a wooden statue of Kuan-yin (13C); and a recumbent Ram (late 6C).—**R15** contains examples of Japanese art and sculpture.—**RR16–17** are concerned with the arts of Indonesia and Oceania, in which one can hardly overlook the 19C Fertility statue from Bali.—**RR18–19** contain numerous artefacts from Africa.

Bears Wrestling with Monkeys; Pahari region, India, c 1725 (Reitberg Museum)

In **R20**, on the 2nd floor, is an impressive collection of Swiss masks, many from the backward Lötschental, used during the twelve nights after Christmas, in Shrovetide plays, Carnival, etc.

E. SE Zürich; the Bührle Foundation

A short distance S of the Grossmünster and on the E bank of the Limmat, here crossed by the Quaibrücke, is the Bellevue-platz.—The *Kronenhalle Restaurant* at No. 4 Rämistrasse contains an extensive collection of modern and contemporary art.

Further S is the **Opera-house** (1891), recently modernised, where took place the first performances of such works as Alban Berg's 'Lulu' (1937), Hindemith's 'Mathis de Maler' (1938) and Schoenberg's 'Moses and Aaron' (1957).

From the BELLEVUE-PLATZ one may take the No. 4 tram from the Bahnhofquai or No. 2 from Paradeplatz (half-way down the Bahnhofstrasse) to the Wildbachstrasse stop in the Seefelstrasse. There turn uphill to the E to Zollikerstrasse, where at No. 172 is the ****Bührle Foundation**.

Here is displayed a remarkable collection of paintings collected by Georg Bührle (1890–1956), never exhibited during his lifetime, and opened to the public in 1960.

GROUND FLOOR: *Rembrandt*, Portrait of Saskia (1636); *Greuze*, Portrait of Laurent Pêcheux; *Ingres*, Portraits of M. Devillers, and of Mme Ingres; *Fragonard*, Portrait of his wife, and of Hubert Robert; *Courbet*, Portrait of Leboeuf, the sculptor; *Degas*, Mme Camus at the piano, and Comte Lepic and his children; *Corot*, A girl reading; *Strozzi*, St. Catherine of Alexandria; Venetian scenes by *Canaletto*, and *Guardi*; *G.-B. Tiepolo*, The bath of Diana; *Goya*, Procession in Valencia; Landscapes by *S. van Ruysdael*, and *Cuyp*; *Terborch*, Interior; *Rembrandt*, Still life with game; works by *David Teniers the Younger*; *Philips Koninck*, Landscape with hunter; *Hals*, Portrait of a youth; *Van Goyen*, Seascapes; *Toulouse-Lautrec*, Messalina, Portrait of François Gauzi, and of Georges-Henri Manuel, Lovers, and Confetti; *Renoir*, Little Irène; *Gauguin*, Sunflowers on a chair; Boy with a red waistcoat, and Self-portrait painting; *Mary Cassat*, Mother and child; *Berthe Morisot*, Portrait of Mme Albine Sermicoli; also a small collection of 12–16C woodcarvings.

On the staircase and on FIRST FLOOR: *Delacroix*, Self-portrait in 1830, and other works; *Chagall*, The Russian marriage; *Signac*, The modistes; and several works by *Soutine, Braque, Dufy, Matisse, Vlaminck, Derain* and *Gris*; *Patinir*, Baptism of Christ (two versions); *Courbet*, The hunter (self-portrait), and Winter scene; *Fantin-Latour*, Self-portrait; and works by *Pissarro* and *Daumier*; *Monet*, Waterloo Bridge, A meal Chez Sisley, and The garden at Giverny; *Boudin*, two Views; *Renoir*, Portrait of Sisley, La source (nude), and Spring bonnets; *Manet*, Garden scene, The suicide, and The Grand Duc (bird); *Gauguin*, Idylle à Tahiti, and A peasant; *Van Gogh*, Self-portrait (1887), The sower, The old tower; *Cézanne*, Landscapes; *Puvis de Chavannes*, Le fils perdu; *Sisley*, three landscapes; *Bonnard*, Portrait of Ambroise Vollard; *Vuillard*, Self-portrait in 1912, and Nude on a sofa.—On upper stair: *Rouault*, The box; *Modigliani*, Nude; and several *Picassos*.

Also in this SE sector of Zürich, at Höschgasse 3, leading down from Seefeldstrasse to the lakeside, is the *Bellerive Museum*, an annex to the Museum of Applied Arts, and often the site of exhibitions.—Hence one may return towards the centre via the Seefeldquai and Utoquai.

24   Zürich to Lucerne via Zug

Total distance, 55km (39 miles). No. 4. 30km **Zug**—25km **Lucerne**.

Maps: M 216; BL 32, or 5008, 5011.

A motorway from a point W of Zürich to meet that already constructed NW of *Zug*, which follows the W bank of the *Zuger See*, will eventually provide a rapid route. The present main road is that described below.

An alternative to the first part is to take the N3 motorway S to the *Horgen* exit, thence making the steep climb SW over a ridge to meet the No. 4 at *Sihlbrugg*. This passes, near the summit, the village of *Hirzel*, birthplace of Johanna Spyri (née Heusser; 1829–1901), author of 'Heidi'.

Another route, which will in part approximately follow the new road, is that leading due W from Zürich to (9km) *Birmensdorf*, there turning S through *Bonstetten* and *Hedingen*, both with late Gothic churches of the characteristic local type, to (10km) *Affoltern*, and then on through *Mettmenstetten*, with good wood-carvings in its church, and *Knonau*, with a late Gothic church (c 1519) and early 16C castle. At (13km) *Cham*, on the N bank of the *Zuger See*, with a Baroque church and the chapel (on Carolingian foundations) of its castle, we bear left along the shore to (5km) **Zug**.

Following the No. 4 SW from Zürich, which skirts the lower slope of a long ridge, at 10km industrial **Adliswil** (16,400 inhab.) is by-passed. The road later passes below the *Albishorn* (913m) to approach (13km) *Sihlbrugg*.

4.5km NW, at **Kappel**, is a notable Cistercian *Abbey-church* (13–14C), founded in 1185 and colonised from Hauterive (Fribourg). It contains 14C glass and wall-paintings and late 13C stalls; the conventual dependencies have been secularised. A monument on the Hausen road (to the N) commemorates the *Battle of Kappel* (1531), a sanguinary defeat for the Protestants, in which Zwingli, aged 47, was killed.
   For the road from Sihlbrugg to the *Ägerisee* see Rte 25A.

We shortly fork left through **Baar** (also by-passed), a textile town of 15,200 inhab., with a *Rathaus* of 1676 and a quaint Romanesque church-tower with a 17C cupola, to enter the N outskirts of Zug itself.
   ZUG (425m; 21,600 inhab.; 11,100 in 1930; 4800 in 1880), pron. Tsoug, the capital of its canton, with several factories in its vicinity, preserves its picturesque old centre to the S of the more modern town. Well sited at the foot of the *Zugerberg*, a high wooded plateau rising to 1039m, it overlooks the **Zuger See**, 14km long and some 4.5km wide, with an area of 38.3km^2, the S bank of which is commanded by the Rigi; see Rte 22B.

The early history of Zug is shrouded in mist, although some have assumed it to be Roman *Tugium*. Its canton, the smallest of the Confederation, consists of the districts immediately surrounding its lake and the Ägerisee to the SE; and its name has been fancifully derived from 'Fischzug', meaning 'a haul of fish', but the word *Zug* is notoriously one of the most varied in meaning in the language. It was bought by the Habsburgs in 1273 and part of it was pledged as a marriage-gift for Edward I's daughter, Joanna, betrothed to Hartmann of Habsburg (son of Rudolf I), but his death in 1281 preceded the marriage. The battle of Morgarten (1315) was fought on the territory of Zug and in 1385 the canton joined the league of Swabian cities against Leopold, so that it shared also in the victory of Sempach in 1386. Zug resisted the Reformation and in 1843 joined the reactionary Sonderbund. Louis-Philippe d'Orléans and his sister Adélaïde spent part of their exile here. In 1435, 1594 and again in 1887 it suffered from landslides. Its 'Kirschwasser' enjoys some reputation, as do the local 'Zuger Rötel' (red trout).

At the S end of the Bahnhofstrasse, the main thoroughfare, is the Post-Platz, with Cantonal Offices, etc. overlooking a lakeside promenade, which provides a view of the peaks of the Bernese Oberland as well as of the Rigi and Pilatus. Continuing S, the once-walled enceinte or 'Dorf' is entered, four towers of which are preserved on the hillside, together with a short stretch of wall. In the centre is the Kolinplatz (with a memorial to Peter Kolin, who fell at Arbedo in 1422; cf.), overlooked by an ancient gateway and watch-tower, the *Zeitturm* (its blue and white painted tiles being the colours of the canton). Passing through the Zeitturm we enter the *ALTSTADT, with a number of quaint old houses of the 16C onwards, some well-restored, including the **Rathaus**, with woodwork of 1507.

To the N of the Aegeristrasse (leading E from the Kolinplatz) is the *Chapel* of a Capuchin nunnery (1595), approached by a covered stairway, and containing an Entombment of the same date by Denys Calvaert. A short distance beyond is the *Kapuzinerturm* of 1526.

To the SE, at a higher level, stands *St. Oswald (1478–1515), dedicated to St. Oswald of Northumbria (died 642), some of whose relics were brought to Zug at the time of its foundation. There are curious sculptures on the buttresses, while its fine choir-stalls are dated 1492. The whole is under restoration.

A few paces further uphill is the entrance to the *Burg, the 13C residence of the Habsburg bailiffs, partly half-timbered and recently restored with taste to house what is one of the more attractive of the smaller cantonal *Museums*. It is surrounded by a circle of crenellated walls and inner moat. In the basement are late 15C statues by Ulrich Rosenstein from St. Oswald; an altar of 1525 by Lienhard Rihiner, and several fine silver and gold reliquaries, etc. A lift ascends to the top floor and an attic housing archaeological collections; other rooms (as we descend) contain collections of arms and armour, models and maquettes, and maps and plans explaining the history of the Burg and of Zug itself; costumes, furniture, stoves, and pewter, stained-glass, and portraits, including some by Johannes Brandenburg (1661–1729) and J.K. Moos (1774–1835), both natives of Zug.

A short distance S is the *Pulverturm*, NE of which is the *Huwiler-turm*. Several other streets of the older town deserve exploration for the imposing mansions they contain.

For the road S, skirting the E bank of the lake, see Rte 25A.

Circling the N end of the Zuger See through *Cham* (see above), we bear away from the lake, on the W bank of which, on a promontory, stands the castle of *Buonas*.—Although the No. 4 continues SW direct to Lucerne through *Gisikon* (near which was fought a battle during the 'Sonderbund War' of 1847, which led to the capture of Lucerne by the Federal troops), later skirting the *Rooter Berg* (840m), it is preferable to join the motorway some 3.5km SW of Cham. This is followed for 5.5km, with a view ahead of the Rigi, bearing SW at the exit to (2km) *Küssnacht*, for which, and for the road hence along the N arm of Lake Lucerne, with the Pilatus rising ahead and the Bürgenstock on the far bank to the S, see Rte 22B in reverse.—For (14km) **Lucerne** itself see Rte 21.

25   Zürich to Andermatt, or the Gotthardtunnel

A. Via Zug, Schwyz and Altdorf

Total distance, 109km (67 miles). No. 4. 29km **Zug**—No. 25.
17km—No. 4. 9km **Schwyz**—4km. **Brunnen** lies 2km W—No. 2.
16km **Altdorf**—6km. Turn right for 1km onto N2. 22km
Göschenen—No. 2. 5km **Andermatt**. Remain on the N2 for the
Gotthardtunnel.

Maps: M 216, 217; BL 32, 33, 37, 38, or 5001, 5008, 5011.

For the first part of this road see Rte 24, above.

From (23km) the *Sihlbrugg* crossroads a road leads S via *Unterägeri* to (21km)
Sattel, 9km N of Schwyz. This climbs towards *Schönbrunn*, once noted for its
springs, from which the stalactite caverns known as the *Höllgrotten*, in the gorge
of the *Lorzenlobel* to the NW, may be visited. The road passes close to *Menzingen*
(left), with a church of 1625.—*Unterägeri* (729m), an industrial village and resort,
lies at the foot of the little *Ägerisee* (7.2km²), the E bank of which we skirt past
Oberägeri, with the *Rossberg* (1580m) rising to the SW to reach a monument
commemorating the *Battle of Morgarten*, a decisive defeat inflicted in 1315 by
the Confederates upon Duke Leopold of Austria, the first victory of the Swiss over
their Habsburg overlords. The road climbs over a ridge (views) to a left-hand
turning for *Sattel*; see Rte 25B.

Driving S from Zug along the E bank of its lake, with the Rigi rising
steeply ahead beyond its S shore, at 13.5km we enter *Arth*, with a
church of 1695 retaining its Gothic tower, and turn left for adjacent
Goldau. The former village and its adjacent hamlets were entirely
destroyed by a huge landslide on 2 September 1806, when part of the
Rossberg (NE; 1580m) fell away after heavy rains; some of the
desolation caused is plainly seen where the face of the mountain bears
the scar, and the valley is strewn with boulders, since covered with
trees and vegetation. The present village is a lower terminus of the
cogwheel railway to a point not far from the *Rigi-Kulm*; see Rte 22B.
   One may follow either the No. 2 SE along the S bank of the nearby
Lauerzer See, or the N4 motorway skirting the N bank of the lake,
somewhat diminished in size by the landslip, which caused a wave
high enough to sweep over the islet of *Schwanau*.—**Schwyz** (see Rte
25B) lies 3km SE of the lake, where we briefly join the motorway,
making our exit 3km further S for **Brunnen**; see Rte 22B. The lakeside
town is also by-passed by the motorway, which here pierces a buttress
of the *Fronalpstock* to merge with the *Axenstrasse* after 2km, for which
see Rte 22B likewise.
   At 12km the turning is reached which joins the road to the N2, which
drives S up the valley of the Reuss and parallel to the No. 2 as far as
Amsteg; see below. We continue ahead to (2km) Altdorf.
   ALTDORF (458m; 8200 inhab.), capital of the mountainous canton
of *Uri*, one-tenth of which is covered by glaciers, is mainly famous as
being the place where, traditionally, William Tell shot the apple from
his son's head, and the legend and cult is strongly impressed on the
history of the canton. Although there were several 'Tell' ballads, etc.,
known in the last decades of the 15C, the first printed version was in
Etterlin's 'Chronicle' of 1507. Schiller's version dates from 1804.

Uri was one of the Forest Cantons foremost in the struggle for independence, being in fact the first Swiss district to assume the form of a canton. It clung tenaciously to its old faith at the Reformation. It held considerable possessions in the valleys of the Ticino until forced out of them after the declaration of the Helvetic republic in 1798. It was also the theatre of the memorable campaign of 1799 (when Altdorf itself experienced a destructive fire), in which the armies of France, Austria and Russia, dispossessing each other by turns, fought and manoeuvred in its lofty mountain passes.

A colossal bronze *Statue* of Tell, by Kissling (1895), stands in the central RATHAUSPLATZ at the foot of a modernised 13C tower, which is said to mark the site of the lime tree to which the child was bound and on which Gessler's cap was hung. To the NW stands the *Church of St. Martin* rebuilt 1810, containing a Descent from the Cross by Denys Calvaert of 1600. To the NE, at a higher level, is a *Capuchin friary*, founded 1579 and the oldest in Switzerland. The *Bannwald* on the hillside is preserved to protect the town from the avalanches which threaten it every spring. A few minutes' walk SE from the central square is the mid 16C *Jauch Haus*, with a stepped gable, which was Gen. Suvarov's headquarters in 1799. There is a regional *Museum* at Gotthardstrasse 18, to the S.

At *Seedorf*, on the far side of the motorway, is the small castle of *A Pro*, a ruined 13C tower and a quaint old nunnery, beyond which rises the *Uri-Rotstock* (2928m; see Rte 22A).—SW of Altdorf lies *Attinghausen*, the birthplace of Walter Fürst, one of the three conspirators of the Rütli (cf.); it gives its name to an ancient family whose castle ruins remain. Baron Werner of Attinghausen figures in Schiller's 'William Tell'.

From Altdorf to *Engelberg* via the *Surenenpass*; see Rte 22A. For the road over the *Klausenpass* to *Glarus* and *Näfels* see Rte 32 in reverse.

Bürglen, a village picturesquely perched on a knoll by this latter road 2km SE of Altdorf, is the traditional birthplace of William Tell. The chapel of 1582 said to occupy the site of his house was decorated in 1758 with paintings of his exploits. The late 17C church stands above a Romanesque crypt; the 13C tower, at a lower level, was the residence of the bailiffs of the Fraumünster in Zürich, of which Bürglen was once a fief. It is the base for ascents of the *Rossstock* (NE; 2461m), the *Bälmeten* (2414m) and *Hoch Fulen* (2506m), both to the S; from the last one may descend to the NE to *Unterschächen*; see Rte 32.

The No. 2 skirts *Schattdorf* and ascends the narrowing valley, with the *Bristen* (3072m) rising ahead, to (7km) *Erstfeld*, above which, in 1962, workmen excavating for an avalanche barrier unearthed a remarkable Celtic gold Treasure (c 400 BC; now in the National Museum, Zürich), probably lost or hidden by a trader crossing the Gotthardpass.—To the W opens the ERSTFELDERTAL, the torrent of which descends from a tarn below the *Schlossberg* (3133m), *Gross Spannort* (3198m) and *Krönten* (3108m); see also Rte 22A.

The road now climbs more steeply below the rocky wall of the *Windgälle*, rising to 3188m above *Silenen*, with castle ruins; those of *Zwing-Uri* are not far beyond.—7km *Amsteg*, a village at the foot of the MADERANERTAL, with its numerous waterfalls, in which the Kärstelenbach descends from the great *Hüfifirn*, between the peaks of the Windgälle and Bristen.

Several ascents may be made and passes crossed from the hamlet of *Bristen* itself, beyond which the road ends, or from *Balmenschachen*, overlooked by the *Gross-Ruchen* (3138m), some distance further up the valley. From Balmenschachen the *Hüfi Hut* is approached, at the foot of the *Düssi* (3256m) and near the *Hüfi Glacier*, remarkable for the purity of its ice and the beauty of its ice-fall. A track ascends SE from Balmenschachen to circle E of the *Fruttstock* (2838m) to approach via the BRUNNITAL and its glacier, the high *Brunnipass* (2739m), for *Disentis*; see Rte 38. the *Oberalpstock* (3328m) is ascended from the col.—From where the road ends the wild ETZLITAL, to the S, may be climbed to the easy *Chrüzlipass* (2347m), which was traversed by the Russo-Austrian army in 1799, descending thence to *Sedrun*; see Rte 38.

At Amsteg it is preferable to join the motorway, which threads several tunnels below the Bristen, with a view S up the FELLITAL, rich in crystals. At the head of the Fellital is the *Fellilücke pass* (2478m), above the *Oberalppass* (2044m); see Rte 38.

Below, in the REUSS VALLEY, toil the old main road and the railway line, the latter shortly entering the first and longest of a series of remarkable spiral tunnels (the *Pfaffensprung* or 'parson's leap'; 1476m long), which, with a number of viaducts, enable it to coil and climb rapidly—some 562m in 8 km. At 10km we pass (right) *Wassen*, with its conspicuous 18C church, at the E end of the road (No. 11) ascending the MEIENTAL to the *Sustenpass*; see Rte 20.—At 4km the exit for *Göschenen* and **Andermatt** is reached; see below.

The motorway now enters the *Gotthardtunnel*, completed in 1980 after eleven years work, and the longest road tunnel in the world (16.3km). This remarkable engineering achievement provides an essential winter crossing of the range, when the *St. Gotthardpass* is closed to traffic. At its S entrance lies *Airola*, in the upper VALLE LEVENTINA; see Rte 41.

Göschenen (1106m) is a straggling village built at the foot of the Göschenertal (see below), and at the N entrance also of the *St. Gotthard railway tunnel*, almost 15km long and pierced with great difficulty (and with the loss of 277 lives) during the years 1872–82. A monument in the cemetery commemorates these navvies and Louis Favre (died 1879), the chief contractor. On the approach lines there are some 80 tunnels with a combined length of 46km, together with 324 bridges of over 10m span! The traffic is so dense at times that another longer tunnel is projected, at a lower level and further E.

A road ascends the wild GÖSCHENERTAL to the W to (10km) the *Göscheneralpsee* reservoir, beyond which rises the *Dammastock* (3630m). Immediately W of this is the head of the *Rhône Glacier*, together with other peaks of the Winterberg range; while to the NW of the road at the head of the *Flachenstein Firn* rises the *Sustenhorn* (3503m); see Rte 20.

The road climbs steeply from Göschenen to (5km) Andermatt through the deep and gloomy defile of the *Schöllenen* (so-named from the rock-steps or '*scaliones*' of the old bridle-path), the lofty granite walls of which leave only just sufficient room for the road and light railway. We later traverse a rock gallery to reach the *Devil's Bridge* (*Teufelsbrücke*) of 1955, spanning the chasm above the level of the bridge of 1830 to the right. The new bridge cuts out a hairpin bend as it carries us back to the right bank of the Reuss, the falls of which are best seen from the old bridge. Below the latter is a fragment of its 15C predecessor, destroyed in 1799. Just short of the old bridge, to the left, a Greek cross hewn in the rock, with a Russian inscription, commemorates Suvarov's campaign of 1799, when the gorge was twice contested within six weeks. A little further on (fine retrospective views) the road threads a defile by a rock gallery known as the *Urnerloch* ('Hole of Uri'), pierced by Pietro Moretini in 1707. Prior to this, the road was carried on hazardous plank galleries built over the cliff-side! The first wheeled carriage to cross the St. Gotthard, in 1775, was the phaeton of an Englishman, Charles Greville, who apparently spent 18 louis paying a gang of men to help him over the steeper sections; see also p 305.

Passing several masked fortifications and barracks, and the old church of *St. Columba*, mentioned in 766 but rebuilt on its present site in the 16–17C, and with a stone pulpit of 1559, we enter **Andermatt** (1447m), with an attractive main street, likely to be crowded in summer.

The Baroque *Parish Church* of 1695 (between the Unter Reuss and the main street, near the stone-built *Rathaus* of 1559) contains a font of 1582 from St. Columba's. The chapel of *Mariahilf* (1740), on a hillock above the village, commands a good view, and a path hence leads SE to the *Gurschenbach Falls*.

To the SW, on the slopes of the *St. Annaberg*, are trenches and embankments against avalanches.—To the S rises the *Gemsstock* (2961m), a fine view-point reached by cable-car; while to the SE rises the *Badus* (2928m); and to the NE the steep zigzagging road climbs to the *Oberalppass* (2044m).

The resort is also an important defensive strongpoint at a strategic crossroads of Alpine passes, and also on the railway between Disentis and Brig, and several walks in the vicinity may be marked *'verboten'* for military reasons. It lies in the wide URSERENTAL (one which D.H. Lawrence found 'terribly raw and flat and accidental'), the lower part probably a lake within comparatively recent times, but even in pre-Roman days it must have been an important route between the Grisons and the Valais, and the Romans included the latter in the province of Rhaetia (AD 15). Its Christianisation took place early and the inhabitants, at first Romanised Celts, mixing later with Germans from Uri and the Valais, were ruled by imperial bailiffs, an office for a time held by the Habsburgs. The opening of the St. Gotthard Pass in c 1200 led eventually to an alliance between Urseren and Uri (1410), since when the valley has shared the fortunes of that canton.

For roads hence to **Chur**, **Bellinzona** and the **St. Gotthard Pass** itself, and **Brig**, see Rtes 38, 41 and 45 respectively, in reverse.

B. Via Einsiedeln, Schwyz and Altdorf

Total distance, 119km (74 miles). No. 3. 21km *Wädenswil*—5km *Richterswil*—6km *Biberbrugg*. **Einsiedeln** lies 6km SE.—No. 8. 21km **Schwyz**—4km. **Brunnen** lies 2km W.—No. 2. 16km **Altdorf**—6km. Turn left for 1km onto N2.—22km *Göschenen*—No. 2. 5km **Andermatt**. Remain on the N2 for the *Gotthardtunnel*.

Maps: M 215, 217; BL 32, 33, 37, 38, or 5001, 5008, 5011.

For the lakeside road to *Richterswil*, see Rte 31A.

The recommended road is the N3 motorway driving S from Zürich and swinging SE parallel to the No. 3 until reaching, at 30km, the exit (immediately after a tunnel) for Schwyz and Einsiedeln. Here we climb S, after some 6km reaching crossroads at *Biberbrugg*, and turn SE along the valley of the ALPBACH.

The first right-hand turning leads 4km to the large village of *Einsiedeln* (905m), of no intrinsic interest; indeed it has been described as 'of miscellaneous ugliness'. In the 1830s it already had '55 inns and 20 alehouses ... The best is the Ox, celebrated for its extortionate charges, especially during the pilgrimage'. It is therefore preferable to continue ahead at this turning, with a view of the snow-capped peaks of the Glärnisch range, and take the next turning, which leads directly to the huge Benedictine ***Monastery of Einsiedeln**.

It derives its name from the '*Einsiedler*' (hermits) who founded it in 934, the first of whom was a certain Meinrad, who is said to have retired to this wilderness c 828, bringing with him the little 'black Virgin' that had been given to him by a neighbouring abbess. He was murdered by robbers in 861, who were brought to justice in Zürich through their pursuit by the hermit's croaking ravens. It is said that when Conrad of Konstanz was about to consecrate the church in 948 he was aroused at midnight by angelic minstrels and was next day informed by a heavenly voice that in fact it had already been consecrated by Christ. Pope Leo VIII pronounced this a true miracle and by a papal bull (964) blessed the pilgrimage to Einsiedeln. The abbots became princes of the Empire and the monastery was protected successively by the counts of Rapperswil, the Habsburgs and the house of Schwyz. It was sacked in 1314 by the herdsmen of Schwyz, which precipitated Habsburg intervention at Morgarten the following year.

'Paracelsus' (1493–1541) is believed to have been born at Einsiedeln (where his father was a physician) prior to moving to Villach in Austria in 1502. Zwingli was parish priest here in 1516–18 and his experiences perhaps influenced his resolution to reform. Gibbon, who visited the place in 1755, was 'astonished by the profuse ostentation of riches in the poorest corner of Europe; amidst a savage scene of woods and mountains, a palace appears to have been erected by magic: and it was erected by the potent magic of religion'. In 1775 it was visited by Goethe. In 1798 the French revolutionary army plundered the place, but the monks carried off their precious image into the Tyrol for safe-keeping.

The organ of the Klosterkirche at Einsiedeln

The monastery, rebuilt in 1704–70 to the designs of Caspar Moosbrugger of Vorarlberg (died 1723), who had been a lay brother since 1681, is remarkable for its size and situation in this hill-girt basin rather than for its architecture, characteristic of the South German taste of the period. The present edifice is in fact the sixth or seventh raised on this spot since its foundation, the others having been destroyed by fires.

From the Klosterplatz, laid out in 1749, with its *Baroque Fountain* and sweep of arcades, a flight of steps flanked by statues by J.-B. Babel of Otho the Great and Heinrich II, by whose donations the monastery greatly benefited, rises to the convex *West Front*. In the centre of the stark 140m-long facade rise the twin towers (spires in a former building); while between the towers stands a colossal statue of the Virgin and child. In the richly decorated octagonal nave, with stuccowork and pulpit by Egid Quirin Assam, stands the black marble *Lady Chapel* or *Gnadenkapelle* (rebuilt in 1807 after Solari's original had been demolished by the French), containing the late 15C image of the Virgin and child (replacing the smoke-blackened Romanesque statue consumed by a fire in 1465). Notable in the interior are the frescoes painted by Cosmas Damian Assam; two altars painted and decorated by the Carlone brothers; the organ-cases at the crossing, by Babel (1749; organ modern); the wrought-iron choir screen, and the carved stalls by Michael Hartmann of Lucerne. The pink rococo *Choir* itself was re-modelled after 1746 by Franz Anton Kraus, who also painted the Assumption.

The *Fürstensaal*, with its pink, yellow and white decoration, on an upper floor of dependencies entered from the courtyard to the right of the building, is of slight interest. Regrettably, the important *Library*, decorated by J.A. Feuchtmayer, containing about 1300 MSS and 1200 incunables, is rarely open.

Travellers continuing E may regain the No. 3 at (21.5km) *Siebnen*, by crossing the *Sihlsee reservoir* by a viaduct and the *Sattelegg pass* (1190m), beyond which a minor road turns S to the *Wägitaler See*.

From *Unteriberg*, 11km SE of Einsiedeln, one may continue S to *Weglosen* (overlooked by the *Druesberg*; 2282m), from which cable-cars ascend; or by turning SW through *Oberiberg*, may follow a rough road W, later climbing down to *Schwyz*.

Another road leads SW from Einsiedeln to *Alpthal*, beyond which, at *Brunni*, a cable-car (and path) ascends from below the *Klein Mythen* (1811m) and *Gross Mythen* (1899m). SE of the last is the *Rotenflue* (1571m), to which another cable-car mounts from *Rickenbach*, just SE of Schwyz.—A bridle-path also climbs SW from Alpthal to a pass (1414m) at *Haggenegg*, N of the Klein Mythen, thence descending to Schwyz.

Regaining the No. 8 at *Biberbrugg* (6km NW of Einsiedeln), we turn left, climbing to and traversing an upland plateau with a turf-cutting industry, through (7.5km) *Rothenthurm*, a village taking its name from a 13C tower of reddish stone, the relic of a rampart thrown up by the Schwyzers on their frontier. To the left is seen the hamlet of *Biberegg*, cradle of the Reding family which in the 18C boasted 17 generals in foreign service; it was Alois Reding (1765–1808), who in 1798 led his mountaineers against the French and their supporters in this neighbourhood.

We shortly descend to (4.5km) *Sattel*. To the W rises the *Rossberg* (1580m; see *Goldau*); to the SE, the Mythen group (see above); to the SW, the Rigi (cf.). The road provides several fine views ahead as we circle to the S above *Steinen*, birthplace of Werner von Stauffacher of the Rütli Oath (cf.), with a church in part dating from 1318.

9km **SCHWYZ** (516m; 12,000 inhab.; 6500 in 1880), the ancient

capital of its canton, situated at the foot of the symmetrical peaks of
the Mythen (the mitre), and which gives its name to Switzerland, is
a town of some character, preserving numerous 16–18C patrician
mansions.

The inhabitants of this Forest Canton, uniting in 1144 and 1206 with those of Uri
and Nidwalden, formed the earliest basis of the Confederation, later confirmed
at Rütli (cf.). The men of Schwyz were prominent in the popular insurrection of
1 January 1308 and on the field of Morgarten (1315), which took place some 12km
N of the town. It was after this latter success that Helvetia took the name of
Switzerland and the confederates of the three cantons became generally known
as 'Schwyzers'. It was also one of the main recruiting grounds for Swiss
mercenaries during several centuries. In 1798, together with other Forest
Cantons, it was fought over by Austrians, Russians and French.

Above the central town square stands the imposing parish church of
*St. Martin, erected in 1769–74 by the brothers Jakob and Johann
Anton Singer on the site of several predecessors, the earliest dating
back to c 730. Its Baroque interior is tasteful, with a good organ-case
of 1780 by J.F. Schillinger and a Baroque pulpit. In the churchyard
is a two-storeyed ossuary.

On the other side of the square is the *Rathaus* of 1645, altered in the
18C, and daubed with murals; its elaborately decorated council-
chamber contains good marquetry.—Behind it is a 12C *Tower*,
formerly housing archives (see below), and now local antiquities.—Another *Museum* may be visited not far NE of the church, in
a house once belonging to the Reding family.—In the Herrengasse,
W of the church, is the *Kapuzinerkloster*, founded in 1585; a
Dominican nunnery had been founded in Schwyz in 1272. On the
hillside to the N is the former Jesuit monastery of *Maria-Hilf*, now a
seminary.

In the Bahnhofstrasse, leading SW from the square, is the *Tourist
Office*, which supplies a plan pin-pointing the numerous impressive
16–18C residences in the neighbourhood.

A short walk along this street brings one to the **Bundesbriefarchiv**
(or *Swiss Federal Archives*), in a building of 1936. Here one may
inspect the numerous original charters, agreements, etc., not only of
the canton of Schwyz, but also of several other cantons which over the
centuries were to form the Confederation as we now know it. These
include the 'Freiheitsbrief' or Grant of privileges to the inhabitants of
Schwyz of 1240, in which the Emperor Frederick II declared them
'immediate' subjects of the Holy Roman Empire, and therefore free
of control of lesser rulers, and it was to defend this right that the Pact
of 1291 was made (cf. Rütli). Also to be seen is a collection of banners
and flags of Schwyz, including those claimed to have been flown at
Morgarten (1315), Laupen (1339) and Sempach (1386), apart from
several others. A complete list (and explanation in English) may be
requested.

From the nearby village of *Rickenbach*, to the SE, a cable-car ascends to a point
below the *Gross Mythen*, also approached by a safe bridle-path (even if
overlooking precipices). The *Uri-Rotstock* (2818m), to the SW, is the nearest of
the snow mountains conspicuous from the Mythen.

A road ascending S from Schwyz leads SE up the MUOTATAL past (right) the
lower terminus of the funicular to *Stoos* (1275m), from which cable-cars and
chair-lifts rise towards the summit of the *Fronalpstock* (1922m), providing a view
almost as extensive as that from the Rigi, and from which a path descends S
towards *Riemenstalden*; see Rte 22B.—At the village of *Muotathal* itself is a
rococo church of 1790 and 17C conventual buildings. It was down this valley that

Suvarov made a desperate attempt to force a way from Altdorf to meet up with the Russian army at Zürich on 27–28 September 1799, but the trackless E shore of the Urner See barred his progress, and his army was obliged to 'march' over the *Chinzig-Chulm* (2073m) via the HÜRITAL which offers a route to Altdorf for good walkers.—The road climbs SE up the BISISTAL to approach the *Waldibachfall* at the head of the valley, below the *Alpler Horn* (W; 2380m), and the *Jegerstöck* (2573m), to the E, near which a cable-car ascends to the *Glattensee*.—Another road climbs E from Muotathal to the *Pragelpass* (1550m) for *Richisau* and the KLÖNTAL, W of *Glarus*; see Rte 32.

The main road from Schwyz leads SW to meet the N4 after 4km, immediately E of **Brunnen**, for which, and for the *Axenstrasse* to **Altdorf** and on to **Andermatt**, see Rtes 22B and 25A.

26 Zürich to Schaffhausen

A. Via Winterthur

Total distance, 53km (33 miles). No 1. 24km **Winterthur**—No. 15. 29km **Schaffhausen**.

Maps: M 216; BL 27, 28, or 5010.

Following the motorway, drive NE from Zürich. At 22km it approaches the centre of *Winterthur*, but then bear to the right after passing under the railway bridge. Turn left along the Graben to reach the wide Stadthausstrasse, with the Lindstrasse leading N.

WINTERTHUR (439m; 88,750 inhab.; 53,900 in 1930), a thriving industrial town, and with important collections of paintings, was founded at the end of the 3C as *Vitudurum*, the site of the Roman fort being at Ober-Winterthur, to the NE. It was famous for the decorated faïence stoves or poêles manufactured here in the 17–18C. This later gave way to textiles and then the Sulzer locomotives. The *Schweizerische Lokomotiv Fabrik* was founded by Charles Brown, an Englishman.

It was a Habsburg stronghold for two centuries, but was sold to Zürich in 1467, although its chartered liberties were reserved. Its musical society, the *Collegium Musicum*, was founded in 1629.

Among its natives were the artists Johann Ludwig Aberli (1723–86), Anton Graff (1736–1813), Heinrich Rieter (1751–1818), Johann Jakob Biedermann (1763–1830) and Max Bill (1908–); Johann Georg Sulzer (1720–79), the writer on aesthetics; Heinrich Wölfflin (1864–1945), the art historian; and Oskar Reinhart (1885–1965).

Flanking the N side of the Stadthausstrasse is the ***Oskar Reinhart Foundation**, inaugurated in 1951, housed in a building of 1842. GROUND FLOOR: Prints and engravings, including several by *Claude Lorrain*, *Jan Both*, *Joseph Anton Koch*, *Nicolas Berchem*, *Karel Dujardin* and *Ferdinand Olivier*. Note also the bust of Oskar Reinhart by *Otto Charles Bähninger*.

FIRST FLOOR. Rooms to the right: *Fuseli*, three watercolours, and Jealousy; *Wolfgang-Adam Töepffer*, Self-portrait, and other works; *Jacques-Laurent Agasse*, Self-portrait with dog, Westminster Bridge, Children playing, Halt of the mail-coach near Portsmouth, etc.; *Jean-Étienne Liotard*, Self-portrait, and other works; *Édouard Castres*,

Bourbaki's retreating army, etc.; *Alexandre Calame*, Landscapes; *Anton Graff*, The artist and his family, and several portraits; *Caspar Wolf*, a fine series of Landscapes; *Johann Melchior Wyrsch*, Portrait of Pierre-Étienne Fantet.

Rooms to the left: *Wilhelm von Kobell* (1766–1855), Equestrian scenes; *Caspar David Friedrich* (1774–1840), Landscapes, including The cliff; *Franz Krüger* (1797–1857), Prussian outriders in the snow; *Rudolf Friedrich Wasmann* (1805–86), several Portraits; *Ferdinand Georg Waldmüller* (1793–1865), several Landscapes, and Portrait of Anna, Countess Kinsky, among others; *Friedrich Gauermann* (1807–62), Landscape in the Salzkammergut; *Jakob Alt* (1789–1872), Stift Melk; *Ferdinand Olivier* (1785–1841), St. Peter's Cemetery, Salzburg; and watercolours by *Moritz von Schwind* (1804–71) and *Julius Schnorr von Carolsfeld* (1794–1872).

SECOND FLOOR: *Ferdinand Hodler*, Self-portrait, Portrait of Mlle Duchosal, and several Landscapes and other works; *Giovanni Giacometti*, View in Rome, The artist's daughter, etc.; *Alexandre Blanchet* (1882–1961), Portrait of Oskar Reinhart in 1943; *Arnold Böcklin*, The artist's wife, and other canvases; *Albert Anker*, The artist's daughter, Louise, Market at Murten, and other works; *Karl Hofer* (1878–1955), Self-portrait, and Portrait of Theodor Reinhart (1849–1919), the father of Oskar Reinhart, in 1907; *Barthélemy Menn*, Portrait of Louise Gauthier, and other works; *Hans Sturzenegger*, Self-portrait, and portraits of Éduard Morstadt and of his Aunt.

To the N, on the far side of gardens, stands the **Kunstmuseum**, or municipal art gallery. The building also contains *Natural History* collections, a *Numismatic* collection, relief models, and the *Library*. Notable among the paintings are: *Fuseli*, Titania; *J.J. Biedermann*, The Pissevache-Fall; *Kokoschka*, Portrait of Dr Hugo Caro; *Hodler*, Self-portrait, and The Wetterhorn; *Henri Rousseau*, Child and puppet; *Hans Asper*, Portrait of Zwingli; *Van Gogh*, Summer evening near Arles; Portraits by *Anton Graff*; *Brancusi*, Bust of Mlle Pogany; and *Fritz Huf*, Bust of Rainer Maria Rilke.

Also listed among their holdings are a Christ by *Quentin Massys* and representative works by G. *Giacometti, Vallatton, Bonnard, Braque, Marquet, Monet, Pissarro, Renoir, Vuillard, Waldmüller, Lovis Corinth* and 20C Swiss artists.

Immediately E of the Lindstrasse is the *Stadthaus* of 1868 by Gottfried Semper; and a short distance further E, the *Heimatmuseum*, largely of local interest.—Hence one may return W, parallel to the Stadthausstrasse, by following the Obertor and Marktgasse, the main thoroughfare (now a pedestrian precinct) of the older town, in which stands the *Rathaus*, containing the *Kellenberger Horological Collection* and a small collection of art, mostly of the Dutch School.

A few paces S stands the *Stadtkirche*, largely 1264–1515, with a tall belfry of a later date, but it is a building of slight interest. The Baroque organ-case is by J.-A. Feuchtmayer.

Without doubt, the most interesting and important object of a visit to Winterthur is the private collection of art assembled by Oskar Reinhart at **'Am Römerholz'**. This is some distance N of the centre, approached by turning right off the Lindstrasse into the Albanistrasse, and following the signposts.

Here, in his former residence, built in 1915 and later extended, is the Reinhart Collection, which was donated to the Swiss Confederation in 1958 on condition that the paintings were neither loaned, sold, nor added to through purchase or by further donations. Clara Haskil, the pianist, found a welcome refuge here during the Second World War.

Lucas Cranach the Elder, Anna Putsch, wife of Dr Johannes Cuspinian

Among the more remarkable works in the collection are (in approximate order of display, for the collector did not necessarily observe chronological or geographical order): 116, *Renoir*, Nude; 125, *Utrillo*, Snow on the Moulin de la Galette; 181, an early 16C Tournai tapestry of the Shepherd's life; 60, Coronation of the Virgin (*late 14C Florentine*); *Lucas Cranach the Elder*, 36, Portraits of Dr Johannes Cuspinian, c 1503, and (37) his first wife, Anna Putsch (formerly in the collection of Charles I of England); 2, *Pieter Brueghel the Elder*, The Adoration of the Magi in the snow, 1567; 150, *Matthias Grünewald*, Woman lamenting (the hands served as a study for those of Mary at the Crucifixion on the Isenheim altarpiece); 127, *Watteau*, The light repast; 11–14, *Chardin*, The House of Cards, and Still lifes; 83, *Pieter Huys*, St. Christopher (once ascribed to Bosch); 82, *Hans Holbein the*

Younger, Portrait of Lady Elizabeth Widmerpole; 46–7, *Gerard David*, Christ on the cross, and Mary with the body of Christ; 92, *Master of St. Giles*, Portrait of Philip the Handsome, c 1496; 103, *Jan Provost*, The Resurrection; 93, *Quentin Massys*, Portrait of a man aged 51, 1509; 104, *Rembrandt*, A man in front of a furnace, c 1660; 121, Fair-haired woman (*South German*; c 1530), a pendant male portrait hangs in the National Gallery, London; 64, *Geertgen Tot Sint Jans*, Adoration of the Magi; 177, *Rodin*, Seated woman, and (178) Bust of Pope Benedict XV; 167–73, *Maillol*, early sculptures; 174–6, *Renoir*, sculptures of Mother and child, and of Washerwomen.

157–8, *Rembrandt*, ink wash drawings of Christ among the doctors, and The sacrifice of Manoah; 145–7, *Fragonard*, Studies of Don Quixote; 49, *Degas*, Ballet-dancer in her dressing-room; 151–2, *Ingres*, crayon portraits of an Unknown lady, and of Antoine Thomegueux; 154–6, *Picasso*, The harvesters' rest I and II, and Mother nursing her child; 130, *Cézanne*, Bathers; and 144, *Delacroix*, Arab guard-room.

66, *Géricault*, Gén. Letellier on his deathbed, and several Landscapes, etc. by *Courbet*; 95, *Monet*, Melting ice on the Seine; 68, *Van Gogh*, Mackerel; 16, *Constable*, Master James Heys; 94, *Millet*, Collecting apples; 148–9, *Van Gogh*, Les Saintes-Maries, and Garden in Provence; 48, *David*, Portrait of Baroness Pauline Jeanin, one of his twin daughters; part of a remarkable Collection of paintings and drawings by *Daumier*; 27, *Courbet*, The hammock, and (34) Portrait of Gustave Mathieu; 102, *Poussin*, The Roman Campagna; 86, *Claude Lorrain*, Landscape with Hagar and the angel; 84, *Ingres*, Portrait of his second wife; 17, *Constable*, Hampstead Heath; 70, *Van Gogh*, The garden of the hospital at Arles; 98, *Picasso*, Portrait of Mateu F. de Soto; 108, *Renoir*, The milliner; 5, *Cézanne*, Self-portrait, (3) Male portrait, and several Landscapes and Still Lifes; 90, *Manet*, At the café, and (89) Portrait of Mlle Marguerite de Conflans; 119, *Sisley*, Barges on the Canal St.-Martin, Paris; 114, *Renoir*, Noirmoutier; 71, *Van Gogh*, The hospital at Arles (interior), and (69) Mme Augustine Roulin; 123, *Toulouse-Lautrec*, The female clown; 67, *Géricault*, A madman with military propensities; 105, *Renoir*, Arum and conservatory plants; 26, *Corot*, View of Dunkirk; 28, *Courbet*, Sleeping woman; 118, *Rubens*, Lady with a puppy; 109, *Renoir*, Portrait of M. Chocquet, and (110) of Mme Henriot, 113, Reclining nude (in a bad state), 106, The Seine near Paris, and 111, Confiding; 51, *Delacroix*, Greece expiring on the ruins of Missolonghi (sketch for the painting at Bordeaux); 20, *Corot*, Rochefort, 22, Château-Thierry, 19, Harbour in Brittany, and 23, Young girl reading; 63, *Gauguin*, Blue roofs, Rouen; 99–100, *Pissarro*, Landscapes near Pontoise; 120, *Sisley*, At the foot of the Louveciennes aqueduct; 72, *Goya*, Card-players, 74, Portrait of a youth, and (77) of José Pio de Molina, 75–6, Still-lifes; 87, *Eugenio Lucas*, Corrida; 78, *El Greco*, Portrait of the Card.-Inquisitor Fernando Niño de Guevara (a study for the larger portrait in the Metropolitan Museum); 80, *Hals*, Boy reading, and (81) Fisherboy; 117, *Rubens*, sketch for a painting of the Publius Decius Mus series at Vaduz; 73, *Goya*, The washerwoman.

In Frauenfelderstrasse, Oberwinterthur, is the *Technorama der Schweiz*, which is of interest to the scientifically minded, providing an exposition of the technical history of Switzerland from the early 19C to the present.

Some 7km S of Winterthur, approached via *Seen* and *Sennhof*, stands **Schloss Kyburg**, a 10–11C fortress preserving important collections of furniture and arms and armour. The chapel contains 13–15C frescoes. It was inherited by Rudolf of

Habsburg in 1204, and the imperial insignia was kept here from 1273 to 1424.
For the road from Winterthur to *Rapperswil*, see p 260.

Climbing N from Winterthur, the N1 is crossed at 3km, and after 8km
Andelfingen is by-passed. A group of Celtic tombs was discovered at
Andelfingen in 1911, and it has a castle overlooking the Thur. After
2.5km the No. 15 widens to become the N4, which continues N, at
10km reaching a turning for the S bank of the *Rheinfall* and *Schloss
Laufen* (see below) prior to descending to reach the Rhine at (4km)
Schaffhausen.

From the N bank of the Thur at Andelfingen a by-road bears NW via *Marthalen*
to **Rheinau**, a peninsula—once an island—on the Rhine, which here forms the
frontier with Germany, and the site of a Benedictine Abbey dating from the time
of Charlemagne, but occupied since 1867 by an asylum. The *Church*, built over
the grave of St. Fintan (died 827), an Irish missionary, is a typical Baroque
building except for the two late Gothic towers (the N a copy); in the S tower
survives a Romanesque doorway with contemporary sculptures.—The main road
may be regained by circling to the E.

SCHAFFHAUSEN (Schaffhouse in French; 34,250 inhab.; 23,100 in
1930; 12,550 in 1880), capital of its canton, is an industrial town on
the right bank of the Rhine. It preserves its characteristic old centre
in which numerous fine examples of domestic architecture survive,
many displaying decorative oriel windows, while notable among
relics of its medieval defences is the Munot, dominating the N
bridgehead of the river-crossing.

Schaffhausen grew up around the riverside wharfs erected here by the
Benedictine abbey of Allerheiligen (All Saints), founded in 1050, where freight
coming down the Rhine had to be unloaded onto waggons. By the 13C the town
had become a free imperial city. In 1501 it joined the Swiss Confederation in
order to secure itself against the Habsburgs. Its later prosperity (with that of
neighbouring *Neuhausen*, with a pioneering factory producing aluminium as
early as 1888) is largely due to the cheap turbine power generated by the Rhine,
the falls of which, to the W, were also the target for several generations of tourists
and trippers. Considerable damage was inadvertently caused here by American
bombers in April 1944.

Among its natives were the artist Tobias Stimmer (1539–84) and the historian
Johannes von Müller (1752–1809). It was here that Ruskin, as a child, had his
seminal first distant view of the Alps.

Its prosperous canton, the most northerly of the Swiss cantons and the only
one wholly N of the Rhine, forming an enclave in Germany, has a very democratic
constitution, and it was one of the pioneers of the Referendum.

Long flights of steps ascend to the cylindrical late 16C fort known as
the *Munot, the roof of which, approached by a ramp, provides a fine
view over the town. It houses a collection of arms and armour. It was
here, in 1415, having been deposed by the Council of Constance, that
the debauched Pope John XXIII was offered asylum by Friedrich of
Tyrol ('of the empty pockets').

Hence one may cross to the Bachstrasse to enter the old town by
following the Vordergasse W past No. 43, of 1653, to reach the large
five-aisled church of **St. Johann** (12–15C), recently restored. No. 61,
the *Schmiedstube*, dates from 1590, with an original portal and
corner-turret of 1653; No. 65, the *Haus zum Ritter*, has a painted
facade of 1510 (a copy; the original frescoes, by Tobias Stimmer, are
in the museum; see below); No. 73 is the *Altes Rathaus*, restored since
1944, with a panelled room of 1624.—We now reach the Fronwagplatz,
with replicas of two early 16C fountains, and the 16–17C *Grosse*

Haus (No. 24).

Hence the Vorstadt leads N past several picturesque buildings preserving their oriel windows and painted facades, notable No. 17 ('*zum Goldenen Ochsen*'; 1609), and No. 43 ('*zum Grossen Käfig*', or large cage; 1586, its facade painted in 1675), to reach the *Schwabentor*, a relic of the medieval fortifications.

A few steps W of the Fronwagplatz is the lofty *Obertor*, while to the S is the Herrenacker, a square partly destroyed in the air-raid of 1944, from which one may descend to the E to the Beckenstaube and the arcaded W front of the **Münster**, originally the church of the abbey of All Saints, consecrated in 1052 by Leo IX in person, and finished in 1104, but a rather dull Romanesque pillared basilica with a flat roof and single tower. Here formerly hung the bell cast in 1486, whose inscription ('I summon the living, mourn the dead, and quell the lightning') is said to have suggested Schiller's 'Song of the Bell' and the opening of Longfellow's 'Golden Legend'; it now stands in the charming 12C *Cloisters* adjacent.

The monastic dependencies, partly rebuilt since 1944, when several old paintings were destroyed, are entered near the W Front. They accommodate the extensive collections of the ***Allerheiligen Museum**. Among these are finds from the several prehistoric sites in the vicinity, of the Hallstatt period and from Roman times; Medieval antiquities and ecclesiastical art, including the Schaffhausen Onyx, a cameo attributed to the time of Nero; several panelled and furnished rooms are reconstructed here; fragments of the original frescoes from the Haus zum Ritter, by *Tobias Stimmer* (1570); ironwork; ceramics; costumes; MSS and old maps and plans, etc.; sections illustrative of the growth of Schaffhausen's industries, etc., and notable among the paintings, works by Stimmer.

At Baumgartenstrasse 23, a short distance S, is the *Hallen für neue Kunst*, where in a former textile factory is displayed a collection of international contemporary art. It may be visited by appointment out of season.

The 'lion' of Schaffhausen is the ***Rheinfall** or '*Laufen*', the rapids of the Rhine, still among the more impressive of the natural sites of Europe, but less so than they were prior to the erection of far too many buildings in the background when seen from the W or S. The latter viewpoint (4km) is reached by turning right off the Winterthur road to approach *Schloss Laufen*, with a gate-tower of 1546, sited on a promontory above the fall, near which are the belvederes known as the *Känzeli* and *Fischetz*, close to the foaming falls.—By following the Mühlenstrasse W from the river bank at Schaffhausen through contiguous **Neuhausen** (10,650 inhab.), and then forking left at a church (signposted) we may descend through woods to the *Schlösschen Wörth* viewpoint, from which the width of the cataract (150m) is better appreciated. The two main falls are divided by a rock pillar, and are 16 and 21m high respectively (right and left bank); the volume of water discharged is about 700 cubic metres per second, rising to almost 1100m^3 during June and July when the river is swollen by melting snow.

The excursion from the N or right bank may be extended by returning to the above-mentioned church and there turning W, shortly after forking left onto the No. 13 for (10km) **Neunkirch**, an attractive little walled town, 3km beyond which lies *Hallau*, in the vine-clad Klettgau. Not far further W we reach the river Wutach, forming the NW frontier of the canton.—Rural *Schleitheim*, some 9km

N of Neunkirch, on the site of Roman *Juliomagnus*, lies on the main road NW to (73km) *Freiburg*, in Germany.

B. Via Bülach

Total distance, 50km (31 miles). No. 4. 20km. *Bülach* lies to the right—7km *Eglisau*—23km **Schaffhausen**.

Maps: M 216; BL 27, or 5010.

Driving NE from Zürich, we shortly veer N, later passing (left) *Zürich Airport* at *Kloten* (15,850 inhab.). The motorway descends the valley of the Glatt to by-pass **Bülach** (12,300 inhab.), an industrial town with a 16C church of Carolingian foundation in its old centre.—*Regensberg*, a picturesque hilltop village, lies some 10 km SW.—We cross the Rhine at **Eglisau**, a pleasant riverside village, part of which was submerged when the water level of the Rhine was artificially raised. It preserves a few old houses in its Obergasse, and a church of Romanesque origin, with a choir of 1350 containing late 15C frescoes and a baroquised nave.—At 5km *Rafz*, retaining several ancient houses, is by-passed, to reach and briefly cross an enclave of German territory to re-enter Switzerland close to the **Rheinfall** (see above) prior to entering *Neuhausen* and contiguous **Schaffhausen**.

27 Schaffhausen to St. Margrethen (for Bregenz and the Rhine valley) via Stein am Rhein and Kreuzlingen (for Konstanz)

Total distance, 93km (58 miles). No. 13. 19km **Stein am Rhein**—27km **Kreuzlingen**—27km *Arbon*—7km **Rorschach**—13km *St. Margrethen*.

Maps: M 216; BL 28, or 5010, 5014.

Crossing to the S (left) bank of the Rhine, close to a point where in 1799 the Austrian army of the Archduke Karl crossed the river, bear left to (10km) **Diessenhofen**, an ancient little town with a covered wooden *Bridge* (on the site of its predecessor, crossed by the French in 1800 on their way to Hohenlinden). Several relics of its medieval fortifications and numerous 16–18C houses may be seen, together with its church, originally 12C, founded in the 8C.—1km W of the town is the convent of *Sankt Katharinental*, a mid 13C foundation with 18C dependencies and a Baroque church of 1735 containing a large organ-loft.

Just prior to reaching at (9.5km) *Burg* the turning for Stein am Rhein, we traverse *Wangerhausen*, with the late 11C church of a former Benedictine priory (1283–1529), with an early 12C cloister. The ruined castle of *Wolkenstein* lies further N, near *Hemishofen*.—On a hillock just NE of the crossroads at Burg are remains of a Roman castrum.

*Stein am Rhein is a quaint old—and once fortified—town on the N bank of the river, here another small Swiss enclave. The river is spanned by a modern bridge replacing the old wooden structure. The town, very popular with trippers, consists largely of the RATHAUSPLATZ and Hauptstrasse, in which are preserved numerous painted or half-timbered houses of the 16–17C, with their oriel windows, providing several picturesque views. The 12C church contains early 15C murals in its choir; the tower dates from 1596. Adjacent are buildings of the former Benedictine abbey of *Sankt-Georgen*, founded in 1005 and secularised in 1526. It has been restored to house a *Museum* of antiquities; several rooms are decorated with frescoes by Ambrosius Holbein and Thomas Schmid, and with 16C wood-carving.—Conspicuous above the town is *Schloss Hohenklingen* (591m; view), formerly that of the feudal lords of Stein.

At 1km the village of *Eschenz*, possibly the *Tasgetium* of Ptolemy, with an 18C church, is traversed.

FROM ESCHENZ TO FRAUENFELD (14km). The road, climbing steeply over a ridge above the *Untersee*, providing several attractive views of the agricultural region of Thurgau, leads S.—At (10km) *Weiningen*, a right-hand turning leads through *Warth* to the former Carthusian house of **Ittingen** (1461–1848), rebuilt after its partial destruction in the 16C; in recent years its faded charms have been commercialised by a proselytising body.—The road crosses the Thur to enter (4km) industrial **Frauenfeld** (18,600 inhab.; 8800 in 1930), lying on the Murg, its banks once lined with dyeing and printing works. It is the capital of Thurgau, a district formerly an Imperial fief, but occupied by the Confederates in 1460 at the instigation of Pope Pius II. It remained subject to Zürich until becoming a separate canton after the Napoleonic occupation. There is a cantonal *Museum* in the *Schloss*, built round a 13C keep; while in the Freiestrasse, to the S, are a few old houses. To the NE is the church of *St. Laurence*, founded in the 10C, with a Gothic choir.—Hence the road continues up the valley of the Murg to (17km) *Wil*; see Rte 28A.—*Pfyn*, 7km NE of Frauenfeld, was Roman *Ad Fines*, and the limit of the zones of influence between the barbarous Rhaeti and the Helvetii.

From Eschenz the road skirts the S bank of the *Untersee*, the westernmost and narrowest arm of the *Bodensee*, or Lake Constance, from which the Rhine emerges.—3.5km *Mamern*, a small lakeside village, lies below the castle ruins of *Neuberg* (13C), 6km beyond which the ancient town of **Steckborn** is entered. It contains several attractive old houses, a 17C *Rathaus*, the 16–17C *Turmhof*, and a church rebuilt in the 18C, but of Carolingian foundation.

Beyond (3km) *Berlingen*, we see the German island of *Reichenau* and the wide arm formed by the *Zellersee*, with *Radolfzell* at its head.

After 2km a turning climbs shortly to **Schloss Arenenberg**, dating from 1546, and the residence from 1817 of the Duchesse de St.-Leu ('La Reine Hortense', ex-Queen of Holland), who here entertained Mme Récamier, Chateaubriand and Dumas père. She died here in 1837. Her son, Louis Napoleon, lived here before making his abortive attempt to seize power at Strasbourg in 1836. It was later owned by ex-Empress Eugénie, who presented it to the canton in 1906, together with its Napoleonic collections. These include furniture of the period, sculptures by Canova and portraits by Baron Gérard, Winterhalter, etc.

At 3.5km *Ermatingen*, another lakeside village, is traversed, to enter (4km) *Tägerwilen*. Just N of Tägerwilen, overlooking the upper end of the Untersee (where the Rhine enters from Lake Constance), is the 13–14C castle of *Gottlieben*. In 1414 this was the prison of Johannes Huss and Jerome of Prague before their execution by burning, and also, in 1415, of Pope John XXIII (see Schaffhausen).

3km **Kreuzlingen** (16,100 inhab.; 8600 in 1930), an industrial town contiguous with *Konstanz*, from which it is separated by the frontier line only, is of interest for its Stifts-Kirche, *Sankt-Ulrich*, a Baroque building, restored when not rebuilt, having been gutted by fire in 1963. It contains good rococo decoration of 1764 and a remarkable 18C wood-carving of the Passion, incorporating between 250 and 300 individual figures (c 1730).

The old city of **Konstanz** (anglicised as *Constance*), which lies on the S or left bank of the Rhine here, was the seat of the famous ecclesiastical Council of Constance, which met in the Gothic cathedral, and under the presidency of the Emperor Sigismund, condemned to death Huss and Jerome of Prague (see above). In c 1526 it embraced Protestantism and joined hands with Zürich and Berne. It was reconverted at the sword's point by the Spaniards and Austrians, and lost its imperial privileges in 1549, becoming subject to the Habsburgs. In 1805, by the Treaty of Pressburg, it passed to the German Grand Duchy of Baden. Robert Hallam, Bp of Salisbury, who represented England at the Council, was buried in the choir of the cathedral in 1417, having died at Gottlieben castle (see above).

The No. 13 bears SE above the shore of the **Bodensee** (*Lake Constance*), the Roman *Lacus Brigantinus*, 369m above sea level and with a maximum depth of 252m. It is some 67km long (from Bregenz on the Austrian shore to the head of the *Überlingen See*, its NW arm); its greatest breadth is 13.7km, and its total area is 541km^2, forming one of the natural barriers between Switzerland and Germany.

It is subject to sudden rises and falls of obscure origin, apart from normal seasonal variations, and its surface is sometimes rough. Its fishing is good, and the *Blaufelchen* is a species peculiar to it. Traces of several lake-dwellings have been discovered on its banks, which are otherwise of slight interest. Enquiries may be made at Kreuzlingen, Romanshorn, Arbon and Rorschach concerning summer steamer services.

Bottighofen is the first of a number of small lakeside resorts on the main road—and skirted by a railway line—between Kreuzlingen and (20km) Romanshorn; see below. Among them are (2km) *Münsterlingen*, with the 18C dependencies of a former Benedictine convent founded in the late 10C by a daughter of Edward the Confessor, the church of which is a good Baroque building; and 8.5km beyond, *Kesswil*, birthplace of Carl Gustav Jung (1875–1961), the psychologist.

FROM MÜNSTERLINGEN TO ST. GALLEN VIA BISCHOFSZELL (c 40km). This interesting alternative route climbs S through orchards to meet, at 12km, the No. 14 to Romanshorn.—At *Hagenwil*, some 2km SE of this crossroad, is an ancient moated castle.—Continuing S from this junction, *Zihlschlacht* is traversed for (7.5km) **Bischofszell**, a charming little town on a height above the Thur, with a notable pink Baroque *Rathaus* of 1750 by Kaspar Bagnato; a *Church*, once part of an abbey founded in the 11C; and, in addition to a town gate and late 15C *Bridge*, several characteristic mansions.—Hence one may follow a hilly cross-country road direct to *St. Gallen*, or continue S to join the motorway before *Gossau*.

Romanshorn, a small lake-port with a church of pre-Romanesque foundation and *Schloss* formerly owned by the abbots of St. Gallen, lies opposite German *Friedrichshafen*, to the NE. The frontier lies at a midway point in the lake.

8km **Arbon**, Roman *Arbor Felix*, is a small industrial town of 11,350 inhab., containing a few buildings of some note, among them the *Schloss*, rebuilt in the 16C, with a tower probably on Roman foundations, and a neighbouring church with a late 15C choir and 18C nave.—*St. Gallen* lies 13.5km SW; see Rte 28A.

7km **Rorschach** was founded in the 9C by the abbots of St. Gallen as a commercial port on the lake and entrepôt for grain. A *Granary* of 1784 near the harbour has been converted to house a regional *Museum*. The main thoroughfare is the Hauptstrasse, flanked by several 16–18C houses with oriel windows, including the *Rathaus* (No. 29; 1689), and No. 33. Nearby is the *Church*, rebuilt in the 15C and later altered, from which one may approach, at a higher level to the S, the former Benedictine convent of *Mariaberg*; a Flamboyant Gothic cloister of 1519 and other (mid 16C) dependencies are preserved.

Higher still, beyond the motorway, is the *St. Annaschloss* (15–16C).

Beyond Rorschach the road (and also the railway) briefly skirts the shore before veering SE parallel to the Rhine, which here enters the Bodensee, later crossing the motorway to reach (13km) *St. Margrethen*, the frontier village.

The Customs-post is on the far bank of the Rhine, from which one may approach **Bregenz** (24,500 inhab.) capital of the *Vorarlberg*, lying on the far side of the alluvial flat formed by the river, and below the conspicuous *Pfander* (1064m); see *Blue Guide Austria*.—*Lindau* lies 8km further N, not far beyond the Bavarian frontier.

For the road hence to **Chur**, see Rte 29A.

28   Zürich to St. Gallen

A. Via Winterthur and Wil

Total distance, 82km (51 miles). N1. 24km **Winterthur**—No. 7. 29km **Wil**—18km *Gossau*—11km **St. Gallen**.

Maps: M 216; BL 28, 33, or 5010, 5014.

For the road to Winterthur and **Winterthur** itself, see Rte 26A.

Driving NE from Winterthur we pass (just E of *Oberwinterthur*) *Schloss Hegi*, first mentioned in 1225 but rebuilt at the end of the 15C, containing historical collections.—At 6km the motorway is joined. To the N of this junction stands the conspicuous *Schloss Morsburg* (11–13C), also preserving antiquities.—*Frauenfeld* lies 10km NE; see p 242

The N1 continues due E through undulating wooded and agricultural country, later veering SE above the valley of the Murg.

At 19km (at the exit before Wil) a minor road leads S through several villages to (7km) **Fischingen**, with a notable 17–18C *Church* of a Benedictine abbey, founded in the 14C, of which a 16C cloister is also preserved.—Beyond rises the *Hörnli* (1133m).

The peaks of the Churfirsten and the Appenzell mountains come into view as at 5km the exit for Wil is approached.—**Wil** (599m; 16,250 inhab.; 7500 in 1930), now an industrial town, retains its characteristic hill-top Altstadt, with 14–18C houses in the Marktgasse and Hofplatz, notably the arcaded *Baronenhaus* of 1795 and the *Hof*, and the *Toggenburg castle*, containing a local *Museum*. The *Church*, rebuilt in the 15C, but more recently disfigured, contains a few details of interest, including an armoured skeleton of silver gilt; its terrace commands a distant view of the Säntis (see Rtes 29B and 30, and likewise the latter for the road from Wil to *Buchs* via *Wattwil*).

One may continue E by either the motorway or the No. 7 to (18km) **Gossau** (633m; 14,600 inhab.), a small industrial town with an early 18C church of Carolingian foundation, and the terminus of the light railway to Appenzell.—For *Bischofszell*, 9km N, see p 243.—At 7km *Bruggen* is entered, and the suburbs of St. Gallen.

ST. GALLEN (668m; 75,850 inhab.; 34,250 in 1880) is the capital of its canton and the centre of the textile industry of NE Switzerland. It grew up around a powerful Benedictine abbey, which was celebrated throughout the medieval period as a centre of learning. The ancient enceinte just N of the cathedral, built near the largely canalised stream of the Steinach, still preserves several characteristic old streets of interest. The Abbey Library is famous, while its museums are also noteworthy.

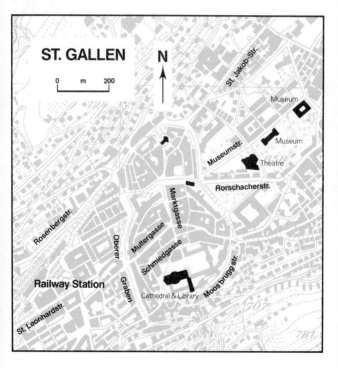

St. Gallus or Gall, from whom the town takes its name, was an Irish missionary who built his hermitage on the banks of the Steinach in the second decade of the 7C. After his death, St. Othmar (720–59), the first abbot, established a school of translators, etc. (notable among whom—in the 10–11Cs—were Ekkehard I and Ekkehard IV). Its reputation grew rapidly. Abbot Gozbert (816–37) founded its library, in which numerous MSS of the Greek and Latin classics were carefully preserved (although it never recovered works lent to cardinals and bishops at the Council of Constance). Notker Balbulus ('the Stammerer'; 840–912), who fled here c 860 from Jumièges (near Rouen), was partly responsible for developing the sequences which were later to form the basis of Gregorian chant. The musical theorist Notker Labeo (died 1022) also worked at St. Gallen.

A. Das Fürstl. Closter.
B. Das Münster.
C. S. Laurenty.
D. Der Spital.
E. Das Rathhaus.
F. Das Kornhaus.
G. Die Metzig.
H. S. Mangen.
I. S. Catharina.
K. Die Wage.
L. Das Bruel thor.
M. Blate thor.
N. Schibenr thor.
O. Muolter thor.
P. Der Grun thurn.
Q. Müller thor.
R. Spijer thor.
S. Zeughause.
T. Des Aptes thor.
V. Schü haus.

Early engraving of St. Gallen

The abbey was fortified against further Magyar incursions after 926, and offered some protection to the town, which later became a free imperial city, its abbots being made princes of the Empire in 1204, exchanging 'a love of piety and knowledge for worldly ambition, and the thirst for political influence and territorial rule'. As so often happened, the increasingly venal abbots were frequently at odds with the burghers, who in the 14C wrested a share of government from them, and in 1454 St. Gallen joined the Swiss Confederation. At this period the district of *Appenzell* (cf.) was also part of the canton, but broke away and became autonomous in 1513. In 1524 certain Lutheran reforms were brought about by Joachim von Watt (Vadian or Vadianus; 1484–1551, a native of the place and a friend of Zwingli), who returned here in 1518 after being Rector of the University of Vienna.

The abbey was devastated during the 'Toggenburg War' of 1712 and in 1798 was deprived of its temporal powers, being suppressed a few years later. Twenty-six English spinning-mules started production in its empty halls in 1800, and from these beginnings St. Gallen's economic importance grew, becoming

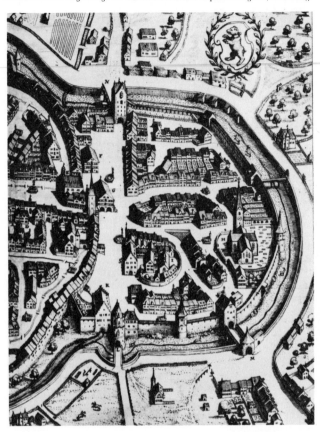

the expanding centre for the production of linen, cotton, muslins, laces and embroideries, the last being produced in the surrounding districts. Since 1845 it has been the seat of a Roman Catholic bishop, and from 1963 the site of a newly built Graduate School of Economics, Business and Public Administration, attended by some 2000 students, the successor of one established here in 1898.

The main road from the W, on entering the town centre, skirts the N side of the *Railway Station* to reach the Blumenbergplatz, NW of the old enceinte, the W side of which is bounded by the Oberer Graben. The first main street to the right, the St. Leonhardstrasse, leads shortly to the *Tourist Office*.

In the parallel Vadianstrasse is the **Gewerbemuseum**, where two floors are devoted to the Iklé and Jacoby collections of old lace and embroidery, together with sections concerning the once important but now extinct linen industry of the vicinity.

One may turn into the Altstadt from the E side of the Graben, following the Multergasse, or a street turning off immediately to the left, to reach the Marktgasse, where we turn right. On reaching the *St. Laurenzenkirche* (13C, but rebuilt in a neo-Gothic style in the mid 19C), turn right along the Schiedgasse, in which there are several characteristic houses, among them Nos 15 and 21, and then left up the Gallusstrasse, in which No. 22 is the *Haus zum Greif.*

Opposite rises the W front of the ***Cathedral**, the former abbey church, a huge edifice in the rococo taste of 1755–69 by Peter Thumb and J.M. Beer, on the site of several former buildings. Both its towers are unusually placed at its E end. The well-proportioned interior preserves carved choir-stalls and confessionals by J.M. Feuchtmayer; a fine wrought-iron choir-screen of 1771 by J. Mayer, painted green and gilt. The elaborate stucco-work and frescoes in the cupola are by Christian Wenzinger. The ornate *Pulpit* and huge *Organ* are notable.

On the S side, in the inner quadrangle, is the ***Abbey Library** or *Stifts-Bibliothek* (usually closed in November), its main room likewise in the rococo taste, with its ceiling painted by Josef Wannenmacher. There are frequent bibliographical exhibitions taken from its 200 MSS and 1650 incunables, apart from books and numismatic collections.

St. Gallen; the Library

Among the treasures are an 8C Virgil; a 10C German psalter; the Gospel of Sintram (9–10C), bound in Tuotilo's ivory tablets; a version of the Nibelungenlied (13C); 8C Irish Gospels; and a Plan of the abbey from c 820, a rare example from the Carolingian period.

From the N side of the cathedral one may cross the spacious KLOSTERPLATZ, passing (left) the former *Arsenal*; other wings of the 17–18C abbey dependencies now house archives and cantonal offices.

Bearing NE, we shortly reach the *Schlössli* (1590), at the E end of the Spisergasse, and turn right and then left into the Burggraben. After a few paces, cross the latter and skirt the S side of a park, and then cross the Rorschacherstrasse to reach the *Stadttheater* (1968), an interesting example of modern architecture.

Adjacent to the E is one of the two large **Museum** buildings (the former *Kunstmuseum*), at present in the process of radical modernisation, which will be linked to the *Historisches Museum* further E by an underground passage. At present the latter accommodates many of the town's collections, including several reconstructed panelled rooms, etc.; also collections of furniture; arms and armour; musical instruments; costumes; medieval sculpture; ecclesiastical silver; numismatic collections; town plans, and a maquette of St. Gallen in 1642. Among more recent sculpture are examples of the work of *Barye, Gustinus Ambrosi* and *Jean Tinguely*.

Among paintings, only a proportion of which are on display, notable are: *Friedrich Herlin* (c 1435–c 1500), Adoration of the Kings, and Nativity; an *anon. 15C* German Crucifixion; *Martin Drolling*, Kitchen interior; Portraits by *Félix Maria Diogg* (1764–1834), *Anton Graff, Angelika Kauffmann, Emanuel Handmann, Hans Sturzenegger* (of Hermann Hesse, and others) and *Millet*. Also *Monet*, Palazzo Contarini, Venice; and representative works by *Van Goyen, Courbet, Waldmüller, Corot, Arnold Böcklin, Giovanni Giacometti, Ferdinand Hodler, Félix Vallottan, Pissarro* and *Sisley*, and collections of naïve paintings by Appenzeller and Toggenburger artists.

At No. 27 Museumstrasse is the *Kirchhoferhaus*, containing archaeological collections, furniture, and other objects of local interest.—A short distance NE is the *Vadiana*, with some 400 incunables and 500 MSS, many of interest for the history of the Reformation.

Turning W along the Museumstrasse, we re-enter the older town behind the 16C *Waaghaus*, facing the Bohl, extending W to the Marktplatz.—To the N between the two stands the *St. Mangenkirche*, a 9C foundation, rebuilt in the 12C and altered in the 19th.—The Oberer Graben lies a few paces W of the Marktplatz.

B. Via Rapperswil, and Wattwil

Total distance, 93km (58 miles). Take the motorway to (33km) **Rapperswil**—No. 8. 25km *Wattwil*—25km *Herisau*—10km **St. Gallen**.

Maps: M 216; BL 33, or 5011, 5014.

Rte 31C describes the road along the N bank of the *Zürichsee* to *Rapperswil*, and that town likewise.

Hence the No. 8 leads E through **Jona** (12,150 inhab.), with the 13C

Kapelle St. Dionys preserving 15C murals. It climbs gently, with
several extensive views towards the SE, notably between (12km)
Sankt Gallenkappel, with a Baroque church of 1755, and (6km) the
Rickenpass (780m), above which rises the *Tweralpspitz* (1332m). The
road descends into the Toggenburg valley to *Wattwil*; see Rte 30.—At
Lichtensteig, 2km N, we turn E, steeply mounting in zigzags below
(right) the *Köbelisberg* (1046m), with a view to the left of the ruins of
Schloss Neu-Toggenburg, before descending through attractive
wooded hills via (9km) *Sankt Peterzell* to (11km) *Waldstatt*.

Appenzell, 12km SE, may be approached hence via *Hundwil* or by following a
longer route via *Urnasch*, 7km S; see Rte 29B.

Turning N, one may fork right at 3km to **Herisau** (771m; 14,150
inhab.), an old town, referred to as early as 837, and since 1876 the
capital of the half-canton of *Appenzell Ausser Rhoden* (see Appenzell), the upper town preserving several old buildings, among
them the *Rathaus*. The adjacent *Church*, although mentioned in 907
and with a 14C belfry, dates from the early 16C. Two of the
surrounding heights are topped by ruined castles, the *Rosenberg* and
the *Rosenburg* (which, according to the story, were once connected
by a leathern bridge). Herisau was the home from 1675–97 of
Johannes Grob, the satirist.
    Bearing NE, we approach the W suburbs of **St. Gallen**; see above.

29   St. Gallen to Chur

A. Via St. Margrethen (for Bregenz), Buchs and Vaduz (Liechtenstein).

Total distance, 109km (67 miles). No. 7. 26km *St. Margrethen*.
Bregenz lies 12km NE—N13. 30km *Haag* exit.—No. 13. 6km *Buchs*.
Schaan lies 3km E and **Vaduz** 3km S of Schaan—8km
Balzers—2km N13.—15km *Landquart* (for Klosters and
Davos)—15km **Chur**.

Maps: M 216, 218; BL 33, 38, 39, or 5012, 5014, 5015.

It is perhaps preferable to join the N1 motorway leading NE from St.
Gallen unless visiting (12km) *Rorschach*; see Rte 27. The motorway
bears E above the *Bodensee* (cf.), with a view across the lake towards
Friedrichshafen in Germany, and below the wooded hills at the NE
extremity of the canton of Appenzell; see Rte 29B. We later veer SE,
skirting the Rhine, which here enters the lake, to (26km) *St.
Margrethen*, the frontier village.

The Customs-post is on the far bank of the river, from which one may approach
Bregenz (24,500 inhab.), capital of the *Vorarlberg*, lying on the far side of an
alluvial flat produced by the Rhine before its canalisation. Above the town rises
the conspicuous *Pfander* (1064m); see *Blue Guide Austria.—Lindau* lies 8km
further N, not far beyond the Bavarian frontier.

The road turns S, passing, 2km W at the next exit, *Berneck*, a village
of some character surrounded by vineyards on the lower slopes of the
Meldegg (NW; 884m).—*Altstätten* (see Rte 29B) lies 12km SW of this

exit, the road passing through several villages with their former castles.

To the E rise the hills of the Bregenzerwald and Vorarlberg, while in the distance to the SE the view is dominated by the Rätikon massif (*Schesaplana*; 2964m).

At 7km a road crosses the embanked Rhine to the adjacent village of *Diepoldsau*, now almost isolated on a loop of the river which still forms the frontier.—*Hohenems* lies 2km beyond, below the *Hohe Kugel* (1645m); see *Blue Guide Austria*.

11km *Oberriet*, where the Appenzell hills approach the road and near which a Neolithic site has been excavated, is perhaps the best place to cross the Rhine to visit **Feldkirch**, 13km SE; see *Blue Guide Austria*.

The old road (No. 13) skirts the foot of the hills, passing through a number of villages below the *Höher Kasten* (1795m) and other summits in the Alpstein range, above which rises the Säntis (2503m), further W; see Rte 29B. The *Alvier* (2343m) is prominent ahead. Until the 17C this district belonged to the barons of *Hohensax*, whose castles, reduced to ruins by the Appenzellers, may still be noticed on the W heights of the valley.

After 4km the N extremity of Liechtenstein is reached, its W frontier formed by the Rhine, while a range of mountains, rising to the *Gallinakopf* (2198m) and *Uchsenkopf* (2286m) marks its E limits; to the S its border is formed by the *Naafkopf* (2570m) and *Falknis* (2562m); but see below.

At 12km one may turn off the motorway 4km E of *Gams* (see Rte 29B), forking immediately left to approach (6km) **Werdenberg**, the castle of which, on its height, was the former seat of a powerful line of counts who sold their domains to Glarus in 1517. The village has a group of ancient wooden houses, preserving curious mottoes, clustered at one end of an ornamental lake. The view from its S shore is attractive.

Adjacent to the E is **Buchs**, a small town and railway junction of slight interest, above which rises the *Buchser Berg* (1111m), ascended by a steeply zigzagging road. It provides good views and a base for excursions into the massif further W.

Buchs lies immediately W of a bridge across the Rhine (which flooded the area in 1927) to *Schaan* in Liechtenstein. 4km S of Schaan is Liechtenstein's capital, **Vaduz**. For the roads leading S from Buchs see below.

The **Principality of Liechtenstein** is 157km² in area, 27km from N to S, and 9km at its greatest width. It is composed of eleven communes with a total population in 1983 of 26,500 (7500 in 1901), of whom over one third are foreigners. In 1960 it was 16,650, of whom 25 per cent were foreigners.

In 1608 Charles of Liechtenstein, who had been Governor of Bohemia, was elevated to the rank of prince by the Emperor Rudolf II. At Prague, after the battle of the White Mountain (November 1620), he offered to pardon those rebelling Protestants who came forward—some 730 of them—and then had their estates confiscated in whole or in part. Until 1719, when the Lordship of Schellenberg and County of.Vaduz (which had been bought from the Hohenems family in 1699 and 1712, respectively) were merged, the house lacked any territory over which to rule. Even so, the first time a Liechtenstein visited his principality was 1842. It was virtually a dependency of Austria until 1919. In 1921 it entered into a Customs Treaty with the Swiss Confederation and in 1959 Switzerland assumed its diplomatic representation abroad. Its currency is Swiss, and its postal administration is amalgamated with that of Switzerland, although its stamps are different, which has allowed it to profit from the acquisitive propensities of some 100,000 subscribing philatelists. The tune of its National Anthem is that of 'God save the King'!

Francis Joseph II (1906–) succeeded to the title in 1938 when his uncle renounced the throne, and he was instrumental in removing a proportion of the family collection of paintings from Austria to Vaduz. Female suffrage was conceded in 1976. The prince regnant is Hans Adam, born in 1945, who since 1985 has exercised most princely powers. Among foreign countries with representatives in Liechtenstein are Monaco and San Marino.

In 1923 about 70 per cent of the peasant population was engaged in agriculture; it is now less than 4 per cent of the working population. Several minor industries have developed, including the manufacture of pharmaceutical products and dental prostheses. Protestations of innocence with regard to the use of the country as an address of convenience by international companies and financial organisations cannot conceal several undesirably anonymous aspects of its spiralling commercial and economic activities. There were already some 30,000 'boites' here a decade ago.

Its most famous native was the composer Joseph Rheinberger (1839–1901).

At present the only object of any great interest in **Vaduz**, apart from the *Postal Museum*, is the **National Museum**, containing collections of local archaeology; a maquette of the principality at 1: 10,000; a winged altarpiece of 1490; collections of ecclesiastical silver, and Gothic and Baroque sculpture; arms and armour; a numismatic collection; watercolours of the area by Moriz Menzinger (mid 19C); a painting of the Siege of Vienna in 1683; and items of folk art.

Only a small proportion of the works of art belonging to the Liechtensteins are at present on view to the public, among them several huge canvases by *Rubens* (which may well be on display abroad). It is hoped that within a few years the projected Museum, to be erected in a central position in Vaduz, will exhibit the collection as a whole. Other notable canvases in the collection, and seen recently at the exhibition of Austrian paintings of the Biedermeier period, include: *Peter Krafft*, The battle of Aspern, in which Prince Johannes I von Liechtenstein took part; *Friedrich von Amerling*, Portrait of Peter Fendi, Self-portrait, and portraits of children of the Liechtenstein family; *Joseph Rebell*, View in the Gulf of Salerno; *Thomas Ender*, Glacier-scapes, and View near Sorrento; *Waldmüller*, Sicilian scenes, Views near Mödling, and other landscapes; *Friedrich Gauermann*, Landscapes at Zell am See; and *Franz Ebel*, Young girl in a mountainscape.

Other works in the collection—not yet on public view—include: *Bernardo Daddi*, Flight into Egypt; *Piero di Cosimo*, Virgin and child with St. John; *Raphael*, Male portrait; *Rubens*, Portrait of a child (1616), Bearded man, Toilet of Venus, Portrait of Jan Vermoelen, and The sons of the artist; *Hans Mielich*, Portrait of Count Ladislaus zu Hag with his leopard; *Bernard Strigel*, Georg Tannstetter and his wife; *J.B. Lampi the Elder*, Portrait of Antonio Canova; *The Master of Mondsee*, Christ before the scribes; *Lucas Cranach the Elder*, St. Eustace, and The sacrifice of Abraham; *Barthel Beham*, The future Maximilian II aged two, and Portrait of Duke Ludwig X of Bavaria; *Monogrammist AG*, A youth; *Hans Hoffmann*, St. Eustace (after Dürer); *Bartholomaeus Spranger*, Self-portrait; *Angelika Kauffmann*, Ferdinand IV of Naples with his family; *Anton Hickel*, The Princess de Lamballe; *Leopold Stober*, The artist and his family; *Amerling*, Portrait of Bertel Thorvaldsen.

Also an extensive collection of paintings by the Dutch and Flemish Schools, among them works by *Salomon van Ruisdael, Claes Berchem, Van Ostade, Jan Steen, Van Goyen, Philips Wouverman* and *Rembrandt* (Self-portrait of 1652), etc.

Among sculptures are: *Tilman Riemenschneider*, St. Helen finding the True

Cross; *Georg Raphael Donner*, two plaques; *Canova*, Bust of the Roi de Rome; and *Giovanni da Bologna*, bronze equestrian statuette of Ferdinando I de Medici.

A road climbs from the N end of the town to the picturesquely sited *Schloss* (no admittance), rebuilt in the 16–17C after its destruction in 1499, and restored c 1900 and again since 1939 as the main residence of the Liechtenstein family.—The road goes on to *Triesenberg* (884m), a village with a good view over the Rhine valley and a local *Museum*.

Climbing steeply, a road threads a short tunnel to reach an upper valley, the SAMINTAL, off which are the MALBUNTAL and the winter-sporting resort of *Malbun* (1599m)', from which a lift ascends the N slope of the *Sareiser Joch* (2000m).

One may descend from Triesenberg in zigzags to *Triesen* (3km S of Vaduz) to approach (4km) *Balzers*, with the 14C *Schloss Gutenberg*, whence one may leave the principality by crossing the *Engpass* to the S, E of the *Fläscherberg*. The pass is defended by the fort of *Luzisteig*, named after the legendary King Lucius of Britain who, having become a missionary, entered the Grisons by this route in AD 176.—For *Maienfeld*, 8km beyond, see below.

Alternatively, one may cross the Rhine to regain the motorway 12km S of Buchs; or, on reaching the old main road, turn left through *Trübbach* (see below).

Driving S from Buchs, the old road provides a view (left) of *Schloss Liechtenstein* (see above) above *Vaduz*, and a splendid panorama ahead of the Grisons, after (6km) *Sevelen* passing the ruined 13C castles of *Herrenburg* and *Wartau*, to reach (7km) *Trübbach*.

At 3km the site of a Roman.villa discovered in 1967 is passed, 1km prior to entering **Sargans**, an ancient village, strategically sited at a junction of valleys and the seat of a countship until 1483. It is overlooked by its 13–15C *Castle*, containing a local *Museum*, above which rises the *Gonzen* (1830m), with an iron-ore mine at its foot.

For the valleys SW of *Sargans*, see Rte 31A.

The N13 veers SE beyond Sargans, shortly by-passing the old spa of **Bad Ragaz**, at the mouth of the wild gorge of the Tamina and fed by the thermal waters of *Pfäfers*.

The springs are said to have been discovered in the 11C by a monk of Pfäfers while hunting, and the first bath-house was erected in 1242. They were described by Paracelsus c 1535, and were recommended by Merian in 1642 to those whose limbs had suffered on the rack! Ragaz itself originally belonged to the abbots of the Benedictine monastery of Pfäfers, whose residence became the *Hof Ragaz Hotel* in 1840. Friedrich von Schelling (1775–1854), the philosopher, died here and is buried in the cemetery of its Baroque church.

On a height to the NW are the ruins of the castle of *Freudenberg*, destroyed during the war between the Confederation and Zürich (1437).—A cable-car mounts SW from just S of Hof Ragaz to a height of 2220m on a spur of the *Graue Horner* massif, rising to the *Pizol* (2844m), further SW, and commanding superb views of the Rhine valley and its flanking mountains.

An interesting excursion from Bad Ragaz is that up the wooded TAMINATAL to the S, enclosed by narrow cliffs only just allowing room for the road and the torrent beside it. After threading a rocky archway, *Bad Pfäfers* is eventually reached, with buildings dating from 1704, beyond which the extraordinary

*Taminaschlucht is entered, little more than a cleft in the rock, in which the hot springs rise (waterproofs desirable). The earliest patients, in the 14C, were let down into the gorge by ropes and lodged in chambers supported by beams projecting from the rock.—The return to Ragaz (but see below) may be made by ascending by marked paths to the village of Pfäfers, with the 17C church and dependencies of the once important monastery (founded in 720 and suppressed in 1838), finely sited on a platform overlooking the Rhine valley. Hence one may follow the road down to (4km) Ragaz, passing near (right) the ruins of the castle of Wartenstein.

The road climbing S from Pfäfers leads up the valley, which later opens out, to (11km) Vättis (943m), a small resort below the Vättnerchopf (NW; 2616m) and the Simel (SW; 2354m), beyond which a track ascends to the Kunkelspass (1357m) above Tamins; see Rte 38.—The road climbs W from Vättis to the Gigerwaldsee reservoir, in the savage CALFEISEN VALLEY below the Ringelspitz or Piz Barghis (3247m). The S bank of the reservoir may be skirted to St. Martin, W of which rises the Surenstock or Piz Sardona (3056m), and SW, the Trinserhorn or Piz Dolf (3028m) and, beyond, the Piz Segnas (3099m).

Due E of Bad Ragaz, to the left of the motorway, lies **Maienfeld**, an ancient little town with a 13C tower, and the Schloss Salenegg, a typical 17C mansion of the Grison nobility. On a height to the SE, above Jenins, is the ruin of Aspermont; to the N rises the Falknis (2562m). It was the neighbourhood of Maienfeld that formed the background to the story of 'Heidi' in the novels of Johanna Spyri (1827–1901).

The road now enters the canton of Graubünden, or the Grisons; see p 264. In May 1911 its authorities decided to refuse permission for its roads to be used by motor vehicles, and the restriction was not entirely lifted until June 1925.

The next exit from the motorway, here commanded by the Pizalun (W; 1478m), is at Landquart, a little town at the mouth of the PRÄTTIGAU, up which climbs the Rhaetian railway to Klosters and Davos; see Rte 33.—SE is the medieval castle of Marschlins, with its four towers, reconstructed in 1633; and further S, the 12C ruins of Falkenstein.—To the NE, at Malans, is Schloss Bothmar (16–18C).

The N13 continues to skirt the Rhine past (left) Zizers, with a large and impressive Schloss, and (right) Untervaz (with the ruins of Neuenberg, and Rappenstein), both approached from the next exit. Above Untervaz is the ridge of Calanda (2806m).—Further S, on the far bank of the Rhine, are the ruins of Liechtenstein and Haldenstein. To the SW rises the Dreibundenstein (2160m); to the SE, the Gürgaletsch (2441m); and to the E, the Montalin (2266m).

Turning off the motorway, the N suburbs of **Chur** are shortly entered; see Rte 33.

B. Via Appenzell, Altstätten and Buchs

Total distance, 112km (69 miles). At 15km there is a right-hand turning for (5km) **Appenzell**—10km **Altstätten**—No. 13. 29km Buchs—20km Sargans—7km Bad Ragaz—6km Landquart (for Klosters and Davos)—15km **Chur**.

Maps: M 216, 218; BL 33, 38, 39, or 5012, 5014, 5015.

Ascending SW from the centre of **St. Gallen**, the line of the partly cogwheel light railway is followed round the W flank of the Fröhlichsegg (998m), at 6km reaching a junction.

Some 2km W is the *Brücke*, a remarkable concrete bridge spanning the *Urnäsch gorge* to approach, 5.5km beyond, the village of *Hundwil*, which shares with Trogen the honour of being the meeting-place or *Landsgemeinde* of the Ausser Rhoden of canton Appenzell.

2km E of the crossroads lies *Teufen*, now by-passed by the main road which bears SE through *Bühler*; see below.

FROM TEUFEN TO BERNECK (28km). This hilly cross-country road leads E to (5.5km) *Spiecher*, a small resort. 2km beyond Spiecher is **Trogen** (also approached directly from St. Gallen by light railway), the seat of government of the *Ausser Rhoden of Appenzell* from 1597 to 1876, with an 18C church. The *Landsgemeinde* meets here on the last Sunday in April of even years.—S of the village is *Pestalozzidorf*, a group of chalets originally built in 1944–57 to house and educate orphans from the war-battered countries of Europe, and still caring for those of other nationalities.—10.5km NE lies *Heiden*, a small resort near several view-points; it was here that Henri Dunant (1828–1910), a founder of the Red Cross, retired in penury before receiving the Nobel Peace Prize in 1901, and here he died.—Hence one may climb down via *Oberegg* and *Reute* and, after crossing a col, to *Berneck*, 10km E; see Rte 29A. A by-road leads S from Reute, later descending to (7.5km) *Altstätten*.

From *Bühler*, with typical Appenzeller houses, the main road leads to (7km) *Gais*, a small resort below the *Gäbris* (1251m), providing a notable view SW towards the Säntis and its massif.—For the road from Gais to *Altstätten*, see below.

Bearing SW over a ridge (927m) we descend into its pastoral valley, watered by the Sitter, to enter (5km) **Appenzell** (775m; 4900 inhab.), the village capital of the *Inner Rhoden* of the canton of *Appenzell*, a highland region which has played a considerable part in Swiss history.

Its name (*Abtszell*, or *Abbatis Cella*) is derived from the country seat established here by the abbots of St. Gallen, with whom the Appenzellers were constantly feuding from the 13th to the 15C, their liberties only secured after several serious skirmishes. The Reformation led to a division of the canton in 1597 into the *Inner Rhoden*, mainly Catholic and pastoral, and the *Ausser Rhoden*, largely Protestant and industrial (see *Herisau*). Primitive institutions have survived here in all their naïve simplicity; women are still denied the vote; the stolid males are keen on displaying their muscular prowess by wrestling, hurling and kindred sports; the goat's milk 'whey cure' is still practised. It was described by Murray as 'a dull and dirty village ... consisting of old and ill-built houses, with two convents, and a modern church, hung with several flags'.

The *Church* was in fact founded in the 11C and retains its 16C choir, but the nave was rebuilt in 1823. The pulpit, organ-case and main altar are notable; the modern glass is not. The crypt contains some late 15C glass. The main street preserves several picturesque houses, among them the colourful herb-painted facade of the *Löwen-Drogerie*. The *Rathaus* dates from 1561.

A road leads SE and then S through *Weissbad* and other attractively situated villages to (7.5km) *Wasserauen*, a base for excursions into the surrounding mountains, on whose slopes whortleberries grow in profusion. A lift mounts hence to the *Wildkirchli*, once a chapel near a cavern, approached along a ledge, in which remains of the giant cave-bear, the Alpine wolf and the cave-lion, all belonging to a pre-glacial period, together with traces of human occupation, have been discovered. Above rises the *Ebenalp* (1640m). Another peak reached by lift from *Brülisau*, SE of Weissbad, is the *Hoher Kasten* (1795m; extensive views), while a path from Brülisau climbs S to skirt the tarns of *Sämtisersee* and, beyond, the *Fälensee*, towards a pass E of the Altmann; see below.

A path climbs SW from Wasserauen below the *Hundstein* (2156m) and past the picturesque *Seealpsee*, to approach the **Säntis** (2503m), the dominating summit of the range (more easily reached from Schwägalp; see below, and Rte 30), to the SE of which rises the *Altmann* (2436m), while between the two the *Rotsteinpass* (2120m) leads down to *Unterwasser*.—The *Zwinglipass* (2011m), to the E of the Altmann, leads down to *Wildhaus*; for both villages see Rte 30.

A road ascends W from Appenzell via *Gonten*, between the *Hundwiler Höhi* (1306m) and the *Kronberg* (S; 1663m), reached by a lift, to (11km) *Urnäsch*, 7km S of Waldstatt (see Rte 28B), from which one may follow a road S up a mountain-girt valley, climbing over a col to (10km) *Schwägalp*. Hence a funicular mounts to near the summit of the **Säntis** (2503m), with its observatory, and commanding an extensive *View over the Bodensee, the Grisons and the Bernese Alps. A road descends W to (10km) *Neu Sankt Johann*, on the No. 16; see Rte 30.

From *Gais*, 5km NE of Appenzell, one may follow the road E, partly following the line of a cogwheel light railway, via *Stoss*, with a chapel commemorating the battle of 1405, when a handful of Appenzellers (reinforced, according to the story, by their red-smocked women) beat an Austrian force of at least 1200. The descent in wide curves, providing splendid views across the Rhine valley towards the Bregenzerwald, is made to (10km) **Altstätten**, an old town of some character, preserving a partly arcaded Marktgasse, a neo-Classical late 18C church and several picturesque corners.—At *Oberriet*, 8km S, reached by following the No. 13, we meet the N13 motorway skirting the Rhine, for which see Rte 29A.

30   Wil to Buchs via Wattwil: the Toggenburg

Total distance, 59km (36 miles). No. 16. 18km **Wattwil**—41km *Buchs*.

Maps: M 216; BL 28, 33, or 5014, 5015.

Driving S from **Wil** (see Rte 28A), the road ascends the upper valley of the Thur, known as the *Toggenburg*, traversing several industrial villages, above which rise green pastures and attractive fir-clad slopes.

It was once governed by its own counts, but when the line became extinct in 1436 Zürich and Schwyz disputed its possession in the first internicine war of the Swiss cantons. The abbots of St. Gallen who later purchased the district were often at odds with its inhabitants, who temporarily drove them out during the 'Toggenburg War' of 1712.

18km *Lichtensteig*, founded c 1200, preserves a dignified Hauptgasse with 16–18C mansions built over arcades, among them the *Rathaus*, near which is a regional *Museum*.

For the roads climbing steeply E and ascending SW from Wattwil see Rte 28B.

2km **Wattwil** (613m) is a small textile town, above which (W) is the Capuchin convent of *Santa Maria zu den Engeln*, with a 17–18C church. After traversing the town we veer SE, by-passing *Ebnat-Kappel*, with a spired early 18C church, several old houses and a *Museum* containing old musical instruments, etc.—To the SW rises the *Tanzboden* (1443m) and, further S, the bold peak of the *Speer*

(1950m); the latter may be ascended hence, the climb being eased by a lift from *Krummenau*, further SE, where a natural rock-bridge spans the Thur.

12km **Neu Sankt Johann**, a village named after the Benedictine abbey founded here in 1150, with a notable *Church* of 1644 by Alberto Barbieri.

A road hence ascends the LUTEREN VALLEY to the E via *Rietbad*, below the *Stockberg* (1781m), with flora of interest, to (10km) *Schwägalp*, from which the *Säntis* (2503m) may be reached; see above.

The industrial village of *Nesslau* is next traversed, a defile is threaded, and the *Giessenfälle* is passed to reach (5km) *Stein*, beyond which the seven jagged peaks of the Churfirsten stand out prominently. The road circles to the E, with the bold outline of the *Wildhuser-Schafberg* (2373m) looming ahead, to enter (8km) *Unterwasser*, a small resort lying at 906m, below the *Säntis* (N; 2503m), and a base for the ascent of the *Churfirsten* by good paths and a funicular, which approaches the summit of the highest peak, the *Hinterrugg* (2306m). The road continues to climb, to (3km) **Wildhaus** (1090m), at the foot of the *Schafberg*, a resort and base for the ascents of the Säntis and—mainly over high pastures—the Hinterrugg, and for the *Zwinglipass* (2011m), E of the *Altmann* (2436m), to *Brülisau*; see Rte 29B.

The hamlet of *Lisighaus*, to the W, was the birthplace (an ancient wooden structure may be visited) of Ulrich (or Huldrych, to use his own spelling) Zwingli (1484–1531). Of peasant stock, he was educated at Basle and was present as an army chaplain at the battles of Novara and Marignano (1513 and 1515). Under the influence of Erasmus and later of Luther, he established a Reformed Church in Zürich in 1523; he was killed at the battle of Kappel (cf.).

The road descends steeply to the E down the wooded *Simmitobel* gorge, making a sweeping zigzag before reaching (9km) *Gams*, with a view ahead of the N part of Liechtenstein. Turning right, the road skirts the foothills on the W side of the Rhine valley through *Grabs* and *Werdenberg* to (5km) adjacent *Buchs*; see Rte 29A.

31 Zürich to Chur

A. Via the N3

Total distance, 118km (73 miles). 34km *Rapperswil* exit—24km *Näfels* exit—35km *Sargans* exit—10km *Landquart* (for Klosters and Davos)—15km **Chur**.

Maps: M 216, 218; BL 32, 33, 38, or 5011, 5012, 5015.

The motorway avoids the crowded W bank of the *Zürichsee* (see Rte 31B) and is a convenient road to follow, driving at first due S and then veering SE above the lake. It is the most rapid route for those making directly for the Grisons and is also recommended for travellers to *Einsiedeln* or *Schwyz*; see Rte 25B.

At 36km the exit for *Rapperswil*, on the far bank of the lake, is reached (see Rte 31C), approached hence by crossing a narrow spit of land and a viaduct virtually dividing the Zürichsee from the

Obersee to the E.

The motorway later circles to the N to meet at 15km the junction where it will eventually join that bearing SE from Zürich to Rapperswil before skirting the N bank of the Obersee.—To the E the *Speer* (1950m) is prominent.

The N3 skirts the *Linthkanal*, joining the Obersee to the *Walensee*. Until the turn of the 19C the Linth, brawling down from Glarus, ran directly into the Obersee, spreading destruction in time of flood; but by a masterly series of works undertaken in 1807–27 by Conrad Escher (later Escher von der Linth), it was turned into the Walensee, whence the surplus water was carried off by a canal.

At 5km an exit is provided to *Schänis*, on the far bank, with the restored church (12–18C) of a convent of Carolingian foundation. Under the choir of 1507 is a Romanesque crypt, but most of the interior has been baroquised. Near by is a chapel flanked by a cylindrical Romanesque tower.—After 4km narrows are reached just W of the Walensee, with the ruins of two castles which once defended it; to the right opens the valley of the Linth.

Näfels lies 4km to the S and *Glarus* 8km beyond; see Rte 32.—To the N of the next exit (2km E) is *Weesen*, a village charmingly situated at the W extremity of the Walensee. It has a 17C church of 13C foundation and a Benedictine convent of 1690. The massacre of the Swiss garrison here in 1388 was avenged by the Austrian defeat at Näfels (cf.). The *Speer* (1950m) may be ascended hence.

A minor road mounts steeply to (6km) *Amden*, from which the *Mattstock* (1936m) may be climbed. Further E lies the hamlet of *Kapf*, beyond which rises the *Leistchamm* (2101m).

The motorway at present (1986) merges with the No. 3, which skirts the precipitous S bank of the *Walensee*, threading several short tunnels. An extension to the N3 is being constructed at a higher level, on the *Kerenzer Berg*; this will later descend to meet the section completed near *Flums*; see below.

The grand but gloomy *Walensee is one of the more imposing of Swiss lakes due to the sheer cliffs which rise above its N shore in regular stratified layers. Above them are pastures on the S flank of the *Churfirsten ridge*; see Rte 30. The lake itself is some 15km long, 2km wide and 24km² in area.

From *Murg*, about half-way along the S bank of the Walensee, one may enter the picturesque MURGTAL, at the upper end of which lies the *Murgsee* (1820m); above rises a rocky cirque of peaks culminating in the *Bützistock* (2496m). A road climbs SE from Murg to *Quarten* (which, like several other place-names in the area, probably dates from a medieval numbering of pasture-lands) and *Oberterzen*, whence lifts ascend to *Tannenbodenalp* (1342m), and then to the SW to approach a series of peaks, rising to the *Gulmen* (2317m); see also *Flums*, below.

Just beyond the E extremity of the lake lies *Walenstadt*, a dull little garrison town. Above it to the N rears the *Hinterrugg* (2306m) and to the E the *Gamsberg* (2385m).—SE of the town, on a rocky height, stands the *St. Georgs-Kapelle*, 12C with 15C additions, but on Roman foundations.

At 12km the road bears SE up the SEEZTAL, passing the ruined castle of *Gräpplang* and by-passing **Flums**, an ancient place. Its *Church* has a Romanesque nave and tower, 15C choir, and a crypt over the remains of two earlier churches on a Roman site.

A very steep mountain road zigzags SW to *Tannenbodenalp* (see above), providing approaches to the mountains here, while another track leads off this up the SCHILSTAL towards the *Spitzmeilen* (2501m) and *Magerrain* (2524m); see also Rte 32.

To the E rises the *Alvier* (2343m); ahead lie the Grisons. At 11km the exit for *Mels* (right) is reached, with a Capuchin monastery founded in 1651, and also *Sargans*, below the *Gonzen* (N; 1830m), for which see Rte 29A, and for the road hence to Chur.

From Mels a by-road climbs SW up the WEISSTANNENTAL, with the rugged range of the *Graue Horner* (*Pizol*; 2844m) rising to the SE. From near the head of the valley a path ascends to the *Risetenpass* (2189m) for *Matt*; and further S, the *Foopass* (2223m) for *Elm*, both in the SERNFTAL; see Rte 32. Between the two rises the *Ruchen* (2611m).—From *Wangs*, just SE of Mels, cable-cars rise towards the *Schwarze Horner* (2645m).

B. Via Wädenswil and Näfels

Total distance, 124km (77 miles). No. 3. 21km *Wädenswil*—5km *Richterswil. Einsiedeln* lies 12.5km S.—12km *Lachen*—20km **Näfels**—16km N3.—10km *Walenstadt* exit—13km *Sargans* exit—12km *Lanquart* exit (for Klosters and Davos)—15km Chur.

Maps: M 216, 218; BL 32, 33, 38, or 5012, 5015.

The old road, skirting the W and S banks of the *Zürichsee*, traverses a district which—at least as far as *Horgen*—has become somewhat overbuilt.—6km *Kilchberg*, the home from 1875 of the poet and novelist Conrad Ferdinand Meyer (1825–98). He is buried in the cemetery of *St. Peter's* church, of Romanesque foundation, but rebuilt in 1444. It contains Baroque decoration and glass by A. Giocometti. Thomas Mann (1875–1955), who had lived his last 15 months at Kilchberg (at No. 39 Alte Landstrasse), is likewise buried here; see also Küsnacht.

3km *Thalwil* (15,400 inhab.; 7950 in 1930), a textile town, is traversed, and then *Horgen* (16,600 inhab.), 5km beyond. The latter contains a Baroque church of oval plan (1782; by J.J. Haltiner), with rococo decoration by Andreas Moosbrugger.

A less cluttered reach of the **Zürichsee** is approached, although the railway track skirts its length between the road and its bank. The lake itself is 39km long, and varies between 2 and 4km in breadth, with an area of 90km^2.—Another 7km brings one to industrial **Wädenswil** (18,500 inhab.; 9500 in 1930); several houses of the old town are preserved, together with a mid 16C castle enlarged in the early 19C.—4km *Richterswil*, likewise industrial, was the residence of a certain Dr J. Hotze, who here entertained J.G. von Zimmerman, Lavater, Goethe, and Pestalozzi.

The road now veers due E, traversing several villages, to (7km) *Pfäffikon*. Near the lake is a 13–14C castle of 10C foundation.

Offshore lies the island of **Ufenau**, with an ancient church and chapel, the former the site of a 1st or 2C Roman temple and the burial-place (grave unknown) of Ulrich von Hutten (1488–1523), the knightly satirist and friend of Luther. Zwingli obtained eleventh-hour asylum for him here after the death of Franz von Sickingen, with whom he had formerly taken refuge from the supporters of Leo X.

After 1km the turning for *Rapperswil* is reached. The town is conspicuous on the far side of the lake, the narrows of which had been crossed by a 1300m long wooden bridge in 1358; the present dike dates from 1878.

5.5km *Lachen*, a village on a marshy bay of the *Obersee*, has an imposing Baroque *Church* designed by Caspar Moosbrugger. The road now bears away from the lake to (4km) *Siebnen*.

Hence a by-road climbs up the narrow WÄGITAL via (7.5km) *Vorderthal* and *Innerthal* (940m), on the N bank of the *Wägitaler See*, a small reservoir encircled by mountains, from the far end of which a path crosses a pass into the KLÖNTAL; see Rte 32.

The No. 3 veers S parallel to the motorway, which it is preferable to join at (10km) *Bilten*, unless visiting *Näfels* and *Glarus* (see Rte 32), for which we continue on the old road, at (3.5km) *Nieder-Urnen* turning right for Näfels.—See Rte 31A for the continuation of the road to **Chur**.

C. Via Rapperswil

Total distance, 126km (78 miles). No. 17. 31km **Rapperswil**—9km *Lachen*—No. 3. 20km *Näfels*—16km N3—10km *Walenstadt* exit—13km *Sargans* exit—12km *Landquart* exit (for Klosters and Davos)—15km **Chur**.

Maps: M 216, 218; BL 32, 33, 38, or 5012, 5015.

The sub-route FROM WINTERTHUR TO RAPPERSWIL (36km) is first described, for those wishing to take in *Winterthur* en route from Zürich. Driving SW and then S along the KEMPTTAL, the road then bears SE up the wide valley to (25km) *Pfäffikon*; lake-dwellings have been found on the bank of its marshy lake. It is an industrial village of ancient origin; its church, of Carolingian foundation, was rebuilt in the 15C.—At *Irgenhausen*, just to the S, are the well-preserved walls of a *Roman castrum* of the 3C, with foundations of eight towers. We get occasional views ahead of the Glärnisch Alps.—By passing (right) **Wetzikon** (15,850 inhab.), a motorway is met after 9km, which likewise by-passes (right) *Bubikon*, with a Commandery of the Knights Hospitallers founded in 1192 by Count Toggenburg and rebuilt in the mid 15C (*Museum*); the church contains frescoes of interest.—At *Rüti*, E of the road, there was once an important Premonstratensian convent and the church contains the tomb of the last Count of Toggenburg (1364).—The motorway is being continued to the SE to meet the N3 E of the *Obersee*. We turn off shortly for *Rapperswil*; see below.

An alternative rapid approach to Rapperswil to that described below is the road climbing SE from Zürich, extended beyond (8.5km) *Zumikon* by a motorway, which later provides a view NE over the *Greifensee* towards the industrial town of *Uster* (23,700 inhab.; 9650 in 1930), and ahead towards the Glärnisch Alps. On the far bank of the lake lies the village of *Greifensee*, with a castle taken by the Confederates in 1444 after heavy fighting. A curious little triangular church of 1350 has been built into an angle of the town wall. It was the birthplace of Johann Jakob Bodmer (1698–1783), the writer and translator of 'Paradise Lost' into German.

The No. 17 skirts the residential E bank of the *Zürichsee* past *Zollikon* (12,150 inhab.) to (6km) **Küsnacht** (12,750 inhab.), site of a Commandery of the Knights Hospitallers founded in 1358, with a Romanesque and 15C church, and preserving several old houses. Thomas Mann lived at Schiedhaldenstrasse 33 from the autumn of 1933 to the spring of 1938, and in 1953 and the first four months of

1954 at adjacent *Erlenbach*, before moving across the lake to Kilchberg.

8km **Meilen** (10,450 inhab.), with a 15C church on Carolingian foundations. Wagner completed his 'Die Meistersinger von Nürnberg' when staying with the Wille family at *Haus Mariafeld*. Above the town rises the *Pfannenstiel* (853m).

The road passes several lakeside towns—including *Stäfa* (10,550 inhab.)—below vine-clad slopes to (12km) *Feldbach*, with an attractive group of early 16C houses, 3km above which lies *Hombrechtikon*, preserving several 16–18C half-timbered houses.

2.5km **Rapperswil**, a busy little town containing several characteristic streets (notably the Hintergasse) and squares—notably the central HAUPTPLATZ with the early 15C *Rathaus*—lies on a promontory commanded by its 13–14C *Castle*, with a triangular courtyard. The castle contains a *Museum* devoted to Polish refugees and the history and culture of their country, for a small Polish community had established themselves here in the mid 19C. The heart of Kosciusko was sent hence to Warsaw in 1927. The neighbouring church on this ridge, the *Lindenhof*, is also 13–14C, but is of slight interest since reconstructed after a fire in 1882. In the Herrenberg, E of the church, is a small regional *Museum*, beyond which is the Obere Halsgasse, whence one may return to the Hauptplatz by a parallel street. Below the castle is a relic of a Capuchin convent founded in 1603.

For the road to *Wattwil*, see Rte 28B.

The main road gains the shore of the *Obersee* E of the town at *Wurmsbach*, with a Cistercian convent founded in the 13C; its church was altered in the 17C.—Beyond (10km) *Schmerikon* we turn right onto a section of completed motorway crossing the *Linthkanal* (cf.), which here enters the lake, to reach the N3 5.5km S; see Rte 31A.—At *Uznach*, just beyond this turning, are the ruins of a castle destroyed by Rudolf of Habsburg in 1266. To the SE rises the *Speer* (1950m).

32   Näfels to Glarus and Altdorf via the Klausenpass

Total distance, 61km (38 miles). No. 17. 8km **Glarus**—16km *Linthal*, for *Braunwald*—23km *Klausenpass*—24km **Altdorf**.

Maps: M 216, 218; BL 33, 38, or 5008, 5015.

Näfels (437m), a small industrial town near the mouth of the LINTH-TAL, is famous for the battle which took place here in 1388, in which the Swiss, numbering some 600 men of Glarus, defeated a much larger force of Austrians, their respective losses being 54 and 2500!

The *Church* is a handsome Baroque building of 1778–81 by J. Singer, with rococo decoration in its interior. In the main street is the *Freuler-Palast* of 1645, well-restored, and containing several rooms preserving Renaissance wood-carving, and a cantonal *Museum*. A number of good 17–18C houses may be seen in Näfels and contiguous *Mollis*, to the E beyond the *Linthkanal* (cf.). Mollis was the birthplace of Heinrich Loris, better known as Henricus Glareanus (1488–1563), the poet and musical theorist, and disciple of Erasmus.

A steep road climbs W from Näfels to the little *Obersee*, prettily situated among woods at the foot of the *Brünnelistock* (2133m); to the SW of Näfels rises the *Wiggis* (2282m).

Travellers wishing to regain the N3 NE of Mollis may follow a picturesque road along the flank of the *Kerenzer Berg*, overlooking the *Walensee*, via *Filzbach*, from which a lift ascends towards the *Nüenchamm* (1904m), and a path approaches the tarns at the foot of the formidable *Mürtschenstock* (2390m), a rocky peak pierced near its summit by a natural arch.—The road goes on through *Obstalden*, a small resort situated on a spur above the Walensee, to the bank of which the road later descends; see Rte 31A.—A by-road climbs SE from Mollis to a point below the *Nüenchamm* and the *Fronalpstock* (2124m) further S.

The No. 17 leads S from Näfels via (5km) *Netstal*, somewhat exposed to avalanches, 3km beyond which lies **Glarus** (489m; 5900 inhab.), a small textile town and the capital of its alpine canton, one of the smallest in Switzerland, consisting of the basin of the Linth and its tributaries. It is almost cut off from its neighbouring cantons by an encircling chain of high mountains, culminating in the *Tödi* (3614m) which marks its SW border; it has been described as 'a microcosm of Switzerland'.

Its name is corrupted from that of St. Hilarus, Bp of Poitiers, to whom was dedicated the first church here (c 650) by his disciple St. Fridolin, an Irish monk. The men of Glarus secured their independence by defeating a Habsburg army at Näfels in 1388; see above. Zwingli was parish priest here in 1506–16 and later served in two campaigns as chaplain to the mercenary contingents of the district; see Wildhaus. The Tschudi family for centuries filled the chief public offices of Glarus, its most distinguished member being Ägidius Tschudi (1505–72), the intolerant Catholic author of the 'Chronikon Helveticum', in which he painstakingly elaborated the William Tell legend. The last witch trial in Europe took place here in 1782, when a serving-maid was beheaded.
   The Reformation was accepted by most of the inhabitants of the canton before 1530, but owing to later friction each confession was allotted its own cantonal assembly by a settlement in 1683. The *Landsgemeinde* takes place annually in May; the first took place in 1387. It was the first canton—only in 1972—to institute female suffrage, the principle being nationally agreed the previous year, although not yet accepted by the Inner-Rhoden of Appenzell.

The *Föhn* or S wind which sometimes sweeps down the valley with great violence has caused disastrous fires, notably in 1861 when Glarus was almost destroyed. The town was then entirely rebuilt, although the *Haus Brunner im Sand* of 1770 survived, as did a few others in the Landsgemeindeplatz and elsewhere.
   Few of its public buildings are of interest, although the *Kunsthaus* contains paintings by Swiss artists and sections devoted to the history and natural history of the canton, including some remarkable fossil fish found in the slate quarries of Elm.

Glarus is overlooked to the SW by the *Vorder Glärnisch* (2328m), part of a finely grouped massif rising further SW to the *Ruchen* (2901m), the *Vrenelisgärtli* (2904m) and the *Bächistock* (2914m), but the most accessible view-point in the vicinity is the *Schwammhöchi* (1100m), reached by a by-road climbing W.—The same road goes on to skirt the N bank of the *Klöntaler See* (also approached via *Riedern*), extending W below the grey cliffs of the *Glärnisch*, to enter the narrow KLÖNTAL, where Salomon Gessner (1730–88), who idealised Nature in his poetry, used to spend his summers. Beyond the hamlet of *Richisau* is the *Pragelpass* (1550m), crossed by Suvarov's army in the autumn of 1799 when descending into the MUOTATAL for *Schwyz*; see Rte 25B. It was probably also the scene of the first ski tour in Switzerland, made in the opposite direction by two Norwegians in January 1892.

The main route follows the LINTH VALLEY to the S, known for its green Schabzieger cheese, with the view of the Tödi rising above the head of the valley to the SW, to (6km) **Schwanden**, a large industrial village at a junction of valleys. It was a man of Schwanden who in 1697 brought the first potatoes to Switzerland, from Ireland. In the *Freiberg*, to the S, was established in 1569 a reserve for chamois, to provide two animals for each man of canton Glarus on marriage.—A road leads S, beyond which a lift mounts to a small reservoir, with the *Kärpf* (2794m) rising ahead.

FROM SCHWANDEN TO ELM (14.5km). A road circles to the SE up the narrow SERNFTAL past *Engi*, with its slate quarries, of interest to geologists for the numerous fossils found there.—10km *Matt*, with a church of Romanesque foundation, from which the CHRAUCHTAL ascends to the *Risetenpass* (2189m), leading into the WEISSTANNENTAL; see Rte 31A.—4.5km *Elm*, a small resort and mountaineering centre at the foot of the *Piz Segnas* (E; 3099m), was in part destroyed by a landslide in 1881 from the Tschingelberg slate beds. Several passes lead hence: the *Foopass* (NE; 2223m), N of the *Surenstock* or *Piz Sardona* (3056m), into the Weisstannental (see Rte 31A); the *Pass dil Segnas* (SE; 2627m), into the FLEMTAL above Flims; and the *Panixer Pass* (SW; 2407m), to *Reuen*, W of Ilanz; see Rte 38. This last pass, partly approached by road to the hamlet of *Wallenbrugg*, lies some distance W of the *Vorab* (3028m) and SE of the *Hausstock* (3158m), dominating the head of the Sernftal. The Panixer Pass was crossed by Suvarov and the remnants of his army on the 6–8 October 1799, the culminating feat of his remarkable retreat. From Wallenbrugg one may also climb W over the *Richetlipass* (2261m) to *Linthal*; see below.

From Schwanden, the main road leads SW up the LINTH TAL proper, traversing several villages, passing (left) the *Doppelfall*, to approach (10.5km) *Linthal* (662m) in full view of the snow mountains ahead, the highest peak among them being the *Tödi* (3614m). A steep funicular mounts NW to *Braunwald* (1256m), a well-sited resort facing the Hausstock massif and, with the Clariden range extending SW, the base for several ascents in the area.

A road climbs due S of Linthal for 5km, with a view (right) of the *Sträjenbach* waterfall, to *Tierfehd*, near the *Pantenbrücke*, S of which is the *Limmernsee* reservoir, below the *Muttenstock* (3089m) and the *Kistenpass* (2638m), above *Breil/Brigels*; see Rte 38.—From the Pantenbrücke one may follow a path ascending SW up the ravine of the *Sandbach* below the *Selbstsanft* (3029m) for a closer view of the *Tödi* (3614m; first ascended in 1824) and the *Bifertenfirn* below *Piz Urlaun* (3359m); the *Bifertenstock* (3421m; further E) and the *Clariden* (SW; 3267m), with its glacier, and—between that peak and the Tödi—the *Sandfirn*, below the *Sandpass* (2781m). These peaks form the watershed between the valleys of the Linth and the Vorderrhein.

Beyond Linthal the main road starts to climb W in a series of steep zigzags past the *Fätschbachfalle*, to reach the *Urner Boden*, below (right) the *Ortstock* (2717m) and the *Chamerstock* (S; 2124m). Ascending this high pastoral valley to the SW, flanked by the ridge of the *Jegerstock* (N; 2573m) and the *Gemsfairenstock* (S; 2972m), we later thread the gorge of the *Klus* and again climb in zigzags to (23km from Linthal) the **Klausenpass** (1948m), dominated to the N by the curious rock hump of the *Märcherstöckli* and by the *Chammli*, a spur of the *Clariden* (3267m), almost due S.

The road descends almost due W past the *Klausenpasshöhe*, providing several fine views S across to the spur running SW from the Clariden and the peaks of *Chammliberg* (3214m), the *Schärhorn* (3295m), the *Klein-* and *Gross-Ruchen* (3138m) and the *Grosse*

Windgällen (3188m). *Aesch* lies in the valley below the *Staübifall*. A
rock gallery is threaded below the *Schächentaler Windgällen* (2764m)
and later, beyond *Urigen*, the road descends in a wide zigzag to
(12.5km) *Unterschächen* (995m), a mountaineering centre beautifully
situated at the foot of the BRUNNITAL, above which tower the cliffs
of the Ruchen and Grosse Windgällen. The road continues to descend
the SCHÄCHENTAL below the *Spitzen* (S; 2404m), the site of a
landslip in 1887, passing several ski-lifts near *Springen*, to reach
Burglen. The No. 2 is met just S of **Altdorf** (see Rte 25A), with a view
ahead of the *Uri-Rotstock* (2928m) and adjacent peaks.

33   Chur to Klosters, Davos and the Flüelapass, for Susch, Scuol/Schuls and Martina (for Landeck)

Total distance, 124km (77 miles). No. 3. 15km *Landquart*—No. 28.
31.5km **Klosters**—10.5km **Davos**—31km **Susch**—No. 27. 22km
Scuol/Schuls—17km *Martina. Nauders* lies 8km E and **Landeck**
43km NE.

Maps: M 218; BL 39, or 5002, 5017.

CHUR (**Cuera** in Romansch and **Coire** in French; 595m; 32,050 inhab.;
15,550 in 1930), capital of the **Grisons**—or the **Graubünden**—is an
attractively situated town near the confluence of the Plessur with the
Rhine, and long an important hub of communications. It preserves a
fine cathedral and its regional Museum is of some interest; both are
in the older enceinte, SE of the newer town.

Roads from the Oberalppass (beyond which are the Furka and St.
Gotthard); the San Bernardino, and Splügen; the Julierpass (and the
Bernina and Maloja passes beyond); and also the Abulapass, can
converge on Chur, and that from the Flüelapass descends to meet the
valley only 15km N. To the NW it is commanded by the *Haldensteiner
Calanda* (2806m); to the NE by the *Montalin* (2266m); and to the S by
a spur of the *Dreibündenstein* (2174m).

The *Curia Rhaetorum* of the Romans, it was known to have been the seat of a
bishop in 452, although the see was probably founded a century earlier. Its
prelates soon dominated the district, becoming princes of the Holy Roman
Empire in 1170. Its burghers eventually threw off the episcopal yoke in 1464 and
in 1524 accepted the Reformation, as did the majority of the canton during the
next few years.

The canton, the largest (some 7100km²), is also the most sparsely populated
in Switzerland (24 per km²), being predominantly Alpine in character. It is
named after 'the league of the Greys' (see below), and consists of a network of
mountain valleys—the flora of the upper valleys being extraordinarily rich—the
streams descending which drain into the Rhine, the Danube and Po. About 35
per cent of its inhabitants speak German, some 20 per cent speak Italian and
approx. 25 per cent (at least 40,000) among themselves speak *Romansch* or the
Ladin dialect, derived from the 'lingua rustica' or vernacular Latin of the Roman
Empire.

This is divided into four or five dialects: in the Vorderrhein valley (from just
W of Chur to the Oberalppass) *Sursilvan* is spoken; in the lower part of the
Hinterrhein valley (N and S of Thusis), the variant of *Sutsilvan*; in the
Oberhalbstein valley (from Lenzerheide to the Julierpass), *Surmiran*; and in the
Albula valley, the Ober-engadine, Unter-engadine, and Val Müstair, two

variants of Ladin (*Puter* and *Vallader*), except in the vicinity of the main resorts. Needless to say the inhabitants of these valleys also speak either German or—to a lesser extent—Italian. Despite attempts to preserve the language and its scanty literature, both here and in pockets of NE Italy, erosion continues.

The natives of the canton, apparently of Celtic stock, were thoroughly Romanised—the Grisons representing the S part of the province of Rhaetia. Its interest for the Romans—and throughout the course of its history—was determined by its position as a channel of communication through which the richer lands of the South might carry their merchandise into Northern Europe. In the 6C Rhaetia passed into Frankish hands and in 916 it was in part incorporated into the German Empire.

Its medieval history is a record of the gradual enfranchisement of its inhabitants from the ecclesiastical and civil magnates by whom they were oppressed. In 1367 the *League of the House of God* (Lia da Ca Dè) was formed, and in 1395 that of the *Upper* or *Grey League* (Lia Grischa), renewed in 1424, followed in 1436 by that of *The Ten Juristictions* (Lia dellas Desch Dretturas, or Zehngerichtenbund). The three are said to have united at Vazerol in 1471 to establish the *Triple Perpetual League*, although the first satisfactorily recorded account refers to a meeting in 1524 at Ilanz. The nobles were overpowered and many of their castles destroyed. In 1497 the three made common cause with the Swiss Confederation in the struggle for independence and it was men of the Grisons who won the battle of the Calven Gorge in 1499.

The *Valtellina*, acquired in 1512, was ruled as a dependency for some 300 years, during which period, in 1620–39, the Engadine family of Planta sided with the Spaniards and the Salis family of the Val Bregaglia with the French. In 1799 the cantons of the Triple Perpetual League were incorporated into the Helvetic Republic, and in 1803 the Grisons became the 18th canton of the Swiss Confederation.

For centuries the Graubündner have emigrated, acquiring a reputation as pastry-cooks and confectioners, etc., but they usually returned to their native province on retirement, where they confected their graffito-decorated mansions. One of the earliest descriptions of the area is an 'Account of the Grisons' by John Leonhardi (London; 1711).

Several roads converge on the POSTPLATZ, a short distance S of the *Railway Station* and *Tourist Office*, and on the NW side of the Altstadt, which still preserves mainly 15–17C buildings.

Immediately NE of the square is the **Kunsthaus**, deserving reformation, but containing: Three girls singing, and a Self-portrait of 1780, by *Angelika Kauffmann* (1741–1807), born at Chur (see below) and one of the original members of the Royal Academy in London; *Ferdinand Hodler*, Cliffs overhanging the Rhône; *Giovanni Giacometti*, Self-portrait, and portrait of Alberto Giacometti in 1921; numerous drawings and sculptures by the latter; several works by *Augusto Giacometti*, including a Self-portrait; and representative paintings by *Giovanni Segantini*.

The Poststrasse leads S, passing (left) the arcaded *Rathaus* (15C), behind which, at No. 57 Reichsgasse, was Angelika Kauffmann's birthplace; see above. We shortly reach a small square, SW of which is a market-place surrounded by restored houses, and just beyond, an esplanade skirting the Plessur. A few paces to the W are the *Obertor* and the adjacent *Pulverturm*, relics of medieval fortifications.

To the E end of the square stands *St. Martins-Kirche*, 15C with a 16C tower, but of Carolingian foundation. The characteristic Kirchgasse leads behind the church to the recently reformed ***Rhaetian** or **Rätisches Museum**.

GROUND FLOOR: The Splügen-Chiavenna coach; carved and painted furniture and boxes, etc.—Stairs descend to the BASEMENT past a bronze pitcher (5–4C BC) to reach the Archaeological section, with Neolithic steles, Bronze Age implements, Iron Age ceramics,

jewellery, fibulae, terra sigillata, glass, votive altars, Roman bronze
statuettes, helmets of the late La Tène period, etc.—FIRST FLOOR:
Paintings, including Views of Chur, and Maps, on the stair. Medieval
arms and armour; silver; furniture; dies and coins; weights and
measures; pewter; gold plaques from an altar of c 600; sections of a
marble screen from the cathedral; finds from the cemetery of Bonaduz
(mid 4–5C).—SECOND FLOOR: 18–19C arms; 16–17C crossbows,
etc.; peasant costumes; furniture and linen, etc.; glass; pottery; and
examples of wood-carving and metalwork; a Testament in Romansch
printed at Scuol in 1743; Roman and Greek pottery and glass,
etc.—THIRD FLOOR: 19C furniture; musical instruments, etc.

Hence, ascending through the *Torturm*, the *Bischöflicher Hof* or
Bishop's Court is entered, dominated by the *Cathedral, built between
1178 and 1272 on the site of an older church. Some 8C masonry from
this is said to be incorporated in the present edifice, which was
probably erected over a Roman temple. The building, the plan of
which is unsymmetrical—the nave and its vaults being out of align-
ment with the choir—shows a combination of Gothic methods and
forms of construction with Romanesque details; the carvings and
sculpture reveal a strong Italian influence.

The *interior*, restored in the 1920s, preserves several quaint capitals
above its massive piers. At the W end of the N aisle is the tomb of
Jürg Jenatsch (died 1639; see p 275) and the Katharinenaltar (c
1500); in the S aisle the sarcophagus of Bp Ortlieb von Brandis (died
1491). In the S transept is a 15C chapel with a carved Pietà and
Lombardic ornamentation (8C) on the altar; the altarpiece is dated
1545. The *Choir*, some 15 steps higher than the nave, contains late
Gothic stalls and a richly carved *Winged-altar* by Jakob Russ (died
1490). At the foot of the steps is a stone tabernacle of 1584. The vault
of the *Crypt* rests on a single pillar supported by a man squatting on
a lion. A second crypt or apse lies to the E of the first. The *Treasury*
contains a rich assortment of cult objects, and charters of
Charlemagne (773) and Louis le Débonnaire (831), etc.

To the N is the *Bishop's Palace*, rebuilt in the 18C, skirting which
one may ascend the vine-clad hill to the SE, where above a small
cemetery (views) is the over-restored church of *St. Luzi*, partly 12C,
preserving a crypt of Carolingian foundation. A few paces N is the site
of what was probably the 6C funerary chapel of the first bishops of
Chur.

From the N side of the Bishop's Palace, where the *Marsölturm* is
believed to represent a Roman precursor, one may descend NW along
several characteristic lanes, and later (right) past *St. Regula* (1500) to
reach the Grabenstrasse; turn left to regain the Postplatz.

At No. 31 Masanserstrasse, leading N at this turning, is the *Natural History
Museum*, devoted to the rich flora and fauna of the Grisons.

For the roads from Chur to **Andermatt** and **Bellinzona** see Rtes 38 and 37
respectively; for that via Lenzerheide, Tiefencastel and the Julierpass for
Silvaplana and **St. Moritz**, see Rte 35 in reverse.

FROM CHUR TO AROSA (31km). The narrow and winding road ascends steeply
to the SE through a defile, and follows the valley to the E high above the
narrow-gauge railway line which threads several tunnels at a lower level. To the
N rises the *Hochwang* (2533m), while to the SE, beyond the high-lying village
of *Tschiertschen*, is the *Weisshorn* (2653m); ahead is the *Tiejer Flue* (SE; 2781m).
At (22km) *Langwies*, situated amid rich pastures, a track leads E up to the
Strelapass (2350m) for *Davos*. The road turns S. To the N rises the *Mattjisch Horn*
(2461m), with flora of interest, to the E of which another path climbs NE to the

Durannapass (2117m), descending to *Küblis* in the Prättigau. Below us is a remarkable 290m-long railway viaduct spanning a tributary of the Plessur. We climb again to enter (9km) **Arosa** (1739m), a well-sheltered and well-equipped resort long favoured by the English, surrounded by pine-woods, and clustering round two small lakes. In the older part stands an interesting example of a late Gothic mountain church.

Ski-lifts mount to the W, providing approaches to several peaks, among them the *Hornli belvedere* (2513m), while to the S ascends the WELSCHTOBEL VALLEY, dominated by the *Arosa Rothorn* (W; 2980m), the *Lenzer Horn* (SW; 2906m), the *Guggernell* (S; 2810m) and, to the E, the *Sandhubel* (2764m). At the head of the valley is the *Furcletta Pass* (2573m), leading to *Alvaneu*; while due E of Arosa is the *Maienfelder Furgga Pass* (2440m) from which a path descends into the Zügen valley S of *Davos*.

For the road N from Chur to (15km) **Landquart** see the latter part of Rte 29A, in reverse. At Landquart we turn abruptly E below *Malans*, above which rises the *Vilan* (2376m), following the line of the Rhaetian railway, and shortly enter the defile of the *Klus* below the ruined castle of *Fracstein*. This forms the entrance to the district known as the PRÄTTIGAU (in Romansch the *Val Pratens*, or valley of meadows), watered by the Landquart, and noted for the beauty of its woods, orchards and pastures. To the N rises the Rätikon range, separating the valley from the Vorarlberg, in Austria, and, further E, the upland vale of Montafon.

5km *Seewis*, on a height to the N (where in 1622 Protestant peasants slew Fidelis, a Capuchin monk who was a leader of the Counter-Reformation), is a convenient base for the ascent of the *Schesaplana* (2964m), on the frontier to the NE.—The road passes the ruined castle of *Solavers*, and *Grusch*, at the foot of the TASCHINASBACH VALLEY, with several picturesque old houses.—From (5km) *Schiers*, a road climbs to *Schuders* (1272m), from which the ascents of a number of peaks in the *Rätikon massif* are made, passing en route hamlets preserving old wooden houses of some interest.—10.5km *Küblis* (814m) lies at the entrance of the ST. ANTÖNIENTAL.

The village of *St. Antönien* itself is 11km NE. Beyond it rises the imposing limestone cliffs of the *Sulzfluh* (2817m); to the NE and E are the *Gruobenpass* (2232m), for *Schruns*, and the *St. Antonier Joch* (2379m), for *Gargellen*, both in Austria. To the SE rises the *Madrisa* (2826m).

Conters, reached by a steep road climbing SE from Küblis, is on the path leading to the imposing *Durannapass* (2117m) and *Langwies*, 9km N of Arosa; see above.

The main road continues to climb, with snow mountains appearing ahead, past *Saas*, with a characteristic church-tower, which was practically wiped out by an avalanche in 1722, and at 9.5km reaches *Klosters Dorf*, providing a good retrospective view down the valley. To the NE is the *Schlappiner Joch pass* (2202m), for *Gargellen*.

1.5km **Klosters** (1179m) is an old established and attractively sited resort, long frequented by the English and a good centre for excursions. It lies in a sheltered position below the *Parsenn* (SW), to which ski-lifts mount, and with a view E towards the *Silvrettagruppe* on the Austrian frontier. Its parish *Church*, altered in 1634, and once that of a Premonstratensian foundation, preserves 16C murals in its apse.

A road leads E to *Monbiel*, from which tracks and paths ascend towards the Silvretta massif, notable among which are the *Silvrettahorn* (3244m), with its glacier, and the *Verstanclahorn* (3298m); to the S of the latter, and further W, is the *Piz Buin* (3312m), among several other peaks above 3000m. At *Alp Novai* one may follow a track SE up the VEREINTAL towards the *Flesspass* (2453m),

below the *Platternhörner* (3220m) and W of the *Piz Linard* (3411m); another pass
leads SW past the *Jöriseen* tarns to meet the No. 28 not far W of the *Flüelapass*;
see below.

The main road climbs steeply S from Klosters through woods to the
watershed, and descends past the little *Davoser See* to (10km)
Davos-Dorf, extending SW up the wide mountain valley to contiguous
Davos-Platz (1558m; 10,450 inhab.), a full-blown tourist resort, which
has grown very considerably since it was described by R.L. Stevenson
as 'a village of hotels'. Its dry sunny situation, sheltered from cold
winds, and its clear air made it for some time one of the more important
sanatoria in Europe for the cure of consumption, but in recent decades
it has again expanded as a winter-sports centre.

It was first heard of in 1160 as a mere mountain pasture or 'Alp', the meaning
of *Tavau* in Romansch, and was settled in the 13C by immigrants from the upper
Rhône. In 1860 it had less than 2000 inhabitants. In 1865 a Dr Alexander
Spengler, praising its health-giving qualities, did much to promote its rapid
growth; the first winter visitors from England arrived here in 1869. A Colonel
Napier introduced skis to Davos in 1888.
  John Addington Symonds (1840–93) practically made it his home from 1877
until shortly before his death in Rome, and most of his books were written here,
including his charming account of it in 'Our Life in the Swiss Highlands' (1891).
It was likewise described in his 'Essays of Travel' by Robert Louis Stevenson,
who spent two winters here (1880–82) and issued from the 'Davos Press' his
'Moral Emblems'. Thomas Mann conceived 'The Magic Mountain' ('Der Zauer-
berg'; 1924) when visiting Davos in 1912. James Elroy Flecker died here in
January 1915. In 1894 Conan Doyle, whose wife was consumptive, began his
'Brigadier Gerard' series here, and laid out the original golf-course for his own
amusement. Llewelyn Powys (1884–1939), author of 'Swiss Essays' (1947), died
here. The only Swiss resorts remaining open in winter before 1900 were Davos,
Grindelwald and St. Moritz.

The church at Davos-Dorf dates from the early 16C; that of Davos-
Platz has a choir and tower of 1481 with a spire added a century later,
and contains glass by A. Giacometti. The *Rathaus* (1564) was largely
rebuilt in 1930.

From Davos-Dorf a funicular climbs towards the *Weissfluhjoch* (2693m), below
the *Weissfluh* (2843m). From *Schatzalp* (1861m), with a *Snow and Avalanche
Research Station*, just above Davos-Platz, a lift ascends to near the *Schiahorn*
(2709m) and the *Strelapass* (2350m) for *Langwies*, N of Arosa; while others
approach the *Jakobshorn* (SE; 2950m).
  On either side of the Jakobshorn are two valleys, partly served by roads, the
DISCHMATAL (N) leading SE towards the *Piz Vadret* (3229m) and other peaks
and glaciers in its vicinity; and the SERTIGTAL, with the *Hoch Ducan* (3063m)
and *Piz Kesch* (3418m) beyond, among other summits rising to over 3000m. At
the head of the two valleys are the *Scalettapass* (2606m) and the *Sertigpass*
(2739m) with the VAL FUNTAUNA between them.

FROM DAVOS TO TIEFENCASTEL (31km). The road leads SW up a narrowing
mountain-flanked valley past the old hamlet of *Frauernkirch*, and later threads
tunnels in the defile of the *Zügen* (so-named from the 'tracks' of the avalanches
by which it has been swept). We later climb along the N side of the picturesque
Landwässer gorge, with a view of the narrow-gauge railway-viaduct (with a
central arch 210m wide), and later descend, with a view (right) of the ruins of
Belfort, to meet the Albulapass road 4.5km before reaching *Tiefencastel*; see Rte
35. For the road hence to Chur via *Lenzerheide* see the sub-route on p 280, in
reverse; for that to La Punt-Chamues-ch. see p 274, likewise in reverse.

From the N end of Davos we turn E up the FLÜELATAL, soon veering
to the SE, steadily climbing through a somewhat dreary landscape to
(14km) the **Flüelapass** (2383m), its road constructed by 1867, between

the *Flüela-Wisshorn* (N; 3085m) and, to the S, the *Schwarzhorn* (3147m).

The Schwarzhorn commands one of the finest panoramas in Switzerland, including the Silvretta massif to the NE, the Piz Vadret (SE), the Bernina (in the distance), Piz Kesch (S), the Corn da Tinizong (SW), the Valais and the Bernese Alps (in the distance), the Lenzerhorn (W), the Tödi and Glärnisch Alps, the Schesaplana (NW), the Lower Engadine, and a retrospective view towards Davos.

The road now descends the stony VAL SUSASCA, providing several fine views, among them (right) up the VAL GRIALETSCH, dominated by the *Piz Vadret* (3229m) and its extensive glacier, and later climbs down between the *Piz Murtera* (N; 3044m) and *Piz dal Ras* (3025m) in steep loops to the valley floor at (14km) Susch, with a view ahead of the *Piz Arpiglias* (3027m).

Susch (1426m), a small village, much of which was burnt by a fire in 1925, was once of strategic importance, and one of the low hills surrounding it bears the ruined keep of *Chaschinas*. Another old tower and a large early 16C church are notable.

For the road hence to Zernez and **St. Moritz** see Rte 34.

The road bears NE down the long **Unter Engadine** (or *Engiadina Bassa* in Romansch), the lower part of the Engadine valley, one of the most attractive and unspoilt in the country. The Engadine, from the Maloja Pass beyond St. Moritz to Martina, is approx. 100km long, and the predominant language—except in the main tourist centres—is Romansch. We follow the left bank of the Inn or En, which eventually, after passing through Innsbruck in Austria, flows into the Danube at Passau in Germany.

At (3.5km) *Lavin*—its name alluding to ˙its exposure to avalanches—the VAL LAVINUOZ opens to the left, overlooked by the *Piz Linard* (3411m), the highest of the Silvretta Alps, the majority of which form the frontier range further N.—At the next hamlet, at the entrance to the VAL TUOI, we get a glimpse of the *Piz Buin* (3312m) at its head. Several villages in the Lower Engadine are perched at a higher level than the main road, basking in the sun, among them near here being *Guarda* and the hamlet of *Bos-cha*, both commanding extensive views S towards the *Piz Nuna* (3124m) and *Piz Plavna Dadaint* (3166m), etc.

8km **Ardez**, containing several characteristic 16–18C houses and a 16C church, commands a fine view down the valley towards Schloss Tarasp (see below) and is dominated by the ruins of 13C *Steinberg*.—To the right opens the VAL SAMPUOIR, with the *Piz Laschadurella* (3046m) at its head.

At the head of the VAL TASNA, which is shortly passed to the left, is the *Pass Futschöl* (2768m), just E of the *Augstenberg* (3230m), leading over to *Galtür* in the Austrian Paznauntal.

The road climbs down towards the river, with the high-lying village of *Ftan* (1633m) above us to the left, preserving a number of old houses and a 17C church with a separate belfry. To the right rises the *Piz Pisoc* (3174m).—A right-hand turning leads shortly to *Bad Tarasp*, a small spa in a somewhat confined site, with springs known since the 15C. SE of Bad Tarasp, on terraces on the far bank of the Inn, lies the resort of *Vulpera*.

W of Vulpera, at a higher level, occupying the summit of a conical hill, stands ***Schloss Tarasp**, dating from the 11C and an isolated Austrian possession as late as 1801. It was rebuilt in the early 17C but then fell into ruin and was restored early this century. It contains a good collection of furniture, etc., and may be visited; enquire at the tourist office at Scuol.

Schloss Tarasp, Engadine

At 10.5km (from Ardez) the road by-passes **Scoul** (or **Schuls**, 1243m), which should be entered. It is the main town of the Lower Engadine and lies on a plateau above the N bank of the Inn. The lower town or *Unter-Schuls* preserves—near the high bridge—a conspicuous church rebuilt in the 16C, several characteristic 17C houses, and a *Museum* devoted to the region in the 'Clostra' or 'Chagronda', near the lower covered wooden *Bridge*.

Hence a minor road, later a track, climbs steeply up the S bank of the Inn and then the VAL S-CHARL, watered by the Clemgia, in part following a gorge, the W bank of which is an enclave of the *National Park*; see Rte 34. Further SE is the *Cruschetta Pass* (2296m) below the *Piz Sesvenna* (3205m), on the Italian frontier NW of *Tubre* (formerly Taufers im Münstertal), just NE of Müstair; the VAL MÜSTAIR may also be reached via the *Pass da Costainas* (2251m); see Rte 34.

SE of Scuol rises the *Piz Lischana* (3105m), with its glacier, a stiff climb rewarded by a magnificent panorama, from the Tödi to the W to the distant Dolomites.

The main road continues NE from Scuol, but a minor road may also be followed through high-lying *Sent*, an attractive village partly rebuilt after a fire in 1921, with a 16C church, frescoed houses, an 11C tower and a ruined 15C church with a Romanesque tower, and of Carolingian foundation.

A bridge later crosses the Inn to *Sur En*, at the foot of the VAL D'UINA, traversed by a track, partly blasted along the side of a cliff, and then threading the imposing ravine of *Il Quar*, to reach the frontier *Passo di Slìngia* (2309m) for *Burgusio* or *Màlles Venosta/Mals*.

8km *Ramosch*, a village at the foot of the VAL SINESTRA, with the *Piz Arina* (2828m) to the N and the *Piz S-chalambert-Dadaint* (3031m) to the SE. It preserves an interesting early 16C church with a fine tower and a ruined fort.—The road circles to the N, with a view of the *Muttler* (N; 3294m) on the Austrian frontier. Several hamlets are passed, among them *Strada*, above which rises *Piz Lad* (SE; 2808m)—marking the meeting of the Swiss, Austrian and Italian frontiers—to approach (9km) *Martina* (1035m), the main frontier village (Customs).

The actual frontier is formed by the Inn bridge, beyond which a very tortuous road climbs in zigzags to (8km E) *Nauders* (1394m), on the road NE down the Inn valley to (44km) **Landeck**; see *Blue Guide Austria*. Nauders also lies only 4km N of the Italian frontier (Customs) at the *Reschenpass* or *Passo di Rèsia*, for *Merano*; see *Blue Guide Northern Italy*.

FROM MARTINA TO SAMNAUN (20.5km). The road is continued along the left bank of the Inn to (6km) *Vinadi*, where one may also cross into Austria to meet the main road between Nauders and Landeck at the *Kajetanbrücke*, 4km beyond, after threading the *Finstermünz* defile. The narrow road, now little more than a track, ascends steeply into the VAL SAMNAUN parallel to the frontier. The mountain-encircled enclave, with a wild grandeur and remoteness not found in the broader valleys of the Engadine, is now a tax-free area. The main village is *Compatsch*, with a 16C church; the upper hamlet of *Samnaun* lies at 1840m, from which the *Zeblasjoch pass* (2539m) leads into the FIMBERTAL and to *Ischgl* in Austria.

34 Susch to Zernez (for Müstair) and St. Moritz; and Pontresina (for the Passo del Bernina): the Ober-Engadine

Total distance, 39km (24 miles). No. 27. 6km **Zernez**—27km. *Samedan* lies to the right—6km **St. Moritz**. **Pontresina** lies 4km SE of the Samedan crossroads.

Maps: M 218; BL 39, 44, or 5013, 5017.

From **Susch** (see p 269) we turn S through a wooded defile threaded by the Inn, which opens out as **Zernez** is approached, a pleasantly situated village lying at the junction of valleys at 1473m and a good centre from which to explore the neighbouring National Park and the Val Müstair; see below.

On a slope to the NE is the *Church*, rebuilt in 1607 but retaining a Romanesque tower and containing elaborate stucco-work in its choir. There are several 16C houses in the village; the *Schloss Planta-Wildenberg* was the home of the Planta family for 450 years from 1400. A medieval tower stands outside the centre.

The view N is particularly fine, with the *Piz Linard* (3411m) rising beyond the Inn narrows, and with the nearer *Piz d'Arpiglias* (3027m) and *Piz Nuna* (3124m) to the NE; to the NW are the *Piz dal Ras* (3025m) and *Piz Arpschella* (3032m), while immediately to the W is the *Piz d'Urezza* (2906m).

FROM ZERNEZ TO MÜSTAIR (48km). Driving SE on the No. 28 past *Offices of the National Park* (which can provide detailed walking maps and other information), we shortly climb steeply above the Spöl, the main Swiss affluent of the Inn and one of only two streams entering the country from Italy. For the Val Cluozza see below. To the S rises the *Piz Terza* (2686m), with the *Piz Murtèr* (2836m) beyond, while to the NE is the *Piz Laschadurella* (3046m). A reservoir lies in the valley below. After c 8km the road enters the NW edge of the **Swiss National Park**, perhaps better described as a 'Reserve', established in 1909 to provide a protected zone for its flora and fauna.

The extent of the park, which scenically ranks with the most imposing parts of the country, but which is of very irregular shape, is 143km². Shooting, fishing, plant-collecting, flower-picking, wood-cutting, lighting fires, camping, or leaving any form of rubbish, etc., are strictly forbidden and the penalties for any infringement of the statutory prohibitions are rightly severe. Guards and keepers are constantly on the watch. Visitors are requested not to stray from the many marked paths without special permission.

Geologically, the park is of interest, containing within its bounds both the primitive crystalline of the W Alps and the characteristic dolomites of the E Alps, but its geological formation is difficult to interpret on account of extensive denudation, with streams, ridges and valleys running in every direction. The summits of its peaks are very much of equal altitude, with over 100 between 2880 and 3200m. Its fauna includes chamois, red deer, roe deer, marmots, martens, foxes, eagles, and many game birds. Ibexes, which had become extinct in Switzerland, were re-introduced in 1920. There are no wolves. The last bear was shot in 1904 and the last lynx in 1872. The flora is rich and varied, including many of the rarest Alpine plants.

The VAL CLUOZZA, to the W of the Piz Terza, one of the most striking parts of the park, may be entered immediately SE of Zernez, beyond which rises the stratified *Piz dal Diavel* (3062m). A fatiguing path ascends to the SW between the *Piz Quattervals* (3165m) and the glacier-buttressed *Piz Serra* (2095m) to the S, descending into the VAL MÜSCHAUNS below the symmetrical *Piz d'Esan* (3127m) and then into the wooded VAL TRUPCHUN, to gain the main road (No. 27) at *S-chanf*, 14km SW of Zernez.

The views as the road descends, with the majestic *Piz del Diavel* (3062m) prominent to the right, are very fine, and after 4km we reach the *Punt la Drossa*, at the N entrance of a tunnel into the duty-free enclave of the VALLE DI LIVIGNO, one of the few segments of Italian territory N of the watershed.—*Livigno* itself, a long straggling village, lies 12km S, beyond the *Lago del Gallo*, and in recent decades has been developed as a winter-sports centre.—The main road circles to the NE along the VAL DEL FUORN or OFEN , said to derive its name from an iron foundry worked here in the 17C, with views of the jagged peaks to the N of the *Piz del Fuorn* (2906m); and to the NE, the *Piz Nair* (3010m) and *Piz Tavrü* (3168m); to the S is *La Schera* (2578m).

Beyond a hotel, the road ascends steadily up the valley, watered by the Ova dal Fuorn, to reach the E edge of the park at a height of 1968m (good retrospective views). It soon gains the **Ofenpass** (or *Pass dal Fuorn*; 2149m), commanding a wonderful *View down the VAL MÜSTAIR, the Romansch-speaking valley which descends in steps to the frontier. The *Piz Umbrail* (3033m) and the Ortler group rise to the SE. The road climbs down steeply in several zigzags to (6km from the pass) *Tschierv* (1660m), the highest village, below which *Fuldera* and *Valchava* are traversed. The church of Valchava, with a slender onion-domed tower, contains a small Baroque organ. The VAL VAU leads to the SW.—7.5km **Santa Maria**, the prosperous narrow-streeted main village, has a 15C Gothic church with several tombstones of interest. It was the birthplace of Simon Lemm (Lemnius; 1511–50, at Chur), the satirist and poet, who crossed swords with Luther.

Hence a very steep road, little more than a track, climbs in zigzags due S up the VAL MURANZA to (16km) the **Pass Umbrail** (2501m; the highest of the Swiss road passes; also known as the *Giogo di Santa Maria*; Customs), on the Italian frontier. It provides a view of the glaciers of the Ortler group. 3km E is the **Stèlvio Pass** (2757m), the road completed in 1835. *Bormio* (see *Blue Guide Northern Italy*), lies 17km SW of the former pass; the latter was held by Austrian troops during the First World War, it being then on the Austro-Italian frontier.

The main road descends NE below the lofty wall of mountains to the E to (4km) **Müstair**, the frontier village, the lower part at 1247m, where stands the ancient Benedictine convent traditionally thought to have been founded by Charlemagne, from which it takes its name—Münster or Müstair. The convent itself is under restoration, and contains a small collection of Baroque images, Carolingian carved stones, etc. The adjacent *Church, retaining its triple apse, was largely rebuilt in the 15C but preserves several marble tombstones and 8–9C frescoes, in several cases unfortunately repainted; among them are the Martyrdom of St. Andrew, the Pantocrator, Salome (Life of the Baptist), the Stoning of St. Stephen (see 274), etc. The relief of the Baptism of Christ and the early 12C stucco statue of Charlemagne will also be noted.

The frontier lies 1km beyond (Customs). The road hence descends through a *gorge of the Calven*, where in 1499 the Swiss defeated the Austrians and won their practical independence of the Empire. At 12km the main road at *Sluderno/Schluderns*, in the upper valley of the Adige, is reached. For *Merano*, 52km E, see *Blue Guide Northern Italy*. For *Nauders*, 31km N, just beyond the Austrian border, see the last section of Rte 33.

The No. 27 leads SW from Zernez, shortly climbing into the upper valley of the Inn or En, known as the **Ober-Engadine**, which lies at an altitude of between 1500 and 1800m (roughly between 5000 and 6000 feet).

Its flora is rich and varied and its climate severe, an advantage for winter-sports. The predominant language, except in the larger centres, is Romansch. It is largely a straight level trough, with a maximum width of c 1.5km, and it contains several lakes in its upper end. To the SE it is bounded by the Bernina range and to the NW by the Albula group, while of its several lateral valleys, the most important is the Val Bernina, leading SE from Pontresina.

Driving SW, the *Piz Vadret* (3229m) rises to the W, and the *Piz Kesch* (3418m) to the SW; to the S is the *Piz d'Esan* (3127m), near the W edge of the National Park; see above.

11km *Capella*, from which a path climbs NW up the VAL SUSAUNA to the *Scalettapass* (2606m) for *Davos*; see Rte 33.—3km *S-chanf*. A path ascends SE to the *Pass Chaschauna* (2694m; fine views) for *Livigno*; see above.—2km **Zuoz**, once the main village of the Upper Engadine. It was the original home of the Planta family and preserves

Müstair; detail of The Stoning of St. Stephen, fresco in the church of St. Johann

the 13C tower of their ancestral mansion, and several 16C houses in the vicinity of the DORFPLATZ. Its slender-spired church, of Romanesque origin, was rebuilt in the early 16C.

The ruins of *Guardaval* are shortly passed, and at 4km *La Punt-Chamues-ch* is entered. SE lies the VAL CHAMUERA, on either side of which rise the *Piz Mezzaun* (N; 2963m) and the *Munt Müsella* (2630m).

FROM LA PUNT-CHAMUES-CH TO TIEFENCASTEL: THE ALBULAPASS (40km). This minor route is described as an alternative to the much better engineered road over the *Julierpass*; see Rte 35. Some distance beyond the pass it follows the line of the *Albula Railway*, a narrow-gauge line to Thusis via Filisur and Tiefencastel (with a branch from Filisur to Davos), built at the cost of £920,000 between 1898 and 1903, which included the piercing of numerous tunnels and the construction of several viaducts. The narrow road climbs steeply NW and veers W along the VAL D'ALVRA to (9.5km) the **Albulapass** (2312m), one regularly used from the 13C. To the E rises the *Piz Uertsch* (3268m); to the S, the *Piz de las Blais* (2930m), below which is the S entrance to the main railway tunnel below the range. Shortly beyond the pass the steep and somewhat tortuous descent commences, passing the *Palpuogna lake* (left) to the hamlet of *Preda*, below the *Piz Muot* (N; 2670m), with the *Piz Ela* (3339m) prominent to the W. The road is now frequently crossed by the railway, which here threads a number of loops and spiral tunnels in overcoming the difference in level as it descends to (13.5km) *Bergün* (*Bravuogn* in Romansch; 1367m), an old village with a 12C church and slender tower. A path climbs NE hence to the *Sertigpass* (2739m; see p 268), while to the W rise the dolomitic peaks of the *Corn da Tinizong* (3172m) and *Piz Mitgel* (3159m). We later traverse *Filisur* (1032m), the junction for the line to Davos, dominated by the *Muchettu* to the E (2623m), while ahead to the NW rise the *Lenzer Horn* (2906m) and *Aroser Rothorn* (2980m). The road now bears due W to meet at 12.5km that from Davos to *Tiefencastel*, with the massive ruin of *Belfort* on the far side of the valley; see p 268.

The railway and car-carrier, which tunnels below the Albula range, enters the Engadine at *Bever*, now by-passed by the main road, and turns SW to (7km) **Samedan** (1705m), the junction, a village preserving a number of stone houses and the *Haus Planta*, another residence of that ancient and influential family, whose crest (a bear's paw) is much in evidence. The birthplace of Jürg Jenatsch (1596–1639), a hero of the Grisons' struggle for independence, is pointed out. The church in the village centre, with its slender belfry, is 18C; to the W, at a higher level, is a late Gothic church containing the tombs of the Plantas.

To the SE, the *Muottas Muragl* (2568m), and beyond, the *Piz Muragl* (3157m), above Pontresina, are prominent; and to the NW, the *Piz Pradella* (2856m), and *Piz Ot* (3246m), among other summits of the range.

The old road from Samedan goes through (3km) **Celerina** (*Schlarigna* in Romansch), the lower end of the '*Cresta Run*', beyond which we climb above the *Charnadüra gorge* to reach the upper town of St. Moritz. This approach is more interesting than that by the new road, which veers S at Samedan and after 2km turns abruptly W near *San Gian*, an isolated church with a Romanesque choir, painted wooden ceiling of 1478 and 15C N Italian frescoes. It later skirts the partially wooded banks of the *Lake of St. Moritz* (Lej da San Murezzan), perhaps its most attractive feature.

Pontresina lies some 2km SE of this turning, the left-hand fork ascending through the village; the main road by-passing it to climb the VAL BERNINA; for both see pp 276–8.

ST. MORITZ (1822m; *San Murezzan* in Romansch), the cosmopolitan metropolis of the Engadine, consists of two distinct parts, the upper and older resort, or *Dorf*, which grew up on a sheltered and sunny slope around the church, and *St. Moritz-Bad* (1775m), SW of the lake. Of the church, only a late 16C leaning tower remains; not long before its demolition the church had been put to the practical use of a garage for the parish fire-engine. The lower town was reputed for its chalybeate spring, visited by Paracelsus in 1537, where the old Kurhaus was built in 1856. Votive offerings of the Bronze Age have been found there. Its importance as a winter-sporting centre is largely explained by the fact that it enjoys four or five months of cold, clear and dry weather in winter, almost without rain or thaw, and these ideal conditions have been exploited to the full.

It was first referred to in 1139; but it was not until 1835 that it was first resorted to in winter by visitors—for its climate rather than for its waters. In 1838 its three inns were referred to as accommodations 'of the homeliest kind'; its population was but 160, but it was 'rising in repute ... as a watering-place'. The first hotel of any consequence was not established until 1856–59 by Johannes Badrutt, who, by inviting a group of English there some years later, opened the floodgates ... by 1880 a curling match was in progress, with stones brought from Scotland, and soon after 'bandy', or ice-hockey, was introduced. In 1884 the artificial sleigh or toboggan run, the *Cresta Run*, was built on the initiative of three Englishmen; in 1886, providentially, a second spring was discovered; in 1896 the huge *Palace Hotel* was inaugurated; in 1903 the *Ski Club Alpina* was founded; by 1907 a cable-car was in operation, ascending to Muottas Muragl; in 1926 the Olympic Ski Jump was opened; in 1969 took place the first so-called *Ski Marathon* (held in mid March). The population of St. Moritz rises to 12,000 in the season, when in the exclusive *Corviglia Ski Club* hubris is at its headiest. It is now a terminus for the *Glacier Express* to Zermatt via Andermatt, a well-promoted 7½-hour scenic railway journey, and the *Palm Express*, via Ascona. Regular post-buses ply hence via Chiavenna to *Lugano*; see Rte 36.

Vaslav Nijinsky briefly settled at St. Moritz during the winter of 1917–18 before being diagnosed insane, giving his last charity performance at the Hotel Souvretta on 19 January 1918.

From the main crossroads, the Post Platz, on the E side of the upper town, one may follow the Via dal Bagn downhill—with a pleasant view over the lake—past the *Engadiner Museum*, largely devoted to the history and folk art of the region. A short distance beyond is the *English Church* (1871).—Climbing uphill hence, one may visit the *Segantini Museum*, in the form of a cupola, devoted to the art of Giovanni Segantini (1858–99).—Continue downhill to approach *St. Moritz-Bad*, spread out along the far bank of the Inn, which feeds the lake, embellished by a most up-to-date establishment known as the *Heilbadzentrum*, erected at vast expense and inaugurated in 1976.

Among the main peaks visible from St. Moritz-Dorf are: the *Piz Albana* (3100m) and *Piz Polaschin* (3013m) to the SW; the towering *Piz Julier* (or *Güglia*; 3380m), to the W; *Piz Nair* (NW; 3057m), *Piz Padella* (N; 2856m), *Piz Languard* (E; 3262m), *Piz Rosatsch* (3123m), *Piz Surlej* (3188m) and *Piz Corvatsch* (3451m), the last three in eschelon towards the S; the ridge-topped *Piz de la Margna* (up the valley to the SW; 3159m) and, in the distance beyond, the *Pizzo Cengalo* (3370m) and *Pizzo Badile* (3308m), marking the Italian frontier.

Several ascents may be made from St. Moritz-Dorf via the Chantarella and Corviglia funiculars, and from near the Heilbadzentrum in the lower town; also from neighbouring Celerina and from Punt Muragl, on the road to Pontresina.

For the road SW hence to *Maloja* and *Soglio* see below.

Pontresina (1805m) is less conventional and more of a village resort than St. Moritz, but likewise has all the usual winter-sporting facilities and it is also a good mountaineering base. It stretches along the steep slope above the Bernina torrent, facing SW towards the entrance of the Val Roseg. Its name probably means 'bridge over the Resina' (a brook in the village), although in the earliest records it appears as 'Pons Sarisina' and 'Pons Sarracenus'.

There were sufficient summer visitors by 1879 (including Mrs Gaskell, whose 'Wives and Daughters' was written here) for an *English Church* to be erected in the lower part of the village in that year. The railway arrived in 1908. Although several characteristic old houses survived a fire in 1718, its main building of interest (enquire re admission at the *Tourist Office*) is the little church of *Santa Maria, approached by a path from the upper town. It was largely rebuilt in the mid 15C, but retains its original 12C tower; inside there are wall-paintings of c 1230 and 1495. There are several English graves in the graveyard. Adjoining is an old tower known as *La Spaniola*, a name which ante-dates any association of the Spaniards with the district. The valley of the Inn served in the early 17C as one of the main routes of Spanish troops, etc., between Lombardy and Habsburg Austria.

Among excursions from Pontresina is that to *Muottas Muragl* (2453m), reached by funicular not far beyond the lower end of the village, and providing a fine general *View of the peaks and valleys of the district. Among the most prominent are (from S to N) the *Piz Zupò* (3996m) and **Piz Bernina** (4049m), both on the Italian frontier, the latter, the highest peak in the Bernina Alps, first ascended in 1850 by Herr Coaz of Chur, while in 1861 the first English mountaineers reached the summit. This is followed by the *Piz Tschierva* (3546m), *Piz Surlej* (3188m), *Piz de la Margna* (3159m), *Piz Julier* (3380m), *Piz Nair* (3057m), *Piz Ot* (3246m), *Crasta Mora* (2935m) and the snowy *Piz Kesch* (3418m). Below us lie Pontresina, St. Moritz, Celerina, Samedan and Bever; and to the SW the lakes of the Upper Engadine. A path descending to Pontresina may be followed with ease. SE of Pontresina, reached by path, rail, or by car (turning off the Bernina road) is *Morteratsch*, to the SW of which is the viewpoint of *Chünetta* (2083m), commanding a superb *View of the *Vadret* or *Morteratsch glacier*, surrounded by the *Munt Pers* (SE; 3207m) and *Piz Palü* (3905m), *Piz Zupò* (3996m), *Crast Agüzza* (3854m), *Piz Bernina* (4049m; see above), *Piz Morteratsch* (3751m) and *Piz Misaun* (3249m), among other peaks. In 1864 Prof. Tyndall almost lost his life in an avalanche when attempting to scale the Morteratsch. An attractive path leads SW up the VAL ROSEG (pron. Rosedge), with its splendid Arolla pines, to reach a hotel among green pastures surrounded by an amphitheatre of mountains, among them (from the E) the *Piz Chalchaga* (3154m), *Piz Misaun* (3249m), *Piz Tschierva* (3546m), *Piz Roseg* (3937m), *Piz Sella* (3517m), *Piz Glüschaint* (3594m), *Il Chapütschin* (3386m), *Piz Corvatsch* (3451m), *Piz Surlej* (3188m) and *Piz Rosatsch* (3123m). The hotel was once much closer to the foot of the glacier, which has receded; between its arms rises the green alp of *Piz Aguagliouls* (3118m). A better view of the imposing ice-falls is obtained from the *Alp Ota* (2257m), reached by a path above the left bank of the Roseg.

The ascent of the **Piz Languard** (3262m), rising almost due E of Pontresina (on the summit of which Johan Addington Symonds and Janet Catherine North exchanged engagement rings on 16 August 1864), presents few difficulties, few peaks of this height being so easily surmounted in good weather and with ordinary precautions. The path ascends near the church of Santa Maria through pinewoods to the *Alp Languard*, later climbing in zigzags. The *View is illimitable, embracing among the higher peaks the *Piz Kesch* (NNW; 3418m), *Piz Linard* (N; 3411m), the *Wildspitz* (NE, in Austria; 3772m), the *Ortler* (E, in Italy; 3905m); *Il Gran Zebrù* (just S of the last, and formerly the *Königspitze*; 3851m); to the S, the *Piz Palü* (3905m), *Piz Zupò* (3996m), *Piz Bernina* (4049m); *Piz Julier* (W; 3380m), *Piz Bever* (3230m), just N of the last, and *Piz d'Err* (3378m), beyond Piz Bever; *Piz Ot* (NW; 3246m) and the *Piz d'Ela* (3339m), to the right, beyond Piz Ot; while *Monte Rosa* (4634m) is visible to the SW, but not prominent.

FROM PONTRESINA TO TIRANO (50km). The main road (No. 29), completed in 1864, ascends SE up the VAL BERNINA, closely following the line of the *Bernina Railway*, constructed in 1906–10 and the highest 'adhesion' (i.e., ordinary) railway in the Alps (except for a section of the Jungfrau line), attaining a height of 2255m: for boldness of construction and magnificence of scenery it has few rivals. The descent on the S side of the pass, where the line runs some distance W of the road as far as Poschiavo, is in part negotiated by a series of hairpin bends, and travels beneath several avalanche galleries. It commands remarkable views of the *Palü Glacier*, and from *Alp Grüm*, down into the Poschiavo valley, prior to making the corkscrew descent.

At 5km the road passes the turning for *Morteratsch* (see above), shortly after obtaining both a fine retrospective view and then a view of the *Morteratsch Glacier*, surrounded by a dazzling array of snow-clad peaks, and later of the *Bernina Falls*. To the left rises the *Piz Albris* (3166m). The group of houses known as the *Bernina Suot* is passed.

They lie at the foot of the VAL DAL FAIN (Hay Valley), noted for its flora, through which a path climbs to the *La Stretta pass* (2476m), at the S end of the VALLE DI LIVIGNO (see p 272), from which a road crosses the *Forcola di Livigno* (2315m) to meet the Bernina road beyond its pass.

At 6.5km we pass the lower terminus of a cable-car ascending SW to the *Diavolezza Pass* (2973m), between the *Munt Pers* (NW; 3207m) and the *Piz Tròvat* (3146m), providing an outstanding *View* of the Bernina massif and its glaciers. Another lift shortly rises to the *Piz Lagalb* (SE; 2959m), likewise commanding a fine panorama.—We skirt the banks of the three Bernina lakes (Lej Pitschen, Lej Nair and Lej Bianco), the narrow strip of land beneath the last two being the watershed between the Danube and the Po. *Lago Bianco* is dammed; beyond it is the glistening glacier below snow-capped *Piz Cambrena* (3604m).

The **Bernina Pass** (2328m), with its adjacent hospice and tarn, is crossed, the road having been constructed in 1842–64. It provides a splendid view of the mountain-encircled upper VAL POSCHIAVO, with (from E to W) the *Piz Paradisin* (3302m), beyond which is the *Passo da Val Viola* (2489m) for Bormio; the *Scima da Saoseo* (3264m), *Piz Sena* (3075m), *Piz Cancian* (S; 3103m), *Piz Varuna* (3453m), the *Sasso Rosso* (3481m), *Piz Cambrena* (3604m) and the *Piz Palü* (3905m), beyond. The road descends steeply in a series of wide curves to (14.5km) *San Carlo*, a village with a red-roofed church-tower, 2km beyond which Poschiavo (1021m) is entered, dominated by the stony *Sassalb* (E; 2892m).

Poschiavo, although long in dispute between the bishops of Chur and Como, has belonged to the Grisons since 1486. The two earliest books printed in Ladin (see p 264) were produced here, in 1522 and 1560, and the Landolfi printing press in Poschiavo, in operation between 1549 and 1615, did much to disseminate Reformation literature in Italy until suppressed by the Pope. It is noted for its carnations and does a brisk trade in Valtellina wine. The town is thoroughly Italian in character and contrasts strongly with the communities on the far side of the Bernina. Several old houses, with their coats-of-arms and vaulted portes-cochères, are preserved. The collegiate church of *San Vittore* (1497) has a good portal and rose-window, and an ossuary adjacent. The Protestant church dates from the mid 17C. Not far from the *Hotel Abrici*, in the Piazza Communale, is a regional *Museum*.

The road continues down the Val Poschiavo, at 4km skirting the *Lago di Poschiavo*, and the Bergamasque Alps come into view. The S end of the lake, above which towers the *Gandi Rossi* (E; 2831m), provides a good retrospective view up the valley. Several waterfalls and rapids are passed on the descent to (6.5km) *Brusio*, with two churches, lying amidst tobacco, maize, and corn-fields, beyond which is the *Piattamala defile*, which is threaded to reach (3km) *Campocologno*, with electrical works supplying the Bernina railway, and the Italian frontier (Customs).

Passing the early 16C pilgrimage church of *Madonna di Tirano*, with a fountain of 1780, the VALTELLINA is entered, with its luxurious vegetation, and (4km) **Tirano** (430m; 8500 inhab.). The older town of Tirano, on the W bank of the Adda, preserves the mansions of the Visconti, Pallavicini and Salis families, etc.

For roads hence to *Bormio* and the *Stelvio Pass*, and to *Sondrio*, *Lecco* and **Milan**, see *Blue Guide Northern Italy*.

35 St. Moritz to Chur via the Julierpass, Tiefencastel and Lenzerheide

Total distance, 76km (47 miles). No. 27. 6km *Silvaplana*—No. 3. 42km *Tiefencastel*—10km *Lenzerheide*—18km **Chur**.

Maps: M 218; BL 38, 39, 44, or 5002.

From **St. Moritz** (*Dorf*, or *Bad*; see Rte 34), we bear SW, shortly passing the lake or *Lej da Champfèr*, dominated by the *Piz Surlej* (3188m), with the *Piz Corvatsch* (3451m) further S and, to the SW, the *Piz da la Margna* (3159m).

6km **Silvaplana** (1815m), a pleasant little resort with a 15C church, lies on a level near fields of wild crocus in spring, while its pine-girt lake or *Lej da Silvaplauna*, with a cascade on its far bank, forms an attractive feature against the background of mountains. Across the lake to the E, reached by a bridge, lies *Surlej*, a village once partly destroyed by a rock fall. Surlej is the lower station for cable-cars rising to 3295m on the NE slope of the *Piz Corvatsch* (3451m), also providing an approach to the *Fuorcla Surlej* (2755m), both commanding remarkable views of the Bernina massif and its glaciers. The lake is dominated to the W by the *Piz Polaschin* (3013m) and, further S, the *Piz Lagrev* (3165m).

For the road beyond, via *Sils Maria* to the *Maloja Pass* and **Chiavenna**, see Rte 36.

The road climbs steeply immediately above Silvaplana, at first in zigzags, into the OVA DAL VALLUN, and in 7km reaches the **Julierpass** (2284m). The road was completed in 1826; fragments of Roman columns mark the former pass. Lying between the *Piz Julier* (NE; 3380m) and the *Piz Lagrev*, it provides a good retrospective view of the Bernina massif.—We climb down in two series of zigzags to (9km) *Bivio* (1769m), with the *Piz Platta* (3392m) rising ahead.

The hamlet lies at the lower end of the partly paved bridle-path climbing S to the **Septimerpass** (or *Pass da Sett*; 2310m), now of slight importance, but said to have been used by the Romans. In medieval times it was more frequented, largely because, with the Muretto Pass, it lay entirely within the jurisdiction of the Bp of Chur and so offered an untroubled passage into the subject Valtellina.

The road continues to descend through a somewhat barren district, later skirting the reservoir of *Marmorera*, and passing (left) the picturesque tower of the castle of *Splatsch*, among other ruins. NW rise the *Piz Forbesch* (3262m) and *Pic Arblatsch* (3204m); to the NE, the *Piz d'Err* (3378m) and *Piz Calderas* (3397m).—2.5km *Mulegns*, beyond which the narrow upper valley of the Romansch-speaking OBERHALBSTEIN is threaded past (4.5km) *Rona*, with its woods and waterfalls, and *Tinizong*, with an Italianate church of 1643 with a Romanesque tower. To the NE rises the jagged *Corn da Tinizong* (3172m).

5km **Savognin** (1207m), the main village and resort of the valley, has three churches, of which *St. Michael's* is octagonal in plan. It was the home of the artist Giovanni Segantini in 1886–94. The neighbouring ruined castle of *Patnal* is on the site of a Roman camp. To the NE rises the *Piz Mitgel* (3159m); to the W, the *Piz Curvèr* (2972m). Cable-cars ascend from just W of the village towards the summit of the *Martegnas* (2670m) and above *Radons*, SW in the VAL NANDRÒ. Paths hence climb W into the VAL FERRERA; see Rte 37.

The road passes near several small villages, among them *Riom*, W of *Cunter*, with ruins of the episcopal castle of *Raetia Ampla* (13C), and *Salouf*, with a well carved altarpiece of 1500 in its church.—Passing below the precipitous *Crap Ses*, we descend rapidly to (9km) **Tiefencastel** (*Casti* in Romansch; Roman *Imacastra*). The village, with a conspicuous white church, its facade painted in the Italian manner, is of little interest in itself, but is picturesquely situated at the confluence of the Albula and Julia.—Near the hamlet of *Mon*, on a height to the SW, is an early Romanesque church containing 14–15C murals; but more important is that of **Mistail**, reached by a path below the village leading NW, where *•St Peter's*, with its three semi-circular apses, dates back to the second half of the 8C and is perhaps the best-preserved building of its period in Switzerland. It contains 14–15C frescoes (Italian) and German ceiling-paintings of the 16C.

For the roads up the *Albulapass* and to *Davos*, see pp274 and 268, in reverse.

FROM TIEFENCASTEL TO THUSIS (13km). Cross to the N side of the valley and turn left above Mistail, with a retrospective view of the Piz Mitgel. The road shortly enters the first of a series of tunnels piercing the precipitous S side of the wild ravines of the Albula (in part known as the *Schyn Pass*), also threaded by the Albula railway; see p 275. Passing above the ruins of the castle of *Campi*, and *Schloss Baldenstein*, we by-pass *Sils im Domleschg*, with a view of the *Heinzenberg* ahead, to meet the N13 motorway immediately E of *Thusis*; see Rte 37.

The road climbs almost due E and then abruptly NW to (5km) *Lantsch/Lenz*, with a number of painted houses, passing en route near the farm of *Vazerol*, where a monument commemorates the alleged union of the three Rhaetian Leagues in 1471; see p 265. The road provides good retrospective views of the *Corn da Tinizong* (3172m) prominent to the SE, and of the valley of the GELGIA through which the road has passed.

We now cross a tract of heath, with the *Lenzer Horn* (2906m) rising to the E, to enter (5km) **Lenzerheide** (1473m), a well-sited resort, which developed from the old Grisons village of Lai, taking its name from the wooded Lenzerheide or Planüra, the plateau connecting the Stätzer Horn, the Parpaner Rothorn and the Weisshorn; it claims to be the birthplace of skiing in Switzerland. Lifts ascend W to near the summit of the *Piz Scalottas* (2323m), providing a superb view; to the E rises the *Aroser Rothorn* (2980m). We shortly pass the little *Heidensee* or *Igl Lai*, and a lift mounting E to the *Parpaner Rothorn* (2861m), and climb through *Valbella* to the *Lenzerheidepass* (1547m), descending thence through *Parpan*, its *Schlössli* preserving late 16C decoration, to (7km) *Churwalden*. Its 15–16C church, that of a former Premonstratensian abbey and possibly dating in part from the 9C, contains a well-carved S German altarpiece of 1477. Lifts ascend the lower slopes of the *Fulbergegg* (2529m), to the W.

Passing (right) the ruins of *Strassberg*, we continue to descend the valley of the Rabuisa through *Malix* to enter (10.5km) **Chur**; see Rte 33.

36   St. Moritz to Lugano via the Maloja Pass and Chiavenna

Total distance, 126km (78 miles). No. 27. 6km **Silvaplana**—10.5km *Maloja*—32.5km **Chaivenna**—S 36. 20km—S 340D. 29km *Menaggio*—S 340. 28km **Lugano**.

Maps: M 218, 219; BL 43, 44, 48, or 5007, 5013.

This route describes an alternative approach to the Ticino from the Upper Engadine to that via the *San Bernardino Pass*; see Rte 37. The route is also followed by a regular Swiss post-bus service. For details of the Italian towns passed through on this route see *Blue Guide Northern Italy*.

See the first section of Rte 35 for the road to *Silvaplana*. The main road skirts the N bank of the lake or *Lej da Silvaplauna*, at 3.5km reaching a left-hand turning for **Sils-Maria**, 1km S, a small resort attractively sited between the lake and the *Lej da Segl* (Romansch for Sils), further SW. It was the residence of the philosopher and critic Friedrich Nietzsche (1844–1900) during the years 1881–88, and his home, near the Edelweiss hotel, contains souvenirs of his life.

A cable-car ascends just E of the village to a viewpoint on a ridge of the *Piz Corvatsch* (3451m), rising to the SE, and, beyond, the Bernina massif.—Paths ascend the VAL FEX to the S past *Crasta*, with a little Romanesque chapel containing relics of frescoes, to the glacier at its head. To the E· rises *Il Chaputschin* (3386m), *Piz Glüschaint* (3594m), *Piz Tremoggia* (3441m), *Piz Fora* (3363m) and *Piz Led* (3087m).

The main road is regained at adjacent *Sils-Baselgia*, with a church of medieval origin transformed in the 17C. We skirt the N bank of the *Lej da Segl*, with a view beyond the far bank of the Fex glacier and, further W, of the *Piz de la Margna* (3159m).

7km **Maloja**, a small resort at the upper extremity of the Engadine, is crossed, just W of which is a fine belvedere providing a plunging view down the VAL BREGAGLIA. T.H. Huxley (1825–95) was a visitor to Maloja; the artist Giovanni Segantini (1858–99) is buried here.

We shortly cross the **Passo del Maloja** (1815m; the watershed between the Danube and the Po), on the old track between the *Septimerpass* (NW; 2310m; cf.) and the *Passo del Muretto* (2562m), to the SE.

This last may be reached by ascending the VAL FORNO, and provides a good view of the *Monte Disgrázia* (3678m); the pass leads over to *Chiesa* in Valmalenco; see *Blue Guide Northern Italy*. To the SW of the Val Forno, in which lies the small lake of *Cavloc*, is seen the long ice-stream of the Forno, exhibiting all the phenomena of more famous glaciers, the cirque at its head framed by the peaks of the *Cima di Rosso* (3366m), *Monte Sissone* (3330m), and the *Cima di Castello* (3388m).

A bridle-path leads NW from Maloja to skirt a small tarn below the *Piz Lunghin*

(2780m), which is the source of the Inn/En. It then crosses a pass at 2645m to reach the *Septimerpass*, and continues ahead to the *Forcellina Pass* (2672m), descending thence to *Juf* (2126m; see p 285), the highest hamlet in the AVERSERRHEIN valley. From Juf a road leads via *Crôt*, after 25km meeting the N13 some 11km NE of *Splügen*.—Another high-level path leads W from *Casaccia*, below the Maloja Pass, and between the *Gletscherhorn* (3107m) and *Piz Duan* (3131m), to circle to the NW and descend the MADRISSERRHEIN to meet a track S of *Crôt*; see above.

The main road descends from the pass in several steps or terraces approached by a number of hairpin bends at first cut into the cliffs below *Piz Lunghin* (NW; 2780m), passing (right) the ruined church of *San Gaudenzio*, and climbs down again through *Casaccia* (see above), continuing its descent into the fertile VAL BREGAGLIA, the Roman *Prae-Gallia*. Sections of the Roman road which ran from Chiavenna to Chur by this route, still traceable, were in use during the Middle Ages. The later road, completed in 1840, has been improved recently. We pass (left) a cable-car mounting to the dam of the *Lago da l'Albigna* (2163m). Most of the peaks to the S, marking the frontier, with their glaciers, rise to over 3300m; to the N looms *Piz Daun* (3131m). The change in vegetation shows an extraordinary contrast, due to the descent of over 800m in 16km, and it soon becomes decidedly more southern in character.

13.5km **Vicosoprano**, a village once the main centre of the valley, is by-passed; it stands on the lowest of the three terraces which form the 'Sopra Porta' half of the valley. It preserves several old houses, a late 16C town hall, a medieval tower and 17C church, and, across the river, an older but altered church with a 13C tower. In 1870 the area was devastated by floods bringing down rocks and other debris from the surrounding mountain gorges.—2.5km *Stampa*, birthplace of Augusto Giacometti (1877–1947), the artist, and Alberto Giacometti (1901–66), the sculptor, some works by whom may be seen in the regional *Museum* installed in the *Ciäsa Grande*.

The road shortly skirts a hill surmounted by the ruins of *Castelmur*, once the key to the valley, here divided into 'Sopra' and 'Sotto Porta' by the *Porta*, a rocky gateway and tunnel, which brings one suddenly from a pine into a chestnut region. The prominent church of *Nossa Donna*, with its Romanesque belfry, and of Carolingian foundation, was desecrated by Protestants in 1552 and restored in the 1860s.

The villages of *Promontogno* and *Bondo*, standing at the mouth of the picturesque VAL BONDASCA, are by-passed. Bondo contains the 18C Baroque residence of the English branch of the Salis family and a church, partly Romanesque, preserving late 15C murals.

At the head of the valley, with its glacier, rise the *Piz Badile* (3308m) and *Piz Cengalo* (3370m) to the S; and to the E, the *Sciora-Dafora* (3169m), the *Sciora-Dadent* (3275m) and *Piz Cacciabella* (2980m).

A road to the right ascends to **Soglio**, a high-lying village providing a fine view of the Bondasca glacier and of the splintered peaks above it. It was the chief seat of the powerful Salis family from 1300 onwards, but their magnificent palace was burned by the Spaniards in 1621. Another mansion, the *Casa Battista*, remarkably Jacobean in style, and more recently the *Hotel Willy*, once had Rainer Maria Rilke as guest.

We descend to *Castasegna* (6.5km from Stampa), the last Swiss village (Customs).

After traversing *Villa di Chiavenna*, the first Italian village, the campanile of *Santa Croce* is seen, and the road crosses *Piuro*, once a thriving town, overwhelmed by a landslide in 1618. To the N is a fine waterfall.—10km **Chiavenna** (325m; 7100 inhab.), Roman *Clavenna*, charmingly situated in the valley of the Mera, was perhaps so-called as being the key to the Julier, Septimer and Splügen passes; for the last see Rte 37. Above the turreted *Palazzo Balbiani* rises the *Paradiso* (view), a rock with botanic gardens on its slopes; 16C *San Lorenzo*, with an octagonal baptistry, has a massive detached campanile.

We turn S down the valley on the S 36, traversing *Novate Mezzola*, and at 20km turn right onto the S 340D; the S 36 continues ahead to skirt the E bank of Lake Como (motorway/autostrada under construction) to (44km) *Lecco*.

The N shore of **Lake Como** (or *Lago di Como*) is skirted to (12km) **Gravedona**. The square *Palazzo Gallio* (late 16C) has four corner turrets; to the S is *San Vincenzo*, with a very ancient crypt; while near by is 12C *Santa Maria del Tiglio*.—3.5km *Dongo*, where Benito Mussolini, the fascist 'Duce', was captured by partisans prior to his execution on 28 April 1945.—A road, later a track, ascends hence to the *Passo di San Jorio* (2014m), on the frontier with Switzerland E of Carena and Bellinzona.—The almost impregnable *Rocca di Musso*, an early 16C stronghold from which Gian Giacomo Medici once terrorised the district, is passed. To the W rises *Monte Bregagno* (2107m), while prominent beyond the far bank of the lake is *Monte Legnone* (2609m).—The 10C castle of *Rezzónico* is passed before entering (13.5km) *Menaggio*, a small resort providing a view of *Bellagio* on its promontory between the two southern arms (or legs) of the lake. The main road continues to skirt its bank to (35km) **Como**, 7km SE of *Chiasso*; see Rte 40.

At Menaggio we turn W, at c 8km skirting the reedy *Lago di Piano* to reach *Porlezza*, 4km beyond, on the E extremity of the *Lago di Lugano*. We follow its N bank below *Monte dei Pizzoni* (1303m), traversing several villages, among them *San Mamette*, with a 12C campanile.—At 9km Customs are passed at the frontier and *Gandria*, the first Swiss village, is soon entered, beyond which rises the sunny slope of *Monte Brè* (925m). Passing through *Castagnola*, below which, lapped by the lake, is the *Villa Favorita*, the E suburbs of **Lugano** are reached; see Rte 40.

37 Chur to Bellinzona via the San Bernardino

Total distance, 114km (71 miles). No. 13. 9km *Reichenau*—N13. 15km *Thusis* crossroads.—25km *Splügen* exit—65km (via the *San Bernardino tunnel*) **Bellinzona**.

Maps: M 218; BL 38, 43, or 5002, 5007.

For **Chur** see Rte 33. Hence the N13 motorway is followed SW up the Rhine valley, on the floor of which are numerous mounds supposed to be the remains of the prehistoric landslide at *Flims*. At 7km the road passes under the No. 19 (see Rte 38) at *Richenau*, with an old *Schloss* of the Planta family, where Louis Philippe lived and gave lessons in 1793 under the name of 'Professor Chabot'. It lies at the confluence of the VORDERRHEIN and the HINTERRHEIN, the latter valley opening to the S, into which we turn.

At the adjacent exit from the N13 one may take the old road through (2km) **Bonaduz**, where the chapel of *St. Georg* contains 16C frescoes, and *Rhäzüns*, where *St. Paul's* preserves 14–16C murals. The castle, of ancient foundation, dates mainly from the 16–17C. For the road hence to *Ilanz*, see Rte 38.

Rhäzüns stands at the entrance of the narrow but fertile DOMLESCHG (*Vallis Toliliasca*), the name given to the floor and E side of the valley, the W slope of which is the *Heinzenberg*. We get a good retrospective view of the *Ringelspitz* (3247m). On the pillar-like rock on the far bank of the river are the ruins of *Nieder-Juvalta*, while high up on the E is the church of *Feldis*, above the valley side there pierced by a motorway tunnel.—At (6.5km) *Rothenbrunnen*, on the far bank, are the ruins of *Ober-Juvalta*. The highest of the peaks rising above is the *Stätzer Horn* (2574m). Among other ruins of feudal castles on this bank, some of which were destroyed in a revolt of peasants against their bailiffs in 1541, are those of *Ortenstein*, with a nearby chapel containing 13C frescoes; two at *Paspels*; and above *Rodels*, the *Rietberg*, where in 1621 Pompejus Planta, leader of the Catholic faction, was murdered by Jürg Jenatsch, pastor of *Scharans*, further up the valley (in 1639 Jenatsch was himself assassinated at Chur).—At (4.5km) *Cazis* is a fine early 16C church of a Dominican convent, and *St. Martin*, with a Romanesque tower. To the SW the pyramidal *Piz Beverin* (2998m) comes into view; to the SE, beyond Tiefencastel, the *Piz Mitgel* (3159m); and to the S, the *Piz Curvèr* (2972m). Passing below the castle of *Tagstein*, at 3km the small market-town of **Thusis** (723m) is traversed, to join the motorway.

For the road hence up the wild Albula valley to (13km) *Tiefencastel* see the latter part of Rte 35, in reverse.

The motorway, which has meanwhile turned S through a tunnel, leads up the valley along the right bank of the Hinterrhein, here partly 'corrected' and embanked, which has enabled much land to be reclaimed for cultivation. The motorway also provides a view of the several castle ruins listed above, together with that of *Ehrenfels*, passed immediately E of (15.5km) Thusis.—Also, high above the mouth of the Via Mala, which we now enter, the *Hohenrhätien* or *Hoch Realta*, known to have existed in the 11C.—A steep mountain road climbs W above the NOLLA VALLEY from Thusis to the *Glaspass* (1846m) below the conspicuous *Piz Beverin* (2998m), which leads into the SAFIENTAL.

The celebrated *•Via Mala* has since 1967 been threaded by the N13, which has virtually superseded the older road cut through the *Verloren loch* in 1473, and first made strong enough to take carriages by Poccobelli, an engineer from the Ticino, in 1818–23. The limestone cliffs, rising to a height of almost 500m and at places barely 10m apart, were pierced by tunnels and galleries between rock ledges high above the foaming torrent below, spanned by bridges, the first and second of which were constructed in 1738–39. Eventually one emerges into the open valley of the SCHONS, once filled by a lake, lying between the *Piz Beverin* (2998m) and the *Piz Curvèr* (E; 2972m), while ahead to the SW rises the *Surettahorn* (3027m).

It is worthwhile to make our exit here to visit the *•Church of Zillis*, in which the restored 12C ceiling-paintings are amongst the oldest and most complete series of their kind in existence, comprising 153 square panels.—Several high-lying pastoral villages with their church-towers are seen on the upper slopes of the valley. The main village is *Andeer*, shortly crossed by the old road, where one may regain the motorway. However, it is an interesting experience to follow the former road ascending in zigzags and providing a better idea of what it was like not so long ago to thread the romantic gorge of the *Roffla Schlucht*, down which the Rhine descends in a picturesque cataract.

Detail of the painted ceiling in the church of St. Martin, Zillis

The N13 passes through a tunnel to reach (15km from Thusis) an exit for the VAL FERRERA.

This high valley is not much frequented. A mountain road climbs S through *Ausserferrera*, with its waterfall, and (8km) *Innerferrera*, overlooked to the SW by the *Surettahorn* (3027m) and to the S by the *Piz Miez* (2835m). The road then ascends SE through tunnels past the foot of the VALLE DI LEI, with its reservoir, which is in Italian territory although entirely on the N slope of the range. The *Pizzo Stella* (3163m) rises at its head, near which is a pass reached from *Piuro*, 4km E of Chiavenna (see Rte 36). *Cröt* is entered after 8km, at the junction of the MADRISERRHEIN (S) and AVERSERRHEIN, in which lies *Cresta*, a small village encircled by mountains, among them the *Piz Platta* (3392m) to the NE and the *Tscheisch* (3109m) to the S. The road ends at (9km) *Juf* (2126m), which claims to be the highest permanently occupied hamlet in Europe, above which rises the *Stallerberg* (2579m; view).

For the passes to the SE see p 282.

The main road veers SW to enter the pastoral RHEINWALD valley, with a small reservoir overlooked by the village of *Sufers*, and at 11km reaches the turning at the village of *Splügen* (1457m) for its pass; see below. A bridle-path between the two villages is said to be a section of Roman road, which passes the ruined castle of *Burg*, not far E of the church at Splügen.

To the SE rises the *Seehorn* (2762m), below which are the three *Suretta* tarns; the *Surettahorn* (3027m), marking the frontier, rises further to the S, while to the SW is the pyramidal *Piz Tambò* (3279m). To the NW is the *Barenhorn* (2929m), just E of which is the *Safierberg pass* (2486m) into the SAFIENTAL. To the N are the dolomitic peaks of the *Teurihorn* (2973m) and *Alperschällihorn* (3039m).

FROM SPLÜGEN TO CHIAVENNA (39km). The road ascends in a series of zigzags to the S, at 9km reaching the **Splügenpass** (2113m; Customs), on a narrow ridge between the Piz Tambò and the Surettahorn, forming the frontier with Italy. The pass was known to the Romans and the route from Curia (Chur) to Clavenna (Chiavenna) is mentioned in the 'Antonine Itinerary' (early 3C). The most famous crossing of the pass was that of Marshal Macdonald, when, despite stormy weather and bad snow conditions, he succeeded in conveying an army of infantry, cavalry and artillery to Chiavenna (26 November–6 December 1800) to protect the left flank of Napoleon's Army of Italy, losing 100 men and 100 horses in the snow en route.—The road (S 36) descends to *Monte Spluga* and skirts the reservoir now filling its desolate basin, beyond which, with views SW to the *Pizzo Ferre* (3103m), with its fine glacier, and the *Cima di Balnisco* (2851m), among other towering peaks, we continue to climb down through snow galleries above the Liro ravine. At (13km) *Pianazzo* the resort of *Madesimo*, 2km NE, up a side valley, is by-passed, and a grand waterfall is passed, before a further steep descent is made to (5km) *Campodolcino*. The E bank of the Liro is followed down the barren VALLE SAN GIÀCOMO, strewn with reddish rocks, passing the tall white campanile of *Gallivaggio* against its background of chestnut woods and precipices, to the village of (8.5km) *San Giàcomo*, beyond which the valley widens and the vegetation becomes more luxuriant. For **Chiavenna**, 3.5km beyond, see Rte 36.

The N13 continues W from Splügen, with the huge *Zapport Glacier* in the distance, and with the *Rheinwaldhorn* (3402m) rising beyond, first climbed by Placidus à Spescha in 1789.—At 9.5km is an exit for *Hinterrhein* (1620m), the highest village in the valley and still Rhaetian in aspect, with its characteristic barns and ancient church.

Hence a path climbs W to the *Zapport Hut*, a base for several ascents in the area, and the *Ursprung*, a grey torrent ('Rheni luteum caput') bursting from the ice at the foot of the glacier, and the source of the Rhine, but an excursion hardly repaying the trouble.

The motorway plunges into the **San Bernardino Tunnel** 1.5km beyond Hinterrhein, which pierces the range below the Pass. It was opened in 1967 and is 6.6km long, reaching a height of 1644m. The **Pass** (2065m), approached by climbing for 8km in numerous sharp zigzags, lies between the *Marscholhorn* (2967m) and the *Piz Uccello* (2724m) to the E. Its summit is partly occupied by the tiny *Lago Moësola*, the source of the Moësola. The head of the pass is grander and less dreary than some other road passes, and commands several striking views—particularly from a large white rock reached by a path from the hospice—among them the jagged peaks and glaciers of the Ádula group to the W.

Formerly known as the *Vogelberg* (*Mons Avium*, or *Passo Uccello*), from its neighbouring peak, it was renamed in the 15C after St. Bernardino of Siena (1380–1444), who preached in the district. It seems to have been known to the Romans, but its medieval history is relatively unimportant. In 1799 it was crossed by the French army of Gén. Lacourbe. The road was constructed in 1818–23 by

Poccobelli (responsible also for that at the Via Mala), and most of the cost was advanced by the King of Sardinia.

The road descends steeply in zigzags to (7km) the village of *San Bernardino* (1608m), with a conspicuous domed mid 19C church, also approached from an exit at the S exit of the tunnel.

Although the old road (No. 13) may be followed down to the floor of the mountain-flanked VALLE MESOLCINA, the motorway, a masterpiece of civil engineering, provides a preferable descent in sweeping curves, over impressive viaducts and traversing half a dozen short tunnels, with a fine view of the hill-top *Castelo di Misox* or **Mesocco**, passed to the left at 17km. This divides the valley into two halves, the lower decidedly southern in character, with pomegranates, vines and mulberries, apart from its chestnut woods. *Santa Maria* at Mesocco contains good mid.15C murals. Some idea of the abruptness of the S side of the Alps may be gathered from the fact that we are now approx. at the same altitude as Chur. The beautiful waterfall of *Buffalora* is shortly passed on the right, one of several in this stretch of the valley, in which fig-trees now make their appearance. The picturesque ruin of *Norántola* is later seen (right), and then several villages on reaching the valley floor, among them *Grono* (right at 18km), with its Romanesque campanile, and the medieval *Torre Fiorenzana*, at the foot of the narrow and picturesque VAL CALANCA.

From *Rossa*, its main village (1069m), 20km N at the head of the Val Calanca, the *Pas Giümela* (2117m) leads W to *Malvaglia*, in the VAL BLENIO; see Rte 41.

Roveredo, preserving several old mansions, is shortly by-passed. The prior of Roveredo and eleven old women were burned for witchcraft by San Carlo Borromeo in 1583.—At 8km crossroads are reached near the site of the *Battle of Arbedo* (see Rte 41), where we turn left to enter the N suburbs of **Bellinzona**, 4km beyond; see Rte 39.—The right-hand turning (No. 2) leads N to the *St. Gotthard*; see Rte 41. The N2 motorway, joined W of the crossroads, by-passes Bellinzona for **Lugano**; see Rte 40.

38 Chur to Andermatt via Flims, Disentis/Mustér and the Oberalppass

Total distance, 93km (57 miles). No. 13. 9km *Reichenau*—No. 19. 12km *Flims-Dorf*—11km **Ilanz**—30km **Disentis/Mustér**—31km **Andermatt**.

Maps: M 218; BL 38, or 5001, 5002.

From a point 7km W of **Chur** (see Rte 33), bear right across the Rhine and continue W above the left bank of the VORDERRHEIN. The remarkable limestone rock-formations in the gorge here are the result of erosion on a prehistoric landslide.

From *Bonaduz*, some 2km SW of the bridge over the Vorderrhein (see the first part of Rte 37), one may follow an alternative mountain road to *Ilanz*, 21km SW. This leads W above the right bank of the river, passing through three short tunnels, and climbs to the village of (8km) *Versam*.

Hence a rough road climbs almost due S up the unfrequented SAFIENTAL to (15.5km) *Safien Platz*, with its waterfall, from which the *Glaspass* (E; 1846m) leads to *Thusis* and from which the *Piz Beverin* (SE; 2998m) may be approached, providing a fine mountain panorama. The track continues a further 6.5km to *Thalkirch*, between the *Bruschghorn* (E; 3056m) and the *Piz Tomül* (SW; 2946m), from which one may ascend the *Safierberg Pass* (2486m) for *Splügen* (see Rte 37) or W over the *Tomülpass* (2412m) to *Vals* in the VALSERTAL; see below.

From Versam, one may continue W above the ravine of the Rhine, with its hacked and shattered brecciated walls, and emerge into a more open valley; the formations of the mountains change from limestone to primitive rock, the scenery taking on a different character.—13km *Ilanz*; see below.

On approaching (4km) *Trin*, the ruins of *Hohentrins* are passed to the left, an 11C castle in the foundations of which are the remains of a 6C church. The road shortly bears right to reach *Mulin*, with its waterfall. To the N rises the *Ringelspitz* (3247m).—A small lake is passed on approaching (7km) **Flims-Dorf** (1081m), an old village preserving several houses of interest, and adjacent *Flims-Waldhaus*, a modern resort at a higher level, well situated amid larch and beech forests in the vicinity of several small lakes.

Numerous lifts ascend N and NW from Flims, among them to just below the *Cassons Grat* (2637m; view), N of which rises the *Trinserhorn* or *Piz Dolf* (3028m), the *Surrenstock* (3056m), and *Piz Segnas* (3099m), just W of which is the *Pass dil Segnas* (2627m) leading over to *Elm*; see Rte 32. Others mount from a point some 3.5km SW of Flims-Waldhaus, and just right of the main road, to a height of 2477m (view), below the *Vorab* (3028m).

The road descends through (5.5km) *Laax*, a small resort, near its ravine, the *Laaxertobel*, from which a by-road climbs W to *Falera*, a high-lying village with a quaint old church commanding a fine view. After a further 5.5km descent the Rhine is reached, the river being spanned by a bridge to Ilanz. **Ilanz** (698m), an attractively sited village at the entrance of the LUMNEZIA VALLEY, with the *Piz Mundaun* (2064m) rising to the SW, was mentioned in a charter of 765 as 'the finest town on the Rhine'.

It was the capital of the 'Grey League' (see p 264), and in 1526 was the seat of conference of the Three Rhaetian Leagues which resulted in the grant of equal privileges to both Protestants and Roman Catholics. It is the centre of the district known as the *Bündner*, or Grisons Oberland, the inhabitants of which are mostly Romansch speaking.

Several imposing 16–17C mansions testify to its former importance and two towers of its fortifications are preserved. The *Parish Church* was completed in 1518; that of *St. Martin*, on a height to the S, is probably older.

FROM ILANZ TO VALS (21km). The road soon crosses to and follows the right bank of the Glogn past ruined *Castelberg*, and several ravines are bridged before turning up the VALSERTAL, which narrows to a gorge beyond the hamlet of *St. Martin*. It continues to climb to *Vals*, a small spa in a sheltered and well-wooded site, and the base for several ascents in the area, and also for the *Valserberg Pass* (S; 2504m) leading to *Hinterrhein*, just below the San Bernardino; see Rte 37. One may continue SW to (7.5km) the mountain-girt *Zervreilasee*, a reservoir which submerged the hamlet of that name, beyond which rises the *Zervreilerhorn* (2898m), while to the S is the *Fanellahorn* (3124m), and further SW, the *Güferhorn* (3383m).

FROM ILANZ TO VRIN (21km). The more westerly road up the LUMNEZIA VALLEY runs along the hillside, passing the *Frauentor*, a gateway successfully defended by the women of the valley in 1352 against Count von Monfort, while the men were fighting on the heights above. The name Lumnezia or LUNGEZ TAL, which also includes the Valsertal to the E (see above) is one of the more beautiful valleys of the Grisons, richer in meadow and pasture than in forests, and the cherry blossom is a notable feature in spring. Romansch is spoken in the Vrin branch, but a colony of 'Walsers', or German-speaking immigrants from the Valais in the mid 13C, inhabit the Vals.—We traverse several villages including after 10 km *Igel* with, in its church, a remarkable carved altarpiece of c1500, to reach (4.5km) *Lumbrein*, with an old castle. Then one continues to climb to **Vrin** (1448m) and beyond to other hamlets. It is a base for several ascents in the area, among them the *Piz Cavel* (W; 2946m), *Piz Ault* (SE; 3121m), *Piz Terri* (SW; 3149m), *Piz Scharboda* (3122m) and the *Frunthorn* (3030m) to the S. The *Pass Diesrut* (SW; 2428m) leads into the VAL SUMVITG.

From the N bank of the Rhine at Ilanz the No. 19 continues its ascent of the valley, on both banks of which, at a higher level, are a number of villages and ruined castles, among them—near the road—that of *Grottenstein*. To the N rises the *Hausstock* (3158m); further W is the *Muttenstock* (3089m).—At *Waltensburg/Vuorz* is a ⋅church of c 1100 containing interesting murals, some mid 14C. In the neighbourhood are the extensive ruins of *Jörgenberg* (to the E) and the 12C fortress of *Kropfenstein*.

Above *Breil/Brigels* is the *Kistenpass* (2638m) leading into the LINTHAL; see Rte 32. Breil itself is best approached by climbing to the right after 11.5km.—Soon after passing (left) the ruin of *Ringgenberg* we enter (6.5km) *Trun*, at the foot of the VAL PUNTEGLIAS, at the head of which is its glacier, below *Piz Urlaun* (3359m), beyond which is the *Tödi* (3614m; see p 263), while to the E is the *Cavistrau* (3252m).

3km *Rabius*, whence one may cross the Rhine to enter the wild VAL SUMVIGT, with its lofty mountain wall, in which the hamlet of (6.5km) *Tenigerbad* serves as a base for ascents. To the S rise the *Piz Vial* (3168m) and, further W, *Piz Medel* (3211m).—The main road continues to climb past the *Russeiner Tobel* (right), while to the left opens the VAL MEDEL; see below.

9km **Disentis/Mustér** (1142m), one of the main centres of this long valley, where it is joined by the road from the Lukmanierpass, has been reputed since the turn of the century for its radioactive waters, but its main architectural attraction is the huge Benedictine Abbey (largely rebuilt and/or restored in 1846), which dominates the place. It is said to have been founded c 700 and sacked in a Saracen raid in 940, but it was of some importance in the 16–17Cs. It has several times been destroyed or burned, lastly by French troops in 1799. The crypt of the *Abbey Church* (1695–1712) consists of the relics of an earlier church of c 1000. The 17C parish church contains a late 15C altarpiece.—Several Baroque chapels may be seen in the vicinity. Father Placidus à Spescha, an early alpinist, was a monk here.

A cable-car mounts NW towards the summit of *Piz Ault* (3027m), which provides several fine views, to the E of which is the *Cavardiras Pass* (2739m), leading into the upper MADERANERTAL; see Rte 25A. The *Oberalpstock* (3328m) rises just NW of the Piz Ault.

FROM DISENTIS TO BIASCA VIA THE LUKMANIERPASS (62km). The road first threads the *Medelserschlucht*, a narrow and romantic ravine enlivened by cascades, on emerging from which we climb to (5.5km) *Curaglia*, a small resort below the *Piz Muraun* (E; 2897m), while to the SE rises the *Piz Medel* (3211m), with its glacier, and other peaks of the massif. The road continues to climb past several hamlets, and the *Fumatschfall* (right), where the savage VAL CRISTALLINA opens to the S, at the head of which is the *Pass Cristallina* (2398m), leading to *Campo* (Blenio), above *Olivone*. To the W rises the *Piz Gannaretsch* (3040m). Skirting the *Lai da Sontga Maria* reservoir, the **Lukmanierpass** (or *Passo del Lucomagno*; 1914m) is reached, a flat watershed between the cantons of Grisons and the Ticino. Crossed by Otto I in 965 and by Frederick Barbarossa in 1164 and 1186, it has been comparatively little used in modern times. The carriage-road was made in 1871–77, but the project of piercing a railway tunnel here was abandoned in favour of the St. Gotthard.—To the E rises the *Scopi* (3190m); to the W, the *Rondadura* (3016m). The descent into the VALLE SANTA MARIA is gentler than the ascent, with the *Rheinwaldhorn* (3402m) conspicuous to the SE. The road climbs down in a series of loops to (19.5km) **Olivone** (889m), a striking view of which we get on the final descent. It is a well situated village near the head of the VAL BLENIO, lying beneath the grand precipices of the *Sosto* (NE; 2221m). The scenery of the valley, watered by the Brenno, which is now followed to the S, is remarkable, and several of its villages have churches containing Romanesque details and late-medieval wall-paintings. Characteristic is that of *San Carlo di Negrentino, with 12–13C and 16C frescoes, approached from (9km) *Acquarossa* and *Prugiasco* (where first enquire for the key). From *Leontica*, at a higher level to the W, a cable-car mounts to near the 'col at *Bassa di Nara* (2123m), leading into the LEVENTINA; see Rte 41. The road passes along the comparatively luxurious valley, with its vines growing on granite trellises, its mulberries, chestnuts and walnuts, to (5km) *Motto*, where the main road bears left through **Malvaglia**, with several old houses and a church of Romanesque origin with a tall 12C campanile; the right-hand by-road passes the ruins of the castle of *Serravalle* to regain the main road further S.—Malvaglia is a base for ascents in the range to the E of the valley, among them the *Cima Rossa* (3161m).—The debris of a great landslide of 1512 is shortly passed to approach **Biasca**, below the *Pic Magn* (2329m), for which see Rte 41.

Climbing SW from Disentis, the VAL TAVETSCH is soon entered, a fertile vale forming the uppermost part of the Vorderrhein valley, of which we get a good retrospective view.—8.5km *Sedrun*, its church with a Romanesque belfry. The river here is little more than a mountain torrent.

A path ascends N to the *Chrüzlipass* (2347m), leading into the MADERANERTAL; see Rte 25A.—A road climbs S to the *Lai da Nalps reservoir*, below the *Piz Gannaretsch* (3040m), to the S of which rise the *Piz Rondadura* (3016m) and *Piz Blas* (3019m).

The *Piz Badus* (2928m) becomes prominent ahead, as we climb through *Tschamut*, some distance beyond which a left-hand turning ascends to the *Lai da Curnera reservoir* below *Piz Paradis* (2884m), and a path mounts towards several tarns in which the Vorderrhein rises.

The old road climbs in a series of zigzags to (12km) the **Oberalppass** (2044m), the boundary between the Grisons and the canton of Uri, beyond which is its lake (right) and the view of the St. Gotthard range. Another series of zigzags soon leads one down to (10.5km) **Andermatt**, in its high valley, for which see Rte 25A.

For roads hence to **Bellinzona** and **Brig** (in the Valais) see Rtes 41 and 45, in reverse; and for that to **Interlaken** via **Meiringen**, Rte 40, likewise in reverse.

39   Bellinzona to Locarno and the Valle Maggia

Total distance, 19km (12 miles).

Maps: M 217, 219; BL 42, 43, or 5007.

BELLINZONA (229m;16,750 inhab.;4050 1880), capital of the canton of **Ticino** (*Tessin*, in German), overlooked by its three picturesque castles, confirming its medieval importance as the key to the passes of the St. Gotthard, Lukmanier and San Bernardino, is an ancient town of some character, too frequently by-passed by travellers hurrying on to the lakes or to Italy.

Roman *Castrum Bilitonis*, and the site of a fortress named *Blifio* from the 6C, it was acquired by the Dukes of Milan in 1242 and in the late 15C was promised to his Swiss allies by Louis XII when duke of Orléans and claimant to Milan; a promise he later refused to honour. By the Treaty of Arona (April 1503) Bellinzona and the Blenio valley was handed to Uri, Schwyz and Nidwalden. It was chosen as the cantonal capital in 1878, having previously shared the honour with Lugano and Locarno, each holding the position for six years.

The canton, the only wholly Italian-speaking one of the Swiss Federation, in which it was incorporated in 1803, was during a later period of its history disturbed by the struggle between the Ultramontane and Radical Catholics. It had a reputation for its architects in the 16–17Cs, among them being Francesco Borromini, Carlo Maderno, G.P. Tencala and Domenico Fontana; and later, Domenico Gilardi (1788–1845), who worked in St. Petersburg.

View of the Castello Grande, Bellinzona

The PIAZZA DEL SOLE, at the S end of the Via Henri Guisan, the central section of the main thoroughfare, is overlooked to the W by the isolated **Castello Grande** (or *San Michele*, or *Vecchio*), long an arsenal, and in the process of a radical restoration, and will then be open to the public. Dominated by its two 28m-high towers, this is the most extensive of the three castles, built after 1445 by the Duke of Milan. It finally fell to the Swiss in 1508, being occupied by the bailiff of Uri. It replaced a former fortification founded in the late 4C and extended in the 6th.

The Via Codeborgo leads S to the Piazza Collegiata, from which steps ascend to the entrance of its large **Church** (*Santi Pietro e Stefano*; 1517–1764), recently restored. Abutting its N side is the mid 18C *Oratory of Santa Maria* (normally closed, but entirely frescoed within).

From behind the church, flights of steep steps and paths climb to the hilltop **Castello Montebello** (or *Svitto*, once belonging to Schwyz; or *San Martino*), the main tower of which has since 1974 been imaginatively fitted up to house an *Archaeological and Historical Museum*. It commands a pleasant view over the town.

Further SE, at a higher level (230m above Bellinzona), and approached by a winding road ascending from the E end of the Via Ospedale (turning off the Via Lugano), is the **Castello di Sasso Corbaro** (or *Santa Barbara*, or *di Cima*), built in 1479 and formerly controlled by Unterwalden. It contains a local *Museum of Folk art*, Costumes, etc.

Continuing S from the Piazza Collegiata, the arcaded PIAZZA NOSETTO is shortly entered, on the S side of which is the courtyard of the *Town Hall* or *Palazzo Municipale*, built in 1924 in a neo-Lombardic style, incorporating some 15C capitals, etc. Adjacent, in the Via Camminata, is the *Tourist Office*. The Via Camminata leads to the Piazza Indipendenza, and the church of *San Rocco* (14–15C).

Hence the Via Lugano leads S, and some five minutes' walk brings one to (right) the Franciscan church of *Santa Maria delle Grazie* (late 15C), with 15–16C frescoes of the Crucifixion showing many similarities with those of Luini in Santa Maria degli Angioli at Lugano.—By passing under the railway bridge a few paces S in the Via Lugano and turning uphill to the N, we reach **San Biagio**, a 13C basilica with a 14C fresco on its facade and 15C frescoes inside. The road skirts the railway to reach the Dragonato stream, where turn left and then right to regain the town centre.

For the road to **Lugano**, see Rte 40.

Crossing the river Ticino, and the motorway immediately W of the town, turn left through *Monte Carasso* (above which the chapel of *San Bernardo* contains 15–17C frescoes). The road passes several other villages below the lower slopes of the *Cima dell'Uomo* (2390m), with a view SW over the valley, here called the *Piano di Magadino*, towards Lago Maggiore and the frontier range further W, to (14km) *Gordola*.

FROM GORDOLA TO SONOGNO (25km). The alpine VAL VERZASCA, which this by-road traverses, is usually visited from Locarno and its lower reaches are more spectacular than the upper. The road climbs steeply through several short tunnels along the E bank of a reservoir to (6km) *Vogorno*, with a good view ahead of the hamlet of *Corippo* plastered against the mountain-side like a martin's nest, which may be reached by a track at the head of the reservoir. The road goes on to thread a defile before the valley opens out at (5.5km) *Lavertezzo*, with a picturesque medieval *double-Bridge*.—*Brione*, 6.5km beyond, is the main village, 7km N of which the road peters out at *Sonogno* (918m), with the *Madone Grosso* (or *Madom Gröss*; 2741m) rising to the NE. A path leads NW over the *Passo di Redòrta* (2181m) to *Prato-Sornico*, in the VAL LAVIZZARA; see below.

Continuing W from Gordola, *Minusio* is traversed, where the German poet Stefan George (1868–1933) died, now little more than a suburb, with adjacent *Muralto*—where Paul Klee (1879–1940) died—of (7km) Locarno.

LOCARNO (198m; 14,100 inhab.; 5600 in 1920; 2850 in 1880), well situated on a bay of the most northerly reach of Lago Maggiore, and with a mild and sunny climate, is perhaps the most attractive of the larger lakeside resorts of the Ticino, particularly in winter.

Although granted privileges by Frederick Barbarossa in 1186, it did not enter the orbit of Switzerland until 1512, when it was taken by the men of Uri, Schwyz and Unterwalden after a fruitless assault a decade earlier, and it remained a subject bailiwick until 1798. Many of its inhabitants embraced the reformed religion in the early 16C, but in 1555, by a decree of the Swiss Diet, they were sent into exile, being forced to cross wintry passes in order to reach the refuge of the Grisons, and the town stagnated. It later had a reputation for violent crime. From 1815–78 it was one of the three alternating capitals of the canton. Here in October 1925 took place the *Pact of Locarno*, a well-intentioned attempt to control possible future German aggression. In 1917 James Joyce convalesced here, whence he sent the first part of 'Ulysses' to Ezra Pound for perusal.

Lago Maggiore, the Roman *Lacus Verbanus* and the second largest of the Italian lakes after Garda, is 64.3km long, but only about one fifth of its total extent of 214km^2 is Swiss territory. Its main affluent is the Ticino, but also important is the Maggia, which flows into the lake just W of Locarno, while on its E side, near Luino, is the Tresa, which drains the Lago di Lugano.

These and numerous other tributaries, largely fed by mountain snows, subject the lake to sudden floods. The *tramontana* blows regularly from the N in the early morning, followed after 10.00 or so by the *inverna* from the S. The lake's usually placid surface can be made unexpectedly rough by the *maggiora*.

The main centre is the PIAZZA GRANDE, at the E end of which is the quay (with lake steamers) extended to the E by attractive lakeside gardens. The N side of the Piazza is flanked by picturesque old houses built over arcades, continued along the Via Fr. Rusca, from which several narrow alleys ascend towards the old Via Cittadella. The Via Fr. Rusca ends at the **Castello**, formerly a seat of the Visconti and after 1513 of the Swiss bailiffs. It was begun in 1342, but was partly demolished in 1531. It now houses a local *Museum*, together with a collection of paintings by Hans Arp.

At the W end of the Via Cittadella stands 14C *San Francesco*, with monolithic granite columns.—Higher up the hill is *San Antonio* (17C), beyond which is the cemetery chapel of *Santa Maria in Selva*, with relics of 15C frescoes.—Further E in the Via Cittadella is the *Chiesa Nuovo* (1613), with a St. Christopher painted on its facade.

Of more interest is Romanesque *San Vittore*, in Muralto, approached by ascending the Via Ramogna from near the E end of the Piazza past the funicular station (see below) and *Railway Station*, and turning right along the Via della Colleggiata. The 12C church, founded in the 9C, preserves a crypt displaying early sculptured capitals (11C) and several other features of interest; on its tower is an early Renaissance relief of St. Victor (1462), brought from the castle.—Turning S across the railway, one may descend to regain the lakeside gardens.

S of the Piazza extend the more modern quarters, laid out on a grid plan, beyond which is a residential district.

The funicular mounts to the Franciscan monastery and 17C Church (altered in the 19C) of the *Madonna del Sasso*, sited on a precipitous spur above the town. Founded in 1480, it is approached by a corridor displaying terracotta groups and contains a Flight into Egypt by Bramantino. The view it commands is extensive. It is also reached by a road zigzagging up from opposite San Antonio. The ascent may be continued to the *Cardada* (1350m) for a wider view, and on to the *Cimetta* (1672m).

FROM LOCARNO TO ASCONA AND BRISSAGO (10.5km). Driving W, the neck of the delta of the Maggia is shortly crossed, where fork left to (3km) Ascona; the right-hand fork traverses *Losone* and climbs to the old village of *Arcegno*, with its granite houses crowded in a narrow mountain rift.—**Ascona**, a characteristic old lakeside town developed as a tourist resort, is best visited out of season. *SS. Pedro e Paolo* (1530), with its tall campanile, contains monolithic columns and two paintings by Giovanni Serodine (1594–1632).—In *Santa Maria*, to the E, are 15–16C wall-paintings; S of Santa Maria is the *Collegio Papio*, with a 16–17C cloister. The *Municipio*, of the same period, has a pleasing arcaded front. Several old mansions are preserved, notably (near Santa Maria) the *Casa Borrani*, with a facade of 1620. Georg Kaiser (1878–1945), the German dramatist, who emigrated to Switzerland in 1938, died here.

The road goes on to adjacent *Porto Ronco*, high above which lies **Ronco**, a picturesque village, once the home of Erich Maria Remarque (1898–1970), author of 'All Quiet on the Western Front', who is buried in the cemetery.—Offshore lie the verdant islands of *Brissago* and *San Pancrazio*, with a *Botanical Garden*, and a smaller islet with ruins of a Romanesque church.—9km **Brissago**, the frontier village, has a 16–17C parish church with an octagonal cupola, and is surrounded by ancient cypresses. Nearby, in the *Villa Myriam*, lived Leoncavallo when composing 'Il Pagliacci' (1892). Nearer the frontier, at *Ponte di Valmara*, is the larger church of *La Madonna del Ponte* (1531), by Giovanni Beretta.—On the opposite shore lies the Italian village of *Pino*; inland rises *Monte Limidario* or *Gridone* (2188m), marking the frontier, which is shortly reached (Customs), with *Cannobio* 5.5km beyond.

For Cannobio and the lakeside road on to (12.5km) *Verbania* see *Blue Guide Northern Italy*, and likewise for the main road hence up the Valle d'Ossola to (40km) *Domodóssola*.

For the road from Locarno to **Brig**, in the Valais, via Domodóssola and the *Simplon Pass* see Rte 46, in reverse.

FROM LOCARNO TO (28KM) BIGNASCO AND FUSIO, 17km beyond. The **Val Maggia**, with its main tributaries, the Valle di Campo and Val Bavona, is, as its name implies, the largest of the valleys that open to the N of Lago Maggiore. Its lower reaches form a broad straight trench between lofty precipices on either side, which are streaked by numerous waterfalls; higher up the scenery becomes bolder, and after Bignasco the valley is known as the Lavizzara. Driving NW, at 4km we bear right at *Ponte Brolla*, where the Domodóssola road turns left; see Rte 46, in reverse.

However, as the excursion hence up the VALLE ONSERNONE is usually made from Locarno, it is described here. The side valley is entered by turning right at *Cavigliano*, 3km W, the narrow winding road climbing rapidly, just prior to (11.5km) *Russo* passing the remarkable overhanging rock known as the *Sasso della Caurga*. The road goes on to (8km) *Spruga*, from which a path ascends to the frontier below the *Pilone* (2192m).—A turning 1km beyond Russo leads into the VALLE DI VERGELETTO and (3km) the small resort of *Vergeletto*, surrounded by wooded hills. A track 2km beyond climbs N past the small *Lago di Alzasca* into the Valle Maggia near *Someo*; another path at the head of the valley, beyond which rise the *Piz di Madei* (2551m) and *Piz dell'Alpe Gelato* (2613m), leads over the *Passo della Capegna* (1978m) to *Cimalmotto*; see below.

The main road up the Maggia valley by-passes most of the characteristic villages, among them **Maggia** itself, where *Santa Maria delle Grazie in Campagna* preserves 16C frescoes, and (14.5km) *Someo*, shortly beyond which is the *Soladino Fall* (left).—6.5km *Cevio*, a granite-quarrying village, with the richly sculpted chapel of the *Madonna del Ponte* (1615), lies at the foot of the VALLE DI CAMPO, with a mountain road climbing up to (17km) *Cimalmotto*; see above. To the NW of the latter rises the *Piz Quadro* (2793m).

From a point 9km up the valley one may turn N into the VALLE DI BOSCO-GURIN. The inhabitants of the secluded village of *Bosco Gurin* have the distinction of speaking the Germanic dialect of the Valle Formazza to the W of the frontier, from where they emigrated in the 15C. To the NW rises the imposing *Wandfluhhorn* (or *Pizzo Biela*; 2863m), below which there is a pass to *Foppiano*, in Italy.

Above Cevio the valley narrows as we approach (3km) **Bignasco** (443m), a characteristic village and base for excursions into the Ticino Alps. It is charmingly situated at the junction of the Val Bavona, leading NW towards the grim precipices of the *Basòdino* (3272m), and the VAL LAVIZZARA (NE), where the view is closed by the summit of the *Piz Campo Tencia* (3072m).

The deep wooded glen of the VAL BAVONA, one of the most attractive of Alpine valleys, may be followed to (10.5km) *San Carlo*, a hamlet at 938m, lying below the Basòdino with its glacier to the W. Lifts mount to *Robliei*, near one of several small reservoirs and tarns between the *Marchhorn* (W; 2962m) and the *Cristallina* (2912m), to the W of which its pass (2568m) leads into the VALLE BEDRETTO W of Airola; see Rte 41.

Turning NE up the main valley above Bignasco, at 8km opens the wild VAL DI PRATO, at the head of which is the Piz Campo Tencia, and from which the *Passo di Redòrta* (2181m) leads SE to *Sonogno*; see p 292.—At (2km) *Peccia* the valley again divides, the VALLE DI PECCIA ascending to the left, while the Val Lavizzara grows yet narrower and steeper. Along it the mountain road zigzags to (7km) *Fusio* (1289m), the last village, and a base for ascents in the area.

A path climbs NE to the *Passo Campolungo* (2318m) into the VALLE LEVENTINA, while a road circles to the NW, skirting the *Lago Sambuco* reservoir to (14km) the beautiful *Lago di Naret* and its adjacent tarns below the *Poncione dei Laghetti* (2616m). The *Passo di Naret* (2438m), W of the reservoir, leads to the *Passo di Cristallina* (see above) or to the VALLE BEDRETTO, overlooked to the E by *Il Madone* (2756m).

40 Bellinzona to Lugano and Como

Total distance, 58km (36 miles). No. 2. 28km **Lugano**—30km **Como**.

Maps: M 219; BL 43, 48, or 5007.

Driving SW from **Bellinzona** (see Rte 39), industrial *Giubiasco* is traversed to reach the entrance to the N2 motorway, which it is preferable to follow up the N flank of the *Cima di Medeglia* (1260m), rising steeply above the flat *Piano di Magadino*, the W spur of which has recently been pierced by a tunnel, avoiding the former climb up to the *Monte Ceneri Pass* (554m; see below), although the old No. 2 is not a difficult ascent and provides a better view from the summit.

At a point just W of the motorway entry, and before the No. 2 starts to climb, the right-hand fork continues W (off which one may later turn right for Locarno) to (9km) *Vira*, on the S bank of *Lago Maggiore* (see p 293). From Vira a steep road climbs to **Fosano**, a hamlet with a little church containing 16C frescoes, and commanding an extensive *View across the lake towards Locarno and the Maggia valley beyond.—Hence a winding and zigzagging road (built during the 1914–18 war when the village was cut off from traffic by the closing of the Italian frontier) leads some 15km S, between *Monte Tamaro* (1962m) and *Monte Gambarogno* (1734m) to *Indemini*, preserving a number of characteristic Ticino houses.—The lakeside road beyond Vira may be followed parallel to a railway line to (8.5km) the frontier village of *Zenna* (Customs); for the road beyond to (15km) *Luino* see *Blue Guide Northern Italy*.

The motorway and main road descend from Monte Ceneri into the valley of the VEDEGGIO and follow its lower course, known as the VAL D'AGNO, in part industrialised, later climbing over a ridge to descend again past the *Railway Station* of Lugano, there turning sharp right along the Via Cantonale and Corso Pestalozzi to reach the *Parco Civico*. The view E across the town towards Monte Brè, now thickly plastered with villas, is somewhat disillusioning.

LUGANO (278m; 27,800 inhab.; 15,200 in 1930; 6950 in 1880), the largest town of the Ticino, is situated at an elbow of the very irregularly shaped Lago di Lugano and on the E flank of Monte San Salvatore. It has spread rapidly to the N and E beyond the torrent of the Cassarate and has thus dissipated much of its former charm. The views it commands to the S and SE across the lake are very fine, and several streets and alleys of the old centre retain their Italian character. Its main attraction for the connoisseur is now the collection of paintings at the 'Villa Favorita' at *Castagnola*, the lakeside suburb below Monte Brè.

Lugano was taken from Milan by the Forest Cantons in 1512 and was ruled as a subject district until the dissolution of the old Swiss Confederation in 1798. It vigorously repulsed an attempt to bring it under Italian domination, choosing rather to remain 'free and Swiss'; and in 1803 became part of the new canton of Ticino. In 1822 Anthony Panizzi (1797–1879), later the influential Librarian of the British Museum, fled here en route for London, and here he published a pamphlet condemning the judicial iniquities of the Prince of Modena's regime. In 1838 its population was 4500. From 1848–66 it was Giuseppe Mazzini's headquarters during the struggle of the Italians to throw off the Austrian yoke in Lombardy. Élisée Reclus sought refuge here in 1871–74, when exiled after the Paris Commune. Lugano shared with Bellinzona and Locarno the privilege of being the cantonal capital for alternate periods of six years until 1878, when Bellinzona became the fixed capital.

The *Lago di Lugano, also known as that of *Ceresio*, is largely comprised of three main reaches and its total area is 49km^2, of which 25km^2 is politically Swiss. Its length (from Agno to Porlezza) is 35.5km and its width is never more than 3.25km. None of the streams which feed into it is of much importance and the surface level is therefore more constant than that of its larger neighbours.

It was, however, one of the most polluted lakes of Europe until equipped with purifying installations. Its waters drain into Lago Maggiore via the river Tresa. Except for the noontide *breva*, the lake is not exposed to periodic winds, but the tempestuous *caronasca* occasionally sweeps its central reach from the W. The scenery of its shores, except for the bay of Lugano, is far wilder and more desolate than on the greater lakes.

The *Parco Civico* was originally the grounds of the *Villa Ciani* (1840), now housing the **Municipal Museum**, adjacent to which is the modern *Palazzo dei Congressi*.

Among the more notable paintings in the museum are: *attrib. Cranach the Elder*, St. Andrew; *attrib. G.-B. Moroni*, Portrait of M. Ricci, the missionary; *G.A. Petrini*, Jacob's dream, and other works; *C. Tencalla*, Communion of St. Anthony; *Carlo Bossoli* (1815–84), two Views of Lugano; works by *Antonio Ciseri* (1821–91), *Edoardo Berta* (1867–1931), *Giuseppe Foglia* (1888–1950) and other artists from the Ticino; *Hodler*, Alpine scene; and representative works by *Augusto Giacometti, Boudin, Rodin, Renoir, Matisse, Pissarro* and *Douanier Rousseau*; and bronzes and drawings by *Francesco Messina* (1900–).

From the SW corner of the park one may follow the lakeside Riva Giocondo Albertolli to the PIAZZA MANZONI and PIAZZA RIZIERO REZZONICO, between which is the *Municipio* or *Town Hall* (1845). Just N of this is the characteristic arcaded **Piazza della Riforma**, the main centre and a pedestrian precinct, from which a number of narrow alleys diverge. From its NW corner one may approach the small PIAZZA CIOCCARO, from which a funicular ascends to the *Railway Station*. The stepped Via Cattedrale climbing NW brings one shortly to the terrace (left; view) on which the **Cathedral**, or *San Lorenzo*, stands. Its facade, in the Lombard-Venetian style, has three good portals; the central one dates from 1517. The interior preserves some 14–16C frescoes.

Returning to the Piazza Cioccaro, walk SE to reach the N end of the Via Nassa, just beyond the S end of which stands the plain Franciscan church of *•**Santa Maria degli Angioli**, founded in 1499 and restored in 1930 (including the frescoes). The most remarkable of the frescoes, occupying the arch between the nave and the choir, is the huge depiction of the Passion and Crucifixion (1530) by Bernardino Luini (c 1475–1532); below are figures of St. Sebastian and St. Roch. In the first chapel on the right is a Madonna and child with St. John; on the left wall of the nave, a Last Supper. A fresco of the Flight into Egypt in the fourth chapel to the right is attrib. to the School of Bramantino.

Hence the esplanade of the Riva Vincenzo Vela leads back to the Piazza R. Rezzonico.

Some distance E of the Parco Civico, reached by following the Viale Castagnola through the suburb of *Cassarate*, where the main road bears right, the Via Pico (turning left) leads shortly to the lower terminus of the funicular climbing up the flank of **Monte Brè** (925m; view), also approached by a road ascending in zigzags, which continues to the high-lying village of *Brè* (800m).

The Castagnola road soon reaches (right) the entrance to the '**Villa Favorita**', the home of the **••Thyssen-Bornemisza Collection** (open from Easter until mid October). Enquire at the Tourist Office at the E end of the Riva Giocondo Albertolli for times of admission.

The building was acquired in 1932 from Prince Friedrich Leopold of Prussia by Baron Heinrich Thyssen-Bornemisza (1875–1947), and a gallery was later added. His father, August Thyssen (1842–1926), had founded a great iron and steel works near Mühlheim, and collected 'Old Masters'. The collection was considerably expanded and numerous 19–20C European paintings were bought, the family tradition being carried on by the present baron, Hans Heinrich (born 1921), who opened the collection to the public in 1948. The paintings by the 'Modern Masters', shown at the Royal Academy in London in 1984, are *not* displayed here; when not on show elsewhere, they are at Daylesford House in Gloucestershire.

On STAIRCASE: *Piero di Cosimo*, Virgin and child with angels; *Master of the André Madonna*, Virgin and child with musical angels; *G.B. Tiepolo*, Death of Hyacinth; *Traversi*, Fainting woman—Below steps: Female head (Roman; 1C); clay model of St. John, by *Benedetto de Maiano*; *Guercino*, Christ and the Samaritan women at the well; and *Fuseli*, The tomb of Rosicrucius. The furniture throughout should not be overlooked.

R1 *Ugolino da Siena*, Crucifixion with the Virgin and St. John; *Vitale da Bologna*, Crucifixion; *Master of the Magdalen altarpiece*, Virgin and child; *Lorenzo Veneziano*, Triptych; *Lorenzo Monaco*, Virgin and child with angels; Byzantine ivories.

R2 *Hans Baldung Grien* *Adam and Eve; *Derick Baegert*, five sections from a Crucifixion altarpiece of 1477; *Hans Wertinger*, Portrait of 'Ritter Christoph'; *Master of the Lyversberg Passion*, Deposition, Entombment, Descent into Limbo, and Resurrection; *Master of Grossgmain*, St. Jerome; *Michael Pacher*, Virgin and child with Saints Catherine and Margaret; *Bernhard Strigel*, Annunciation, and Annunciation to Saints Anne and Joachim.

R3 *Barthel Beham*, male and female Portraits of members of the Stüpf family; *Altdorfer*, Portrait of a young woman; *Sebald Bopp*, Wedding portrait of a lady wearing the Order of the Swan; *Dürer*, Jesus among the scribes; *Hans Holbein the Elder*, Male and female portraits; *Holbein the Younger*, Portraits of Thomas Cromwell, Henry VIII (the only one entirely executed by the artist); *Wolf Huber*, Adoration of the Magi; *Hans Burgkmaier the Elder*, Deposition; *Hans Maler*, Crucifixion, and Christ in limbo; *Michael Wolgemut*, Portrait of Levinus Memminger.

R4 *Hans Cranach*, Hercules as Omphale's slave, Bearded man; *Lucas Cranach the Elder*, wings of an altarpiece depicting Saints George and Christopher, on the reverse of which are Saints Anne and Elisabeth, with the donors, George and Barbara of Saxony, Virgin and child with grapes, Reclining nymph, Portrait of a young woman; *Hans Baldung Grien*, Portrait of a lady; *Christoph Amberger*, Portrait of Mattheus Schwarz the Elder.

R5 *Dieric Bouts*, Virgin and child; *Jacques Daret*, Nativity; *Gerard David*, Crucifixion; *Jan van Eyck*, Annunciation (diptych); *Juan de Flandes*, Portrait possibly of Joana la Loca (the Mad) or her sister, Catherine of Aragon, Pietà with Saints John and Mary Magdalen; *Master of the Legend of St. Lucy*, Triptych of the Lamentation over Christ, with Saints Donation and Adrian in the wings together with donors; *Master of the Virgo inter Virgines*, Calvary; *Memling*, Male portrait; *Rogier van der Weyden*, Virgin and child enthroned, and Male portrait.

R6 *Joos van Cleve*, Self-portrait; *Jan Gossaert (Mabuse)*, Adam and Eve; *Maerten van Heemskerk*, Lady with spindle and distaff; *Lukas van Leyden*, Card players, St. Paul; *Master of Flémalle (Robert Campin)*, Portrait of Robert de Masmines; *Jan Mostaert*, Redeemed souls, the donor perhaps Mary of Burgundy; *Van Orly*, Rest on the flight into Egypt; *Van Reymerswaele*, Calling of St. Matthew; *Jan van Scorel*, Virgin and child with two donors; *Van Valckenborch*, Massacre of the Innocents.

R7 *Jan Brueghel the Elder*, Christ in the tempest; *Cornelis Ketel*, Portraits of a lady and gentleman aged 56 and 58 respectively; *Adrien Key*, William I of Orange (1579); *Paul Bril*, Rest on the flight into Egypt; *Anthony Mor*, Portrait of Jan Baptist Castilan; *Momper*, two Landscapes.

R8 *Ferdinand Bol*, Self-portrait; *Van Goyen*, Ice-skating near Dordrecht; *Nicolaes Maes*, The naughty drummer; *Aert van der Neer*, Landscapes; *Rembrandt*, Stormy landscape, Self-portrait (c 1643); *Pieter Jansz Saenredam*, Facade of St. Mary's church, Utrecht.

R9 *Herrit Dou*, Girl with a candle; *Willem Claesz Heda*, Still life; *Willem Kalf*, Still lifes; *Pieter de Hooch*, Dutch interior; *Salomon van Ruysdael*, Alkmaar from the sea; *Jan Siberechts*, The ford; *Gerard Terborch*, Portraits, and Man reading a letter.

R10 *Berckheyde*, Townscapes in the Hague and Amsterdam; Landscapes by *Cuyp*, *Jacob van Ruisdael*, and *Salmon van Ruysdael*.

R11 *Adrein Brouwer*, Peasants drinking; *Frans Hals*, Portrait of a lady; *Pieter Neefs the Elder*, Church interior; Tavern scenes by *Jan Steen*, *Van Ostade* and *David Teniers the Younger*.

Carpaccio; Young Knight in a Landscape

Ghirlandaio, Portrait of Giovanna Tornabuoni

R12 *Jan van de Cappelle*, Seascape; *Van Dyck*, Portrait of Jacques Le Roy (1631); *Govert Flinck*, Male portrait; *Van Goyen*, The beach at Scheveningen; *Frans Hals*, Family group; *Hobbema*, Trees; *Pieter de Hooch*, Interior of the Town Hall, Amsterdam; *Nicolaes Maes*, Portraits of a lady and gentleman; *Van de Velde the Younger*, The Dutch fleet at anchor; *Cornelis de Vos*, Portrait of Antonia van Eversdyck.

R13 *Bartolomeo Veneto*, Portrait of a Patrician; *Gentile Bellini*, Annunciation; *Jacopo Bellini*, St. Jerome; *Jacopo Bassano*, Pastoral scene; *Carpaccio*, Young knight in a landscape; *Palma Vecchio*, Virgin and child with saints, 'La Bella'; *Sebastiano del Piombo*, Ferry Carondolet with his secretaries; *Titian*, Portraits of Antonio Anselmi, and the Doge Francesco Venier, St. Jerome; *Veronese*, Lady with a lapdog.

R14 *Antonello da Messina*, Male portrait; *Colantonio*, Crucifixion; *Daddi*, Crucifixion; *Duccio*, Christ and the Samaritan woman at the fountain; *Giovanni di Paolo*, Virgin and child with angels; *Piero della Francesca*, Portrait of Guidobaldo da Montefeltro; *Pietro da Rimini*, Nativity; *Uccello*, Crucifixion with the Virgin, the Evangelist, the Baptist and St. Francis.

R15 *Fra Angelico*, Virgin and child with angels; *Bartolo di Fredi*, Golgotha; *Bramante*, Ecce Homo; *Ghirlandaio*, •Portrait of Giovanna Tornabuoni; *Gozzoli*, St. Jerome with a monk; *Luini*, Virgin and child with St. John; *Bartolomeo Montagna*, St. Jerome; Bust of a young woman by *Gian Cristofero Romano*.

R16 *Fra Bartolomeo*, Holy Family with St. John; *Bonfigli*, Annunciation; *Boltraffio*, Portrait of a lady; *Bronzino*, Cosimo de' Medici in armour; *Lorenzo Lotto*, Self-portrait; *Mazzola*, Portrait of Alessandro de Richao; *Pontormo*, Portrait of a lady; *Raphael*, A youth; *Ercole de' Roberti*. The Argonauts leaving Colchis; *Andrea Solario*, Male portrait; *Cosmé Tura*, The Baptist on Patmos; *Zoppo*, St. Jerome.

R17 *Bernardo Bellotto*, Bridge across the Brenta; *Canaletto*, 'Il Bucintoro', Venice; *Longhi*, Tickling; *Marieschi*, View of Santa Maria della Salute.

R18 *Boucher*, Mme Boucher fixing her garter; *Chardin*, Still life; *Fragonard*, The seesaw, Portrait of Mlle Duthé; *Lancret*, The swing, The Earth (representing one of the elements); *Antoine Le Nain*, Children singing and fiddling; *Nattier*, Mme Bouret as Diana; *Roslin*, Architect and his wife.

R19 *Caravaggio*, St. Catherine; *Houdon*, Bust of Daubenton; *Vouet*, Rape of Europa; *Claude Lorrain*, The flight into Egypt; *François Clouet*, The 'billet doux': *Valentin de Boulogne*, David with the head of Goliath; *Sebastien Bourdon*, Holy Family with angels; and a Tureen by *François Thomas Germain*.

R20 *Goya*, Ferdinand VII, El tío Paquete, and Portrait of Ascencio Julia Florida; *El Greco*, Mater Dolorosa, and other works, and two wooden busts of saints; *Murillo*, Virgin and child appearing to St. Rose; *Velazquez*, Maria Anna of Austria; *Zurbarán*, Crucifixion, St. Elizabeth of Thuringia, (St. Agnes has been sold!); *Ribera*, St. Jerome.

FROM LUGANO TO BOGNO: THE VAL COLLA. From Cassarate bear N and then NE along the flank of Monte Brè to *Dino*, with a Romanesque campanile, and *Sonvico*, thence across a ridge into the VAL COLLA. This may be followed to the village of *Bogno* (961m) at its head, and there climbing slightly to wind W along the sunlit N side to *Tesserete*, with an old campanile. Just W of Tesserete is *Ponte Capriasca*, the church of which contains a good copy of Leonardo's 'The Last Supper' (c 1550, referred to by restorers of the original). One may either return to Lugano along the W side of the hills above the CASSARATE VALLEY or from Tesserete along the W side of the valley.

FROM LUGANO TO MORCOTE, AND THE CIRCUIT OF ITS PENINSULA. Driving S along the lakeside through the suburb of *Paradiso* and below *Monte San Salvatore* (912m), the small Italian enclave of **Campione** is seen across the lake, in which the chapel of *St. Peter* (1327) and the cemetery chapel of *Santa*

Maria dei Ghirli, with its frescoes (a Last Judgment on the facade and 13C examples inside), are of interest.—We pass under the motorway for *Melide*, the birthplace of Domenico Fontana (1543–1607), architect of the Royal Palace at Naples. At the E end of the causeway lies *Bissone*; see below. Continuing ahead, a string of hamlets are traversed to reach a turning climbing to *Vico Morcote*, its church of 1625 preserving a fine marble bas relief.—**Morcote** itself lies at the extremity of the peninsula, and is still perhaps the most picturesque village on the lake. Characteristic is the tall campanile of the church of *Madonna del Sasso* (14C), adorned with 16C frescoes.—Morcote may also be approached from Paradiso by climbing over the W flank of *Monte San Salvatore* (to which a funicular ascends, and the view from which impressed Wordsworth) to **Carona**, where *San Giorgio*, of Romanesque origin, contains 15–16C frescoes. The road continues along the E side of *Monte Arbòstora* (835m) to Vico Morcote.—*Brusino-Arsizio*, on the opposite bank to the SE, lies below the chapel-crowned *Monte San Giorgio*, which divides the two arms of the lake; *Porto Ceresio*, to the SW, is on the Italian shore.—Circling round the peninsula, the E bank of this W arm is followed through several villages to crossroads at its head.

Hence one may either return to Lugano past the small *Laghetto di Muzzano*, or continue the excursion by turning left past the aerodrome through *Agno* to the Italian frontier at *Ponte Tresa* (Customs), on a land-locked bay overlooked by *Monte Caslano* (526m). A road runs along the N bank of the Tresa, the effluent of the lake, and marking the frontier, later crossed to reach *Luino*, on Lago Maggiore; see *Blue Guide Northern Italy*.—The comparatively unspoilt villages of the *Malcantone*, a district of wooded valleys and vineyards NW of Ponte Tresa, may be explored, among them *Cademário*, with the little 12C church of *Sant' Ambrógio*, with 13–15C wall-paintings.

The motorway may be regained a short distance SW of Lugano, which briefly leads down a valley W of *Monte San Salvatore* below (right) *Montagnola*, the home of Hermann Hesse in 1919–26, before bearing SE through a tunnel under the ridge to cross the '*ponte diga*' or causeway, its foundations laid on a natural rock bar, between *Melide* (see above) and **Bissone**, on the far bank of the Lago di Lugano. The *Tencala mansion* (1600) was built by Giovanni Pietro Tencala. It was the birthplace of Stefano Maderno (1576–1636), the sculptor, the architect Francesco Borromini (1599–1667), and the Gaggini family of sculptors.

Road, railway and motorway bear S above the SE arm of the lake, with *Monte Giorgio* on the far shore. To the left is *Rovio*, where the 11C chapel of *San Vigilio* preserves Romanesque frescoes of Byzantine inspiration.—*Capolago* is shortly reached, the terminus of the rack-railway up **Monte Generoso** (1701m), long reputed for its rich flora, the rocky crest of which commands a panoramic *View* of the Alps. There is an *Alpine Garden* at *Bellavista*, on its S flank, also approached by a road climbing up from Mendrisio.

The view extends from Monte Viso or Monviso (to the SW beyond Turin) past the Gran Paradiso, to Monte Rosa and the Mischabel massif. To the N above the Ticino Alps rises the Bernese Oberland, with the Tödi and the Rheinwald group to the right. To the NE is Monte Disgrazia, with the Bergamasque Alps further S. In the opposite direction lies the plain of Lombardy.

Just W of Capolago, the birthplace of Carlo Maderno (1556–1629), the architect, is the village of **Riva San Vitale**, where the *Bapistery* (restored), just S of the main square, with its octagonal vault and apsidal choir, dates from the 6C, and is unique in Switzerland. To the N, the octagonal cupola of 16C *Santa Croce* is conspicuous.

The next exit on the motorway is that for Mendrisio, to the E, but by turning right and then back over the motorway, one shortly reaches (left) the interesting 12C church of *San Martino*, of Carolingian foundation and with Paleo-Christian remains under the choir. Hence, by passing below the railway and turning right, Mendrisio may also be reached.

The older town of **Mendrisio**, the main centre of this enclave, is dominated by the large church of *Santi Cosma e Damiano* of 1875 built on the site of its predecessor, the adjacent tower being its belfry. Several patrician residences may be seen, including the *Palazzo Pollini* (1720) and the *Palazzo Torriani-Fontana* (16–17C). The 15C cloister of a former Servite convent is N of the church.—At Via Carlo Maderno 19, in neighbouring *Rancate*, is the *Giovanni Züst* collection of 17–19C paintings by artists of the Ticino.

The main road bears SE through *Balerna*, with a much altered church of early Romanesque foundation, NE of which lies *Morbio Inferiore*, with a conspicuous Baroque church, to reach industrial *Chiasso*, the frontier town and railway junction.

The motorway by-passing Mendrisio circles E to skirt the bank of the Breggia between Balerna and Chiasso to the frontier crossing (Customs), there traversing a short tunnel into Italy, with a brief view of the SW extremity of an arm of *Lago di Como*, on the banks of which extends Como.

For **Como** itself, a manufacturing town with a population approaching 100,000, but with a centre preserving to a marked extent its Roman street plan, and with a late 14C *Cathedral*, mainly of marble, among several other buildings of interest, see *Blue Guide Northern Italy*; likewise for the shores of its lake, and *Milan*, some 45km S.

41 Bellinzona to Andermatt via Biasca and the Gotthardtunnel or pass

Total distance, 83km (51 miles). No. 2. 21 km **Biasca**—9km **Giornico**; there preferably entering the N2—28km *Airola* exit—20km *Göschenen*—No. 2. 5km **Andermatt**. From Airola to Andermatt via the pass is 27km.

Maps: M 218; BL 37, 42, 43, or 5001.

Driving N from **Bellinzona** (see Rte 39), at 4km the N13 motorway is crossed near the *Battlefield of Arbedo*, where in 1422 some 3000 Swiss made a gallant but unavailing stand against 18,000 Milanese. Continue up the valley of the Ticino, here known as the RIVERA. *Claro* is shortly by-passed, on a crag to the E of which stands a small Benedictine nunnery founded in 1490; to the NW rises the pyramidal *Piz di Claro* (2727m).

17km **Biasca** (301m), lying at the foot of the VAL BLENIO (see p 290), is overlooked to the SE by the Romanesque basilican church of *Saints Peter and Paul* (12–13C, but of earlier foundation), containing 13–16C frescoes. Enquire in the village for the key before making the stiff climb to the church.

The road now bears NW up the VALLE LEVENTINA (*Vallis Lepontina*) parallel to the N2 motorway under construction. This may be entered just prior to (9km) **Giornico**, but it is well worth while to enter the village first, and cross the river, with an old bridge, to visit *San Nicolao, a short distance downstream. The Romanesque basilican church, dating from the second half of the 12C, is one of the finest in the Ticino. Apart from its sober campanile, it preserves a typical entrance in the Lombardic tradition, a raised choir with late 15C frescoes, and a small crypt.—*Santa Maria di Castello* (12–13C), on the far side of the railway, on a hill once fortified, likewise contains 15C frescoes. It was near Giornico that in 1478 the Swiss gained a decisive victory over a Milanese army, although outnumbered by ten to one!

It is recommended to turn back and take the motorway to Airolo and the S entrance to the Gotthardtunnel (see below), but the No. 2 is also described.

Beyond Giornico we climb and thread the steep *Biaschina ravine*, a left-hand turning in which leads to *Chironico*, with an early two-apsed Romanesque church containing 14–16C frescoes and a 14C tower.—A mountain road leads NE above the valley to *Dalpe* and *Prato* to regain the main road at *Rodi-Fiesso*; see below.

11.5km *Faido*, the main village of the valley, preserves several characteristic 16C houses. Beyond it the defile of the *Dázio Grande* is traversed. The former road, at a lower level, was twice swept away by floods in the 1830s.—5.5km *Rodi-Fiesso*, from which village a mountain road climbs steeply SE to *Prato* and (5km) *Dalpe* (1192m), a base for ascents in the *Piz Campo Tencia* group to the SW, rising to 3072m, and also for the path to the reservoir of *Lago Tremorgio* and the *Passo Campolungo* (2318m) to *Fusio*; see Rte 39. Prato has a fine example of a Romanesque campanile typical of this district. In the vicinity are traces of a Roman road.

At 1.5km beyond Rodi-Fiesso we meet the motorway, below which the old road continues to climb, later threading the *Stalvedro gorge*, which in 1799 was stoutly defended by a small French force against Suvarov's Russians before they were forced to retreat W up the Valle Betretto to cross the Nufenenpass. Ruined fortifications are passed in the gorge, some built by the Lombards in the 8C.

From an exit of the N2, a mountain road climbs right above the valley through *Quinto*, with the six-storey 12C tower of its 17C church, of pre-Romanesque foundation, to *Piora*, by *Lago Ritóm*, a reservoir overlooked from the N by *Piz Taneda* (2667m), one of several fine view-points, to the NE of which rise *Piz Blas* (3019m) and *Piz Rondadura* (3016m). A path leads E up the VAL PIORA to the *Lukmanierpass*; see p 289.

The motorway, now veering slightly N of W, commands imposing views of the remarkably engineered road climbing to the St. Gotthardpass, built out over the steep mountainside, and of the numerous snow-clad peaks rising due W, among them the *Piz Rotondo* (3192m). Traversing a short tunnel, the exit for Airolo and the road over the pass (see below) is reached, prior to plunging into the ***Gotthardtunnel**, completed in 1980 after eleven years' work, and at present the longest road tunnel in the world (16.3km). It is an essential route in winter, when the St. Gotthardpass is closed to traffic. The exit is immediately E of *Göschenen*; see Rte 25A, and for the road down the valley of the Reuss to **Altdorf**. For the rail tunnel see p 230.

Airolo (1139m), the Romanesque campanile of its church being preserved, is a base for excursions and ascents in the St. Gotthard Alps.

2km S is the start of a cable-car mounting to the *Sasso della Boggia* (2065m), commanding fine views. NE is the VAL CANARIA, with *Piz Ravetsch* (3007m) at its head. SE is the *Passo Sassello* (2334m), leading to *Fusio*, while to the SW, off the Valle Bedretto road, paths climb to the *Passos del Naret* and *di Cristallina*; see latter part of Rte 39.

FROM AIROLO TO ULRICHEN (36km). The road ascends the VALLE BEDRETTO to the W, in which the Ticino rises. To the NW is the *Pizzo Pesciora* (3122m), with its glacier on its flank, and the adjacent *Witenwasser Stock* (3082m), while further W is the *Piz Rotondo* (3192m). At 9km the village of *Bedretto* is passed, its church tower protected against avalanches by an angular buttress. Beyond *All'Acqua* a path climbs S to the frontier pass of *San Giacomo* (2313m) from which a military road descends into the VAL FORMAZZA past the *Lago di Toggia* reservoir; see *Blue Guide Northern Italy*.

The road climbs to (14km) the **Nufenenpass** or *Passo della Novena* (2478m), opened to traffic in 1969, between the *Piz Gallina* (3061m) to the N and the *Grieshorn* (2929m) on the frontier, just W of which is the *Griespass* (2479m), an old 'wine pass' between Switzerland and Italy, near the *Griesser reservoir* at the foot of the smooth *Griesgletscher*. It provides a good view of the peaks of the Bernese Oberland and the Valais. The road descends rapidly down the AGENENTAL to (13km) *Ulrichen* (1346m) in the GOMS; see Rte 45.

The *old* road over the *St. Gotthardpass** can still be used, but the new road (or tunnel; see above) is recommended, not only as an outstanding example of Swiss engineering, but also because its passage is much gentler. The old road climbs up in 28 zigzags, several times passing under or over the No. 2, and passing a rock inscribed 'Suvarovii Victoriis' in memory of the forcing of the pass by the Russians in 1799. The gully known as the VAL TREMOLA, or 'valley of trembling', has now lost most of its terrors for the wayfarer; it gives its name to 'tremolite', a translucent mineral, pieces of which may be found in the rocks.

The *St. Gotthard Hospice*, which entertained thousands of poor travellers until the opening of the railway in 1882, is now an annex to the hotel. The earliest hospice was built on this wild height in the 14C; its successors have more than once been swept away by avalanches.

The **St. Gotthardpass** (2108m), a saddle in the granite chain, was formerly one of the most frequented passages over the Alps. In 1402 Adam of Usk crossed in an ox-waggon with his eyes blindfolded. Joseph Addison, 'shivering among the eternal frosts and snows', wrote to William Congreve from here in 1702. It was first crossed in a phaeton by an Englishman, Charles Greville, nephew of Sir William Hamilton, in 1775. The road was improved in 1820–30, but lost much of its importance with the opening of the rail tunnel, until the growth of vehicular traffic necessitated the construction of the road tunnel. The No. 2 is frequently used during summer (June–mid November) for the spectacular views it commands. (In 1983 some 10,300 vehicles crossed the pass; 112,300 traversed the tunnel.) The area is of exceptional interest to botanists and geologists.

The road now descends not far E of the *Lago di Lucendro reservoir*, and then between the *Winterhorn* (W; 2661m) and the *Blauberg* (2619m), shortly—at the *Mätteli inn*—enjoying a good view N as it climbs down to **Hospental**, named after a former hospice, founded in the 13C. An old tower (restored) above the village dates from this period.

For the road SW hence to the *Furkapass* see Rte 45.—**Andermatt** lies 2km NE; see Rte 25A. For the road hence to **Chur** see Rte 38, in reverse.

42 Montreux to Aosta

A. Via Martigny and the St. Bernard tunnel or pass

Total distance, 116km (72 miles). No. 9. 13km. *Aigle* lies 2km SE.—15km **St. Maurice**—14km **Martigny**—No. 21. 39km to the N entrance of the **St. Bernard tunnel**—S 27. 35km **Aosta**.

Maps: M 217, 219; BL 41, 46, or 5003.

For **Montreux**, **Chillon** and (5km) *Villeneuve* see pp 102–3 and 104.

FROM VILLENEUVE TO MONTHEY VIA VIONNAZ (20km). Just S of the town turn right to (3km) *Noville*, with a restored church containing traces of 14C frescoes. Noville lies on the flat alluvial estuary of the Rhône, crossed 4km further SW. Ahead is an unattractive view of quarries and cement-works above *Porte du Sex* and *Vouvry*, approached by turning left immediately on crossing the river. For the road hence along the S bank of *Lac Léman* see Rte 2B.—A road climbs W from Vouvry to *Miex*, whence a bridle-path leads NW over to the hamlet of *Tanay* and its lake. *Le Grammont* (2172m) rises to the N, providing a magnificent view over Lac Léman, while to the SW are *Les Cornettes de Bises* (2432m), just S of which is the *Col de Verne* (1814m) leading to *La Chapelle-d'Abondance* in France.—5km *Vionnaz*, a village from which a road zigzags beyond *Revereulaz*, whence a path climbs to the *Col de la Reculaz* (1803m), W of the *Tour de Don* (1998m), among other frontier peaks which may be ascended.—The villages of *Muraz* and *Collombey* are passed between Vionnaz and (8km) *Monthey*; see p 307, and the road thence to *Champéry*.

The N9 motorway provides a rapid route from a point just S of Villeneuve to (31km) the elbow of the RHÔNE VALLEY 2km NE of Martigny, although the by-pass E of St. Maurice is not yet (1986) completed.

Our route follows the No. 9, which crosses the motorway immediately S of *Villeneuve* and shortly traverses *Roche*, below *Mont d'Arvel* with its marble quarries. An *Organ Museum* has been installed since 1983 in the former *Relais du Grand St. Bernard* (18C); it contains several restored instruments of interest. There is a view ahead of the Dents du Midi massif.

At 8km the main road turns right, but it is worthwhile driving ahead through **Aigle** (417m), Roman *Aquilea* and long a feudal stronghold. It is a pleasant little town surrounded by vineyards. Its large medieval *Castle* of 11C foundation now houses *Museums* devoted to Wine and Salt. Near by is the former abbey-church of *St. Maurice*, founded in 1143, with a late Gothic tower. In 1526 Guillaume Farel, the preacher, was sent here by the Bernese at the start of the first Protestant mission to French-speaking Switzerland.

A rack-railway mounts to *Leysin*, for which, and for the road NE up the valley of the Grande-Eau to **Château-d'Oex**, see sub-route on p 131, in reverse.

Regaining the main road below the *Signal de Plantour*, at 3km we bear right 1km prior to *Ollon*.

FROM OLLON TO (9KM) VILLARS AND (15KM) BEX. The road climbs steeply SE before turning NE and ascending in zigzags to *Chesières*, almost contiguous with Villars, on the far side of the Petite-Gryonne. **Villars-sur-Ollon** (1231m) is a well-sited resort, in view of the Grand Muveran, the Dents du Midi and the chain of Mont Blanc, etc. A cable-car mounts to the *Roc d'Orsay* (1951m); the

Col de Bretaye (1806m), to the N, with its tarns, is reached by rack-railway. W of the col rises *Le Chamossaire* (2113m), providing a splendid panoramic view. Hence one may descend to the village of *Les Diablerets* to the NE or to *La Forclaz* to the N; see p 131. Les Diablerets may also be approached by road direct from Villars via the *Col de La Croix* (1778m).

The climb down to Bex passes (left) a lift to *Les Chaux* (1754m) and a mountain road leading E to *Solalex* (1462m). A path hence leads to the *Pas de Cheville* (2038m), with a view of the Pennine Alps as far E as Monte Leone. The *Les Diablerets* massif, with its summit (3210m) immediately to the N of the pass, dominates the area. From near the hamlet of *Derborence* (1449m), not far SE of the pass, with a small lake formed by a landslip in 1749 which destroyed 40 chalets, a road descends via *Conthey* to a point just W of Sion, and a path climbs down to *Ardon*; see Rte 43.—The resort of *Gryon*, enjoying a splendid view of the Muverans and the Dent de Morcles, is passed prior to continuing the descent in zigzags above the *gorge of the Avançon* to *Le Bévieux* and to *Bex* 2km SW; see below.

From Le Bévieux a mountain road climbs SE to *Les Plans-sur-Bex* (1095m), a hamlet in a green hollow at the foot of the *Grand Muveran* (3051m), and beyond to the *Pont-de-Nant*, below its precipices, with the *Alpine Botanic Garden* of Lausanne University. SW rise the *Dent de Morcles* (2969m); to the NE is the *Col des Essets* (2029m), beyond which is that of Cheville; see above. Another track climbs SE from Les Plans to *Javerne* (1666m), below the *Croix de Javerne* (2097m), commanding a panoramic view.

W of Ollon is a low hill on which stands the hamlet of *St. Triphon*, with a 9C tower, passed as the No. 9 veers almost due S, with the *Grand Muveran* (3051m) and *Dent de Morcles* (2969m) in view to the SE, and to the SW the *Dents du Midi*, rising to 3257m.—A left-hand fork shortly leads to adjacent **Bex** (pron. Bé), a small spa, associated with Senancour's novel 'Obermann' (1804), pleasantly situated in a well-wooded plain between the hill of *Montet* to the N and the ruined *Tour de Duin* to the S. A rack-railway ascends hence to *Villars*; see above.

Salt was first obtained by evaporation from the springs at Bex in 1544, but it was not until 1823, when these were failing, that the rock-salt of *Le Bouillet* (above Le Bévioux, 2km NE) was mined. The salt was dissolved in fresh water in subterranean reservoirs to produce the brine, which was then conveyed in firwood pipes to the boiling-house and evaporation sheds of Le Bévioux. Apparently Victor Hugo, Tolstoy and Rimski-Korsakov visited the spa in its heyday.

For *St. Maurice*, 4km S, see below. Relics of Roman *Tarnaiae* may be seen at neighbouring *Massongex*, by-passed.

FROM BEX TO CHAMPÉRY VIA MONTHEY (18km). This DETOUR may conveniently be made by turning right immediately S of Bex via (8km) **Monthey**, almost due W, an industrial town of 11,300 inhab. (4900 in 1930) at the mouth of the VAL D'ILLIEZ. The fair complexion of the children in this valley has suggested that its inhabitants may be of Scandinavian origin. In the chestnut woods above Monthey are erratic blocks, mainly granite, supposed to have been deposited there by a former glacier. The road ascends SW above the Vièze to (4km) *Troistorrents*.

Just before entering the village, a right-hand turning climbs in steep zigzags (with retrospective views of the seven peaks of the Dents du Midi) to (10km) **Morgins**, a resort lying at 1305m among Alpine meadows and pinewoods. The French frontier lies only 1.5km N near a lake and the *Pas de Morgins* (1369m; Customs), whence one may descend via *Châtel* to (8.5km) *La Chapelle-d'Abondance*; see Blue Guide France. N of Morgins rise *Le Corbeau* (1992m; reached by lift) and, further E, the *Pointe de Bellevue* (2042m). A track ascends SW up the valley to a point just below the pass of *Portes du Soleil* (1950m), above *Champéry*; see below.

Shortly beyond Troistorrents a waterfall is passed (right), and *Val d'Illiez*, the main village of the valley, is traversed, the site of a daughter-house of N.D. d'Abondance. The ascent becomes less steep, while the elaborately decorated older chalets, with projecting gables sheltering large leaning crosses, are characteristic and differ greatly from the plainer ones of the Valais.—8km **Champéry** (1064m), a well-sited resort under the flank of the *Roc d'Ayerne* and opposite the crags of the Dents du Midi, consists largely of one main street. Its church of 1725 has a square tower crowned by a curious lantern. Of the numerous view-points within easy reach perhaps the best is the *Galerie Defago*, constructed above the right bank of the Vièze.

The principal ascent from Champéry is that of the **Dents du Midi**, the highest of its peaks, the *Haute Cime* (3257m) being first scaled by the vicar of Champéry, M. Clément, in 1784. The *Cime de l'Est* (further NE; 3178m) is only slightly lower but, like other summits in this massif, only fit for practised alpinists. They are usually ascended via the *Chalets de Bonavau*, beyond which a ravine is climbed by the staircase of the *Pas d'Encel* to the *Cabine de Susanfe* (2102m). To the E of this is its col (2494m) leading to the reservoir or *Lac de Salanfe* (1925m). To the S of the col rises the *Tour Sallière* (3219m), just W of which is *Mont Ruan* (3054m), where while prospecting for gold in 1834, Jacques Balmat, aged 72, lost his life. He had acted as porter to Dr Paccard, who made the first ascent of Mont Blanc in 1786.—Several other ascents—some aided by lifts—may be made from Champéry, including that to the *Portes du Soleil* (NW; 1950m), for *Morgins*; to the *Col de Bossetan* (SW; 2289m), below the *Dents Blanches* (2639m), for *Samoëns*; to the *Col de Coux* (W; 1921m), for *Morzine*; and—more difficult—via the *Col de Sageroux* (S; 2395m), below the *Dent de Barme* (2659m) for *Sixt*, for which, and for Samoëns, and Morzine, see *Blue Guide France*.

St. Maurice lies immediately W of the No. 9. It occupies the site of Roman *Agaunum* and owes its name to the unauthenticated tradition that it was in the vicinity that the *Theban Legion* (so-called because it was raised at Thebes in Egypt), under the command of the warrior saint, Maurice, suffered martyrdom by order of the Emperor Maximian Herculeus in 287 because they refused to serve against their fellow Christians in Gaul. The old *Bridge* spanning the Rhône here, erected at the end of the 15C, may rest on Roman foundations.

The **Abbey of St. Maurice**, at the N end of the town, overlooked by cliffs, has its origin in a chapel on the site of the martyr's tomb, founded at the end of the 4C by St. Theodore, first bishop of the Valais, while the monastery was established in 515 by St. Sigismond. It has belonged to the Augustinians since 1128, and since 1840 its abbot has borne the title of Bishop of Bethlehem in partibus (the see had been at Clamecy, near Vézelay, from 1188 until the Revolution). The abbey was ravaged by fire in 1560 and damaged by a landslide in 1611. The upper part of the 12C tower (on a 10C base) was destroyed in 1942 by another rock-fall, since when it has been restored.

The **Church** was entirely renovated in 1613–27, and has not been improved by the recent addition of glass, etc. Of more interest are the foundations of its several predecessors, recently excavated immediately below the cliff, in which the original chapel, the 6C basilica, the Carolingian church of the second half of the 8C, and early Romanesque rebuilding, have come to light. The *Treasury* contains an engraved Roman sardonyx vase made into a reliquary, a golden ewer of Byzantine origin given to Charlemagne, the skull-reliquary of St. Candidus, and several other early examples of ecclesiastical art.

Driving S, we pass below (left) the *Dent de Morcles* (2969m) and a spur of the Dents du Midi, to by-pass *Evionnaz*, beyond which (right) is the *Pissevache waterfall*. A short distance beyond is the entrance to the *Gorges du Trient*, little more than a fissure in the mountain-side.

On a plateau above the valley lies *Salvan*, a small resort from which a mountain road climbs N to the hamlet of *Van-d'en-Haut.* A path ascends to the *Lac de Salanfe* reservoir below the Dents du Midi, and thence along its N bank to the *Col de Susanfe* (2494m; see above) or SW to the *Col d'Emaney* (2463m) between the *Tour Sallière* (W; 3219m) and the *Luisin* (2786m) to *Emaney,* in the upper *Gorges du Trième.* Another pass, that of the *Col de Barberine* (2481m), leads SW from Emaney to a track along the E bank of the *Lac d'Emossan* reservoir to meet the road above *Finhaut;* see Rte 42B.

We now reach the 'elbow' of the Rhône valley, which makes an abrupt turn to the NE. Passing below the cylindrical tower of *La Bâtiaz,* on its commanding rock, a survival of a castle built in 1260 by Peter of Savoy and destroyed in 1518, we enter (14km) Martigny.

MARTIGNY (467m; 11,300 inhab.; 4800 in 1930), a small industrial town, Roman *Octodurum* or *Forum Claudii Vallensium,* derived its importance from its strategic position at the junction of the Simplon route with those from the Grand St. Bernard and Col de la Forclaz, from Chamonix. Its asparagus and apricots are reputed.

The modern town is of no great moment. Near the central square is a 17C church and one or two 16C houses. To the SW, approached by the Ave du Grand-St.-Bernard and turning along the Rue d'Oche, is (right) the *Promenade Archeologique,* the site of excavations, just E of which stood the *Forum.* By turning right in the Rue du Forum, the ***Pierre Gianadda Foundation,** or *Museum of Gallo-Roman Octodurûs,* is approached.

It was inaugurated in 1978 by Léonard Gianadda in memory of his brother, killed in an air crash. The imposing building, a stoutly buttressed edifice, was constructed over the foundations, which remain in situ, of a Roman temple possibly dedicated to Mercury, discovered two years previously. Around this are displayed a number of Roman relics (or replicas of them) found in Martigny. Together with its gardens, the museum has also been the site of several important exhibitions of art and sculpture, and it is a venue for concerts.

Adjacent is a *Vintage Car collection,* in which superb examples of some 40 automobiles are displayed, among them a Jeanperrin of 1899, a Delauney-Belleville of 1917, built for the Tsar but never delivered, and a Hispano-Suiza of 1936.

A short walk S, beyond the railway, brings one to the comparatively small late 1C Roman *Amphitheatre,* still under excavation; it held c 5000 spectators and was in use until the end of the 4C.

For the road hence to the Col de la Forclaz, for **Chamonix,** see Rte 42B, below; for the road from Martigny to **Brig** via **Sion,** see Rte 43.

Passing through *Martigny-Bourg,* the No. 21 bears SW and then circles to the E up the valley of the Drance to (5.5km) *Les Valettes.*—A mountain road ascends the narrow *Gorges du Dunand* to (11.5km) *Champex;* see below.—The main road threads a defile to reach (6.5km) *Sembrancher* (712m), an old village. Its Baroque church is surmounted by a Gothic belfry with an octagonal spire.

FROM SEMBRANCHER TO MAUVOISIN (24km). We climb almost due E up the VALLÉE DE BAGNES, watered by a branch of the Drance to (5.5km) *Le Châble,* the main village of the valley, with the ruins of a castle and abbey. *La Ruinette* (3875m) and the *Glacier du Giétro* are conspicuous to the SE.—Hence a narrow by-road climbs steeply in zigzags to the NE to (9.5km) **Verbier** (1500m), a resort sheltered from the N by the *Pierre Avoi* (2473m). Several lifts mount towards neighbouring peaks, among them *Mont Gelé* (E; 3023m), beyond which rises *Mont Fort* (3329m). A mountain road climbs N to the *Croix de Coeur pass* (2174m) above *Riddes,* in the Rhône valley.

The main road, now narrower, climbs steeply below the huge *Glacier de Corbassière*, descending from the *Grand Combin* (S; 4314m); to (12.5km) *Fionnay*, a small resort in an amphitheatre of peaks. The *Alp de Louvie* (N; 2250m) commands a splendid view of the Grand Combin and Mont Blanc ranges. It is a base for ascents S into the former massif and also of Mont Fort, the *Roseblanche* (3336m) and *Le Parrain* (3259m), to the NE, etc.—Just S of Mont Fort the *Col de Louvie* leads to the *Barrage de la Grande Dixence*; see Rte 43.—Beyond Fionnay the road threads wild cliffs, later passing the lofty *Pont de Mauvoisin* (1698m) to (6km) *Mauvoisin* itself (1824m), a mountaineering base between the precipices of *Le Pleureur* (NE; 3704m) and the *Pierre à Vire* to the S. To the E rise *La Ruinette* (3875m) and the *Mont Blanc de Cheilon* (3870m). Below the latter is the *Glacier du Giétro*, which in 1818 blocked the valley and caused a disastrous flood. It would have been more calamitous had not M. Venetz, a local engineer, cut a tunnel through the ice barrier to reduce the increasing water level behind it. When the dike burst it took only 1½ hours for the water to reach Martigny, sweeping away some 34 people, although they had been warned of the impending danger. The glacier has greatly receded since then, and its outflow forms an attractive cascade. A path follows the W bank of the *Mauvoisin* reservoir towards the *Cabane de Chanrion* (SE), a base for the ascent of the *Grand Combin* and *La Ruinette* (among other peaks). Whymper asserted that no other Alpine mountain of the same height as La Ruinette could be ascended so easily, and that few had a superior view (of the Grand Combin, etc.). To the SW a path climbs to the *Fenêtre de Durand* (2797m), on the Italian frontier, an ancient pass into the VALPELLINE, mentioned as early as 1252, and said to be the route by which Calvin escaped in 1541 after his unsuccessful attempt at reforming the Aostans. There are some remains of earthworks thrown up by the Duke of Savoy in 1688 to prevent the return of the exiled Waldensians. The col commands a fine view of the Testa del Rutor and other mountains to the SW beyond Aosta. A road is met some distance SW, which descends via *Ollomont* and *Valpelline* to *Aosta*; see Rte 42B, and *Blue Guide Northern Italy*.

The main road from Sembrancher turns S up the VALLÉE D'ENTREMONT to (5.5km) *Orsières*, a village huddled below the confluence of the two branches of the Drance, with a Romanesque tower to its church.

FROM ORSIÈRES TO FERRET (15km). 2.5km SW is the hamlet of *Som-la-Proz*, from which a by-road zigzags steeply NW to (8km) *Champex* (1468m), a mountain-girt resort with a small lake. It is S of *La Catogne* (2598m), ascended from Champex for the view, and NE of *La Breya* (2374m), approached by a lift. The Dents du Midi are seen to the NW. Champex is a base for ascents of the NE peaks and glaciers of the Mont Blanc massif, here forming the frontier. Among them are the *Aiguille d'Argentière* (3900m) and, further S, marking the meeting of the Swiss, French and Italian frontiers, *Mont Dolent* (3820m). A path climbs W from Champex to the *Fenêtre d'Arpette* (2665m) for the *Col de la Forclaz*; see Rte 42B.—The mountain road up the VAL FERRET ascends steeply through several hamlets serving as bases for ascents, to (10.5km) *La Fouly*, with a view W of the glacier in the remarkable rock basin between Mont Dolent and the *Tour Noir* (3836m), further N.—2km *Ferret*, a hamlet beyond which the road deteriorates. From Ferret two paths diverge; that to the SW climbs to the *Col Ferret* (2537m) on the Italian frontier between Mont Dolent and the *Grand Golliat* (3238m). The view SW looks down the Italian VAL FERRET and up the VAL VENI beyond to the Col de la Seigne, 30km distant; while to the right the masses of the Grandes Jorasses and the Aiguille du Geant, streaked with glaciers, conceal the summit of Mont Blanc. To the NE the Grand Combin and Mont Vélan are prominent. At *Pré de Bar* (2062m), a hamlet just below the col on the Italian side, a track, later a road, descends to (14km) *Entrèves*, a village with an old castle not far N of *Courmayeur*; see Rte 42B.—The left-hand path ascends to the little *Lacs de Fenêtre*, often frozen in summer, where by keeping to the right, the *Fenêtre de Ferret* pass (2698m) is reached, on the frontier, with a view of Mont Blanc to the W, and of the Graian Alps to the S. A steep descent brings one to a point a short distance below the St. Bernard Hospice; the left-hand path at the lakes later meets the road at the col; see below.

At Orsières the main and improved ascent towards the **Grand St. Bernard** pass commences, which now by-passes the villages en route. The pass is more remarkable for its historical and romantic associations than for its scenery, which, although interesting, is less impressive than that on most other great passes.

Known and used by Celts and Romans, its ancient name was *Mont Jovis* (*Mont Joux*), from a temple of *Jupiter Poeninus* which once stood on the Plan de Jupiter. It was only in the 12C that it acquired its present name. The pass was much frequented by pilgrims and clerics bound to or from Rome, and between 774 and 1414 it was crossed twenty times by medieval emperors, among them Frederick Barbarossa in 1162. It has been estimated that by the latter part of the 18C some 8000 crossed the pass annually. Several hundreds of thousands of French and Austrian troops did so during the French Revolutionary campaigns; the most famous passage being that made by Napoleon in person (as depicted in David's painting), who on 14–20 May 1800 led 40,000 men by this route into Italy, a month later defeating the Austrians at Marengo. Each regiment took three days to cross the pass, halting the first night at Bourg St. Pierre, the second at St. Rhémy or Étroubles, and the third at Aosta.

At 8.5km *Liddes* is by-passed, to the NE of which rise *Mont Brûlé* (2569m) and *Mont Rogneux* (3084m), while to the SE, below the Grand Combin massif, is the *Glacier de Boveire*.—At 6km *Bourg St.-Pierre* (1632m) is by-passed, with a Romanesque church tower, while near by is a Róman milliary column of the time of Constantine. At the upper end of the village is an *Alpine Botanic Garden*, at its best towards the end of June. It is also a mountaineering centre, particularly for ascents in the Grand Combin massif to the NE, rising to 4314m, and of *Mont Vélan* (SE; 3731m), marking the frontier. The road leaves the *Défilé de Saraire* to the right, and—now under snow galleries—skirts a small reservoir. At 7km, at a height of 1915m, it enters the **Tunnel du Grand St. Bernard** (toll; Customs). It was pierced in 1958–64 and is 5.9km long, its lower exit being at 1875m; see below.

The road over the pass—from which a lift mounts to *Super-St.-Bernard* (SE)—enters the wild *Pas de Marengo*, beyond which are the *Hospitalet* refuge huts. It continues to climb, later in bold zigzags (below these is the rough track traversed by Napoleon), to reach the **Col du Grand St. Bernard** (2469m) after 6.5km.

The *Hospice*, one of the highest habitations in Europe, is a massive stone edifice exposed to storms from the NE and SW, being sheltered by the *Chenalette* and by the *Mont Mort* to the SE. It is now composed of two buildings, that dating from c 1560 which replaced its predecessor destroyed by fire, and one completed in 1898.

The hospice was supposedly founded in the 11C by St. Bernard of Menthon, archdeacon of Aosta, although the earliest known documents (1125) called it after St. Nicolas. It possessed property in England, Hornchurch in Essex being given to it by Henry II but later passing to New College, Oxford. By 1215 it was regularly manned by Austin canons from Martigny, and it flourished financially until the Reformation. Napoleon quartered a garrison of 40 men here for some months which somewhat taxed its resources. Since 1925 it has been managed by some dozen canons and lay brothers or 'aumoniers', who in the rescue of snow-bound travellers were assisted by the famous St. Bernard dogs. The breed is said to be a cross between the Pyrenean sheepdog and the Newfoundland and some 30 of them are still on the strength. But, as has recently been said, 'Nothing better illustrates the transition from a life-saving institution to a tourist attraction than the hospice on the Great St. Bernard pass'.

The older *Hospice* may be visited. It contains a chapel of 1686, in which there is a monument to Gén. Desaix, who fell at Marengo; a library; a reception room with a piano presented by Edward VII; and a *Museum* displaying miscellaneous objects, bronze statuettes, Roman and later coins, etc., found in the area. Adjacent is the old mortuary, in which the bodies of frozen travellers were once placed. Behind the hotel are the kennels for the dogs. Near by are the Customs houses.

The narrow road from the pass descends in several curves, later passing under the No. 21 to (11.5km) *St. Rhémy* (1619m), the highest hamlet on the Italian side, to join the main road 3km beyond.

The main road, on making its exit from the tunnel—but still under snow galleries—shortly circles to the W and then curves round to the E to merge with the upper road at 9km. The youths of (4km) *Étoubles* and St. Rhémy exercised the right, between 1658 and 1915, to act as guides and snow-sweepers on the road instead of doing military service. There is an impressive retrospective view up the valley closed by the *Grand Golliat* (3238m) and other peaks, while to the S rises *Mont Fallère* (3061m). After 6km we get a fine view NE up the VALPELLINE and traverse *Gignod*, with a 15C church tower. Aosta is approached through a country of trellised vines, with *Mont Emilius* (3559m) and the *Becca di Nona* (3142m) rising ahead.

Aosta (581m; 36,900 inhab.), a town of great antiquity, retains its ancient centre, less than 2km square, surrounded by Roman walls and containing numerous Roman and medieval survivals. Unfortunately it has been spoiled by industrial expansion in the immediate vicinity. For its history and monuments see *Blue Guide Northern Italy*; for the road hence via the *Tunnel du Mont Blanc* to **Chamonix** and Martigny, see Rte 42B in reverse.

B. Martigny to Aosta via Chamonix and the Tunnel du Mont Blanc

Total distance, 104km (64 miles). 24km *Le Châtelard*—N506. 18km **Chamonix**—29km *Courmayeur*—S 26. 33km **Aosta**.

Maps: M 219; BL 46, or 5003.

For a more detailed description of those parts of France and Italy through which the route runs see *Blue Guide France* and *Blue Guide Northern Italy*.

From *Martigny-Bourg* (2km SW of **Martigny**; see Rte 42A), the road climbs right towards the *Bâtiaz tower* and then SW, later ascending in zigzags, with fine retrospective views up the Rhône valley, with the Bietschhorn and Balmhorn in the distance, to (13km) the *Col de la Forclaz* (1526m). A lift mounts hence towards *Mont de l'Arpille* (N; 2085m). The road descends steeply S towards the *Glacier du Trient* (reached by a path), and then swings N through (3.5km) *Trient*, a small resort below the **Col de Balme** (SW; 2204m), which so impressed Wordsworth when he crossed that pass with Robert Jones in August 1790.

A path climbs to this frontier pass, which provides a *View of the whole of *Mont*

Blanc from the valley of Chamonix to its summit (4807m), and a retrospective view of the Diablerets and the Blümlisalp, with the mountains of the Bernese Oberland beyond; an even more extensive panorama is obtained by walking up the slope of the Croix de Fer to the N, but the ascent to the summit is dangerous. The path climbs down to the upper terminus of a lift by *Charamillon* and continues down the valley of the Arve—with a view of the *Glacier du Tour*—to meet a road at *Le Tour* (1453m), 3km from *Argentière*; see below.

At 4km, after passing through a short tunnel, a right-hand turning leads to **Finhaut** (1224m), a small resort above a gorge, commanding fine mountainscapes, including the Aiguilles Rouges to the SW and the Aiguille du Tour (SE).

The village is a base for ascents further W, approached by the road to the *Col de la Gueulaz*, above the *Lac d'Emosson reservoir* (1930m). A path along its S bank leads to the *Lac du Vieux Emosson* (2205m), or, by skirting the W bank to the N, to the *Col de Tenneverge* (2484m), above the *Cirque du Fer à Cheval* and the road to *Sixt* and *Samoëns*; see Blue Guide France.

At (1.5km) *Le Châtelard* the French frontier is crossed (Customs) and the road descends past *Vallorcine*, with a view of *Mont Buet* (3099m) rising to the W, and the *Cascade de Bérard*, at 6.5km crossing the *Col des Montets* (1461m), providing a good view of the Mont Blanc massif, to (3.5km) **Argentière** (1257m). This is a well-sited winter-sports centre, near the foot of its glacier, at the head of which rises *Mont Dolent* (SE; 3820m), at the meeting of the Swiss, French and Italian frontiers. Lifts mount SE towards the *Aiguilles Vertes* (rising to 4122m); to the W are the *Aiguilles Rouges* (*Aiguille du Belvédère*; 2965m).

The road veers SW to (8km) **Chamonix-Mont-Blanc**, as it is officially styled, once a typical Alpine village (1037m) in an almost inaccessible valley, and now a flourishing tourist resort with a resident population of 9300, but with some hundreds of thousands of visitors a year. The piercing of the tunnel and construction of motorways have made it much more accessible. Its chief characteristic is the number of hotels of all sizes it contains, but all man-made constructions are dwarfed and overshadowed by the mighty mass of Mont Blanc looming up to the SE.

The inscribed stone of Prarion attests that the area was known to the Romans and in the Middle Ages the valley of the Arve paid tribute to a powerful Benedictine priory founded here at the end of the 11C. This was burned down in 1758 and in 1786 the inhabitants of the district purchased their freedom.

Chamonix was 'discovered' in 1741 by a group of Englishmen staying at Geneva. Among them were Richard Pococke, recently returned from his travels in the East, and William Windham, author of 'An account of the Glaciers or Ice Alps in Savoy', and it is to the latter's glowing account of its charms that the valley owes the foundation of its popularity. Since 1760, when De Saussure first offered a reward for the ascent of Mont Blanc, the history of Chamonix has been bound up with the mountain; see below. Thomas 'Buck' Waley, the Irish eccentric, visited the place in 1792, and it attracted many distinguished visitors during the early 19C, including Chateaubriand (who disliked it), Shelley, Byron, Southey, Wordsworth and Faraday (who praised it highly), while its fame was finally sealed for the English by the approval of Ruskin. Most visitors walked up to the *Montenvers*, where a cabin known as 'Blair's Hut' stood until 1812; it had been erected some decades earlier by Charles Blair, an Englishman living in Geneva.

The town itself is of slight interest, although the main 'Place' is a centre of considerable animation in the mornings when guides and the guided assemble for the day's excursion. Opposite the *Railway Station* is a little *English Church*, beside which are the graves of Capt. Arkwright and other victims of Mont Blanc; beyond the *Gare du Montenvers* is the *New Cemetery*, in which lie Edward Whymper (1840–1911), the alpinist, and Louis Lachenal (died 1955), the conqueror of Annapurna.

For general information about excursions and ascents apply to the *Tourist Office* just W of the town centre, near the main church. A variety of cableways and ski-lifts, etc. mount to several surrounding peaks, among them *Le Brévent* (2526m) to the N and the *Aiguille du Midi* (3842m), almost exactly above the tunnel. A rack-railway ascends from the Gare de Montenvers to approach the *Mer de Glace*, a remarkable sweep of glacier.

Mont Blanc (4807m), the loftiest of the Alps, and the highest peak in Western Europe, is the culminating summit of the great mountain chain which divides the valley of Chamonix from the valley of Courmayeur. The chain forms a watershed between the basins of the Rhône and the Po and a partition wall between France and Italy. On every side Mont Blanc is surrounded by lesser peaks and by pointed '*aiguilles*', some of which still defy the climbers' skill; down its slopes stream huge glaciers.

Indeed, in the Middle Ages Mont Blanc seems to have been generally known as '*Les Glacières*' or '*La Montagne Maudite*', and Bp Burnet, in 1685, refers to it as 'the hill called Maudit or Cursed, two miles in perpendicular height, and of which one-third is always covered with snow', while in 1742 Peter Martel of Geneva refers to it as Mont Blanc. Until 1760 its rocks and glaciers were deserted except by chamois hunters and searchers after crystals, but in that year Horace Bénédict de Saussure (1740–99) made his first visit to Chamonix and was so impressed by the majesty of the mountain that he offered a reward to whoever made the first ascent to the summit.
  Numerous unsuccessful attempts by local men led in 1783 to a more organised expedition by Marc-Théodore Bourrit, precentor of the cathedral at Geneva, and Michel Gabriel Paccard, doctor of Chamonix. In 1784 the *Bosses* were attained; in July 1786 the *Rochers Rouges*, this time by Jacques Balmat. Finally, on 8 August 1786, Balmat and Paccard reached the summit. De Saussure himself made the ascent on 3 August 1787, six days after which Col Beaufoy made the first English ascent. An accident in 1830, when Dr Hamel and his party were swept away by an avalanche, led to the abandonment of the old route, and in 1827 a new route through the *Corridor* was first successfully made (the frozen remains of Dr Hamel's party were discovered in 1861 at the foot of the Glacier de Bossons, where Capt. Arkwright's body was found in 1897, 31 years after his death.) The first woman to climb Mont Blanc was Mlle Henriette d'Angerville (1838), for although the summit had been attained by Marie Paradis of Chamonix in 1809, she was carried by her companions for a great part of the way! The route usually followed nowadays (via the *Bosses du Dromadaire*) was discovered in 1859 by the Rev. C. Hudson and his party. The first ascent from Courmayeur was made in 1864. The first winter ascent was made on 31 January 1876 by Miss Arabella Straton, who later became Mme Charlet, having married her guide.
  The ascent normally occupies two days, and the route from Chamonix is the most frequented and easiest.
  The •*View* from the summit (when not obscured by cloud) is remarkable rather for its extent than for any feature of individual beauty. The Alps are visible from Dauphiny to the Bernina; the Jura appears like a relief plan, with the plain of the Saône stretching out behind it to the Côte d'Or. The Lombard plain is hidden by intervening ranges, but the line of the Appenines extends SE beyond the limit of vision.

3km SW of Chamonix is the turning for (4km) the N entrance of the **Tunnel du Mont Blanc**, bored between 1957–65. It is 11.6km long and ascends from 1274m on the French side to 1381m on the Italian, where the Customs houses are grouped, and has a capacity of 450 vehicles an hour (toll).—The S exit is above *Entrèves* in the VAL FERRET, 5km beyond which the road by-passes the resort of **Courmayeur** (*Cormaggiore* in Italian) and after a further 5km meets the road descending from the *Col du Petit St. Bernard* (SW) at *Pré St.-Didier*, a small resort with an 11C church tower.

At 4.5km *Morgex*, the principal village of the VALDIGNE, the upper valley of the Dora, is traversed. Its church preserves 6C elements. The 13C tower of *Châtelard* is passed to the left and later—with retrospective views of Mont Blanc—the village of *Derby* to the right with its medieval houses, is by-passed. The road threads the gorge of the *Pierre-Taillée*, and passes (left) *Avise*, with three old castles.

13.5km *Arvier*, with a 13C castle, stands at the foot of the VALGRISENCH (SW), one of several valleys ascending to the S of the road, which during the next 9km passes *Villeneuve*, with a ruined 12C castle; that of *Sarriod* (mainly 14C); *St.-Pierre*, with a restored castle on an isolated rock; and *Sarre*, with a 13C castle rebuilt in 1710.

5km **Aosta**, for which see the last paragraph of Rte 42A, above; likewise—but in reverse—for the road ascending thence to the *Grand St. Bernard Tunnel* and *Col*, and descending the N side of the range to *Martigny*.

43 Martigny to Brig via Sion, Sierre and Visp

Total distance, 81km (50 miles). No. 9. 28km **Sion**—15km **Sierre**—29km **Visp**—9km **Brig**.

Maps: M 217; BL 41, or 5003, 5009.

From **Martigny** (see Rte 42A) we drive NE along the No. 9 or N9 motorway, which at present (1989) merge after 14km, although the extension of the latter is projected. Conspicuous on the N flank of the RHÔNE VALLEY is the ruined castle of Peter of Savoy at *Saillon*.—The village of **St. Pierre-de-Clages**, its triple-apsed 11–12C *Church with an octagonal tower and spire, is passed to the left, and above rises the *Haut de Cry* (2969m), before traversing (6km) *Ardon*, at the foot of the *Pas de Cheville*; see p 307.

After 4km, below *Conthey*, the Morge is crossed. Since the 14C this had been the boundary between the Upper (or Episcopal) and Lower (or Savoyard) Valais.

A road leads 23km up the valley to the N, threading the wild ravine of the Morge, to the *Col du Sanetsch* (2251m), between the *Sanetschhorn* (W; 2924m) and the *Arpelistock* (3035m), and to a small reservoir 5km beyond, from which a path climbs down to *Gsteig*, 10km S of Gstaad; see Rte 7A.

To the right opens the pastoral VAL DE NENDAZ, at the head of which rises *Mont Fort* (3329m); see Rte 42A.

4km **SION** (*Sitten* in German; 22,900 inhab.; 8650 in 1930), the capital of the *Valais* and the see of a bishop since c 580, is finely situated at the foot of two castle-crowned hills rising abruptly from the valley floor. Unfortunately, the recent growth of Sion has, to a certain extent, dispelled the picturesque impression, but its old centre and the hill-top church of N.D. de Valère are still of considerable interest.

View by Matthäus Merian of Sion (1642).

The bishops of Sion (Roman *Sedunum*) were from 999, by a grant of Rudolf III of Burgundy, also counts of the Valais. They were frequently at odds with the counts of Savoy, from whom the Lower Valais was appropriated in 1260. Matthias Schinner (1465–1522), the most famous bishop, was head of the anti-French or Imperial party in the Valais and Lombardy. He visited England in 1516, as an envoy from the Diet of Berne, to dissuade Henry VIII from marrying his sister Mary to Louis XII of France, and obtained large sums from Henry for his anti-French crusade. One of his predecessors, Bp Ermenfroy, had crowned William the Conqueror at his second coronation at Winchester, in 1070. Jules Verne wrote much of 'Around the World in Eighty Days' here (published 1873).

The name **Valais** (*Wallis* in German; *Vallese* in Italian) derives from the Roman *Vallis Poenina*, or Upper Valley of the Rhône. Hemmed in by the two largest snow-ranges in the Alps, one fifth of the canton—the third largest of the Swiss cantons—is covered by glaciers. Several of the upper slopes of the valley are devoted to winter sports, while the warm lower slopes produce excellent wine. Access was provided by the passes of the Grand St. Bernard (guarded by the Pennine Procurator), the Simplon and the Furka. The Valaisans in the lower valley speak French; those in the upper part—beyond Leuk, some 24km NE of Sion—speak German, reflecting the former division between the Burgundians and Alemanni. It was the French department of Simplon from 1810–14; Chateaubriand was named envoy but never took up the post. In 1815 it was integrated into the Swiss Confederation, but remained a poor area during the first half of the 19C until opened up by the construction of the railway through the Simplon in 1860. With the growth of Zermatt and other resorts, Sion prospered, and with the recent improvement of the Simplon Pass the valley has become an important thoroughfare.

The Rue de Lausanne leads into the centre. A few steps to the N, beyond the Rue de Conthey, stands the early 16C church of ***St.**

Théodule, with a well-vaulted choir and preserving several details of interest, but spoilt by modern glass.—Just beyond is the **Cathedral**, a 15C building, partly Romanesque and partly Gothic, with a 9th or 10C belfry and a conical spire. The somewhat over-restored but interesting triptych of the Tree of Jesse (16C) is found in the choir.—To the NW is the *Tour des Sorciers*, part of the medieval fortifications.

From an arcade on the S side of the Rue de Conthey one may enter the *Maison Supersaxo* (1505), notable for its remarkable Renaissance ceiling.—To the E is the main street, known as the Rue du Grand-Pont because a stream flows beneath it, preserving several old houses of interest, among them, opposite, the 17C *Hôtel de Ville*.

Beside it, the Rue des Châteaux climbs steeply to the **Majoria** (or *La Marjorie*; left), rebuilt after a fire in 1529 and restored in 1947. This served for some time as the bishop's palace, and now houses the

The organ (1390) in the church of Valère; see p 318

Musée cantonal des Beaux-arts, with paintings by Raphael Ritz (1829–94), among local artists, and, among later works, those by Marguerite Burnat-Provins (1872–1932) and Ernest Bieler (1863–1948) are notable.

To the right is the ***Archaeological Museum**, with a good collection of Roman glass, jewellery and bronze statuettes; bronze fittings for a door of a villa; parts of a bronze statue of Jupiter (2C); the head of a three-horned bull (from Martigny); and several interesting anthropomorphic steles (3200–2400 BC). In the basement are collections of terra-sigillata, amphorae, Etruscan figurines, Roman sculptured busts (from Martigny); finds from the Halstatt and La Tène cultures, and Valasian type bracelets, etc.

The street continues uphill to a car-park, whence the left-hand path mounts steeply to the ruined episcopal castle of *Tourbillon* (1294), burnt in 1788, which commands an extensive view.—Of more interest is the right-hand path which climbs past a chapel of 1310 to the *Castle of Valeria* or *Valère*, containing the curious ***Church of Notre-Dame**, formerly the cathedral. The church is largely 13C but with a 10th or 11C choir on a higher level, possibly on the foundations of a Roman temple. The choir contains several remarkable capitals, among them one depicting Jonah and the whale (?); there is also a painting of the Adoration of the Magi of c 1420. Note also the fresco of the Martyrdom of St. Sebastian on the S wall, the 17C choir-stalls, and in particular the restored ***Organ** of 1390, which is one of the oldest to survive in working order; there are occasional recitals.

Adjacent is the *Musée Historique*, a curious collection housed since 1883 in a warren of former canonical dependencies. The 12C silver reliquary bust is of interest, and there are collections of medieval boxes and chests and arms and armour.

5km N of Sion lies *Savièse*, with a well-vaulted 16C church.

A road climbing NE eventually leads direct to (20km) *Crans* (see below), off which at 9km a narrower road ascends above the valley of the Liène to (14km) the *Lac de Tseuzier* reservoir (1777m). Along the W bank of the reservoir a path continues below the *Six des Eaux Froides* (2905m) and later beneath the cliffs of the *Wetzsteinhorn* (2782m) to the *Rawil Pass* (2429m), a broad saddle commanding a splendid retrospective view of the mountains beyond the Rhône valley, especially of the Weisshorn, N of Zermatt. The track then descends steeply to *Iffingen*, high up in the valley above *Lenk*; see Rte 7A.

FROM SION TO EVOLÈNE (26km). The road climbs SE in zigzags to (8.5km) *Vex*, and follows the W side of the valley into the VAL D'HÉRÉMENCE via *Hérémence*, with an interesting church by Walter M. Förderer (1971).—At 15.5km we reach the ***Grande Dixence reservoir** (1965; with an immense concrete wall 284m high, 75m long, and 22m thick at the top), the tallest gravity dam in the world, with an active storage capacity of 400 million m³. The dam stretches between the *Rosablanche* (SW; 3336m) and the *Aiguilles Rouges* (SE; 3646m). At its head rises the *Mont Blanc de Cheilon* (3870m), which may be approached by following a path along the W bank of the reservoir.—Another road leads S from Vex up the fertile VAL D'HÉRENS, but keeping to the left bank of the Borgne before turning E and briefly tunneling below the *Pyramides d'Euseigne*, earth pillars protected from erosion by the flat stones which cap them.—7km *Euseigne*, a village among walnut trees, is passed through, and in 10.5km **Evolène** (1371m), the main village of the valley is entered. This small resort and mountaineering centre provides a fine view SE towards the *Dent Blanche* (4357m) and its glaciers. Ascents from Evolène include the *Sasseneire* (NE; 3254m), reached from the *Col de Torrent* (2918m); the *Becs de Bosson* (N; 3149m); the *Tsa de l'Ano* (SE; 3368m), and N of the latter, the *Couronne de Bréona* (3159m).—3.5km *Les Haudères*.

Two mountain roads ascend hence: that to the SE leads 7km to the mountaineering village of **Ferpècle** (see below), while 12km to the SW lies

Arolla, towards which the view is impressive. The pyramid of *Mont Collon* (3637m) rises behind the *Arolla Glacier*, with the snow dome of the *Pigne d'Arolla* (3796m) on its right. Prominent on the jagged ridge which shuts in the valley on the E is the slender *Aiguille de la Tsa* (3668m), with the *Dent de Perroc* (3676m) further N.—**Arolla** itself (1998m) is a beautifully sited resort among the woods of larches and Arolla pines ('Aroles'), characteristic of the valley.

Among the easier and most attractive walks in the neighbourhood is the excursion to the tiny *Lac Bleu* to the NW (above *Satarma*), which may be approached direct across the Praz Gras pastures and past the *Cascade des Ignes*. The lower part of the *Arolla Glacier* may also be reached without difficulty. Among ascents usually made from here, other than those listed above, are the *Évêque* (3716m), just S of Mont Collon, while among passes are the *Col de Bertol* and *Col d'Hérens* (3462m) for *Zermatt*; and to the W of Arolla, the *Col de Riedmatten* (2919m), from which a bridle-path descends along the W side of the *Grande Dixence reservoir*; see above. The *Col de Collon* (3130m), SE of the Évêque, is an easy frontier pass. Through the shrinkage of a glacier here, the skeletons of a man and a chamois came to light in 1921, with a rifle and coins dating to before 1850. *Mont Brulé* (3585m) rises to the E. On the Italian side one may climb down to *Prarayer* (2005m), the highest hamlet in the VALPELLINE, a wide valley leading down to *Aosta* following the course of the Buthier torrent; see *Blue Guide Northern Italy*.

From Ferpècle (see above), below its impressive combe, dominated by the *Dent Blanche* (SE; 4357m), one may ascend the steep right bank of the torrent between the *Dents de Veisivi* (W; 3418m) and the *Grand Cornier* (3962m), to the *Glacier de Ferpècle* and the *Col d'Hérens* (3462m), from where the descent to the E to *Zermatt* may be made either via the *Zmutt Glacier* or the longer but easier route via the *Schönbielhütte*.

From Sion, the main road continues up the valley, with a view ahead of the Bietschhorn to (15km) **Sierre** (533m; *Siders* in German; 13,050 inhab.; 4950 in 1930), where we reach the language frontier. Sierre preserves a few old mansions and the 17C château of the Courten family, transformed into a hotel, in which Rilke stayed briefly until shortly before his death in 1926; but see below. The 16C castle of the bailiffs of the bishops of Sion, in the main street, has been spoiled by rebuilding. Overlooking the town to the E is an old watch-tower.

FROM SIERRE TO MONTANA AND CRANS (14–16Km). A funicular and two roads climbing in zigzags ascend NW to the contiguous resorts of Montana and Crans (c 1475m). The more easterly road passes near the small 13–14C castle of *Muzot*, in which Rilke was offered a congenial home by his Swiss patron Werner Reinhart and where in three weeks of February 1922 he wrote the 'Die Sonette an Orpheus' and completed the 'Duineser Elegien'. The castle of *Venthône* is then passed before reaching the dry upper wooded slopes where **Montana**, and then **Crans**, bask in the sun in the vicinity of several small lakes, commanding a magnificent mountain panorama to the S beyond the Rhône valley.

Several cable-cars mount thence: to the *Cry d'Err* (2258m) and on to just below the *Bella Lui* (2548m); to *Les Violettes*, and on to the *Pointe de la Plaine Morte* (2927m), above its glacier; and from further NE to the *Petit Mont Bovin*, SE of *Mont Bovin* (2995m). To the NE rise the *Schnesshorn* (3178m), *Schwarzhorn* (3105m), and the *Wildstrubel* (3244m), among other summits.

FROM SIERRE TO ZINAL (27km). On crossing the Rhône, turn right to climb in zigzags into the VAL D'ANNIVIERS or EIFISCH-TAL, one of the more attractive tributary valleys of the Rhône, with its green meadows, interesting flora and its fir-clad and deeply furrowed slopes below the chain of mountains to the E, several of which are over 3000m.—16km *Vissoie*, the main village of the valley. 5km above lies *St. Luc*, and 6km N of the latter, the high-lying village of *Chandolin* (1934m). To the E rises the *Bella Tola* (3025m), a comparatively isolated peak providing a fine mountainscape.—5km *Ayer*, from which a path mounts E to the *Forcletta Pass* (2874m) for *Gruben* in the parallel TURTMANN-TAL.—**Zinal** lies 7km further S at 1675m, a secluded hamlet and the base for several ascents in the vicinity.—Prominent to the S is the dark peak of the *Besso* (3668m), between the Zinal and Moming glaciers: the *Alpes de la Lé* and *d'Ar Pitette*, to the S, are fine view-points.

The *Roc de la Vache* (SE; 2581m) is the usual excursion, while to the NW is the *Corne de Sorebois* (2896m). The *Frilihorn* (NE; 3124m) is another easy climb. Other ascents are the S summit of the *Diablons*, to the E (3592m); more difficult is its N summit, while to the SE is the *Tête de Milon* (3693m). To the N of the Alp de la Lé rises the view-point of the *Garde de Bordon* (3310m). A favourite excursion from Zinal is to the *Mountet Hut* (2886m; S of the Besso), situated in an amphitheatre of glaciers and snow-peaks and best seen from the *Roc Noir* (3011m) in the midst of the *Zinal Glacier*. To the E rises the *Zinalrothorn* (4221m); to the SE, the *Ober Gabelhorn* (4063m). The passes from here to *Zermatt* are exposed to falling stones and are for experts only.—One may return down the valley by bearing left to *Grimentz*, at the foot of the VAL DE MOIRY, with its reservoir; beyond is the *Glacier de Moiry* below the *Grand Cornier* (3962m) and the *Dent Blanche* (4357m).

The Rhône is crossed just E of Sierre, and then one reaches the *Pfynwald*, a stunted forest whose Latin name ('ad Fines') records the division between the French and German languages in the Valais. There was a skirmish between the French and Valasians here in 1799.—9km *Susten*, at the foot of a curious rocky glen known as the ILLGRABEN.—On the far bank, at a higher level, lies **Leuk** (731m), a quaint old town with a conspicuous tower (1541) of the episcopal castle founded in 1254, and a *Rathaus* in the *Schloss*, rebuilt in 1543. The *Church*, rebuilt in 1497, preserves its Romanesque tower, and contains some good 17C wood-carving.

FROM LEUK TO LEUKERBAD (14km). The road first climbs in a wide circle to the E, later crossing the *Dala gorge* to a point not far N of the old road from Sierre, which traversed a narrow ledge, partly roofed, known as the '*Felsengalerie*'. In 1799 this was defended for several weeks by the Valasians against the French. High above the E bank is the village of *Albinen*, now served by an upper road but formerly approached from the road by a series of rough ladders (*Leitern*) fastened to the cliff and by which the peasants clambered to their homes.—**Leukerbad** (1402m), an old spa and resort, lies in a cirque of imposing cliffs conspicuous above which are the *Rinderhorn* (3453m), and beyond, further NE, the *Balmhorn* (3699m). Its hot saline springs, known since Roman times, were patronised by Bp Schinner of Sion, who rebuilt the bath-houses, several times since destroyed by avalanches. Mark Twain, in 'A Tramp Abroad', amusingly described the former scene at the baths, where valetudinarians were obliged to spend long hours submerged up to their chins, the tedium being relieved by bathing in common, with floating tables sustaining coffee-cups, reading-matter, and even chess-boards.—Lifts mount SE, from which one may climb the *Torrenthorn* (2998m) for the views it commands, among them the Mont Blanc massif to the SW, and the Weisshorn to the S, the Lötschental to the NE, and the entire chain of the Pennine Alps from the Mischabels (SE) to the Dents du Midi (SW).

FROM LEUKERBAD TO KANDERSTEG BY THE GEMMIPASS. A cable-car now ascends to a point just E of the pass, which was previously only gained by climbing a very steep path which zigzags abruptly upwards. This is still one of the wonders of early Alpine tracks. It was constructed in 1736–41, and may still be used by the hardy on the ascent (2½ hours) or descent. The top of the vertiginous precipice is reached at the **Gemmipass** (2314m), 900m above Leukerbad, commanding a superb view of the Alps from the Mischalbehörner and Monte Rosa to the Matterhorn, the Dent Blanche, and the Weisshorn.

The plateau here is rich in flora, particularly in June. To the W rises the *Wildstrubel* (3244m) above its glacier, to the S of which is the *Schneehorn* (3178m); to the NW is the nearer *Steghorn* (3146m), just E of which is a pass approached by a path climbing W of the *Daubensee* for *Adelboden*, below the *Engstligenalp*; see Rte 17B. After skirting the E bank of the lake, frozen over most of the year, with the *Rinderhorn* (3453m) rising to the E, bear right, away from the *Felsenhorn* (2782m; noted for its flora). The descent passes the

Schwarzbachfall before reaching *Kandersteg*; see Rte 17B.

From Susten, the main road continues E through (6km) *Turtmann*.

Its valley is threaded by a road ascending steeply S through (10km) *Oberems* to *Meiden*, 11km beyond, at 1822m. At the head of the valley is the *Turtmann Glacier*, with the *Weisshorn* (4505m) rising further S. The *Turtmann Hut* (2519m) at the foot of the *Brunegg Glacier*, is the base for several ascents, among them the *Barrhorn* (E; 3610m), commanding a superb view of the Zermatt valley; the *Brunegghorn* (SE; 3833m), etc.

At 3km we reach a turning for (2km) *Gampel*, on the N bank of the Rhône.

FROM GAMPEL TO GLETSCHERSTAFEL (21KM): THE LÖTSCHENTAL. The valley, a narrow trough between the Bernese and Valasian Alps, and watered by the Lonza, was long a backward cul-de-sac, known only for its terrifying Carnival masks and traditional folk festivals when old costumes were worn. It was comparatively little visited until the hamlet of Goppenstein was built during the construction of the *Lötschberg railway tunnel*. The tunnel, 14.6km long, and bored in 1906–12, provided a rapid connection between Berne and the Valais. The Simplon tunnel (between Brig and Iselle) had been pierced between 1898 and 1905; see Rte 46. The road threads a defile before climbing to (7km) *Goppenstein* (1216m), at the S end of the tunnel. Here, there is a terminus for the shuttle-service of car-carriers, with another at Brig; see below.—4km *Ferden*, from which a path climbs NW to the *Lötschenpass* (2690m), one of the medieval passes between the Valais and Berne, on which a cross is mentioned as early as 1352, and from which the GASTERNTAL may be reached; see Rte 17B. The valley bends to the NE and its scenery becomes grander. Passing through a short tunnel, *Kippel* is reached, with several picturesque houses and a parish church of 1740. Adjacent *Wiler* was rebuilt after a fire in 1900.

To the E rises the *Bietschorn* (3934m), appearing as a pyramid from afar, but in fact culminating in small rocky peaks. It was first climbed by Sir Leslie Stephen in 1859.—*Ried*, a hamlet of old blackened wooden chalets, is passed to reach (5km) *Blatten* (1540m), N of which is the ridge of Petersgrat, and the *Tschingelhorn* (3576m), with its glacier. Further E is the *Lauterbrunner Breithorn* (3785m), while to the S of the latter (and E of Blatten) rises the *Lötschentaler Breithorn* (3785m), E of which is the *Nesthorn* (3824m). The road climbs to (5km) *Gletscherstafel*, which among other hamlets is a base for ascents in the area. Beyond, paths ascend to the foot of the much crevassed *Langgletscher* and the *Schinhorn* (3797m) as well as other peaks, while further NE is the *Sattelhorn* (3741m), beyond which extends the *Grosser Aletschfirn* to the Konkordiaplatz.

From the turning for Gampel the main road bears almost due E, with a view across to the N slope of the valley along which the railway curls through numerous short tunnels and crosses the several valley mouths in a series of viaducts before gently descending to *Brig*.—4km. In the cemetery of the hilltop mid-13C *Burgkirche* at **Raron**, on the far bank of the Rhône Rainer Maria Rilke (1875–1926) is buried.

7km **Visp** (651m), now important as the junction for the road approaching, and rail for, Zermatt, is an old village which from 1250–1365 belonged to the Italian counts of Biandrate. It preserves an old church tower and a few mansions of the nobility who once lived here. Conspicuous to the S is the glacier-clad *Balfrin* (3796m), dividing the two branches of the Vispa torrent.

For the routes from Visp to **Zermatt**, and *Saas-Fee*, see Rte 44.

10km SE of Visp, reached by a steeply climbing road, is the high-lying village of *Visperterminen* (1336m), with a chapel, dating from 1652, containing an organ of 1619. The local 'Heidenwein' (heathen wine) is produced from the highest vineyards in Switzerland. From here a path climbs over a ridge below the *Gebidem* (N; 2317m) into the GAMSATAL, where the torrent descends to the

Rhône in an almost impassable gorge. Then the path crosses the N end of the Fletschhorn ridge by the *Bistinenpass* (2417m) to reach the *Simplon Hospice*; see Rte 46.

The valley becomes more populated beyond Visp as (9km) **Brig** is approached. On the W outskirts of Brig, to the right of the road, is the large parish *Church* of *Glis* (i.e. ecclesia), at present undergoing restoration, which contains both late Gothic and early Renaissance elements in its choir, a mid 17C nave and a belfry of 1519 on a Romanesque base. The old Simplon road turned right at this point.

For *Brig* and the road from there to *Locarno* via the *Simplon pass* see Rte 46; for the road hence to *Gletsch* and the *Furkapass*, for **Andermatt**, see Rte 45.

44 Visp to Zermatt: The Matterhorn

Total distance, 34km (21 miles). 28km *Täsch*—6km (by rail) **Zermatt**.

Maps: M 217, 219; BL 42, 46, 47, or 5006.

For **Visp**, see last section of Rte 43, above.

It should be noted that motor vehicles may not enter Zermatt, but must be parked at Täsch, 6km N, from which a railway shuttle-service runs. Zermatt may also be conveniently approached by the narrow-gauge Furka Railway from Brig or Visp. It is also the W terminus of the train known as the *Glacier Express*, a 7½ hour scenic excursion, which ascends the upper valley of the Rhône, descends the Vorderrhein valley and then climbs SE to St. Moritz, and vice versa; and also of the *Palm Express* to St. Moritz via Ascona.

The road drives due S up the valley of the Vispa, at *Neuebrück* passing an old bridge, and climbs to (7km) *Stalden*, picturesquely sited above the confluence of the Saaser Vispa and the Matter Vispa, with a view ahead of the *Balfrin* (3796m).

FROM STALDEN TO SAAS-FEE (18km). The SAASTAL was colonised by Italians from the Val Anzasca in the 13C, although the Teutonic influx from the upper Rhône valley has left the district German speaking, with only a few Italian place-names remaining. The road bears left up the valley, later passing several cascades descending from the *Fletschhorn* (E; 3993m) to (12km) *Saas-Balen* (1483m), below the NE foot of the Balfrin, a projecting peak of the Saas-Grat. The curious and picturesque little *Church*, by J.J. Andermatten, with a lofty circular nave, semi-circular choir, and tower, dates from 1812.—Beyond a rocky defile the valley expands to form a mountain-girt basin and at 4km *Saas-Grund* is entered, the main village of the valley, deriving its name from the Italian '*sasso*' or rock. A lift ascends NE to near the *Weissmies Hut*, a base for ascents of the *Fletschhorn, Lagginhorn* (4010m), and the *Weissmies* (4023m).

A road climbs steeply SW to (4km) **Saas-Fee** (1792m), a well-sited resort immediately behind which is the *Fee Glacier*, descending from the Mischabelhörner group, the culmination of the enormous Saas-Grat ridge, separating the valleys of Saas and Zermatt. The German dramatist Carl Zuckmayer settled here in 1958.

Several lifts mount to points below the glacier, etc. Among the main ascents in the area are the *Allalinhorn* (SW; 4027m), and the *Alphubel* (4206m; NW of the last), between which the *Alphubeljoch* (3782m) provides a pass into the *Mellichenbach* above Täsch. The *Nadelhorn* (4327m), the *Ulrichshorn* (3925m), and *Balfrin* (3796m) rise to the W and NW, while between the Alphubel and the Nadelhorn are the *Täschhorn* (4491m), and the *Dom* (4545m); see below.

From Saas-Grund one may continue S up the valley through (4km) *Saas-Almagell* (1673m) to reach, 7km beyond, the *Mattmarksee reservoir.*—From Saas-Almagell, a path climbs E to the *Zwischbergenpass* (3268m), below the Weissmies, for the ZWISCHBERGENTAL and *Gondo* (855m), the frontier village on the Simplon road; this may also be reached at the hamlet of *Gabi* (1228m) by following a track NW from the hamlet of *Zwischbergen.*—Another pass climbs SE from Saas-Almagell up the *Furggtäli* to the *Antronapass* (2838m), a passage of very ancient use, with relics of a paved track between the *Latelhorn* (NE; 3198m) and the *Jazzihorn* (3227m), crossing the frontier and descending past a small reservoir into the VAL DI ANTRONA for *Antronapiana*; see *Blue Guide Northern Italy.*—A path skirts the W bank of the *Mattmarksee* reservoir, below the *Schwarzberg glacier*, and the *Rimpfischhorn* (4199m), to the head of the valley below *Monte Moro* (2984m). The dam was completed in 1969, but on 30 August 1965 part of the *Allalin Glacier*, which had advanced, broke away and engulfed the building site, killing 88.

The *Monte Moro Pass* (2868m), on the frontier, provides a view of the whole E face of **Monte Rosa** (or the *Dufourspitze*; 4634m) and the basin of the MACUGNAGA far below our feet. This pass has been in use since at least the 13C; colonies of Italians moved into the Saas valley in 1250 and German-speaking settlers from the Valais are recorded at Macugnaga in 1262; both valleys were under the suzerainty of the Counts of Biandrate. The first mention of a way over the pass is made in a treaty of 1403 between the inhabitants of the valleys concerning the upkeep of the road. It was much used in the 16C by pilgrims bound for Varallo.—For *Macugnaga*, to which a lift descends, see *Blue Guide Northern Italy.*

From Stalden, the road for Zermatt bears SW, climbing high above the deep rocky gorge, with occasional views of the narrow-gauge railway on the far slope.—At 8.5km a left-hand turning ascends steeply to the high-lying resort of (8km) *Grächen* (1615m).—*St. Niklaus* (1127m), the main village of the valley is soon entered, its church with a curious bulbous steeple (17C, on a Romanesque base). The valley then contracts as the foaming torrent of the Vispa is skirted, and we later get a view of the pyramidal *Weisshorn* (SW; 4505m) above the *Bies Glacier*. Prof. Tyndall, who made the first ascent in 1861, described the view from the summit as the finest in the Alps.

E of (11km) *Randa*, rises the **Dom** (4545m), the loftiest mountain in the *Mischabelhörner range* and the highest mountain *entirely within* Swiss territory, since the Dufourspitze of Monte Rosa (4634m) is on the Italian frontier.—To the SW the *Zinalrothorn* (4221m) rises above the *Hohlicht Glacier*.

4km *Täsch* (1450m), overlooked to the E by the *Alphubel* (4206m), which with other peaks in the vicinity may be approached from the *Täschütte* in the valley to the SE, is the terminus for motor vehicles, with a huge car-park. The rail shuttle-service takes us the final 6km to Zermatt, where we get our first view of the majestic pyramid of the Matterhorn to the SW.

ZERMATT (1616m) is a first-class resort and mountaineering centre, attractively placed on a level site among pine-woods, and with a rich and varied flora.

In 1838 Murray suggested that the place had already 'been affected by the influx of strangers', for 'many mineralogists, botanists and entomologists come here to collect rich harvests in the neighbourhood'. However, there were few winter visitors: T.S. Kennedy described it in January 1862 as presenting a scene of almost utter desolation ... Not a person was in the streets, hardly a light in the houses, and the two inns barred up and forsaken'. John Ball (1818–89), the first President of the Alpine Club (1857) and editor of 'Peaks, Passes and Glaciers' (1859), visited Zermatt in 1845. Although Monte Rosa had been scaled in 1855, undoubtedly the first tragic ascent of the Matterhorn in 1865 did much to bring the name of Zermatt to a larger public. Intimately connected with the growth of the place was the enterprise of Alexandre Seiler (died 1891), who acquired his first hotel here in 1854, the 'Monte Rosa'. In 1881 'The Zermatt Pocket Guide' was published, compiled by William Martin Conway (1856–1937), the alpinist and art critic. There was a typhoid epidemic here in 1963.

The old name of Zermatt was *Preborno* or *Praborgne*. At the end of the 15C the name '*Matt*' is found and the form Zermatt was used by De Saussure in 1789; all these names, including that of the Matterhorn itself, are taken from the meadows ('*prés*', or '*Matten*') which surround the village.

Zermatt consists mainly of a single crowded street running SW from the *Railway Station;* the older village is near the far end, where wooden chalets survive. On the right is the *Mont Cervin Hotel*, with a small *Alpine Museum* adjacent, containing numerous souvenirs of alpinists, including the broken rope of the 1865 disaster, and a relief of the Matterhorn and Monte Rosa by X. Imfeld (died 1910). Close by is the little *English Church* of St. Peter's (1870), in which the Rev. Charles Hudson (an army chaplain in the Crimea, described by Leslie Stephen as 'as simple and noble a character as ever carried out the precepts of muscular Christianity without talking its cant') is interred; he had first been buried in the local cemetery, together with Douglas Hadow (whose body was later removed to England), and Michel-Auguste Croz; that of Lord Francis Douglas was never found: see Matterhorn, below. Further up the main street is the *Monte Rosa Hotel*, with a bronze plaque commemorating Edward Whymper (1840–1911; buried at Chamonix) on its facade.

Among the several excursions which may be made from Zermatt, the most rewarding are the following: the **Gornergrat**, approached by a rack railway (station opposite the main Railway Station), first climbing SE to the Riffelberg, the W end of a long ridge culminating in the Stockhorn to the E. Near the *Riffel Alp Station* stands the *Holy Trinity Church*, built for the English clientele of the Hotel here, opened by Seiler in 1884 and burnt down in 1961. A monument commemorates Thomas W. Hinchliff (1825–82), part-founder, first secretary and President (in 1874–77) of the Alpine Club. The ascent continues past the halts of *Riffelberg*, and *Rotenboden*, to (9km) *Gornergrat.

Its belvedere commands a splendid view of the glacier and the icefields stretching for almost 20km between the Matterhorn and the *Cima di Jazzi* (3803m), and a panorama of snow peaks, including *Monte Rosa* (SE; 4634m), the *Weisshorn* (NW; 4505m) and the *Mischabelhörner* (NE; the *Dom* rising to 4545m); the summit of the *Stockhorn* (3532m) may be reached by the adjacent cableway.

Monte Rosa is the name given to a group of peaks which stands at the angle of two great ridges, one running W to the Matterhorn, the other N to the Mischabelhörner. The name appears to have been originally 'Monte della Rosa' ('roisa' or 'ruise' being patois for glacier in the Aosta valleys).

The main summit, the **Dufourspitze**, takes its name from Gén. Dufour (died 1875), who was in charge of the first scientific cartographical survey of

Switzerland. It is the highest *peak* in the country, although its E slope is in Italy. The neighbouring *Grenzgipfel*, formerly thought of as the highest crest, was first ascended in 1851 by the Schlagintweits. The '*Allerhöchste Spitze*', as the Dufourspitze was then called, was climbed in 1855 by five Englishmen, including the ill-fated Charles Hudson. Winston Churchill and T.S. Amery scaled it in 1894. Most of the peaks to the S were first attained from the Italian side; the *Punta Giordani* was climbed as early as 1801. Some have been named after their conquerors, such as the *Zumsteinspitze* (in 1820), and *Punta Gnifetti* (or *Signalkuppe*), in 1842.

To the W of Monte Rosa rises the *Liskamm* (4527m), notorious for its treacherous ice-cornices, and further W, the *Zwillinge* or 'Twins' (4092m, and 4228m). The *Cima di Jazzi*, due E of the Stockhorn, and the highest point of the ridge between Monte Rosa and the *Strahlhorn* (4190m), may be ascended without difficulty, and provides a view over the colossal precipices which descend sheer into the VAL ANZASCA, and the rock wall on the E side of Monte Rosa.

Another excursion may be made to the SW, aided by a cableway, to the **Schwarzee** (2583m), where the adjacent ridge provides a good *View of the Matterhorn* and of the whole length of the *Gorner Glacier*. A still finer *View* is commanded by the *Hörnli*, reached by a steep climb to the lowest buttress of the NE ridge of the Matterhorn.

The ***Matterhorn** (4478m; *Mont Cervin* in French; *Il Cervino* in Italian), an isolated and sharply tapering pyramid dominating the area, has long exercised a powerful fascination for mountaineers and has taken a heavier toll in fatal accidents than any other peak in the high Alps. It is a fatiguing climb, but with the help of skilled guides and with the aid of ropes and iron railings fixed at the most difficult points, mountaineers of no great pretension may make the rewarding ascent to the summit.

In 1857 the Abbé Gorret, of Ayas, reached the *Tête du Lion* on the SW ridge of the Matterhorn and in 1862 Prof. Tyndall worked further up the ridge to a point since named after him; however, it was not until 14 July 1865 that the summit was attained, this time via the NE ridge. The ascent was made by Edward Whymper, Lord Francis Douglas, the Rev. Charles Hudson and Douglas Hadow, with Michel-Auguste Croz of Chamonix and Peter Taugwalder senior of Zermatt, as guides. On the descent Hadow slipped, knocking Croz over and dragging Douglas and Hudson over the precipice. Taugwalder withstood the shock and the rope parted so that the remainder of the party were saved. The bodies of Hadow, Croz and Hudson were later discovered. A few days after the disaster an ascent was made up the NW face, and in 1867 a direct route up from *Breuil* (SW, in Italy) was achieved. Thomas Hardy wrote a poem on the Matterhorn in 1897.

A cableway mounts S from the Schwarzsee to the *Trockner Steg*, and is continued by another reaching a height of 3820m (the highest in Europe, inaugurated in 1980), near the summit of the *Klein-Matterhorn* (3883m; first ascended in 1792 by De Saussure). The *Breithorn* (E; 4164m) an easy climb from the last station, rewarded by a magnificent *View* extending from the Bernese Alps to the Gran Paradiso, with Mont Blanc to the left of the Matterhorn, and the Liskamm and Monte Rosa to the E. To the W is the frontier *Théodulpass* (3317m), one of the easiest and most frequented of the high glacier passes of the Alps. Sir John Herschel, the astronomer, made the first ascent of the Breithorn from the pass in 1821.

A bridle-path descends N from the Schwarzsee to the *Staffel Alp*, well sited at the foot of the stony *Zmutt Glacier* amid forests of Arolla pines, in full view of the N side of the Matterhorn. To the NW rises the *Dent Blanche* (4357m); to the SW the *Dent d'Hérens* (4171m). The return to Zermatt may be made by following a path E along the N bank of the Zmuttbach torrent via the old hamlet of *Zmutt*, or above its S bank to *Zum See*.

Among other excursions are those towards the *Findelen Glacier* to the E, at the head of which rises the *Cima di Jazzi* (3803m).—NW of Zermatt one may ascend its gorge to the *Trift Inn*, below and S of the *Mettelhorn* (3406m), from where there is a splendid view. To the NW rises the *Zinalrothorn* (4221m); to the W, the *Unter Gabelhorn* (3392m) and *Ober Gabelhorn* (4063m).

45 Brig to Andermatt via Gletsch and the Furkapass

Total distance, 80km (50 miles). No. 19. 37km *Ulrichen*—11km *Gletsch*—32km **Andermatt**.

Maps: M 217; BL 37, 42, or 5001, 5004.

For **Brig** itself, see Rte 46.

Crossing to the N or right bank of the Rhône, here known as the *Rotten*, **Naters** (673m) is entered, a village of ancient origin, formerly of interest for its curious houses built on stilts and for an *Ossuary* of 1514 containing thousands of skulls, beside its 17C church with its 12C tower and Baroque high altar. The tower of a 13C castle and the ruins of another of the same date may also be seen.

A road climbs N to (9km) *Blatten*, from where a path ascends to *Belalp*, a mountaineering village (2130m) commanding a splendid view of the *Aletsch Glacier* to the NE, and the long chain of the Pennine Alps. It was visited by Ruskin in 1844 and by Spurgeon in 1865, while in 1877 Prof. John Tyndall (1820–93) built a chalet here. To the N towers the *Sparrhorn* (3021m); to the NW rises the *Unterbächhorn* (3554m) and, beyond, the *Nesthorn* (3824m). To the E is a reservoir filling the upper end of the wild *Massa gorge*.

We drive NE parallel to the *Furka-Oberalp Railway*. This railway, partly rack-and-pinion, opened in 1926 (the lines were laid by 1914, but the First World War caused the line E of Gletsch, together with the Furka Tunnel, to be abandoned), and joins the Rhaetian Railway at Disentis; see Zermatt or St. Moritz concerning the 'Glacier Express'. The Upper Valais is here known as the '*Goms*'.

7.5km *Mörel*, from where cableways mount to *Riederalp*, below the *Riederhorn* (W; 2230m). From Riederalp one may visit the lower end of the *Aletsch Glacier*, the morain of which is easily crossed to *Belalp*; see above.—Other lifts mount from further along the road to *Bettmeralp* (1957m), a recently exploited resort near a small lake.

The road starts to climb more steeply to (8.5km; just beyond *Lax*) a right-hand turning ascending to the BINNTAL, reputed for its flora and rare minerals.—2km ***Ernen** is a village of characteristic houses, with a *Rathaus* of 1770 and a *Church* founded in 1214.—Matthias Schinner, the powerful bishop of Sion, was born at adjacent *Mühlebach*.

The road goes on through a tunnel to (7km) *Binn*, a small resort preserving several old blackened chalets, below the frontier range. To the S the LENGTAL leads to the *Ritterpass* (2764m), below the *Helsenhorn* (3272m), to the E.—To the E of Binn, at the head of the Binntal, rises the *Ofenhorn* (3235m), to the S of which is the *Albrunpass* (2409m) leading into Italy, crossed by troops as early as 1425. For the VALLE ANTIGORIO and VAL FORMAZZA, see *Blue Guide Northern Italy*.—To the N of Binn is the *Eggerhorn* (2503m), which may be climbed for the view.

2km Fiesch (1049m), a small resort preserving several characteristic dark-brown chalets, lies at the entrance of a side valley blocked by the retreating *Fiescher Glacier* which descends to an unusually low altitude.

Mountain roads, and a cableway, with an intermediate station at *Kühboden*, ascend from Fiesch to below the summit of the *Eggishorn* (NW; 2927m), which offers a splendid mountainscape and unrivalled view of glaciers. Conspicuous among these glaciers is the **Grosser Aletsch-gletscher**, the largest in the Alps, 115km² in area, 27km long and about 1.7km broad. The *Aletschhorn* (4195m) rises to the NW at the head of a tributary glacier, and further to the N, the *Dreieckhorn* (3811m), with the *Jungfrau* (4158m) beyond. To the N is the *Wannenhorn* (3906m) and beyond to its E, the *Finsteraarhorn* (4274m).—From the Kühboden station, a road leads to the *Märjelensee*, a small lake bordering the glacier, often dotted with miniature icebergs; it empties itself intermittently through a sub-glacial channel. The surface of the glacier is gently inclined and smooth, with very little debris. The *Konkordia Huts*, on the icy expanse of the *Konkordiaplatz* which extends beyond, may be approached from here, but guides or expert knowledge are indispensable for any ascents from the huts.

The road climbs again beyond Fiesch, the second 'step' up the Rhône valley—the river is here little more than a mountain torrent —to (6km) *Niederwald*, the village birthplace of César Ritz (1850–1918), the famous hotelier.—6km *Reckingen*, with a fine Baroque church of 1745, lies at the foot of the BLINNENTAL, at the head of which rises the *Blinnenhorn* (3374m).

3km **Münster** (1388m), said to be named from a medieval Benedictine monastery, is the main village of the Upper Rhône valley, also known as the *Goms*, and lies at the foot of the MINSTIGERTAL, above which rises the *Löffelhorn* (3095m) on the Aargrat ridge. It is an attractive place, preserving a number of dark wooden houses characteristically huddled together and a handsome white-painted *Church* dating from 1491 and altered in 1666 and 1750 in the Baroque taste. It contains an altarpiece of 1509 and an elaborate pulpit and font.

4km *Ulrichen* (1346m) is notable for two 'victories' over the Bernese who crossed the Grimsel in 1211 and 1419. It is believed that the German-speaking natives of the Upper Valais are themselves descended from invaders from beyond the Grimsel, for they differ in race as well as language from the people of the Lower Valais.—The *Gross Sidelhorn* (2879m), to the N, is easily climbed from here, while to the NE is seen the snow pyramid of the *Galenstock* (3583m) above the Rhône Glacier.

For the road up the AGENENTAL to the *Nufenenpass* for *Airolo* see Rte 41.

Obergesteln is shortly passed. This village was partly overwhelmed by an avalanche in 1720, and.was burnt down in 1868; the rebuilding was mainly in stone and its appearance is therefore unlike other villages in the region. A mountain road and path mount N to the *Grimselpass*.—5km *Oberwald* (1368m), the highest village in the Upper Valais, with an early Baroque church, is the last station before the rail (and car-carrying) tunnel, or *Basistunnel Furka*, used when the upper route is impassable. 14.5km long, and completed in 1982, it is the world's longest narrow-gauge tunnel.

The road now climbs in wide zigzags past the *Rhônefälle*, providing a sudden view ahead of the Rhône Glacier and a distant retrospective view of the Weisshorn, to (6km) **Gletsch** (1757m), where the Furka and Grimsel routes meet. For the *Grimselpass* (2165m), reached by another series of zigzags, and the road to *Innertkirchen*, see the sub-route on p 195, in reverse.

The main road climbs again in steep zigzags to reach, after 11km, the summit of the **Furkapass** (2431m), with a magnificent view over the **Rhône Glacier**, 11km long, between 1·3km wide, and 20km² in extent.

Nineteenth century view of the Rhône glacier.

It descends from a great height to form a beautiful and impressive ice-fall, at the foot of which the river rises. The glacier is much shrunken, and has withdrawn several kilometres within recorded history; however this regression seems to have been arrested. The glacier is seen at its best in early summer, when the slopes beside it are bright with Alpine flowers. Just before reaching the pass, one may turn off to the *Hôtel Belvédère*, strikingly situated on the very edge of the glacier, commanding a full view of its extraordinary ice-falls; adjacent is an ice-grotto.

The *Furkapass*, named from being a 'fork' between two peaks, was opened to wheeled traffic in 1867, and is one of the highest road passes in Europe (2431m). The railway passes below it in a tunnel at this point. The pass is often wrapped in mist, but otherwise the views it commands are very grand.

The road now descends, with a view of the smaller but deeply crevassed *Tiefen Glacier*, above which towers the *Gletschhorn* (N; 3305m), and to the W, the *Galenstock* (3583m), with its steep snow-slope and cornice. To the S is the stream of the Furkareuss. The road winds down to (12km) *Realp* (1538m), a village lying in a desolate site at the foot of the pass. It is now protected from avalanches by artificial works, for on one occasion in the 18C the whole village was swept away. Goethe spent the night here at the Post Inn, then a Capuchin hospice, in 1779.

A mountain road leads S to *Oberstafel*, from where a path climbs to a pass (the *Passo di Cavanna*) at 2613m, not far E of the *Witenwasseren Stock* (3082m) to enter the VALLE BEDRETTO W of Airolo; see Rte 41.

At 6km **Hospental** (1452m) is reached, where the road from the *St. Gotthardpass* descends from the S, a resort named from a former hospice founded in the 13C, the date also of the restored tower above the village. The impressive Baroque *Church* (1711) is by the same architect as that at **Andermatt**, 2km NE, for which see the latter part of Rte 25A.

For the roads hence to **Chur** and **Bellinzona** see Rtes 38 and 41, respectively, in reverse.

46 Brig to Locarno via the Simplon Pass and Domodóssola

Total distance, 115km (71 miles). No. 9. 24km **Simplon Pass**—21km to the Italian frontier—S 35. 21km **Domodóssola**—S 337. 30km *Ponte Ribellasca*—19km **Locarno**.

The longer road from Domodóssola to Locarno via *Verbenia* and the W bank of *Lago Maggiore* may also be followed; an additional distance of 86km or 37 miles; the latter part is described in reverse in Rte 39. See also *Blue Guide Northern Italy*.

Maps: M 219; BL 42, 43, 47, or 50.07.

The route is also followed by a regular train service.

Brig (684m) lies at the confluence of the Saltina with the Rhône and owes its importance to its position at the junction of the road up the Valais to the Furkapass with that over the Simplon; it is likewise at the N entrance of the Simplon rail tunnel, and not far from the S exit of the Lötschberg rail tunnel. The rail up the valley reached Brig in 1878.

Its most conspicuous building is the grandiose 17C *Schloss Stockalper, built by the local Maecenas, with three towers crowned by bulbous cupolas and a handsome triple-arcaded courtyard. Several of its rooms may be visited, including the *Chapel* with its oriel window, while an upper floor houses a local *Museum*.

Several other mansions erected over past centuries by families rich from the profits of trading with Italy may be seen, while the *Church* of the former Jesuit college (1662) is of some interest. In the central square is the little chapel of *St. Sebastian*; opposite is a statue commemorating Georges Chavez, the Peruvian pilot who first flew over the Alps—from Brig to Domodóssola—but who crashed and was killed on landing (29 September 1910).

Although a hospice was built on the **Simplon Pass** in 1235, the pass does not appear to have been very important, except as a route for merchants, until Napoleon chose it as the route for his—primarily military—road connecting the Rhône valley with the Lombard plain. This complex undertaking, decided upon immediately after the passage of the Grand St. Bernard (cf.) and the battle of Marengo, was begun on the Italian side in 1800, and on the Swiss a year later; it was completed in 1808. This mountainous section was the last part of the great carriage-road, 182km long, which then led from Geneva to Sesto Calende, NW of Milan. Nicolas Céard (1747–1821) was its chief engineer, and at one time over 30,000 men were employed on its construction. Much has been done in recent years to improve it further; its sinuosities have been brilliantly engineered and several refuges have been provided. According to Sir Henry Holland, when Caroline of Brunswick crossed the Simplon in 1814, one of the conveyances for the party was an old London and Dover mail-coach which had been purchased, still with its former destinations on its panels.

The railway traverses the **Simplon Tunnel** almost immediately on leaving Brig. It is the longest rail tunnel in the world (19.8km); its first gallery was bored in 1898–1905. Although a subsidiary gallery, connected by cross-shafts, formed part of the original construction, this was not enlarged to take a second track until 1912–21. The maximum elevation is only 705m; it is therefore the lowest of the great Alpine tunnels; there are 2134m of mountain overhead where the main range is pierced. Car-carrier trains between Brig and Iselle are frequent; the frontier is crossed about half-way through the tunnel.

Simplon; the Ganter Bridge

Driving S from Brig, the road almost immediately makes the first of its abrupt turns—to the NE—away from the *Glishorn* (2525m), and then swings S again, climbing steeply and traversing four short tunnels. It then turns due E, spanning the Gantertal by *Ganter Bridge* (1980), 678m long, supported by two huge concrete piers. The *Bortelhorn* (3194m) rises ahead. At the hamlet of (15km) *Berisal* it again veers abruptly SW below (left) the *Wasenhorn* (3246m) and climbs again through *Rothwald*. The road from this point to the summit was much exposed to avalanches, and now has protective galleries. The road now ascends S through two short tunnels before making its final curve to the W to (9km) the **Simplon Pass** (or *Passo del Sempione* in Italian; 2005m), a broad plateau providing a good retrospective view of the *Aletschhorn* (4195m), and of the Fletschhorn group to the S, while to the E rises *Monte Leone* (3553m).

Just beyond the pass stands the *Simplon Hospice*, built by Napoleon as barracks in 1811 but left unfinished until it was acquired by the monks of St. Bernard in 1825. Their hospitality should not be abused. Further along the road, on the right, is the former *Hospice*, maintained by Knights Hospitallers from 1235 to 1470 and in 1653 acquired by Caspar Stockalper of Brig, who built its square tower.

The road circles to the SE on the descent, with a view SW of the *Rossboden Glacier* descending from the Fletschhorn. At 9km the village of *Simplon* is now by-passed, before bearing E and climbing down through 600m-high precipices into the *Gorge of the Gondo* to (11km) *Gondo* itself. This is the frontier village (Customs), previously described as a 'cluster of miserable hovels at the foot of the Zwischbergen Tal', only remarkable for the eight-storey tower erected by the Stockalpers as a refuge for wayfarers.

The Italian frontier is crossed 1km beyond at *Paglino* (Customs); soon after one passes a fine waterfall to the right.—3km *Iselle*, the first station S of the rail tunnel, beyond which the railway traverses a short spiral tunnel before entering *Varzo*, with a church of 1440, by-passed by the road at 5km.—From here a minor road ascends NW up the VALLE CAIRASCA to *San Domenico* (1410), below the *Nature Reserve* of *Alpe Veglia*. The main road circles to the S along the VAL DIVEDRO to (8km) *Crévoladossola*, a village at the foot of the VALLE ANTIGORIO, extended by the VAL FORMAZZA to the *San Giacomo Pass*; see *Blue Guide Northern Italy*. By continuing due E and then SE, one soon meets the direct road from Domodóssola to Santa Maria Maggiore and Locarno, which is equally well approached via Domodóssola, only 5km S.

Domodóssola (271m; 19,700 inhab.) is a characteristic Italian town of Roman origin, with an old arcaded market-place. In the *Palazzo Galletti* is a *Museum*, with a room illustrating the construction of the Simplon Tunnel. The town was engagingly, if somewhat unfairly, described in the first edition of Murray's Hand-Book to Switzerland as Italian to its very stone; 'Houses with collonades, streets with awnings, shops teeming with sausages, macaroni, and garlic, lazy-looking, loitering lazzaroni, in red nightcaps, and bare, mahogany-coloured legs, intermixed with mules, burly priests, and females veiled with the mantilla, fill up the picture ...'

For a fuller and up-to-date description see *Blue Guide Northern Italy*, and likewise for the road S, from which one may turn W up the VAL DI ANTRONA for *Antronapiana*, and further S, up the VALLE ANZASCA to *Macugnaga*, below the E wall of *Monte Rosa*; see also Rte 44.

At (21km) *Cuzzago*, one may bear left for (19km) *Verbania*, on the *Lago di Maggiore*, the NW shore of which may be followed via *Cannobio* to re-cross the frontier 12km SW of *Locarno* (see Rte 39), providing an alternative route—on main roads—to that described below.

The S 337 closely follows the line of the railway, opened in 1923, and repaired since flood damage put it out of action in 1978. At (4.5km) *Masera*, with an old church tower, we enter the VALLE VIGEZZO, frequented by artists since the 19C and known as the 'Valle dei Pittori'.—12.5km **Santa Maria Maggiore**, the main village, is finely situated in an upland basin, a native of which was Giovanni Maria Farina (1685–1766), the inventor of 'Eau de Cologne'. To the W, in the distance, are the peaks of Monte Rosa, better seen from the *Piana di Vigezzo* (1724m), the upper station of the cableway, the lower terminus of which is passed to the left of the road to (2.5km) *Malesco*.

From here a rough mountain road leads SE to the gorge and waterfall of the *Orrido di Sant'Anna*, and descends to (24.5km) *Cannobio*.

At 9km we cross into Switzerland by the bold *Ponte della Ribellasco* (Customs), with *Monte Limidario* (or *Gridone*; 2188m) rising to the E.—Beyond *Cámedo* we descend through a district known as the CENTOVALLI from the numerous side-streams which here feed the Melezza.—12km *Intragna*, a village with a prominent church tower, was the original home of the Gambetta family, from which the grandfather of Léon Gambetta emigrated to Genoa.

For the VALLE ONSERNONE, which opens to the left, see Rte 39.—The Mággia is shortly crossed at *Ponte Brolla*, from where turn right for **Locarno**, passing a right-hand turning for neighbouring **Ascona**; for both see Rte 39, and for **Bellinzona**, 19km further E.

INDEX

Topographical names (including some beyond the frontier) are printed in Roman or bold type; the names of notable people are in *italics*, including—in brackets—the dates of the principal Swiss artists and certain foreign artists working in Switzerland; while subjects are in CAPITALS.

In an attempt to keep this index within reasonable bounds, not every château, Schlösser, peak, pass, glacier, river, lake, waterfall, gorge and valley has been included.

Places named after saints (St., Sankt, San, or Santa) are listed in alphabetical order.

Typeset by MCL Computerset Ltd, Ely, Cambs, England